D0945457

The Socialist Left
and the German Revolution

The Socialist Left
and the German Revolution

A HISTORY OF THE GERMAN INDEPENDENT
SOCIAL DEMOCRATIC PARTY, 1917–1922

DAVID W. MORGAN

Cornell University Press

ITHACA AND LONDON

Cornell University Press gratefully acknowledges a grant from the Andrew J. Mellon Foundation that aided in bringing this book to publication.

Copyright © 1975 by Cornell University

All rights reserved. Except for brief quotations in a review, this book, or parts thereof, must not be reproduced in any form without permission in writing from the publisher. For information address Cornell University Press, 124 Roberts Place, Ithaca, New York 14850.

First published 1975 by Cornell University Press.
Published in the United Kingdom by Cornell University Press Ltd., 2-4 Brook Street, London W1Y 1AA.

International Standard Book Number 0-8014-0851-2
Library of Congress Catalog Card Number 75-5393
Printed in the United States of America by York Composition Co., Inc.

329.9
M826

JN
3970
.S6
M66

To Alan Bullock, Gerald Freund,
James Joll, and Wallace T. MacCaffrey,
teachers and friends

Contents

Preface

The German Independent Social Democratic Party (known from its German initials as the USPD) came and went in the brief space of five and a half years, between April 1917 and September 1922. This would be a short life to justify a substantial book had not these years been among the most eventful in modern German history and had not the USPD for much of this time stood close to the center of the public stage. The party was born in 1917 by painful schism from the Social Democratic Party (SPD), Germany's largest party and the foremost embodiment of the European socialist movement. Its creation expressed both the continued alienation of many socialists from the German social and political order, even during the World War, and the unrest bred in the lower classes by the misery and misgovernment of the war years. When revolution came to Germany in November 1918 the socialists picked up the reins of government; and if it was ultimately the right-wing socialists, with their eyes turned to parliamentary democracy, who did most to determine the outcome of the revolutionary months, the smaller group of Independent Socialists also left their mark, if only by the expectations they helped to arouse but could not satisfy. Driven out of power, radical socialism regrouped and grew, to the point where at its peak, in 1920, the USPD was the second largest party in the country. Yet the movement was fragile. At the end of 1918 a split produced a third working-class party, the Communists; and still another schism in October 1920 deflated the USPD while elevating the Communists to the status of a real power in working-class politics. By the end of 1920 three substantial parties struggled to gain the heritage of the German socialist movement. After two years of effort the remaining Independents, seriously disoriented by the course of events since 1918, threw in their lot again with the large party on their right, the mother party—the SPD. A small faction carried on the party name, but for practical purposes the life of the USPD was over.

In part, this book is a study of left-wing socialists in a revolutionary epoch; it examines their perceptions of what was happening around

them, their sense of duty and opportunity, and their practical responses, both novel and traditional. The behavior of Independent Social Democracy and its various factions has often been criticized, by the left as well as the right, as unrealistic, irresponsible, inconsistent, and crippled with indecision; and it was often any or all of these things. More to the point for our present purposes, however, the Independents' behavior is usually explicable in terms of their characteristic orientations—their theoretical views, their temperaments, their understanding of the revolution, their conceptions of proper political and revolutionary practice. Indeed, it is often hard to see how the radical socialists could have acted otherwise without repudiating their political past. This is not to deny either that they were often faced with difficult choices or that they sometimes produced significant innovations, notably in their use of workers' councils. Rather, the point is that the left-wing socialists of 1918 and later were particular kinds of men with particular preconceptions, which strongly influenced their comprehension of their situation and their interaction with it; to understand the operation of these factors is one of the most important tasks confronting the student of the movement.

This book is also a study in party history. The Independent Social Democratic Party was more than just a name for a segment of the socialist spectrum; it was an organization, with a structure and weight of its own. Surprisingly little attention has been paid to the role of the parties in the German revolutionary period, in spite of Arthur Rosenberg's often-quoted attempt to show that the party alignments of the period frustrated the actual political will of the socialist groups.[1] I will argue here that the two Social Democratic parties, and not the workers' and soldiers' councils, were the basis of the revolutionary regime in most of Germany, including the critical city, Berlin; and that in spite of a certain fluidity in party allegiances in the postrevolutionary period, and tensions between party factions, the bonds that united the members of a given party were often as important as any other factor in determining the course of socialist politics. The powerful emotional principle of party unity thus becomes an important part of the story, as does the role of party leadership and organization. The traditions of unity and leadership were unusually strong in German Social Democracy, to the extent that even dissident radicals were generally unable to cast off their inherited attitudes completely. The party history of the revolution is, therefore, one of the keys to the history of the revolution as a whole.

Finally, the book may contribute to a broader understanding of the

1. Arthur Rosenberg, *Geschichte der Deutschen Republik* (Karlsbad, 1935), pp. 30–31.

German political scene out of which the Weimar Republic emerged. The socialist left was, of course, only a fragment of that scene, but it shared in the conduct of public affairs for several months after the revolution, and it labored under the burdens of the past in ways that may be illuminating for the more general study of the era. The antagonisms the left felt, and those it aroused, in a kind of vicious circle, were among the most important factors preventing the consolidation of the Republic in its formative years. Moreover, the experiences of the Independent Social Democrats and their responses to these experiences left a mark on the working-class parties of the later Weimar years, long after the party itself had become defunct. The Communist Party drew much of its organizational strength and even its leaders—notably Ernst Thälmann— from the Independents after 1920; and the reunited Social Democratic Party after 1922 owed much of its ambivalence toward the Republic it had been largely responsible for creating to the influx of Independents.

The approach outlined in the preceding paragraphs gives the present work a somewhat different cast from much recent research into Germany's revolutionary epoch. For one thing, American students of German socialism who closely examine the motives and dynamics of the USPD may relinquish the special sympathy that (according to one sharp-eyed critic) they have tended to feel for the socialist left, as supposedly the most determined advocate of democratization in Germany.[2] Such sympathy rests on a misperception. Certainly the critique of German society by early twentieth-century Marxists still has force; and certainly democracy, in the standard Western sense of the word, was a central ideal of left-wing socialism (as distinguished from the growing Communist movement) throughout this period. But such perceptions and ideals, which even nonsocialists can honor, were embedded in the total life and attitudes of a political faction whose practices could not, in the end, offer much prospect of establishing an open, democratic social and political order. Left-wing socialism, embodied in these years in the Independent Social Democratic Party, was tied to a particular political constituency, fettered by adherence to unattainable ideals and a misunderstanding of the revolution it helped to sponsor, and hampered by leadership that was, on the whole, as unimaginative as that of the SPD. The socialist left was committed to the ideology of the class struggle, one of the most fruitless, debilitating legacies of the old order. Finally, it was condemned to the position of a small minority and thus caught in the classic dilemma of democratic socialism: in its pursuit of both

2. Klaus Epstein, "Three American Studies of German Socialism," *World Politics*, 11 (1958–59), esp. 629 and 650–51.

democracy and socialism the socialist left lost its impetus—lost even its sense of direction—and achieved neither.

For similar reasons the much-debated democratic potential of the council system (workers' councils and later factory councils) appears in a different and less promising light when considered in the context of the constraints on socialist politics that are brought out by a study of the USPD. Two arguments in particular, sometimes used by the retrospective advocates of the councils, deserve re-examination. The first, that the impulses of the masses in the German revolution were essentially democratic, is misleading, for the democratic sentiments that were unquestionably present, and forcefully expressed, were mingled with other loyalties, commitments, and ideological presuppositions—particularly in the case of the Independent Socialist militants, but also among the followers of the SPD. There was no common conception of "democracy." Probably none of the contending socialist groups of 1918 had a vision of the democratic reforms necessary in Germany that would satisfy historians of our own day; if any did, it faced an impossible task in trying to convince the others. Thus the democratic impulse was dissipated in fundamental conflicts of purpose. The second argument— that the councils themselves might have served as a means of transcending the differences between the older political and industrial organizations of the working class—is not supported by the realities of the revolutionary years. The parties and trade unions, with their strengths, weaknesses, and mutual antagonisms, were the established institutions of the German labor movement as it entered the revolution, and the councils were never strong enough, or likely to become so, to overcome the shortcomings of the movement and channel its energies into a purposeful democratization of society. For that, the German labor movement would have had to have been different—not just in the persons or orientations of its leaders, but also in its historical experience. The working out of this historical experience among the left-wing Social Democrats in the revolutionary years is the central subject of this book.

The approach adopted requires the minimum of attention to the theory or formal doctrine of the Independent Socialists. The doctrine itself was scanty, since, apart from the ideals of the council system, the ideological formulations used within the party were nearly all either derivative (like the Leninism gradually adopted on the extreme left), marginal to the party's real orientation (like the writings of Karl Kautsky on the extreme right wing), purely conventional, or purely instrumental and therefore ephemeral. In any case, the formal doctrines of a large political movement, while they express the movement's needs and its conception of itself, do not dictate behavior; political behavior on a

large scale—behavior of individuals is another problem—takes its shape from attitudes, formulas, and traditional modes of action. Any mass party moves within an accepted framework of modes of comprehension and action, a framework that may change, even quite radically, but gradually, in a process of interaction with changing circumstances. This changing but still continuous framework is the focus of the account that follows. Although theory itself and the problems of the relationship between theory and action are rewarding fields of study, the present work deals above all with daily politics, in an attempt to contribute to an understanding of what left-wing socialism, gathered into a political party, did and suffered in the era of revolution after 1917.

It is a pleasure to be able at last to record formally my gratitude for assistance received over the many years this book was in the making. During the first stage of the work, which took place at Lincoln College, Oxford, my research was supported by the Marshall Aid Commemoration Commission; at later stages I received generous support from the Warden and Fellows of St. Antony's College, Oxford, and from Wesleyan University. The archivists and staff of nearly a dozen archives have provided assistance, often beyond the call of duty: the International Institute of Social History in Amsterdam; the Institut für Marxismus-Leninismus in Berlin; the Archiv der Sozialen Demokratie at the Friedrich-Ebert-Stiftung in Bonn–Bad Godesberg; the Staatsarchiv in Dresden; the Bundesarchiv's Militärarchiv in Freiburg i.B.; the Bundesarchiv in Koblenz; the Staatsarchiv in Magdeburg; the Deutsche Zentralarchiv, Historische Abteilung II, in Merseburg; the Deutsche Zentralarchiv in Potsdam; the Staatsarchiv in Potsdam; and the Library of Political Studies in New York. The librarians of many of these institutions have also been helpful, as have those of the Wiener Library, the British Library of Political and Economic Science, the Sterling Library of Yale University, and others too numerous to name. Special thanks are due Anne Abley of the St. Antony's College library and William Dillon of Wesleyan University's Olin Library for their kind assistance in procuring books from other libraries for me to consult.

Advice and encouragement from others are the most pleasant of all debts to acknowledge. Alan Bullock and James Joll both stood godfather to the work in an earlier guise and provided numerous helpful insights. Kenneth W. Morgan, Jeffrey Butler, and Susanne Miller offered suggestions that have contributed to the work's readability, while Susan Osborne's admirable editing trimmed away much unclarity and redundancy. Hartfrid Krause kindly supplied some materials in his possession and allowed me to consult an unpublished manuscript. Karen Bovard

helped compile statistical material. The comments of Allan Mitchell and Werner T. Angress aided me in eliminating errors and in improving various formulations as well as the general presentation of the work. Robert Wheeler's careful critique of the manuscript at an earlier stage not only helped me to remove careless errors and questionable assumptions but forced me to rethink the whole portrayal of the factional alignments of the USPD, a contribution of inestimable importance. Finally, the help of Elizabeth Levering Morgan has been important to me in more ways than I can express here.

DAVID W. MORGAN

Middletown, Connecticut

Abbreviations

ADGB	Allgemeiner Deutscher Gewerkschaftsbund (General German Federation of Trade Unions)
AfA	Arbeitsgemeinschaft freier Angestelltenverbände (Association of Free White Collar Unions), later Allgemeiner freier Angestelltenbund (General Free Federation of White Collar Workers)
ASD Bonn	Archiv der Sozialen Demokratie, Friedrich-Ebert-Stiftung, Bonn-Bad Godesberg
BA Koblenz	Bundesarchiv, Koblenz
BA-MA Freiburg	Bundesarchiv-Militärarchiv, Freiburg i.B.
DZA Merseburg	Deutsches Zentralarchiv, Historische Abteilung II, Merseburg
DZA Potsdam	Deutsches Zentralarchiv, Potsdam
e	evening edition
ECCI	Executive Committee of the Communist International
IISH Amsterdam	International Institute of Social History, Amsterdam
IML Berlin	Institut für Marxismus-Leninismus, Zentrales Parteiarchiv, Berlin
KAG	Kommunistische Arbeitsgemeinschaft (Communist Alliance)
KAPD	Kommunistische Arbeiterpartei Deutschlands (German Communist Workers Party)
KPD	Kommunistische Partei Deutschlands (German Communist Party)
m	morning edition
MdI	Ministerium des Innern (Ministry of the Interior)
RMdI	Reichsamt/Reichsministerium des Innern (Reich Ministry of the Interior)
SAG	Sozialdemokratische Arbeitsgemeinschaft (Social Democratic Alliance)
SPD	Sozialdemokratische Partei Deutschlands (German Social Democratic Party)
StA	Staatsarchiv

15

USPD, USP   Unabhängige Sozialdemokratische Partei Deutschlands (German Independent Social Democratic Party)

VKPD   Vereinigte Kommunistische Partei Deutschlands (United German Communist Party)

VSPD   Vereinigte Sozialdemokratische Partei Deutschlands (United German Social Democratic Party)

The Socialist Left and the German Revolution

CHAPTER 1

The Division of German Social Democracy

In April 1917 the leaders of the main opposition groups from within the German Social Democratic Party (SPD), driven out of the mother party, met to found a new organization. In the eyes of many of them, the new foundation was a wartime expedient, a base from which they could continue to agitate for views proscribed in the SPD. Its members were still part of the mystically united Social Democratic movement, whose formal unity would be restored—with a due settlement of accounts—after the war. This spirit determined the choice by the new organization's founding congress of a name that expressed attachment to the movement's heritage: the German Independent Social Democratic Party (USPD).

The new party outlasted the expectations of its founders; when the war ended nineteen months later, the party, instead of disappearing, began the most vigorous phase of its existence, which was to last for nearly four more years. During its five and a half years of life, the USPD underwent transformations its founders could hardly have foreseen and painfully gave birth—not once but twice—to sizable forces of Communists, practitioners of a kind of politics scarcely within the experience of most socialists in 1917. The USPD's rhetoric and formal aspirations moved a considerable distance from those that were traditional in the old party from which it had originated. Nevertheless, the party's origins were unmistakable. The Independent Social Democratic Party was unambiguously the descendant of the old Social Democratic Party of 1914—in organization and practices, in ideology, aspirations, and hesitancies, and in personnel. The story of the USPD is a part, if at times an aberrant part, of the history of German Social Democracy from Ferdinand Lassalle and Karl Marx through August Bebel to Kurt Schumacher and Willy Brandt.

To understand the tradition inherited by the new party in 1917, we must look back to the last period of normality in the still united Social

Democratic Party, the years before the outbreak of World War I, and from there trace the outlines of the process of divergence that ultimately drove the socialist left to found a party of its own.

German Social Democracy in 1914

The prewar German Social Democratic Party was one of the most remarkable institutions of its time. Under constant harassment from the semiautocratic governments of Germany since its beginnings in the 1860's, the party had experienced almost uninterrupted growth and consolidation. Its unity, discipline, and organizational strength were the envy of the other socialist parties of Europe. Its doctrinal orientation, founded on the discipleship of Karl Kautsky and others under Friedrich Engels, tended to be accepted as defining orthodox Marxism for the Socialist International. Before the outbreak of the war the SPD had become the largest party in the German Reichstag, the largest vote-getter by far in national elections, and, with its one million enrolled members, the largest organized political party in the world. Despite its size, however, the party had never exercised a share of power at any level of government, and its prospects of doing so in the foreseeable future were slight.

Any account of the old SPD must begin with its organization. Organization played an important role in the German labor movement in this, its most vigorous phase—indeed, critics have charged the party with "fetishism of the organization."[1] Organizational work strengthened the structures that would (in the eyes of their supporters) lead to the emancipation of the proletariat; at the same time it served as an outlet for the energies of able members of a social class whose other paths to advancement were largely blocked. Party work was an elevating aspect of life for many simple members and functionaries; for the editors and officials it was an all-absorbing task,[2] a "substitute for [the] political action" that seemed precluded by the circumstances of Imperial Germany.[3] The party was turned in upon itself and its own affairs, its perspective constricted by concern for its own operations. The "party," meaning the established forms and procedures of the political labor movement, became very nearly the highest value of all.

1. See, for instance, Thomas Nipperdey, *Die Organisation der deutschen Parteien vor 1918* (Düsseldorf, 1961), pp. 325 and 327.
2. An affecting account of what the prewar party meant to its active members appears in Eugen Prager, *Geschichte der U.S.P.D.: Entstehung und Entwicklung der Unabhängigen Sozialdemokratischen Partei Deutschlands* (Berlin, 1921), pp. 14–15. I use the term "functionary" to refer to volunteer party or union workers on the lower level, rather than to paid officials.
3. Helga Grebing, *Geschichte der deutschen Arbeiterbewegung: Ein Ueberblick* (Munich, 1966), p. 116.

The party organization itself was a legitimate source of pride, the first great model of a mass party founded on individual, dues-paying membership.[4] At the base of an elaborate pyramidal structure, largely completed in the years just before the war, were the ordinary members, attending monthly branch meetings; above them came the constituency parties (in nearly all of Germany's 397 Reichstag constituencies), the 38 administrative districts, the state (*Land*) organizations (principally in the South German states and Saxony), and, finally, the party's central institutions. Up the pyramid passed money (from dues) and political wishes, while downward came political guidelines, propaganda materials, and subsidies for agitation. It was the very pattern of a functioning, nationwide mass party.

The structure was participatory and democratic—formally, and to some extent in reality. An active member could make himself heard in his local party and, if willing to assume responsibility, might become a minor officeholder, or functionary. On the constituency level, where most of the real work of the party was done (organization, agitation, workers' education, and above all conduct of election campaigns), the rank and file could use its democratic rights to determine policy and elect leaders, perhaps giving the organization a particular factional alignment in the party—left or right, or (to use the socialist terminology) radical or reformist. At the center, the elected national leadership was accountable to annual party congresses, where the major questions of party doctrine and strategy were resolved—the great showcase of party democracy.

By 1914, however, the machine had become too big and complex for its formal democracy to operate well. The role of salaried officials necessarily increased; they came to predominate at the center, to control most of the district offices, and to exert increasing influence in constituency organizations as their numbers grew there. The increasing practice of hiring full-time officials had unforeseen political consequences. The traditional practice of the socialist (and trade-union) movement was to choose salaried officials on the basis of their energy and presumed administrative ability, and without examining closely their political views; once in office, these officials were regarded with loyalty rather than suspicion and were very difficult to remove. The administrative power of the party was thus in the hands of men chosen mostly on nonpolitical grounds and largely unaccountable for any political bias exercised with reasonable discretion. Nor was the broader impact of bureaucracy on

---

4. The classic survey of the SPD's party organization is Nipperdey, ch. 7; see also Carl E. Schorske, *German Social Democracy, 1905–1917: The Development of the Great Schism* (Cambridge, Mass., 1955).

political practice perceived by the party. Robert Michels' classic theoretical work on the subject, based on observation of the SPD, was written at this time;[5] but its lessons were lost on most party members, who failed to recognize that the party, though ostensibly committed to a revolutionary challenge to the existing order, was creating within itself a powerful body of men who tended, because of the nature of their work, toward orderly procedures, avoidance of risk, accommodation with the powers that be, and general moderation. Activities that were, in theory, auxiliary to the party's goals—such as managing finances, improving the efficiency of agitation, and conducting election campaigns —were the raison d'être of the bureaucracy and easily became the sole preoccupation of many bureaucrats. To be sure, there were highly radical party secretaries, and some of the radical party organizations, such as that of Leipzig, were as thoroughly bureaucratized as any reformist organization. Such cases, however, were exceptions and only tended to obscure the fact that the growth of bureaucracy meant increased resistance to risk, radical change, or any attempt to implement the far-reaching ideals that the party professed.

What was true of the party bureaucracy was true a fortiori of the Free (that is, socialist) Trade Unions, the party's close and influential ally.[6] The unions were a massive force, with a 1914 membership of two and a half million, as compared with one million for the party, and 2,384 salaried local and district officials to the party's 157.[7] This force was by no means unconditionally at the service of the party. The leaders of the unions were party members and professed the ideology of class struggle, but they insisted on having complete freedom to conduct their own affairs. As early as 1905–1906 the unions had been able to prevent the party considering seriously the possibilities of a general strike, thus setting themselves squarely athwart the path of revolutionary action as understood at the time.[8] In taking this action the General Commission of Free Trade Unions was only reflecting the tendency of union leaders, whether Social Democrats or not, to concern themselves with the pain-

5. Robert Michels, *Zur Soziologie des Parteiwesens in der modernen Demokratie* (Leipzig, 1911). Schorske, pp. 118 and 126–27, points out that the particular functions assigned to the SPD bureaucracy—especially membership growth and electoral victories—and the context within which it worked determined its character; the Communist Party bureaucracy in Germany in the 1920's, for instance, fits Michels' model much less well.

6. Unless otherwise stated, the term "trade unions" refers to the Free Trade Unions. There were other trade-union organizations in Germany, but their combined membership was scarcely a third of that of the socialist unions.

7. Dieter Fricke, *Zur Organisation und Tätigkeit der deutschen Arbeiterbewegung (1890–1914)* (Leipzig, 1962), pp. 51 and 250.

8. See Schorske, pp. 49–53.

fully constructed apparatus and procedures that served their members' daily needs and guaranteed the size of their following and to push problems of radical change, particularly violent, disruptive change, into the background.[9] Since the union organization had the status of a powerful equal partner of the party, while its leaders were active in the party at all levels—they made up 21 percent of the SPD's Reichstag delegation in 1912[10]—and increasingly found sympathy among the growing party bureaucracy, the union element operated as a formidable conservative force in party councils.

Yet these strong everyday concerns and inward-looking tendencies of the German labor movement remained allied with a revolutionary perspective, with an awareness that the party's final goal was the creation of a socialist order. This revolutionary orientation—nominal for some members, but intensely real for others—was as distinctive an aspect of the party as its organization, with which it inevitably stood in a kind of permanent tension. In its formal framework the ideology was Marxist; indeed, it embodied—even defined—the full range of the Marxist orthodoxy of the epoch of the Second International (1889 to 1914). This ideology met the needs of a generation (perhaps the last one) which could still assume that bourgeois society was a transitory historical phenomenon about to yield the stage to the more progressive domination of the working class. But it also met the needs of a mass party with complicated institutional ramifications in the real life of the contemporary working class.

At the center of the doctrine was the class struggle.[11] The working class, both the creation and the natural enemy of the capitalist social order, was growing in size and strength and approaching the day when it would assume political power and reconstruct society along socialist lines. Marx had characterized the seizure of power as a revolution. His orthodox successors of the prewar generation, led by Karl Kautsky, continued to use the term "revolution," but, with their sense of the his-

9. On the union leaders' attitude toward theory see Theodor Cassau, "Die sozialistische Ideenwelt vor und nach dem Weltkriege," in *Die Wirtschaftswissenschaft nach dem Kriege: Festgabe für Lujo Brentano,* ed. M. J. Bonn and M. Palyi, 2 vols. (Munich and Leipzig, 1925), I, 135–36.

10. A further 21 percent had strong ties to the unions; see *Die Reichstagsfraktion der deutschen Sozialdemokratie 1898 bis 1918,* ed. Erich Matthias and Eberhard Pikart, 2 vols. (Düsseldorf, 1966) (hereafter cited as *Reichstagsfraktion*), I, lvii–lix.

11. For the party's ideology before the war in the context of its total orientation, see, especially, Schorske; Hans-Josef Steinberg, *Sozialismus und deutsche Sozialdemokratie,* 2d ed. (Bonn–Bad Godesberg, 1972); Erich Matthias, "Kautsky und der Kautskyanismus," in *Marxismusstudien,* 2 (1957), 151–97; Dieter Groh, *Negative Integration und revolutionärer Attentismus* (Frankfurt on Main, 1973).

torical dialectic weakened by a long period of social stability and economic progress, they played down the violent connotations. The barricades disappeared altogether from the historical vision of many Social Democrats; most of the rest—including the dominant center bloc of the party—came to consider revolutionary upheaval and bloodshed as at most an incidental accompaniment to the majestic progress of the proletariat and perhaps entirely avoidable. In any case, violence and upheaval were not the business of the party. The party's task was to unite the working class and teach it its historic role as the future creator of socialism. As an awakened, united working class was realized, historical circumstances—unforeseeable in detail—would ensure that the new class overthrew the old.[12] The party, as guide, educator, and organizer of the proletariat, would help the workers construct the socialist order.

Class struggle required class consciousness; the working class (or at least its active elements) must remain detached and hostile within the bourgeois order while waiting for its moment to come. This prescription was not wholly visionary; for as a result of such factors as the delayed industrial revolution, an aggressive business class, the Bismarckian barriers to a democratic political evolution, severe restrictions on workers' access to higher education and social prestige, and systematic social and governmental bias against socialists of all persuasions, Imperial Germany had conspicuously failed to integrate its working class effectively into the national community. The resulting alienation was far from purely ideological. Many Social Democratic leaders of moderate views, notably the trade unionists, were not so much repelled by existing German society as conscious of having been repulsed by it. In other words, if the Social Democrats were the outcasts of German society two causes were at work: many had chosen to reject society's basic principles; at the same time all were deliberately driven off by the ruling classes. It is difficult to disentangle the two motives (which must have been mixed in most individuals) because they found the same conventional ideological expression in the party's doctrine of class struggle.[13] Only the wrench of changed circumstances after 1914 revealed the different premises on which a common front against the existing order had been based.

Class unity—a corollary of class consciousness—had until then been

12. See Steinberg, p. 61.
13. See Peter Nettl, "The German Social Democratic Party 1890–1914 as a Political Model," *Past and Present*, no. 30 (April 1965), p. 70; Ossip K. Flechtheim, "Die Anpassung der SPD: 1914, 1933 und 1959," *Kölner Zeitschrift für Soziologie und Sozialpsychologie*, 17 (1965), 584–86. On the failure of integration see Guenther Roth, *The Social Democrats in Imperial Germany: A Study in Working-Class Isolation and National Integration* (Totowa, N.J., 1963), esp. chs. 7 and 8.

strong in the German labor movement, one of its deepest commitments. Indeed, the party's dominant ideological orientation, the Kautskyan version of Marxist orthodoxy—embodied above all in the Erfurt Program of 1891—was noteworthy for the efficiency with which it served this aim.[14] Admittedly, the unity of German socialism may have been, in some respects, more formal than real; but in an era when the socialists of many other countries, including England and France, found unity impossible, it was a considerable achievement, highly valued by all German socialists. After all, the party had to address itself not only to those alienated workers of some industries and large cities who were attracted by the perspective of a sharp class struggle, but also to other, less radical blocs of workers, such as trade unionists interested primarily in tangible benefits, or members of the craftsman class who felt their political and social disenfranchisement keenly. A vision of the triumph of socialism at some future date was not enough to hold all these groups. The party found itself in the business of advocating reforms, both those directly affecting the life of the workers (such as the eight-hour day) and those designed to secure a more democratic political order (such as universal suffrage in Prussia). Such efforts were seen as a way of dramatizing to the workers the inequities of the existing order and demonstrating how unresponsive bourgeois society was to just demands. In this way the revolutionary and reformist perspectives were forced into conjunction. Self-contradictory as the combination may seem in retrospect, it was little challenged at the time since it seemed to work: it aided the growth of the party.

Some tensions did arise in practice from the juxtaposition of aims; for whereas the commitment to reform implied that any opportunities for exerting influence on the government should be seized, the principles of class struggle forbade close collaboration with organs of government or other parties. To some degree the party's position on such matters was dictated by past decisions that amounted to shibboleths. The party held that Social Democrats should not hold office under the existing governmental system; since this view was shared by the governments of Germany the issue was not a live one. Nor should the party's parliamentary delegations approve the granting of funds to a capitalist government; in this case, the prohibition was violated repeatedly in the Diets of the South German states, the only part of the country where socialists could sometimes really influence government policy. Beyond these principles

14. See Matthias, "Kautsky," esp. p. 165. The critique of Matthias in Steinberg, pp. 75-86, challenges many points of Matthias' argument, but the central thesis still appears sound.

parliamentary guidelines were unclear. By 1914 most Social Democratic leaders had turned away, in some measure, from the old practice of "pure opposition" under which Social Democracy made its proposals purely for demonstrative effect and entered into no agreements with other parties, though it might vote for other parties' proposals on occasion. There was rich material here for conflict between those socialists who stressed the opportunity to win benefits for the working class and those who saw in socialist displays of electoral strength (especially the great electoral victory of 1912) harbingers of a real struggle for power and not occasions for compromising the party by parliamentary horse trading. The former group, the reformists, were by 1913 often able to mobilize a majority in the party's Reichstag delegation; but the issue was far from settled before war broke out.

The party's attitude toward elections also revealed the tension between ideology and practice. Official party doctrine did not hold that the transition to socialism could be accomplished by means of a parliamentary majority; yet well before 1914 successful election campaigns had become a key element in the party's self-image of growing strength, and a great part of the party's energies were devoted to them. In most German states and municipalities the electoral system was carefully rigged to make sure that the Social Democrats could never win a parliamentary majority—most conspicuously in Prussia, where the SPD held only ten Diet seats in 1914. And although the Reichstag was elected by universal manhood suffrage, a mere parliamentary challenge was unlikely to topple the Bismarckian order. There were, however, orthodox Marxist arguments for full exploitation of such electoral opportunities as existed: the agitational possibilities of an election campaign, the opportunity to display the growing strength of the movement, the chance to use the parliamentary rostrum for propaganda, even the means provided of observing the nearing of the proletarian revolution and timing the party's actions accordingly.[15] Electoral agitation became, in fact, the most conspicuous and perhaps most strenuous of all the party's activities; among the duties of party officials it ranked with the growth and consolidation of party membership. Members of nearly all persuasions vigorously seconded the emphasis on electoral success, in which they took great pride.

The outspoken internationalism of the German Social Democrats provoked little disharmony in the pre-1914 period. The orthodox view was that German workers were more truly a part of the international social-

15. These ideas go back at least to Engels' 1895 preface to Marx's *The Class Struggles in France;* see Marx and Engels, *Selected Works,* 2 vols. (Moscow, 1962), I, 129–30.

ist and labor movement than of German society under the capitalist order. The ideological commitment was bolstered by certain practical aspirations: trade-union internationalism, for instance, which aimed at coordinating trade-union practice in matters of common interest; and above all prevention of war in Europe, a goal that was to be achieved somehow by the Workers' International. Whatever the various motives, participation in the Second Socialist International was a conspicuous part of the SPD's public life, without distinction of faction. The possible problems of such participation were lessened in that the International rarely took binding decisions and never attempted to enforce them; that its resolutions on policy questions commonly followed the lead of the German party; and that the SPD's organization, unity, and doctrinal orthodoxy were widely admired in the brother parties. German socialists were proud of their leading role in the International, and this pride had something to do with the intense involvement many felt in its idealism.

This schematic presentation of the condition of the SPD before 1914 makes it apparent that the party, for all its great achievements, existed in a curious state of suspension. Its traditions, and its desire not to lose the support of a sizable body of genuinely radicalized workers, had kept the party from committing itself to a purely gradualist policy of attempting to achieve socialism through practical reforms—a course rendered highly problematical in any event by the intransigence of the still un-shaken Bismarckian state. On the other hand, the vision of upheaval and total transformation, of a final confrontation with the existing powers of German society, was much weakened, not to say compromised, by the day-to-day practices of the socialist movement. While official doctrine continued to uphold this ideal, the notion of seizing power had never been given specific content applicable to the German situation; the indistinct future was left to take care of itself. Such fundamental ambiguities were of little concern to the many socialists interested only in the growth and unity of the party; indeed, they served these goals efficiently. They were profoundly disquieting, however, to many others in the party who believed that significant opportunities for reform, or for revolutionary preparation, were being missed, especially in the years just before the war. Ultimately they permitted the broad, orthodox center bloc of the party, the seat of unity and continuity, to pull apart in pursuit of different emphases within the established tradition. As a result, in 1914 there were, broadly speaking, four important factions within the SPD, each trying to fix the party to a future course embodying its own ideas.[16]

16. The following discussion is strongly influenced by Schorske's work. Though

The two extreme positions are the easiest to identify and had existed as factions for the longest time. The extreme right will be of little concern here. Consisting of a fairly small group of intellectuals known as revisionists, who held that violent social revolution was neither likely nor desirable and sought to adjust formal doctrine accordingly, and a much larger group called reformists, who were impatient with talk of revolution, indeed often with theory in general, and wished to commit the movement wholly to an active policy of reform, this fairly sizable right wing included many of the most prominent trade unionists and much of the official leadership of the party in South Germany. It represented the oldest of the continuing challenges to orthodoxy, having been the defiant object of official party disapproval since the early 1890's. Only in the last few years before the war, as the other extreme of the party came to worry the central leadership more, did the right wing begin to achieve a measure of respectability to go with its strong, if minority, power position.

The extreme left was smaller and, as a distinct faction, a newer phenomenon. It had separated itself from the orthodox center by stages. The process began about 1905 in reaction to the party's hesitant attitude to the idea of a general strike—and in particular to its concession to the conservative trade unions of virtual veto power—at a time when the general strike was coming to be regarded as the given revolutionary form for a mass socialist party. By 1910, the year of Rosa Luxemburg's definitive breach with Karl Kautsky, the emergence of a distinct left wing, usually called the left radicals, was quite clear. The group was not homogeneous; the Bremen left radicals, followers of Johann Knief, Karl Radek, and others, held different views from the group in Berlin, led mainly by Rosa Luxemburg; and Karl Liebknecht, the enfant terrible of the SPD's Reichstag delegation, held different views again. The wide dispersal of centers of left radical strength—Bremen, Berlin, Stuttgart— made cohesiveness difficult, and at the local level the extreme left often continued to function as part of a broader left-wing group. The adherents of the extreme left were distinguished, however, by their sense of urgency (a response to the general European malaise that preceded the outbreak of war); by their belief that the real business of the party was to foster a revolutionary spirit, to the exclusion if necessary of other traditional party functions; and by their dissatisfaction with the complacent, ponderous workings of the great party machine. They were in-

dated in some particulars, this book remains the most illuminating study of the origins of the wartime opposition and the later USPD in the factions of the prewar SPD.

tensely theoretical, bringing new life into German Marxist doctrine. At the same time they were active as agitators among the workers, whose role they saw as being to override the constricting, passive elements in the Social Democratic tradition and, in the not too distant future, to create a socialist society.

Between the two extremes lay the great middle bloc of the party, the so-called Marxist Center, comprising all those—the official leadership and the great mass of the rank and file—who were basically satisfied with the party, its traditions, and its practices, as they understood them. Naturally, a considerable range of views was possible under this heading. The Center customarily acted as a bloc in voting down the presumptions of either the right wing, which had presented important challenges at party congresses up to 1903 and occasionally thereafter, or the radical left wing, which comprised the principal opposition at some of the later congresses. Some issues tended to divide the bloc, however, and in the congresses from 1910 on the outlines of a possibly serious fissure were drawn. Although in retrospect the party's trend toward reformism may seem clear, this was by no means apparent, and was certainly not acceptable, to a sizable part of the Center for whom the traditions of Marxist defiance of the existing order were the very essence of the party. The heart of the revered leader August Bebel (if not always his practical policies) was with this group; his cochairman after 1911, Hugo Haase, certainly belonged to it; and the party's authoritative master in matters of doctrine, Karl Kautsky, was, even if he appeared to be weakening on some points, still its guiding star. The group stood, above all, for the spirit that had, in its members' eyes, made the party great and that guaranteed the party's role as the future midwife of socialism.

This broad grouping, which we may call the left Center, was accustomed to leading the party—indeed it identified itself with the party. Only after about 1910 did this group realize that it no longer had the party under its general control, that it would have to enter a factional struggle to impose its views. At about this time, too, while another large bloc of the Center was drifting slowly in the direction of moderation and accommodation with other parties and the government, the left Center was making its first timid movements in the other direction. Like the left radicals, the members of the left Center sensed—in an attenuated fashion and without apocalyptic expectations—the advent of new obligations and opportunities for the party. They endorsed the general strike as a party weapon even though they had no clear notion of its precise nature. They wanted the party to use mass action—including street demonstrations, even in defiance of the police—to force reform of the Prussian franchise. They tried to get the party to reinforce its internationalism

and antimilitarism, even if only verbally. But even when the left Center and the left radicals joined forces, in the Reichstag delegation's meetings or at party congresses, they usually found themselves outvoted. Similarly, even their combined efforts were not always enough to prevent small but symbolic inroads being made into the party tradition of separatism: despite opposition from the left, the party executive entered into an electoral agreement with the Progressive Party in 1912; and in the following year the Reichstag delegation supported a taxation bill.

The fourth grouping in the party, consisting of the more moderate part of the old Marxist Center, was hardly conscious of being a faction at all. If the left Center was the guardian of the party's rhetoric and symbolic practices, the right Center, though also subscribing in a general way to the party's formal ideals—its "official radicalism," as Rosenberg calls it[17]—stood for the tendencies growing out of its actual daily practice. The intraparty voting results indicated that the right Center occupied the middle ground, being able to form a majority either as part of the Center bloc—as it still did on many matters—or by combining with the right wing. The group's position in the bureaucracy and the party executive was strong, especially when, after Bebel's death in 1913, Friedrich Ebert became cochairman; and relations with the trade unions were good. Unless the left Center (or unexpected events) should somehow reverse recent trends in the party, it seemed in 1914 that the party's center of gravity, and probably its future, lay with the right Center.

The development of distinct factions in the SPD, and especially the divisions within the Center bloc, posed a challenge to the party's comfortable synthesis of reformist and revolutionary perspectives greater than any faced since that synthesis had received its elaboration at the turn of the century. The Center, guarantor of the party's continuity and cohesion, was falling apart; and if the right Center seemed to enjoy the more favorable position, greater support in the party machine, and possibly larger numbers, the left Center, with its eminent leaders and its command of so many of the party's orthodox arguments, was still a formidable force. To be sure, the bonds uniting the old partners of the Center were by no means severed at the start of 1914; and pride in party unity worked to discourage a serious breach. Nor were the factional alignments of 1914 necessarily permanent. Had war not broken out, resolution of the interfactional tensions might have been a slow process, and what the outcome might have been is hard to judge. The

17. Rosenberg, *Geschichte*, p. 18.

party was not granted a period of quiet, however, in which to work out its problems. A great war was about to begin.

The Impact of War

The greater part of the SPD was emotionally and intellectually unprepared for war. There was no doubt about the party's obligation to oppose the outbreak of war by all means at its disposal, and this it did in the last days of July 1914.[18] Its followers responded well, though not in a way that involved anything like a revolutionary threat—after all, nothing in the party's past suggested that it would or could attempt direct, illegal obstruction. But then, on July 31, the government ended opposition by declaring martial law and imposing censorship, and the following day war was declared; at this point the party entered uncharted territory.

Socialists had thought about what they must do during a war; but their thinking had resulted in several different and mutually inconsistent prescriptions, none of them precise. On the one hand, a 1907 resolution of the International obliged member parties "to intervene in favor of [the war's] speedy termination and with all their powers to utilize the economic and political crisis created by the war to rouse the masses and thereby to hasten the downfall of capitalist class rule."[19] Essentially contradicting this resolution, which did not distinguish among warring powers but attempted to set socialist parties equally against all governments making war, older socialist traditions suggested that the International collectively should take sides either against the most reactionary belligerents or (which was not necessarily the same thing) against the aggressive powers.[20] But another principle, not strictly a socialist ideal but permitted by prewar orthodoxy—the principle of defense of the nation—was embraced throughout Europe. Indeed, a dispassionate observer of the European socialist movement, and particularly of German and French movements, might have predicted that the principle of national defense, supported by ordinary patriotic emotions, would dominate the behavior of the parties when war came. A number of circumstances in Germany in August 1914 ensured that these motives would prevail.

First, the war was perceived by most German socialists as a war against Russia—against "Russian despotism," as the socialist declaration

---

18. Details in *Geschichte der deutschen Arbeiterbewegung: Chronik,* issued by the Institut für Marxismus-Leninismus beim Zentralkomitee der SED, 3 vols. (Berlin, 1965–67) (hereafter cited as *GdA: Chronik*), I, 286–87.

19. Text in James Joll, *The Second International, 1889–1914* (London, 1955), pp. 196–98.

20. Schorske, pp. 67–68 and 80–84.

in the Reichstag had it.[21] Early Russian mobilization sparked this idea, and clever news management by the German government during the crucial days encouraged it. Insofar as German socialists could accept this view it made their choice easy, for war against tsarist Russia had been sanctioned by their leaders from Marx onward as a kind of socialist crusade against reaction.[22] Second, the overwhelming majority of workers accepted the war as necessary at the outset, most supporting it warmly. This response rendered any notion of socialist action against the war purely theoretical, or at best a long-term prospect; moreover, a determinedly antipatriotic attitude by the party might seriously have endangered its standing with the working class. Finally, the government obviously stood ready to use its powers under martial law against the party if it attempted to obstruct the war effort. The movement as such, of course, could not be destroyed by government action, but the organization could be; and the party without the organization had become unthinkable to most Social Democrats.

Doubtless the motives of the Social Democratic leaders in the first days of August 1914 were mixed. Some of these men were moved especially by considerations of principle, some by concern for the future of the party, some by the patriotic emotions of the moment.[23] The overwhelming majority, however, decided to support the war effort. On August 3 the Reichstag delegation caucused and, after heated debate, voted by seventy-eight to fourteen to support the government's request for war credits.[24] The next day, in a formal session of the Reichstag, the senior chairman of the party, Hugo Haase (himself opposed to voting the credits), delivered the party's declaration explaining and qualifying its decision, which culminated in the ringing words: "Here we make

21. *Verhandlungen des Reichstages* (hereafter cited as *Reichstag*), vol. 306, p. 9. On the general problem of the SPD's initial decision see also A. Joseph Berlau, *The German Social Democratic Party, 1914–1921* (New York, 1949), pp. 70–75; Groh, ch. 7.

22. See Jürgen Kuczynski, *Der Ausbruch des ersten Weltkrieges und die deutsche Sozialdemokratie* (Berlin, 1957), pp. 70–77.

23. The problem of individual motivation has been seriously addressed only by Susanne Miller in "Zum dritten August 1914," *Archiv für Sozialgeschichte,* 4 (1964), 515–23; see also the interesting but scanty comments in Groh, pp. 678–81. Two men who voted for war credits in 1914 but later became Independent Social Democrats have left accounts of their motives: Wilhelm Dittmann, in his untitled memoirs (typescript in IISH Amsterdam), pp. 423 and 435; and Eduard Bernstein, "Entwicklungsgang eines Sozialisten," in *Die Volkswirtschaftslehre der Gegenwart in Selbstdarstellungen,* ed. Felix Meiner (Leipzig, 1924), pp. 45–46.

24. Meeting recorded in *Reichstagsfraktion,* II, 3–4, with numerous other relevant sources cited in the footnotes. For the names of the minority, not all of which are known with certainty because of conflicting sources, see *ibid.,* I, clxxxviii and cxc.

good what we have always emphasized: In the hour of danger we will not abandon our own Fatherland." Thereupon the party's deputies voted unanimously (as custom prescribed) for the proposed credits.[25]

Whatever the motives of August 3 and 4, in the months that followed support of the war effort became settled policy for a majority of the SPD leadership. Considerations of expediency—the desire not to risk alienating the party's electors—still played a part in this stand. So too did a kind of "unimaginative patriotism" on the part of the majority, which, although it only rarely became outright chauvinism, made it difficult for them to understand the attitudes of either foreign socialists or the SPD's own minority.[26] The majority also had a set of more or less reasoned beliefs to support its position: that Germany was fighting a defensive war; that the only real choice was between victory and defeat; and that Germany and the German workers must win rather than lose. In the face of overriding necessity, discussion of who started the war, or what the war aims of the Imperial government might be, was a luxury. Within the majority, most viewed the prospect of an annexationist peace settlement with grave misgivings and opposed the idea of making expansion a precondition for settlement—which could only prolong the war. In the latter part of the war, after the collapse of tsarism in Russia, the majority came to regard a compromise peace settlement, without victory or defeat, as possible and made it part of their program; but their overriding aim was still to avoid a German defeat at all costs. Their own indispensable contribution, as they saw it, was to keep the workers attached to the national cause, which in turn made a united national front imperative. To this end they repeated their symbolic action of voting war credits, whenever these were requested, throughout the war.

In the same spirit the party officially continued to observe the so-called civic truce (Burgfrieden) proclaimed at the outbreak of war. Under this truce partisan political activity was suspended; in a broader sense there was implicit agreement that potentially divisive issues would not be raised publicly, or at least not in an aggressive manner. Such restraint was accepted as a duty by the leaders of the socialist majority. They would not risk contributing to the disruption of the war effort and were, therefore, determined to avoid fostering dissatisfaction among the workers—and especially to avoid setting the workers against the government. Thus the SPD of the early war years was, in its externals, scarcely recognizable as the verbally aggressive party of the years before 1914.

25. *Reichstag,* vol. 306, pp. 8–9. Groh, pp. 694–95, examines the reasons why no one broke discipline.
26. The phrase is from Joll, p. 187.

The wholehearted endorsement of the united national front by so many leading socialists gave the party an unprecedented respectability, which in turn affected its relations with the governing circles of Germany.[27] The party began to be consulted before measures were introduced in the Reichstag; audiences with the chancellor became common. The Prussian government for the first time permitted a few Social Democrats to assume minor local government positions. To be sure, the "new orientation" expressed itself principally in the smoothing over of frictions and the handling of grievances; very little progressive legislation resulted from all the party's efforts (though the trade unions had more success) and no fundamental political reforms were achieved until the last, desperate weeks of the war. But even this marginal involvement with the government left its mark on the Social Democratic leadership. Slowly and undramatically the majority of the party's leaders became committed to seeking influence within existing institutions, whatever the disappointments and compromises involved, rather than pursuing the risky, perhaps speculative vision of a total change of system.[28] This commitment suited the prewar practice of these leaders in many respects; wartime patriotism and the opportunity to break through the barriers previously raised against Social Democracy now oriented them toward more or less standard political roles within the existing social order.

The effect of the war on the trade unions was just as pronounced. The unions promptly declared the suspension of all strike activity for the duration; indeed, this action was taken on August 2, before anyone knew what the party would do. The unions soon found themselves involved, too, in many new duties.[29] Starting with relief work—provision for the dependents of soldiers, later for their widows and orphans and for disabled veterans—they became an important adjunct to state and municipal authorities in the distribution of food in the cities; they acted as an intermediary between state and workers in improving working conditions for war production; they finally gained a voice in the overall control of war production through regular negotiation with management and the military.[30] The unions thus not only warmly supported the war effort but, by the middle of the war, were deeply involved in it.

27. For other consequences of the *Burgfrieden*, see Berlau, p. 76.
28. In effect, "the state ceased to be considered as an instrument of class struggle" (*ibid.*, p. 88). See the shrewd comments on this point (apparently by Emil Lederer) in the unsigned "Sozialpolitische Chronik" in *Archiv für Sozialwissenschaft und Sozialpolitik,* 39 (1914/15), 636–41, and 42 (1916/17), 334 and 336–37.
29. For surveys of union activities see Siegfried Nestriepke, *Die Gewerkschaftsbewegung,* 3 vols. (Stuttgart, 1920–21), II, 41–60; Heinz Joseph Varain, *Freie Gewerkschaften, Sozialdemokratie und Staat* (Düsseldorf, 1956), pp. 73–78.
30. Gerald D. Feldman's *Army, Industry and Labor in Germany, 1914–1918* (Princeton, 1966), takes this last point as a major theme.

These developments were important both in themselves and for the part they played in provoking a strong opposition movement within the SPD as the war dragged on. The opposition arose not only from dissatisfaction with the party's official policy toward the war and the war effort but also from fundamental objections to the civic truce, restiveness with the passivity of the party organization, and indignation at the increasing involvement of Social Democratic leaders in the workings of the state and the shift in attitudes such involvement implied. In other words, the general tendencies of the party were at least as important in creating an opposition movement as were differences over specific policies toward the war. This analysis is supported by a consistency in the prewar and wartime factional patterns, and especially (for our purposes) by the continuity of two of the factions: the left radicals, a grouping that carried over, with relatively little change in character, into the war period; and the more amorphous group surrounding the prominent leaders of the left Center, who were destined to become the true fathers of the USPD.[31]

In the emerging opposition the left radicals had a certain priority. They immediately saw the war as an outgrowth of imperialism and monopoly capitalism, and no other considerations mattered to them. As socialists had fought such evils in peacetime, so must they fight the same evils in a new guise; the circumstances might be altered, but in such a way as to intensify the class struggle, not attenuate or suspend it. This perspective was so self-evident to Karl Liebknecht, Rosa Luxemburg, and their associates that they could only view what had happened to the party in August 1914 as a virtual collapse or, as Arthur Rosenberg has put it, "an act of hara-kiri."[32] For them the SPD's war policy was not just a temporary disorder, an error that must be corrected, but an unforgivable treason against the socialist cause, a disaster marking the bankruptcy of the old party and its ideas. They had been critical for some time of the old, balanced, orthodox, rather passive traditions of class struggle and of the party's "fetishism of the organization," but they had not expected such a catastrophe. Now they repudiated the greater part of these traditions completely, saying that "the old program and the old party can no longer be the basis of our further activity, that the decisions of German party congresses taken before August 4, 1914, can

31. The opposition did not include substantial numbers of revisionists, as Arthur Rosenberg, *The Birth of the German Republic, 1871–1918* (London, 1931), pp. 118 and 121, and Berlau, pp. 66 and 146, mistakenly suppose. The men whom Berlau cites as "examples"—Eduard Bernstein, Kurt Eisner, and August Erdmann —are in fact the only revisionists among the scores of leading Independents whose prewar orientation is known.

32. Rosenberg, *Birth,* p. 119.

no longer provide the foundation for our new tasks."[33] The movement needed to be renewed from the ground up, starting with a new spirit among the masses that would force a transformation of ossified party institutions. This struggle—to be carried on in all European countries—would culminate in the creation of not only revitalized parties but also a new, more rigorous International, one capable of effective action in future European crises. And a hard struggle it would be, given that the left radicals had few sympathizers among the established leaders of the movement or its bureaucracy. Franz Mehring, summoning up the spirit of the days of the Anti-Socialist Law, proclaimed the slogan: "*With* the leaders if they will lead, *without* the leaders if they remain inactive, *in spite of* the leaders if they resist."[34]

As to the war itself, the left radicals offered only the most extreme of solutions: the capitalist order must be overthrown in the belligerent countries. There could of course be no question of joining the national defense; for the working class of each country, "the main enemy is at home!"[35] The group dismissed the notion of a compromise peace settlement among the cutthroat capitalist powers—the program of the left Center—as illusory; even if it were achieved, such a peace would not alter the intensified capitalist exploitation the left radicals foresaw for all countries after the war. The only way out was insurrection. This goal, in the early part of the war, was not so much a real vision as an attempt to restore to the proletariat a conception of its own independent initiative; the program was advanced "not as a political expression of wants but as a process of political stimulation."[36] The idea of revolution to end the war could not have more than abstract reality even for the extreme left until the first demonstration strikes of 1916, and not for most other radical militants until the Russian revolution of March 1917. Until then the antiwar policies of the left radical movement had the character of nothing more than vehement protest.

Radical protest had its place in Germany during the war, and the left radicals found support among small but active cadres of party functionaries and sympathy among a broader section of the rank and file. Not only left radicals could admire the courage of the group's leaders,

33. Fritz Heckert in USPD *Parteitag,* April 1917, p. 61. (All published proceedings of conferences and congresses are cited in this short form; full particulars are given in the Sources at the end of the book.)
34. New Year's greeting to the Independent Labour Party, in *Labour Leader,* Dec. 31, 1914.
35. "Der Hauptfeind steht im eigenen Land!" leaflet by Liebknecht reprinted in Karl Liebknecht, *Gesammelte Reden und Schriften,* 9 vols. (Berlin, 1958–71), VIII, 225–32.
36. J. P. Nettl, *Rosa Luxemburg,* 2 vols. (London, 1966), II, 680.

most particularly that of Karl Liebknecht, whose single-minded attempt to use the Reichstag as an agitational forum was among the best-known political phenomena of the war and whose imprisonment in May 1916 made him the outstanding martyr of the socialist left. The left radicals were able to convert such sympathies into a limited amount of local organizational strength. Ultimately, however, their ideas and practices were too extreme to produce the hoped-for resonance in the German labor movement. When, in time, the left centrist opposition began to express itself with the openness that had earlier been the preserve of the left radicals, it was able to neutralize much of the latter's early popularity. Even among most Independent Socialists—to say nothing of the socialists further to the right—the far left found themselves finally with the reputation, not of pioneers, but of reckless adventurers.

The bulk of the opposition in the early part of the war, led by parliamentarians, party officials, and journalists of the old left Center, had a sharply different orientation. Like the left radicals, left centrists had a conception of the party and of themselves as socialists that was tied to the idea of the class struggle, an enduring antagonism to the existing order, and a sense of separateness within that order. But the Marxist radicalism of the moderate section of the opposition drew its inspiration from the past, not from innovative theories of mass action or, still less, any millenarian sense of the approach of the socialist revolution. The leaders were party men, devoted to the movement as expressed in the party—particularly to the Marxist spirit and principles that they felt to be the heart of the party, but also to the party's auxiliary goals, its gradualist methods, and its massive organizational achievement. They had been out of sympathy with some of the party's policies before the war and disliked its war policies even more; but, unlike the left radicals, they did not see these differences as requiring a radical break with the past or a complete reordering of the party's priorities. They fought for a restoration rather than a revolution in party affairs. But ultimately they were willing to risk a break rather than abandon their own convictions about what the SPD was and must continue to be.

The issue of support for the war effort, the ostensible point of conflict between the party's majority and minority, was thus part of a struggle for the soul of the movement. It was also a very real and emotional issue in its own right. About every four months the government would bring to the Reichstag a request for war credits. By old Social Democratic tradition a vote of funds was equivalent to a vote of confidence in the government; and for the stricter Marxists, such as Haase, the Imperial government could under no circumstances deserve such a vote of confidence. For others of the minority, as for many in the ma-

jority, the issue was whether Germany was engaged in a necessary or justifiable war that socialists could support. If the war was to be regarded as defensive in any meaningful sense, an assurance was needed that the government had not provoked it, had no war aims other than the maintenance of Germany's present frontiers, and was doing its best to secure promptly a peace that would be just and therefore lasting. At first, many succumbed to the pressure to believe that Germany was innocent and Russia the aggressor; at least thirteen, and probably seventeen, of the twenty-six deputies who later joined the USPD's Reichstag delegation favored supporting the war effort in August 1914.[37] But socialists who, for other reasons, tended to be suspicious of the government could not be satisfied for long. Indications that the Reich was waging a war of aggrandizement began to accumulate. Doubts about the origins of the war also spread; by the end of the war most Independent Socialists believed that the German government was largely responsible for its start. As for ending the fighting, the Berlin government, despite its advantageous military position, seemed to be making no serious attempts to negotiate a peace. The conviction grew among the opposition that the war had reached a military and diplomatic stalemate, that the belligerent powers, unable to achieve outright victory, were paralyzed by their imperialist war aims and unable to take any constructive steps toward peace.

The minority thus came to believe that mobilizing the masses to put pressure on the government not only held no dangers for the national cause but was necessary in the best interests of all nations, Germany included. A lasting settlement, they believed, could only be found through an agreement based on the status quo ante bellum; frontiers should be changed, if at all, only by the exercise of self-determination by the peoples concerned; and the settlement should be strengthened by new international conventions, in particular by courts of arbitration.[38] International socialism's task was to hold high the banner of international understanding and induce, or if necessary force, the belligerent governments to accept such a peace.

Thus, after an initial period of hesitation, the minority recalled their

37. See the list in *Reichstagsfraktion*, I, clxxxviii; the sources conflict, and while I have regarded Liebknecht's list as the most reliable the matter is not certain. On the strength of statements in *Volksblatt für Halle und den Saalkreis* (hereafter cited as *Volksblatt* [Halle]), Nov. 10, 1917, Adolf Albrecht may be classified as definitely opposing the voting of credits in August 1914.

38. This program was elaborated most fully in preparation for the abortive Stockholm conference of the International in 1917 and may be found in *Reichstag*, vol. 310, pp. 3590–92. See also the USPD's counterresolution to the Peace Resolution of July 1917, *ibid.*, vol. 321, p. 1757.

obligation "to intervene in favor of [the war's] speedy termination." After re-establishing their credentials (severely damaged in foreign eyes by the SPD's war policies) as leaders of the International, they hoped to take the lead in reviving the moribund institutions of the International as instruments of peace. How the International was to perform this function was far from clear given that its prewar role had been principally symbolic, or at best hortatory, and that no machinery existed for coordinating members' policies. The opposition agreed, however, that the antiwar parties and minorities of all countries must assert their solidarity by collaborating. At international conferences in Zimmerwald (September 1915) and Kienthal (April 1916), the opposition launched efforts for international cooperation against the war, making this activity a central part of its program.

Ultimately, however, the opposition's program to end the war through international action, however urgently propagated, was but an expressive fiction—just as the left radicals' insistence that the war could only be ended by proletarian revolution and the majority's expressed belief in the honest intentions of the German government were fictions.[39] All served to justify political orientations based on divergent conceptions of the proper mission of the German socialist movement. The specific, unavoidable issues of wartime placed an unremitting strain on socialists, forcing many into choices they would probably have preferred to avoid and hardening the dividing lines between factions. The end result was schism.

Schism

The break did not occur, however, until 1917, for schism was something few German socialists could contemplate lightly. In retrospect, events between August 1914 and April 1917 can be seen as stages in the breakup of the party, as the increasingly unmanageable divergence of goals, intensified by the war, led to a breach along the obvious line of fissure—that dividing the Marxist Center into its right and left wings. At the time, socialists, insofar as they could sense the prospect of division, felt it to be unnatural rather than unavoidable, a severe threat to their conception of the movement. As for the socialist left, then experiencing in its challenge to Imperial Germany a heroic period, the story of the developing schism is one of tactical camouflage, worry, and indecision—and ultimately of desperation and impotent fury. Eighteen

39. As late as July 3, 1918, Scheidemann said in the Reichstag, "There has been no government in Germany during the war which has not shared our [the SPD's] views almost completely"; *ibid.*, vol. 313, p. 5708.

months had passed before the factional conflict permeated the party organization, another bitter year before the breach was irremediable.

One reason for the delay lay in the initial collapse of the party's internal life. Wartime conditions, and more particularly the suspension of partisan activity, had a drastic impact on the SPD's party life. At the local level, it was "almost completely extinguished" and recovered only slowly.[40] For one thing, the loss of party members to military call-up was startlingly high; by September 1914 some 33.8 percent of the national membership had been called up, and by March 1916 party membership was down by 60 percent, or over 650,000, from the prewar level, the armed services being primarily responsible for the decline.[41] Among those who remained enthusiasm for party work was much diminished at first, and such meetings as were held tended to be poorly attended. Preoccupation with the war was doubtless the principal reason;[42] but in any case the party, constrained by the civic truce and the state of siege, could offer little to hold its following beyond appeals to loyalty. The press was subdued, public assemblies infrequent and tame; elections, normally one of the party's major functions, were suspended (except for by-elections and some municipal elections) for the duration of the war; and wherever socialists did show an inclination to resume their customary agitation the military authorities were quick to ban assemblies or suspend party newspapers. The air at the middle and lower levels of party organization during the first years of the war was, accordingly, predominantly one of retrenchment, the atmosphere of a holding operation.

Well into 1915, leading Social Democrats who opposed official party policy showed remarkable self-restraint. Concerned with unity, they

40. Berlin police report of August 26, 1914, DZA Merseburg, Rep. 77 Tit. 332r Nr. 126, p. 4. For conditions in Bremen see Erhard Lucas, *Die Sozialdemokratie in Bremen während des ersten Weltkrieges* (Bremen, 1969), pp. 35–36, for the cities of the lower Rhineland, Henri Walther and Dieter Engelmann, "Zur Linksentwicklung der Arbeiterbewegung im Rhein-Ruhrgebiet unter besonderer Berücksichtigung der Herausbildung der USPD und der Entwicklung ihres linken Flügels vom Ausbruch des 1. Weltkrieges bis zum Heidelberger Parteitag der KPD und dem Leipziger Parteitag der USPD (Juli/August 1914–Dezember 1919)," 3 vols. (Ph.D. dissertation, University of Leipzig, 1965), I, 55–56.

41. *Mitteilungs-Blatt des Verbandes der sozialdemokratischen Wahlvereine Berlins und Umgegend* (hereafter cited as *Mitteilungs-Blatt*), Oct. 14, 1914; SPD *Parteitag,* Oct. 1917, p. 10.

42. During the first year of the war the working-class districts of Berlin celebrated the birthdays of the kaiserin and kaiser (which was unprecedented), as well as military victories, with displays of flags: police reports in DZA Merseburg, Rep. 77 Tit. 332r Nr. 126, pp. 6, 7, 25, 56, and 86; Kurt Koszyk, *Zwischen Kaiserreich und Diktatur: Die sozialdemokratische Presse von 1914 bis 1933* (Heidelberg, 1958), pp. 62–63.

seem to have sensed from the start that the issues raised by the war
could disrupt the party.[43] They refrained at first, therefore, from actively propagating their views. Like almost everyone else, they expected
the war to be short; once it was over, the conflict over principle and
propriety could be fought out in a calmer atmosphere and without interference from the censors. In the meantime their activity, such as it was,
was virtually private, being conducted in limited discussion groups or
conventicles and within the Reichstag delegation.[44] No display of dissatisfaction was made for nearly a year in the party publications controlled by the opposition—such as *Vorwärts* in Berlin or Karl Kautsky's
influential *Neue Zeit*—except in the most indirect fashion, or in the
Reichstag until the growing minority within the delegation abstained
from the third vote of war credits in March 1915. Even the most radical
left centrists—those who, like Georg Ledebour of Berlin and Robert
Dissmann of Frankfurt on Main, launched immediately into energetic
agitation and organization—confined their efforts to party circles. The
left radicals were not held back by scruple, but their following was small
and their work necessarily slow, dangerous, and largely underground,
with only rare moments of public drama such as Karl Liebknecht's lone
vote against war credits in the Reichstag in December 1914. The public
at large, and even much of the party, could be only vaguely aware of
the undercurrent of dissent.

By the spring of 1915, however, circumstances were forcing the minority to take a more active line. For one thing, the party opposition
was growing, spurred on by rank-and-file restiveness with wartime
conditions and by the evidence of Germany's annexationist aims; as
Haase remarked, referring to the party declaration of August 4, 1914,
"We declared ourselves then against a war of conquest, today we have
that war."[45] At the same time the leaders of the moderate opposition

43. See, for instance, Kautsky's views, in *Neue Zeit*, Aug. 21, 1914, p. 846, and
Die Internationalität und der Krieg (Berlin, 1915), pp. 2–5.
44. On the internal party controversy during 1914 and 1915, which is relatively
well known and will not be treated extensively here, see the classic memoirs, such
as Philipp Scheidemann, *Der Zusammenbruch* (Berlin, 1921) and *Memoiren eines
Sozialdemokraten*, 2 vols. (Dresden, 1928), and Karl Liebknecht, *Klassenkampf
gegen den Krieg* (Berlin [1919]); Dittmann memoirs, which incorporate also his
minutes on the meetings of the Reichstag delegation; and the documentation in
sources such as Prager and *Reichstagsfraktion*. There is a concise secondary account in A. J. Ryder, *The German Revolution of 1918: A Study of German Socialism in War and Revolt* (Cambridge, 1967), pp. 48–58.
45. Quoted in Dittmann memoirs, p. 629; see also the minutes on the debates on
annexationism in the Reichstag delegation in May, *ibid.*, pp. 544–68. For the
sources of popular unrest see the opening section of the following chapter. The
gradual spread of opposition can be seen in the number of later Independent Social-

felt themselves squeezed between what Kautsky later called "the ruthless elements on the right and left," while the attitude they themselves regarded as the sole correct one for the party was finding no voice at all.[46] On the one side the party leadership was deeply committed to the patriotic cause, and through it to accommodation with the existing political order—indeed, many of the party's most influential revisionists were consciously attempting to ensure that the wartime direction of the party's policies should become a permanent commitment to gradualism.[47] On the other side, the left radicals were enjoying a clear field, largely because of the quiescence of the moderate opposition. Left centrists might ally themselves with the far left on occasion, and were accustomed to defending it from the hostility of the party's right wing, but they did not approve of either its ideas or its tactics. Left radicals were too absolutist in their approach to the war issue, too abrupt in their declaration of the death of the old International, too radical in their prescriptions for reconstructing the party, and above all too reckless of party unity in their single-minded pursuit of their goals.[48] Even so radical a socialist as Ledebour found Liebknecht's impetuosity too much to accept and quarreled bitterly with him (not for the last time) in November 1914.[49] Yet disaffected party militants had no one to turn to except the left radicals, who accordingly gained greatly in prestige. With the ranks of the discontented in the party swelling it would have been folly for the moderates to leave them to the agitation of the extremists. The more hesitant part of the opposition had to act.

The dam burst in June 1915. First came an aggressively critical petition to the party executive on June 9, sponsored not only by the regulars of Liebknecht's circle but also by such figures as Ledebour, Joseph Herzfeld, and Heinrich Ströbel from the radical part of the left Center and bearing the signatures of nearly a thousand officials and functionaries of the labor movement.[50] On June 21 the *Leipziger Volkszeitung*

ists in the Reichstag delegation who did not join the movement against war credits until March 1915 (Dittmann, Simon, Zubeil), August 1915 (Brandes, Büchner, Cohn, Erdmann, Raute, Wurm), or even December 1915 (Hüttmann, Jäckel, Ryssel).

46. Letter from Kautsky to Victor Adler, Feb. 28, 1917, in Victor Adler, *Briefwechsel mit August Bebel und Karl Kautsky* (Vienna, 1954), p. 635.

47. See, for instance, *Das Kriegstagebuch des Reichstagsabgeordneten Eduard David 1914 bis 1918*, ed. Susanne Miller with Erich Matthias (Düsseldorf, 1966).

48. A typical example of left centrist disapproval of left radical efforts to organize themselves separately within the party is the resolution of the Berlin party leadership in *Mitteilungs-Blatt*, June 9, 1915.

49. Liebknecht, *Klassenkampf*, p. 90.

50. Text in *Dokumente und Materialien zur Geschichte der deutschen Arbeiterbewegung*, issued by the Institut für Marxismus-Leninismus beim Zentralkomitee

carried a milder yet inherently more dramatic document: the manifesto, "The Need of the Hour," by the party's senior chairman and two most respected theorists, Haase, Kautsky, and Bernstein.[51] Both were circulated widely as handbills, and their publication was followed by bitter debate at the upper levels of the party and in the party press, which finally threw off its restraint. From this point, the dispute in the leadership about the party's future was conducted in the open.

There were no immediate organizational consequences, not even in the Reichstag delegation, which maintained its outward unity (apart from the inconspicuous abstentions of the minority on war credits bills) for another six months. All recognized that a public division in the delegation would pose a real threat of schism in the party; and the restive minority—which numbered thirty-six by August, or just under a third of the total—could hope to capture control of the delegation in time. Yet many in the minority could not be easy in their consciences, or in their relations with their constituents, as long as they held back from the important gesture of voting against the government. Nor could they carry through their program of consolidating the opposition around the left centrist position (in contrast to the left radical position) as long as they appeared halfhearted to the radical part of the rank and file. Kautsky helped some over their dilemma with a theoretical rationale for breaking discipline, published in *Neue Zeit*.[52] Others were no doubt moved more by direct pressure from restive party militants; it was surely no accident that ten of the first eighteen left centrist deputies to break away lived in Berlin, where the local organizations were strongly opposed to the party leadership, or that others of the eighteen had such radical constituencies as Remscheid and Gotha to deal with.[53] Events in

---

der SED, series 2, vols. 1–3, and vol. 7 (no series) (Berlin, 1957–58, 1966) (hereafter cited as *Dokumente und Materialien*), I, 169–85. On the background see Heinz Wohlgemuth, *Die Entstehung der Kommunistischen Partei Deutschlands 1914 bis 1918: Ueberblick* (Berlin, 1968), pp. 107–8.

51. "Das Gebot der Stunde," text in Prager, pp. 72–74. On the background see letter from Bernstein to Edmund Fischer, June 26, 1915, in the Edmund Fischer papers (DZA Potsdam), 1, p. 51; Bernstein, "Der Riss in der Sozialdemokratie," *Die Zukunft*, April 21, 1917, p. 71; Dittmann memoirs, p. 576. A good discussion of its impact is contained in Walther and Engelmann, I, 93–104.

52. Issues of Oct. 29 and Nov. 5, 1915.

53. Büchner, Ledebour, Stadthagen, and Zubeil represented Berlin constituencies, while Bernstein, Cohn, Haase, Herzfeld, Kunert, and Wurm lived there while representing constituencies elsewhere (see Appendix 2). In at least two cases pressure from the deputy's constituency is demonstrable: for Zubeil, see StA Potsdam, Pr. Br. Rep. 30 Berlin C Polizeipräsidium, Tit. 95 Sekt. 7 Lit. T Nr. 1, vol. 1, p. 296, and vol. 2, pp. 192–93; for Ryssel, see Kurt Schneider, "Der politisch-ideologische Differenzierungsprozess in der Leipziger Arbeiterbewegung während des ersten Weltkrieges" (Ph.D. dissertation, University of Leipzig, 1964), pp. 131–32.

the delegation meetings and the plenum early in December precipitated matters; the minority at this time felt cut off from influence in the delegation's decisions and betrayed by the majority's spokesmen.[54] The culmination came on December 21, when, after forty-four delegation members (40 percent of the total) had voted against war credits in the party's private deliberations, seventeen of them, instead of leaving the Reichstag chamber before the vote, remained to join the left radicals Liebknecht and Otto Rühle in voting against the war credits bill, giving a declaration to justify their action.[55]

The actual division into two socialist Reichstag delegations, though clearly foreshadowed in December, came only three months later, on March 24, 1916, when eighteen members, after defying discipline once again, were expelled from the SPD delegation and formed the Social Democratic Alliance (SAG); (Liebknecht and Rühle, expelled two months earlier, remained aloof).[56] This development was the last critical step in the open separation of majority and minority at the very top of the party, though by no means the end of what was ultimately a much more serious, though less obvious, struggle for the allegiance of the party's organization and following. Early in 1916, as the various party organizations passed resolutions for or against the minority's actions in the Reichstag, the opposition's efforts to win the party over to its views were still in an early stage.

These efforts had begun to be widely felt in the party's lower reaches nearly a year earlier, in fact as soon as the opposition received the needed leadership from the previously hesitant left centrists in the late spring of 1915. At that time the district executive of the powerful Lower Rhineland district (including Düsseldorf, Essen, and Elberfeld-Barmen) came out in support of the opposition in a sharply worded open letter to the party executive; the important Leipzig party backed the stand of its Reichstag deputy, Friedrich Geyer; and other district and local organi-

54. The critical moment came when the minority was denied a speaker in a foreign policy debate in the plenum and the speaker for the majority allowed a highly questionable statement by the chancellor to pass unchallenged. For the effect of this incident on the decision of a part of the minority to break discipline, see Dittmann memoirs, pp. 673–75 (including the text of a handbill put out by the minority); *Die Bildung der Sozialdemokratischen Arbeitsgemeinschaft* (n.p. [1916]), pp. 6–11; Bernstein, "Der Riss," p. 73; *Hugo Haase: Sein Leben und Wirken,* ed. Ernst Haase (Berlin, n.d.), pp. 231–32.

55. *Reichstag,* vol. 306, pp. 507–8. Bernstein, who missed the vote through illness, associated himself with the group as its eighteenth member. The eighteen were identical with the original members of the SAG, as given in Appendix 2.

56. The events of March 24 are recounted by the two sides in *Bildung der Sozialdemokratischen Arbeitsgemeinschaft,* esp. pp. 14–15, and *Material zur Fraktionsspaltung* (Berlin, 1916), esp. pp. 11–15. See also Dittmann memoirs, pp. 743–49. On Liebknecht's attitude see *Dokumente und Materialien,* I, 336–37.

zations followed suit.[57] Opposition speakers and newspapers were no longer hindered by scruple from agitating against the increasingly unpopular state of siege and the government's management of food supplies, and the agitation helped consolidate opposition support among the workers—insofar as the military governors allowed them to reach the workers at all. At the same time, as they resumed their international connections the dissidents began to receive psychological support from abroad, starting at the conference at Zimmerwald (Switzerland) in September 1915.[58] A majority of the delegates at the Zimmerwald conference represented unofficial party minorities; the delegations were arbitrary in composition, and the resolutions and meetings were little publicized because of censorship. Yet this conference, and its successor at Kienthal in April 1916, gave color at last to the minority's ideal of upholding international socialism during the war. The opposition thereby gained impetus as it began to organize itself.

But if the ponderous, still-cautious left centrist opposition was now in motion, the left radicals, and especially the Liebknecht-Luxemburg faction whom from this point we may call the Spartacists, were still the most vigorous wing of the opposition.[59] They were, in fact, at the peak of their activity and influence in 1916 and early 1917. They had put their advantage as the first outspoken opponents of the war to good use, building themselves strong positions in the party organizations in Stuttgart, Braunschweig, and parts of Berlin (especially the Teltow-Beeskow organization) and achieving significant minority positions in Düsseldorf, Leipzig, and elsewhere. Spartacist influence was pre-eminent among the antiwar youth, thanks in part to the special interest of Liebknecht and others in youth work. The group enjoyed outstanding agitational and

57. For the Lower Rhineland see leaflet in ASD Bonn, Collection Flugblätter 7; for Leipzig, see police report in StA Dresden, Kreishauptmannschaft Leipzig 2527h, pp. 96–97 and 101. For a resolution of the Braunschweig district executive, see *Volksblatt* (Halle), July 7, 1915; a Delphic notice in the same issue of this paper suggests that the Halle district executive had adopted a similar resolution but was unable to get it past the censor.

58. The most satisfactory account of the so-called Zimmerwald movement is still Merle Fainsod, *International Socialism and the World War* (Cambridge, Mass., 1935); see also the extensive documentation printed in Olga Hess Gankin and H. H. Fischer, ed., *The Bolsheviks and the World War: The Origin of the Third International* (Stanford, 1940), and Horst Lademacher, ed., *Die Zimmerwalder Bewegung*, 2 vols. (The Hague, 1967).

59. Other left radical factions enjoyed a certain prominence in Dresden, Hamburg, and, above all, Bremen, where they controlled the constituency organization. We shall be primarily concerned here, however, with the Spartacists (so called after the "Spartacus Letters" they issued periodically), the most numerous and widely distributed faction, for they were the left radicals who eventually entered the USPD; they also supplied the early leadership of the Communist Party.

theoretical leadership and had an impressive output of illegal publications. Early in 1916 the far left consolidated its organization and doctrine through national conferences in January and March and a national youth conference in April.[60] The actual number of left radicals may have been small, especially among the leading cadres of the SPD, but the group's influence and potential for growth in these months were considerable.

During the spring of 1916 the struggle for dominance within the opposition was therefore sharp. Immediately after the Reichstag vote of December 1915 the Haase-Ledebour group began to present itself as the true focus of antiwar opposition, only to meet with vigorous objection from the Spartacists, to whom the opposition of the "December men of 1915" appeared belated, still halfhearted, and based on an uncertain theoretical understanding of the war.[61] At this point the informal alliance of the more radical non-Spartacists with the Liebknecht group (in effect since June 1915) broke up, and sharp controversy ensued. In order to assert itself effectively, the moderate opposition turned for a time to illegal publications of its own, at least in Berlin.[62] At the outset the most emphasized point of difference concerned the future of the International, the moderates advocating the centering of antiwar action on what was left of the International, while the Spartacists, in effect, called for a new International combining only the truly revolutionary forces of socialism.[63] Later, other issues became more prominent; the Spartacists demanded, for example, that local organizations should cut off dues payments to the party executive as a demonstration against the latter's misuse of its powers, a gesture that the moderates saw as having little meaning and as likely to lead to schism in the organization.[64] Behind all surface issues, however, lay an organizational conflict; the Spartacists were determined not to sacrifice their independence of action and propaganda to a group they did not trust, while the moderates were exasperated at the refusal of

60. Wohlgemuth, pp. 139–45, 151–57, and 166–68.
61. Liebknecht, *Klassenkampf*, pp. 91–92; *Spartakusbriefe*, vol. I (Berlin, 1926), pp. xi (Meyer's introduction), 64–67, 87–88, 99, and 110.
62. A series of illegal pamphlets, appearing approximately every month, began with *Lose Blätter* on March 18, 1916, and ended in July with the arrest of the printer and the two prominent Berlin party officials who had been responsible for them (one of whom was Emil Eichhorn); see IML Berlin, Reichskanzlei 8/8, p. 72. Illegal publications of left centrist origin were not common, and the *Lose Blätter* series is the outstanding instance.
63. See the Spartacist *Leitsätze* in *Spartakusbriefe* (1926 ed.), pp. 83–86, and the answering handbill of the moderates in Lademacher, II, 452–56; Robert Wheeler, "The Independent Social Democratic Party and the Internationals: An Examination of Socialist Internationalism in Germany 1915 to 1923" (Ph.D. dissertation, University of Pittsburgh, 1970), pp. 23–29.
64. *Spartakusbriefe* (1926 ed.), p. 98.

the far left to take their place as disciplined members of a united opposition bloc.[65]

The result of the struggle within the opposition was, in the long run, a kind of victory for the SAG and the relatively moderate line. To be sure, the attempt to assimilate the forces of the far left to the moderate position, or at least to bring them to accept the discipline of majority votes within the opposition, was a failure; and the left radicals also continued to hold those organizational positions they had already captured. Elsewhere, however, the growth of working-class dissatisfaction with the war during 1916 and 1917 tended to work to the benefit of other forces— the left centrists, with their far greater organizational resources and greater access to the press, and the new factory-based opposition groups;[66] in the mass opposition then coalescing the Spartacists were more admired than followed. The Spartacists were especially vulnerable, too, to repressive action. In the latter half of the war almost all their leaders spent time in jail, Liebknecht and Luxemburg continuously; and nearly all their legal publications, including all the sympathizing daily papers, were lost to seizure by the party majority or suppression by the police. These losses were serious; they made of the Spartacists an almost wholly underground faction, save where the group already had a foothold in the local organization. Theirs was a dangerous existence, and one that made it difficult for them to be heard by the workers. The benefit accrued to the more cautious and respectable SAG.

The most important of the SAG victories over the Spartacists in this period came at the general assembly of the Greater Berlin party in June 1916, when the Spartacist following proved far less numerous than had been feared.[67] On the same occasion the opposition, cooperating for the purpose, turned out the old, promajority leadership of the Greater Berlin

65. See, for instance, Liebknecht, *Klassenkampf,* pp. 91–92; the handbill by Ledebour and Adolph Hoffmann, "Die Differenzen in der Opposition," reprinted in *Aus Flugschriften und Flugblättern der Parteiopposition* (n.p., n.d.), pp. 4–6; letter from Mehring to Henke, June 15, 1916, in Alfred Henke papers (ASD Bonn), I, item 32. On the original point of conflict, whether the left radicals might have separate representation in the councils of the Zimmerwald movement, see Lademacher, II, 452–56.

66. This phenomenon and its importance for the opposition are discussed in the following chapter.

67. On this victory see the letters from Haase to Dittmann, July 26, 1916, in Dittmann memoirs, pp. 770–72; from Haase to Alfred Gottschalk, July 2, 1916, in *Hugo Haase,* pp. 123–25; and from Ledebour to Dittmann, July 7, 1916, in the Wilhelm Dittmann papers (ASD Bonn), Mappe: Photokopien von Briefen, vor 1918, I, item 85. The background is given in Manfred Kitze, "Die Berliner Arbeiterbewegung vom Ausbruch des ersten Weltkrieges bis zur Grossen Sozialistischen Oktoberrevolution unter dem Gesichtspunkt ihrer Linksentwicklung in den Wahlvereinen" (Ph.D. dissertation, University of Halle-Wittenberg, 1966).

organization with ease. This struggle against the party majority was of course the main struggle. Most often victory over the majority was much harder to achieve than in Berlin.

The opposition's immediate goal was to win over a majority of the party to its view, or, in more practical terms, to win control of enough local organizations to be sure of a majority at the next party congress. The contest for control of the local organizations was one in which the combined opposition—the SAG, the left radicals, and the more reserved opposition (those whose leaders remained in the SPD Reichstag delegation)—could hope to do fairly well. Indeed, in June 1916, Emil Eichhorn, a well-informed observer, calculated that if all the constituency organizations believed to sympathize with the opposition were to send united delegations to a party congress these delegates would amount to a majority.[68] The division of the factions at the party conference in September bore out most of his calculations, even though, for technical reasons, the opposition mustered only 118 delegates to the party executive's 182.[69] This result at least dispelled the impression of some party leaders that the opposition was a mere clique. Indeed, it gave some plausibility to the minority's ambition to become a majority in the party.

But this perspective had two serious defects. First, the opposition was divided; a significant part of it, headed by some twenty-three members of the remaining SPD Reichstag delegation, was not prepared to go as far as the SAG in organizing separately for their cause. Influential men, including Adolf Braun of the Northern Bavarian organization and Paul Reisshaus of the Thuringian organization, voted with the minority but had no intention of risking a break with the party majority. Second, the attempt to gain dominance over the party through control of its grass-roots, democratic aspects came up against the great weight of entrenched bureaucratic interests. The party executive was a committed party to the dispute, the more so since Haase had been forced to resign in March 1916;[70] it had the loyal support of all but about ten of the thirty-odd members of the party committee, and of a similar proportion of the district secretaries (in many cases the same persons).[71] Even the local party

68. DZA Potsdam, RMdI 13581, pp. 86–87.

69. See the delegate list and the results of the roll-call vote in SPD *Reichskonferenz*, Sept. 1916; and Hans Block's article in *Sozialistische Auslandspolitik,* Sept. 27, 1916, esp. pp. 1–2.

70. Within the twelve-man executive Haase had the support of only secretary Luise Zietz, who concerned herself mainly with women's affairs, and associate member Robert Wengels, a popular but not influential figure in the party. These two did not resign until February 1917.

71. At the meeting in January 1917 that in effect expelled the minority, ten members of the party committee voted against the party executive, and only seven

secretaries were generally more conservative than the functionaries of their organizations, and so were the trade-union officials; these people wielded measurable influence. As of the summer of 1916 the bureaucracy had hardly begun to bring its weight to bear. It did so now.

The most bitter field of conflict between the opposition and the forces of the party executive soon came to be control of the party press. At the beginning of 1916 the opposition could express its views in about twenty-three newspapers, not counting papers like those in Nuremburg and Essen that tried to mediate between the factions; by the time of the foundation of the USPD, in April 1917, control of seven of these had passed into the hands of the majority, after a bitter local crisis in each case. The precedent was the case of Stuttgart, where in November 1914 the left radical editors had been forced out (leading to a breach in the Württemberg party organization, the first anywhere in Germany).[72] On that occasion the conservative state executive had acted; in 1916 and 1917 it was most commonly the party executive itself that intervened, often by using the power that past financing gave it over the business side of press operations. The first to fall, in April 1916, were the editors of the Duisburg paper, left radicals who had been advocating starving the party executive of dues revenue.[73] In December the Bremen paper was brought under control when its two left radical editors were dismissed and its two left centrist editors (one of them Alfred Henke) were isolated in an editorial board controlled by the majority.[74] In February 1917 the oppositional editors of the Elberfeld and Königsberg papers were removed from their posts; in April the young Curt Geyer was dismissed as editor-in-chief of the Würzburg paper, while the left radicals lost their last outpost in the daily press when the Braunschweig paper passed into majority hands.[75] But the most spectacular and bitter loss was that of *Vorwärts* itself, in October 1916.[76] The installation of an editor-in-chief from the party executive (Hermann Müller) followed an ultimatum from the censor, but the affair developed in such a way as to leave the minority-controlled

of these belonged to the committed minority that formed the USPD; see *Mitteilungs-Blatt*, Jan. 28, 1917.

72. Wilhelm Keil, *Erlebnisse eines Sozialdemokraten*, 2 vols. (Stuttgart, 1947–48), I, 306–22; Koszyk, pp. 48–54.

73. Walther and Engelmann, I, 128–36.

74. Lucas, *Sozialdemokratie in Bremen*, section C, esp. pp. 79–82.

75. The Danzig and Zittau papers were also lost by the opposition before the foundation of the USPD. The Stettin paper was lost later, in September 1917; the Düsseldorf paper was temporarily lost, from May to November 1918; and others, notably the Halle paper, very nearly went the same way.

76. The party executive's side of the story is given in *Zum Vorwärts-Konflikt* (Berlin, 1916), esp. pp. 19–30, the opposition's in the issues of *Mitteilungs-Blatt* for Nov. and Dec. 1916.

Berlin organization with the firm belief that the party executive had merely used the censorship issue as a lever to pry the opposition's most effective press organ out of its hands. Whether or not this was the intention, it was certainly the effect of the party executive's action, and great bitterness followed in Berlin and the SAG. Haase, for one, called it "the shabbiest thing I have experienced in politics."[77] More than any other single event, the seizure of *Vorwärts* inaugurated the final phase of the SPD's organizational conflict.

To this point the opposition had been cautious about taking any action that could be interpreted as preparation for a split in the party, or as an excuse for the party executive to commence expulsions. Once outside the party, there was a real danger that the opposition might become a mere "sect" (the standard socialist term).[78] Departure from the party would mean being cut off from the possibility of influencing the politics of the SPD and, to some extent, from agitating among its members. It would also mean leaving behind a large number of the more timorous (or more loyal) opponents of the party executive—those who had not even gone so far as to align themselves with the SAG—and thus splitting the opposition. A new party would be weak in newspapers and organization at the very time it most urgently wanted to influence the course of events. And it would have to deal with the problem of the intransigent left radicals, who would cast a larger shadow in a diminished opposition than they did in the party as a whole.[79] These considerations, and the force of the ideal (or habit) of party unity, had led even radical members of the opposition to moderate their behavior in the hope of avoiding a final breach.

Thus, apart from the long-standing existence of parallel organizations in Württemberg the party entered 1916 organizationally united; even the division of the Reichstag delegation in March did not cause normal organizational relations to be severed elsewhere in the party. But the strains were beginning to tell. The left radicals were urging that dues should not be paid to majority-controlled district organizations and the party executive, and by the second half of the year the idea had taken hold in some of their strongholds, notably Duisburg, Bremen, and parts of Berlin. The party executive responded by, in effect, encouraging the growth of new parallel organizations in areas where the old ones had become

---

77. *Hugo Haase,* p. 130.

78. See the warnings by Haase and Richard Lipinski of Leipzig in "Bericht über die gemeinsame Konferenz der Arbeitsgemeinschaft und der Spartakusgruppe vom 7. Januar 1917 in Berlin," appended to USPD *Parteitag,* April 1917, pp. 89 and 92.

79. Over a quarter of the delegates to the opposition's conference of Jan. 7, 1917, voted with the left radicals; see *ibid.,* p. 118. They had met in a separate conference the day before to concert their policy; Wohlgemuth, p. 196.

refractory.[80] Pressure from some of their followers, and their own indignation at the party executive's move to silence or subordinate the opposition, caused some fraying in the caution and organizational loyalty of the more responsible leaders of the minority. In this context the *Vorwärts* affair seemed to indicate an all-out offensive by the party executive, against which the minority must organize if it was to survive as a force in the party, let alone capture control of it. By the end of the year even so respectable an organization as the Leipzig party was building up a war chest by withholding, on various pretexts, contributions normally paid to the party executive.[81] Then, on January 7, 1917, the opposition made the risky move of holding a full national conference. The party executive seized the occasion to take a step that had gradually come to seem imperative; on January 16 it announced, with the support of the party committee, that those who adhered to this party-within-the-party must consider themselves no longer members of the SPD. The schism was finally formal and complete.

The leaders of the opposition must have known at once that they had been forced, in effect, to found a new party. To all outward appearances, however, they drew back from this conclusion and continued to conduct their struggle with the supporters of the party executive as though it were still an intraparty matter.[82] Indeed, on the local level the issue of allegiance often was fought out in the old familiar manner in party assemblies and leadership elections. Where supporters of the executive— Majority Socialists, as they became known—had a firm local majority or firm control of the apparatus they generally proceeded quickly to expel the opposition; where they were in the minority they soon established new organizations. Where the SAG supporters were in command they contented themselves with attacking the SPD leadership, endorsing the actions of the SAG, and waiting. In a few districts, notably Northern Bavaria and Thuringia, the leadership ignored the party executive's hardline policy of expulsion and set itself to preserve unity—with some success, to the cost of the future USPD.[83] But most of the party was soon

80. A detailed account of the most discussed case, that of the Berlin constituency of Teltow-Beeskow, is contained in Kitze, pp. 116–29 and 147–56.

81. Police report cited by Günther Gorski, "Die revolutionäre Arbeiterbewegung 1917/18 in Leipzig und die russische Februar- und Oktoberrevolution," *Jahrbuch für Geschichte der deutsch-slawischen Beziehungen,* 2 (1958), 10. The Düsseldorf and Berlin parties did the same; see DZA Potsdam, RMdI 13581, p. 126, and Koszyk, p. 99.

82. Haase actually went so far as to tell a Berlin assembly on Feb. 11 that "we refuse to found a new party!" *Mitteilungs-Blatt,* Feb. 18, 1917. None of the declarations of the SAG leadership during the first three months of 1917 spoke openly of a new party.

83. See Prager, p. 132; *Mitteilungs-Blatt,* March 4 and April 15, 1917.

forced to realize that the time for equivocation was past. When the party executive expelled the entire Leipzig district organization, when it established its own organizations in one after another of the Berlin constituencies, when it severed relations with the existing organizations in Braunschweig, Bremen, Erfurt, Königsberg, and other major cities, schism was a fact.

On April 6, 1917, the opposition assembled in Gotha for still another conference to decide on the appropriate organizational forms to unite the opposition.[84] Even then the awesome prospect of founding a breakaway party had its effect on many delegates, and their reservations found expression in the debate over a name for what was inevitably going to be a new party. Forty-two of the delegates, including Bernstein, Kautsky, and Kurt Eisner, wanted to hold as tightly as possible to the claim that they were the temporarily victimized representatives of the true party tradition and preferred a name such as "German Social Democratic Party, Opposition." But more venturesome spirits, led by Herzfeld, Henke, Ledebour, and Dissmann, won seventy-two votes for their choice, "German Independent Social Democratic Party."[85] With this decision the opposition conference had unmistakably turned into the founding congress of a new party.

It was hardly a promising start for the new party, this small assembly behind closed doors in remote Gotha, with the doubts of a substantial part of the delegates all too much in evidence.[86] The new party began life on the defensive, the product as much of expulsion as of the search for an independent path. Those who aligned themselves with it in April 1917 were conscious of facing formidable obstacles in their effort to bring Social Democracy back onto its true course; they were making a leap of faith. It was far from certain, early in 1917, that the USPD would live as long, and have as much influence even during what remained of the war, as it did.

84. These were the terms in which the conference was announced by the leadership of the SAG; see *Mitteilungs-Blatt,* Feb. 18, 1917.
85. USPD *Parteitag,* April 1917, pp. 49–50; Haase is listed as voting with the minority, but cf. Prager, p. 146.
86. The readers of the opposition-oriented Halle *Volksblatt,* for instance, did not learn that their leaders had founded a new party for them until April 13, five days after the conference ended. The USPD never published the minutes of its founding congress; what we now have is a (not very reliable) condensed transcript issued in 1921 by Emil Eichhorn, by then a Communist, who seems to have thought to shame the Independents by his publication.

CHAPTER 2

The New Party (1917)

In its first manifesto, the USPD party executive declared that "the old Social Democracy has arisen anew."[1] As a reflection of the ideals of the centrist leadership faction of the new party these words are illuminating;[2] but as a statement of fact they were far off the mark. The USPD was unmistakably an offshoot of the old Social Democracy in every respect, from its leaders to its ideology. The old SPD, however, had been able to lay claim to being the comprehensive national organization of the politically active elements of the working class, a circumstance that had dominated its self-image, its strategy and tactics, and its prospects. The USPD, a much more confined party, could make no such claim. It was something unprecedented in German socialism, the first separate party of the socialist left.

As such the USPD not only spoke with a different voice than the old party but was also subject to internal pressures of a kind the SPD had not known for a generation or more. Among the moderate left and far left factions that had founded the new party, the representatives of centrist doctrinal orthodoxy were no longer comfortably in the middle but were a faction on one wing—albeit initially the dominant one. Given the nature of the party's following in such disturbed times—times of war and revolution that first forced the foundation of the party and then kept it alive—the tendency toward further radicalization was a basic fact of party life from the start.

Here, in the tension between tradition (represented by the centrists) and elemental popular radicalism, lay the basis for much of the instability that marked the history of the USPD. Since the party was also organizationally incoherent—decentralized, regionally imbalanced, and

1. *Mitteilungs-Blatt,* April 22, 1917.
2. Those elements in the USPD whose outlook was inherited from the left Center of the old SPD will be referred to hereafter simply as "centrist." The usage was contemporary, employed critically by other socialists who considered themselves truly "left," and has been perpetuated in the Leninist vocabulary. I use it here without deprecatory overtones.

53

excessively tentative in its central leadership—it faced a continuing struggle against disintegration.

Radical Socialism and Popular Radicalism

The analysis so far has focused primarily on the two best-known leadership groups on the socialist left, the Spartacists and the centrists. While this bipolar picture may be an adequate approximation of the opposition's early evolution, at least at the level of visible factional alignments, it is less accurate after the opposition's emergence as a complex independent force in 1916 and the beginning of mass action in that year. Both inside and outside the party there was a groundswell of discontent and rebellion among German workers, which found its outlet finally in the general strikes of 1917 and 1918. By the time the USPD was founded, this popular unrest had bred an inchoate socialist radicalism of a strength unknown for decades in the German labor movement.

The causes of the discontent were not primarily political; workers were dissatisfied with the war, with their working conditions, and above all with the falling standard of living.[3] Shortages of food, coal, and other necessities arose soon after the start of the war and grew worse through its first three years, especially in the great cities; and the shortages were accompanied by a severe inflation of prices. Wages in most cases could not keep up, and meeting a family's basic needs became a daily preoccupation, while what the government should do about it became the liveliest public issue of the war.[4] For workers the hardships of private life were aggravated by dissatisfaction at work, for even where wages did manage to keep up with inflation—as they did in the armaments industry —hours of work were arbitrarily lengthened and the pressure on the labor force was intensified, the factory legislation protecting workers having been suspended for the duration of the war. In nearly every respect the workers' lot worsened. Meanwhile, the reluctant, inefficient application of state controls permitted a flourishing black market to grow and thereby allowed the well-to-do to avoid hardships that were inescapable for the poor and enabled a conspicuous class of speculators and profiteers to make fortunes.

3. On the sources of discontent see also Gerald D. Feldmann, Eberhard Kolb, and Reinhard Rürup, "Die Massenbewegungen der Arbeiterschaft in Deutschland am Ende des Ersten Weltkrieges (1917–1920)," *Politische Vierteljahresschrift,* 13 (1972), 86–89; and Rosenberg, *Birth,* pp. 90–91.

4. The increasing severity of the food crisis, and the public response to it, is vividly conveyed in the regular reports of the Berlin Police President to the Prussian government, collected in DZA Merseburg, Rep. 77 Tit. 332r Nr. 126. For the debate in the press and the Reichstag, see Berlau, pp. 92–100.

Such circumstances were bound to encourage social radicalism. Similar conditions—perhaps not so intense, particularly with respect to food shortages—prevailed in other countries without resulting in the general strikes that Germany experienced, but in Germany the confidence in the national cause that could have made the sacrifices bearable tended to flag. The war, fought deep in foreign countries, ceased to seem urgent, while the autocratic, class-bound government at home was not adept at sustaining the ideal that the war was in the interests of the whole people. As the war dragged on into its second, third, fourth, and finally fifth years, an ever-growing part of the lower classes became restive, and only the right-wing working-class leaders' determined loyalty to the war effort kept the alienation of the rank and file from being more actively expressed.

Primarily nonpolitical in origin, social radicalism was at first nonpolitical in many of its more important manifestations, such as disconnected strikes and food riots.[5] But it also found quasi-organizational expression in the labor movement in two significant and related ways: in the formation of a factory opposition movement in the large cities and, especially, in the armaments industry; and in the emergence of a strong, militant and radical (yet non-Spartacist) force within the socialist opposition. By 1917 the antiwar socialists were split, not just between centrists and Spartacists, but into at least three camps. The rise of the radicals (as we shall call them) between the extreme left and the moderate centrists was important for each of the other factions of the USPD and for the party as a whole.

The factory opposition movement had as its basis the large number of workers—generally in the very largest plants, which in wartime meant the armaments industry—who objected to the industrial truce imposed from above by the trade-union leadership at the start of the war. This opposition was expressed by shop-floor union functionaries (shop stewards) and some middle-level union officers, more rarely and hesitantly by paid union officials. In normal times such dissent would have worked itself out within the unions, but with the military authorities keeping a sharp eye on labor, ready to conscript troublemakers, the opposition took on an underground character and proved in time to be susceptible to political radicalism. The impact of the factory opposition was great; with normal channels of complaint dammed up and trade-union leaders all too obviously involved in the evolution of government labor policy, the movement was able to assume much of the authority usually exer-

5. A chronicle of these events, which were not mentioned in the press at the time, is available in *GdA: Chronik,* vols. 1 and 2.

cised by the unions. Like the unions, the new organizations maintained a degree of separateness from their party, in this case the USPD; their strength did not depend on the party, and they collaborated with it only when they wished.[6]

The political character of the factory opposition, as it developed, varied from place to place. In the great Stuttgart plants, the predominant brand of radicalism was Spartacist; in Bremen, too, left radicals had the main influence, but left radicals who refused to compromise by joining the USPD. These groups were able to mobilize the Stuttgart and Bremen factories at critical moments in 1918 and 1919.[7] In Braunschweig and Düsseldorf the Spartacists were strong, but not necessarily predominant —just as in the local parties. In Leipzig, where practically the entire socialist movement went over to the opposition, the factory movement seems to have had unusually close ties to the party, as it did in Frankfurt on Main, where, under Robert Dissmann, the political opposition kept in close touch with the factories.[8] In Halle the connection with the party was through Wilhelm Koenen, who was both a party figure and one of the organizers of the shop stewards' movement there.[9] In Berlin, the best documented case, the "Revolutionary Shop Stewards" were particularly suspicious of the politicians, not least of the Spartacists; their leader, Richard Müller, carefully kept the Spartacists at arm's length, and the group did not take up relations with the USPD leadership until the end of 1917.[10]

6. Only for Berlin do we have extensive inside accounts of the movement's development; see the memoirs of two of its leaders, Richard Müller, *Vom Kaiserreich zur Republik*, 2 vols. (Vienna, 1924), esp. I, 55–59 and 125–26, and Emil Barth, *Aus der Werkstatt der deutschen Revolution* (Berlin [1919]), pp. 10–20; and Paul Blumenthal's recollections in *1918: Erinnerungen von Veteranen der deutschen Gewerkschaftsbewegung an die Novemberrevolution (1914–1920)* (Berlin, 1958), pp. 98–124. For some of the scanty sources on parallel movements in other cities see the notes to the next paragraph.

7. For Stuttgart, see the account of the revolution at the end of ch. 3, below; the factories whose men came out on November 4 tended to support Spartacist-sponsored actions well into 1919, including the general strike of March 31–April 8, 1919. For Bremen, see Lucas, *Sozialdemokratie in Bremen*, p. 85; Peter Kuckuck, "Bremer Linksradikale bzw. Kommunisten von der Militärrevolte im November 1918 bis zum Kapp-Putsch im März 1920" (Ph.D. dissertation, University of Hamburg, 1970), pp. 4–5 and 64.

8. The Leipzig strike of April 1917 was organized and carried out jointly by the party and the factory radicals; see K. Schneider, pp. 171–72 and 175–77. For Frankfurt see Erhard Lucas, *Frankfurt unter der Herrschaft des Arbeiter- und Soldatenrats 1918/19* (Frankfurt on Main, 1969), pp. 14–15.

9. Wilhelm Koenen in *Zu einigen Fragen der Novemberrevolution und der Gründung der Kommunistischen Partei Deutschlands: Protokoll der theoretischen Konferenz der Abteilung Agitation-Propaganda der Bezirksleitung der SED-Halle* [Halle, 1959], p. 19.

10. R. Müller, *Kaiserreich*, I, 102 and 126.

The leaders of the factory opposition could not, of course, mobilize the workers at will, either for their own purposes or for those of a political group. Some, in fact, were markedly cautious, exercising their limited authority over the workers only when they were certain of a broad following.[11] They could, however, help focus their fellows' discontent on particular issues and give it a political aspect; and they could sometimes develop an elemental expression of unrest into an impressive demonstration. The first such incident to attract general attention was the partial strike in Berlin, Braunschweig, and Bremen in June 1916 protesting the penitentiary sentence imposed on Karl Liebknecht; the numbers involved were not great, but the coordination between different factories and several cities compelled notice.[12] In April 1917 another, much larger protest strike took place; and a third instance, in January 1918, held suggestions of a full general strike and thus of a direct political threat.[13] In the intervals between, especially during the summer of 1917, there were local actions on a similar factory basis. The potential of such actions was important to all groups on the socialist left in the latter half of the war: the elemental popular force required by the programs of the left seemed to have assumed a definite form, if a form over which the political leaders had very little control.

The factory opposition movement was concentrated in the great munitions plants and shipyards, where social radicalism was strongest and could be most effectively expressed; it was, accordingly, largely a phenomenon of the metalworking trades and became a central feature of the Metalworkers' Union. This union, alone of the larger ones, had a significant number of paid officials and leading functionaries who were militantly opposed to the general trade-union policy of collaboration with the government; indeed, contacts through the union appear to have given the factory opposition such national coherence as it had.[14] At the union's annual conference in June 1917, despite the wartime restrictions on union democracy, over a third of the delegates supported a resolution criticizing the policies of the central trade-union leadership, the general commission.[15] This was, however, the high-water mark of organized challenge to official union policies during the war. In other unions (excepting

11. See, for instance, *ibid.*, I, 80–81 and 130–31.
12. *Ibid.*, 62–64; *Spartakusbriefe* (1926 ed.), pp. 144 and 149; *Spartakus im Kriege*, ed. Ernst Meyer (Berlin, 1927), p. 142.
13. The strike movements are discussed in the following chapter.
14. R. Müller, *Kaiserreich*, I, 60, 100, and 125.
15. Fritz Opel, *Der Deutsche Metallarbeiter-Verband während des ersten Weltkrieges und der Revolution* (Hanover and Frankfurt on Main, 1957), pp. 66–67. The principal spokesman for the opposition at this conference was Robert Dissmann, who had formerly been an official of the Metalworkers' Union.

a few smaller ones) the challenge was far feebler; and the principal source of those practices that the radical rank and file found offensive, the general commission itself, was quite unmoved by the criticism. In the last years of the war, then, the factory opposition, however influential locally, was frustrated within the union organizations. Breakaway unions were not the answer; since a united front vis-à-vis the employers was such an obvious condition of union effectiveness, the inhibitions against splitting were significantly stronger than in the party. There was no way of expressing dissatisfaction short of individual withdrawal from the unions—a course against which the USPD leadership felt it necessary to warn workers in April 1918.[16] An outlet came only with the birth of the workers' council movement at the end of 1918, a development to which great numbers of radicalized, frustrated workers were ready to respond.

The factory- and union-based opposition had a close political counterpart in the growing radicalism within the party itself. The circumspection of most senior leaders of the opposition was alien to many left-wing party functionaries and activists, including many who did not consider themselves left radicals. These radicals did not share their nominal leaders' strong reliance on the old methods and traditions. Like the Spartacists, they were dissatisfied with the old party and wanted to give a new spirit to the German class struggle; while they had a definite sense of continuity with the old party, they were more open to new ideas and methods than the representatives of classic centrism proper. Eventually, as the radicalizing effect of the war seemed to create opportunities for effective action, they began to consider whether it might not be possible to make a revolution.

Through 1917, and in many cases probably until the end of 1918, the radicals seem to have had little sense of forming a distinct faction. It takes definite issues to coalesce factions, but the USPD's opportunities for practical action were so limited, and its chance to debate internal theoretical differences so restricted, that the formation of factional alignments was retarded. Certainly a lively sense of the differences within the party existed, even apart from the Spartacist extreme; but the leadership took care not to exacerbate them, and such papers as the *Leipziger Volkszeitung* and the Halle *Volksblatt,* which by mid-1919 were firmly entrenched on opposite wings of the party, were carefully avoiding taking up factional positions as late as the end of the war.[17] The radical

16. *Volksblatt* (Halle), April 18, 1918.
17. The Berlin *Mitteilungs-Blatt,* Ernst Däumig's paper, was an exception, departing from a middle line during the summer of 1917 to take up an unambiguous

tendency in the party was accordingly formless and difficult to identify, at least until 1918, when the sense of impending revolution, and the example of Russia, began to give a more precise outline to this wing of the USPD.

The foremost members of a new class of leaders that was forming to represent the radical tendency in party councils and the party press can be readily identified, however. Many were relatively young and less impeded by prewar commitments, not newcomers to Social Democracy but rising junior officials whose careers were accelerated by the opportunity to speak for a new temper in the party; typical of this group were Curt Geyer of Würzburg and Leipzig, Wilhelm Koenen of Halle, and Walter Stoecker of Cologne, all later eminent in the party. Some were older, party figures of not quite the first rank who became prominent through their response to changed circumstances; Otto Brass of Remscheid and Ernst Däumig of Berlin belonged to this class. In 1917 their names were still not widely known; in the revolution and its aftermath they were to come into their own.

Among the established socialist leaders who came to the USPD there were also a few certified radicals. Chief among them was the aging firebrand, Georg Ledebour. Despite his advanced years—he was sixty-four when war broke out—Ledebour had a strong streak of impetuous radicalism. Erect, sharp tongued, and willful, he was popular with the militants of his Berlin constituency, where he had agitated tirelessly since the early days of the war; by the end of 1917 he had even been accepted into the inner circle of the shop stewards' movement. Ledebour's vision of a socialist's duty did not permit of hesitation or compromise; by 1918 his aims had become unambiguously revolutionary. Alfred Henke, the next most prominent radical among the first Independents, was altogether different. Editor-in-chief of the *Bremer Bürgerzeitung* since 1906, Henke was a left radical of long standing who had begun to separate himself from this group only about 1912, when he was first elected to the Reichstag. In the opposition, and later the USPD, he was verbally one of the most radical leaders of the party left; but he remained a loyal party and organization man, which set limits to his extremism in practice. Robert Dissmann of Frankfurt on Main, aged only thirty-five when war broke out, was probably the best-known radical bureaucrat in the old party—he had nearly been elected to the party executive as a left-wing candidate at the 1913 party congress. For Dissmann, a former (and future) trade-union official, radical activism was always indis-

---

position on the party's left wing; see, for example, the programmatic editorial of April 7, 1918.

solubly linked with the recognized organizations of the working class, the party and the unions, and in vital party or union matters he had no time for speculative or visionary politics. He was, therefore, in his own way, as loyally tied to the main bloc of the labor movement as any centrist, though remaining an outspoken radical in many matters.[18]

In the first year of the USPD's life the centrists were no more a definite faction within the party than were the radicals. The typical centrist (more readily definable than the typical radical) displayed a rhetorical and ideological hostility to the existing order that was bolstered by a doctrine of revolution, even if a rather remote revolution requiring no party action; close adherence to the practiced forms of working-class activity and their traditional ideological justification, which amounted at times to nearly total absorption in the internal life of the movement; and an habitual inclination to be circumspect in practice. But most centrists were also flexible, and as the impatience of their constituents grew the centrist leaders showed themselves responsive to pressure. Many radicalized centrists became scarcely distinguishable from radicals of advanced Marxist convictions or those radicalized by factory conditions during the war.

The process of radicalization had begun even before the foundation of the USPD. Karl Kautsky, the archetypal centrist, was a key figure in the coalescence of the opposition in 1915; but by 1917 he was conscious of being far out on the right wing, and he joined the USPD only with reluctance.[19] Though he remained true to the party until its reunification with the SPD in 1922, Kautsky was a conspicuous (though respected) outsider in its ranks. Some of his disciples, however, were more influential in the USPD, most importantly Rudolf Hilferding.[20] A subtle and creative Marxist theorist, Hilferding was more concerned with day-to-day tactics than Kautsky and correspondingly more willing to subordinate his theoretical understanding to the necessities of practical politics as he saw them. As editor-in-chief of the USPD's Berlin newspaper, *Freiheit,* from November 1918 (he had previously been away at the war), Hilferding became the guiding spirit of the faction that wanted the

18. On Ledebour, see Ursula Ratz, *Georg Ledebour 1850–1947: Weg und Wirken eines sozialistischen Politikers* (Berlin, 1969). On Henke, see Karl-Ernst Moring, *Die Sozialdemokratische Partei in Bremen 1890–1914* (Hanover, 1968), and Lucas, *Sozialdemokratie in Bremen.* On Dissmann, see the memoirs of his closest associate, Toni Sender, *The Autobiography of a German Rebel* (New York, 1939). On these and other leading party figures, see also Appendix 4.

19. Karl Kautsky, *Mein Verhältnis zur Unabhängigen Sozialdemokratischen Partei,* 2d ed. (Berlin, 1922), p. 8.

20. See the biographical sketch in Wilfried Gottschalch, *Strukturveränderungen der Gesellschaft und politisches Handeln in der Lehre von Rudolf Hilferding* (Berlin, 1962), pp. 13–31, also pp. 70–85.

party to take the long perspective and view itself as the repository and guarantor of the most valuable traditions of the Marxist labor movement, ready to help guide the revolution when it came but not charged with overturning capitalism at once by any and all means. Yet even the clearsighted and sceptical Hilferding repeatedly twisted and turned during his years as an Independent, endorsing or failing to contest major policy decisions with which he was not in agreement; thus even in his case classic centrism displayed itself imperfectly. Indeed, in this most representative centrist party of the era of the First World War, classic centrism was on the defensive from the outset.

Hugo Haase represented another kind of modified centrism, which, intransigent toward the right but (unlike Kautsky) open to radical innovations, had great impact on the USPD.[21] Haase, a lawyer of simple origins, was a man of strict Marxist principle and strongly attached to the doctrines and tactics of the prewar socialist movement. Noted for decency and self-sacrifice, he led largely by example and argument. However strict his principles for his own conduct, he was a conciliator, just, even-tempered, cautious, even somewhat secretive, and little inclined to insist on a dogmatic unity of views. His own views were definite, and there were points beyond which he would not go, but on the whole he preferred holding his followers together to trying to impose his ideas. For Haase, the party was the vehicle for socialist transformation of the despised capitalist order, the guide and chief support of the workers in their struggle. In turn, the militant part of the working class was the party's true foundation. As the unruly, radicalized workers who made up a conspicuous part of the USPD's constituency turned their thoughts to mass action, Haase and centrists like him followed; they did not lead, nor did they ever accept all the militants' ideas, but they permitted themselves to be shifted perceptibly from the traditions that had originally led them to oppose the majority and found their own party.

The orientation characterized here was by no means confined to leading parliamentarians or party intellectuals but existed at every level in the party and in all walks of life represented by party members. It was stronger among those whose outlook had been formed in the prewar decades and among trade unionists and party officials concerned with the practical needs of established institutions, weaker among the mass of new socialists who came to the party after the war and among

21. See the biographical preface to *Hugo Haase;* Kenneth R. Calkins, "Hugo Haase: A Political Biography" (Ph.D. dissertation, University of Chicago, 1966); Ernest Hamburger, *Juden im öffentlichen Leben Deutschlands* (Tübingen, 1968), pp. 426–44; Werner T. Angress, "Juden im politischen Leben der Revolutionszeit," *Deutsches Judentum in Krieg und Revolution 1916–1923,* ed. Werner E. Mosse (Tübingen, 1971), pp. 174–84.

workers in large factories. But there were whole organizations that continued to live by the old principles, with the assent of nearly all their members. An example was the sturdy little Gera party in Thuringia.[22] The massive Leipzig organization of the USPD was ruled, except for a few months in the revolutionary period, by its version of the old socialist tradition. And so, significantly, was much of the party press.

Creating another complication, the Spartacus group were members of the USPD until the end of 1918. The Spartacists constituted a kind of organized faction, but not an exclusive one. Their views overlapped with the less systematic radicalism of part of the rank and file in a way that makes it impossible to disentangle the two; even the break when the Spartacists formed the Communist Party at the end of 1918 was probably not a neat separation of Spartacists from radicals.[23] The line dividing the Spartacist faction from the still more extreme groups to their left—those who left the SPD early and refused to join the USPD—was also blurred. These difficulties of definition may suggest that Spartacism was in fact a distinct phenomenon only with respect to its cadres, the inner core of which J. P. Nettl has called a "peer group," because of its closeness and sympathy of views.[24] This core included not only Luxemburg, Liebknecht, Clara Zetkin, Franz Mehring, and Leo Jogiches but also such younger adherents as Paul Levi, Ernst Meyer, and August Thalheimer, all of whom played important roles in postwar Communist history. The core shaded off into a network of provincial correspondents, largely self-selected, who were more or less trusted to do the underground work of the movement. There may have been several hundred of these true Spartacists. In the few large cities where their movement was centralized—Berlin, Leipzig, Stuttgart, Braunschweig, Duisburg—were a total of perhaps a few thousand workers who looked to them for leadership; elsewhere, it was lonely individual work.

When the USPD constituted itself in April 1917 a majority of the Spartacist cadres decided to attach themselves to the new party provided it would let them follow their own path and defend their own ideas; indeed, given these conditions, some of them might have preferred to remain in the SPD.[25] As Jogiches explained in a circular of Decem-

22. See Walter Pöhland, "Die Entwicklung der Arbeiterbewegung in Ostthüringen unter besonderer Berücksichtigung der Herausbildung des revolutionären linken Flügels der USPD" (Ph.D. dissertation, University of Halle-Wittenberg, 1965), pp. 98–100.

23. See also Kitze, pp. 100–1.

24. Nettl, *Rosa Luxemburg*, II, 678.

25. For a discussion of Spartacist attitudes toward the problem of unity see *ibid.*, II, 656–58.

ber 1916, they must stay with the main body of the opposition in order to influence "a whole mass of working-class elements who belong to us intellectually and politically and follow the SAG only because of lack of contact with us or because of ignorance of the actual relationships inside the opposition, or for other incidental reasons."[26] The USPD could also serve as a sort of temporary refuge—the state authorities could not deal as effectively with an ill-defined left wing of a legal party as with a separate Spartacist organization.[27] Finally, some Spartacist leaders hoped to drive the centrists into greater activism than they might choose by themselves.[28]

Not all of the left radicals were willing to sacrifice the distinctness of their movement to Jogiches' calculations; after all, ambiguity created for the police might confuse the workers as well. The left radicals of Bremen, Hamburg, and Dresden, determined to raise their own banner as a separate and pure movement, chose to remain outside the USPD. Recent Marxist-Leninist writers, drawing on the organizational teachings of Lenin, have also condemned the Berlin Spartacist leaders' decision to go with the Independents as wrong and harmful to the interests of true revolution.[29] These objections are not persuasive. With local exceptions, the Spartacists did remain weak, but there is every reason to believe that Jogiches was right, that they and their cause benefited more from the protection of the USPD and the opportunity to agitate among its members than they would have from uncompromising separateness. Arguably, even the foundation of the Communist Party at the end of 1918 was mistaken, or at least premature.[30] Given the traditions of the German labor movement, its radicalization, both during the war and after, found expression, not in breakaway splinter groups, but within the broad Social Democratic movement, with its vague and malleable institutional framework and ideology. From 1917 until 1920 it found its home in the USPD.

26. *Spartakusbriefe* (1926 ed.), p. 156.
27. "Schutzdach" was the term used. See the Spartacist circular of Feb. 13, 1917, in *Spartakus im Kriege*, pp. 163–65; and the *Der Kampf* article of Feb. 24, 1917, printed in *Dokumente und Materialien*, I, 567.
28. See Mehring's letter to the Bolshevik leadership, printed in *Leipziger Volkszeitung*, July 4, 1918, in which he admits that the hope proved false.
29. *Geschichte der deutschen Arbeiterbewegung in acht Bänden*, issued by the Institut für Marxismus-Leninismus beim Zentralkomitee der SED (Berlin, 1966) (hereafter cited as *GdA*), II, 274; III, 33 and 170.
30. Jogiches voted against the decision of Dec. 29, 1918, to found the Communist Party, and Paul Levi came to share his view in retrospect. See *Berichte zum Zweiten Kongress der Kommunist[ischen] Internationale* (Hamburg, 1921), pp. 22–23.

The Organizational and Regional Balance

The USPD was characterized for most of its life by strong divergencies among leaders and members; but in 1917 this tendency, while foreshadowed in the ideas and (as we shall see) the actions of its internal groupings, was fully evident only in the peculiar character of its Spartacist left wing. More obvious at the time were certain other characteristics of the USPD which were later to interact with its ideological factionalism to give the party its peculiarly fragile quality: the feebleness of its central institutions and the imbalance among its divergent regional organizations.

The new party gave itself an exceptionally weak national organization. The socialist militants who assembled in Gotha in April 1917 to establish a new party had found themselves in the wilderness because they insisted on their right to agitate for minority views, and they had become habitually mistrustful of the restraints of central direction. Many of the delegates had also recognized the bureaucratic tendencies of the old party as a threat to radical socialism.[31] There was need for some kind of central leadership, and in the circumstances the offices were necessarily conceded to the Berliners and the Reichstag delegation; Haase and Ledebour became cochairmen, Wilhelm Dittmann and Luise Zietz fulltime secretaries in the central office. Clearly, however, what was wanted of them was flaming speeches, as well as assistance in the form of information and contacts, but not directives. The Spartacists were especially determined to insist on a free hand; they would join the party only if local organizations could have virtual independence and only if their group remained free to pursue its own agitation.[32] For the sake of unity the Berlin leaders reluctantly conceded the substance of these demands. In practice the concessions did not much diminish the role of salaried officials or strengthen the voluntary, democratic side of the organization; the only significant departure from the old organizational forms was the much diminished authority of the center. But the price was exaggerated difficulty in executing the center's decisions, even when such decisions were democratically reached and of unimpeachable radicalism. It does not seem to have occurred to the radicals that this could be a serious flaw in a revolutionary party.[33]

---

31. USPD *Parteitag,* April 1917, pp. 18 (Dittmann), 27 (Gustav Laukant), and 32–33 (Dissmann).

32. *Ibid.,* p. 20 (Fritz Rück).

33. See also Schorske, pp. 320–21, and Hans Manfred Bock, *Syndikalismus und Linkskommunismus von 1918–1923* (Meisenheim on Glan, 1969), pp. 59–62. Nettl, "The German Social Democratic Party," pp. 74–75, argues that the German

The USPD explicitly took the old organizational statute of the SPD as its basis, though with modifications.[34] Its party executive, composed of chairmen, secretaries, and associate members—later a treasurer as well—differed from the old model in that just two of its original seven members (the secretaries, Dittmann and Zietz) were salaried.[35] The control commission, comprising seven members headed by the venerable Wilhelm Bock, was empowered to hear complaints against the executive and appeals against the latter's rulings, just like its counterpart in the SPD. The USPD's auxiliary council (*Beirat*), however, was not a large-scale consultative body like the SPD's party committee but was intended as a policy-making body coordinate with the party executive, indeed as an equal part of an expanded party executive. Its seven members, drawn from the different regions of the country, were to be a counterweight to the influence of the Berliners. To what extent this intention was realized is difficult to say, as we have no minutes of the meetings of the auxiliary council with the party executive and no information about the internal procedures followed. Available evidence suggests that, at least during 1919 and 1920, it was summoned frequently to Berlin, probably half a dozen times a year or more.[36] But whether it operated as a check on the party executive is doubtful; apart from a case in January 1918 there is no recorded instance of corporate opposition between the two bodies before September 1920, nor of reversal of the party executive's preferred policies by the auxiliary council.[37] In practice, then, the auxiliary council may have come to occupy only a consultative position, though in a party so loosely united as the USPD the right to be consulted was one the party executive had to take seri-

Social Democrats, unlike Lenin, never saw the connection between questions of organization and questions of policy.

34. The USPD's "Organisations-Grundlinien" are printed in USPD *Parteitag*, April 1917, pp. 47–49. I have ignored the constantly changing nomenclature used by the USPD for its central institutions and given each an English name that will be used consistently throughout.

35. The initial provision that the salaried members of the party executive were not to take part in its votes seems to have been a dead letter from the start. By 1920, when the executive had seven salaried members (out of twelve), including the two chairmen, the rule would have been completely unworkable, but it had undoubtedly been long forgotten.

36. In these years some half a dozen important leadership decisions were identified in the press as issuing from meetings with the auxiliary council, generally with the control commission in attendance as well. The pattern suggests that such meetings must have been reasonably frequent.

37. In January 1918 the auxiliary council played a role in pressing the Reichstag delegation to inaugurate the movement for a general strike, while the executive was inclined to oppose it; in September 1920 executive and council were on different sides on whether to accept the Twenty-One Conditions for admission to the Communist International.

ously. The council was, however, too small to be representative; for this reason, doubtless, the control commission came to be convoked regularly at the same time as the council. The three bodies, meeting together, became the normal organ for the most important policy decisions on matters arising between party congresses.

For still broader consultation the party executive had recourse to national conferences of representatives from the district organizations and the party press. Such meetings had several advantages from the leadership's point of view: they could be convoked on fairly short notice without all the elaborate preparations required for a party congress; the proceedings could be kept confidential; and the participants, having no specific powers under the party statute, could neither force decisions on the party executive nor hold votes on possibly divisive issues. The disadvantage was that resort to such conferences tended in time to be seen as evasion of the leadership's duty to hold proper party congresses.[38]

Ironically for the democratic aspirations of the USPD, party congresses, the democratic core of socialist policy-making, were a lasting sore point for the party. The USPD never managed to return to the normal socialist practice of regular annual party congresses; indeed, the congress of January 1922 was the first and only one not designated a "special" congress.[39] During the war the party could hardly have managed to assure the representative participation and open discussion essential to such a congress, and no attempt seems to have been made to hold one. But the paramount factor discouraging such meetings was factional conflict, which made every full-scale discussion of internal differences a threat to party unity. The USPD never held a congress without some of the participants wondering whether the course of the debates would not force them to leave the party. Under these conditions the leaders tended to hold congresses only when they could not be avoided. And each became a distinct moment of crisis for the party.[40]

38. The national conferences (*Reichskonferenzen*) of May, June and Sept. 1919, Jan. and Sept. 1920, and Feb. and July 1922 are discussed in their contexts below. Only for the conference of Sept. 1920 was a stenographic report published; of the others, only that of Sept. 1919 was reported reasonably fully in the party press. Some others, for example those of Sept. 1918 or Dec. 6, 1918, were not reported in the press at all.

39. At a "special" (*ausserordentlich*) congress the party executive did not have to deliver a full business report, with detailed statistics on the party's membership and press, revenues and expenditures; indeed it never did this, not even at the sole "regular" congress.

40. Similar considerations may have contributed to preventing the implementation of one of the more striking features of the party statute, the provision that critically important issues were to be submitted to a referendum of the membership for decision. This provision was invoked only once, to make sure that the delegates

Below the central institutions the structure of the party remained essentially unchanged. The organization continued to be founded on the constituency—because of the electoral system and long habit—and the district. The principal difference was in altered practices: the districts, and often the constituency parties as well, had unprecedented autonomy. In part this autonomy was anchored in the party statute; the party executive was prohibited from imposing its choices as district or local party secretaries or paying their salaries directly, and from acquiring property rights in party newspapers or printing offices through subsidies from the central party treasury. More important, the USPD had been assembled from the bottom up, by a federation of the breakaway district and local organizations; these had conceded a minimum of their autonomy to the new party center. The atmosphere of the USPD was federalist in the extreme.

The USPD was born with a tiny, harassed central office, a chaotic provincial organization, and quasi-conspiratorial habits. The effect on the party's collection and release of statistics was crippling; the leadership was unable to assemble accurate data until well after the end of the war, and even then was reluctant to issue information to the public. We have no membership statistics for the USPD as a whole that would meet ordinary standards of accuracy until 1920 or 1921. At no time before the revolution, however, can the USPD's membership have rivaled that of the SPD. The only membership figure released by the Independents during this period was 120,000, in September 1917, and this was probably exaggerated, perhaps substantially.[41] Later a figure of "about 100,000" was officially given as the party's membership at the time of the revolution;[42] a figure of this order, or somewhat less, can probably be accepted. The party's numbers in the Berlin and Leipzig strongholds were declining over this period, and, with recruitment difficult in wartime and conscription continuing to eat into its following, the same may have

---

to the Halle congress in October 1920 were elected directly by the membership as representing one side or the other of the controversy (see ch. 11 below). This requirement came as a surprise; the statutory provision had been virtually forgotten.

41. *Volksblatt* (Halle), Sept. 14, 1917. Any figure ending in so many zeros is a rough estimate, and inevitably an optimistic one.

42. Zietz in USPD *Parteitag,* March 1919, p. 50. Däumig later mentioned a total of 70,000 for the time of the revolution, when he was working in the central office; see *Freiheit,* Dec. 28, 1919, and USPD *Parteitag,* Oct. 1920, p. 107. Ernst Drahn, "Sozialdemokratie," in *Handwörterbuch der Staatswissenschaften,* 4th ed., VII (Jena, 1926), 534, holds that 100,000 was probably the maximum membership during the war; while the well-informed Walter Rist, "Der Weg der KPD.," *Neue Blätter für den Sozialismus,* 3 (1932), 84, offers a figure of 90,000 for 1917–18, with no indication of his source.

been true of the party as a whole.[43] By contrast, the SPD's official membership figure for March 1917 was 243,061, a credible total, though several thousand must be deducted for late defections not reflected in the figure; a year later it was 249,411.[44] The USPD seems, therefore, to have taken over between a quarter and a third of the wartime membership of Social Democracy.

The USPD's membership was geographically concentrated, to an extent unusual even for a working-class party. This peculiarity, which characterized the party throughout its short history, was especially pronounced at the start. Only six of the SPD's thirty-eight former district organizations were captured by the opposition—Greater Berlin, Leipzig, Halle, Erfurt, Braunschweig, and Frankfurt on Main. A further twenty constituency organizations came to the new party, but in only two districts—Lower Rhineland and Thuringia—were these enough to give the USPD real regional strength.[45] A few dozen disconnected local organizations complete the picture. Berlin, the Leipzig district, and the Düsseldorf–Elberfeld area (the Lower Rhineland district) made up probably half of the national membership; and fully two-thirds of the party executive's income from dues during the USPD's first year came from these three districts.[46] Elsewhere, whole areas of Germany were practically untouched by the new party. For reasons to be discussed shortly,

43. A decline of 24 percent in the membership of the large Leipzig-Land constituency organization from April 1917 to October 1918 is documented in *Jahresbericht des Vorstandes und Sekretariats des Sozialdemokratischen Vereins für den 13. sächsischen Reichstagswahlkreis* (Leipzig, 1917), pp. 12–13, and *Halbjahresbericht des Vorstandes u[nd] Sekretariats des Sozialdemokratischen Vereins für den 13. sächsischen Reichstagswahlkreis* (Leipzig, 1918), p. 10. Most of the loss occurred before April 1918. For Berlin see *Mitteilungs-Blatt*, July 21, 1918. Some organizations, in places like Stettin and the Frankfurt area, were growing, but it is doubtful if their gains offset the losses in the largest party centers.
44. SPD *Parteitag*, Oct. 1917, p. 10; SPD *Parteitag,* June 1919, p. 54.
45. The basis for a list of defecting organizations is Ebert's report in SPD *Parteitag*, Oct. 1917, p. 235; from this list the constituency organizations of Weimar (erroneously included) and Bremen (which went to the left radicals, not the USPD) should be deleted, while Hof should be added. Detailed membership figures for 1913 are in SPD *Parteitag*, Sept. 1913, pp. 54–71. The amended list includes 57 constituencies, instead of the 62 claimed by the USPD (*Volksblatt* [Halle], Aug. 1, 1917; Hof would make 63); but as the USPD never issued a list we are forced to rely on the SPD's enumeration.
46. In Berlin 28,000 (*Mitteilungs-Blatt,* July 1, 1917); in the Lower Rhineland about 10,000 (USPD-Niederrhein *Parteitag*, April 1919, p. 8); in the Leipzig district the figure for 1917 must have been about 15,000, or midway between the figures available for 1916 and 1918 (SPD *Parteitag*, Oct. 1917, p. 10, and USPD-Sachsen *Landesversammlung*, Aug. 1919, p. 12). A copy of the party's accounts for the year ending March 31, 1918, fell into the hands of the Düsseldorf police: IML Berlin, Reichskanzlei 8/13, pp. 24–28. These are the only detailed accounts we have for the entire history of the party, and they do not include membership figures.

there was little the party could do to alter this exaggerated imbalance during the remaining months of the war. The USPD began as a regional party, its national significance depending largely on its considerable local and regional importance in certain areas, and it never entirely overcame this limitation.

Berlin was the most important component for the original USPD, in part because of the sheer size of the city—with some two million inhabitants in 1914 and nearly four million after the extension of its boundaries in the fall of 1920, Berlin was the only German city of over a million, and its prewar party membership (120,000) was correspondingly high.[47] Equally important, the central leadership of the socialist parties was immersed, willy-nilly, in the atmosphere of the Berlin party. Appropriately for a city with many large factories and a rapidly growing and not very stable proletariat, the party there was traditionally radical. While the established leaders of the Greater Berlin district and of a few of its eight constituency organizations remained loyal to the policies of the SPD party executive, the antiwar trend was strong in constituency meetings from the start of the war and was encouraged by *Vorwärts,* a centrist newspaper (insofar as the censors allowed) of high quality.[48] By the summer of 1916 the opposition had ousted all the party executive's adherents from key positions, so that the entire organizational structure (though by no means all of the members) passed to the USPD the following spring. The spirit was one of advanced radicalism. Although few of the radical militants ultimately followed the Spartacists, a majority of the Berlin party's influential members displayed a left-wing tendency, reflected in the popularity of the intransigent Ledebour and the election of the strident Adolph Hoffmann as chairman for Greater Berlin in 1916.

For all its radical tone, however, the Berlin organization's impact in the USPD appears to have been more psychological—in persuading the national leadership to edge leftward (or to appear to do so)—than organizational. In part this may have been because the Berlin organiza-

47. SPD *Parteitag,* Oct. 1917, p. 10. The Greater Berlin organization incorporated the six city constituencies plus the Teltow-Beeskow and Niederbarnim organizations, which covered most of the city's industrial suburbs. The Teltow-Beeskow party and two of the city organizations ranked third, fourth and fifth in membership among all the constituency organizations in the SPD in 1913. Decision-making was centralized to a high degree in the Greater Berlin central organization by 1914, and this remained the case in the USPD.
48. On constituency meetings, see the police reports in DZA Merseburg, Rep. 77 Tit. 332r Nr. 126; StA Potsdam, Pr. Br. Rep. 30 Berlin C Polizeipräsidium, Tit. 95 Sekt. 7 Lit. A Nr. 11a, vols. 3 to 20. *Vorwärts* had some unusually able editors, among them Rudolf Hilferding (until May 1915), Ernst Däumig, Heinrich Ströbel, and the prominent Spartacist Ernst Meyer.

tion produced no significant leaders during the life of the USPD; after Hoffmann, a succession of second-rank bureaucrats held the top positions. If the party executive operated in the shadow of the radical Berlin membership, the Berlin leaders clearly felt the shadow of the national leadership. However radical their spokesmen, the Berlin members never set themselves in opposition to the more moderate central leadership during, and even after, the war. At critical points—most notably in June 1916 and December 1918—the radical Berliners failed to put forward a line of their own and favored the position of the official moderates rather than that of the Spartacists.[49] Overall, the Berlin party organization was less of an actor in internal party matters than many smaller party districts.

The second most important stronghold of the USPD, Leipzig, did have independent weight in the party. Germany's fifth largest city had one of the oldest socialist traditions in Germany, and in 1914 one of its two consituency organizations, Leipzig-Land, which embraced the outlying working-class districts, was the second largest constituency party in the SPD, having over 40,000 members.[50] In Leipzig, too, the party tradition was radical, but with a difference. The dominant element was not working-class discontent but rather a long-standing, doctrinaire, conventional acceptance of the formulations of centrist Marxism. Reinforced by the policies of the *Leipziger Volkszeitung,* the Leipzig version of Marxist radicalism penetrated most of the city's far-flung socialist institutions, including many trade unions and a good part of the consumer cooperative movement. Consequently, as the war proceeded, the opposition was able to mobilize nearly all of the Leipzig labor movement.

Leipzig had a small but active Spartacist minority, which was prominent early in the war; and even non-Spartacists sometimes displayed an aggressive strain of radicalism.[51] The well-entrenched leadership, however, under the remarkable Richard Lipinski, who administered the Leipzig district organization, and to a considerable extent the local Leipzig party as well, from his position as district chairman, was essentially centrist. Lipinski was the party man par excellence, a sturdy socialist but committed to maintaining the coherence and effectiveness of the organization over which he presided; for him, socialist activism always took a back seat when the security or unity of his party was threatened. After a

49. The two cases are mentioned on pp. 47–48 above and pp. 206–7 below.
50. *Bericht des Vorstandes und Sekretariats über das verflossene Geschäftsjahr 1913/14 des Sozialdemokratischen Vereins für den 13. sächs[ischen] Reichstagswahlkreis* (Leipzig, 1914), pp. 10 and 12.
51. See K. Schneider, especially the early chapters.

phase early in the war when Lipinski was visibly reluctant to lead his organization into open opposition, he showed himself a master at maintaining contact with his membership's wishes, even if this meant leading strike demonstrations in person.[52] His careful course was supported by other prominent local socialists, including the increasingly influential Fritz Seger, local editor of the *Leipziger Volkszeitung,* and, most important, by the newspaper itself. The *Volkszeitung*'s tone in 1917 and 1918, when it was the most widely read paper in the USPD, was of somewhat radicalized centrism, leavened by articles representing all shades of opinion, from Karl Kautsky to Franz Mehring and Clara Zetkin. The key editors, however, were predominantly centrist, and the paper, like the Leipzig organization, proved to be a bastion of the USPD's right wing.

Such strong leadership together with a long tradition of being on the left in the party were guaranteed to ensure the adherence of the Leipzig party organization to the USPD. The one-sidedness with which the Leipzig party split off is nevertheless noteworthy. When the SPD founded its counterorganization in Leipzig in March 1917 it was able initially to rally only 80 members out of the more than 12,000 remaining to the Leipzig organization; in the Leipzig party district as a whole—four constituencies—the SPD's April 1916 membership of 19,552 had shrunk to 428 a year later.[53] No other metropolitan area had such a one-sided majority for the left; and though the SPD recovered somewhat after the war, the Independent organization in Leipzig had an unparalleled, lasting solidity in its local support. For the party in general, and its more moderate forces in particular, this fact was important.[54]

The directly adjoining Halle district was very different. It was a sprawling rural region, with one large industrial city, several smaller manufacturing towns, significant deposits of brown coal, copper, and potash, and a few giant electrical and chemical installations rising abruptly out of the farmlands. Halle itself, a city of just under 200,000, had about a third of the district's organized Social Democrats in 1914.[55] With a total membership of only 26,089 in 1914 the district had not been one of the more prominent in the old SPD. In the USPD, how-

52. Evidence of Lipinski's early backwardness is collected *ibid.,* pp. 96, 126–28, and 131, and in *Dokumente und Materialien,* I, 94–95.

53. StA Dresden, Kreishauptmannschaft Leipzig 2527h, pp. 170, 231–32, and 258; SPD *Parteitag,* Oct. 1917, p. 10. A year later, in April 1918, the SPD's membership for the district was still only 572; see SPD *Parteitag,* June 1919, p. 54.

54. Leipzig's influence within Saxony was even more marked; as seat of the state party executive (under Lipinski) it subsidized and dominated politically the smaller Saxon districts, except for Dresden.

55. *Volksblatt* (Halle), Dec. 12, 1914.

ever, which took over the district organization and all eight constituency organizations, the district was to become the second strongest in the party, with a peak membership of perhaps three times the prewar figure.[56] It also became the most important stronghold of the party's left wing.

The sources of this upsurge of social radicalism in the Halle district have never been closely studied, but some explanations may be suggested. The work forces of the vast new plants that, attracted by ready access to water and brown coal, were invading the area just before and during the war, were plainly important. These new plants caused a sudden rapid expansion of the industrial labor force, much of which was either not rooted in the area or not accustomed to factory work, especially in such huge plants; the greatest of them, the nitrate works at Leuna, was established in the fields south of Merseburg in 1916 and employed 15,000 workers before the end of the war. Under certain conditions the workers of these plants could become the shocktroops of radicalism.[57] The miners, too—especially the copper miners of the Mansfeld region around Eisleben—became radicalized during the revolution as they experienced a kind of liberation from the oppressive domination of the mine-owners; they quickly turned to the most radical, activist forms of socialism. Both the new chemical workers and the newly political miners put their weight behind the radical policies favored by the district leadership.

The third source of radicalism, and the backbone of its organizational strength, was more conventional: the party organization and factories of Halle. That the Halle party should have supported the antiwar opposition was natural enough; the local party tradition was to the left, as were the editors of the *Volksblatt* under editor-in-chief Paul Hennig. Less easy to explain is how the Halle organization came to attach itself so firmly to the radical wing of the USPD. Many influential local leaders, such as Hennig and Reichstag deputy Adolf Albrecht, were centrists and party men; the newspaper, indeed, appeared motivated more by pacifism and

56. The district claimed a membership of 82,000 on the eve of the schism of October 1920; see *Die Internationale* (Left USPD), Oct. 27, 1920.
57. The best survey of this phenomenon seems to be that of the district governor in a report of April 13, 1917, in DZA Merseburg, Rep. 77 Tit. 1059 Nr. 3 Beiheft III, pp. 71–75. See also Eberhard Schulz, "Rolle und Anteil des linken Flügels der USPD im ehemaligen Regierungsbezirk Halle-Merseburg bei der Herausbildung und Entwicklung der KPD zur revolutionären Massenpartei (1917–1920)" (Ph.D. dissertation, University of Halle-Wittenberg, 1969), pp. 16–20. On how the radicals organized the Leuna workers, see Wilhelm Koenen in *Vorwärts und nicht vergessen: Erlebnisberichte aktiver Teilnehmer der Novemberrevolution 1918/1919* (Berlin, 1960), pp. 377–83.

less by social radicalism than even the *Leipziger Volkszeitung.* On the other hand, Halle was a center of the metalworking industry, so often the breeding ground of left-wing militancy. In Halle's case the factory movement was tied unusually closely to the party, mainly through the agency of the young provincial editor of the *Volksblatt,* Wilhelm Koenen. Koenen, who arrived in his Halle job in 1911 aged twenty-five and held three important elective posts in the labor movement there by 1914, was both a convinced radical Marxist and an unusually resourceful organization man, probably the most formidable organization man of the far left wing (the workers' council wing) of the USPD. But while the war lasted, the Halle party was still far from being entirely Koenen's party. It took the district's special postwar experience of the councils and the socialization movement to mold the Halle organization into the monolithic radical phenomenon it later became.[58]

The fourth center of USPD membership strength, the Lower Rhineland district (focused on the western Ruhr and the heavy industrial cities to the south of it), had yet another character. Here the opposition had dominated the entire organization and party press early in the war, and though the party executive's counteroffensive of 1916 and 1917 had cost the opposition control of the district treasury and several newspapers, the USPD finally took six of the most important constituency organizations (Düsseldorf, Solingen, Remscheid, Elberfeld-Barmen, Essen and Hagen), comprising over four-fifths of the district's membership, and three newspapers (in Düsseldorf, Solingen, and Remscheid).[59] The district organization of the USPD was not strong, partly because repeated arrests frustrated all attempts to stabilize the district leadership while the war lasted, partly because the Düsseldorf organization, the natural leader of the district, was afflicted with an unruly membership that kept it in permanent crisis well into 1919.[60] The most influential spokesman for the district came to be a relatively inconspicuous functionary from the little metalworking town of Remscheid, Otto Brass, a radical but an organization man with strong roots in the realities of the working class. But for all its weak cohesion, this district, with its large numbers (it consistently made up about 10 percent of the USPD's total membership)

58. See chs. 5 and 7, below.
59. Data from Otto Brass's report in USPD-Niederrhein *Parteitag,* April 1919, pp. 6–8; in contradiction to Brass, however, I have credited the Essen organization to the USPD, since the SPD conceded it and the USPD claimed it in 1917. See SPD *Parteitag,* Oct. 1917, p. 235; *Volksblatt* (Halle), Aug. 1, 1917; the account in Walther and Engelmann, I, 207–8, is ambiguous. Of the newspapers, the Düsseldorf *Volkszeitung* fell to the SPD in April 1918 but returned to the USPD during the revolution.
60. USPD-Niederrhein *Parteitag,* April 1919, p. 5; Dittmann memoirs, p. 641.

and its collection of important socialist centers, was necessarily one of the most significant in the party.

The few other district organizations of the USPD that brought some strength from the old party were not comparable to those already mentioned. In the ducal state of Braunschweig, for instance, the entire district organization went to the Independents, leaving the Majority Socialists with a few hundred members; Braunschweig, however, though its postwar political history was to have its spectacular moments, was politically a second-rate entity, a congeries of exposed enclaves in Prussian territory, and small—the USPD's wartime membership there cannot have exceeded 5,000.[61] In Thuringia, at that time still a geographical expression for a hilly region of scattered old manufacturing towns comprising eight petty princely states with a Prussian government district (Erfurt) lying among them, the USPD made off with the whole of the Erfurt district organization, five other constituency organizations, and the newspapers in Erfurt, Nordhausen, Gotha, Gera, and Greiz. The combined Thuringian organization was numerically of some importance in the USPD—it may have brought some six or seven thousand members to the party in 1917 and grew rapidly after the war—and it became politically significant after the formation of a united Thuringia (minus the Prussian territories) in 1920. But as a district organization it was little more than a fiction; its strongholds were interspersed with equally vigorous Majority Socialist organizations in towns (such as Weimar) where the USPD initially had scarcely a foothold; and it was divided by the differing political circumstances of the petty states and by ideological differences among the local parties—from the militant radicalism of Gotha to the sturdy centrism of Gera and Greiz.[62] Finally, there was the strange case of the Frankfurt on Main district, the only instance of the whole hinterland of a district coming to the USPD without the dominant city organization. The impulse here, offsetting the influence of the right-wing *Frankfurter Volksstimme,* was provided by the prodigiously energetic Robert Dissmann, the district secretary, who converted all opposition to the party executive into organizational strength for the opposition.[63] The Frankfurt party district, with Hanau and Höchst as its cen-

---

61. The SPD's Braunschweig membership was 5,926 in March 1916, 335 a year later; SPD *Parteitag,* Oct. 1917, p. 10. There was apparently a general attrition of about 20 percent in overall socialist membership in this year, so that fewer than 5,000 are likely to have gone to the USPD.

62. On Gera see n. 22 above: on Gotha, Ulrich Hess, *Die Vorbereitung und Durchführung der Novemberrevolution 1918 im Lande Gotha* (Gotha, 1960), and Ewald Buchsbaum, "Die Linksentwicklung der Gothaer Arbeiterbewegung von 1914 bis 1920" (Ph.D. dissertation, University of Halle-Wittenberg, 1965).

63. The critical phase of the Frankfurt split, with the arguments of both sides,

ters in addition to a newly founded Frankfurt organization, made up the core of a new, larger Southwest district for Dissmann to administer; and he made it one of the few in the party to grow significantly before the end of the war.[64]

These seven district organizations constituted the backbone of the USPD, making the existence of the party in some measure secure. But the remaining thirty district organizations of the SPD were largely unshaken, suffering the defection of only small groups of members. The old party did lose control of the Bremen organization, but to the left radicals, who in Bremen remained aloof from the USPD; the newly founded Independent organization there, with Alfred Henke as spiritus rector, was locally considerable but under pressure from the parties on either wing from the start. The two big Königsberg constituencies came to the USPD, but the Independents, despite their strong base there, were slow to make an impression on the rest of the province of East Prussia; and the same was true in Pomerania, where the USPD captured the strongest constituency party, that of Randow-Griefenhagen (outside Stettin). In Württemberg, the belated accession of the radical breakaway organization formed in 1914 brought pockets of support to the Independents; the membership there was small, however, and, as a predominantly Spartacist organization, its value to the USPD was problematic.[65] In Dresden, where the opposition, under the leadership of newspaper editor Hermann Fleissner, had challenged the majority for dominance during 1915 and 1916, the split left the USPD a tenacious but small minority.[66]

In no other major city did the USPD have even as much of a foothold as in Dresden. In Hamburg, Cologne, Munich, and Breslau—in size the second, third, fourth, and seventh cities of Germany—the new party was little more than an underground sect. In all of Prussia east of the Elbe the Independents had no daily newspaper and were hardly visible outside of the Berlin, Königsberg, and Stettin areas during the war. The same was true of the vast Prussian province of Hanover, of the Rhineland apart from the Düsseldorf-Elberfeld area, and of Westphalia (including most of the Ruhr mining district), where USPD mem-

was reported extensively in the opposition press in the summer of 1916 and may be followed in (among others) *Volksblatt* (Halle), July 3, 10, 12, 13, and 19–21, 1916. See also Koszyk, pp. 55–58, and Dieter Schneider and Franz Neuland, *Zwischen Römer und Revolution* (Frankfurt on Main, 1969), pp. 54–56.

64. *Mitteilungs-Blatt,* July 28, 1918.

65. The Württemberg organization joined the USPD only in October 1917. Its membership at the time of the revolution was later given as 2,000; see *Freiheit,* Nov. 6, 1919 (m).

66. Ernst Lorenz, *5 Jahre Dresdner USP: Ein rückschauendes Betrachten anlässlich des fünfjährigen Bestehens der Partei* (Dresden [1922]), pp. 9–13.

bership in December 1918 was a negligible 2,000;[67] of Grand Ducal Hesse, of Baden, and of the whole of southern Bavaria, where in May 1918 the USPD had a single local branch (Munich) with about 400 members.[68] Across great stretches of the country there were no USPD organizations, and where locals did exist they boasted a few dozen, at the most a few hundred, members.

The party organization of the USPD reflected this heavily unbalanced membership picture, being powerful in a few great centers and feeble or nonexistent in much of the rest of the country. A year after its foundation, the USPD had established itself organizationally in just over 140 of the 397 constituencies of the country.[69] These were grouped into 22 districts, as against the former 38, by drastic consolidation where the party was weak. Robert Dissmann's new Southwest district, for instance, included not only his former Frankfurt district but five others as well.[70] Consolidation had also produced a single district for the North Sea coast, from Bremen to Kiel, with its seat in Hamburg and Alfred Henke as secretary.[71] The Lower Rhineland district organization had to take over care of the practically nonexistent organizations for Westphalia and the Middle Rhineland.[72] But these at least had a solid core, whereas the consolidated Silesia district—comprising four former districts—had but two constituency organizations and existed mainly on paper.[73]

The case was even worse with the party press. The USPD took over fourteen of the eighty-odd daily papers of the SPD and three weeklies (the Berlin *Mitteilungs-Blatt,* the Stuttgart *Sozialdemokrat,* and Rudolf Breitscheid's *Sozialistische Auslandspolitik,* which, after Kautsky's dismissal from *Neue Zeit* in September 1917, served unofficially as party journal).[74] Some of the dailies were of considerable regional, or even

67. *Freiheit,* Oct. 15, 1919 (e).

68. Karl-Ludwig Ay, *Die Entstehung einer Revolution* (Berlin, 1968), pp. 194–95.

69. Data from the USPD treasurer's report of April 1, 1918, in IML Berlin, Reichskanzlei 8/13, p. 27.

70. See Dissmann's reports in *Mitteilungs-Blatt,* esp. July 28, 1918.

71. *Partei-Mitteilungen für die Organisationen der Unabhängigen Sozialdemokratie Deutschlands, Bezirk Waterkant,* Aug. 11, 1917. This was the first and only issue of an intended weekly bulletin. See also Lucas, *Sozialdemokratie in Bremen,* p. 93.

72. USPD-Niederrhein *Parteitag,* April 1919, pp. 22–23; *Freiheit,* Oct. 15, 1919 (e).

73. IML Berlin, Reichskanzlei 8/13, p. 27; see also Wolfgang Schumann, *Oberschlesien 1918/19: Vom gemeinsamen Kampf deutscher und polnischer Arbeiter* (Berlin, 1961), pp. 53 and 114.

74. See the list circulated by the German Admiralty on Sept. 26, 1917, in *Militär und Innenpolitik im Weltkrieg 1914–1918,* ed. Wilhelm Deist, 2 vols. (Düsseldorf, 1970), II, 1060, which is complete except for the omission of the *Oberfränkische Volkszeitung* (Hof) and Breitscheid's *Sozialistische Auslandspolitik.*

national, significance, including the *Leipziger Volkszeitung*—effectively
the USPD's central organ until November 1918—and the Düsseldorf,
Erfurt, and Halle papers. But they formed two limited regional concentrations; apart from the three Rhineland papers, all the others appeared in a strip of Central Germany running from Pirna (near Dresden)
in the east to Nordhausen and Gotha in western Thuringia, with the
Halle district on the northern edge and Hof as a small Bavarian append-
age. The devoted militant elsewhere might occasionally subscribe to the
Leipzig paper, or more likely to the weekly *Mitteilungs-Blatt* from Berlin, but more probably read the local press of some other political shad-
ing or no newspaper at all. It was a truism among German socialists that
organizational work could never go beyond a fairly primitive level without the help of a local newspaper; in the USPD's circumstances, loss of
existing support had to be feared if members could not be reached
through the press. But attempts to remedy the situation were generally
vain. Henke's Coastal district succeeded in putting out a bulletin for its
members in August 1917, but the authorities killed it after the first issue.
The same happened in Königsberg.[75] Other projects, notably Kautsky's
attempt to found an *Internationale Neue Zeit* to carry on his life's work,
never got as far as the first issue.[76] Only in Nuremberg, in July 1918, was
a weekly paper established that survived, and it lived only because its
stubborn sponsors printed it on wrapping paper when none of the ra-
tioned newsprint was forthcoming.[77] Effectively, the USPD press, and
hence to a large extent USPD influence, remained confined to its original strongholds.

The opposition's success in one city and lack of success in the next
cannot be explained simply by local party tradition—even if we had a
reliable way of measuring local party tradition—for the influence of
strong leaders or vigorous minorities is often evident.[78] The case of
Robert Dissmann in the Frankfurt district organization has already been
cited. In some parts of the country, notably northern Bavaria and parts

75. Koszyk, p. 91. The Königsberg paper managed two issues before it was
suppressed.
76. See the material in the Karl Kautsky papers (IISH Amsterdam), G 10.
77. Klaus-Dieter Schwarz, *Weltkrieg und Revolution in Nürnberg* (Stuttgart,
1971), p. 252.
78. Schorske's interesting attempt to correlate wartime and prewar radicalism in
local parties (pp. 282–83) treats the political bias of an organization's delegation
to prewar congresses as a mirror of the political complexion of the organization,
though congress delegates were then still widely elected without particular regard
to their faction; and in any case the lines of schism in 1917 were influenced by
many factors beyond general tendencies among the membership. Cf. the criticism
of Schorske in Nipperdey, pp. 337–38. Schorske's point is generally true all the
same, but he has used misleading data; an adequate demonstration would require
direct investigation of local circumstances.

of Thuringia and the Lower Rhineland, influential party leaders who placed party unity above their own sentiments kept their flocks safely in the SPD. The influence in particular of newspapers, which often represented more the views of their editors than of any settled majority in the local party, should not be underestimated; in Stuttgart the original dominance of the opposition—quite a radical opposition—faded away gradually after it lost control of the *Schwäbische Tagwacht* in November 1914; similarly the fortunes of the Majority Socialists in Berlin improved markedly after *Vorwärts* was seized for their cause in October 1916. Overall, the correlation of newspaper policy with local party policy is very close.[79] In every town where the newspaper went to the USPD the party organization went as well. And there was no significant Independent center in the Reich, with the exception of Dissmann's Frankfurt district, where the local party paper had not been opposition-oriented for at least the early part of the war.

The cause of the USPD's failure to extend its influence significantly while the war lasted, despite the workers' increasing receptivity to socialist radicalism, was the state of siege. The military authorities had been harassing the party left—and not always only the left—since the early months of the war, censoring and intermittently suspending its press, restricting public assemblies and even closed party meetings, systematically preventing leading figures from delivering speeches, opening mail, arresting people who led demonstrations or distributed leaflets, conscripting the militants in the factories, and imposing preventive detention where none of these other measures was effective. With the formation of the USPD the authorities at last had a well-defined target for their efforts to suppress subversion. On June 14, 1917, the minister of war addressed a circular to the military commands in Germany, laying upon them the responsibility to employ all means "suitable for checking the influence of Independent Social Democracy on the populace."[80] As this command reached the local police during the summer, the state of siege took on an edge directed specifically at the USPD.

Though the circular was secret, its results were quickly obvious.[81]

79. Nipperdey, p. 338, holds that the editors' views generally determined local party attitudes, rather than vice versa. This is plausible; but there were some prominent counterexamples before the war (Berlin, Stuttgart), and some species of mutual influence between editors and local militants was probably more common than any simple one-way effect. The matter needs more detailed local investigation than we now have.

80. *Militär und Innenpolitik,* II, 761–64. See two follow-up memoranda in DZA Potsdam, Reichskanzlei 2439/1, pp. 226–27 and 314.

81. See Haase's letter to Chancellor Michaelis, Aug. 20, 1917, in DZA Potsdam, Reichskanzlei 2439/1, pp. 208–14. Many of the following particulars are taken from this letter.

Not only the party's scheduled public assemblies but also its regular party meetings were commonly forbidden or made practically impossible by the stringent conditions attached to permission. Except in the case of the little Nuremberg weekly, all attempts to extend the party's press were frustrated, usually with reference to limited supplies of newsprint—though such shortage did not prevent the Majority Socialists from founding new papers in Leipzig, Halle, and Düsseldorf. Luise Zietz, Emil Eichhorn, Sepp Oerter, and others were banned from speaking anywhere; others, Haase among them, suffered local or regional bans of the same sort—Henke, for instance, in the Coastal district of which he was party secretary. Conscription of opposition militants became more common, often in the wake of strikes but sometimes as a preventive measure.[82] Searches of USPD offices and the homes of its leaders were frequent. The *Leipziger Volkszeitung* was even threatened with permanent closure.[83]

This harassment was still restrained by an attenuated adherence to concepts of the rule of law, and more directly by fears that the socialists, perhaps with liberal and Catholic support, might make trouble in the Reichstag if persecution of a political party became too blatant. But the impact on the attitudes of the more party-minded leaders of the USPD was considerable. Their party, in addition to its other difficulties—its uneven distribution, its weak center and poor communications, its tenuous coherence—was threatened with outright extinction if it ever gave the military cause for action. While the war lasted, the USPD, for all its aggressive rhetoric and its sense that the hour of socialism might be approaching, was on the defensive, a party of enclaves, united mainly by force of circumstance, looking to a hopeful future but living in an exceptionally uncertain present.

82. An extreme example is provided by the case of Wilhelmshaven, a naval port where an attempt was made to found a local USPD group early in 1918; the leader was sent to prison for three years, and all sixty of his comrades were called up by the army. See *Die Auswirkungen der Grossen Sozialistischen Oktoberrevolution auf Deutschland,* ed. Leo Stern, Archivalische Forschungen zur Geschichte der deutschen Arbeiterbewegung, vols. 4/I–4/IV (Berlin, 1959) (hereafter cited as *Auswirkungen*), III, 1117–20.

83. See the protest letter of the editors in DZA Potsdam, RMdI 12277, pp. 235–47.

CHAPTER 3

Toward Revolution (1917–1918)

The issue that dominated the life of the new Independent Social Democratic Party in 1917 and 1918, directly or indirectly, was mass action—eventually revolution itself. The party had not been founded in this expectation; while all Independents held that the long class struggle was in an active phase, and intended to fight the war and the autocratic and militaristic forces behind it, few can have imagined at first that revolution might become a reality in Germany in the foreseeable future. There were active revolutionaries in the USPD from the start, but they were not in command of the party; nor was it their efforts that, in November 1918, brought down the old regime, which, on the contrary, died of its own infirmities when the populace was confronted with the fact of a lost war. Indeed a substantial part of the USPD responded only reluctantly to the radical activism that was growing within the party during the latter part of the war. Yet the events of 1917 and 1918 made the USPD the political vehicle of the emergent revolutionary forces in the German labor movement and the central revolutionary party of the postwar period of upheaval. Its deficiencies as a revolutionary party were all too obvious: divided purpose, organizational weakness, the prevalence of skepticism and timidity and narrow traditionalism in the party, including much of the national leadership. By 1918, however, the terms of debate in this divided party were dictated by the hazy prospect of radical upheaval, toward which the party increasingly oriented itself, and finally by the onset of revolution.

The groundwork for this unanticipated development was laid by the revolution in Russia, which, taking place in March, preceded the formation of the USPD by a few weeks and which had a vague but powerful impact on the thinking of advanced socialists everywhere. Rosa Luxemburg spoke for more than the Spartacists when she said: "The Russian events are of a mighty, incalculable significance, and I regard what has happened there up to now as only a small overture. Things there must pass over into the grandiose, that is in the nature of the case. And an

echo in the whole world is inevitable."[1] In the USPD, the Russian revolution served as an overture to the serious adoption of ideas of mass action and revolution in the party.

The echo raised on the activist left was naturally the clearest. Events in Russia gave faith to those Germans who had the will to revolution, and over the course of the following summer the prospect of a serious challenge to the Imperial regime came to dominate the thoughts of the radicals. The effect on the party was divisive, for some radicals, taking up a position antithetical to that of the centrists, began to see revolution as unconditionally necessary and all other hopes as futile unless predicated on social revolution.[2] The clash of views was not yet so sharp in practice, since the centrists were quite prepared to go the first step— mass action—with the radicals; but the spirit of the two sides was different and the latent divergence dangerous. The political precepts of many militants were growing more like those of the Spartacists, though disagreements over method remained important. Däumig, Ledebour, and other experienced Social Democrats held that the first necessity was to organize carefully for the revolution and construct a definite chain of command.[3] Others, including the Spartacists, thought of the coming revolution as a great groundswell; accordingly, intensive agitation was their only concern. There was friction here, but enough of a bond for the Spartacists and the radicals to function in some matters as a united revolutionary wing in the USPD.

The more moderate sectors of the party were also enthusiastic about the March revolution in Russia. The minority's Reichstag delegation sent a warm message to the Russian socialists, the "vanguard of socialism and international solidarity," while Haase declared that "the mighty world-historical event of this revolution not only completely alters the political and social life of this country [i.e. Russia], but reaches out beyond its frontiers."[4] The Russian revolution gave a new impulse to the centrists' peace program, both because it showed the efficacy of mass action and because a democratic Russia seemed likely to be anxious to end the war with a just peace—a peace without annexations or indemnities and founded on self-determination, to use the formula of the Petrograd workers' and soldiers' council. For such a peace, the democratization of the Reich was also highly desirable, and now seemed more

1. Letter to Clara Zetkin, April 13, 1917, Clara Zetkin collection (IML Berlin), NL 5 III—A/14, p. 3.
2. See, for example, the editorial in *Mitteilungs-Blatt*, Oct. 28, 1917.
3. On Däumig's views, see the police report of March 1917 in *Auswirkungen*, II, 388. Cf. R. Müller, *Kaiserreich*, I, 80–81.
4. Both quotations from *Reichstag*, vol. 309, pp. 2887–88.

likely than ever before; having witnessed the fate of the tsar, surely the ruling classes in Germany would have to concede important domestic reforms.

But most leaders of the USPD did not believe that Germany could or would experience revolution while the war lasted. The strength of the antirevolutionary forces, especially the military, was regarded as too overwhelming; the most that could be done was to prepare the ground by agitation for the upheaval that must surely come sometime after the end of the war, the return of the troops and demobilization, and the end of the state of siege. Even before the end of the war revolutionary socialism could be strengthened to the point of being a decisive force in resisting the war effort and pressing for far-reaching democratization. On this base the revolutionary movement could build after the restoration of civil freedoms.[5] Moreover, the centrists feared that adventurous revolutionary actions might give the military authorities occasion to cripple the movement decisively before the real struggle began. There must and would be mass action, but for sensible, attainable goals.

Whatever the reservations held, the idea of a genuinely activist radicalism was in the ascendent once the Russians had led the way, and the following unruly months saw the left-wing socialists trying to work out the consequences of their changing perspective. The USPD was embarked on its ambivalent career as a party of radical mass action.

The USPD and Mass Action

Mass action was under way in Germany in the spring of 1917, though not in response to the wishes of the socialist left. The impulse came from simple misery. The winter of 1916–1917, the third winter of the war, brought the worst hardships the German populace had yet suffered, indeed the worst they were to know in the whole war. Food was exceptionally difficult to obtain—Düsseldorf, for instance, went seven weeks without potatoes;[6] while coal, heating oil, and winter clothing were also in short supply. Starting in February, Germany experienced a series of strikes, demonstrations, and disorders focusing on the shortage of food.[7] When the government announced that the daily ration of bread, the re-

---

5. See the editorial in *Mitteilungs-Blatt,* May 27, 1917 (when it was still expressing orthodox party attitudes); the USPD's presentation to the organizing committee in Stockholm in July 1917, as reported by a police agent, in *Auswirkungen,* II, 567–68; Wheeler, "Internationals," p. 55. Russian socialists also understood this to be the USPD's view; see Abraham Ascher, "Russian Marxism and the German Revolution, 1917–1920," *Archiv für Sozialgeschichte,* 6/7 (1966–67), 394 and 396.

6. Report in DZA Potsdam, RMdI 13581, p. 188.

7. See the table in *Dokumente und Materialien,* I, 702–4.

maining staple that had carried people through the winter, would be reduced, widespread disturbances on the date of the reduction were predictable.[8]

The great April strike of 1917—Germany's first major strike about something other than the usual trade-union issues—was thus the culmination of a movement in which the socialist leaders had no hand.[9] Even the coordination of action in the cities where the strike began simultaneously, on April 16—Berlin, Leipzig, Danzig, Magdeburg, Braunschweig, and a few smaller cities—was effected, not by the socialists, but by a uniform reduction of the bread ration the day before. Certainly the factory opposition leaders generally took over the strike leadership.[10] And contacts through the network of the political opposition played a role; in particular, a brief meeting of radical delegates at the USPD's founding congress in Gotha encouraged a few Leipzig Independents to take the lead in organizing the strike there. But only in Leipzig was the strike associated from beginning to end, not merely with the improvement of food supplies, but with political aims, such as the restoration and extension of civil liberties and an immediate declaration of German readiness to enter into peace negotiations on socialist principles.[11] In Berlin, after the strike had already been under way for two days and was about to be broken off, the leading Independents entered the lists and attempted to persuade the workers to adopt the Leipzig demands and remain on strike until the demands were met. They had only meager success.[12] Elsewhere, even in such radical centers as Halle and Braunschweig, the strike was nothing more than a well-organized protest at the shortage of food.

The April strike was nevertheless a significant event; after it everyone had cause to take mass action seriously, including the government. Indeed, industrial unrest revived in June (from much the same causes)

8. See, for instance, the predictions of the commanding general of the Ruhr area in a letter of March 22, 1917, in IML Berlin, RMdI 9/11, pp. 84–86.

9. There is no full account of this strike, though the military reports in *Militär und Innenpolitik*, II, 724–35, add up to a kind of survey. For Berlin see Heinrich Scheel, "Der Aprilstreik 1917 in Berlin," in *Revolutionäre Ereignisse und Probleme in Deutschland während der Periode der Grossen Sozialistischen Oktoberrevolution 1917/1918*, ed. Albert Schreiner (Berlin, 1957), pp. 3–88; for Leipzig, see K. Schneider, pp. 171–213, with documents in an appendix, pp. xxxiv-xlvi.

10. In both Berlin and Leipzig the strike call came from regular assemblies of the Metalworkers, in Berlin against the wishes of the union leadership.

11. K. Schneider, pp. 171–72, 175–77, and xxxvii-xxxix (Lipinski's speech to the strikers). For the demands of the Leipzig strikers, see *Dokumente und Materialien*, I, 612.

12. Police report of April 19, 1917, IML Berlin, RMdI 9/11, p. 112; military memorandum of May 7, 1917, *Auswirkungen*, II, 511–12. See also Scheel in *Revolutionäre Ereignisse*, pp. 52–55.

and gave its stamp to the summer. It proved unexpectedly hard, however, for the Independents—mainly but not exclusively the radicals and Spartacists—to give these strikes any focus or political coordination, and their strenuous efforts to foster political action among the skeptical workers had only local success during the summer. The first effort, a veiled call by the USPD's Reichstag and Prussian Diet delegations for demonstrations and strikes on May Day, seems to have met with virtually no response.[13] A strike in Leipzig on July 16 attracted only a few participants, even though the party involved itself at the last minute; and a broad strike movement planned for August 15 ultimately made itself felt only locally, in the Halle district and Braunschweig.[14] These efforts provoked efficient countermeasures by the authorities, in particular waves of arrests and conscription; significantly, in neither Leipzig nor Halle did the workers turn out in numbers for the great strike of the following January. Soon the uncoordinated summer unrest was past. By September all was quiet, so quiet indeed that even moderate Independents were exasperated by the lassitude of the masses.[15]

Autumn, however, brought a new impulse from outside. Early in September, after negotiations lasting nearly five months had failed to result in a general conference of the Socialist International, representatives of parties of the Zimmerwald group assembled in Stockholm for a conference of their own. In their impatience delegates turned to the old idea of an international general strike, which should serve as a declaration of support for the Russian revolution and as the first step toward ending the war by simultaneous pressure on all the belligerent governments. Only Haase is known to have voted against this plan, on grounds of impracticality. He was unceremoniously overridden; his colleague Ledebour was one of the strike's most enthusiastic supporters. A manifesto was drafted that was, however, to be published only with the consent of

13. Text in *Volksblatt* (Halle), April 26, 1917. The government's files contain no evidence of real May Day strikes in any city. General Groener's claim to have convinced Haase to damp down May Day strikes is, however, not to be taken seriously; see his testimony in Hans Herzfeld, *Die deutsche Sozialdemokratie und die Auflösung der nationalen Einheitsfront im Weltkriege* (Leipzig, 1928), pp. 351–52. Not only would this have been out of character for Haase, but also the USPD did issue its (oblique) appeal for strikes and Haase was in no position to control the results.

14. For Leipzig, see K. Schneider, pp. 220–25. For the background to the strike of Aug. 15, *Auswirkungen*, II, 678, and StA Potsdam, Pr. Br. Rep. 30 Berlin C Polizeipräsidium, Tit. 95 Sekt. 7 Lit. A Nr. 11b, vol. 2, pp. 115–16. For Halle, see *Auswirkungen*, II, 654–56; Schulz, "Rolle und Anteil," pp. 53–59; Koenen, in *Zu einigen Fragen*, p. 134. For Braunschweig, see R. Müller, *Kaiserreich*, I, 89.

15. Haase letter of Oct. 1, 1917, in *Hugo Haase*, p. 150.

Zimmerwald supporters in all the belligerent countries—England, France, and Italy not having been represented at Stockholm.[16]

Despite some hesitations, the USPD apparently felt itself bound by this decision to make an effort of some sort. Contrary to rumors circulating in Germany at the time, there seems never to have been a definite date for the strike, and there is no evidence that in the two months between the Stockholm meeting and the Bolshevik revolution the USPD's plans passed an early preparatory stage. Word spread through the organization that some action was in the offing, though few were told what was intended.[17] Ledebour proclaimed the necessity of an international general strike from the podium of the Reichstag, naturally without being specific.[18] But the response in the country was not encouraging.

One, though not the whole, reason was no doubt that some leading Independents did not have their hearts in the proposed action.[19] Most centrists firmly believed that the initiative for political action of this sort had to come from below and that it was fruitless for the party to try to sow the seeds of activism for some tactical reason of its own. But in the autumn of 1917 they also had strong practical reasons for caution. In August there had been disturbances on some of the ships of the German fleet, and the government's investigation had shown that the leaders of the mutiny were also proselytizers for the USPD who had been in contact with leading Reichstag deputies in the party. The Admiralty jumped to the conclusion that the Independents were inciting mutiny in the armed forces—an unlikely charge in the case of the deputies concerned, Haase, Dittmann, and Ewald Vogtherr, though some lower-ranking members of the party were certainly engaged in activities of this sort.[20] Some government cir-

16. Angelica Balabanoff, "Die Zimmerwalder Bewegung 1914–1919," *Archiv für die Geschichte des Sozialismus und der Arbeiterbewegung,* 12 (1926), 402–6; idem, *Erinnerungen und Erlebnisse* (Berlin, 1927), pp. 167–70; Wheeler, "Internationals," pp. 59–62. Sketchy and incomplete minutes of the meetings are available in Lademacher, I, 456–73. Ledebour claimed to have first proposed the international general strike; see his testimony in Georg Ledebour, ed., *Der Ledebour-Prozess* (Berlin, 1919), p. 23, and his account in a series of newspaper articles from 1931 in the Georg Ledebour papers (ASD Bonn), second article.

17. *Auswirkungen,* II, 713–14; IML Berlin, Reichskanzlei 8/8, p. 304.

18. *Reichstag,* vol. 310, p. 3856.

19. Ledebour was unable to convince a majority of the USPD Reichstag delegation to approve the Stockholm plan; see *Ledebour-Prozess,* p. 24.

20. See the conclusions of the later Reichstag investigating committee, in *Die Ursachen des Deutschen Zusammenbruches im Jahre 1918,* Series 4, 12 vols. (Berlin, 1925–29) (hereafter cited as *Ursachen*), IX/I, xxi–xxiv; and those of a historian certainly not sympathetic to the USPD, Erich Otto Volkmann, *Der Marxismus und das deutsche Heer im Weltkrieg* (Berlin, 1925), pp. 176–82. See also the interesting reconstruction in Daniel Horn, *The German Naval Mutinies of World War I* (New Brunswick, N.J., 1969), esp. pp. 82–93, 112–23, and 131.

cles were anxious to use the occasion to suppress the USPD altogether. For some time the matter hung in the balance, although the evidence against the party leaders was so flimsy that the government's legal advisers, as well as the leaders of all the other parties, advised against taking action.[21] During this crisis the party executive, over Ledebour's protests, sent Luise Zietz on a hasty trip to Stockholm with a plea to delay publication of the inflammatory manifesto.[22] Chancellor Michaelis, in a fit of pique, brought the charges into the open in the Reichstag on October 9; since they still could not be substantiated, more discredit was brought upon the government than the USPD. Though the legal investigation continued for a few more months, and party secretary Zietz found herself in jail for a time, the critical danger for the party was past.

The Bolshevik revolution in Russia on November 7, later to have so divisive an impact on the party, at first united it for action, not least because the coup was accompanied by a powerful appeal for an immediate general peace. In a manifesto of November 11 the party executive greeted this "event of world-historical importance" and called on the German workers to stage mass antiwar demonstrations.[23] The masses, however, failed to act. On the following Sunday—the usual day for demonstrations —there were no more than small, isolated protests; in Berlin the planned meetings were forbidden by the police, and only a few thousand dared to defy the ban.[24] Under pressure from the militants, the party took the matter in hand at the center and attempted to organize a wave of demonstrations across the country for the following Sunday, November 25, with the aid of handbills prepared in Berlin. This activity was necessarily secret, but in many places the local USPD threw its weight behind the plan as far as it dared. But once again police measures were sufficient to disperse the limited number of bold spirits who turned out.[25] The result was just the sort of fiasco that those who were against trying to force the pace had predicted.

Following this plain defeat there was a lull, caused partly by the Bol-

21. *Ursachen*, IX/I, 80–90; Wilhelm Deist, "Die Unruhen in der Marine 1917/18," *Marine-Rundschau*, 68 (1971), 232–37.

22. Balabanoff, "Die Zimmerwalder Bewegung 1914–1919," *Archiv für die Geschichte des Sozialismus und der Arbeiterbewegung*, 13 (1928), 232, and *Erinnerungen*, pp. 172–73. The manifesto was eventually issued in the aftermath of the Bolshevik revolution and caused very little stir.

23. *Leipziger Volkszeitung*, Nov. 12, 1917.

24. See two Berlin police reports in *Dokumente und Materialien*, II, 23–24, and *Auswirkungen*, II, 765–66.

25. For the text of the handbill, see *Auswirkungen*, II, 770–71. For the demonstrations in Berlin, *ibid.*, II, 779–81; in Stettin, IML Berlin, Reichskanzlei 8/13, pp. 1–2; in Leipzig, Gorski, pp. 46–47; in Halle, Schulz, "Rolle und Anteil," pp. 63–64.

sheviks themselves: on November 27 the Soviet government announced that it would seek a separate peace with Germany. This disconcerting news strained the radical socialists' sympathy; it would be hard to call on the German workers to launch an attack on the German Imperial regime if even Bolshevik Russia were to give up the struggle. The Independents, especially the centrists, were also dismayed at the idea of a probably imperialist peace settlement in the East, which would sow the seeds of new wars, while the German military would intensify its efforts on the Western front.[26] The Independents would have liked to dissuade the Bolsheviks, and made vain attempts to get to Stockholm for consultations.[27] But ultimately the only way to do this would be to promise revolution in Germany, and in December 1917 this could scarcely be regarded as likely. The Majority Socialists, and apparently most German workers, welcomed the prospect of even a partial peace that would bring the end of fighting and privation nearer; misgivings were brushed aside.

At this point the German negotiators at Brest-Litovsk made it clear that they intended to inflict a damaging settlement on Soviet Russia, under which Germany would win effective control of great tracts of the former Russian Empire. These terms outraged many socialists, crystallizing a growing dissatisfaction with Chancellor Hertling's new government and with the tribulations of another wartime winter; together these factors aroused active protest against the government and its endless war in a broad section of the working class. Suddenly the USPD had a more receptive audience than ever before.

Under these circumstances the USPD undertook the only large-scale, coordinated subversive action the party ever carried out—the general strike of January 1918. This action was directed toward a just peace, not revolution.[28] There continued to be skeptics in the party executive, but even they were already half-committed to early mass action, and under

26. See for example Ströbel's article in *Leipziger Volkszeitung,* Jan. 4, 1918; for the views of the Spartacists, see Peter Lösche, *Der Bolshewismus im Urteil der deutschen Sozialdemokratie 1903–1920* (Berlin, 1967), pp. 107–9.

27. *Leipziger Volkszeitung,* Dec. 19, 1917, and Jan. 3, 1918. They were unable to get passports. According to Ledebour, the party instead sent a telegram to the Bolshevik representatives in Stockholm telling them they could count on the support of the USPD if they signed a general peace but that the party reserved its position on any treaty signed with the Central Powers alone; *ibid.,* Jan. 26, 1918.

28. The USPD's organization was more responsible than has been generally recognized for encouraging and coordinating the strike. On the origins of USPD involvement see Barth, p. 21; R. Müller, *Kaiserreich,* I, 101; Blumenthal in *1918: Erinnerungen,* pp. 110–12; the confidential Spartacist report in *Auswirkungen,* III, 1131–32; the judicial interrogation of Kurt Eisner, *ibid.,* III, 1245; also the sources given in the following notes. The available information clearly refutes the assertion in Rosenberg, *Birth,* p. 122, that the USPD "refused to take part in illegal activities."

the pressure of their followers in Berlin (especially the shop stewards' committee) and of their auxiliary council they finally agreed to put the party's weight behind an appeal for a general strike. For the party executive itself to issue such an appeal, however, would be to court dissolution of the party, and so the responsibility was passed to the Reichstag delegation, which enjoyed a tenuous parliamentary immunity. The delegation was equally cautious, arguing that the USPD's fight against militarism would be crippled if they were all arrested,[29] and the manifesto of January 10 confined itself to a broad hint:

Should there fail to be mighty manifestations of the will of the working population, it could seem as if it were in agreement with these machinations [at Brest-Litovsk], as if the mass of the German people had not yet had enough of the terrible misery of this war. . . . Only a peace without annexations and indemnities, on the basis of the right of self-determination of nations, can save us. The hour is come to raise your voices for such a peace! It is your turn to speak![30]

Oblique though the manifesto was, the party leaders were determined to put it to use, even if cautiously. Word of the decision to act spread through trusted circles in the USPD organization within a few days, and the three-day strike was understood to be set for January 21–23, though it was later postponed for a week.[31] All preparations were left to local organizations, in keeping with the party's federal structure, except that the delegation's manifesto was printed and circulated to all parts of the country from Berlin, together with the recommended timetable of action.[32] In the end one more impulse from outside was needed, and it came in the form of news of the Austrian general strike of January 14–20. By the end of the following week the Kiel shipyards were on strike,

29. The minister of war in fact demanded the arrest of the delegation after the strike; DZA Potsdam, Reichskanzlei 547, pp. 158–59. According to Ledebour (*Ledebour-Prozess*, p. 24) only he, Henke, Herzfeld, and Zubeil of the twenty-five delegation members wanted an open appeal for a general strike.
30. "Ihr habt jetzt das Wort!" Text in *Auswirkungen*, III, 954–55; the tortured language of the translation reflects that of the original.
31. Interrogation of Eisner, *ibid.*, III, 1246; Dresden police reports, *ibid.*, II, 917–18, and III, 938–39, and DZA Potsdam, Reichskanzlei 548, p. 229; Berlin police report in DZA Potsdam, Reichskanzlei 547, p. 162. For the suggestion that party leaders may have carried the word to some local organizations under cover of speaking tours, see Werner Boldt, "Der Januarstreik 1918 in Bayern mit besonderer Berücksichtigung Nürnbergs," *Jahrbuch für Fränkische Landesforschung*, 25 (1965), 29. Ledebour apparently presented the strike to the Independents of Franconia as part of an international general strike; *ibid.*, pp. 8 and 29–30. See also Wheeler, "Internationals," pp. 69–70, for other indications that the strike was thought of as international in some cities.
32. On local preparations in the Rhineland, see Helmuth Stoecker, *Walter Stoecker: Die Frühzeit eines deutschen Arbeiterführers 1891–1920* (Berlin, 1970), pp. 144–46. For Berlin, see *Auswirkungen*, III, 1113–16.

and the Spartacists had published the conspiratorial decision that "On Monday, January 28, the general strike begins!"[33]

The organizing force behind the strike that began in Berlin, Nuremberg, and Hamburg on January 28, and in Mannheim, Danzig, Munich, Cologne, and elsewhere in the following days, was the Independent Socialists, either through their recognized leaders or through organized groups working within the party. In general, however, the workers did not regard it as the USPD's strike; in most places the Majority Socialists were also taken into the strike leadership as a matter of course, whether the Independents liked it or not. In Berlin, Ebert, Scheidemann, and Otto Braun were added to the strike committee on the first morning (over the vehement protests of Ledebour) by a vote of the factory delegates.[34] In Nuremberg the SPD stood aside for the first day of the strike and then stepped in, effectively taking over the strike from the organizationally weak Independents.[35] The strike would have happened with or without the SPD, but some prominent Majority Socialists were clearly not unhappy about it and hoped that it would force the government onto a more progressive course.[36] Impatience with the government was strong as far to the right as the General Commission of the Free Trade Unions, which instead of helping the government to control the strikes declared itself neutral. A conference of union leaders on February 1 blamed the strike on the blindness of the government; their statement, too extreme to pass the censor, was the closest the trade-union movement came to open protest during the war.[37]

The strikers' demands were comprehensive. In Berlin a seven-point program was put forward in which a rapid peace settlement, according to the now-familiar socialist formula, occupied pride of place. This time —in contrast to the Leipzig demands of April 1917, which the Berlin program otherwise closely resembled—the demand for adequate food supplies receded into second place. Restoration of civil liberties came next, with the revival of prewar laws protecting labor. The other demands were for release of all political prisoners; universal, equal, direct, and secret suffrage in Prussia; and general democratization of the German

33. Heading on a Spartacist handbill, *Dokumente und Materialien*, II, 71–73.
34. *Zum Massenstreik in Gross-Berlin* (n.p., n.d.), pp. 5–6. This anonymous SPD pamphlet is by Scheidemann.
35. Boldt, pp. 7–12; Schwarz, pp. 236–50. The Nuremberg Independents waited (in vain) for further guidance from Berlin after the strike broke out; Boldt, pp. 8, 26, and 30, and Schwarz, pp. 239–45.
36. *Zum Massenstreik*, pp. 3 and 11–13; contemporary report on the mood of the socialists in *Ursachen*, V, 103–8.
37. Printed in *Zum Massenstreik*, pp. 13–14. See also the chancellor's interview with two leaders of the general commission on Jan. 31, in DZA Potsdam, Reichskanzlei 548, pp. 68–73.

state governments. With variations of emphasis, these demands were made in other cities as well; as far as we can tell, therefore, these were the political concerns of the workers, or at least of the workers' immediate leaders, at the start of the last year of the war. They constituted a desire for peace, liberty, and democracy—radical democracy but not, as yet, socialist democracy.[38]

The January strike was a landmark for the German labor movement. In Berlin some 300,000 workers struck, including those in nearly all of the large factories;[39] in Hamburg and Kiel the shipyards were shut down; the whole industrial labor force of some small cities, such as Fürth and Luckenwalde, joined in the work stoppage. Those who took part experienced their first political general strike, an action with more revolutionary overtones than anything the modern German labor movement had known previously. Haase saw it as "the greatest event in the history of the German working class."[40] Everyone understood it as evidence that Germany, too, could have a revolution.

Yet the strike had serious shortcomings. Geographically, there were notable gaps. In Leipzig, where the factories were full of Independents, there were few stirrings on the appointed date; when the news from Berlin roused some inclination to strike on the following days, the authorities quickly discouraged the militants with sharp countermeasures.[41] On the lower Rhine, despite extensive preparation, strikes took place in only a few localities, and these were small. The movement in Halle was tiny. The workers in Munich and Dresden made no move until Berlin had led the way, and even then most remained at work. In fact, although many more cities were affected than in the previous April, the strike was overwhelmingly one of the workers of Berlin and the northern shipyards. Thus, even at this point of general unrest among German workers, dis-

---

38. For the Berlin demands, see *Dokumente und Materialien*, II, 75; for Kiel, *ibid.*, II, 78–79; for Schweinfurt and Cassel, DZA Potsdam, RMdI 13582, pp. 156 and 157. Rosenberg, *Birth*, pp. 209–10, judges that these demands largely coincide with the purposes of the Reichstag majority bloc (see the following section of this chapter). In this he seems to overrate the democratic impulses of the Reichstag majority and to underrate the radicalism of the democratic vision held by many workers and the USPD—as he generally underrates the radical implications of the USPD's outlook; see *ibid.*, pp. 121–22 and 178. See also Walter Tormin, *Zwischen Rätediktatur und sozialer Demokratie: Die Geschichte der Rätebewegung in der deutschen Revolution 1918/19* (Düsseldorf, 1954), pp. 30–33.

39. 300,000 is the figure most commonly given, but estimates range between the tendentious extremes of 180,000 (the government's figure, in *Reichstag*, vol. 311, p. 4173) and 650,000 (a strikers' handbill, in *Dokumente und Materialien*, II, 105).

40. *Hugo Haase*, p. 157.

41. Leipzig police reports in *Auswirkungen*, III, 1021–22 and 1074–76; Gorski, pp. 52–56.

content could still not be systematically converted into rebelliousness or the leadership and spark be provided that would encourage action. The problem was to recur.

The worst failing of the strike was its apparent purposelessness. As originally conceived, the strike was to be a demonstration lasting three days, not a trial of strength with the government; other actions of the same kind would follow.[42] In theory such a strike would bring gains even if none of the strikers' demands were met. But in the main strike center, Berlin, the necessary self-restraint was quickly lost in the consciousness of strength and in exasperation at the unbending line taken by the authorities.[43] The government refused to deal with the strike committee, while the military authorities turned to repression. The strike leaders succumbed to the provocation and tried to continue the strike until the government should at least agree to negotiate. Meanwhile there were violent episodes. But the strike had reached its peak and started to crumble; the outcome was a plain defeat for the strikers.

As a result, it proved much harder than expected to follow up the first action with preparations for new ones. The workers were discouraged, the military active in reprisals. In Leipzig and Berlin there was systematic conscription of all who could be shown to have had a part in fomenting strikes. The factory opposition in Berlin was seriously weakened by the arrest or call-up of many of its leaders, including Richard Müller; a reserve leadership had been prepared for this eventuality, but it could not hope to be effective immediately.[44] And while the rebels were recuperating, Germany's war position took an apparent turn for the better. The settlement with Russia became an accomplished fact, which was in general a source of relief. And the successes achieved by the German offensive on the Western front began to mount up, giving rise to hopes that the war might finally be won. The spirit that brings political mass actions did not rise again until October, when the obvious military and political crisis came.

For a time, mass action rested. In the ten months since the birth of the USPD, the idea of the mass demonstration strike had become firmly identified in the minds of activist workers and the socialist left as the form of radical action for their time—whether revolutionary action, as

42. See a handbill from the early days of the strike, *Auswirkungen,* III, 987–88.
43. Later strikers' handbills, *ibid.,* III, 1016, 1029, and 1081.
44. R. Müller, *Kaiserreich,* I, 111 and 126; manuscript by Emil Barth (Müller's successor), "Die Revolution vom Januar 1918 bis März 1919," in the Emil Barth papers (ASD Bonn), II, item 274, pp. 6 and 9. Government sources indicate that several thousand strikers were called up in Berlin alone; *Militär und Innenpolitik,* II, 1169n. In Jena the strike committee was arrested and the whole local USPD leadership called up by the army; Pöhland, pp. 127–28.

some saw it, or radical political pressure. The January strike was the culmination of this development. The USPD had found the model that, in all its ambiguity, indeed its ineffectuality, was to dominate the party's thought throughout the coming years of upheaval.

Party Tactics: Drift toward Radicalism

For a party that regarded itself as a continuation of Social Democracy, mass action could not be an exclusive concern, and the other issues that confronted the USPD during 1917 and 1918—from parliamentary by-elections to relations with the SPD—repeatedly posed problems with implications for the general orientation of the party. Increasingly, these issues brought to light dissension at the top of the party that prevented it from doing much more than drift with the tide of events. On the whole, this drift led it ever more into intransigent radicalism.

The divergence of aims within the party leadership found expression in the persons of the two party chairmen, Haase and Ledebour. The difference between the two, implicit in their activity within the opposition since the early months of the war—Haase the pacifier, Ledebour the intransigent agitator—had affected party policy at least since the Stockholm conference, when Haase had resisted Ledebour's advocacy of a timetable for international mass action.[45] Ledebour headed the faction that was preoccupied with stirring up more strikes and demonstrations, virtually to the exclusion of such other party considerations as recruitment of members, parliamentary tactics, or movement toward a socialist united front. He was not prepared to make any concessions to the right-wing socialists and trusted in coming revolutionary events to unite the working class by converting the workers to the true faith as represented by the USPD. Given his overriding contempt for the leaders of the SPD, Ledebour could envisage a closing of proletarian ranks in no other way. In this he differed from Haase, and while Ledebour might triumph at Zimmerwald meetings Haase still had the greater weight in the councils of the party. While prepared to share in revolution, to help guide and take responsibility for it, Haase held that the task of the party leaders was not to try to "make" revolution, but rather to strengthen the political organization of the working class for the day when revolution might come. Such an aim demanded concern with those questions that Ledebour brushed aside: the size, position, and orientation of the USPD within the workers' movement as a whole. The USPD would do what it could toward encouraging revolution, in propaganda and cadres, but its

45. See the sources cited in n. 16 above.

greatest contribution would be the organization of a large, powerful Marxist party.

Some sketchy evidence indicates that these differences were fought out in February and March of 1918 inside the Reichstag delegation.[46] The first question was whether to begin preparations for a new strike movement at once, as the elated radical wing of the delegation wished. The plan had the support of a number of party activists, with whom the Reichstag deputies were now in closer touch than before—Ledebour himself had become a regular member of the inner councils of the Berlin factory opposition.[47] This time, however, the skeptical centrists had the more realistic appreciation of the mood of the workers. The pressure from below that had forced the delegation to act in January was lacking in March and for a long time afterwards, as even the radicals had to recognize in time.[48] The centrists felt confirmed in their belief that revolutionary morale was an imponderable that they could not easily manipulate, and they were reluctant to risk the very existence of their party again for the sake of a transitory great moment. In these circumstances the radicals, to their frustration, could not win a majority of the party leaders for their policy of raising mass action to the status of the party's overriding, almost its sole concern.

The radicals were more successful with the delegation's posture on the question of the proper uses of parliaments and elections for a revolutionary party. The debate about "parliamentarianism" (as the whole complex of activity was called) was an old one in Social Democracy, and in a party of the socialist left, in agitated times, it was bound to arise with new force.[49] Many activists saw the party leaders, bound by old habits, as giving too much of their attention to "high politics" in the Reichstag and state Diets, as though they believed that the key decisions would be made there—a heresy historically stigmatized by Marxists as "parliamentary cretinism."[50] The critics expected the masses in the

46. Our knowledge of these debates depends wholly on two reports from the Berlin political police in March, in DZA Potsdam, RMdI 12255, pp. 442–43, and IML Berlin, Reichskanzlei 8/13, p. 3. These accounts, however, fit the other information we have about the party's personalities and problems at the time. See, for instance, a newspaper account of a public quarrel between Haase and Ledebour after a Reichstag session in February, in DZA Merseburg, Rep. 77 CB S Nr. 482 adh. II, p. 251.

47. Word seems to have gone down through the party organization in February that there would be another strike, perhaps on May 1; see the Dresden police report in *Auswirkungen*, III, 1285–86.

48. For an account of the course of popular unrest during 1918, see the last section of this chapter.

49. For the context of this debate in the old SPD, see above, pp. 25–26.

50. The phrase goes back to Engels. For a contemporary use see *Spartakusbriefe* (1926 ed.), p. 72.

streets to settle the outcome of the war and begrudged the energies ex-
pended on parliamentary work. In addition, their experience since 1914
had taught many party militants—especially the radicals, who reacted
to the generally moderate stand of the Reichstag delegation—to be suspicious of what the leaders were doing in Berlin.[51] The debate on the
issue did not follow factional lines exactly; the radical Alfred Henke as
well as Ledebour himself attached considerable importance to parliamentary work.[52] But rising young radicals without parliamentary experience tended to regard their elders as corrupted by the system, and such
young radicals were becoming important in the USPD.

With feeling running high, the left tended to reject compromise or
bargaining of any sort, feeling only contempt for any attempt to exert
influence other than by mass action. This attitude was incomprehensible
to the centrists, with their skeptical caution and disinclination to burn
their bridges; and in this they had the whole weight of party tradition behind them. Their classic counterargument was that parliamentary activity
offered significant opportunities for the party, that all means could be
used to advance the revolution, provided that each was employed in due
measure.[53] The argument was unanswerable; but it was also vague enough
to serve as a cover permitting the leaders to carry on as before, and this,
at least, the radical temper of the party prevented. Increasingly, the
party abandoned that part of its tradition which prescribed positive politics where possible in matters of reform. By 1918 the party delegation
in the Reichstag had largely ceased to offer motions or amendments that
had any real chance of success, preferring to lay down far-reaching programs for propaganda purposes. Party spokesmen's speeches were rarely
directed to the deputies in the hall, more often "out the window" to the
workers.[54] The USPD leaders were settling into a largely self-imposed
isolation and reorienting themselves, rhetorically at least, toward revolution.

An early casualty of this posture of intransigence was the possibility
of tactical collaboration with the Majority Socialists, or rapprochement
with a part of them. Many Independents still anticipated reunification of
the socialist movement once the war was over; the influential Wilhelm
Dittmann of the party executive, for instance, regarded "the lasting divi-

51. See the criticism voiced at the USPD's founding congress by Heckert
(USPD *Parteitag*, April 1917, p. 62), Beisswanger (p. 69), Karsten (pp. 74–75),
and others.
52. See Ledebour's speech, *ibid.*, pp. 52–53.
53. This attitude was still expressed editorially in *Mitteilungs-Blatt* as late as
May 12, 1918.
54. A classic example is Ledebour's speech of July 3, 1918, which was eventually shouted down by other deputies; *Reichstag*, vol. 313, pp. 5709–13.

sion of Social Democracy" as "inconceivable."[55] Reunification was out
of the question while the issue of support for the war effort continued to
divide the parties, and even partial cooperation was becoming steadily
more difficult with the growth of the radical faction inside the USPD.[56]
But at the same time, the SPD was experiencing difficulties that a flexible
attitude on the part of the USPD could exploit.

There had been subtle shifts in SPD policy since the breach. The old
party leaders had never been wholly uncritical of the government, and as
the war dragged on the SPD became increasingly open in its demands
for progressive measures and political reform. Just as the opposition had
been driven into the open partly by the radicalism of the Spartacists, so
the SPD had to compete with the opposition after the March 1916 split
in the delegation, and especially after the USPD was constituted a year
later. Simultaneously, the party gradually lost confidence in the government, which was ever more dependent on the Supreme Army Command.
For the most part, the SPD's demands were for domestic reforms: more direct taxation, especially of war profits; improvement in the state's system
of purchasing and distributing food; and above all introduction of a fully
democratic franchise in Prussia. Finally, in the spring of 1917 the SPD
formally adopted a peace program that was virtually identical to that of
the USPD—indeed, among the right-wing parties of the Reichstag the
formula of a return to the status quo ante bellum, modified by self-
determination, became known as the "Scheidemann peace" after the man
who became cochairman of the SPD in Haase's place.[57]

By mid-1917, then, the SPD publicly occupied much the same political ground as the opposition had held a year before, but its methods
were significantly different. A majority of SPD leaders maintained that
the party could and must pursue its ends through influence and parliamentary pressure, without attempting to mobilize mass pressure so long
as the war lasted. For patriotic reasons, they continued to refrain from
publicly doubting the government's war aims, and this restraint alone
would have sustained the antagonism between them and the Independents. The breach widened in the summer of 1917 when the SPD decided to join with the Catholic Center Party and the Progressive Party
to form a stable majority in the Reichstag, a move that necessarily involved compromises, not all of them consistent with socialist doctrine

55. Dittmann memoirs, p. 795.
56. See, for instance, the party's official rebuff to the SPD's (probably insincere)
public approach in the fall of 1917, in *Mitteilungs-Blatt,* Nov. 11, 1917, and
especially the accompanying editorial.
57. See the careful summary of these developments in Matthias' introduction to
Der Interfraktionelle Ausschuss 1917/18, ed. Erich Matthias with Rudolf Morsey,
2 vols. (Düsseldorf, 1959), I, xv–xviii and xxiv–xxv.

and tradition. The original purpose of the alliance was to coordinate pressure on the government, but obviously, should Germany move toward a parliamentary system, the majority bloc would be a potential government coalition. The USPD was unanimous in regarding socialist participation in a capitalist government as unthinkable.

It was by no means certain that matters would go so far, for the nascent coalition was inherently unstable, and many SPD deputies were uncomfortable in their new harness. In the delegation, those of the old opposition who had not seceded were joined by malcontents who wanted to oppose the government openly on certain issues, regardless of the sensibilities of the allied parties. This group had the support of Scheidemann, of the editor-in-chief of *Vorwärts*, Friedrich Stampfer, and of many of the rank and file.[58] They were very restive during the last winter of the war; as already mentioned, a number of Majority Socialists privately welcomed the general strike in January. The treaty of Brest-Litovsk, submitted for ratification in March, provoked a trial of strength; the SPD delegation was hopelessly divided, and the weak policy of abstention finally carried the day against opposition from both sides.[59] Party leaders hoped to avoid further conflicts in the ranks by concentrating all efforts on the long-standing grievance of the Prussian three-class voting system.[60] But progress on this matter in the Prussian Diet was exceedingly slow, and furthermore the issue failed to fire the imagination of the workers. Several times the party came close to abandoning the other majority parties in the Reichstag and openly opposing the government, being held back only by the determined leadership of Friedrich Ebert and like-minded colleagues.

Haase and others of the Independents would have liked to capitalize on the crisis in the old party by winning as many as possible of the malcontents for the USPD. The party was at this time uncomfortably aware that the old party remained much stronger than it; a series of humiliating defeats in by-elections that the USPD might have hoped to win made it plain that the workers were very slow to rally around the new party.[61] Growth in the USPD Reichstag delegation, too, had been limited—eight

58. Edwyn Bevan, *German Social Democracy during the War* (London, 1918), pp. 207–10, gives a good account of the emergence of this tendency in the autumn of 1917.

59. *Reichstagsfraktion*, II, 386–92; Scheidemann, *Memoiren*, II, 151.

60. See the views of Heilmann and Scheidemann, reported in DZA Potsdam, Reichskanzlei 548, pp. 10–11 and 47.

61. Especially disappointing were the results in Niederbarnim (Berlin), the constituency of the deceased Independent Arthur Stadthagen, where a Majority Socialist easily defeated the USPD's Rudolf Breitscheid in March 1918; see *Mitteilungs-Blatt*, March 24, 1918, and the two following issues.

new converts since March 1916.[62] Early in 1918, however, eleven members of the SPD delegation broke discipline to join the Independents in bringing in a motion critical of the government,[63] and Haase thought he saw the chance to win over as many as fifteen deputies for the USPD; with their following, these deputies would have significantly strengthened the USPD in Thuringia and northern Bavaria and would have put the party in a better position after the war to claim to represent the true Social Democratic inheritance. But to attract these cautious centrists the USPD would have to moderate the image that the activities of the radicals and Spartacists had given it and refrain from what might be called revolutionary adventurism.[64] This consideration had been another reason for blocking the proposals of Ledebour's faction after January, but the radicals in their turn were able to block Haase's plan. They expected the strength of their party to grow through action, not political horse trading; and though they could not induce a majority of the delegation to organize revolution they were able to insist on the party's behaving in an outwardly extremist manner. There were no further recruits from the SPD delegation.[65]

Another attempt at conciliation, this time by the Majority Socialists, had no better success. The blind resistance of the old order to significant constitutional reform caused many Majority Socialists to think of open opposition and even of sponsoring mass demonstrations. If they were to follow this course, some sort of accommodation with the Independents would be highly desirable. The initiative for negotiations came, not from the party leaders of the SPD, but from below, most importantly from certain Berlin officials of the Metalworkers' Union, apparently under pressure from their members.[66] In June the USPD turned down a request for a joint approach to the government about improving food supplies and reducing working hours in the munitions industry, saying that past experience of working with the SPD, notably during the January strike, had been discouraging.[67] When the same trade unionists approached the parties later in the summer about possible joint mass demonstrations for peace and equal suffrage in Prussia, neither party responded helpfully. The SPD, replying on August 29, was the more conciliatory, stating its formal conditions for collaboration: all parlia-

62. Particulars are in Appendix 2.
63. *Volksblatt* (Halle), March 1, 1918.
64. Police report on delegation debates in DZA Potsdam, RMdI 12255, pp. 442–43.
65. IML Berlin, Reichskanzlei 8/13, p. 3. See above, n. 46.
66. Eduard Bernstein, *Die deutsche Revolution* (Berlin, 1921), pp. 26–27; Hermann Müller, *Die November-Revolution: Erinnerungen* (Berlin, 1928), pp. 45–46.
67. IML Berlin, Reichskanzlei 8/8, p. 349.

mentary means must be exhausted before extraparliamentary pressure was exercised (though the latter phase would begin in autumn at the latest, if it was needed); collaboration must be arranged in detail, in formal negotiations between the two parties, and the call to action must be formal and open, not conspiratorial. These terms were directed against the known predilections of the Independents, whose reply on September 18 all but killed the collaboration attempt. For the USPD, the only acceptable partners for action were those "who meant to carry out a purely proletarian policy, that is, an all-out class struggle aimed at putting an end to the regime and bringing about peace." In other words, the Majority Socialists must adopt the aims and methods of the Independents. To show its acceptance of proper proletarian policies, the old party must meet three USPD demands: it must reject war credits, refuse to take part in any bloc with nonsocialist parties, and recall any party members serving in offices of state.[68]

Collaboration did not lie this way. The Imperial system was entering its final crisis, and politics were pulling the two socialist parties sharply, though only temporarily, apart. On September 23 an SPD party conference decided to make a bid for membership in the government, and on October 2 this was accomplished.

The Debate on Bolshevism

The Independents were not engaged solely in tactical issues in the last year of the war; one of the liveliest and most illuminating debates in the party in 1917–1918 concerned an apparently remote issue: the attitude socialists should take toward what the Bolsheviks were attempting in Russia. Even before the Bolshevik seizure of power in November 1917 differences of opinion about their intentions were evident in Germany; Kautsky, for instance, thought a seizure of power untimely, while the organ of the Berlin radicals gave its approval in advance.[69] After November the debate grew more heated, to the point of bitterness. Plainly what was really being discussed was not Russia but the future of the German revolution and European socialism.[70]

For the more radical part of the USPD, including the Spartacists, the issue was simple. Däumig's paper stated:

That which has so often been presented theoretically to the workers in assemblies and writings as the goal of the proletarian class struggle, that which

68. Details of these negotiations are in Bernstein, *Die deutsche Revolution*, pp. 27–28.
69. Kautsky in *Neue Zeit,* Aug. 31, 1917, pp. 505–12; *Mitteilungs-Blatt,* Sept. 30, 1917.
70. For what follows see also the account in Lösche, esp. pp. 120–26 and 144–52.

appeared to many people to lie in the mists of the future: In Russia it has been reality for five weeks—the socialist proletariat has captured political power, has the powers of the government in its hands, and is proceeding to realize all the great socialist and democratic goals.[71]

The admirable achievement of the Bolsheviks was an important example for the German workers, who would soon, the more advanced radicals believed, have to carry through their own socialist revolution. The struggles of the Bolsheviks were thus of immediate relevance: "We are not mere spectators of events in Russia, we participate in them with full fervor. We mean to learn from what happens there and then apply the lessons fruitfully to the coming struggles for the salvation of humanity from the claws of capitalism."[72]

Given their perspective, the radicals did not want to hear criticism of Bolshevik policies; criticism in detail was irrelevant to the main point and served only to encourage the enemies of both Russian and German revolutions. In fact, for all the talk of learning from the Russians, there was little thought of copying their methods; the only Russian practices followed in Germany in November 1918 were the workers' and soldiers' councils and, to a lesser extent, the Red Guards.[73] But the radicals were ready to justify even those aspects of the Russian scene that they hoped to avoid in Germany—the suppression of the opposition and its press, the harassment of rival socialist parties, the disintegration of the economy. In any case, information reaching Germany from Russia was taken (rightly) to be incomplete and unreliable, so awkward details could be dismissed as distortions; much of the Bolshevik controversy in Germany was stalemated over disagreement about basic facts.[74] And, it was said, the revolution in (advanced) Germany would naturally take a different course than in (backward) Russia, while the victory of the revolution in Western Europe would allow the Russian soviet system to modify its more questionable features. Such were the basic ideas of the most powerful left-wing critic of the Bolsheviks, Rosa Luxemburg, who believed that the German revolutionaries should learn from both the virtues and the mistakes of the Russians.[75]

The radicals saw that the Russian revolution was seriously threatened

71. *Mitteilungs-Blatt,* Dec. 16, 1917.
72. Speech by Däumig, reported in *Auswirkungen,* III, 1494.
73. On the question of how far the German councils were influenced by the Russian example, see Tormin, pp. 26–29, 31–33, and esp. the summary on p. 130; also Eberhard Kolb, "Rätewirklichkeit und Räte-Ideologie in der deutschen Revolution von 1918/19," in *Vom Kaiserreich zur Weimarer Republik,* ed. Eberhard Kolb (Cologne, 1972), p. 169.
74. This point is made in *Leipziger Volkszeitung,* July 20, 1918.
75. Rosa Luxemburg, *Die russische Revolution* (Berlin, 1922), esp. ch. 1; "Die russische Tragödie," *Spartakusbriefe (Neudruck)* (Berlin, 1920), pp. 181–86.

by problems arising from the backwardness of Russia, as well as by foreign intervention. The predominant view of Western socialists was that the Soviet regime must fall if there were not a general revolution in the West European states.[76] But while the skeptics criticized the Bolsheviks for counting on a revolution that could not come in time to save them, many radicals took the view that, if a revolution in Germany was necessary to save the socialist experiment in Russia, then there must and would be a revolution.[77] The urgency with which the militants worked in the January strike and afterwards reflected this assessment. But most other socialists, whatever their sympathy with the Bolsheviks, were preoccupied with domestic problems. Rosa Luxemburg wrote bitterly that the Russians "will not be able to maintain themselves in this witches' Sabbath . . . because Social Democracy in the highly developed West is made up of the most miserable cowards who will look on calmly while the Russians bleed to death."[78] And indeed the mass of German workers could not be moved to action by the strategic necessities of the world revolution.

Those among the Independents critical of the Bolsheviks were far fewer than the enthusiasts but as impassioned as the latter and even more articulate. The critics included some who had applauded the February revolution in Russia less because it was a revolution than because it established a system in Russia that they expected to be peace-loving, progressive, and democratic (here, too, we see hopes for Germany reflected in evaluations of the situation in Russia). "The Russian people," wrote Kautsky in April 1917, "has exchanged absolutism for democracy."[79] If all went well, the existence of such a regime in Russia would encourage the democratization of the Central Powers and lead to an early and lasting peace in Europe. The Bolshevik coup put an end to these prospects, and did so in what was (in the critics' eyes) the chimerical hope of building socialism in Russia. Kautsky was convinced that Russian economic and social conditions precluded socialism for the time being; the country was simply too backward.[80] The small, primitive proletariat and the illiterate peasantry were not an adequate foundation for

76. See Däumig's comment, reported in *Auswirkungen*, III, 1493–94; Rosa Luxemburg's view is quoted below. See also Haase, in *Interfraktionelle Ausschuss*, II, 22, where he speaks of the impossibility of building socialism in an overwhelmingly agrarian country.

77. Ledebour even proclaimed this from the podium of the Reichstag; *Reichstag*, vol. 313, pp. 5712–13.

78. Rosa Luxemburg, *Briefe an Karl und Luise Kautsky* (Berlin, 1923), p. 210.

79. *Neue Zeit*, April 6, 1917, p. 10.

80. This was a constant theme of Kautsky's, from his article in the *Leipziger Volkszeitung*, Nov. 15, 1917, onward.

socialism, conceived in the old Social Democratic manner as a higher stage of civilization. The attempt to set up a one-class government would lead instead to civil war and defeat, to black reaction and a tremendous setback for the Russian socialist movement; the potentialities of the February revolution would not be realized.[81]

The critics objected especially to the means the Bolsheviks used—in fact had to use because of the weakness of their popular support in the country. One hostile commentator summed up the regime's work as "attempting to introduce socialism in the most backward land in Europe, basing its power on bayonets and machine guns."[82] Worse still was the passivity, or even admiration, with which many German socialists greeted reports that the Bolsheviks were suppressing the opposition press, and even other socialist parties, and introducing terror. This attitude was a complete break with the mainstream of Social Democratic thought, which had assumed that, except for perhaps a brief spasm of violence, the socialist revolution would proceed by peaceful and orderly means, means that accorded with the end—the development of a society of brotherhood and cooperation. Such a transition would be possible because the victorious socialist movement would represent the will of the great mass of the people and would have numbers and a program so obviously superior that repressive measures would scarcely be needed. Marx's famous expression "the dictatorship of the proletariat" was interpreted to refer to a "circumstance which necessarily springs from pure democracy when the proletariat is predominant."[83] A dictatorship in the normal sense—rule by a minority through the continuous exercise of force—would stifle the unfolding of the free capacities of the individual within the collective that was seen as the mainspring as well as the goal of socialism. A dictatorship like that of the Bolshevik party could never lead to socialism, only to defeat and possibly to the perversion of the whole European socialist movement.

In many Independents the enthusiasm of the radicals combined uneasily with the doubts of Kautsky and his friends. As Hilferding wrote about the Bolsheviks, "One's heart is on their side, . . . but one's mind just will not go along."[84] A majority of the party executive (including

81. Letter from Hilferding to Kautsky, July 21, 1917, Kautsky papers, D XII 579.

82. Alexander Stein in *Sozialistische Auslandspolitik,* Jan. 23, 1918. This passage was written at the time of the dispersal of the Constituent Assembly in Russia, which was received unfavorably by nearly all German socialists; see Lösche, pp. 129–37.

83. Karl Kautsky, *Die Diktatur des Proletariats* (Vienna, 1918), p. 21.

84. Letter from Hilferding to Kautsky, Dec. 3, 1917, Kautsky papers, D XII 631.

even Ledebour) belonged to this group of skeptical supporters of the Bolsheviks, and the party's official attitude reflected their ambivalence.[85] The older Independents were familiar with the Bolsheviks' harsh ways from before the war and had felt the Bolshevik contempt for such men as themselves during the war. Formally, the USPD supported the Bolsheviks firmly, though the Russians' negotiation of a separate peace, mentioned above, imposed a strain on this policy for a period; but there was always an undertone of reserve, a feeling that Bolshevism was suited to Russia, perhaps, but not to Germany. Such reticence is shown in an official party comment of September 1918 on the Soviet regime: "Efforts of the Russian communist parties [sic] to carry through socialism are sure of the approval and support of the class-conscious German workers. Success for these efforts would be of the greatest significance for the ultimate victory of socialism in the whole world."[86] It followed that socialists abroad had a duty to oppose capitalist counterrevolution in Russia, and specifically foreign intervention; this duty was performed with conviction by the USPD throughout its existence, with all the means the party had at its disposal.

The party leaders were thus concerned not so much to endorse the Bolsheviks as to see to it that the Russians were left alone to work out their own problems. This principle was applied even to criticism of the regime, on the grounds that public criticism from the Independents would merely strengthen anti-Bolshevik and antisocialist forces inside and outside Russia and be a further divisive element in the already fragile USPD.[87] Such considerations lay behind the party leaders' declara-

---

85. For Ledebour's views, see his telegram to a Swedish newspaper, printed in *Volksblatt* (Halle), Nov. 12, 1917. Ledebour emphasized the peace program of the new government, wanted it to find as broad a basis as possible among the socialist parties, and was reserved about the idea of parceling out land to individual peasant proprietors.

86. *Auswirkungen*, IV, 1564; the censors prevented publication of the declaration. It was in all likelihood the product of the conference called by the USPD in September 1918 to debate the issue of Bolshevism; see Alexander Stein's article in *Freiheit*, Jan. 28, 1922 (e); Heinrich Ströbel, *Die deutsche Revolution: Ihr Unglück und ihre Rettung*, 3d ed. (Berlin, 1922), pp. 157–58. The conference, about which nothing appeared in the party press, probably coincided with the meetings of the Reichstag delegation known to have been held on Sept. 11 and 12; see *Leipziger Volkszeitung*, Sept. 14, 1918, and a police report in StA Potsdam, Pr. Br. Rep. 30 Berlin C Polizeipräsidium, Tit. 95 Sekt. 7 Lit. D Nr. 3a, vol. 6, pp. 237–38, where reference is made to a meeting of the USPD "party committee" on Sept. 11. The declaration quoted above was in the hands of the censors no later than Sept. 15; see DZA Merseburg, Rep. 77 Tit. 949 Nr. 1b, p. 711.

87. See Haase's letter to Kautsky, Aug. 6, 1918, *Hugo Haase*, p. 162. According to Stein (*Freiheit*, Jan. 28, 1922 [e]), Haase criticized the Soviet regime's foreign policy and governmental terrorism at the conference in September; but he said nothing publicly about Bolshevik rule until well after the end of the war.

tion that they were "opposed to any criticism of the Bolsheviks at present."[88] Kautsky himself exercised unusual restraint, considering the importance he attached to the matter, and wrote only three articles against the Bolsheviks in the first nine months they were in power.[89] But few others were so restrained, and the debate could not be suppressed by fiat. The *Leipziger Volkszeitung,* itself inclined to favor the Bolsheviks, printed diatribes from both sides with fine impartiality. The subject of Soviet Russia was a popular one at party meetings, and the membership apparently preferred to hear hopeful rather than critical accounts;[90] indeed, though such tendencies cannot be demonstrated, uninformed sympathies in the USPD were probably then, as later, generally pro-Bolshevik. Those who believed that Bolshevism was a calamity for European socialism could not be expected to remain silent, and bitter controversy broke out in the summer of 1918, in spite of all the party executive's efforts. A flurry of articles in *Sozialistische Auslandspolitik* in August led in September, despite a personal plea from Haase, to publication of Kautsky's classic polemic, *Die Diktatur des Proletariats.*[91]

Probably few members except the party intellectuals understood what the controversy was really about; and despite the antagonism aroused by debate on the issue, the conflict was probably not yet a dangerous one for the party.[92] In any case, abstract debate of this kind could preoccupy the party only during periods of relative inactivity and frustration, and events were soon to occur that would absorb the USPD's attention fully until the middle of 1919. Revolution was coming upon Germany.

Revolutionary Preparations and Final Crisis

Following the January strike, popular militancy had declined sharply; as in April of the previous year, a "safety valve" seemed to have opened to draw off the excess pressure.[93] When the echoes of the strike died away—by March or April at the latest—the revolutionary sentiment the radicals had believed they perceived in January was no longer there, or at best dormant. In only a handful of cities was even an attempt made to

88. *Leipziger Volkszeitung,* July 4, 1918.
89. According to Kautsky himself, in his *Franz Mehring und die deutsche Sozialdemokratie* (n.p. [1918]), p. 6.
90. For example, Alexander Stein's anti-Bolshevik arguments were poorly received at a meeting of Aug. 7, 1918, in Berlin; IML Berlin, Reichskanzlei 8/8, pp. 358–61.
91. Letter from Haase to Kautsky, Aug. 6, 1918, *Hugo Haase,* p. 162.
92. Although, as Breitscheid noted in *Sozialistische Auslandspolitik,* Oct. 31, 1918, the Majority Socialists were then counting on this factor, among others, to cause a split in the USPD.
93. The image comes from Volkmann, *Marxismus,* p. 139.

celebrate May 1 with the traditional strikes and demonstrations. A few weeks later, an event that at another time might have brought a sharp popular response—the mutilation of the franchise reform bill in the Prussian House of Deputies—passed without any popular protest.[94]

However, bitterness and discontent remained, and not long afterward unrest showed itself again in the factories. As before, the specific causes of dissatisfaction were such matters as wages, working hours, and food supplies, the most important single item undoubtedly being a new cut in the bread ration on June 16. As in January, the restraining hand of the Majority Socialists was weakened by their own disaffection, caused this time by a severe political crisis over the forced resignation of Foreign Secretary Kühlmann at the end of June. The result was a number of local strikes, and for a time feeling ran high.[95] When activism declined again after July, much of the feeling remained. Moreover, reports were reaching the government, from Halle, Düsseldorf, Hamburg, and elsewhere, that local unrest was being channeled into preparations for a general strike.[96] Memories of the January strike gave point to the argument of radical shop-floor leaders that the next action must be a great, united effort with political goals, a trial of strength that might not come soon but would, if possible, have real political impact.

More information is available on underground preparations in Berlin than elsewhere, though the indications are that the story was similar in at least some other cities. After being decimated by selective conscription following the January strike, the radicals in the factories regrouped under a new leader, Emil Barth. Barth, a metalworker and middle-rank trade-union functionary who had been invalided out of the war, was given to bombast and self-dramatization, but he was courageous and a good organizer, and the movement under his leadership appears to have become more purposeful than before. By summer it had restored contacts with all the great factories; thus its inner committee had an unusually good view of the state of feeling in the factories as preparations took place for the next great strike.[97]

94. Military survey on May 1, IML Berlin, RMdI 9/12, p. 114; on the Prussian franchise issue, see IML Berlin, Reichskanzlei 8/8, p. 343. See also the trade-union leaders' appraisal of the workers' mood in *Dokumente und Materialien*, II, 143–49.

95. See the emotional accounts of the crisis by Scheidemann, Ebert, and David in a meeting of July 6; *Interfraktionelle Ausschuss*, II, 421–44. A list of the strikes is given in *Dokumente und Materialien*, II, 716–18.

96. IML Berlin, RMdI 9/12, pp. 168 (Düsseldorf) and 184 (Hamburg); *Auswirkungen*, III, 1415 (Halle) and 1470–71 (Essen and Wilhelmshaven). These reports are from June and July.

97. R. Müller, *Kaiserreich*, I, 126–27; Ledebour in *Ledebour-Prozess*, p. 28; Barth, pp. 24–33, gives his own highly colored account.

In effect, Barth's organization was developing into a revolutionary committee, basing its preparations on the principle of "one great blow." Past experience had convinced the radicals that another partial, unsuccessful action would only set the movement back for months again; accordingly nothing should be attempted until they were sure of a very large following, and pressure should be allowed to build up until the masses were ready to act together. If timed and managed properly, a strike then could do more than intimidate the government; it could turn into a insurrection—and this became the acknowledged goal of the committee's activity.[98] The members agitated and extended their cadres, even collected arms and formed small commando units to deal with the police.[99] But the strategy was essentially a waiting one, and the time was not yet ripe; there were no political strikes or mass demonstrations of any consequence in Berlin during the summer.

The Berlin Independents supported this strategy; indeed, Däumig joined the revolutionary committee during the summer and became one of its leaders. The Spartacists, however, were opposed. They did not like this administrative approach to revolution, which gave the leaders all the initiative and robbed revolution of its spontaneous popular vigor; nor did they think the grandiose scheme would ever work. Their strategy, by contrast, was to exploit every opportunity, however small, where the workers showed readiness for action, in the expectation that successive strikes and demonstrations would cumulatively exacerbate the situation and produce a wave of revolution. Barth, though hostile to the method, summed it up well:

Only in battle, in bloody battle is revolutionary energy generated, is the proletariat hardened. . . . A rising of a thousand and bloody defeat brings on a rising of ten thousand, again defeat; bitterness, hatred, the will to fight on the one side, on the other revulsion from one's own actions, doubt, conversion. A new rising of a hundred thousand, etc., until the final victory.[100]

These "revolutionary gymnastics" had a good revolutionary pedigree, perhaps as good as the "one great blow"; but unfortunately for the Spartacists not many German workers were receptive to their tactics. Weakness in the factories forced the Spartacus group back to sheer propaganda. In this, however, its output was formidable, and its illegal literature was notable as the only propaganda at that time explicitly calling for work-

98. R. Müller, *Kaiserreich,* I, 129–32.

99. Barth, p. 33. Walter Bartel, *Zeitschrift für Geschichtswissenschaft,* 12 (1962), 814–15, gives details from the recollections of some Berlin workers who took part in these preparations.

100. Barth, p. 30. Cf. R. Müller, *Kaiserreich,* I, 129, and the more sympathetic treatment in Paul Frölich, *Rosa Luxemburg* (London, 1940), p. 287.

ers' and soldiers' councils and a socialist dictatorship of the proletariat.[101] The Spartacists thus helped shape workers' expectations about the nature of the revolution once it occurred.

The Soviet Russian Embassy was also active in revolutionary preparations. Ambassador Adolf Joffe and his staff arrived in Berlin on April 20, 1918, and immediately cultivated relations with all factions of the German socialist movement that might possibly help promote a revolution, from the small splinter groups of the extreme left to the right wing of the Independents. The USPD party executive maintained cordial relations with the Embassy, and several party members, including Rudolf Breitscheid and Emil Eichhorn, joined a number of Spartacists on the staff of the Embassy and its adjunct, the Soviet news agency.[102] Since the German socialists were later reticent about these fraternal contacts, it is difficult to know how much effect they may have had; indications are that the presence of these representatives of successful socialist revolution acted as a constant spur to the radicals. Rather more is known about such other Embassy activities as the importing of printed propaganda materials, apparently through the Soviet diplomatic couriers, and the distribution of large sums of money for revolutionary purposes.[103] None of this assistance went to the USPD's regular party organization, which had no use for left radical tracts and politely but firmly refused to accept financial aid.[104] A large sum of money found its way (probably indirectly) to Barth, who used it for the purchase of arms.[105] More went into Spar-

101. Tormin, pp. 37–40.
102. The general outline of the Russian Embassy's activities is well known; see John W. Wheeler-Bennett, *Brest-Litovsk* (London, 1938), pp. 348–60, and Joffe's account, recorded by Louis Fischer, *The Soviets in World Affairs,* 2 vols. (London, 1930), I, 75–76, and *Men and Politics* (New York, 1941), p. 26. See also the military counterintelligence reports of May 28 and July 1, 1918 (printed in Volkmann, *Marxismus,* pp. 309–12), and Oct. 15, 1918 (IML Berlin, Reichskanzlei 8/13, pp. 39–65); and Winfried Baumgart, *Deutsche Ostpolitik 1918* (Vienna, 1966), pp. 338–41. Haase gave a brief account of the party executive's dealings with the Embassy in *Freiheit,* Dec. 19, 1918 (m).
103. See especially IML Berlin, Reichskanzlei 8/13, pp. 40–41 and 50–54; DZA Potsdam, Reichskanzlei 5/7, pp. 332 and 339.
104. See Haase's statements in *Freiheit,* Dec. 9, 1918 (e), and at the first postwar party congress (USPD *Parteitag,* March 1919, p. 242), and Bernstein's comment on the reasons in *Die deutsche Revolution,* pp. 23–24.
105. Joffe and Barth exchanged declarations about this at long range in December; *Freiheit,* Dec. 9, 1918 (e), Dec. 10, 1918 (m), Dec. 11, 1918 (m), and Dec. 19, 1918 (m). Barth's denial that the Embassy was the source of his funds was singularly unconvincing. I know of only one other confirmed instance of Russian money passing into the hands of Independents (other than Spartacists): Oskar Cohn, USPD Reichstag deputy, was entrusted with large sums of money by the departing ambassador on Nov. 6 and spent them for such purposes as founding

tacist hands; and the illegal leaflets were distributed through the Spartacist organizations.[106] In a modest way the Embassy succeeded in strengthening the resolve and resources of the German revolutionaries, before itself being expelled from Germany a few days before the workers took to the streets.

By the summer of 1918 radical propaganda was affecting soldiers at the front as well as workers, thanks to the devastating effects of the spring campaign on the morale of an already desperately weary army. Radical agitation among the troops on a large scale late in the summer of 1918 was a consequence rather than a cause of the decline of discipline that was already under way;[107] and its effect was to reinforce the longing for an end to the fighting at any price. More and more soldiers were unwilling to die in a cause they saw to be lost. Whatever the responsibility of the left socialists for the growth of war-weariness, by October it appeared inexorable, though not yet incapacitating the armies; and to the socialists the breakdown of military discipline signaled not only the imminent end of the war but also the eventual helplessness of the state against insurrection.[108]

There is ample evidence of revolutionary agitation by elements within the USPD and by factory radicals in association with USPD local organizations; but we do not know enough to draw firm conclusions about the role of the regular party organization in these preparations. The party remained formally committed to mass action, at least as far as this was necessary to bring peace, and police reports show that local militants in many cities agitated in the belief that the party executive would determine the suitable moment for nationwide action, as it had done in January;[109] but it seems likely that the party leaders played only a passive role, at least until September. Indeed, insofar as there were national preparations for action, the threads probably ran together in the hands of the Berlin revolutionary committee rather than the party's central

---

party newspapers, but independently of the party executive; see *Freiheit,* Dec. 20, 1918 (m), and Dec. 27, 1918 (m), and *Verhandlungen der deutschen verfassunggebenden Nationalversammlung* (hereafter cited as *Nationalversammlung*), vol. 326, pp. 337–39. It is likely that there were other cases.

106. Meyer in *Ursachen,* V, 116, and his introduction to *Spartakus im Kriege,* p. 20. German Communists normally had very little to say about the material support they received from the Russian Communists, in 1918 or later.

107. Volkmann from the army point of view (*Marxismus,* pp. 192–96) and R. Müller for the revolutionaries (*Kaiserreich,* I, 113) agree that the breakdown in discipline preceded the intensified radical propaganda.

108. Evidence that this hope circulated in USPD circles can be found in *Auswirkungen,* IV, 1612 and 1702–3.

109. Reports from Halle and Essen in *Auswirkungen,* III, 1415 and 1470; from Düsseldorf in IML Berlin, RMdI 9/12, p. 168.

offices.[110] The party executive—except for Ledebour and Däumig—was deliberately kept ignorant of the revolutionary committee's aims until the end of October and encouraged to look on Barth's organization as merely a useful network of party supporters in the factories.[111] The party leaders were still anxious for mass action, and not averse to actual revolution, in which they came to believe during the last month of the war; they were willing to encourage this movement in any way that did not risk the party's dissolution; but as far as we know they still did not believe either in the possibility of preparing and proclaiming a revolution or that the masses would be ready until after the war. The party was revolutionary in its aims, revolutionary in its agitation, but proposed to leave the practice of revolution to the workers themselves. Locally, of course, the USPD often was more directly involved with revolutionary preparations; but the central party organization, for all its bustle, apparently watched the coming of revolution with characteristic centrist fatalism.

Before the general political crisis at the end of September began to stir all classes out of their passivity, the effects of the radicals' preparations were hardly visible. Indeed, the radicals had their day only after the revolution started in November; other causes played a greater part than their work in promoting the overthrow of the old regime. Until then, while radical agitation certainly contributed to the intensity of a crisis that was not of their making, radical leaders were actually reining back their most impatient followers as they waited for the great moment to arrive.

The SPD's activity in the summer and autumn was far more dramatic. The Majority Socialists had never been happy with the faintly parliamentarized government of Count Hertling, and its weak, drifting conduct of affairs soon alienated its most hopeful advocates in the party. But the need for a united war effort continued to hold the delegation back from open opposition; moreover, most of the party's leaders were convinced that the best long-run prospects of reform and democratization lay in clinging to the bloc with the Center Party and the Progressives, even at the cost of frustration and growing unrest within the party. By September, however, it was apparent in informed circles that the war must be lost by spring at the latest, making immediate purposeful action by the government essential, and pressure from all sections of the party left the leaders with no choice but to win tangible concessions quickly or leave

---

110. See Barth, p. 47, on his committee's connections outside Berlin.
111. Barth, pp. 43–44. See also Dittmann's memoirs, p. 830, where he refers to the shop stewards' committee as "unsere Vertrauensleute in den Betrieben"; similarly Zietz in USPD *Parteitag,* March 1919, p. 51.

the bloc. The only hope of a reasonable, negotiated peace seemed to lie in taking the direction of affairs out of the hands of the expansionists and the military, adopting the socialist (or Wilsonian) peace program, and implementing fundamental political reforms, notably of the Prussian franchise, to show the world that Germany would not be a danger to a democratic Europe. Equally important, German workers must be convinced that rapid progress was being made, or disillusion and defeat could lead to bloody revolution, Bolshevism, and "Russian conditions." In these circumstances the delegation could no longer be restrained; it would almost certainly have brought down Hertling's government had not the Supreme Army Command anticipated it by a few days.[112] The bloc partners reluctantly acquiesced, and under the firm leadership of Ebert the SPD found itself, not in opposition as the left wing wanted, not even a floating parliamentary supporter of the new government, but a fully committed member of Germany's first formal government coalition, with the task of achieving a political reconstruction that would enable the nation to meet the coming calamity.

The SPD had committed itself to this course before the end of September, that is, at a time when a new government could be expected to have several months to implement its programs before having to negotiate peace. General Ludendorff's panic, which forced the new chancellor to sue for an armistice at once, condemned the experiment to futility. The short, desperate life of Prince Max of Baden's cabinet was not what the Majority Socialists had envisaged. Measures were pushed through that should have been popular: the appeal for an armistice on Wilson's terms disarmed socialist criticism; revision of the constitution made regular parliamentary governments possible; the greater part of the political censorship was abolished by stages; and a general political amnesty freed Karl Liebknecht and Wilhelm Dittmann, among others, from prison. But these accomplishments were too little, too late, too slow, and too wrapped up in the old forms to be appreciated by either the Entente or the German people. The request for an armistice had cut the time terribly short; the government and the Reichstag took the road of reform

112. The SPD's part in the September political crisis can be followed best in *Interfraktionelle Ausschuss*, vol. 2, and *Reichstagsfraktion*, II, 419–60. A concise secondary account based on this material is contained in the preface to *Die Regierung des Prinzen Max von Baden*, ed. Erich Matthias and Rudolf Morsey (Düsseldorf, 1962), pp. xi–xvi; see also Eberhard Kolb, *Die Arbeiterräte in der deutschen Innenpolitik 1918–1919* (Düsseldorf, 1962), pp. 24–30 and 35–36. Ebert and Scheidemann made clear their party's determination to bring down Hertling on Sept. 23 (*Interfraktionelle Ausschuss*, II, 679–80, 682–83, and 685) after a session of their party committee; and they held to this decision under severe pressure from the Center and Progressive leaders (*ibid.*, II, 701n and 709).

with an air of haste and panic that increased rather than allayed uncertainty and unrest.[113]

The suddenness of the crisis caught the Independents, like everyone else, by surprise, and those in a position to appreciate the magnitude of the imminent disaster were appalled.[114] The USPD even tried to help, after its fashion; Haase sanctioned the government's armistice appeal in a Reichstag speech and, by identifying the appeal with the USPD's longstanding program, put the party's supposed international reputation squarely behind Germany's efforts to win a fair peace. Claiming sole right to speak for peace-loving forces in Germany, the Independents demanded justice from the Entente in the name of future European brotherhood.[115] At the same time the moderate Independents could not fail to appreciate the introduction of the parliamentary system for which Social Democrats had fought so long.[116] But they were not prepared to help the government in any other way. In their domestic agitation they dismissed the new government as a halfhearted, incompletely liberal regime that could not hope to convince the world of its bona fides; it was a "fig-leaf of absolutism," in Liebknecht's phrase.[117] A manifesto of October 5 set out minimum goals that ought to have been part of even a modest nonsocialist government's program but were not among the announced aims of Prince Max's cabinet, including amnesty for political prisoners, termination of the state of siege, introduction of a proportional electoral system, radical alteration of the treaty of Brest-Litovsk, and evacuation of Russian territory.[118] Some of these policies were in fact implemented by the government, but any faint hope among centrists that the government could or would move with the necessary élan to effect a radical transformation of public life was soon disappointed. Within a few weeks all Independents had written off the new experiment. There was nothing left but a return to mass action, and as soon as possible.

113. On the development of public unrest in Germany toward the end of the war, see Kolb, *Arbeiterräte,* pp. 15–24.

114. Hans Peter Hanssen, *Diary of a Dying Empire* (Bloomington, Ind., 1955), p. 315; Hetta Gräfin Treuberg, *Zwischen Politik und Diplomatie: Memoiren* (Strasbourg, 1921), p. 231; and Gustav Mayer, *Erinnerungen* (Zurich, 1949), pp. 299–300, record encounters with leading Independents at this time. Mayer's account of Haase's views directly contradicts the well-known portrayal in Prince Max of Baden, *Erinnerungen und Dokumente* (Stuttgart, 1927), pp. 342–43 ("Now we have them!"); Mayer is much the more plausible.

115. Haase speech of Oct. 5, *Reichstag,* vol. 314, p. 6154; party manifesto of Oct. 5, *Auswirkungen,* IV, 1586–87.

116. See the articles on this subject in *Sozialistische Auslandspolitik,* Sept. 26, Oct. 3, and Oct. 10, 1918.

117. Quoted in Tormin, p. 54.

118. Printed in *Auswirkungen,* IV, 1588–89.

However, the aggressive policy of the Majority Socialists since August had effectively, if temporarily, disarmed the Independents. The SPD's large following among the workers could not be persuaded to support the projects of the socialist left while the SPD was on the offensive and seemed to be having some effect; and without these workers no mass action was possible. Consequently the USPD seems to have decided in September to adopt a waiting policy until the coming sessions of the Reichstag and Prussian Diet should demonstrate the futility of Majority Socialist attempts to reform the Imperial system by parliamentary means.[119] If the SPD did not itself then go into opposition, its followers would probably be ready for action even without party sanction, as in January. The advent of Prince Max's government delayed this prospect; many Independents were as ready to call out the masses against it as against its predecessor, but the chances of doing so successfully were minimal at first. However, the greater the hopes placed by the workers in the new government, the greater the impact of the disillusionment that must follow.

Meanwhile preparations went ahead. On October 11, at a meeting with representatives from the provinces, the party executive seems to have finally committed itself to calling a nationwide strike when the time was ripe.[120] There were two foreseeable ways in which this might happen, both reflected in USPD agitation during October. The hesitations and half-measures of the awkward government coalition might drive the workers, with or without the Majority Socialist leaders, into opposition; or there might be a sudden reversal of feeling if the government should try to break off armistice negotiations and continue the war. There was a lively fear among the workers, and not just radical workers, prompted by a wave of new call-ups and by right-wing press campaigns, that the army and others committed to national prestige would somehow force the politicians to carry on the war to the bitter end. These suspicions were only confirmed by the prolonged delay in getting the kaiser to see the need to abdicate, and finally by his virtual flight to Supreme Headquarters on October 29. The Independents' agitation played on these fears; there is every reason to believe that the party could and would have promoted powerful mass action against any last-ditch defense plan. Sentiment among the Independents on this issue, the last stage of their long campaign for peace, was united.[121]

119. *Ibid.*, IV, 1569–70 (from a police agent in Elberfeld).
120. *Ibid.*, IV, 1612. From Däumig's evidence about sentiment in the party leadership ten days later (USPD *Parteitag*, March 1919, pp. 227–28), the commitment may have been grudgingly made.
121. See *Leipziger Volkszeitung*, Oct. 26, Nov. 2 and 5, 1918 (manifestoes against carrying on the war, the last by the party executive); Ströbel's article in *Sozialistische Auslandspolitik*, Oct. 31, 1918; Haase's letter of Nov. 1, 1918, *Hugo*

In general, the last phase of USPD agitation before the revolution was marked by a new rhetorical extremism. In part this was merely the result of new freedom; the government, in its desire to be seen to be liberal, was doing its best to limit the repressive operation of the state of siege. In some areas, notably the Rhineland, vaguely revolutionary agitation could be conducted openly in meetings and demonstrations.[122] Partly, too, the new radicalism was the product of a sense of impending world upheaval. Phrases like "world revolution" and "socialist republic" entered the vocabulary of even the milder Independents, because such things began to seem likely, and passed on into the rhetoric of the revolution itself. The Independents in the Reichstag spoke as prophets of an imminent new world order; Haase and Ledebour proclaimed the inevitability of military defeat and predicted that the collapse of militarism would be quickly followed by that of capitalism.[123] What this new order would be was unclear; the patry leaders apparently persistently refused to make any plans for the postrevolutionary period, trusting that events would determine the path.[124] But their agitation helped ensure that when the revolt came it was generally taken to be the socialist revolution.

The overthrow of the established authorities in Germany, spreading from city to city between November 4 and 10, was seldom the work of the revolutionary apparatus; accordingly, the importance of such revolutionary preparations as there were tends to be underestimated. The network was intended for serious use and was probably at least as effective as that which had helped coordinate the January strike. If it was not put into action, this was because the leaders were not convinced that working-class unrest had yet reached the point where a strike call would succeed. Everyone understood that a general strike in the circumstances would amount to a serious attack on the authority of the state, which the state would presumably attempt ruthlessly to suppress; a high degree of

Haase, p. 169; *Auswirkungen*, IV, 1707 and 1708 (police reports on party sentiment in Leipzig and Berlin); StA Potsdam, Pr. Br. 2A Regierung Potsdam, I Pol. Nr. 1043, p. 124 (on the party's intentions); IML Berlin, RMdI 9/24, p. 23 (quoting Luise Zietz in a Hamburg assembly of Oct. 26); Lucas, *Frankfurt*, p. 16 (on Dissmann's activity in Frankfurt on Main).

122. *Auswirkungen*, IV, 1607–9 (account of a USPD assembly in Düsseldorf, Oct. 14, 1918); *ibid.*, IV, 1664 (report of a Düsseldorf official, Oct. 23, 1918); Dittmann memoirs, pp. 850–52, on his own speaking tour of the Rhineland at the end of October. See also Helmut Metzmacher, "Der Novemberumsturz 1918 in der Rheinprovinz," *Annalen des Historischen Vereins für den Niederrhein,* 168/169 (1967), 151–53.

123. *Reichstag,* vol. 314, pp. 6181–90 (Haase, Oct. 23, 1918) and 6226–37 (Ledebour, Oct. 24, 1918).

124. Barth, p. 35. Kolb, *Arbeiterräte,* p. 41, points out that the revolutionary committee is not known to have had any plans for the period after the revolution either.

restiveness was therefore necessary to move ordinary workers to such an undertaking. The well-informed revolutionaries were surely right in their estimate that this feeling was not there until the last days of October, in most places after that. As late as November 2 the revolutionary committee in Berlin—including a majority of the factory opposition leaders as well as party leaders—felt obliged to abandon its provisional plan to call the action for November 4, fearing that the workers in the provinces, and even many in the factories of Berlin, were not yet ready.[125] Instead, action was set for November 11, and messengers were dispatched to other cities to announce the date. Presumably the Independents would indeed have made their concerted attack on the old system on that date; but by then the revolution was over.

That virtually no resistance would be offered by the old regime was unforeseen. The troops on which the government would depend in the last resort shared the disillusionment of the general populace as the war drew to its disastrous close, growing increasingly unwilling to give their lives in a lost war or in defense of a doomed regime. The effects were most visible in the staging areas behind the field armies, where vandalism, dereliction of duty, and desertion assumed alarming proportions during October. The weakening of the garrison troops in the city barracks was less obvious—the revolutionaries could not be sure what they would do—but their commanders knew that they were growing less reliable day by day.[126] Nor was the government willing to order the firm, decisive military action that might have discouraged the timorous revolutionaries at Kiel and elsewhere; by its very nature, and especially because it included Social Democrats, it was committed to conciliation, to playing for time while trying to accomplish enough reform to build up political confidence among the people. Contrary to the fears of the Independents,

125. Participants' accounts of the meeting (or meetings) of Nov. 2 are numerous; Barth, pp. 46–51; R. Müller, *Kaiserreich*, I, 138–39; Dittmann memoirs, pp. 854–55; Ledebour on many occasions (with variants), see *Ledebour-Prozess*, pp. 28-29, *Allgemeiner Kongress der Arbeiter- und Soldatenräte Deutschlands vom 16. bis 21. Dezember 1918 im Abgeordnetenhaus zu Berlin* (Berlin [1919]) (hereafter cited as *Allgemeiner Kongress*), p. 47, and Ledebour papers, third article; Liebknecht's diary, printed in *Illustrierte Geschichte der deutschen Revolution* (Berlin, 1929), pp. 203–4; Wilhelm Pieck, *Gesammelte Reden und Schriften*, 3 vols. (Berlin, 1959), I, 416–19. According to the last two, the new date was set not on Nov. 2 but at a later meeting on Nov. 6 (Liebknecht) or 7 (Pieck); cf. *GdA: Chronik*, II, 25.
126. R. Müller, *Kaiserreich*, I, 137–38; *Der Dolchstossprozess in München, Oktober/November 1925: Zeugen- und Sachverständigen-Aussagen* (Munich [1925]), p. 45 (testimony of Colonel Mantey about the Berlin garrison). Hermann Müller points out (*November-Revolution*, p. 49) that the Berlin garrison turned to the Majority Socialists for leadership after the revolution, thus showing their defection had not been caused by radical agitation.

the government was strong enough to enforce its will on the generals, to whittle away their powers in the name of civil liberties and countermand their military orders in the hope of compromise. The effect, however, was to sow fatalism and disillusion among the generals and allow the slow dissolution of discipline among the garrison troops.[127] The soldiers and their commanders became convinced that no effective resistance would be offered; and once the workers realized this too, all was over.

In some cities the paralysis of the old order was already far advanced in the early days of November, and how the planned revolt might have gone is suggested by the course of events in the one place it was tried, in Württemberg. The provincial organization of the Independents there was very radical, with a Spartacist, Fritz Rück, serving as chairman. Rück seems, however, to have used not the USPD organization but a parallel Spartacist network when a strike was scheduled for November 4, a decision apparently based on misapprehension of the plans of the Berliners.[128] The strike was successful in some of the largest Stuttgart factories, and a large demonstration followed, which the royal officials did not dare to resist. A workers' council was formed, and demands were presented to the royal government; but no trial of strength was attempted.[129] This uneasy dualism endured for two days, and the small city of Friedrichshafen staged a similar rising in sympathy; but the rest of South Germany was slow to follow.[130] At this point Rück and the other principal leaders of the strike were arrested (on November 7); the decapitated movement thereupon dissolved, so that when, two days later, the Württemberg monarchy collapsed before the spreading national wave of revolution the SPD was able to take effective control of the situation in Stuttgart.[131] Although a failure, the attempt was thus a very near miss; the degree of success achieved with limited Spartacist resources, at a time when the revolution had not gathered momentum, is striking.

On the day originally chosen for action by the Berlin revolutionary committee, November 4, the events usually regarded as the start of the German revolution took place in the extreme north of Germany, in the naval port of Kiel, where the admiral in command of the city had to

127. How the possibilities of military resistance to insurrection were slowly eaten away by disaffection below and procrastination above is brilliantly set out in Volkmann, *Marxismus,* pp. 215–24 (Kiel), 224–30 (the spread of the revolt in North Germany), and 238–43 (Berlin).

128. See Rück's diary, *Illustrierte Geschichte,* p. 184.

129. Kolb, *Arbeiterräte,* pp. 63–64. The demands were based on those of a conference of Spartacists and left radicals on Oct. 7; see *Auswirkungen,* IV, 1723–26, and *Illustrierte Geschichte,* p. 183. On the whole affair, see also Keil, II, 27–37.

130. *Auswirkungen,* IV, 1744–50 and 1755.

131. *Illustrierte Geschichte,* p. 194; Kolb, *Arbeiterräte,* p. 65.

yield his powers to mutinous sailors.[132] Contrary to the Independents' expectation "that the industrial workers in the great cities and centers of industry would raise the banner of rebellion first,"[133] the decisive impulse came from the navy and started in the northern ports. The USPD was of little importance there;[134] the workers played a subordinate role, and although some of the sailors were influenced by radical propaganda they were clearly acting under no one's direction but their own.[135] Even after the city was in their hands, the sailors' public demands amounted to little more than a set of enlisted men's grievances, with no socialist overtones.[136] When Gustav Noske, the SPD Reichstag deputy, arrived from Berlin he was able to bring the situation under control within a few days.

Before order could be restored in Kiel, however, the revolt had spread, partly because of the sailors' missionary zeal, partly because of their desire to forestall any punitive expedition from neighboring cities.[137] Their fame preceded them. The arrival of the sailors during the next few days in armed, businesslike bands in cities as far afield as Braunschweig and Frankfurt on Main was the signal for local radical forces to rouse themselves. Nearly everywhere the conservative forces proved so demoralized as to be able to offer no more than token resistance, and garrison troops came over en masse, loyal elements among them melting quietly away. Generally the appearance of the workers in the streets merely confirmed that the issue was already settled, though sometimes pockets of resistance provided targets for the energies of the revolutionaries. The workers' leaders would then join representatives of the garrison in setting up a workers' and soldiers' council, whose first act was normally to call on the citizenry to preserve public order. Then came hesitation and uncertainty. No one but the extreme radicals was sure at first that these local revolts were part of a revolution; the very word was largely avoided, and the rebels still spoke of forcing the abdication of the kaiser and the conclusion of peace. In fact these revolts were the decisive acts of revolution, because they finally tipped the balance of confidence, teaching the work-

132. The story has often been told; see the admirably concise recent account and analysis in Kolb, *Arbeiterräte*, pp. 71–75.

133. Dittmann memoirs, p. 860.

134. *Ibid.*

135. See the pamphlet by Lothar Popp (chairman of the Kiel USPD) and the sailors' leader Karl Artelt, *Ursprung und Entwicklung der November-Revolution 1918* (Kiel, n.d.), pp. 11–12. Noske and Artelt address themselves directly to this question in *Ursachen*, IX/II, 69–72 and 579–81.

136. Text in *Dokumente und Materialien*, II, 281–82.

137. For a chronicle and analysis of this phenomenon, see Kolb, *Arbeiterräte*, pp. 75–85; maps of the revolt's progress are in Tormin, following p. 148; an impressive regional case study (of the Rhineland) is Metzmacher, "Novemberumsturz."

ers that they could succeed and undermining the authorities' belief that they could resist.

With the sailors carrying the spark of revolt, it seems to have made little difference whether the cities they came to were strongholds of the USPD or devoid of Independents. In Kiel the USPD was small though radical, in Lübeck, Wilhelmshaven, and Cuxhaven no more than a sect; in Hanover and Cologne, the first inland cities to be affected, the party was negligible. In Hamburg, to be sure, an enthusiastic USPD assembly on November 5 helped create the atmosphere in which a band of sailors carried out their coup, and left radical orators led the crowds the next day to face down the commanding general and finish the job.[138] These circumstances gave the left-wing socialists greater representation in the postrevolutionary government of Hamburg than their numbers would have justified. In Bremen, where the socialist movement tended to the left, the workers' leaders were on the alert, but it was sailors who carried the day.[139] Even in these cities no one could suppose that the revolution was a planned radical insurrection.

In Munich, by contrast, it was just that; there, the socialist republic of Bavaria was established during the night of November 7–8. Just as the Munich revolution was unique in being a deliberate and successful seizure of power, so was the Munich USPD unique within the Independent Socialist party, and it requires fuller discussion in a later chapter. There are no indications that Kurt Eisner, the Munich leader, was guided in any way by the national policy of the party; his action, growing out of local conditions, was a perfectly judged and executed exercise in which a small minority neutralized the garrison and then swept aside the Bavarian monarchy in the space of a few hours. Bavaria's geographical position and particularist political tradition made it possible to conceive of such a stroke without concern for whether the rest of the Reich would follow, and this factor should be taken into account. But whether or not Bavaria was concerned about the Reich, radicals elsewhere, and even neutral observers, were much impressed by the socialist color of the revolution in Munich. In the words of the *Frankfurter Zeitung*, "What yesterday was still an almost politically indifferent military movement in northern Germany has overnight become a political convulsion in Munich. . . . A new age has come."[140] The example of this small

138. Dittmann memoirs, pp. 856–60; Richard Bünemann, "Hamburg in der deutschen Revolution von 1918/19" (Ph.D. dissertation, University of Hamburg, 1951), pp. 66–96.

139. Kolb, *Arbeiterräte*, pp. 78–79.

140. Quoted in Allan Mitchell, *Revolution in Bavaria, 1918–1919: The Eisner Regime and the Soviet Republic* (Princeton, 1965), p. 102.

outpost of the USPD contributed greatly to the final, decisive wave of revolution in Saxony and Prussia.

The revolution toward which the USPD had oriented itself, in part actively, in part timidly, over the past year had arrived. What this party, weighted down with traditions, consciousness of weakness, and divergence of purpose, could make of the opportunity remained to be seen.

CHAPTER 4

The Revolutionary Regime in
Berlin (November 1918)

The Independents were ready for revolution, in their different ways. They were not prepared for the postrevolutionary period. The overthrow of the Imperial system in November 1918 was readily comprehensible to them as the advent of the long-awaited social revolution. This revolution, according to their traditional thinking, was to be an attack on class domination and economic oppression, on autocratic remnants in the political order, and on social and economic privilege. They knew the enemy, therefore, and had some idea of the principles of the new order to be established—full political democracy, social ownership of industry, classless education, and the like. They did not, however, have any notion of the specific policies or methods the revolutionary forces should adopt or of the machinery appropriate for carrying them out.

The lack of a concrete revolutionary program was not necessarily crippling; with more imagination, ruthlessness, verve, and certainty the Independent Socialists might have helped turn the German revolution into something quite different from what it became, learning their tasks as they went, as the Bolsheviks did.[1] Although such factors as the lost war and the returning armies, food shortages, the desperate state of the economy, a powerful bureaucratic tradition, and the political inexperience of the populace imposed limits, the course of events was not fixed in advance.[2] But the Independents (and not only they) carried their old luggage with them into the new era. The dominant group of leaders, and their many followers throughout the country, had been trained by their

1. For this reason, the censorious tone of Kolb's discussion (*Arbeiterräte*, pp. 42 and 45) of the USPD's unpreparedness seems misplaced. Closer to the mark is Tormin, p. 137, who notes that the critical fact about the socialist parties in the revolution was "not so much . . . what they or their leaders *did*, but rather . . . what they *were*."

2. On the question of the possibilities of change in the revolution, see the excellent survey of the recent literature in Helga Grebing, "Konservative Republik oder soziale Demokratie? Zur Bewertung der Novemberrevolution in der neueren westdeutschen Historiographie," in *Vom Kaiserreich* (ed. Kolb), pp. 386–403.

whole political experience to be careful, methodical compromisers, for all their far-reaching aims; rather than striking out boldly, they were accustomed to reckon with the mood of their following and of the masses. The more radical Independents had the same qualities, if in different measure; and they, too, were creatures of their milieu, the dissatisfied but by no means déraciné elements of the solid German working class. The Independents struggled with their revolutionary tasks—and increasingly with each other as well—within limits imposed by their whole political past.

The first phase—roughly until the end of the year—saw the Independents trying to make something of the revolution they had experienced. Some set to work to build on the original revolutionary impulse by government action, attempting to unite the working class behind the revolutionary advances by constructing a purposeful alliance of the two party leaderships. These months saw the nearest approach to harmony between the leaders of the two parties of any time between 1916 and 1920; the collapse of the alliance was a new failure of German socialism that decisively influenced the early development of the Republic. Other Independents rejected this course and set their socialist hopes on grassroots organization, specifically on the characteristic institution of the revolution, the workers' and soldiers' councils. This group showed more initiative and determination, also more of an eye for the pursuit of power; but their experience was ultimately no more happy. Still others drifted, with revolutionary rhetoric and emotions but without definite purpose. And the revolutionary opportunities, whatever they may have been, passed away.

Advent of the New Regime

The capital city, Berlin, was not a leader in the insurrection of November 1918. Spontaneous, activist radicalism was probably nowhere very high until the end of October or even later; certainly not in Berlin.[3] The Spartacists, sponsors of such street demonstrations as took place, had little success in their attempts to build up spontaneous, self-perpetuating action. The leaders of the shop stewards' committee bided their time, waiting impatiently. In the end, for all their daring and the hard work of preparation, their single most important decision was *not* to attempt the rising on November 4, as intended. This conclusion was reached on November 2, before there was any news of the trouble build-

3. As late as Oct. 29 the police president of Berlin perceived no growth of radical influence; *Auswirkungen,* IV, 1696–97 and 1708. According to Ebert's sources of information (*Regierung des Prinzen Max,* p. 499), the situation in the factories became dangerous only after new military call-ups began on Nov. 1

ing up in the fleet off Kiel, when a meeting of representatives of the Berlin factories decided by a close vote, twenty-one to nineteen, that a rising could not muster enough support. Barth, Däumig, and Ledebour were apparently reluctant to accept this decision, but Haase, Dittmann, and others successfully insisted on restraint until the workers at large were ready to act. Action was put off for a week, until November 11 (like November 4, a Monday).[4]

Thus the leaders of the Independents in Berlin, while looking (with varying degrees of enthusiasm) toward revolution, were unprepared for the suddenness of the final collapse. They were not, however, completely inactive.[5] On November 4 an official party manifesto called on the workers to resist prolongation of the war, by action if necessary;[6] and mass meetings were announced for the evening of November 7, with the ostensible purpose of celebrating the anniversary of the revolution in Russia but possibly to encourage the workers to spontaneous action. If so the plan was not tested, for the meetings were banned.[7] The Majority Socialists were even busier, as they felt the situation getting out of hand. The cabinet was in a permanent state of crisis from November 6, with the SPD threatening to abandon it unless enough visible reforms, notably the abdication of the kaiser, could be forced through to stave off collapse and violence. The party had already hedged its bets; party leaders met regularly with their own shop stewards' committee, using these contacts to press for patience and understanding among their restive followers but also to keep the way open for a bid for the leadership of any protest movement that proved too strong to be headed off.[8]

Revolution came to Berlin on November 9. What with the news of risings in one German city after another, and particularly of events in Munich, and the paralyzed government's delay in obtaining the kaiser's abdication and an armistice, all the socialists seem to have realized that the moment had come; even the Majority Socialists, though resisting up to the last moment, called on their followers to join the general strike that broke out that morning.[9] Appeals to strike and revolt had gone out

4. The sources for this meeting are cited in ch. 3, n. 125. The vote is given in some of the sources as 22 to 19. This was the first shop stewards' meeting to which Haase and Dittmann were invited.

5. The best source for the activity of the USPD leaders in these days is Liebknecht's notes, in *Illustrierte Geschichte*, pp. 203–4.

6. *Leipziger Volkszeitung*, Nov. 5, 1918.

7. The banning of the meetings was discussed at length in the cabinet; see *Regierung des Prinzen Max*, pp. 572–81.

8. These meetings are mentioned *ibid.*, pp. 492 (Nov. 4), 575–77 (Nov. 7), 581 (Nov. 7), 597–98 (Nov. 8), and 617 (Nov. 9). According to a report in SPD *Parteitag*, June 1919, p. 10, the meetings were held daily.

9. On the SPD's last-minute change of front, see Scheidemann, *Zusammenbruch*,

during the previous night from the revolutionary committee, which was in some disarray;[10] and their apparatus helped organize (and to a small extent arm) the crowds of workers who streamed toward the center city from their places of work. But it was the workers' action more than theirs, and it was over within hours; shortly after noon the abdication of the kaiser was announced, followed by the resignation of Prince Max of Baden's cabinet. The Imperial regime had fallen.

Though the revolution had met remarkably little resistance, the socialists had more than enough to do in trying to organize their hundreds of thousands of followers and establish a new order. This activity inevitably turned into a contest between the two wings of socialism. The Independents—or rather those who controlled the revolutionary committee—had the apparent advantage. They had more organized followers in the city than the Majority Socialists and had been the most active group in the factories throughout the war; they were the acknowledged party of revolution, the men of the hour for the Berlin factory workers. But the SPD was still very much a force. For all the USPD's following in the working class of the great industrial centers, among other classes and in the nation at large they were seen as a mere radical faction, and probably a passing one at that, while the Majority Socialists were regarded as the legitimate representatives of the lower classes. The leaders of the SPD had become during the war mediators between the working masses and the other sections of German society; Ebert's emergence as chancellor-for-a-day on November 9 aptly symbolized this. So the SPD came to stand for a revolution on behalf of the whole people. In Berlin, as elsewhere, the SPD had a broad residual support that would show itself after the first furore had died down.

More immediately advantageous for the SPD was the attitude of the city's large garrison. Many soldiers collaborated willingly in the revolution, and vaguely socialist aspirations of national renewal were widespread among them in the weeks after the revolution. But the soldiers, with few exceptions, had had little contact with prerevolutionary agitation; most had no flaming revolutionary expectations; and indeed many were not from the working class. They turned first, therefore, to the better-known and more moderate of the two parties of the revolution, and the Majority Socialists made the most of the opportunity. Led by

---

pp. 206–7, and *Memoiren*, II, 293–96; Wels' testimony, in Herzfeld, p. 332; Brolat's account, given by Heinrich Schäfer, *Tagebuchblätter eines rheinischen Sozialisten* (Bonn, 1919), p. 38; *Reichstagsfraktion*, II, 518–19.

10. Three separate appeals seem to have gone out; see Barth, pp. 52–54; *Dokumente und Materialien*, II, 324–25; *Ledebour-Prozess*, p. 30; Ledebour papers, seventh article. The account in Pieck, I, 424, conflicts somewhat with the others.

Otto Wels, a member of the party executive, prominent Majority Socialists moved in personally to exert their influence on the garrison.[11] As a result, when elections for soldiers' councils were held in the barracks on November 10, the field was clear for the Majority Socialists; the radicals were not even represented at many of the barracks assemblies. Those elected were not solidly Majority Socialists; many were nonparty, though predominantly of moderate inclinations. But the SPD had gained an ascendancy among the regular garrison troops that was to be very important over the next two months.

The USPD radicals had their troubles in the factory elections as well. Their established position was undercut by a movement to bring about collaboration of the two socialist parties under the watchword "parity." This improbable slogan, "parity," meaning that the membership of the workers' councils should be divided evenly between the two parties, became one of the central themes of the German revolution, and not only in Berlin. The idea seems to have arisen spontaneously, though it was certainly encouraged by the Majority Socialists;[12] in any case, it was taken up with genuine enthusiasm by the masses of simple workers, who apparently wanted a reunification of the socialist movement now that the war was practically over and certainly wanted to avoid fratricidal strife. As a result, even in factories where radical shop stewards had been the acknowledged leaders for years, "Social Democratic officials who had been driven out of the factory with blows the day before, because they did not want to join the general strike, were now elected as members of the workers' council."[13]

The elected delegates assembled on the afternoon of November 10 in the Zirkus Busch and established a balance of forces that lasted for over a month.[14] The assembly had been summoned by the radical shop stewards, was dominated by them and presided over by Richard Müller; but there was no escape from the principle of parity. When the revolutionary committee tried to get itself confirmed as the executive council of the

11. Wels, in Herzfeld, p. 332; H. Müller, pp. 48–49; R. Müller, *Kaiserreich*, II, 41–42; Otto Braun, *Von Weimar zu Hitler*, 2d ed. (New York, 1940), p. 16; Schäfer, pp. 45–48 (according to R. Görlinger).

12. See the editorial "Kein Bruderkampf" in *Vorwärts*, Nov. 10, 1918; also Wels' speech to the Majority Socialist workers' delegates that afternoon before the Zirkus Busch meeting, reported in H. Müller, p. 69. H. Müller, pp. 62–63 and 69–70, notes that the SPD factory organization was effective in spreading the idea. On the sources of the sentiment, see Kolb, *Arbeiterräte*, p. 87.

13. R. Müller, *Kaiserreich*, II, 36.

14. There are good accounts of the meeting, *ibid.*, II, 36–40, in Bernstein, *Die deutsche Revolution*, pp. 46–47, and in J. S. Drabkin, *Die November-Revolution 1918 in Deutschland* (Berlin, 1968), pp. 165–67. Summary minutes of the meeting are published in part in Gilbert Badia, *Les Spartakistes* (n.p., 1966), pp. 84–90.

Berlin workers' and soldiers' councils, unruly soldiers threatened to break up the meeting. Majority Socialist representation had to be accepted, whereupon the Spartacists refused to serve. The result was the election of six workers' deputies each from the SPD and the Independents, all of the latter associated with the revolutionary committee and including Ledebour, Däumig, and Richard Müller. The total was then brought up to twenty-four by adding twelve soldiers' deputies.[15] Parity was not applied in this case since the soldiers declared themselves nonpartisan; there were no more than three radicals among them, the rest being led by a capable Majority Socialist Reichstag deputy, Max Cohen.[16] In this "supreme organ of the revolution," formed under their auspices, the radicals controlled at best a third of the votes.

Preliminary maneuvering for position in the Reich government had been going on simultaneously, with similar results. The course of the negotiations, however, was very different; for in the case of the central government the SPD had the initiative.

The actions of the SPD party leaders on November 9 were improvised; but the results were a brilliant success. When early reports from the factories showed what the day was to bring, the SPD at once made a formal approach to the USPD on a coalition socialist government for the country. They could get no reply from the small number of Independents who could be found.[17] Shortly after noon, still without a reply, Ebert went to Prince Max with a delegation and arranged to take over the reins of government.[18] Ebert's was a bold move, for his position among the rebelling masses in Berlin was still uncertain. It proved strong enough. He could have been overthrown easily by force, but no one seems to have considered this, and the SPD's key mediating position in the political spectrum meant that nearly all the forces of public opinion

15. The more familiar total of 28 was reached a few days later by cooptation, the ratio remaining the same at 7:7:14; see H. Müller, p. 92.

16. R. Müller, *Kaiserreich,* II, 53 and 143; Max Cohen's recollections are in *Vossische Zeitung,* Dec. 19, 1928, clipping in the Heinrich Scheüch papers (BA-MA Freiburg), 1, p. 166.

17. Ledebour in *Ledebour-Prozess,* pp. 31 and 33; Dittmann memoirs, pp. 864–65; *Reichstagsfraktion,* II, 518–19. There are indications that Ebert may have been thinking of an all-party government, to include the Independents, not a purely socialist government; see *Der Zentralrat der Deutschen Sozialistischen Republik,* ed. Eberhard Kolb with Reinhard Rürup (Leiden, 1968) (hereafter cited as *Zentralrat*), pp. xiii–xiv; *Die Regierung der Volksbeauftragten 1918/19,* ed. Susanne Miller with Heinrich Potthoff, introduction by Erich Matthias, 2 vols. (Düsseldorf, 1969) (hereafter cited as *Regierung der VB*), I, xxii–xxiv. The Independents, however, chose to understand the offer as referring to a socialist cabinet and discussed it in these terms.

18. Accounts of the conversation by participants are reproduced in *Regierung der VB,* I, 3–18.

were working in his favor. The chief limitation on his freedom of movement was that, operating in Berlin, he had no choice but to give due
place to the Independents. On balance the SPD was, by a slight edge,
master of the situation.

The leaders of the USPD had no ready answer to the suggestion of a
coalition with the Majority Socialists because (so far as we know) they
had given no thought to such a question. Their attention had been turned
toward mass action, and they had shied away from consideration of practical problems that might arise later, expecting instead that the mass
movement would dictate its laws as it went along.[19] Such practical questions were, after all, one more source of tension that might upset the uneasy unity of the party. In any case, the SPD's sudden change of front at
the moment of the revolution took the Independents by surprise. The
first SPD offer on the morning of November 9 was scorned by Ledebour, though Dittmann showed an inclination to accept.[20] Meanwhile
Haase, the party's most respected leader and successful conciliator, was
absent from Berlin until evening.

In these circumstances the top echelons of the USPD were reduced to
the dithering that was to become characteristic of the party's behavior
at critical moments. Not until the afternoon were enough Independents
assembled—assorted members of the Reichstag delegation, the party
executive, the local Berlin leadership, and the revolutionary committee
—to take up the question. Then came hours of debate.[21] Most of the
left wing of the party—led by Ledebour, Däumig, and Richard Müller
—wanted to reject the offer; the SPD leaders were too untrustworthy or
simply too compromised to be proper revolutionary allies; there was
some feeling, also, that the old machinery of the central government
should be bypassed altogether in establishing the new order. The haste
with which the SPD, only yesterday a pillar of the old order, wanted to
set up a provisional government on the model of coalition cabinets suggested to the radicals that the SPD leaders were anxious to choke off
the revolution in its early stages.

More moderate views prevailed. The proposal to abandon and destroy
the Reich's old administrative machinery found no more than lukewarm
support; most Independents could not really conceive of workers' councils as a permanent alternative to a revolutionary cabinet that would
reform the existing state apparatus. Yet the USPD was too weak to form

19. See Barth, p. 35, and R. Müller, *Kaiserreich*, I, 139.
20. Scheidemann, *Memoiren*, II, 298–99; Ledebour in *Ledebour-Prozess*, p. 33.
21. Accounts by participants are, Bernstein, *Die deutsche Revolution*, pp. 34–35;
Barth, pp. 57–59; R. Müller, *Kaiserreich*, II, 27–29; Dittmann memoirs, pp. 867–
70; Pieck, I, 427–30.

a cabinet by itself, and all talk of such a solution was mere daydreaming.[22] The only alternative to joining a coalition was to abstain, in the hope of being carried to power by a further surge of revolution, but at this point such a course was both too visionary and too irresponsible for most Independents. What tipped the balance, as party leaders afterward emphasized, was the unmistakable enthusiasm of the revolutionary assemblies for joint revolutionary leadership by the two socialist parties.[23] To this extent, indeed, the expectation that revolutionary developments would dictate postrevolutionary forms was realized, and the USPD bowed to what it saw as the will of the masses.

But the conditions for partnership caused a further day's delay. An attempt was first made to force far-reaching terms on the SPD: Germany was to be a "social republic," that is, not an ordinary parliamentary one; the entire executive, legislative, and judicial power was to rest "exclusively in the hands of elected delegates of the entire working population and the soldiers"; and the participation of the Independents was to be for three days only, "in order to provide a government capable of concluding the armistice."[24] In short, all power was to be given to the workers' and soldiers' councils, with the heir of the old government retaining only vestigial functions. Clearly the assembled USPD leaders' attempt was to find a formula that would keep the radicals and Spartacists from boycotting the party's action; indeed, Liebknecht is said to have proposed these terms himself.[25] But the SPD, as was only to be expected, rejected the demands, though in terms that left the door open for further negotiation. On the main point they replied firmly: "If by this demand the dictatorship of a part of one class is intended, without the majority of the people behind it, then we must refuse this demand because it contravenes our democratic principles." Instead a constituent assembly was proposed which should decide on the future form of the state.[26]

22. The SPD, despairing of coalition, seems actually to have proposed to the Independents that one of the parties take over, with the other as a loyal opposition; see Hanssen, p. 361 (according to Breitscheid); Schäfer, pp. 43–44 (according to Brolat); Barth, pp. 57 and 60; R. Müller, *Kaiserreich*, II, 29. The only indication that any leading Independents considered such a solution seriously is in a letter of Nov. 26 from Haase to his son, *Hugo Haase*, p. 173.

23. See Haase's statement at the Berlin party assembly of Dec. 15, *Freiheit*, Dec. 16, 1918 (m), and his article in *Freiheit*, Jan. 1, 1919; also Dittmann's memoirs, pp. 870 and 901. There is little evidence that avoidance of civil war was the decisive factor for the USPD leaders (as argued in Kolb, *Arbeiterräte*, p. 159), though this may have been an undercurrent in their thinking.

24. The text is not preserved but can be reconstructed from quotations embedded in the SPD's point-by-point reply, in *Vorwärts*, Nov. 10, 1918.

25. Bernstein, *Die deutsche Revolution*, pp. 34–35; Scheidemann, *Memoiren*, II, 318.

26. *Vorwärts*, Nov. 10, 1918.

The effect—and partly, perhaps, the intention—of the SPD's reply was to drive a wedge into the ranks of the Independents. While the radicals were adamant, most of the USPD leaders were prepared to drop the Spartacist formulation of the powers of the workers' and soldiers' councils; so long as the councils received adequate recognition, their actual functions could be left to later determination. At the moment, the dominant political fact was the popular insistence on the collaboration of the two socialist parties. Haase, when he returned to Berlin during the evening of November 9, was discovered to hold similar views on the basis of his experiences in Hamburg and Kiel, where he had found strong popular pressure for collaboration.[27] Haase's return appears to have stiffened the resolve of the moderates. The next morning, in the absence of most of those originally drawn into consultation, the party executive hammered out new terms that proved acceptable to the Majority Socialists. The narrow conception of the functions of the cabinet was abandoned, and a compromise formula concerning the councils left their role less than clear: "The political power lies in the hands of the workers' and soldiers' councils." Consideration of the SPD's demand for a constituent assembly was specifically put off to a later date.[28]

The price of this compromise was high for the USPD. The party leaders wanted to place Haase, Ledebour, and Liebknecht in the government and thus involve all three factions in the venture. Liebknecht, after an interlude when it did appear that he was going to join the government, withdrew his consent. Ledebour refused from the start, and did not change his mind even when the party of which he was cochairman definitely decided to throw in its lot with the provisional government. These two could be replaced by Dittmann, who still enjoyed something of a reputation as a radical, and Barth, the only shop stewards' leader who could be recruited; but neither had the stature of the man he replaced. Too many of the party activists stood apart, skeptical or hostile, their criticism muted at first only from feelings of party solidarity. Haase, Dittmann, and Barth could not doubt that they had taken up a very exposed position.[29] And as partners they had three former comrades—

27. Dittmann memoirs, p. 870. See also the account in H. Müller, pp. 38–39; Müller returned from the coast with Haase on Nov. 9. But cf. Haase's later claim to the contrary, USPD *Parteitag,* March 1919, pp. 238–39.

28. Text in *Vorwärts,* Nov. 11, 1918. The vote in the party executive was unanimous except for Ledebour; Zietz in USPD *Parteitag,* March 1919, p. 52, and Ledebour in *Ledebour-Prozess,* p. 35. On the reasons for the SPD's immediate acceptance of these terms, see Kolb, *Arbeiterräte,* pp. 116–17.

29. According to Gustav Bauer, who was in a position to know, Haase actually withdrew his party's consent to serve after the SPD-sponsored soldiers' riot at the Zirkus Busch assembly of the councils on Nov. 10 but thought better of it that

Ebert, Scheidemann, and Otto Landsberg—from whom they were divided by attitudes developed during years of conflict and separation and by differences of opinion on the nature of their task that had merely been swept under the rug.

Much thus depended on guidance being provided by the continuing revolution. The Berlin workers, however, were satisfied for the time being to resign their unexpected revolution into the hands of the leaders— the parties, the government, and the Berlin executive council. On Monday and Tuesday, November 11 and 12, they returned to their factories. In the next few weeks the red flags and cockades slowly disappeared from the streets of the city. The ferment was still there beneath the surface; increasing unemployment and a severe shortage of food and other necessities would have seen to that, even had there been fewer radical expectations among the workers and fewer agitators to feed on their frustrations. But at first the city was quiet. Even the Spartacists were unable to do much until more than a week had passed. The inclination to violence did not show itself again until December.

The Problem of the Future of the Revolution

Not surprisingly, the revolution was understood in very different ways by those who experienced it. Vigor and hesitancy, pride and doctrine, and feelings of responsibility were present in various combinations that permit identification of at least four different socialist approaches to the future exploitation of the revolutionary events of November 1918: those of the Majority Socialist leaders and the Spartacists on the two extremes, and between them those of the radicals (as we shall continue to call the more aggressive Independents) and the official, moderate wing of the USPD. The division is not a neat one along the older party or factional lines, for this was a confused period in which perspectives were uncertain and allegiances in flux; many socialists had no very definite conceptions to guide them. But the four approaches outlined below will provide us with a framework for understanding the conflicts within socialism that eventually shattered the hopes cherished on all sides in the first days of the revolution.[30]

For the Majority Socialist leadership, the revolution was already com-

---

same evening; letter from Bauer to Paul Löbe, Nov. 13, 1918, in the Paul Löbe collection (DZA Potsdam), 4, p. 32.

30. Similar investigations by other authors have sometimes enumerated the distinctive approaches differently. Rosenberg, *Geschichte*, pp. 25–31, subdivides both the Majority Socialists and the Spartacists/left radicals for purposes of analysis (which we shall do only in passing). Tormin, pp. 69–71, lumps together the radical Independents and the Spartacists, which can be misleading. Closest to our approach is that of Kolb, *Arbeiterräte*, ch. 6.

pleted, its result enshrined in the work of the provisional government in its first days. The dynasties had been overthrown, Germany had become a republic with, for the first time, a government of the left. On November 11 the war came to an end with the signing of the armistice. The government's program, announced on November 12, ordained that future elections to all legislative assemblies would be conducted under universal, equal, secret, and direct suffrage, without distinction of sex, under a proportional system—the old socialist formula. The same manifesto extended and guaranteed such basic liberties as freedom of the press and assembly, restored the prewar labor laws, and promised welfare measures.[31] These were the first fruits of the revolution, and perhaps its true fruits; the autocratic monarchy was swept away and democratic liberties introduced, the war was terminated and exceptional repressive measures ended. These gains were, for the SPD, legitimate. They had been the aims of nearly all the workers and soldiers who had made the revolution, and the results were acceptable, though not ideal, to most of the rest of the population, even to a large part of the powerful bureaucracy and the army. They were the starting point of a new order.

At this point the thinking of the SPD leaders turned away from revolution—a revolution they would have preferred to avoid in the first place. Indeed, they were prepared to try to prevent further upheaval and disorder; as Sigmund Neumann has observed, the guiding ideas of the old party in the months after November 9 were "avoidance of chaos" and "stabilization of the democratic republic."[32] The country's condition demanded domestic peace, in their view, and with the Bolshevik example before them they feared that continuing revolution could lead to minority dictatorship and civil war. This fear had little basis in the actual strength of the extreme left at the end of 1918 but was an obsession founded on a false analogy between the German and Russian revolutions. It combined, however, with the SPD's sense of responsibility for the nation—embedded in its leaders' outlook since 1914, and especially since the formation of the Reichstag majority bloc in 1917—to lead Ebert and his colleagues to think of themselves as "emergency aides in a national crisis, not as leaders of a revolution."[33]

The central point in the SPD's program in the postrevolutionary weeks

31. Text in *Vorwärts*, Nov. 13, 1918. Haase was the author of the program (Dittmann memoirs, pp. 883–85), which was opposed in the cabinet only by Barth, who wanted farther-reaching measures, such as socialization of industry (Barth, p. 68).

32. Sigmund Neumann, *Die deutschen Parteien: Wesen und Wandel nach dem Kriege* (Berlin, 1932), p. 26.

33. Reinhard Rürup, "Entstehung und Grundlagen der Weimarer Verfassung," in *Vom Kaiserreich* (ed. Kolb), p. 221.

—the only point, it sometimes seemed—concerned the National Assembly. A national constituent assembly elected by universal suffrage could expect to have the moral authority with all classes to reconstitute the state, restore orderly processes of government, and conclude the peace; but for the SPD, such a parliamentary assembly was not only expedient but also represented the sole legitimate form of government. The reserve with which Social Democrats had traditionally regarded parliamentary forms had gone the way of the SPD's feeling of political alienation, both casualties of the war; in their place was a deep commitment to democratic reform by parliamentary means, even if this meant being forced into coalition with nonsocialist parties. This commitment found dramatic expression when Social Democratic ministers entered Prince Max of Baden's cabinet and was in no way changed by the revolution.

Indeed, the revolution led to an upsurge of democratic idealism in the SPD, strengthened by the hopeful belief in some quarters that the revolution would increase socialist electoral support and might even produce a socialist majority.[34] As their party committee proclaimed on November 29, the SPD saw "in the universal, equal, direct, and secret suffrage of all adult men and women . . . the most important political achievement of the revolution and at the same time the means of transforming the capitalist social order into a socialist one, by planned work in accordance with the will of the people."[35] Majority Socialists were tempted by the easy faith that a democratic electoral system would mean the execution of the "will of the people" and that this would suffice to ensure the eventual triumph of socialism.[36] In this view, workers' and soldiers' councils —whether or not one shared the party leaders' view of them as dangerous and essentially undemocratic[37]—became superfluous once they had helped restore order after the days of violence, and there was every incentive to return to parliamentary rule as soon as possible. This optimistic attitude, though not its full logic, proved popular; most revolutionary authorities, whether councils or more formal organs of government, carried on their activities on the assumption that the real business of the new Germany would be transacted by a popular assembly issuing from national elections. The revolutionary regime had something of the spirit of a caretaker regime.

These attitudes, shared by leading Majority Socialists and powerful trade unionists—who had seized the occasion to conclude an advanta-

34. See, for instance, Hermann Müller's speech, *Vorwärts*, Nov. 19, 1918. On the SPD's idealism, see Kolb, *Arbeiterräte*, pp. 169–74.
35. *Vorwärts*, Nov. 29, 1918.
36. Thus also Berlau, pp. 216–17.
37. See esp. Rosenberg, *Geschichte*, pp. 25–26, and Kolb, *Arbeiterräte*, pp. 172–73.

geous collective bargaining agreement with the employers' federations and were thereafter vehemently opposed to further disorder[38]—were crucial to the program of the revolutionary period. The organizations these men commanded embraced the great majority of the organized working class and, as they retained their cohesion in a time of general dissolution, they were one of the few effective nationwide forces that remained. Yet the hold of the leaders on their followers was not quite as firm as it looked. The ordinary workers were strongly influenced by traditional loyalty to their organizations, but they were much slower than their leaders to adopt the full parliamentary democratic faith; indeed, many workers never accepted it without reserve. A vague, conditional belief in parliamentary democracy was perhaps more characteristic of the bulk of the SPD rank and file than the complete commitment that dictated Ebert's course, and these party members never entirely abandoned older Social Democratic conceptions of their party's goals. The party held together; but there were growing pressures on the leadership from below to show a prouder proletarian spirit. Later these pressures were to become politically important.

The sentiments of the other extreme of the labor movement, the Spartacists and their left radical allies, were quite different. They were interested only in the socialist revolution, and a political upheaval that brought the SPD to power was not their revolution at all but only a meaningless shadow play. The sole real achievement of November had been to open the question of the immediate establishment of socialism. In a resolute struggle for clarity the true revolutionaries must build on this opportunity, keep the masses in motion until they perceived their real goals, strive to unmask Majority Socialist policies, and destroy the illusions of socialist unity. In most cities, including Berlin, this attitude led to abstention from the day-to-day work of the revolutionary institutions.[39] The true revolution was still to come, and the only worthwhile task for socialists was to prepare the masses. The Spartacists thus set out once again on a lonely path, well ahead of the masses they hoped to lead, in bold and uncompromising isolation.[40]

38. The text of the agreement is in *Dokumente und Materialien*, II, 393–96; on its origins see Gerald D. Feldman, "German Business Between War and Revolution: The Origins of the Stinnes-Legien Agreement," in *Entstehung und Wandel der modernen Gesellschaft: Festschrift für Hans Rosenberg* (Berlin, 1970), pp. 312–41.

39. In the few cities where Spartacists or left radicals played a role in the councils—Stuttgart, Braunschweig, Hamburg, Bremen, Munich, and several cities of Rhineland-Westphalia—the regular USPD was relatively weak; thus the extreme left could aspire to leadership of the whole socialist left; see ch. 5.

40. This brief sketch of Spartacist views and aims during the first ten weeks of

In this second revolution, according to the leading Spartacists, the masses must play the leading role, not the parties or even the councils. Though the Spartacist slogan "All power to the councils!" and other ideas derived from the Russian experience, most leading Spartacists were not Leninist in their views of the prerequisites for revolution; that is, they did not believe that a disciplined vanguard movement was more important than the spontaneous activity of the masses for the making of a revolution. Rosa Luxemburg expressed quite a different view in her Spartacist program of December 14, which was later adopted as the first program of the German Communist Party. The proletarian revolution, she wrote,

is not the desperate attempt of a minority to model the world after its ideal by violence, but the action of the great million-masses of the people, which is called upon to fulfil its historical mission and transform historical necessity into reality. . . . The Spartacus League will never take over the powers of government except by the clear, unambiguous will of the great majority of the proletarian masses in all Germany, never except by authority of their conscious adherence to the views, goals, and fighting methods of the Spartacus League.[41]

In keeping with this view, the Spartacists emphasized agitation rather than organization. Contrary to what the Majority Socialists may have believed, the immediate aim of the Spartacist leaders was not to seize power but to awaken a great, irresistible wave of socialist militancy that, in some undefined way, would sweep away the old order.

In the German revolution, however, the fervor required by the Spartacist vision was not common, and parties and organizations counted for a great deal. The Spartacists' regular following in November 1918 was tiny—perhaps a few thousand in the whole country—and recruitment, though steady and at times rapid during the weeks after the revolution, could not begin to provide the numbers necessary to the group's ambitions. The disparity was so obvious as to reflect on the credibility of their program; neither the Spartacists' enemies nor many of their followers could take seriously the professed aim of rallying the huge majority of the working class before taking decisive action. Even the leaders were given to moments of intoxication when it seemed that they might throw off all restraints and allow their heedless followers to sweep them along in an attempt to seize power.[42] Their intransigence in practical matters,

---

the revolution draws in part on the outstanding analysis in Kolb, *Arbeiterräte*, pp. 138–57. See also ch. 6, below.

41. *Rote Fahne,* Dec. 14, 1918; see also the editorials of Nov. 20 and Dec. 4, 1918. The loose Spartacus Group had constituted itself as the Spartacus League on November 11.

42. See the editorials in *Rote Fahne* after the demonstrations of Dec. 8, Dec.

the radicalism of their propaganda, their traditional tactics of strikes and demonstrations, their emphasis (also to be found in Rosa Luxemburg's writings) on the necessity for violent conflict—all contributed to the impression that the Spartacists were merely mustering their forces for a well-timed putsch. By their goals, their methods, and their image they thus became separated from the reality of the German revolution in its first months.

The radical Independents, too, were quickly dissatisfied with the revolution; in Ernst Däumig's words, "The German revolution has only taken its first step and must take many more harder and larger ones."[43] But the radicals, unlike the Spartacists, placed a high value on what had been achieved so far. Indeed, they felt a proprietary interest in the revolution; it had, they felt, been *their* revolution, especially in Berlin, and in consequence their feelings of responsibility for the new order bound them to take an active part in it.[44] Above all they were proud of the workers' and soldiers' councils, which, indeed, they came to regard as the only real advance brought by the revolution.[45] The radicals, with their roots in workers' organizations, could not turn their backs on what the workers had accomplished, imperfect though it might be. Whereas the Spartacists were numerically tiny, the radical Independents were a considerable force; in Berlin, as in parts of the Rhineland, in Halle and other important cities, they controlled the local party machinery of the USPD and dominated, or could hope to dominate, the labor movement. From this base they hoped to capture control of the workers' councils and trade unions and, supported by popular pressure, carry through the uncompleted phases of the revolution. In their enthusiasm they permitted themselves to overlook the fact that their movement took in only a small fraction of the national population and that, whatever their local successes, the German revolution could not be carried through by the workers of a few great cities alone. In concentrating on this design they created a confined revolutionary world of their own in the councils and

---

16, and Dec. 21, 1918; also Kolb, *Arbeiterräte,* pp. 149–51. For Spartacist awareness of weakness see the letters published by Ottokar Luban and Hermann Weber in *Archiv für Sozialgeschichte,* 11 (1971), esp. 239 (letter probably by Levi) and 433 (letter by Zetkin).

43. From the minutes of the general assembly of Berlin councils, Nov. 19, printed in *Beiträge zur Geschichte der deutschen Arbeiterbewegung* (hereafter cited as *BzG*), 10 (1968), 1045.

44. See, for example, the editorial in *Mitteilungs-Blatt,* Dec. 8, 1918; Richard Müller in the general assembly of Berlin councils, Dec. 23, IML Berlin, 11/11, "Protokolle der Vollversammlungen der Arbeiter- und Soldatenräte von Gross-Berlin," I, 65. These minutes will be cited hereafter as minutes of the general assembly, with date and archival designation.

45. For example, Däumig in *Republik,* Dec. 8, 1918.

factories of these cities; within this world, in all its ultimate futility, a good part of the USPD lived out its heroic period.

If the councils stood at the center of the radicals' vision, they were accompanied by very little in the way of a program of practical action. As we shall see, even quite radical councils commonly found themselves unable to do much more than maintain proletarian vigilance; and in such cities as Berlin, where the councils had very limited authority, the program of the radicals amounted to little more than a demand for more power for the councils. Until the new year, there was no attempt even to coordinate the work of the radicals in their various strongholds.[46] In place of a program the radicals propagated a profound mistrust of normal parliamentary politics, and thus of the National Assembly so ardently desired by the bourgeoisie and the SPD. They set out instead to give theoretical content to their own alternative.

The earliest full exposition of this new theory came from Ernst Däumig in the form of a draft program submitted to the Berlin executive council on November 13.[47] According to Däumig, the oppression and exploitation of the working class could only come to an end "through the transformation of the German state not into a bourgeois-democratic republic, but into a proletarian republic with a socialist economic basis, in which the working people, i.e. only the workers by hand and brain, exercise public rights." It followed that "the efforts of bourgeois circles to convoke a National Assembly as soon as possible are intended to rob the workers of the fruits of the revolution." Instead, a congress of workers' councils should determine the new constitution "in accordance with the principles of proletarian democracy."

These principles were later elaborated further. "The historical necessity of this council system," said Däumig, was that it "is and must be the given form of organization for the modern revolution"; more, it was the given form for "proletarian democracy" in the postrevolutionary socialist state.[48] It could also be called a dictatorship, since it deliberately disenfranchised the propertied classes, but this did not disturb the radicals, who contrasted it with the bourgeois economic dictatorship they saw in parliamentary democracy.[49] But they preferred to regard their council system as true democracy, a system that involved the great mass of the

46. See Tormin, pp. 65, 88–89, and 131; Kolb, "Rätewirklichkeit," pp. 174–75; Kolb, *Arbeiterräte*, p. 127.

47. Text in R. Müller, *Kaiserreich*, II, 82–83.

48. *Allgemeiner Kongress*, pp. 113–14. Däumig's wording makes it clear that for him the Russian precedent was important, but very little direct reference to Russian institutions was heard among the radicals at this stage, nor were Bolshevik practices treated as a model; see, for example, *ibid.*, p. 116.

49. *Ibid.*, p. 117.

working population in direct self-government, removed the bureaucratic separation of powers, and put legislative, executive, and judicial authority directly into the hands of the people.[50]

Such a vision of the workers' councils was attractive; but the radicals had difficulty from the start in getting the councils themselves to share it. Not many workers were ready yet to see any incompatibility between councils and parliament, and the arguments of the radicals, like those of *Vorwärts* on the other side, made little impact at first. Even the Berlin executive council, despite the efforts of Däumig, Ledebour, and Richard Müller, avoided adopting any far-reaching statement on the rights of the councils.[51] As *Freiheit* noted, in exasperation at the radicals, "A dictatorship against the will of the dictators is an impossibility."[52] For the time being, the radicals could only propagate their views. Thus, in spite of the prominence of the councils on the revolutionary scene in November, not until the following spring did the political theory of the absolute dominance of the workers' councils grow into an effective doctrine with broad working-class support.

Somewhere between the radicals and the SPD were the party leaders of the USPD, trying, as Richard Müller wrote, to inscribe both extremes on their banner.[53] In doing so the centrist leaders seemed to catch the early spirit of the revolution, a spirit pervading much of the Majority Socialist rank and file as well as their own. But the moderates were neither able to provide a convincing rationale for their preferences nor strong enough to implement them; and in time support drifted away from their middle position toward the two poles of sober, conventional politics and the millennial proletarian dictatorship.

The Independent leaders had agreed to join the government on condition that the workers' and soldiers' councils be regarded as the supreme political authority of the revolution and that the National Assembly be postponed to the indefinite future. These were the assumptions of the party's first postrevolutionary manifesto, issued on November 12, which failed even to mention a constituent assembly. The USPD leadership declared that the monarchy had given way to a socialist republic and that the old instruments of state power had been replaced by the councils. These results of the revolution must be confirmed

in order to complete the economic as well as the political liberation of the working class. . . . Filled with the firm belief that our final goal can be at-

50. See the early exposition of these ideas by the Spartacist Heckert, *ibid.*, p. 120; also Däumig, *ibid.*, pp. 115 and 117.
51. See below, pp. 140–41.
52. *Freiheit,* Nov. 30, 1918 (m).
53. R. Müller, *Kaiserreich,* II, 90.

tained, we proceed to the difficult work of ending the evils and suffering of the war, to the reconstruction of the ruined economy, to the thoroughgoing transformation of all areas of our public life, to the elimination of all positions of power held by the old ruling, possessing minority.[54]

This manifesto implied the dictatorship of the victorious proletariat, and neither Haase nor Rudolf Hilferding, editor-in-chief of the USPD's new Berlin newspaper, *Freiheit,* hesitated to call it that.[55] This dictatorship did not, however, accord with the ultrademocratic vision of Ernst Däumig but was conceived more soberly, as a dictatorship of the experienced socialist politicians under the supervision of the workers' and soldiers' councils. Its legitimization came, not from the high ideal of a new form of government, but from the assumption that it was carrying out the wishes of the great majority of the population, or at least acting in their interests.[56] The leaders of the USPD never turned their backs on the parliamentary system, and still less on majority rule. For them the councils were an expedient, a natural but probably temporary outgrowth of a workers' revolution, serving as "the bearers and guarantors of the revolution whose activity had to be sustained until the consolidation of [new] conditions."[57] The councils assured socialist dominance while the country's institutions were revised so that the true will—presumably the socialist will—of the majority could be expressed.

USPD leaders, then, expected a transitional dictatorship, leading ultimately to a constituent assembly, which they accepted in principle.[58] The revolution had left much undone; the composition of the National Assembly was unpredictable, and it seemed best, in the interests of socialism, to "confront the National Assembly with faits accomplis."[59] Like most socialists, they emphasized the need to purge the bureaucracy, reform the army so as to end the autonomy of the officer class, and begin a program of socialization. These fine plans, however, could not be carried out without the aid of the powerful SPD, both in the cabinet and in the councils; and the SPD was reluctant. As its leaders pointed out, if the government proceeded with care, reform and socialization could take

---

54. *Leipziger Volkszeitung,* Nov. 13, 1918.
55. "R.H." (Hilferding) in *Freiheit,* Nov. 18, 1918 (m), and Nov. 23, 1918 (m); Haase, cited in Ströbel, *Die deutsche Revolution,* p. 69. Ströbel is a good guide to right-wing USPD thinking in the months after the revolution, when he was a member of the Prussian provisional government.
56. See Haase's speech to the Berlin general assembly of Nov. 19, *BzG,* 10 (1968), 1047–48.
57. Dittmann memoirs, p. 892.
58. On this conception see also Kolb, *Arbeiterräte,* pp. 158–63; Ströbel, *Die deutsche Revolution,* esp. pp. 56–58 and 65.
59. Dittmann memoirs, p. 892. Cf. the editorial by "R.B." (Breitscheid) in *Freiheit,* Nov. 17, 1918 (m).

years; accordingly, these achievements could not be made preconditions for the constituent assembly without postponing the assembly indefinitely, which would make a mockery of the principle of universal suffrage.[60] In any case, in the Majority Socialist view, structural reforms were the proper province of the people's elected representatives, not of the provisional government.

By the time the various factions had felt their way to the positions described, the question of the National Assembly had become acute. The position of the SPD was plain, though the party rank and file may have had no very clear idea of the implications of the National Assembly; so was the position of the radicals and Spartacists. The USPD leadership, however, was caught in the middle, the fate not only of the revolution but also of the government coalition and the party itself depending to some extent of their decision.

The USPD's problem was that its attitude toward the National Assembly was not only contradictory but also unpopular. The idealism of the revolution was as much national and democratic as it was socialist, and the title "National Assembly" had a fine ring of 1848. The idea was popular, even without the intensive campaign of the Majority Socialist and nonsocialist press in its support. The Majority Socialists argued that the National Assembly was the natural outcome of the overthrow of the monarchy and that it was necessary to the avoidance of civil war, the preservation of the cohesion of the Reich, and the conclusion of peace.[61] Rumors and leaks from sympathetic government circles were also employed to help form public opinion.[62] The arguments were persuasive; where the SPD pressed its point, even in the workers' and soldiers' councils, it was generally successful.

Faced with these pressures, the USPD soon decided that the National Assembly could meet as early as April of the following year, and references to it were allowed to creep into government decrees.[63] As time went by the party line changed. Less emphasis was placed on confronting the National Assembly with faits accomplis, although the provisional government's right and duty to adopt far-reaching measures was still fiercely

60. Gustav Noske, *Von Kiel bis Kapp* (Berlin, 1920), p. 61.
61. *Vorwärts* made one or another of these points almost daily during November, beginning on Nov. 10; see esp. Stampfer's editorial, Nov. 13, 1918, and Scheidemann's article, Nov. 18, 1918.
62. Examples in R. Müller, *Kaiserreich*, II, 80 and 126–30; cf. Kolb, *Arbeiterräte*, ch. 7.
63. R. Müller, *Kaiserreich*, II, 81; according to Haase, USPD *Parteitag*, March 1919, p. 239, it was May. See mentions of the National Assembly in the government program of Nov. 12, *Vorwärts*, Nov. 13, 1918, and in connection with a refusal to let the Reichstag meet, *ibid.*, Nov. 16, 1918.

defended. Rather, the line was: "The constituent assembly—yes, it will come, but it can only come when all technical and political preconditions are fulfilled, when the will of the enlightened people is really expressed in it."[64] The argument for delay rested primarily on concern for democratic elections, democratic both in electoral machinery and in the free choice of a politically enlightened populace.

The Independents advanced some respectable practical reasons for delay: the uncertainty of Germany's future frontiers, the absence of large numbers of soldiers and war prisoners, the need to draw up new lists of voters to include women and all those men who had come of age since the 1912 elections.[65] More important, however, was the party's insistence on a long, thorough election campaign: "We want to bring mature, educated voters to the election."[66] This argument referred in general to the need for people to become accustomed to free political activity and a free press and in particular to the disadvantages under which socialist ideas had labored under the old regime, especially during the war, and the need for time if they were to show their full strength at the polls as the natural choice of an enlightened people. An extended period for agitation was of special importance for the USPD, as the Independents sometimes admitted.[67] They were acutely conscious of having been pariahs for the four years of the war; their antiwar position had led to the full resources of the state and of all the other parties, including the SPD, being used to discredit the party and reduce its influence. The Independent Socialist leaders were convinced that their following was artificially small and that their ideas, to make proper impact, needed several months of free play.

Unfortunately for the USPD, such an argument was unlikely to win sympathy outside the party, and their other arguments were too weak to counterbalance the attractions of a great popular election. In spite of their weak position, the Independent members of the cabinet resisted strenuously when, at the end of November, the SPD demanded elections in January; when the Majority Socialists threatened to resign, however, the Independents had no choice but to give in.[68] They were too well

64. Party manifesto, *Freiheit,* Nov. 27, 1918 (m).
65. *Ibid.;* speech by Barth, reported in *Vorwärts,* Nov. 22, 1918.
66. Haase in *Allgemeiner Kongress,* p. 128.
67. *Ibid.;* editorial in *Leipziger Volkszeitung,* Nov. 27, 1918.
68. Only Barth went so far as to abstain from the vote. See the cabinet minutes of Nov. 29, 1918, in *Regierung der VB,* I, 224–29, esp. pp. 227–28. On Nov. 29 see also Friedrich Ebert, *Schriften, Aufzeichnungen, Reden,* 2 vols. (Dresden, 1926), II, 109; recollections by Landsberg in *Regierung der VB,* I, clxxvi–clxxvii; and notes by Scheidemann in *BzG,* 1 (1959), 368–70 (and the discussion of this source in *Regierung der VB,* I, clxxiii).

aware that resistance to the National Assembly was hopeless and un-popular, and they had not the numerical support or moral authority to carry on without the SPD; in any case, they could only lose by bringing down the government over the apparently petty issue of a date. The best they could achieve was a compromise date of February 16, with the proviso that the decision be subject to the approval of the Workers' and Soldiers' Congress, scheduled to meet on December 16.

With this decision, the USPD leaders' conception of the proper further development of the revolution collapsed. The revolutionary coalition had far too short a life ahead to work in the manner the Independents had advocated, even supposing that its ill-matched partners had been capable of energetic action; and the outcome of its labors would be determined by a national vote that the Independents mistrusted as premature. Fur-thermore, the cabinet's decision—naturally announced without mention of the SPD's ultimatum—meant a defeat for the USPD leaders in the eyes of the party.[69] That Haase and the others should have remained in the cabinet in these circumstances was surely an error, by normal standards of party leadership, but an error that shows how deeply they felt the responsibility to share, even at great political risk, in the guid-ance of the revolutionary situation they had helped to bring about.

The Radicals and the Executive Council

While the constitutional problem, including the future of the workers' councils, was exercising socialists in the abstract, the councils were also the center of lively practical debate. Here again the Independents were divided. For the party moderates, including most of the central leader-ship, the keys to the future of the revolution were established institutions —the party organization on the one hand, organs of the government on the other; the councils could and should act upon these institutions but could not replace them. For the radicals, however, the councils were the essence of the revolution. In Berlin the most vigorous elements of the USPD, such party men as Däumig and Ledebour, as well as militants from the factories, devoted their efforts to making the Berlin councils a decisive revolutionary factor.

The proviso on which the USPD entered the cabinet—that the "poli-tical power" of the Reich be ascribed to the workers' and soldiers' coun-cils—was never formally challenged by either party; indeed, this consti-tutional fiction was solemnly reaffirmed on December 9.[70] The new Reich government, which actually resulted from an agreement between the two

69. Discussed further in ch. 6, below.
70. Joint declaration of the cabinet and the executive council, *Freiheit*, Dec. 10, 1918 (m).

socialist parties and depended on the continuance of that agreement, allowed itself to be confirmed by the council assembly of November 10 in the Zirkus Busch. The new socialist government of Prussia, which had a similar nature, constituted itself in close consultation with the Berlin executive council, head of the local councils. These attributes of sovereignty were conceded without question to the councils.

But some councils claimed more than this, believing that the revolution had vested in them practical powers of legislation and administration. The Berlin executive council decided that it enjoyed dictatorial powers, by delegation of the general assembly of Berlin workers' and soldiers' councils, and issued a manifesto asserting its authority over all government offices, including, until a national congress of councils should meet, those of the Reich and Prussia as well as Berlin.[71] A few days later it tried to exercise these powers. On November 15 it attempted by fiat to subordinate the Supreme Army Command and other hitherto independent military organs to the War Ministry, and hence to the cabinet.[72] The same day the first of several attempts was made to bring departments of the War Ministry under the direct supervision of delegates of the executive council.[73] Another decree provided that local Prussian officials (Landräte) could be deposed by local councils, if necessary by force of arms, if they showed counterrevolutionary inclinations.[74]

But the executive council's pretensions to powers of this sort bore no relation to its capacities or authority. The revolution in Berlin had given the workers' and soldiers' councils no direct participation in any of the existing administrative organs, not even those of the city of Berlin, so the executive council was in no position to rule by decree. Its effectiveness in affairs of state depended entirely on persuasion of, or pressure on, those who actually governed. The allegiance of the garrison troops would have greatly aided the council; but these soldiers had been effectively cultivated by the Majority Socialists and in case of conflict would tend to support the government against the executive council. In fact, on November 13 the soldiers imposed a humiliating defeat on the council when they forced it, with threats of violence, to rescind an order of the previous day creating an elite troop of workers, a "Red Guard," for the defense of the revolution.[75] Nor were the workers much more helpful to the executive council, since most of them expected the leaders to compose

71. *Vorwärts*, Nov. 13, 1918.
72. *Freiheit*, Nov. 16, 1918 (m).
73. *Ibid.*, Nov. 18, 1918 (m); cabinet minutes of Nov. 18, *Regierung der VB*, I, 73–75.
74. *Freiheit*, Nov. 18, 1918 (m).
75. R. Müller, *Kaiserreich*, II, 137–40; H. Müller, pp. 117–20.

their differences rather than fight among themselves. The council's great asset at the outset was its moral authority; but the authority of a government composed of representatives of the two established labor parties was at least as great among the workers and incomparably greater among other classes of society.

On top of this, the council's management of its own affairs was confused.[76] Most of its members appear to have had very modest organizational experience, and none at all in high politics. During the first days of its existence, as important events passed it by, the council was forced to devote itself almost entirely to arguing about first principles and trying to organize itself for effective action. It had no more success in the latter than in the former; the council was constantly being embarrassed by evidence of mismanagement, by the need to concern itself with petty detail, and by the arbitrary acts of one or another of its members. When the council did act, its typical move was an abrupt intervention in the affairs of the Reich, or Prussia, or the city of Berlin, intervention by decree without follow-up. Such actions presumed powers scarcely anyone seriously supposed the Berlin executive council to have; and they diverted the council for nearly two months from the arena of its greatest potential effectiveness—the affairs of the city, and especially the factories, of Berlin.

The executive council's most important deficiency was its failure to develop a corporate will. The real driving force of the council was the radical contingent (about one third of its membership), skeptical in their attitude toward the Reich cabinet and centrally concerned with the problem of political and economic power. The followers of the official SPD line, a like number but led by the able Hermann Müller from the party executive, served as the brakes, their overriding purpose being to prevent the council from taking some drastic step that would bring it into direct conflict with the government.[77] The remaining third of the membership was caught in the middle of the power struggle without really understanding it. Nearly all the members of this group held a higher estimate of the legitimate authority of workers' and soldiers' councils than did the SPD leaders, and in the day-to-day work of the council they often followed the lead of the radicals—as in the case of the decrees previously mentioned. But in a major controversy the middle bloc could not be induced to follow the radicals in opposing the government.

76. The principal sources on the internal affairs of the executive council, apart from the minutes of its meetings in IML Berlin and the Paul Levi papers (ASD Bonn; formerly in the Library for Political Studies, New York, where I consulted them), are the memoirs of Richard Müller and Hermann Müller. See also Kolb, *Arbeiterräte*, pp. 125–27, and *Regierung der VB*, I, cii–cvii.
77. H. Müller, p. 104.

A case in point was the draft program submitted to the council by Däumig on November 13, which the radicals hoped to make the basis of their labors.[78] The decisiveness of Däumig's theses, and the potential they held for conflict with party leaders in the government, were more than the executive council could face. A majority in the council favored Däumig's proletarian belligerence but not his conclusions, and the amended program that was finally adopted retained Däumig's radical premises while still finding a place for the National Assembly (though with a powerful auxiliary role for the councils.)[79] This strange juxtaposition of principles—proletarian revolutionary pride and traditional parliamentary democracy—probably had the merit of representing working-class sentiment in these first months of the revolution; but it also illustrated the council's inability to think any matter through clearly or take up a firm position in the face of controversy.

These were the circumstances of the executive council when, only a week after the revolution, it came into conflict with the government over areas of authority.[80] The executive council stated its view in a memorandum of about November 18:

Until all outstanding questions are settled by the assembly of delegates [of the councils of the whole Reich], the executive council . . . unites in itself the executive authority in both political and military matters. The people's commissioners (the political government of the Reich) regards itself [sic] merely as agent of the executive council.[81]

In this view, the powers of the council were to be unlimited until the national congress met. But the prospect of unlimited interference by the executive council was intolerable to the entire cabinet, including Barth; so long as they were carrying on the business of the Reich, they insisted, they must possess unfettered and undivided executive power. In Haase's view,

the source of all power is in the workers' and soldiers' councils; the government, too, derives its power from this source, it cannot exist without the confidence of the workers' and soldiers' councils. But as long as the workers' and soldiers' councils give their confidence to this government, its administrative measures may not be interfered with, or the entire machine will cease to move.[82]

78. For the substance of the draft, see above, p. 133.
79. R. Müller, *Kaiserreich*, II, 83; H. Müller, p. 128; minutes of the executive council for Nov. 16 and 17, *BzG*, 10 (1968), Sonderheft, 138–50.
80. The conflict is carefully analyzed in Kolb, *Arbeiterräte*, pp. 133–36; *Zentralrat*, pp. xvii–xxii; and *Regierung der VB*, I, xcii–cii. Successive drafts of the eventual agreement may be found in *Regierung der VB*, I, 127–30.
81. *Regierung der VB*, I, 129.
82. Minutes of the joint meeting of Nov. 18, *ibid.*, I, 95.

Haase's conception triumphed, after several days of talks and some bitterness. The agreement of November 22, amounting to a crude provisional constitution, attributed sovereign political power to the workers' and soldiers' councils of "the German Socialist Republic" and conceded the right to exercise this power to the Berlin executive council for the time being.[83] The key to the agreement was in the third clause: "The appointment of the cabinet by the workers' and soldiers' council of Greater Berlin means the conferral of the executive," that is, of all executive authority. The executive council, described as "a provisional organ of supervision [Kontrolle]," had the right to appoint and remove cabinet members, and had to be consulted before the appointment of departmental ministers. Finally, the early convocation of a workers' and soldiers' congress was promised; the following day the council set the date for December 16.

Though the members of the executive council did not realize it at once, this agreement disarmed them almost completely. The cabinet's interpretation of its sole executive authority barred the council from any influence on government business except through a direct approach to the cabinet, as the council learned early in December when its attempts to place agents in the War Ministry were rebuffed.[84] It was apparent by then that the supreme power of the council consisted *only* in its right to alter the composition of the government. And this right was illusory. To tamper with the cabinet would mean destroying the delicate party compromise upon which the government rested; and the parties were at least as important a part of the authority of the revolutionary constitution as the councils themselves. If the majority of the executive council had been unwilling to defy the government in the past, this was the main reason; they were hardly likely to challenge the party leaders in even balder terms.

The remaining days before the Workers' and Soldiers' Congress were depressing for the radicals on the council. They had little influence with the government, or even with the workers' and soldiers' councils of the Reich, many of which tended to ignore the Berliners or attack what they regarded as usurpations of authority. Increasingly, the council lost the respect even of those who supported the idea of council government, for it lacked will and was incapable of inspiring energy in others. During

83. Text in *Freiheit,* Nov. 23, 1918 (e). This is the executive council's text of the agreement; the government's text, differing slightly in wording, may be compared with it in parallel columns in *Regierung der VB,* I, 127–30.
84. Minutes of the executive council for Dec. 2, Levi papers, P 20, p. 4b; cabinet minutes of Dec. 4, *Regierung der VB,* I, 252–53. See also Wolfgang Elben, *Das Problem der Kontinuität in der deutschen Revolution* (Düsseldorf, 1965), p. 40.

its six weeks of supposed authority it did nothing but damage the image of councils among the general public, and hinder the consolidation of a system of councils by its extremism in words and haplessness in action. In the end, the radicals in Berlin labored not only without effect but without credit as well.

Socialist Government in Action

The cabinet, too, had difficulty controlling the governmental machine of which it was supposedly master. In essence the problem was the classic one of how political leaders, especially if they represent novel views, can control the activity of traditional bureaucrats who have full mastery of the technical and procedural aspects of government. The problem was exacerbated by a structural peculiarity of the provisional regime: none of the six cabinet members was actually a departmental minister, these posts being occupied by men (only two of them socialists) who themselves were established public figures, Eugen Schiffer and Hugo Preuss among them. What finally rendered the cabinet's task all but impossible was the pronounced difference of opinion among its members, which made the development of new policies difficult. Operation on the basis of the status quo was not repugnant to the SPD, which was awaiting the National Assembly. The Independents, however, could not afford to permit this if the revolution was to take the direction they wished, and if their participation in the government was to remain politically possible.

The problem of control had been recognized from the start, and the USPD's conditions for entering the cabinet had included a provision intended to overcome the problem: the installation of socialist supervisors (*Beigeordnete*) in the various ministries. These positions were indeed filled, for the most part.[85] But the system did not work well, especially from the USPD's point of view. Kautsky, in the Foreign Office, was gradually cut off from its real business and finally shunted into the congenial task of examining documents on the origins of the war;[86] Eduard David, his opposite number from the SPD, was ill for much of November and December, and in any case hardly differed in his views from Foreign Secretary Wilhelm Solf; so Solf and his officials continued to run the Office undisturbed, as they had under Prince Max. The SPD supervisor in the War Ministry, Reichstag deputy Paul Göhre, was a man of no special competence in military affairs who is not known to have had any influence on the decisions of the Ministry. The USPD never filled its posi-

85. The distribution of these offices and their functioning is discussed in *Regierung der VB*, I, lxi–lxxii, and Elben, pp. 37–40.
86. Elben, pp. 111–12.

tion in the War Ministry; Ernst Däumig, one of the few Independents with military expertise, turned down the post, and, no suitable substitute being found, the party in effect abdicated its right to observe the inner workings of this crucial ministry.[87] The only socialist representative at the Supreme Army Command, SPD Reichstag deputy Carl Giebel, was kept ignorant of the more questionable military projects.[88] Matthias Erzberger's Armistice Commission seems to have had no socialists at all attached to it. Thus the system of control through direct agents failed; indeed, it can hardly be said to have been seriously tried, and the USPD's participation was especially halfhearted.

The significance for the USPD of these questions of personnel lay not only in the realm of policy but also in appearances. The party's participation in the government was based on the explicit premise that the government was essentially socialist; yet the visible representatives of the government were often anything but socialist.[89] Some of the government's most prominent servants behaved in a manner impossible to justify from a socialist standpoint, notably Hindenburg of the Supreme Command, Erzberger of the Armistice Commission, and Foreign Secretary Solf, all of whom were strongly attacked from the left. On top of this, Haase and Dittmann—though not Barth, who, however, was not really a party figure—made the error of leaving the representative functions of the cabinet mainly to Ebert and Scheidemann, who tended to adapt their pronouncements to the need to reassure, not left-wing socialists, but the nonsocialist sectors of German society. The Independent rank and file could not be blamed for wondering at the company their leaders kept or for having reservations about government policy; and this problem contributed greatly to the disaffection in the USPD that first weakened the Independents' voice in the cabinet and finally drove them out of it altogether.

The functioning of the revolutionary government can be analyzed best by examining three significant issues, each of particular importance for the USPD: foreign policy, socialization of industry, and control of the military. In each of these areas important decisions were taken that influenced the later course of events—and influenced in important ways the relation of the government to more radical socialist forces outside it.

Despite Haase's later contention that the foreign policy of the provi-

---

87. Dittmann memoirs, pp. 927–28; *Regierung der VB,* I, 74.

88. For instance, Giebel's regular telephoned reports to the government show no knowledge of the Supreme Command's intention to intimidate Berlin with troops from the front armies; see DZA Potsdam, Reichskanzlei 2500/5, and ch. 6, below.

89. Arguably, the ministers played so large a role that the concept of an all-socialist government was little more than a convenient fiction; see *Regierung der VB,* I, lviii.

sional government had been genuinely socialist,[90] it is difficult in retrospect to discern any coherent foreign policy, let alone a distinctively socialist one. In relations with the Entente, in particular, the socialist cabinet made little mark. The ideas of the Independents in this respect hardly amounted to a foreign policy at all; they believed that if it could only be made clear abroad that the old order had been responsible for Germany's share in the origins and horrors of the war; if it could be shown that the new Germany was building on a real popular base toward a system free of imperialism and militarism, and was thus unwarlike; then the masses in the former enemy countries would force their governments to treat Germany with justice and conclude an equitable peace. Direct approaches to the Entente governments thus were not of the first importance, and a preoccupation with internal politics, combined with exhortations to the masses abroad, could be justified. These views are best known in the extreme form propagated by the Independent Kurt Eisner, minister president of Bavaria; but they were common to all of the party's spokesmen on foreign affairs.[91] The SPD leaders, in contrast, had little faith in such notions and shared the apprehensive but impenitent view of such men as Solf and Erzberger. Though Haase was nominally charged with supervision of foreign affairs, Solf and Erzberger were the real authors of Germany's policy toward the West. Solf in particular did not trouble to conceal his independence, which had become an open scandal by the end of November; his relations with Haase, whom he detested, became so bad that he was encouraged to resign in the middle of December.[92] His successor at the end of the month, Count von Brockdorff-Rantzau, did not alter Solf's policy—but was far better at handling socialist politicians.

Less vital for Germany, but more important for the USPD, was the question of diplomatic relations with Russia, which had been suspended during the last days of Prince Max's government on grounds of Bolshevik interference in German politics. Resumption of relations was taken for granted by both the Russians and the German left and was favored by the Independent members of the cabinet—or so they claimed in retrospect.[93] For those responsible, however, the matter became complex, and

90. In USPD *Parteitag,* March 1919, p. 82.

91. See, for instance, the speeches of Eisner, Kautsky, and Bernstein at the conference of state governments in Berlin on Nov. 25, *Regierung der VB,* I, 164–65, 167, and 169–71; and the party's manifesto "An die Internationale!" in *Leipziger Volkszeitung,* Nov. 14, 1918. On Eisner see the opening section of ch. 5.

92. Details of the controversy are in Elben, pp. 108–13. According to Theodor Wolff, *Through Two Decades* (London, 1936), p. 236, Solf found Haase "loathsome."

93. For an extended treatment of relations with Russia in the first two weeks of the provisional government, see Wheeler, "Internationals," pp. 88–106.

even when Haase took up direct teletype communication with G. V. Chicherin and Karl Radek on November 14 or 15, no settlement was reached.[94] The Russians were offering two train loads of flour for the relief of hunger in Germany, an impressive gesture of solidarity; but Haase was put off by the Russian assumption that the new German government would want to join the Bolshevik regime in an active policy of spreading the advancing world revolution to the countries of the Entente. In particular, Radek wanted permission to agitate among the Allied prisoners of war in Germany. The Entente powers, already touchy on the subject of Soviet Russia, would certainly react sharply to signs of rapprochement between the two socialist states; and ultimately Germany depended on the Entente, not only for a peace settlement but also for adequate food supplies. Finally, the two German socialist parties could not overlook either the Soviet government's obvious preference for the extreme left in Germany or its tendency to go over the government's head to the workers' and soldiers' councils.[95] Thus when the cabinet considered the matter on November 18, Haase's suggestion that they "proceed in a dilatory manner" was readily accepted.[96] Accordingly, the cabinet's policy toward its brother socialist republic continued to be marked by time-consuming démarches on minor questions.

Haase's cold response confirmed the Bolsheviks in their suspicion that the new Berlin government was only a "Kerenski regime," and they ceased to make friendly approaches, turning to the workers' and soldiers' councils instead. On November 29, Sverdlov, on behalf of the central executive committee of the Russian councils, telegraphed the Berlin executive council to announce the dispatch of a delegation to the Workers' and Soldiers' Congress in Berlin.[97] The executive council decided, not without dispute, to welcome the delegation and to bid the government arrange its visas.[98] The cabinet did not concern itself with the matter

94. Transcript of the conversation in Gerhard A. Ritter and Susanne Miller, ed., *Die deutsche Revolution 1918–1919* (Frankfurt on Main, 1968), pp. 271–79. The dating is uncertain. A detailed and fairly accurate account of the conversation was published by an unidentified Russian a year later in *Der Arbeiter-Rat*, 1 (1919), no. 41, 4–5.

95. For examples of Soviet telegrams directed to individuals or workers' councils in Germany see *Rote Fahne*, Nov. 18, 1918, and *Leipziger Volkszeitung*, Nov. 19, 1918.

96. Cabinet minutes for Nov. 18, *Regierung der VB*, I, 98–101. The text of the resulting telegram is given in Scheidemann, *Zusammenbruch*, pp. 225–27. In December of the following year, when relations with the Bolsheviks had become of central importance to the USPD, a high-ranking Majority Socialist leaked the compromising cabinet minutes to the press.

97. Text in *Dokumente und Materialien*, II, 501.

98. Minutes of the executive council for Nov. 29, IML Berlin, 11/1, pp. 206–10 (excerpt in Ritter and Miller, pp. 282–84); and for Dec. 4 (when the invitation

until December 9, by which time the delegation had reached the frontier; at this stage the government decided to request both the council and the Russians to relinquish the plan—"with regard to the situation in Germany"—and refused admittance to the delegates, who included former Ambassador Joffe, Bukharin, and Radek.[99] The following day, after bitter argument, a majority of the executive council backed down.[100] Radek managed to reach Berlin, but in disguise and too late for the Congress. The revolution had already entered a new phase, as the later role of Radek illustrates; there remained nothing for him to do but help build up the Communist movement in Germany with a view to a second revolution.

These episodes were of small importance in Germany, but the rebuff to the eager Bolsheviks was to have lasting effects on their interpretation of events in Germany. In particular, such credit as its opposition to the war had lent the USPD was dissipated, being replaced by bitterness.[101] Haase's coldness was returned with interest during the party's dealings with the Third International more than a year later.

The second significant practical issue before the government was socialization.[102] To those who believed that the overthrow of the old regime had been, or should develop into, the long-awaited socialist revolution, it was self-evident that socialization of industry should be one of the principal tasks of the new government. This view was common to Independents of all shades;[103] but before long, differences developed about the means and tempo of socialization. The more moderate sections of the party were oppressed by the difficulties of postwar economic reconstruction, which made the situation unlike any in which they had envisaged taking power. Machines and men had been worn down to a low rate of productivity; raw materials were scarce. Some socialists employed the conceit that there was hardly anything left to socialize.[104] Many decided

was renewed), Levi papers, P 20, pp. 3–4; DZA Potsdam, Reichskanzlei 2482, p. 78.

99. Cabinet minutes for Dec. 9, *Regierung der VB*, I, 303; announced in *Freiheit*, Dec. 10, 1918 (e).

100. Minutes of the executive council for Dec. 10, IML Berlin, 11/2, pp. 44–51 (excerpt in Ritter and Miller, pp. 284–85); R. Müller, *Kaiserreich*, II, 149.

101. Ascher, p. 411, concludes from a study of the Russian press that "by the end of November the Independents . . . had been relegated to the rubbish heap of history."

102. On socialization see esp. Hans Schieck, "Die Behandlung der Sozialisierungsfrage in den Monaten nach dem Staatsumsturz," in *Vom Kaiserreich* (ed. Kolb), pp. 138–64.

103. See the editorials in *Freiheit*, Nov. 15, 1918 (m), Nov. 16, 1918 (m), and Nov. 19, 1918 (m); and Hilferding's speech in *Allgemeiner Kongress*, pp. 156–61.

104. Kurt Eisner, *Die neue Zeit*, 2 vols. (Munich, 1919), I, 25 and 117; Dittmann in *Allgemeiner Kongress*, p. 22.

that speed of action must yield to smoothness of transition, that perhaps
only a few industries should be touched at first lest further disruption of
the economy produce mass unemployment, a serious decline in the ex-
ports needed to pay for Germany's food supplies, or similar disasters.
The SPD leaders held even stronger doubts, seeming even to have written off the possibility of any real socialization of industry before the
completion of reconstruction; in any case they were not anxious for the
provisional government to act on such an important matter before the
meeting of the National Assembly. Finally, so long as the reparations to
be demanded of Germany by the Allies remained undetermined, to increase the state's share in the national assets seemed unwise.[105] Both
parties were thus glad to turn the planning of a future program of socialization over to a special commission, appointed on November 18.[106]

Simpler party members, encouraged both positively by the radicals and
negatively by governmental inaction, saw the problem differently, as a
question for workers' initiative rather than an issue of the national economy and the central administration. This movement did not really gather
force until the new year, and will be treated in a later chapter in more
detail, but it began in the early days of the revolution. In Berlin, the
executive council for a time tried, tentatively, to encourage workers' control of factories through the trade unions, with a view to forcing the
government's hand, but by November 23 the government and the unions
themselves had made the council recant.[107] The factory radicals carried
the fight into the assemblies of Berlin workers' councils on November
27 and 29, the true beginning of their campaign to encourage the workers' councils of each factory to demand some control over the management of the firm.[108] These demands gained force from a simultaneous
renewal of industrial unrest; the causes of the strikes were low real
wages and general discontent, but part of the unrest was easily channeled into political demands. The government, however, was unsympathetic to what it called "wild socialization" and detailed Barth to
exhort the workers to discipline in the interests of the revolution—temporarily with some effect, especially since the Majority Socialist press
was arguing the same line.[109] But division had shown itself even among

105. Dittmann later insisted that this factor was decisive in the cabinet's failure
to make a start on socialization and noted that it was not possible to discuss this
hindrance openly; Dittmann memoirs, pp. 888–89 and 920. Cf. the objections in
Rosenberg, *Geschichte*, pp. 42–43.

106. Cabinet minutes for Nov. 18, *Regierung der VB*, I, 103–4. The socialization
commission did not report before the departure of the Independents from the
cabinet.

107. R. Müller, *Kaiserreich*, II, 108–10.

108. *Ibid.*, II, 110.

109. See the reports of Barth's speeches to the Berlin workers' councils, *Freiheit,*

those who seriously wanted to begin socializing the economy as early as possible. This was another debate that was to develop its full significance only later.

Compromise, concession, or procrastination prevented problems of foreign policy and socialization from becoming fatal to the internal cohesion of the provisional government. But the third major issue, the military question—how to structure and employ the armed organs of the state in revolutionary times—proved ultimately intractable and finally occasioned the government's collapse.

Here again the German socialists were ill-prepared by their past. Nonviolence ran deep in Social Democratic tradition; though the revolution itself might be violent, it was expected to lead to a national and international society where the use of force would die out. More specifically, there was a deep-seated aversion, born of experience, to use of the police or army in domestic political controversies; and to the extent that a military force was necessary, the party program prescribed a popular militia, an ideal derived from liberal models of the middle of the previous century and already dead in the minds of many socialists.[110] Traditional conceptions were of no help to the German socialists in November 1918, with their socialist government precariously balanced on uncertain popular support and plagued by hostile neighbors. The socialist coalition partners had to derive new prescriptions from circumstances, and their divergent responses were fatal to their collaboration.

The Majority Socialists were prepared to revise their thinking to meet the new situation. In their view the period of legitimate (though regrettable) violence was now over, the necessary foundations for democratic social progress having been established. The new status quo, as they saw it, required defense against attack from either extreme; and in practice they expected more trouble from unruly workers and radical demagogues than from counterrevolutionaries. Any new attempts to shortcircuit the democratic process would be a threat to the rule of the people and to national economic recovery, and thus deserving of rigorous suppression. Moreover, the Majority Socialists took account of the dignity and might of the state they now represented and also shared their countrymen's exaggerated regard for highly trained military men. Under the circumstances, the question of means receded in their eyes before the

Nov. 28, 1918 (m), and Nov. 30, 1918 (m); and the SPD pamphlet, *Soll Deutschland ein Tollhaus werden?* (Berlin, n.d.).

110. On prewar Social Democratic orthodoxy on the military question see Reinhard Höhn, "Wehrordnung und moderne Gesellschaft," in Heinz Karst et al., *Menschenführung, Personalauslese, Technik in Wirtschaft und Armee* (Darmstadt [1954]), pp. 41–75.

problems of effectiveness; if necessary, they were prepared provisionally to rely on the institutions and men of the old state to preserve order in the new.

The Independents were not so sure that the period of transitional upheaval was over. If the masses were still active, then the revolution was not complete, and it was no part of the duties of the provisional government to suppress this unrest and prevent the revolution from unfolding. Rather, the government must seek to understand the discontent and direct it into creative channels, encouraging it to resolve itself into new social forms that would remove the impulse to protest. The state could not disarm itself entirely; normal police functions must continue, and threats of violent reaction or of foreign invasion might ultimately require the use of armed force. But all the armed organs of the state should be converted to conform as far as possible to the spirit of a socialist democracy, that is, to the ideal of citizens under arms, voluntarily performing socially useful duties. Armed forces of this sort would, they believed, be capable of resisting invasion or counterrevolution but could be trusted not to let themselves be misused against a genuinely popular movement.[111]

The quasi-pacifist and fatalist premises of the leading Independents may not have been widely shared, but their antagonism to the old military apparatus was echoed by many militant workers and a large part of the dissolving armed forces. The revolution, while not primarily a rebellion against constituted authority, released much pent-up resentment against certain types of officials, notably the political police and, above all, the officer corps of the army. In the early days of the revolution officers could not safely appear in uniform on the streets of Berlin, especially if they carried side arms. Direct action against officers soon died down, but intense resentment of Prussian military arrogance, exemplified by the officer corps, remained strong and was shared by a much broader spectrum of the common people than most other attitudes of the USPD.

These issues did not all present themselves to the cabinet at the start. The government did, however, have to decide quickly how to deal, at least temporarily, with the immense German armed forces. The main problem was not the home army, for the garrisons in nearly all major cities had been reduced to the point of being barely able to carry out police duties and could probably be demobilized eventually without serious disorder. The real issue was what to do with the army in the field, which had remained more or less intact in the hands of its officers, and ultimately under the authority of the leaders of the autonomous Supreme Army Command, Field Marshal von Hindenburg and General Groener,

111. The fullest discussion of the Independents' views occurred at the climactic cabinet meeting of Dec. 28, *Regierung der VB*, II, 73–131; see ch. 6 below.

representatives of the proud traditions of the officer corps, unbroken by the workers' revolution at home.

The issue was not particularly divisive at first, since the main lines of policy were dictated by circumstances. Armies of millions of German soldiers stood beyond the frontiers of the Reich and would obviously have to be withdrawn as rapidly as possible, a formidable logistical operation, especially considering the possibilities for unrest among the troops. The evacuation in the West had to be carried out within thirty days, by fiat of the Entente. If these large forces abroad disintegrated, Germany might fail in her obligations to the Entente—not to mention suffer horrors in her border regions from the uncontrolled passage of huge armies in dissolution. Under the circumstances there seemed no alternative to retaining the old hierarchy of experienced and highly trained officers, at least during the evacuation.[112]

This course was made easier by the willingness of the leading officers to cooperate with the new order. The army leadership's decision was conveyed to the provisional government at once by telegram and later in the famous telephone conversation between Ebert and General Groener, effective head of the Supreme Command, on the evening of November 10. Groener, who knew and respected Ebert from earlier encounters, wanted to reassure himself that the new government would be non-Bolshevik, that it meant to guarantee public security and order, and that it was willing to help the Supreme Command maintain the cohesiveness of the field armies. Ebert was able to give the necessary assurances, and the basis for limited collaboration was laid.[113]

To turn this general understanding into specific arrangements, and to decide what was to become of the army after withdrawal and demobilization were harder problems. The two wings of the USPD agreed that the

112. See Dittmann's explanation in *Allgemeiner Kongress,* p. 81, and in his memoirs, pp. 880–81. This thinking may have been mistaken; F. L. Carsten, *Revolution in Central Europe, 1918–1919* (Berkeley and Los Angeles, 1972), pp. 25–26 and 76–77, points out that the Austrian armies managed a rapid withdrawal operation even though their military hierarchy had collapsed and believes the same could have been done by the German troops. However, the considerable risk that the Austrians took of necessity would have to have been a deliberate choice in Germany, and the unwillingness of the new government to take it was reasonable. For still another view, see Rosenberg, *Geschichte,* pp. 44–45.

113. The text of the telegram is in Hans Volz, ed., *Novemberumsturz und Versailles,* Dokumente der deutschen Politik (Berlin, 1942), pp. 394–95. The best reconstruction of the content of the Ebert-Groener conversation is Wolfgang Sauer, "Das Bündnis Ebert-Groener" (Ph.D. dissertation, Free University of Berlin, 1957), pp. 60 and 81–82. Groener's later recollection of what Ebert said, on Nov. 10 and later (see his testimony in Herzfeld, p. 384, and his *Lebenserinnerungen* [Göttingen, 1957], p. 467), was patently faulty, as Sauer and numerous others have pointed out.

officers should be supervised by soldiers' councils and the unreliable ones dismissed at once; that the old standing army should be dissolved as soon as possible; and that the new defense forces should be "democratic" in form and thus incapable of becoming organs of state repression. Ebert and his colleagues, however, were not prepared to tamper with the officer corps (which they did not especially fear) until some reliable replacement was available, especially in view of what they saw as a serious threat of violence from the left. The Supreme Command was still more intransigent, its aim being, in Groener's words, "to win a share of the power in the new state for the army and the officer corps, [for] if this succeeded, then the best and strongest element of the old Prussiandom would be preserved for the new Germany in spite of the revolution."[114]

For most of the six weeks before Christmas—starting immediately after the revolution—the Supreme Command held the initiative. Groener, not Ebert, first opened relations between the Supreme Command and the new government. The two telegrams of November 11 and 12 from the government to the Supreme Command, laying down in detail the policies the field army was to follow, in fact originated with Groener; he telegraphed the texts to the government, which subjected them to a light editing and promulgated them with little change in substance.[115] The salient feature of the telegrams was the command that military discipline was to be upheld under the old officers, the soldiers' councils (which in practice were often not formed at all) being given only a secondary, consultative role. The government was convinced these measures were necessary if the withdrawal was not to become a rout, and it held to them, though strenuous efforts were needed to explain their intent to the revolutionaries, who protested vehemently when the orders were published.[116]

These arrangements led to a number of field units returning to their homeland without knowing any more about the revolution, the new government, and the councils than what their officers chose to tell them. When such troops came into contact with hostile and disorderly workers' and soldiers' councils in the Rhineland, after about November 20, the predictable result was conflict. Some officers, misunderstanding or disregarding the attitude of the government, were provoked into trying to

114. *Lebenserinnerungen*, pp. 468–69. On the foundations of Groener's outlook, see also Sauer, pp. 46–50.

115. The Supreme Command's proposals for the two telegrams are in DZA Potsdam, Reichskanzlei 2485, pp. 6 and 8; the telegrams themselves are reprinted in Volz, pp. 399–402. See also Drabkin, pp. 176–77.

116. See the official exegesis printed in *Freiheit*, Nov. 18, 1918 (m). The Saxon workers' and soldiers' councils had declared the order of Nov. 12 to be a surrender of important revolutionary gains; *ibid.*, Nov. 15, 1918 (m).

disband or arrest councils they regarded as interfering with the passage of their troops; and the troops obeyed these orders. To a suspicious onlooker, this was counterrevolution. Protests from the Rhineland, including strong words from the SPD leader, Sollmann, in Cologne, had become so vehement by November 26 and 27 that the government had to call the army leaders to order.[117] A few days later one commanding general was summarily relieved of his command by the government, and a lingering dispute with the Supreme Command about the enlisted man's right to show red flags and cockades was settled by blunt orders from the cabinet.[118] These were the most decisive actions the socialist government ever took against the army leadership, and the Supreme Command, if it was to hold to its policy of trying to insinuate itself into a position of influence, had no choice but to give in, at least outwardly. But little was settled; incidents continued, and the sense of counterrevolutionary danger from the army persisted.

Shortly thereafter the government finally took action on the military question. On December 3 Ebert proposed to the cabinet a people's army (*Volkswehr*) that would police law and order inside Germany, or, in other words, "protect the institutions of the government against attacks." The *Volkswehr* was to be a volunteer force; the officers were to be elected by the men, who would themselves be responsible for enforcing discipline, regulating leave, supervising the mess, and the like.[119] No conditions of party membership were set for recruits, but in other respects the *Volkswehr* constituted a sort of Red Guard or militia at the service of the central government. The cabinet warmly supported the plan, approved a draft by December 6, and promulgated the completed decree with detailed provisions for implementation six days later.[120]

The seed fell on stony ground. By December 12, when the project was formally launched, more immediate issues occupied everyone's attention (as recounted below in chapter 6), and it cannot have been pursued with any great vigor. A few units were formed during the following month, but they never played an important role. The weight of

117. DZA Potsdam, Reichskanzlei 2486/4, pp. 84–94 (telegrams to and from Cologne); IML Berlin, Reichskanzlei 8/19, pp. 159–63 (Remscheid), and Reichskanzlei 8/22, pp. 104–5 (Wermelskirchen); and Drabkin, pp. 322–26.

118. On General von Eberhard's dismissal, see DZA Potsdam, Reichskanzlei 2510, p. 19, and *Freiheit*, Dec. 2, 1918 (e). The matter of red flags was settled in the cabinet meeting of Dec. 3, *Regierung der VB*, I, 250.

119. Cabinet minutes for Dec. 3, *Regierung der VB*, I, 247–49; Ebert, *Schriften*, II, 110. The quotation is from a memorandum by Ebert and Haase of Dec. 18, printed in Herbert Helbig, "Graf Brockdorff-Rantzau und die Demokratie," in *Zur Geschichte und Problematik der Demokratie: Festgabe für Hans Herzfeld* (Berlin, 1958), p. 589.

120. Text in *Freiheit*, Dec. 15, 1918.

the army's, and eventually the government's, interest shifted to another kind of volunteer formation, in which the army command structure and the old military discipline prevailed—the Free Corps.[121] Originally thought of (by the government at least) as volunteer units for the defense of German populations and property on the Polish frontier, the Free Corps seemed acceptable at first to the whole cabinet as an unavoidable necessity.[122] It soon became apparent, however, that the result was old-style armies under the command of officers of the most backward political views. At the time of their resignation, the Independents were fighting a rearguard action against this perversion of their original intentions; after their departure, the government decided on a military solution in the East and full-scale recruitment for Free Corps was formally approved on January 4.

Several weeks after the revolution, then, the military situation was still very much in flux. The potential for conflict between the officer corps and the socialist government was still high, with each side awaiting the end of the withdrawal to begin maneuvering for position. On this issue, the views of the uneasy partners in the cabinet could not be harmonized. The fate of the socialist coalition was to depend on the outcome of the debate over military policy more than on any other issue.

121. Hagen Schulze, *Freikorps und Republik 1918–1920* (Boppard on Rhein, 1969), pp. 23–25.
122. See the cabinet minutes for Nov. 19 and 21, *Regierung der VB,* I, 107 and 118–23.

CHAPTER 5

Patterns of Revolution outside Berlin (November 1918 to January 1919)

The politics of Berlin, the nation's largest city and seat of the Reich and Prussian governments, naturally dominated the revolutionary scene, as they have dominated our account of the revolution thus far. For many socialists elsewhere, the Berlin example served as an inspiration, or a warning, and influenced their response to problems closer to home. Events in the capital were observed as closely as the imperfect communications of the day allowed; on occasion they were imitated. And while resolution of the conflicts in Berlin was awaited, much of Germany marked time.

Much in the revolutionary situation was common to large parts of the country. The framework was everywhere the same: the background of bitterness and privation from the war, the demise of the old forms of political legitimacy, the economic crisis resulting from the end of war production and the continued Allied blockade. The proper role of workers' and soldiers' councils was an issue in every city; such questions as how to control the civil servants, how to organize a reliable armed force, and how far to proceed with economic and social reform were often pressing. And socialist factions parallel to those in Berlin, divided from one another by similar issues and ideologies, existed in most cities.

Yet the revolutionary experience, and the USPD's role, differed widely from one part of the country to another. Socialists generally controlled the postrevolutionary governments in the German cities and states, but past and current circumstances played a large part in determining which group and what spirit predominated. In a few areas superior numbers, unusual leadership, or the fortunes of the revolutionary hours gave the Independents the upper hand. Elsewhere, the USPD was either a junior partner (even if nominally equal) or an almost negligible force. These varied experiences, reflecting the different ways in which the nearly autonomous units of the party had developed before the revolution, also helped determine their direction for the future.

155

A survey of the peculiarities of the revolutionary period, and the USPD's role, in other important cities and regions of Germany, will establish the basis for examining the implications of the USPD's position in the German revolution for the party as it approached the crises of December and January.[1]

Munich and Kurt Eisner

Of the cities where Independent Socialists played a decisive role in the revolution, the case of Munich was the most anomalous. As mentioned earlier, Munich was important in providing the crucial first example of the deliberate overthrow of a dynasty in the name of socialist goals; the unpredictable radical side of Bavarian politics remained a source of inspiration or concern for the rest of Germany to the end of the short-lived Soviet Republic of April 1919. Yet Bavaria, with its largely agricultural economy and strongly reformist socialist tradition, seemed among the least likely places in Germany for socialist radicalism to play an important role. The revolution in the Bavarian capital is an extreme example of the power of circumstance and personality to obscure the real balance of political forces in times of upheaval.

Few would have predicted, as the war neared its end, that the Munich USPD would become a serious political force. Unlike Berlin, and other cities, Munich's socialist opposition grew, not out of the factories or the local party organization, but out of a small study group led by Kurt Eisner and composed chiefly of young people and soldiers.[2] In April 1917 the group was so small that Eisner was opposed to breaking with the Majority Socialists and founded his separate USPD organization only reluctantly.[3] Not until just before the strike of January 1918 did the Independents establish contacts with organized factory workers.[4] The party then made a name for itself for its surprising success in promoting this strike, but efficient government repression negated any advantage the party might have gained. At the end of October 1918 the USPD, with

1. The closest approximation to a complete survey in the recent literature is Kolb, *Arbeiterräte*, esp. chs. 4 and 12, to which the present chapter owes a great deal.
2. On the study group, see Felix Fechenbach, *Der Revolutionär Kurt Eisner: Aus persönlichen Erlebnissen* (Berlin, 1929), pp. 16–19; Erich Mühsam, *Von Eisner bis Leviné* (Berlin, 1929), p. 11; letter from Eisner to Kautsky, March 26, 1917, Kautsky papers, D X 166.
3. Eisner in USPD *Parteitag*, April 1917, p. 26; letter from Eisner to Haase, May 1917, *BzG*, 9 (1967), 473–74; Kurt Eisner, *Die halbe Macht den Räten*, ed. Renate and Gerhard Schmolze (Cologne, 1969), p. 33.
4. Fechenbach, p. 23. On the January strike in Munich, see *ibid.*, pp. 21–28, and the account in Eisner's prison diary, *BzG*, 9 (1967), 476–85.

some 400 members, could speak for only a tiny minority in the Bavarian capital.[5]

Perhaps largely because of the tenuousness of the USPD organization, Kurt Eisner preserved his leadership. A literary-minded intellectual, motivated by an almost aesthetic social idealism, he was by no means a typical party leader, particularly in Bavaria, where political advantage has never lain in being a transplanted Prussian and moreover a Jew. In the prewar party he was accounted a revisionist, although not of the standard gradualist type; he was known especially for his critical studies of the conduct of Imperial Germany's foreign policy.[6] The war, and his conviction that Germany bore the principal guilt for its outbreak and prolongation, turned him into a prophet of the need for immediate and total renewal of German life and institutions. For him, the war was "an ethical problem." "The premise of all peace work in Germany during the war," he later stated, "was the overthrow of the guilty system."[7] As a prophet he proved to have real inspirational gifts. More remarkable, he also displayed a high order of political daring and decisiveness.

Eisner's revolution was a successful putsch, planned only a few days in advance—"On Monday . . . we discussed it, and on Thursday we had done it"—and put into operation by some two dozen of his circle.[8] His decision to resolve the political crisis in Munich by a coup on November 7, with the deliberate intention of bringing social and political regeneration to Bavaria, created a unique situation for the Independents in Munich. Their leader became the charismatic focus (for several weeks at least) of the revolution in the most Catholic, particularist state in Germany. Their party, a minority in the cabinet coalition with the SPD, a tiny minority of the population, and without firm organizational footing among the workers in the capital, was able to negotiate on something approaching equal terms with the genuinely strong Majority Socialists. Without the reflected glory of Eisner, the USPD would have had little to say in Bavaria.

5. Kolb, *Arbeiterräte*, p. 67. On the USPD generally during the war, see Ay, pp. 188–96.

6. The best-informed account of Eisner's career is in the preface to Eisner, *Die halbe Macht*, pp. 14–35. See also Mitchell, ch. 2; Fritz Schade, *Kurt Eisner und die bayrische Sozialdemokratie* (Hanover, 1961); Angress, "Juden," pp. 235–51; and Falk Wiesemann, "Kurt Eisner: Studie zu seiner politischen Biographie," in *Bayern im Umbruch*, ed. Karl Bosl (Munich and Vienna, 1969), pp. 387–426.

7. Fechenbach, p. 20; Eisner, *Schuld und Sühne* (Berlin, 1919), p. 24.

8. Eisner's words are in M. J. Bonn, *Wandering Scholar* (New York, 1948), p. 197; the estimate of the size of Eisner's group is from Mitchell, p. 90. See the accounts of the revolution and its immediate background in Mitchell, pp. 89–109; Willy Albrecht, *Landtag und Regierung in Bayern am Vorabend der Revolution von 1918* (Berlin, 1968), pp. 409–428; and Kolb, *Arbeiterräte*, pp. 67–70.

The socialist government itself, formed on November 8, was not particularly radical.[9] As one critic noted, Eisner vigorously fought "militarism, corruption in the press . . . bureaucratic callousness, secret diplomacy, and self-righteousness"—but not capitalism.[10] Welfare measures of many kinds were introduced, but no attempt was made at socialization—Eisner coined the expression that socialization was impossible "when there is nothing to socialize" in the economically desperate aftermath of a great war.[11] As for the councils, until the government crisis at the end of December their treatment was largely left to Erhard Auer, minister of the interior and leader of the Bavarian SPD, whose attitude was like that of the government in Berlin.[12] In Munich, as in Berlin, the council system was ineffective; the bureaucracy was left unchanged, and no reliable socialist armed force was set up. Plans for a Bavarian National Assembly were adopted, despite Eisner's objections. Eisner himself was occupied chiefly with efforts to change the course of German foreign policy. Convinced as he was that Germany must admit her guilt regarding the war, both for the sake of settling accounts with the past and in order to earn a fair peace, he exhorted the Berlin government to proclaim a break with the past and to dispose of the "compromised" men who continued to conduct the country's foreign policy. He went so far as to suspend relations with the Foreign Office in Berlin and pursued numerous diplomatic feelers that were supposed to lead to better relations with France.[13] These efforts were altogether ineffectual, due not least to the false premise, characteristic of Eisner, that the German people had undergone a democratic, pacific conversion and were genuinely repentant.[14]

Though the actions of the Eisner-Auer government followed a familiar

9. In addition to Eisner the eight-man cabinet included only one regular Independent, Minister of Social Affairs Hans Unterleitner, and one close sympathizer who was probably not a party member, Finance Minister Dr. Edgar Jaffé. The other members were four leading Social Democratic politicians and a nonsocialist expert to run the railways; see Franz August Schmitt, *Die neue Zeit in Bayern* (Munich, 1919), p. 11.

10. Mühsam, pp. 18–19. The works by Mitchell and Schade contain full accounts of the government's activity.

11. Eisner, *Die neue Zeit*, I, 117; see *ibid.*, I, 25, for an earlier version of the expression.

12. Mitchell, pp. 154–55.

13. Eisner's own view of his activities may be found in his speeches of Nov. 28 and Dec. 12, in *Die neue Zeit*, I, 46–49, and II, 32–37. The fullest accounts are Schade, pp. 67–74, and Mitchell, pp. 126–38.

14. Eisner's "Unwahrhaftigkeit" in this matter was pilloried by Walter Rathenau; recorded in Harry Graf Kessler, *Tagebücher 1918–1937* (Frankfurt on Main, 1961), p. 133.

pattern, the same cannot be said of Eisner's political conceptions, and especially not of his views on the place of workers', soldiers', and peasants' councils in the new order. In the first weeks after the revolution Eisner was one of the two outstanding Independents (the other being Däumig) to favor the councils' becoming organs of a new democracy in which the common man could play an active role. Eisner, unlike Däumig, certainly had no admiration for the Bolshevik model, and he had shown no interest in the councils at the time of the revolution.[15] He saw them, moreover, not as an alternative to a parliament, but, rather, as coordinate or supplementary institutions. "The councils," he said, "are the foundations of democracy, the National Assembly, the Diet is the crowning of the edifice."[16] A Diet without councils would mean "an empty, fruitless parliamentarianism," "a formal electoral democracy" in which "the people . . . remains an onlooker, a powerless onlooker."[17] In Eisner's vision, the councils were not legislative or administrative organs;[18] they were simply the mass organizations through which the people were to be drawn into active, critical participation in the political process. He fought for this view in the last days of November and the first days of December, when the decision about the nature and date of elections to a new Diet was before the cabinet, and he lost, not least because the majority of the Congress of Bavarian Soldiers' Councils, meeting at this time, was against him.[19] Thereafter he preached acceptance of the coming elections as a fait accompli; but he went on trying to stir up mass support for councils, which alone, he felt, could permanently infuse a new spirit into Bavaria's political institutions.

Inevitably the ill-assorted partners in the cabinet disagreed over such issues, and by December the work of the government was hampered by severe tensions. The Majority Socialists were just as cautious, bureaucratic, and patriotic as the national party, and even more inclined by tradition to coalition with the bourgeois parties; while the USPD, in Munich as in Berlin, was turning more toward the council system to avert a threatening restoration of something very like the old order. In con-

15. For Eisner's views on Bolshevism see, for instance, *Die neue Zeit,* I, 55–56; for the absence of emphasis on councils in his first utterances after the revolution, see *ibid.,* I, 5–19.

16. *Ibid.,* II, 29–30.

17. Eisner, quoted in Helmut Neubauer, *München und Moskau 1918/1919* (Munich, 1958), p. 25; Eisner, *Die neue Zeit,* I, 63 and 68.

18. Eisner, *Die neue Zeit,* II, 39; Neubauer, pp. 25–26; Mitchell, p. 172. Some scholars do not find this consistency in Eisner but argue instead that his views were changeable and unreliable; see Bernhard Zittel, "Rätemodell München 1918/19," *Stimmen der Zeit,* 165 (1959–60), 31.

19. Accounts of this crisis are in Schade, pp. 74–76, and Mitchell, pp. 160–75.

trast to Berlin, however, the Munich partnership of the socialist parties did not collapse but lasted for another two months. One reason was certainly Eisner's enduring belief in the necessity for socialist unity[20]— prompted, no doubt, by a realistic appraisal of his own party's relative weakness as well as by idealism. At the same time Eisner was able to keep up relations with the radicals, for whose emotions he could feel sympathy even if he was increasingly turning away from their tactics. Nor did his own party turn against him, probably in part because it lacked the independently strong radical wing with a factory base that made life so difficult for the party leadership in Berlin.[21] Incapacity in the Majority Socialist leadership also aided the Independents. In the critical days at the end of December, when the issue of using force against the radicals arose in Munich it was so badly mishandled by Auer and his colleagues that Eisner, arguing much like Haase and Dittmann, was able both to defend his position successfully and to discredit his opposite numbers in the coalition sufficiently to keep them quiet for a time.[22] The Majority Socialists were not decisive enough, and did not feel strong enough, to take the whole burden of revolutionary government on themselves. And so the peculiar government carried on.

The artificiality of the arrangement was demonstrated by the elections to the Bavarian constituent assembly, or Diet, on January 12. They were a fiasco for the USPD; while the Majority Socialists, with a third of the popular vote, nearly replaced the Catholic party as the largest party in Bavaria, the Independents received 2.5 percent of the total vote and 3 of the 180 seats. Their vote was concentrated in a few districts, with fully three-quarters of it coming from Munich and Upper and Middle Franconia; but even in Munich the USPD's vote was barely a tenth of the SPD's.[23] In the elections to the National Assembly a week later, by contrast, the Independents increased their vote by nearly half, doubling it in Munich, while most other parties experienced a slight decline—a sign of the coming radicalization of the socialist electorate. Even so, the party was still the smallest of Bavaria's six significant parties.[24] The

20. Eisner, *Schuld und Sühne*, pp. 16–18; Eisner, *Die neue Zeit*, I, 108–9; Eisner, *Die halbe Macht*, p. 11; Schade, pp. 82 and 83–84.

21. In December both Fritz Schröder, chairman of the Munich USPD, and Richard Kämpfer, editor of its new Munich newspaper, pressed Eisner to resign for the party's sake; interview of Kämpfer with Harold Hurwitz in Feb. 1946, record in possession of Dr. Hurwitz, Berlin. They do not appear, however, to have tried to set the party publicly against Eisner.

22. Mitchell, pp. 198–205. Haase's and Dittmann's arguments on the use of force to suppress radical dissent are given below, p. 196.

23. See the tables in Mitchell, pp. 215–18.

24. *Ibid.*, p. 218; Schade, p. 161.

USPD seemed to have remained, in Mitchell's words, "a small dissident faction of the SPD."[25]

From this time Eisner's influence waned rapidly, so much so that it is hardly proper to speak of an Eisner government after mid-January. The USPD had as many seats in the cabinet as it would have in the Diet.[26] Eisner continued as minister president because no one had an alternative coalition to propose—or wanted to propose one before the Diet assembled, partly for fear of provoking the radicals. But the Majority Socialists, feeling renewed confidence, were increasingly alienated by Eisner's ambiguity about the sovereignty of the Diet, as against the councils, and by his renewed pronouncements on Germany's war guilt. Auer and his associates began to steer more openly toward a normal parliamentary order and in the process weakened Eisner's influence within what was nominally his government. The trend to the right in the government, however, was countered by a trend to the left among the militants of all the socialist parties, especially in Munich. The Independents, pulling away from Eisner's moderating influence, consolidated their alliance with the groups to their left, especially after the Berlin disturbances of early January, and the activity of all these groups increased.[27]

The atmosphere of the last week before the opening of the Diet, scheduled for February 21, was heavy with crisis, with a congress of Bavarian councils meeting in Munich and demonstrators in the streets. On February 20 Eisner told the delegates:

I long to see the socialists, without distinction of faction, finally cease to govern and turn again to opposition. . . . Tomorrow the Diet opens, tomorrow the activity of the councils too shall begin anew, and then we shall see where the forces of life and where the convulsions of a society condemned to death are to be found.[28]

The next day, on his way to the Diet with his resignation as minister president in his pocket, Kurt Eisner was assassinated by a nationalist fanatic and the real crisis of the Bavarian revolution began.

The USPD as Ruling Minority: Hamburg, Bremen, and Braunschweig

In Hamburg, too, the revolution lifted the Independents to a position of disproportionate eminence. Here the organized Independents at the end of the war were neither so few nor so detached from factory support

---

25. Mitchell, p. 341.
26. The point is made in Franz August Schmitt, *Die Zeit der zweiten Revolution in Bayern* (Munich, 1919), p. 7.
27. Mitchell, pp. 245–49. The January disturbances are discussed in ch. 7 below.
28. Eisner, *Die halbe Macht*, p. 35.

as in Munich. Yet in comparison with the rival Majority Socialists, the Hamburg USPD was very weak. The old, highly developed SPD organization in Hamburg suffered less membership decline in the early war years than any other party district in the country, and when the split came it lost only a very small fraction of its members to the USPD.[29] The separate left radical faction, though led by such well-known local figures as Heinrich Laufenberg and Fritz Wolffheim, is said by a participant to have numbered fewer than a hundred active followers.[30] In Hamburg, then, to outward appearances, a weak band of Independents and a negligible left radical sect faced a situation firmly under the control of the strongest local party organization in the SPD.

As in Munich, party strength was outweighed by other factors in the revolutionary hours. For one thing, the Majority Socialist leaders, their hopes fixed on democratizing the city's institutions, lost touch with the far-reaching, emotional aspirations of their followers to an extent not equaled in Berlin. On November 5, after news of the Kiel events reached Hamburg, a spontaneous movement in the shipyards and factories gave rise to demands for full democracy and the abdication of the Hohenzollerns, and the SPD leaders were barely able by procrastination to head off an immediate general strike. That evening, a tumultuous assembly of the USPD with Wilhelm Dittmann as speaker—the party's first public meeting ever in Hamburg—resolved on an immediate general strike and the establishment of workers' and soldiers' councils. When it was discovered the next morning that a small self-appointed band of sailors had disarmed most of the military forces in the city during the night, the Majority Socialists no longer knew how to control the situation.[31]

In the next few crucial days the left had more notion of what it was doing. Most of the Independents were uncertain of the nature of their "revolution," and seem to have avoided the word, but they were committed without reservation to the formation of workers' councils and were the driving force behind this process.[32] The left radicals, more sure of the onset of the socialist revolution, took up street agitation and added to their revolutionary credentials by leading a large crowd to chase away

29. An upper limit to the original membership of the USPD is implied by the decline of SPD membership from 46,937 to 41,687 between March 1916 and March 1917; SPD *Parteitag,* Oct. 1917, p. 10. The actual loss to the Independents was probably much less. Bünemann, p. 20, cites a contemporary estimate that the USPD started with 1,000 members in Hamburg.

30. Bünemann, p. 45.

31. The fullest account of this stage of the revolution is *ibid.,* pp. 57–78; see also Dittmann memoirs, pp. 856–59, for the USPD assembly of Nov. 5.

32. Bünemann, pp. 81–84 and Anlage 6.

the city's commanding general.[33] Both groups also made themselves heard in the socialist press, both old and new. The SPD leaders hung back until events in Berlin put an end to their hopes of a return to orderly processes; and by that time they had missed the chance to throw their weight into the balance in the election of the workers' and soldiers' councils. The new regime in Hamburg settled down under an elected council system in which a coalition of Independents and left radicals had a numerical superiority.[34]

The elected leader of the Hamburg councils, after his return from the western front on November 10, was Heinrich Laufenberg. Although a member of the most doctrinaire and the smallest of the groups involved, the left radicals, he nonetheless remained head of the revolutionary government for over two months, working for socialist unity and yielding on principle more than once in order to keep in touch with popular feeling—more specifically, with the Independents, his main political support.[35] The USPD in turn, having no leader who could match Laufenberg in flair and popularity, yielded the main representative functions and the chairmanship to him. It was a strange alliance, but for two months it worked.

In spite of their radical leadership, the revolutionary councils in Hamburg were in some ways even less effective than elsewhere. Except for a brief interlude, the actual government of the city-state remained in the hands of the old Senate, and thus of the business classes of the city.[36] Appropriate measures for social welfare, economic recovery, and political reform were introduced, but under the circumstances socialization of industry could scarcely be an issue for the councils, though there was lively agitation on the point outside them. In the one area where the councils had untrammeled authority, military affairs, little was attempted until after the Majority Socialists had the soldiers' councils so firmly under their control that radical measures were out of the question.[37]

Gradually the SPD recovered its confidence and mustered its still for-

33. *Ibid.*, pp. 85–88 and 94–96.
34. Richard A. Comfort, *Revolutionary Hamburg: Labor Politics in the Early Weimar Republic* (Stanford, Calif., 1966), pp. 41–44.
35. Laufenberg explained the basis for his stress on unity in *Allgemeiner Kongress*, p. 123, and in his article "Die Räteidee in der Praxis des Hamburger Arbeiterrates," *Archiv für Sozialwissenschaft und Sozialpolitik*, 45 (1918/19), esp. 610–15. See also Kolb, *Arbeiterräte*, pp. 149–50.
36. Comfort, pp. 46–51.
37. *Ibid.*, pp. 51–53. At the end of December the Majority Socialist Lamp'l was elected chairman of the soldiers' council by a margin of nearly two to one over the Independent Reich (*Freiheit*, Dec. 29, 1918), and the leadership was henceforth in his competent hands.

midable strength. Working with an image rather than a program, it took up a stand as "the advocate of orderly processes and good government."[38] From January 1 onward it began to mount counterdemonstrations against those of the radicals, who had previously monopolized public political activity. The next few weeks were a time of confrontation, leading occasionally to violence, a paler reflection of the events in Berlin on which attention was concentrated. In these struggles the powerful position of the soldiers' council, a more effectively disciplined force than anything Berlin ever saw, became evident, leading the Independent Carl Herz to refer to a "dictatorship of the soldiers' council."[39] On January 19 Laufenberg finally gave up his balancing act and abandoned his position, leaving the leadership firmly in the hands of the Majority Socialists. The National Assembly elections on the same day confirmed the need for this change; the SPD garnered 51.3 percent of the Hamburg vote, to 6.7 percent for the Independents (Laufenberg's followers put up no candidates).[40] A few eventful weeks later, after the storming of Bremen by government troops, the politics of Hamburg settled down to a kind of normality in which for some time the USPD, though growing steadily larger and more radical, had only a limited role.

In Hamburg's sister city, Bremen, too, the Independents vied with left radicals for the leadership of the socialist left in the revolution. In Bremen, however, the two groups had a much more securely established position on which to build. The supporters of the SPD's war policies, though strong in trade-union and party offices, had lost control of the city party organization; and the two left-wing factions benefited from the leadership of a number of locally popular figures, headed by the Independent Reichstag deputy Alfred Henke. True, the party organization had passed into left radical, not USPD hands; but the Independents had been able to rebuild, and in the revolution they were accounted the stronger of the two.[41] In any case, though the distinction between the main opposition and the left radicals was sharp in theory—the latter, under Johann Knief, being the harshest of all critics of the USPD's "centrism"—it tended to be blurred among followers in the factories. A coalition of the socialist left, well placed by virtue of its dominance in the Bremen party and its connections in the factories, was the salient fact of the early revolutionary experience in Bremen.

The Bremen Independents had more vigor than their Hamburg coun-

---

38. Comfort, p. 57.
39. *Ibid.*, pp. 54–55. Laufenberg used the same phrase in his "Die Räteidee," p. 619.
40. Comfort, p. 180.
41. Lucas, *Sozialdemokratie in Bremen*, p. 92; Kuckuck, pp. 4–6.

terparts. Their inclinations at this date were distinctly to the left; they too were descendants of the prewar left radical faction, of which Henke had been accounted a member until as late as 1916. Early in 1918, Henke had been one of the few Independents to speak openly about the desirability of revolution.[42] Bremen's revolution, on November 6, was itself unremarkable; once again the sailors neutralized the garrison and completed the demoralization of the old regime. But the Independents and left radicals were prepared to move decisively in the sailors' wake— speeches by Henke and his fellow Independent Adam Frasunkiewicz gave the revolution its political turn.[43] In consequence they quickly won the revolutionary initiative, as in Hamburg; in Bremen, however, the socialist left also had a strong following among the organized workers on which to base its rule. In the workers' council elected on November 7, which ruled until January, their followers had a firm majority.[44]

In Bremen, then, the rule of the radical socialists had a kind of legitimacy, that is, so long as the city accepted the revolutionary dominance of the workers in the factories, as represented in the councils. The new order did not, at first, have any particularly radical practical effects. The government in Bremen was confronted with much the same problems as other city governments in those months, and similar half-measures were chosen in an attempt to meet the worst immediate hardships and gain time until Germany's confused political scene should clear sufficiently to give guidance. Again, the old administration continued to function, though under much closer supervision than in Hamburg.[45] Officers were expelled from the soldiers' councils but, because of resistance from the garrison troops, no Red Guard was formed.[46] Henke, in whom the outspoken radical and the flexible pragmatist were combined, exercised his chairmanship of the workers' and soldiers' council as a moderating force. The councils were active and purposeful in their daily work, but it was chiefly in their mood rather than in their acts that they differed from councils elsewhere in the first weeks of the revolution. Their most dramatic moments occurred over resolutions of no immediate practical effect, such as their overwhelming rejection on November 19 of the idea of a National Assembly, or, equally, the rescinding of this decision ten days later, after

42. Lucas, *Sozialdemokratie in Bremen*, pp. 68 and 98–99. Henke's papers (ASD Bonn) contain a lively correspondence with his old collaborator Karl Radek for the years 1914 and 1915.
43. Wilhelm Breves, ed., *Bremen in der deutschen Revolution* (Bremen, 1919), pp. 10–14.
44. Kuckuck, pp. 5–6. In the action committee of the councils the Independents had nine seats, the left radicals and Majority Socialists six each; *ibid.*, p. 7.
45. Breves, pp. 18–21.
46. *Ibid.*, pp. 29–30.

the opinions of the masses inside and outside Bremen, and especially of the soldiers, had become clearer.[47]

But the situation could not be stabilized at this point; the pressure of radicalism within the ruling groups was too strong. Moreover, pressure was deliberately organized from outside by one of the most effective leaders in the whole of the German extreme left, Johann Knief, who returned to Bremen from prison on November 18.[48] The Bremen left radicals were not just a noisy group of intellectuals; they had long had a functioning shop stewards' organization in some of the largest industrial plants, and this organization lent weight to the campaign Knief mounted to force the workers' and soldiers' council off its moderate course. On November 29 there was a confrontation between the council and a large crowd of demonstrators led by Knief. On this occasion the council conceded nothing of substance.[49] The pressure tactics continued, however, and during December the Independents, too, were drawn into the millenarian atmosphere that the left radicals were seeking to create. By the end of the month the left radicals, with the Independents trailing along behind, were well down the path that led to the proclamation of the Soviet Republic of Bremen on January 10. The story of these events belongs to another chapter.

In the city of Braunschweig, capital and dominant industrial town of the small state of the same name, the USPD was in a ruling position, too. The Independents there had been much stronger than the Majority Socialists in the latter part of the war, and in the revolution the energy was all on their side. The revolutionary shop stewards (radical metalworkers like their counterparts in Berlin) seized the initiative by forming a provisional workers' council on November 8 and so managed the factory elections of November 24 that the Majority Socialists felt compelled to abstain, permitting the radicals to retain their monopoly of power.[50] Nor did they, or the new state government formed from among their members, have qualms about using this power. On November 10 the government issued a decree confiscating all the properties of the deposed duke; the following day it began forming a Red Guard and announced its intention of demobilizing all Braunschweig troops as soon as they arrived home, regardless of what Berlin might order (this intention was in fact

---

47. *Ibid.*, pp. 29–30 and 33; Kuckuck, pp. 30–32 and 51–53; *Freiheit*, Nov. 21, 1918 (m), and Dec. 3, 1918 (m).

48. *Illustrierte Geschichte*, p. 335. For Knief's views at this time see Kuckuck, pp. 17–18 and 24–25; Kolb, *Arbeiterräte*, p. 329; and *Dokumente und Materialien*, II, 491–93.

49. Breves, pp. 30–35; Kuckuck, pp. 30–33.

50. Kolb, *Arbeiterräte*, pp. 93 and 95.

carried out in December).[51] On November 16 it created special tribunals to try those accused of hoarding, black-marketeering, and other economic crimes.[52] These actions, while perhaps not outstandingly radical, had few parallels in the work of the cautious German revolutionaries. They stamped the Braunschweigers as exceptionally bold.

The daring that the Braunschweig Independents showed during the revolution—and up to their sudden turnabout in February—was largely the result of their party's relatively unified radical outlook. In Braunschweig the USPD's Spartacist adherents were unusually numerous and effective, merging well into the party ranks and even exercising a measure of leadership through August Merges, a popular speaker who became the revolutionary president of Braunschweig. The aggressive and unpredictable Sepp Oerter, the party leader, was himself not far removed from left radical views, at least during the weeks following the revolution; as head of the government he took the lead in many of its most sweeping decisions.[53] As a result, clear-cut factional conflicts in the council were avoided until January, and even then the local Spartacists were so reluctant to break with the Independents that the Braunschweig Communist Party was not founded until March. It was an impressively forceful alliance while it lasted.

The Braunschweig radicals were well aware of the incongruence between their course and trends elsewhere in the Reich, especially in Berlin. In fact, to some extent their swift action must be seen as part of a design to consolidate the beginnings of socialism in their own small state so that Berlin would not be able to interfere. Such action was striking enough, but the attempt of Oerter and his followers to arm themselves against Berlin by prescribing general elections was even more unusual.[54] Elections would have provided Oerter's regime with a firm foundation if they had, as Oerter expected, returned a majority for the USPD. But these expectations were disappointed. In the municipal elections of December 15 the USPD won only twelve of thirty-six seats; the SPD had eight seats, giving the two parties together a clear majority, but by December socialist collaboration was growing less, not more, likely.[55] A week later state-wide elections produced a similar small overall socialist

51. Ernst-August Roloff, *Braunschweig und der Staat von Weimar* (Braunschweig, 1964), p. 36; Karl Anlauf, *Die Revolution in Niedersachsen* (Hanover, 1919), p. 99; *Freiheit,* Dec. 31, 1918 (m).
52. Roloff, p. 38.
53. For valuable character sketches of Merges and Oerter see *ibid.,* pp. 31 and 32–33.
54. *Ibid.,* pp. 36 and 41.
55. *Freiheit,* Dec. 17, 1919 (m).

majority, this time with the SPD having the edge, with seventeen seats to fourteen.[56]

These results destroyed one of the unspoken premises of Oerter's government, but the Independent-Spartacist alliance showed its mettle by growing more determined—or so it appeared. During January the Braunschweig councils were the most advanced in Germany, going so far as to socialize some of the large factories in the capital city; and Oerter threatened to dissolve the Diet unless it agreed to work as a loyal subordinate to the councils.[57] But these were only gestures. Braunschweig, with half a million people scattered across half a dozen little territorial islands in the middle of Prussia, was in no position to form the fortress of socialist resistance that Oerter talked about. Oerter and his colleagues knew this and began to fend off pressure from the far left. When the Diet finally assembled, on February 10, and refused to accept a consultative position, it was not dissolved; instead, in an abrupt reversal, Oerter and the Independents formed a parliamentary coalition with the Majority Socialists.[58] The revolutionary regime in Braunschweig, which did more to earn the name of a soviet republic than some cities that claimed the title, proved to be only an episode; and even Oerter's brand of Independents showed that, ultimately, the party could not be wholeheartedly quixotic.

The USPD as Dominant Party: Leipzig and Halle

The most significant instances of Independent rule are provided by Leipzig and Halle, where the USPD was the dominant party not only among socialists but also among the population at large. These were the major cities of that Central German area where Independent Social Democracy—and groups farther to the left—played a potent role in the years we are considering: the western sections of the former kingdom of Saxony, the Merseburg government district of Prussia, and much of Thuringia. Halle in particular became the organizing center and spokesman for a considerable industrial area; while Leipzig dominated the northwestern third of the Saxon state. The activities of the energetic, self-confident Independents of these adjoining regions are thus an important part of the history of the party.

In Leipzig the typical roles of SPD and USPD were reversed; since 1917 the established socialist party in Leipzig had been the USPD, and it required strong principle (or special interests) for a man to belong to the Majority Socialist party. While the Majority Socialists numbered in the

56. Roloff, pp. 43–44.
57. *Ibid.*, pp. 44 and 47–49; Anlauf, p. 100.
58. Roloff, p. 51; Anlauf, pp. 105–6.

hundreds, the Independents boasted the second largest (and incomparably the best organized) city organization in the USPD, together with the newspaper that served as the party's unofficial central organ, the *Leipziger Volkszeitung*. The success of the opposition in Leipzig encouraged a pride in the party that, with good leadership, held together its disparate elements on the basis of good party administration combined with an ideological mixture that (until well into 1919) refused to distinguish clearly between centrist and radical ideas. Under the circumstances, the well-organized but relatively small Spartacist group could pose no challenge to the established leaders. Thus, in Leipzig, where socialism was coming to predominate among the electorate, the USPD was for the time being the main political power.

Seizure of power in Leipzig came late—November 8—and was uneventful; again soldiers and sailors took the lead.[59] Leadership of the revolution fell directly into the hands of the Independents, who at once chose a provisional workers' council from among their party officials and functionaries, without needing to grant the SPD any representation.[60] Elections in the city's factories, held on November 9, resulted in a council that confirmed this monopoly;[61] and the municipal elections of January 26 showed that the Independents had the loyalty of an overwhelming majority of the city's socialists and nearly an absolute majority of voters.[62] The rule of the Independents was thus scarcely challenged in Leipzig until late spring, near the end of the sporadic civil war. Their problems came instead from two other sources: Leipzig's awkward position in the overall Saxon political situation; and conflicts within the Leipzig USPD over policy.

The unquestioned supremacy of the Independents in Leipzig provided them at first with an advantage in Saxon politics, since when the Leipzig delegates joined those of the other major cities of Saxony (where the SPD had had to concede parity in the councils) the socialist left had a

59. Gerhard Puchta, "Der Arbeiter- und Soldatenrat in Leipzig vom November 1918 bis vor dem 2. Rätekongress Anfang April 1919," *Wissenschaftliche Zeitschrift der Karl-Marx-Universität Leipzig,* Gesellschafts- und Sprachwissenschaftliche Reihe, 7 (1957–58), 363–64; Horst Beutel, "Die Novemberrevolution von 1918 in Leipzig und die Politik der Leipziger USPD-Führung bis zum Einmarsch der konterrevolutionären Truppen des Generals Maercker am 12. Mai 1919," *ibid.,* p. 388.

60. *Leipziger Volkszeitung,* Nov. 9, 1918. Such a monopoly was rare; according to Kolb, *Arbeiterräte,* p. 86, only in Bremen, Braunschweig, and Leipzig were the Majority Socialists shut out of power completely by the more radical socialists.

61. *Leipziger Volkszeitung,* Sonderausgabe of Nov. 10, 1918. The workers' delegates in the inner committee were nominated by the party and confirmed by the workers' and soldiers' council; Lipinski became chairman, followed later by Friedrich Seger.

62. *Ibid.,* Jan. 28, 1919.

majority—though an artificial one, as time was to show. On the basis of this balance of forces, delegates from Leipzig, Dresden, and Chemnitz issued a revolutionary declaration on November 14[63] and then, the following day, set up a socialist Council of People's Commissioners for Saxony. The prominent representatives of the extreme left—the Spartacist Fritz Heckert of Chemnitz and the left radical Otto Rühle of Dresden—refused to take part and began that process of withdrawal from responsibility that happened more abruptly in Berlin; Rühle withdrew his followers altogether from the Dresden workers' council on November 16.[64] But even without the far left's support the Independents were able to assert their priority in the distribution of government posts. In the six-man cabinet, Lipinski combined the powers of chairman with responsibility for both interior and foreign affairs; Friedrich Geyer of Leipzig had supervision of finance and commerce; and Hermann Fleissner of Dresden took special responsibility for military affairs.[65]

The Saxon government that ruled from then until January was unusually active in reform, and not only because of the leading position of the experienced, self-confident Leipzig Independents. The actions of the socialists in Saxony were influenced by their awareness of genuine popular support for their movement; in the last Reichstag elections before the war, nineteen of the twenty-three Saxon constituencies had returned socialists, and in the national elections of January 1919 the combined socialist vote in Saxony's three electoral districts ranged between 56 and 65 percent.[66] The part of the SPD that retained a live socialist idealism was both stronger in Saxony (especially in the Chemnitz region) and freer to act without contradicting its democratic principles. Thus the artificial dominance of the USPD was not solely responsible for the rapid legislative achievements of the new government. Reforms in electoral processes and the administrative machinery followed in quick succession, and the councils, though barred from direct exercise of legislative or executive authority, were accorded well-defined rights of supervision beyond anything achieved in most other parts of the country.[67] It was not a radical government; indeed, its sober concern to be practical alienated a part of its following. But it worked within the real political framework of Saxony and in this way foreshadowed the work of the coalition socialist

63. Text *ibid.,* Nov. 14, 1918.
64. Walter Fabian, *Klassenkampf um Sachsen* (Löbau, 1930), pp. 29 and 32; Lorenz, p. 50.
65. *Leipziger Volkszeitung,* Nov. 15, 1918.
66. Unless otherwise specified, data on national elections are taken from the *Statistisches Jahrbuch für das Deutsche Reich* for the appropriate year; see also Appendix 1.
67. Fabian, pp. 34–36.

government that reappeared in Saxony, with much the same personnel, some two years later.

This promising coalition was a casualty of the growing estrangement between SPD and USPD. One cause was the increasingly visible fact that in Saxony as a whole the Independents were much the weaker of the two socialist parties; broadly based elections to the workers' councils in Dresden, on November 24, and Chemnitz, on December 9, showed the Independents to be small minorities and drove them out of their share of power in those cities.[68] After this demonstration of where the real popular support lay, the Majority Socialist leaders were no longer content with the balance established in the first week of the revolution, especially as it became apparent from tensions between the two parties elsewhere, notably in Berlin, that the question of relative party authority could become crucial. Consequently the SPD began to press the Independents for a revision of the first revolutionary settlement, a change that the Independents stubbornly resisted.

Whatever other motives the Independents may have had for their intransigence, it was politically impossible for them to accept a secondary position in the Dresden government. Their followers were already restive. The success of the Saxon coalition had rested on, among other things, a notable degree of tactical restraint by its Independent Socialist members, who themselves had to admit that the coalition's achievements lay mainly in democratic reform and social welfare.[69] At the outset the government had announced that it would cooperate with the Reich government on all important matters.[70] This principle was adhered to, and partly explains why the Saxon regime shied away from socialization of industry.[71] Nor did the government display any idealism about the long-range prospects of the councils.[72] To be sure, Lipinski and his colleagues preserved a much better image than the Independents in the Reich government by performing their full share of representative functions and taking a strong line on issues, such as the army, that they did not have to decide. But their government remained vulnerable to criticism from the left; in the atmosphere developing in December, the participation of the USPD was only possible so long as it maintained its leading position.

Meanwhile, the party in Leipzig was undergoing the first stages of the

68. *Leipziger Volkszeitung,* Nov. 25 and Dec. 10, 1918. In the National Assembly elections in January the SPD won 17 seats in Saxony, the USPD only 3, all in the Leipzig electoral district.

69. Lipinski speech, *ibid.,* Nov. 29, 1918.

70. See the programmatic declaration of the Saxon government, *ibid.,* Nov. 19, 1918, and Lipinski's speech reported *ibid.,* Dec. 4, 1918.

71. See the critical analysis in Beutel, pp. 395–97.

72. See, for example, Lipinski's speech reported in *Leipziger Volkszeitung,* Dec. 4, 1918.

radicalization that characterized Independents nearly everywhere at the turn of the year and later. In Leipzig, radicalism at first meant little more than the old socialist impulse toward an ideologically safe isolation; in this spirit the workers' and soldiers' council called on Haase, Dittmann, and Barth to resign after the Workers' and Soldiers' Congress in Berlin.[73] But other, more genuinely radical currents were growing stronger. The key figure was Curt Geyer, son of the long-time Reichstag deputy Friedrich Geyer. Aged only twenty-eight in 1918, Curt Geyer had earned a doctorate and then become a socialist journalist just before the war, returning to Leipzig in 1917, where his vigor and articulateness, together with his local roots, brought him rapid ascent in the party. Geyer headed the faction in Leipzig which corresponded to that of Ledebour and Däumig in Berlin, both in its belief in the council system and in its desire for the Independents to detach themselves from the Majority Socialists and proceed on their own revolutionary path without compromise. Young Geyer's course was much resented by such older party leaders as Lipinski and Friedrich Seger; but in the winter of 1918–1919 they had no choice but to make concessions to the spirit of radical intransigence that he represented. Geyer's influence grew, on the staff of the *Leipziger Volkszeitung* as well as in the workers' council, and at times the Leipzig USPD could both sound and act as though the radicals were firmly in command. Yet this was not the case; the party machine was still in the hands of men who did not think as Geyer did, and in the spring, when the differences turned into open dispute, they proved the stronger.

Against a background of collapsing socialist unity in Berlin, the coalition cabinet in Dresden was not able to stand up in December and January to the dual pressures of the revived confidence of the Majority Socialists and the growing intransigence of the Independents. On December 27 a workers' and soldiers' council for Saxony met and decided to establish a permanent executive council to oversee the government, divided so as to represent the relative strength of the two parties—which meant seven Majority Socialists and only two Independents. The Independents, with their powerful base in Leipzig, refused to be outvoted in this way and withdrew onto the principle that the all-Saxon council had no such powers, that each locality must be free to administer itself without outside interference.[74] Enunciation of this patently self-serving principle—to which the Leipzig Independents adhered until General Maercker's troops brought them to heel in May—was the beginning of the end for the coalition socialist government in Saxony. On January 17, after a conflict between Lipinski and the all-SPD executive council, the three

73. *Ibid.,* Dec. 24, 1918.
74. *Ibid.,* Dec. 28, 1918.

Independents resigned from the government, and the USPD in effect withdrew into fortress Leipzig.[75]

The position of the USPD in the neighboring district of Halle was equally dominant at the end of the war; only a few hundred stubborn Majority Socialists (many of them union officials) carried on the fight after 1917, and the Independents were energetic enough that a distinct Spartacist element never formed while the war lasted. Events in the revolution reinforced the supremacy of the Independents, who were scarcely affected by the formation of a well-organized but small Communist Party in January 1919.[76] It was natural, then, and by no means wholly unrealistic, that, as Wilhelm Koenen later testified, "we always regarded ourselves as *the* party in the district."[77]

In Halle itself, though the revolution again began with the soldiers (in this case a unit of airmen), the Independents were well prepared to play their role.[78] The Halle factories had an unusually well-established system of factory delegates, dating from the prewar practice of the local trade unions; even in its wartime, oppositional form it included mainly trade-union functionaries and was led by such figures as Wilhelm Koenen of the *Volksblatt* and Karl Kürbs, branch secretary of the city's second largest union, the Factory Workers.[79] The group was active on its own but maintained close connections with the party. The workers' council set up on November 8—nearly solidly Independent, and chaired by the editor Otto Kilian—came from this group. Consequently it gave its attention at first less to politics proper—its control of the city administration was scarcely more effective than elsewhere—than to the immediate affairs of the working class, such as wages and working conditions, where it had some effect.[80] The fairly cohesive leftward orientation of the working class also permitted it to set up a more or less reliable military formation to defend the revolution.[81] The city was securely in the hands of the USPD.

75. *Ibid.,* Jan. 17 and 19, 1919; Richard Lipinski, *Der Kampf um die politische Macht in Sachsen* (Leipzig, 1926), pp. 16–17; Horst Dörrer, "Die Dresdner Arbeiterbewegung während des Weltkrieges und der Novemberrevolution 1918" (Ph.D. dissertation, University of Leipzig, 1960), pp. 192–95.

76. The table of KPD membership in the district about Dec. 1919 in Joachim Schunke, *Schlacht um Halle* (Berlin, 1956), p. 18, indicates a total of 4,704 members in the Halle district, or under a tenth of USPD membership at that time.

77. Koenen, in *Zu einigen Fragen,* p. 35.

78. See the account of the revolution in Gertrud Kling, *Die Rolle des Arbeiter- und Soldatenrats von Halle in der Novemberrevolution (November 1918—März 1919)* (n.p. [1958]), pp. 13–16.

79. Koenen, in *Zu einigen Fragen,* p. 17. The Metalworkers were the largest Halle union, but the local leadership was Majority Socialist until after the end of the war.

80. Kling, pp. 17 and 24–25.

81. *Ibid.,* p. 29.

But the revolutionary system in Halle itself was not the most significant arena of USPD activity, for the district as a whole occupied the attention of the party's leaders. In part, this interest had its roots in the
prewar proselytizing work of the Halle organization in its hinterland and
in wartime relations between the factory opposition movements of Halle,
Bitterfeld, Eisleben, Merseburg, and other industrial towns. But the
growth of war industry, and then the effects of the revolution, had posed
a new problem; the district as a whole was obviously industrialized and
radicalized to a degree not reflected in either the party organization or
the trade unions. Here, then, was a classic opportunity for revolutionary
socialists: missionary work among radicalized but unorganized workers.
The Independents took up the task with unusual energy and imagination.
In the process they developed into a distinctive element within the USPD.

The outstanding characteristic of the Halle district in the revolution
was thus that the most active level of postrevolutionary organization
was not in the industrial cities but over the region as a whole, and
not through the party but through the councils.[82] As in the case of
the Lower Rhineland, which also had a regional organization of councils,
though a much less effective one, the Halle district was an outlying
province that contained no unchallenged metropolis (such as Leipzig in
its district); like the Lower Rhineland, too, the region was dotted with
distinct mining and industrial towns; but in the Halle region socialist
politics were dominated by a single party, the USPD, whose leading men
could give unity to the movement. Within days of the revolution, the
various towns had sent representatives to form a district workers' and
soldiers' council, with Independent Reichstag deputy Adolf Albrecht as
chairman. As one of its tasks the district council assumed the right of
supervision of the affairs of the Prussian district governor (the *Regier-
ungspräsident*) in Merseburg; an eight-man committee of leading Independents took over the task, with district party secretary Koenen becoming full-time commissar in the governor's office.[83] After an early flurry
of activity, the district council continued to meet approximately monthly,
to deal with important matters.[84] These organs were active and effective
within the limits of the council system as it was understood in the first
months of the revolution, and their morale was high. They were, and
were proudly felt to be, a model of the council system.

As well as being the center of a strong council movement, the Halle

82. For a survey of the council movement in the district, see Kolb, *Arbeiterräte*,
p. 109.
83. StA Magdeburg, Regierung Merseburg, C48 Ia Nr. 121, esp. documents of
Nov. 13, 14 and 15, 1918, March 22 and May 3, 1919 (unpaginated); and DZA
Merseburg, Rep. 77 Tit. 1373A Nr. 6, p. 16.
84. Schulz, "Rolle und Anteil," pp. 108–11; Kolb, *Arbeiterräte*, p. 109.

district proved itself the most flourishing regional stronghold of the USPD. The two phenomena are surely connected: the party organization, with its still limited resources, could not have assembled support so rapidly if its leaders, through their work in the councils, had not successfully projected an image of the USPD as the representative party of the district. Their success was shown in the elections to the National Assembly in January, when the Independents polled an extraordinary 44.1 percent of the vote (compared with 16.3 percent for the Majority Socialists), their highest poll in the country. It was thus of great importance for the party that its membership around Halle was oriented toward the councils and belonged predominantly to the party's left wing, pursuing policies comparable to those of the shop stewards in Berlin, although perhaps more preoccupied with the economic system than with politics.[85] The leadership had devolved quickly on younger men, including Bernhard Düwell of Zeitz, Kilian, and Koenen, who combined the radical's faith in a new proletarian world attainable through the council system with practical administrative and political ability. Halle was the paradigm of the development of USPD radicalism.

Not surprisingly, the councils of the Halle region came into conflict with the government in Berlin. The disputes began after the Workers' and Soldiers' Congress in December, when the councils set out to implement decisions of the Congress that the central government was apparently going to ignore. In a letter to the Prussian government of January 2, 1919, about new bureaucratic regulations affecting the councils, the district council showed its teeth:

Should the development of the civil administration be revised retrogressively in this way, and its systematic reconstruction not immediately undertaken, we are threatened with a second revolution, which will not stop at the decorative surface of politics but will find itself forced to make up for what has been criminally neglected in recent weeks, by making a clean sweep of the bureaucratic rubbish of earlier decades. We have the power and will know how to use it if retrograde government from Berlin becomes too bothersome to us.[86]

This was not mere bluster. In January, during the fighting in Berlin, Halle experienced a similar turmoil including the obstruction of troop trains that might be proceeding to Berlin.[87] Defiance spread from there to the more fundamental (from the councils' perspective) issue of socialization

85. Peter von Oertzen, *Betriebsräte in der Novemberrevolution* (Düsseldorf, 1963), p. 134.
86. Printed in Eberhard Schulz, ed., *Dokumente und Materialien zur Geschichte der Arbeiterbewegung im Bezirk Halle, I: 1917–1923* (Halle, 1965), pp. 50–51.
87. Kling, pp. 30–31; Schulz, "Rolle und Anteil," pp. 143–47; DZA Potsdam, Reichskanzlei 2500/3, p. 10.

of the mines, a matter in which Halle followed the lead of the Ruhr.[88] By mid-January the powerful council system of the Halle district was on a collision course with the Berlin government. The story of the ensuing events belongs to another chapter.

Other Patterns of Revolution

The cities and regions discussed above were the most noteworthy of the USPD strongholds in the revolutionary weeks but not the only ones. The USPD was relatively strong in other cities of Central Germany: in Erfurt, for instance, a moderate brand of Independents controlled the old party machine and a new network of councils, in form much like that of the Halle region but in spirit far more inclined to work for a permanent alliance with the SPD;[89] and in Gotha, the small Thuringian state, the Independents, in spite of unusually radical leadership, retained a hold on a popular majority well into 1920.[90] In the Lower Rhineland, too, some cities were ruled by Independent-dominated workers' councils: for example, the twin cities of Solingen and Remscheid, just south of the Ruhr, little USPD strongholds since the founding of the party and the political base formerly for Wilhelm Dittmann and later for Otto Brass; and Düsseldorf, where the socialist left, an ill-defined mixture of Independents, Spartacists, and other left radicals, helped create one of the most violent and unstable situations of any city in Germany.[91] On the strength of these cities the USPD dominated the first district workers' council for the Düsseldorf district, established on November 25.[92] In adjoining Westphalia, locus of most of the Ruhr mining, the USPD had Hagen (but only Hagen) as a base from which to expand its influence.[93] But as later events demonstrate, political developments in this part of Germany did not follow any of the normal party patterns; they will be discussed in chapter 7 as part of the supraparty council movement of the spring of 1919.

More typical were those cities or regions where the USPD had a share in revolutionary power thanks only to the principle of parity or where its minority position left it bereft of real influence. Three instances, each intrinsically important—Dresden, capital of Saxony, Stuttgart, capital of

88. Oertzen, *Betriebsräte*, p. 135.

89. Kolb, *Arbeiterräte*, p. 109; *Freiheit*, Nov. 30, 1918 (e).

90. See Buchsbaum; and Georg Witzmann, *Thüringen von 1918–1933: Erinnerungen eines Politikers* (Meisenheim on Glan, 1958), pp. 14–26.

91. Kolb, *Arbeiterräte*, pp. 307–8.

92. *Ibid.*, pp. 109–10.

93. Hanno Lambers, *Die Revolutionszeit in Hagen* (Hagen, 1963), esp. pp. 46–73.

Württemberg and a center of Spartacist influence, and Frankfurt on Main, the most important city of the Main district and an organizing center of the USPD—will serve as illustrations.

Dresden, as far as socialist politics were concerned, was a Majority Socialist town at the end of the war and remained so.[94] Hermann Fleissner's challenge to the majority's policies had some success in assemblies in 1915 and 1916, but when it was repulsed by a solid phalanx of the local party eminences, including the controlling editors of the newspaper, only a small band followed Fleissner into the USPD (a still smaller number followed Otto Rühle's left radical path).[95] Even after the Independents had managed to play an important role in the revolution and the establishment of the councils, the Majority Socialists remained so clearly the dominant force that they were able to dictate terms. The Independents were taken into the councils as equals only on condition that a full, regular re-election of the councils be held in two weeks' time.[96] For a week or more this evenly divided council operated smoothly, before frictions set in. Then came the blow of the council elections on November 24; the SPD won forty-seven seats on the new council, the Independents three.[97] The role of the Independents in the Dresden revolution was close to negligible for many months thereafter.

In Stuttgart the Independents, led by their strong Spartacist component, achieved greater eminence in the revolution but lost it just as completely. The abortive revolution of November 4–7 (described at the end of chapter 3) had both exhausted the radicals' energies and alerted the Majority Socialists, so that when the monarchy fell on November 9 the SPD picked up the reins in Württemberg. The main exception was the capital city itself, a metalworking center with a tradition of radicalism; there the Independents had been able to constitute themselves as the provisional workers' council. They were too isolated, however, to keep this position by revolutionary right alone, and the factory elections to which they were forced to agree soon removed them from power, giving them just over a quarter of the seats in the new workers' council.[98] Yet

94. See the tables of election results from 1919 to 1921 in Lorenz, pp. 54–56. The SPD by itself had an absolute majority in Dresden in the elections of January 1919, though never again; the Independents got more than half of the SPD vote only in their great electoral triumph of June 1920.

95. *Ibid.*, pp. 5–36.

96. *Ibid.*, pp. 46–49.

97. *Leipziger Volkszeitung*, Nov. 25, 1918; Dörrer, pp. 163–65. These elections were held, not at places of work, but by city ward; they thus amounted almost to regular municipal elections in which the wealthy were excluded from suffrage and only the socialist parties put up candidates. These conditions undoubtedly worked to the benefit of the SPD.

98. Kolb, *Arbeiterräte*, pp. 93, 95–96, and 103–4.

the Independents' activism remained a force to be reckoned with in Stuttgart, and one of their number, the editor Artur Crispien, continued to sit in the Württemberg government, reflecting their share in the revolution, even though his Spartacist colleagues soon resigned.[99] In practice, the state was under the control of the competent if unimaginative Majority Socialist leaders; and in January, long after most of his party had given up their hopes of socialist unity and gone into opposition, Crispien finally had to resign.[100]

The case of Frankfurt on Main was altogether different. The USPD there was headed by the forceful Robert Dissmann, district secretary for the area; Tony Sender, aged thirty, a newcomer to socialist politics during the war, and the trade unionist Heinrich Hüttmann were his most prominent associates. Dissmann and Sender were both outspoken members of the party's radical wing, but their sense of the possible (locally, at least) gave them a certain distinction. Their small organization—said to have had 800 members at the outbreak of the revolution—threw itself wholeheartedly into the revolutionary events and, with the aid of a fairly well developed network of factory supporters, secured a strong place for itself in Frankfurt's postrevolutionary institutions.[101] Their opposite numbers, Frankfurt's Majority Socialists, were rare exceptions in being forthright critics of their party's leadership in Berlin; this made collaboration easier from the start.[102] Somehow, the parity established in the workers' council in Frankfurt endured, surviving the bitterness of the winter and spring, thanks to the sympathy of left-SPD police chiefs and the virtual absence of disorders in Frankfurt, surviving the evidence of the Independents' electoral weakness, and even the election of a new municipal assembly in March.[103] Upholding its independent, critical line but without chal-

99. Some brief comments on his activity are contained in the Artur Crispien papers (ASD Bonn), memoir fragment "Ein Sohn des Volkes" (17-page version), pp. 5–6. For the break between Crispien and the Spartacists, see Keil, esp. II, 97–99; on the Spartacists' resignation, *Rote Fahne*, Nov. 18, 1918. In view of Crispien's later role in the USPD it is interesting to note that he was one of only six Independents who held office in socialist/bourgeois coalition governments during the revolutionary period; the others (apart from a pair of soldiers, one each in Baden and Württemberg) were Adolf Schwarz in Baden, Bernhard Kuhnt in Oldenburg, and a Dr. Bardasch in Mecklenburg-Schwerin.

100. Keil, II, 138; *Freiheit*, Jan. 16, 1919 (e).

101. Lucas, *Frankfurt*, p. 15; Sender, pp. 92–112; D. Schneider and Neuland, pp. 66–75.

102. The local party organization of the SPD was in fact controlled by the party's right wing, but neither the newspaper nor the members of the workers' council followed the organization's lead.

103. Election results in Lucas, *Frankfurt*, p. 83. In the National Assembly elections the SPD won 45.6 percent of the vote in Frankfurt, the USPD 4.5 percent; in the new municipal assembly elected on March 2 the SPD had 36 seats and the USPD 8.

lenging the central government's authority in important matters, it survived the military operations of the spring as well, substantially aided by the fact that Frankfurt lay in the demilitarized zone.[104] The Frankfurt workers' council remained the city's sovereign power until September and did not dissolve until November, a few days after the anniversary of the revolution. Frankfurt was unique in Germany, a place where the two sets of party leaders, each sensing the constraints of their situation and willing to compromise for the sake of the socialist cause, kept alive the spirit of the revolution.

The National Position of the USPD

To look only at the great industrial areas and old socialist centers where the USPD played an important role in and after the revolution is misleading. Some areas of Germany knew the USPD only as a tiny faction, others not at all; as the party leaders well knew, the USPD represented a small minority, not just of the German population, but of the working class.[105] For a brief time after the revolution, they could believe the party to be riding a revolutionary wave that made its numerical weakness irrelevant or that would bring the entire working class quickly to the Independents' way of thinking. Several weeks passed before evidence to the contrary began to accumulate and hard political realities had to be faced. For at least a year thereafter the party's more thoughtful leaders and theoreticians could not escape the fact that the greater part of what they liked to think of as the USPD's constituency, the German working class as a whole, was hostile or indifferent to the party.

Membership of the USPD at the time of the revolution was later given as "about 100,000" and may have been even smaller.[106] Such a number was not large for a party of the USPD's pretensions; the SPD had some 250,000 members, perhaps more. The USPD was growing rapidly—an incomplete survey at the end of January 1919 indicated a national membership of about 300,000.[107] But so was the SPD, whose membership had risen to over a million by March 31, 1919.[108] The evidence does not permit even an approximate analysis of the membership increases of these months, but there are scattered indications of its sources. Much of the apparent growth, in both parties, represented the return of many of the 700,000 members lost during the war, mostly to conscription. Returning soldiers probably rejoined according to the local pattern of the

104. Kolb, *Arbeiterräte*, pp. 292 and 301.
105. See, for example, Prager, p. 183.
106. See ch. 2, n. 42.
107. Zietz in USPD *Parteitag*, March 1919, p. 50.
108. SPD *Parteitag*, June 1919, p. 54.

split, without greatly changing the relative strengths of the parties; in an Independent-dominated city such as Leipzig most, and in Berlin a large part, would have entered the USPD. A steady trickle, at least, of Majority Socialists defected to the USPD, though little is known about these switches except in cases where whole local organizations (invariably small ones, like Vegesack, near Bremen) came over;[109] very few leaders changed parties after the end of the war, and rank-and-file SPD members (unlike SPD voters) may well have been similarly constant. Finally, there were enough new socialists to raise the combined Social Democratic membership (apart from the Communists) to a point 20 percent above the prewar level by early 1919 (and to double the prewar total by mid-1920). There is no documentation on who the new socialists were; the impression, however, is that, apart from a limited number of radicalized intellectuals, the new Independents were previously "indifferent" workers stirred up by the revolution (who tended to reinforce the radical wing of the party), while the Majority Socialists, though drawing some new members from this source, won more from sections of the population previously suspicious of Social Democracy. In any case, however encouraging the USPD's growth might be in itself, the party was probably rather less than holding its own against the SPD during the autumn and early spring.

The elections for workers' and soldiers' councils, involving many workers beyond the party memberships, were especially disappointing for the USPD. At the outbreak of the revolution there was little opportunity for orderly elections, and the Independents were often able to convert their initiative or their readier acceptance of the revolution into an important place in the councils. They also gained from the principle of parity, widely followed in the councils of the cities as a token of socialist solidarity or a hedge against violent dissension. But later voting usually showed the Independents to have been overrepresented. The first shock came from Dresden on November 24, where a 94 percent vote for the Majority Socialists put an end to parity; in the following month the SPD had similar successes in Chemnitz (92 percent) and Plauen (79 percent); and there were many other instances, if less dramatic.[110] By the end of November it could be calculated that the USPD would be in a minority at the Workers' and Soldiers' Congress on December 16; but even though forewarned, the party was disappointed by the final balance of forces. Of the 425 delegates who gave their party affiliation, 292 were SPD supporters, only 94 Independents.[111] Even in Berlin, where the

109. *Leipziger Volkszeitung,* Nov. 22, 1918.
110. *Ibid.,* Nov. 25, Dec. 10 and 23, 1918.
111. *Zentralrat,* pp. xxvii–xxviii; cf. the slightly different figures in R. Müller,

USPD was generally thought to be the stronger party, only 5 of the 13 delegates chosen by the mass assembly were Independents.[112]

General elections in the Reich and the states, coming somewhat later than the council elections, cast an even harsher light on the narrow popular base of the USPD. The elections in the Independent stronghold of Braunschweig, where the USPD won a third of the votes in the capital city on December 15 and less than a quarter in the state a week later, have already been mentioned. When the states of Anhalt and Mecklenburg-Strelitz held general elections on December 15, the Independents were unable even to put up candidates, and the Majority Socialists won an absolute majority in both Diets. The more important South German elections early in January confirmed the trend: in Baden, on January 5, the SPD polled more than a third of the votes, while the USPD failed to win a seat in the Diet;[113] in Württemberg, on January 12, the Independents won only 3 percent of the vote, less than a tenth of the SPD's total; and in Bavaria, on the same day, the USPD vote was even smaller at 2.5 percent. Voting for the National Assembly on January 19, 1919, provided the final and unmistakable evidence; the SPD, with over eleven million, had almost exactly five times as many votes as the USPD and won 163 seats to the Independents' 22. The USPD share of the poll was 7.6 percent.

The elections also showed how localized the USPD's strength was. Of the 22 seats the party earned, 6 came from Greater Berlin,[114] 5 from the Halle region, 3 each from the adjoining Leipzig and Thuringian electoral districts, 2 from the Düsseldorf-East district (the industrial part of the Lower Rhineland), and one each from Braunschweig, Hamburg-Bremen, and Franconia.[115] In the remaining 26 electoral districts—which included the whole of Prussia apart from Berlin and the Düsseldorf, Halle, and Erfurt districts and the whole of South Germany except for Franconia—the USPD failed to win a seat. In only 2 districts, Halle and

---

Kaiserreich, II, 203. Nineteen of the Independents came from the Lower Rhineland, where they turned their majority control into a solid block of delegates, without conceding proportional representation to the minorities as other councils did. Otherwise, the USPD bloc was as large as five only in the Berlin, Leipzig, Thuringia, and Halle delegations.

112. *Freiheit,* Dec. 15, 1918 (e).

113. The discussion of the Baden campaign in USPD-Baden *Landeskonferenz,* Feb. 1919, provides a vivid illustration of how difficult it was for the USPD to make electoral inroads in areas in which it had virtually no organization.

114. By "Greater Berlin" is meant Berlin City and the two Potsdam electoral districts; one of the latter consisted nearly wholly of Berlin suburbs that were incorporated into the city in 1920, while in the other further Berlin suburbs were the principal (though not the only) source of votes for the USPD.

115. The Franconian results were challenged, and in November 1919 the USPD's seat from there (held by Joseph Simon) was awarded to the SPD instead.

Leipzig, did the USPD vote exceed the SPD's; and whereas the lowest share of the poll won by the SPD in any district was 16.3 percent (in Halle), the Independents got more than this in only five cases. In 4 districts the Independents did not even put up a list, and in 9 others their share of the poll was below 2 percent.

The Independents, then, might be strong in certain industrial centers, but in the country as a whole they were a helpless minority. Locally it might seem that the transition to socialism required only an effort of will; nationally it was out of the question for the time being, unless the Majority Socialists should somehow be converted. Such was the USPD's predicament at the end of 1918. Influenced by the atmosphere of the great cities, the leaders of the USPD believed, with varying degrees of intensity, that the war had made socialism not only possible but historically necessary. This sense of urgency, reinforced by popular discontent, made it difficult for them to admit that the logic of numbers pointed toward alliance with the hesitant Majority Socialists, who placed order and parliamentary democracy above all and felt no urgency about socialism. Yet without collaboration the Independents could scarcely influence the course of events at all. The most obvious alternative, a second revolution, was not a real one for the moment; for the Independents, heirs of Social Democratic orthodoxy, still adhered to the traditional principle that a revolution could not succeed unless it involved the great mass of the people. And the great mass was clearly not behind them.

The tension of incompatible commitments to socialism and the authority of the masses was disorienting and debilitating. One way out was to seek refuge in local strength, in defiance of the unsatisfactory outside world; we have observed instances of this in Braunschweig and Leipzig. Another was to slip imperceptibly onto the defensive, trying to stabilize the revolutionary progress at its highwater mark even if the way to further progress did not seem to be open; much of the debate about the councils was conducted by the Independents in this spirit. Finally, the party could withdraw from responsibility altogether and set about rallying the masses to the banner of true socialism, in the hope that this could be done quickly enoug to exploit the existing crisis situation in a revolutionary manner; this was the course chosen by the Spartacist leaders in the first days of the revolution and adopted, more reluctantly, by many Independents later. These trends, in varying combinations, were discernible in the tactics of different USPD factions within a few weeks of the revolution, as the dilemma of the socialist left became clear. For the leaders, the choice was defined by the crises that shook the provisional regime and the USPD in December.

CHAPTER 6

Crisis in the Provisional Government and the USPD (December 1918)

As in all revolutions, the patterns of the German revolution of November 1918 proved less stable than they seemed during the first weeks. Expectations were too disparate; the institutions of the provisional regime were too incoherent, incapable of working together; and the disruption brought by the revolution, on top of that already inflicted on German society by the long war, produced too many natural discontents. The new order in Germany entered its first period of crisis after only a few weeks. December saw the breakdown of the original assumptions of the revolution for most left-wing socialists, leaving them in the new year to try and construct something on the ruins.

The Rise of Unrest

The state of the economy, as much as political conflict, prevented the stabilization of the new order. The country was trying to terminate war production and reintegrate millions of soldiers into the economy at a time when resumption of normal patterns of trade was impossible, raw materials were scarce, food supplies were at or below minimum requirements, and the working population was worn down and bitter. The government had neither the machinery nor the vision to cope with such problems; a spiral of decline set in that was arrested only toward the middle of the following year. Meanwhile, factories closed down for want of orders or raw materials; unemployment grew, especially in the already radical regions of Saxony and Berlin; and a series of strikes in basic industries began at the end of November and continued throughout the winter and spring, first in Upper Silesia, then in the Ruhr, and increasingly in locally important industries across the Reich.

The cause of the strikes of late November and December was less political discontent than accumulated economic grievances, reinforced perhaps by a belief that revolution ought to bring tangible benefits to

183

the workers.[1] The strikes did not yet constitute a challenge to the new socialist government or indicate a desire for a second revolution. They were, however, a threat to orderly progress, and the government—at first with the full support of its Independent members—used exhortation to deal with the problem. Barth, particularly, made widely reported speeches warning against degrading the revolution into a mere movement for better wages,[2] and the SPD press and trade union leaders missed no opportunity to emphasize that selfish demands would interfere with the general national interest in difficult times. The Spartacists and most radicals, on the other hand, seized on the spontaneous movement in the mines and factories as evidence that instability and dissatisfaction were still deep-rooted and capable of being transformed into political protest; and they bent their efforts to encouraging this development.[3] For a time economic crisis combined with political factors to bring success to their agitation.

Economic unrest was in fact running parallel to rising political unrest among the socialist left, amounting to a crisis of confidence in the revolutionary regime that the socialists had at first regarded as their own. By the end of November the new government's lack of revolutionary élan was evident. Many of the flaws in its revolutionary image have already been mentioned: continued collaboration with the old military chiefs; apparent passivity in the face of economic crisis, especially in the matter of socialization; tolerance of Foreign Secretary Solf and his policies; failure to purge or control the bureaucrats. Its worst defect, though, from the point of view of the Independents, was its failure either to raise any standard around which serious socialists could rally or to involve them in a feeling of successful progress toward socialism.[4] What little had been done was explained to the public in such a way as to minimize its political significance. Finally, instead of strengthening the popular revolutionary institutions, the councils, or at least collaborating with them, the government had consistently chosen to work through the established administrative channels. The provisional government appeared to be deliberately stifling any sense of participation in a revolutionary epoch.

1. On Upper Silesia, see Schumann, pp. 104–12; on the Ruhr, Erhard Lucas, "Ursachen und Verlauf der Bergarbeiterbewegung in Hamborn und im westlichen Ruhrgebiet 1918/19," *Duisburger Forschungen*, 15 (1971), 29–105, and Hans Spethmann, *Zwölf Jahre Ruhrbergbau*, 5 vols. (Berlin, 1928–31), I, 89–94 and 121–39.

2. See his speeches reported in *Freiheit*, Nov. 28, 1918 (m), and Nov. 30, 1918 (m); and in *Leipziger Volkszeitung*, Dec. 12, 1918.

3. *Rote Fahne* editorial, Nov. 26, 1918; Rosa Luxemburg's article "Der Acheron in Bewegung," *ibid.*, Nov. 27, 1918; article from the Bremen paper *Kommunist*, in *Dokumente und Materialien*, II, 468–69.

4. See the criticism in *Freiheit*, Nov. 19, 1919 (m and e), and in *Leipziger Volkszeitung*, Nov. 15, 1918; also Ströbel, *Die deutsche Revolution*, pp. 70–71.

Real disillusion came for some left-wing socialists with the announcement on November 29 that elections for the National Assembly would be held in February. The effect was to confirm the suspicion that the only definite steps the government ever took were in line with conventional bourgeois aspirations. Indeed, in view of the Majority Socialists' rationale for an early National Assembly, this step seemed to mark the end of any attempt by the provisional government to give socialist shape to the new Germany. The cabinet appeared to be, and largely was, merely a caretaker government.

As if this were not bad enough, the disaffected socialists also feared a military counterrevolution, a danger to which the government appeared wholly blind. The conflict between the returning armies and local revolutionary authorities in the Rhineland after November 20 first signaled danger. Perhaps encouraged by the approach of field army units, small cliques in various cities began to plot the overthrow of the more radical councils. After a week of rumors there were putsch attempts in Hamburg and Berlin on December 6, and in Chemnitz the following day. In Berlin, where events had the greatest impact on radical thinking, a detachment of soldiers briefly held the executive council under helpless, humiliating arrest; another body of troops attempted to proclaim Ebert president, a proposal Ebert turned aside on formal grounds rather than repudiating it outright; still another unit fired on a Spartacist demonstration, killing sixteen, more than the entire death toll for November 9 in Berlin.[5] It was an ominous eruption of the violence that had been lying beneath the surface of politics in Berlin.

The putsch was ultimately a sadly botched affair, and afterwards the government refused to take it seriously. This was the last straw for the frustrated, humiliated executive council, which made a final attempt to assert itself at a long, emotional meeting with the cabinet on December 7.[6] The council members, convinced that a pattern of counterrevolution was developing, wanted to shake the cabinet out of its laissez-faire attitude toward the political right. But the cabinet, convinced that the radicals were suffering from overheated imaginations, stood its ground, refusing to countenance measures to restrict the freedoms of the political right. All the council could extract from the meeting was a bland communiqué confirming the constitutional arrangements of November 22 between the two bodies.[7] The council, and especially its radical Inde-

---

5. There are good accounts from different viewpoints in R. Müller, *Kaiserreich*, II, 165–75, and H. Müller, pp. 144–47. The details of the whole affair are still obscure.

6. Cabinet minutes for Dec. 7, *Regierung der VB*, I, 286–99.

7. Text in *Freiheit*, Dec. 10, 1918 (m).

pendent members, left the meeting furious and convinced that the government was abetting counterrevolution through practically criminal political negligence if not positive complicity.[8]

Fears of counterrevolution focused, naturally, on the army, whose treatment by the government continued to be one of the greatest sources of dissatisfaction among the workers. Resentment of the old militarism, specifically of the arrogance and privileges of the officer corps, was common to the militants of all socialist factions, with the more sophisticated among them also fearing the potential political power of the military. In the eyes of many common people, the revolution had been directed at least as much against the military hierarchy as against the civil authorities of the Empire, and the ideal of military leaders elected by the troops, or at least carefully checked by them, became part of the popular ideology of the revolution. Numerous halting attempts were made to incorporate such practices into a military system for the future: among others, by the executive council in Berlin soon after the revolution; by representatives of the front troops at their Bad Ems conference early in December; by the Great Soldiers' Council in Hamburg a week later.[9] Most of these attempts were ineffectual; and meanwhile incidents in which troop units sided against the workers' and soldiers' councils continued. The confrontation of old and new orders would have to be resolved.

In default of action by the government, the initiative remained with the Supreme Command, which went ahead with plans to make itself a factor in the internal political situation. The aim was to use the relatively uninfected troops from the front to intimidate or crush radicalism, above all in Berlin, and to ensure a conservative republic that would concede the army its old position of autonomy.[10] By December 6 a new military command under General Lequis had been set up on the outskirts of Berlin to assume command of the returning troops and ready

8. See, for instance, Walter Oehme, *Damals in der Reichskanzlei* (Berlin, 1958), ch. 2, where old and unpersuasive charges that Ebert knew in advance of the putsch are raked over and supplied with circumstantial detail.

9. See the draft guidelines of the executive council in *Regierung der VB*, I, 127–29; the resolutions of the Bad Ems conference in Lothar Berthold and Helmut Neef, ed., *Militarismus und Opportunismus gegen die Novemberrevolution* (Berlin, 1958), pp. 143–44; and the military resolution of the Workers' and Soldiers' Congress (in the following section of this chapter), which was based on the Hamburg guidelines.

10. On the army's aims, see the program in *Die Wirren in der Reichshauptstadt und im nördlichen Deutschland 1918–1920*, Darstellungen aus den Nachkriegskämpfen deutscher Truppen und Freikorps, vol. 6, issued by the Kriegsgeschichtliche Forschungsanstalt des Heeres (Berlin, 1940) (hereafter cited as *Wirren*), p. 28; also Sauer, pp. 139–40.

them for action against radicalism.[11] The operation was well camouflaged as an administrative device to facilitate demobilization, and the government hesitantly agreed to the troops' making a triumphal entry into the city, over several successive mornings, to receive the thanks of the populace for their services to the country. Some nine divisions marched into Berlin between December 10 and 22.[12]

Though the operation promised political trouble with the radicals, the SPD leaders were glad on the whole to see the arrival of such an imposing force. They believed that a government should have and display military might, to discourage unruly minorities; in these days they were becoming worn and edgy over the threat of violence from the left.[13] Moreover, they would not admit that the officers might prove untrustworthy. Ebert, indeed, had been at least partly initiated into the Supreme Command's plans; but, contrary to Groener's later assertions, he seems to have remained ambivalent toward the scheme.[14] He made no overt move to stop it; but both he and the war minister withheld help from the Supreme Command in certain essential measures that formed part of the program, such as disarming the civil population.[15] As for the Independents in the cabinet, they were unhappy but apparently not alarmed (though whether because of ignorance or because they sensed that by this time not even front regiments could be made to serve the purposes of the officers we do not know); accordingly, they cooperated.

Like the attempted putsch of December 6, the Supreme Command's elaborate scheme was a threat that fizzled out, but only after arousing strong emotions. Alert radicals were partly responsible; with representatives of the radicalized Berlin garrison they protested in advance of the first troops' entry into the city and almost convinced the government to place crippling restrictions on the operation.[16] Their most effective weapon

---

11. Lequis had secret orders, for which see the Wilhelm Groener papers (BA-MA Freiburg), "Tagebuch des Ersten Generalquartiermeisters" for Dec. 9; Erwin Könnemann, "Der Truppeneinmarsch am 10. Dezember 1918 in Berlin," *Zeitschrift für Geschichtswissenschaft*, 10 (1968), 1604; Elben, p. 148.

12. See cabinet minutes for Dec. 9, *Regierung der VB,* I, 304–5; and the official explanation in *Vorwärts,* Dec. 10, 1918 (m).

13. See Scheidemann's speech of Dec. 8, reported in *Vorwärts,* Dec. 9, 1918 (m): "Things can't go on like this. Speaking for myself, I can't stand these conditions another week." See also cabinet minutes for Dec. 11, *Regierung der VB,* I, 314–15, where all three Majority Socialists spoke in this vein.

14. Ebert was informed about Nov. 28; see *Wirren,* p. 27, and Sauer, pp. 144 and 146–47. From Scheidemann's notes about Nov. 29 (see ch. 4, n. 68 above) it appears that Ebert informed at least his Majority Socialist colleagues. See also Groener's testimony in Herzfeld, pp. 385 and 390.

15. See the notes of Lequis' chief of staff, Major Harbou, printed in Könnemann, "Truppeneinmarsch," pp. 1604–9; *Wirren,* pp. 28–29.

16. *Freiheit,* Dec. 9, 1919 (m), and Dec. 10, 1918 (m). The three-cornered

was a concentrated campaign of agitation among the newly arrived troops, who, though hostile at first, quickly learned to see the situation in much the same terms as the garrison troops did and either ceased to observe the old discipline or, if they had no political or financial reason for staying with their formations, simply slipped away. Several days before Christmas Lequis could see that his mission had failed;[17] ironically, the pretext for the coming of the troops, demobilization, was the end result of the operation. But the episode heightened tensions, which contributed to the drama of the Workers' and Soldiers' Congress that was about to open.

The Congress of Workers' and Soldiers' Councils

The Reich Congress of Workers' and Soldiers' Councils—the most important political gathering in the interim between the Reichstag and the National Assembly—faced a tense situation when it met in Berlin from December 16 to 20. Such an atmosphere may not have been evident among the majority of the Congress—a solid, organized block of SPD supporters, who outnumbered the other delegates by two to one[18]—but the Independents were acutely conscious of their accumulated grievances and ready to close ranks in a rare display of unanimity, not only against the SPD, but also, as it turned out, against their own party leaders. The Congress, the first national gathering of middle- and lower-level party figures since the revolution, was a turning-point for the USPD. It was dangerous for the party that the gathering was under the auspices of the workers' and soldiers' councils rather than the party, that the delegates' deliberations were guided by the radicals of the Berlin executive council rather than party leaders, and that the dominant sentiment was mistrust of a government in which the party leadership participated; by the end

---

struggle (cabinet, executive council, and Supreme Command) is recorded in *Wirren*, pp. 30–31; Barth, pp. 84–85; cabinet minutes for Dec. 9, *Regierung der VB*, I, 304–5; minutes of the executive council for Dec. 8, Levi papers, P 20, pp. 13–16; and for Dec. 11 (a report by Barth), IML Berlin, 11/2, pp. 69–70. The most detailed account, though heavily biased, is Oehme, pp. 91–100.

17. *Wirren*, p. 33, says failure was obvious by Dec. 19; Sauer, pp. 153, 157–58, and 165, points out that it had been obvious much earlier. By Dec. 23 the Lequis command had only 1,200 infantrymen left at its disposal; Arnold Lequis papers (BA-MA Freiburg), 7, "Bericht des Generalkommandos Lequis über die Vorgänge am 23. und 24. 12. 18.," p. 3.

18. There were 292 Majority Socialists, 94 Independents, 10 United Revolutionaries (Laufenberg's unity faction, including some Independents), and several dozen others—soldiers, liberals, and some who gave no affiliation; *Zentralrat*, pp. xxvii–xxviii; cf. R. Müller, *Kaiserreich*, II, 203, which gives slightly different figures. On the Congress, see also the accounts in Tormin, pp. 94–102, and Kolb, *Arbeiterräte*, pp. 197–205.

of the Congress both the party and the government were headed for serious difficulties.

The most important decision of the Congress was predictable: endorsement of the National Assembly. For weeks it had been apparent that the great majority of workers' and soldiers' councils favored national elections and parliamentary democracy; it was even predictable that a campaign to advance the date of the elections to January would find approval with the delegates.[19] Haase might rehearse his party's arguments about voters being confused or disenfranchised by early elections; Däumig might call the Congress "a political suicide club" for hastening the fate of the councils;[20] still, and by a large majority, the Congress set the election for January 19, the earliest practical date. With this act the "highest organ of the revolution" broke the Independents' last real hope of consolidating a revolutionary system in Germany—that is, without a second revolution; from this date, discussion of a new revolution became serious on the left.

The other major issue of principle before the Congress concerned relations between the councils and the provisional government, which became the subject of bitter debate. The trouble began when, before the USPD spokesmen had even had a chance to address this question, the leaders of the complaisant SPD majority introduced a motion fixing the future relationship of councils and government in much the same manner as relations between executive council and government had been regulated, and pushed it through without debate.[21] Furious at this piece of railroading, the Independents united on the platform of the radicals. Seizing on ambiguities in the motion, they reopened the question. According to the USPD motion, presented by Lipinski of Leipzig, the central council that was to be elected by the Congress would act as a true parliament to which laws must be submitted for approval. It would have not only the right to appoint and dismiss members of the cabinet but also the right of "parliamentary supervision [Ueberwachung]"; and if this right could be interpreted broadly enough, the councils would have for the first time actual confirmed authority, at least until the National Assembly met.[22] Haase, however, opposed this proposal. He offered, with Ebert's grumbling acquiescence, the concession that the central council should have the right to examine all laws before their promulgation and

19. Predicted by *Vorwärts,* Dec. 13, 1918 (e), and Haase, in a speech reported in *Freiheit,* Dec. 16, 1918 (m), among others.
20. *Allgemeiner Kongress,* pp. 127–28 and 114.
21. *Ibid.,* pp. 88–89.
22. *Ibid.,* pp. 126 (Lipinski's speech) and 184 (the text of the motion).

raise objections to them, a right the executive council had never enjoyed; but in the event of an unresolved difference of opinion, the cabinet
was to be free to break the stalemate and act.[23] The only sanction, ultimately, was the right of dismissal—resolving differences by creating a
serious cabinet crisis.

This was not enough for the USPD. Haase remained almost alone
among the Independents present; even Barth defected, and the Independent delegation voted en bloc (and in vain) against the government's position. By now the Independents felt driven into a corner by the SPD's use of
its majority, and the situation brought out all their intransigence. The
USPD delegates decided to abstain from the elections for the central
council, and thus from membership in it, if the council's powers were to
be restricted in this way; of over a hundred delegates present at the
caucus that decided on this course, only one voted against the decision,
which was duly carried out.[24] In effect, the frustrations of the executive
council in its dealings with the government, aggravated by partisan tensions, had led to the USPD abandoning any attempt to make the council
system work on the national level.[25] They had not given up faith in the
system; they returned to their respective cities to try to build up the
councils from the grass roots for a later challenge to the central government. But they left behind them an overwhelming imbalance against their
party at the highest levels of government. Their abstention was equivalent to a vote of no confidence in the coalition in which their own party
leaders—or "their leaders up to now," as an opposition newspaper put
it[26]—played a part. The three Independent cabinet members were
isolated.

Before adjourning, however, the Congress took action in two fields
that gave some encouragement to the Independents. In both cases the
Majority Socialist delegates broke ranks to vote with the left on issues of

23. *Ibid.,* p. 126.
24. According to Ledebour in *Freiheit,* Dec. 22, 1918. Ledebour later wrote
(Ledebour papers, twelfth article) that Richard Müller and Däumig announced at
the beginning of the caucus that they would not serve on the central council whatever the caucus decided, an element of pressure that doubtless contributed to the
result. Haase, Dittmann, Barth, and Hilferding (none of them delegates) all spoke
in the caucus against the decision, but in vain; R. Müller, *Kaiserreich,* II, 210.
25. While one can agree with *Zentralrat,* pp. xxxii, and *Regierung der VB,* I,
cx–cxiii, that the conflict over the powers of the central council was not the only
reason for the USPD's abstention, it is difficult to accept their view that the differences between the USPD motion and the government's position were trivial. The
difference was between the right of objection and the right of veto, between influence and coordinate power, and was critical to the radicals' self-respect whether or
not it would have made much difference in practice.
26. *Republik,* Dec. 20, 1918.

great symbolic importance. The less immediate was the issue of social-ization. Delegates knew that the SPD leaders wished to avoid a resolu-tion on this subject; indeed, attempts were made to have it dropped from the agenda. The Congress rejected this move. Some probably acted on grounds of socialist principle in wanting to take a stand on socializa-tion; others, including Barth, had been convinced by daily contact with workers' delegations and assemblies that the government must move im-mediately, for political reasons, even if only in a declaratory way.[27] Most delegates were not convinced by arguments for further delay, and, after a strong speech by Hilferding, a resolution was unanimously adopted calling for an immediate start on "socialization of all industries ready for it, in particular of the mining industry."[28] Here was a basis of consensus on which the Independents could hope to build.

The second issue on which Majority Socialists broke away was the emotional military question. There were early signs, among them the reception given to the recapitulation of the misdeeds of the returning armies in the Rhineland by Otto Brass of Remscheid,[29] that the delegates were dissatisfied with the government's military policy. Even Barth unex-pectedly took the floor to demand harsher policies toward the military authorities.[30] Action came, however, only after the intrusion of a radical delegation of Berlin soldiers. The Congress adjourned for long committee sessions; on reconvening, it overwhelmingly adopted the proposal pre-sented to it, the so-called Hamburg Points, despite the pronounced reluctance of the SPD leaders.

The Hamburg Points, adopted by what was supposedly the supreme organ of the state, imposed a new military policy on the government.[31] For the most part, the resolution represented a codification of the rebel-lious practices of the revolutionary soldiers; for instance, insignia of rank were to be abolished and the officers forbidden to carry side arms while off duty, "as a symbol of the shattering of militarism and of the abolition of total obedience [Kadavergehorsam]." The men were to elect (and remove, if necessary) their own officers, and the soldiers' councils would be responsible for discipline. The cabinet was to assume com-mand of the armed forces, under the supervision of the central council, thereby ending, it was hoped, the autonomy of the Supreme Command.

27. See Barth's speech, Allgemeiner Kongress, pp. 164–65.
28. Ibid., p. 182.
29. Ibid., pp. 33–36.
30. Ibid., pp. 54–56. Dittmann later claimed that he and Haase had known and approved of Barth's démarche in advance; Dittmann memoirs, p. 911.
31. Text in Allgemeiner Kongress, p. 181. The name comes from the fact that the provisions were modeled on those adopted in Hamburg after the counter-revolutionary scare of Dec. 6.

The resolution concluded with a demand that the standing army be replaced by the embryonic *Volkswehr* as quickly as possible.

Yet even the Hamburg Points, the most forceful and specific of all the resolutions of the Congress, had the force only of a declaration of intent, not of enacted law. The new practices could take effect only after promulgation and implementation by the cabinet, under the somewhat problematic supervision of the newly elected central council. Thus, like all the matters touched on by the Congress, the question was thrown back into the realm of party politics.

Collapse of the Joint Socialist Cabinet

The Congress' resolutions on socialization and the military posed some awkward problems for the Majority Socialists in the cabinet; for the three Independents they were a godsend, in that they gave apparent purpose again to their work in the cabinet. They knew from other party contacts[32] that the line taken by the Independents at the Congress was not an accurate picture of party opinion, especially not in its imposing unanimity, which was the product of special circumstances. In this knowledge they held to their positions and hoped that the formal resolutions of the Congress had given them the leverage to force the pace of change. But, however distorted the picture presented at the Congress, the experience had undercut the position of the party leaders more than they seemed to realize. There was no way they could quickly counteract the spectacle of a leadership isolated from its membership, and the negative impact of this image could not but be stronger than the positive effect of the two Congress votes the USPD wanted to exploit.

The further disposition of the Congress' socialization resolution is obscure. The Independents in the cabinet seem to have loyally supported the decision of the councils, and Barth's indiscreet public promise of immediate action, made to the Ruhr miners, was given political support by his two colleagues.[33] Yet there was no visible action, and as there are no minutes of cabinet deliberations for December 20–23 and no information in the cabinet's files we cannot know why. Probably the overwhelming practical problems again occasioned delay; possibly a voting stalemate occured, as it did on the military question. Probably, too, the Independents, except for Barth, did not give first priority to the issue. When they finally resigned from the cabinet, on December 29, the delay

32. See the next section of this chapter, esp. pp. 200–3 and 206–7.
33. Spethmann, I, 133–34; *Leipziger Volkszeitung*, Dec. 24, 1918. Barth, p. 94, implies that the central council had in effect authorized his declaration; no other evidence supports this suggestion, and the very tone of Barth's promise makes it improbable.

in socialization was among the reasons cited—but only as an after-thought.[34] This issue was only to come to the center of the political stage in the spring.

The issue that essentially brought on the final crisis of the coalition cabinet was the military question. The three people's commissioners from the USPD took their stand on the resolution of the Congress and, with only slight waverings, held out for its implementation in all essentials; Haase and Dittmann were plainly doubtful about parts of it, but their political beliefs required them to regard a decision of the Congress as definitive, and in any case the general tendency of the resolution was one with which they could agree.[35] The Majority Socialist leaders were dubious about the practicality of the resolution as well as worried about the effects on the security of the government if it were implemented in full. Their aversion to the Hamburg Points was strengthened by swift intervention by the officers; in rapid succession, the leading officers of the Supreme Command, the War Ministry, the Admiralty, and the Armistice Commission threatened resignation.[36] In short, a general strike of qualified officers was imminent, which would have forced an immediate, not a gradual reconstruction of the armed forces. On December 20, Groener, at Ebert's invitation, attended a meeting of the cabinet with the new central council, and his combination of threats and technical arguments convinced nearly all those present. It was apparent by the end of the meeting that the three SPD cabinet members and at least the leading voices of the central council were willing to approve a solution exempting the field army and the navy from application of the resolution and to revise the provisions that the officers felt as attacks on their personal honor.[37]

Such a compromise could only be enacted by the cabinet, but with the three Independents adamant this was impossible. Nor could the Hamburg Points be carried out so long as the three Majority Socialists objected. The deadlock was complete, and meantime the Supreme Command

34. Socialization was the last of eight points; see below, pp. 196–97. When Dittmann was reading out the points to the central council he seemed to stop after seven; the minutes then read: "(Zurufe: Die Sozialisierung!) Dazu kommt dann noch die Sozialisierung." Cabinet minutes for Dec. 28, *Regierung der VB*, II, 126; according to Dittmann memoirs, p. 945, the *Zurufer* was Barth.

35. Sauer, the most thoughtful of the students of the military question, concludes (pp. 171–72 and 179) that the Hamburg Points were useless as a serious basis for government policy.

36. *Wirren*, p. 23 (Hindenburg and Groener); DZA Potsdam, Reichskanzlei 2047, p. 133 (the war minister), and Reichskanzlei 2508/4, p. 28 (the secretary of the navy); cabinet minutes for Dec. 20, in *Zentralrat*, p. 26.

37. *Zentralrat*, pp. 25–43, esp. Ebert's summing-up on pp. 41–42. See the official notice in *Vorwärts*, Dec. 22, 1918.

could carry on as it wished.[38] The government's military policy before this had been vague and weak; now it was completely paralyzed on this, the most important issue confronting it.

The final blow to the collaboration of the two parties, again military in nature, was the attack of General Lequis' troops on a revolutionary Berlin formation known as the People's Naval Division, on Christmas Eve.[39] The cabinet, without, so far as is known, any protest from its Independent members, had been working for some time to bring the unruly formation under control; the resentful sailors, in turn, began to listen to more radical leaders and to consolidate support among the Berlin Independents. Suddenly, on December 23, the conflict erupted into a dangerous confrontation, during which the government was held prisoner and incommunicado in the Reichskanzlei for several hours, while City Commandant Otto Wels was seized and held captive by threatening sailors in the royal stables. Ebert summoned troops from the Lequis command to liberate the government; but then he sent them away again, negotiations during the evening having produced the prospect of a peaceful settlement. There followed an agitated telephone call from Lequis' chief of staff, telling Ebert that if he insisted on his rebuff to the fired-up troops they would be unusable in any similar situation in the future; Groener himself later rang up with the same message, and a threat to withdraw the Supreme Command's cooperation.[40] While Ebert, Scheidemann, and Landsberg were under this pressure, word came from the royal stables that Wels' life was in danger.[41] This news tipped the balance, and the war minister was ordered to mount an operation against the sailors.[42] The following morning, after a perfunctory ultimatum, some 800 of Lequis' remaining soldiers began an artillery bombardment of the sailors' headquarters in the palace. The attack failed, appropriately for these sad remnants of an ill-conceived enterprise; after making

38. See Hindenburg's secret telegram and public manifesto, printed in *Freiheit*, Jan. 2, 1919 (e), and Dec. 23, 1918 (e).

39. A good account of the immediate background to the conflict of December 23–24 is Bernstein, *Die deutsche Revolution*, pp. 103–4. On the People's Naval Division in general, see *Wirren*, pp. 17–19; Kurt Wrobel, *Die Volksmarinedivision* (Berlin, 1957); and the Division's own version of its history published in *Republik*, Dec. 29, 1918.

40. DZA Potsdam, Reichskanzlei, 2508/5, p. 41; Elben, p. 148.

41. *Vorwärts*, Dec. 27, 1918 (m); confirmed by the otherwise hostile Walter Oehme in *Freiheit*, Dec. 27, 1919 (m).

42. The precise nature of the orders to the war minister is in dispute, the minister himself maintaining that his orders spoke not only of freeing Wels but of rendering the sailors harmless; Wrobel, p. 135. Cf. Oehme in *Freiheit*, Dec. 27, 1919 (m), and Dec. 30, 1919 (m); *Wirren*, p. 36; *Vorwärts*, Dec. 27, 1918 (m); *Freiheit*, Dec. 31, 1918 (m).

some headway against the sailors, the soldiers had to abandon their efforts when a crowd of Berliners surged in among them during a temporary truce and made further fighting impossible.[43]

The failure to consult the three Independent cabinet members before these military operations in the center of Berlin were ordered was fatal to the socialist coalition. When a compromise settlement with the sailors seemed assured, Haase, Dittmann, and Barth had all gone home for the night; the rest of the crisis had been handled entirely by Ebert, Scheidemann, and Landsberg. The evidence suggests that once the three Majority Socialists had decided to risk bloodshed they were determined not to draw back again until the government had decisively asserted its authority. The Independents could not be relied upon to see the operation through, so they were kept in ignorance. Nothing could better demonstrate how collegiality had finally broken down in the cabinet under the frustrating stalemate of the past week. An even worse instance of this came the next morning when, as artillery fire resounded through the inner city, Ebert disclaimed knowledge of the orders for the operation against the sailors.[44] For the time being, Haase and his comrades did not press the point, though they must have understood fairly soon what had happened;[45] matters had reached a point where the central council would have to be called in to arbitrate, and full explanations could be demanded at that time.

The meeting with the central council took place on December 28, after the holidays. In sessions lasting from noon until past midnight, the council heard a full discussion of the issues dividing the cabinet.[46] About half the time was devoted to trying to clear up the origins of the attack on the sailors, which Ebert and his comrades chose to obscure by suppressing mention of the pressure from Lequis' command and Groener. The Independents could not find even the SPD's censored version of events attractive and concluded that "three members of the government, without consulting the other three, gave undefined full powers [*Blankovollmacht*] to the military camarilla to do whatever they might regard as necessary" toward freeing Wels.[47] Even the central council was disturbed.

From here the debate spilled over into questions of principle about the use of military force in such a situation. The three Majority Socialists

43. The operation is described in *Wirren*, pp. 38–42.
44. According to Dittmann, in *Ledebour-Prozess*, pp. 568–69. The three Independents first learned of their colleagues' story from *Vorwärts* on Dec. 27.
45. For instance, Lequis' chief of staff told Barth on the morning of Dec. 24 that Ebert was the source of his orders; record of the conversation in the Barth papers, I, item 44.
46. Cabinet minutes for Dec. 28, *Regierung der VB*, II, 73–131.
47. Barth, *ibid.*, II, 94.

were unrepentent to the point of belligerence; they had apparently crossed some psychological watershed during the long night of December 23–24. The real issue, they said, was the threat of violence from the left, against which the Independents had made it impossible for the government to act. The government in Berlin was constantly threatened with humiliation by radical minorities, mainly Spartacists, and might succumb any day to a well-organized putsch; indeed, Landsberg's first reaction to the fiasco of Lequis' last forces had been to demand removal of the government to some quieter place where it could function in peace and safety.[48] Ebert and the others were convinced there was no danger from the officers, who never did anything worse than offer to resign,[49] and they showed no more qualms about employing whatever military forces were available against the growing menace from the left.

The three Independents disagreed on every point. Radical dissatisfaction was not something to be suppressed by force; rather it could and should spur the cabinet to remedies: "If we put through serious economic measures and measures of social policy now, before the National Assembly, and not only take care of daily business, but rather bring the great issues to a conclusion, then the Spartacus Group is finished."[50] Only in this way could the government become secure: "A strong and powerful government . . . is only possible if we can base ourselves on the healthy popular forces in Berlin, on the confidence of the masses in Berlin. But to win this confidence, a break with the old system is the necessary precondition."[51] Continued reliance on the old "militarism" not only alienated those who should be the true support of the socialist government, but also endangered that government, for "militarism is the element from which a threat to the gains of the revolution is most likely to arise."[52] This was no time to be rallying the remnants of the old army against Spartacus; the old army should be scattered to the winds and a course struck toward a popular army. As the Independents' formal statement to the central council put it, "the government of the Socialist Republic cannot and must not rely militarily on the generals and the remnants of the old standing army, built on total obedience, but [must rely] only on a volunteer *Volkswehr* to be constructed on democratic principles."[53]

As the debates went on into the evening, nothing had been settled and no settlement by agreement appeared likely. The central council had

48. Cabinet minutes for Dec. 24, *ibid.*, II, 35; for Dec. 28, *ibid.*, II, 88 and 112.
49. Landsberg, *ibid.*, II, 115.
50. Dittmann, *ibid.*, II, 130.
51. Haase, *ibid.*, II, 109.
52. Dittmann, *ibid.*, II, 125.
53. *Freiheit*, Dec. 29, 1918.

heard both sides with some reserve. The Independents finally decided to force a clarification of their position by formally requesting the views of the central council on the questions that had occupied the meeting—above all, on recent military issues and their implications, from the embarrassing operation against the sailors to the general problem of how the socialist government ought to organize and use its armed forces.[54] These matters occupied seven of the eight questions posed; the eighth, an afterthought, raised the question of immediate socialization.[55]

The three Independents thus took their final stand on a narrow range of issues. The result, however, would probably have been the same whatever the issues, for although we have no record of the central council's deliberations on that evening, the evidence suggests that the council felt forced to regard the crisis as a party question: were the Majority Socialists or the Independents to run the government? If the council had reprimanded Ebert, Scheidemann, and Landsberg, as the Independents were asking it to do, the Majority Socialists would almost certainly have resigned. Some members of the council would have liked to try tinkering with the composition of the cabinet (for instance, replacing Barth or Ebert) without breaking up the coalition, but this was not a practical possibility, and in the end the council—Majority Socialist to a man—had to choose an SPD rather than a USPD cabinet.[56]

The choice was not stated directly; but the council's refusal to satisfy the Independents in answers to the eight questions resulted just as surely in the resignation of Haase, Dittmann, and Barth. The answer the Independents wanted was given to only two, relatively uncontroversial questions. On the critical point, the decision to proceed against the sailors with force, the central council tersely gave its approval. On the remaining issues (including socialization) the council requested further consultation with the cabinet.[57]

Just after midnight the three Independents resigned in a dignified final session with the central council. They reaffirmed their belief that the

54. Printed *ibid.*
55. See above, n. 34.
56. For indications of the views held in the council see the preliminary discussion on the previous evening in *Zentralrat*, pp. 66–69; and *Vorwärts*, Dec. 28, 1918 (e). Its separate deliberations on Dec. 28 were not recorded. The Independents in the cabinet maintained afterwards that if there had been even a minority of Independents in the central council the balance would have swung against Ebert and his colleagues; see Haase in *Freiheit*, Jan. 1, 1919, and Dittmann in *Ledebour-Prozess*, p. 557. This supposition is unlikely; the Majority Socialists in the council would surely have felt compelled to vote as a bloc along party lines. For a similar view see Jens Flemming, "Parlamentarische Kontrolle in der Novemberrevolution," *Archiv für Sozialgeschichte*, 11 (1971), 82–83 and 97–98.
57. Text in *Freiheit*, Dec. 29, 1918.

orders given to the military had been an impermissible act for a socialist government. Further delay in socialization and in the regulation of the military was irresponsible, they said, and placed the fruits of the revolution in jeopardy. Then, with courteous wishes for the success of the government, the three Independents left the scene of their seven weeks' work.[58]

Thereby was the keystone of socialist collaboration in the German postrevolutionary regime brought down; as the rest of the structure collapsed over the following weeks, the socialist claim to command the fate of Germany distintegrated. Socialist unity had fractured again, not along the fissure that many later observers have pointed to as natural—that corresponding to the division between Communists and Social Democrats in 1921[59]—but along the lines of established party loyalty. These lines, too, had their basis in certain real differences of attitude and policy, as the foregoing account has shown; to judge that Haase's and Dittmann's views hardly differed from those of the SPD is to be misled by actions conditioned by circumstance (including the effort to make the coalition work) or omissions arising from uncertainty and diffidence.[60] But more than this, party bonds themselves determined the regrouping of socialists. We must now examine how it was that the highly fissiparous USPD came through these times of bitter mutual distrust to survive, for two more years, as the rallying-point of left-wing socialism in Germany.

Crisis in the USPD

The departure of the Independents from the government should have eased the internal tensions of the USPD, for it meant an end to an intolerable situation wherein much of the party opposed a government in which its own leadership participated. This, indeed, was the long-term effect of their resignation. At the time, however, it seemed that the leaders' move to return to their party might have come too late; the USPD was in the midst of a potentially serious crisis, the worst before the intervention of the Communist International in its affairs in 1920.

The decision to enter the cabinet had never been popular in the USPD; indeed, even the party executive's original manifesto explaining its decision was defensive in tone and singularly lacking in conviction.[61] Still, the policy was widely accepted, with reservations, as a necessary

58. Text of the declaration *ibid.;* Haase's parting words are in *Regierung der VB,* II, 141.
59. The locus classicus of this suggestion is Rosenberg, *Geschichte,* esp. pp. 30–31.
60. Cf. *ibid.,* pp. 47–48; *Regierung der VB,* I, lxxii–lxxxiii.
61. Text in *Leipziger Volkszeitung,* Nov. 13, 1918. The need for such an explanation is illustrated by an editorial *ibid.,* Nov. 11, 1918.

evil, and, at the confidential party conferences held at the time, a majority apparently refrained from any direct challenge to the leadership's judgment. The restive radicals who could not agree were held in line by party solidarity. They exercised pressure privately; for instance, the Independents of the Rhineland sent word through their leader, Otto Brass, that they expected the three Independents to enforce the party's will in all matters or resign at once from the cabinet.[62] In public, however, even the radicals generally refrained from direct public criticism of the policy of collaboration for several weeks—in Ledebour's case until after December 6. And the party press—even the radical Berlin *Mitteilungs-Blatt,* until December 1—was silent on the internal differences of the party.[63]

This underground tension was aggravated by dissatisfaction, reaching far beyond the radicals in the ranks of the party, over the leadership's failure to do its allotted work effectively. At the end of the war the USPD had a small central operation adapted to its limited membership, its small income, and conditions of semilegality. Suddenly the party was no longer a struggling movement of the extreme left but was at the center of national politics, with growing membership and the highest of ambitions— and a central organization that could not adapt. In November and December 1918 the central office was grotesquely shorthanded; with three of the four principal members of the party executive—Haase, Dittmann, and Ledebour—fully occupied in the government and the councils, the whole burden of the party's work fell on Luise Zietz and a few salaried assistants.[64] The daily business of the executive suffered, and necessary improvements in party machinery were not made. There were whole areas of the country untouched by the USPD; new local parties and new newspapers needed to be established, together with the host of satellite organizations, such as youth groups, that Social Democracy traditionally provided for its followers. Such things required money, more money than the party had, but everyone felt that shortcomings in the central office played their part in frustrating the party's desire to develop the full-scale apparatus it would need to compete with the SPD.[65]

Much of this criticism was unfair, in view of the founding congress'

62. Letter to Dittmann, Nov. 13, 1918, in Dittmann papers, I, Dokumente und Originalbriefe, item 57.
63. Ledebour in *Freiheit,* Dec. 7, 1918 (e), and Dec. 13, 1918 (e). An exception was the outspokenly radical *Gothaer Volksblatt;* see Buchsbaum, pp. 110–11.
64. Dittmann memoirs, p. 902. Däumig, who had been taken on as secretary in the party executive after Dittmann's arrest in February 1918, resigned shortly after the revolution (the exact date is unknown); he, too, was occupied full time in the councils.
65. See the debate on Luise Zietz's *Geschäftsbericht* in USPD *Parteitag,* March 1919, pp. 47–74.

deliberate decision to limit the powers of the leadership. But local leaders wanted guidance, and here they had a legitimate complaint. Apart from the most radical locals, few party leaders liked the extreme autonomy they had in the absence of effective central leadership; it placed great responsibility on them while momentous events, which they did not fully understand, were occurring, and it was evidently leading to the disintegration of the party. The suggestion of a party congress was not well received in Berlin headquarters, however, even when it came from such a respectable source as the Saxon party conference of November 18.[66] The party leaders did not want to take the best men of the party away from their pressing local affairs for several days in such times, especially not to deal with what the leaders doubtless saw as carping criticism. But behind these considerations probably lay an even stronger reason: a party congress could be dangerous to party unity. Much of the demand for a congress came from the increasingly aggressive left wing—for instance, the Spartacists and the Berlin shop stewards, as discussed below —who were vehemently opposed to existing party policy. The leadership saw no reason to sponsor an assembly at which the recalcitrants could muster their forces, especially since it was convinced it was following the only possible course. The leadership had its way. There were consultations in Berlin with provincial leaders,[67] but in spite of repeated demands the executive refused to call a congress and continued on its course.

The tacit policy of the USPD leadership in November and December, supported by a good part of the membership, was to work with the Majority Socialists to the very limits of the possible in order to keep alive the prospects of the revolution. There were good reasons for such an orientation, no matter how much the Independents might dislike the SPD's policies or its leaders. For one thing, collaboration was necessary if the Independents were to have direct influence in the postrevolutionary institutions. In the country as a whole, as well as most cities, including Berlin, the USPD was simply not strong enough to govern without accepting the SPD into partnership, and the prospect of opposition violated the USPD's sense of its right and responsibility to help rule as the true party of the revolution. Opposition would also mean loss of influence over the course of affairs, for the SPD would certainly seek friends to the right and ally itself with bourgeois parties. Such an alliance would

66. *Leipziger Volkszeitung,* Nov. 19, 1918. The same demand came from the Berlin general assembly (*Freiheit,* Dec. 16, 1918 [m]) and a conference of the party's Coastal district (*GdA: Chronik,* II, 43).

67. Zietz, in USPD *Parteitag,* March 1919, p. 173, refers to three. The consultation on Dec. 6 was apparently a regular national conference; others may have been held on the occasions mentioned in n. 82 and n. 83 below or at the time of the Workers' and Soldiers' Congress. None was discussed in the party press.

abandon the advance toward socialism and turn against the far left; the USPD would be caught ineffectually in the middle, socialist unity would be destroyed, and with it the revolution.

A united front, in the form of common government, was thus seen as imperative by the Haase wing of the party. Dittmann, in a speech delivered at the Workers' and Soldiers' Congress, elevated collaboration to the status of a general principle for the furtherance of the revolution.[68] In being so forthright Dittmann went too far, drawing a great deal of criticism from within his party; but the practice of the Independents in many cities and states was based on the same principle, whether clearly enunciated or not.[69] This was, in fact, the dominant feature of the Independents' work in the early weeks of the revolutionary period, notwithstanding the attention focused on the vigorous and angry radicals.

Sentiments favoring socialist unity had been revived by the ending of the most divisive issue, the war, and the opening of an era in which the socialist movement seemed likely to predominate. Axiomatically, the power of Social Democracy lay in its being representative of the broad masses of the workers, and hence of the majority of the people; this principle precluded division into two camps. The ideal course would have been reunification of the two parties, as was urged by many ordinary members of the USPD and by a number of intellectuals on the party's right wing. Kautsky and his small following cautiously urged fusion, arguing that Social Democracy needed to concentrate its strength in order to carry through the measures of socialist reform begun by the revolution; he expected, moreover, that the excesses of right and left would be curbed by reunification and that the center of gravity of a reunited movement would rest, as before the war, in his own variety of centrism, now condemned to an isolated position in both parties.[70] At the end of December, Bernstein went so far as to rejoin the SPD while retaining his membership in the USPD, hoping (in vain) to set an example for others.[71] But unequivocal calls for reunification came mostly from the

68. *Allgemeiner Kongress,* esp. p. 23.
69. The USPD and SPD were joint members of the governments of all significant German states after the revolution except Hesse, Mecklenburg, and Anhalt—and Braunschweig, where the USPD held its monopoly until February 1919.
70. The strongest expression of Kautsky's views is a manuscript of about Dec. 20, 1918, Kautsky papers, A 83, marked "Nicht veröffentlicht wegen Bedenken Haases." See also Kautsky, "Was nun?" *Der Sozialist,* Jan. 4, 1919; Kautsky, *Mein Verhältnis,* pp. 9–10.
71. *Freiheit,* Dec. 25, 1918. No other prominent Independent followed Bernstein's lead. In March a ruling of the USPD party congress forced Bernstein to choose, and he chose the SPD. For a further year he continued as the principal sponsor of an organization known as the Central Office for the Unification of Social Democracy, which had a negligible impact on the political scene.

SPD, where *Vorwärts* and all but the extreme right wing of the party supported the idea.[72] Unity was easier for them to contemplate; they could rely on greater numbers to give their party predominance, and they were sure that the more objectionable elements of the USPD would remain apart from any united party.[73]

Most Independents were not so ready to see their party split and the bulk of it submerged in the SPD. While paying lip service to proletarian unity, they valued the integrity of their own party, were proud of its past and committed to its future. Too much resentment and suspicion toward the SPD was stored up, and too much indignation at Majority Socialist policies since 1914. For some Independents, including Ledebour, staying clear of the SPD leaders was "a matter of cleanliness";[74] others were put off by the prospect of having their most profound political commitments subject to suppression by majority vote or bureaucratic manipulation, as had happened in the early part of the war. Sentiments of this sort affected many party militants, especially in the cities where the party was strong; the Leipzig party paper thought that "not even a baker's dozen" could be found for fusion of the parties in either Leipzig or Berlin.[75] Consequently, even those leaders most concerned about socialist unity—Hilferding, for one, shared many of Kautsky's views, including his belief that centrists could eventually gain control of a reunited party —could not advocate a course that would mean separation from many important radicals (and even stubborn moderates) and, in effect, re-entry into the SPD as a relatively small faction.[76] More than once rumors of imminent unification were denied.[77] The USPD leaders found themselves arguing that the party still had an important role to play in holding high the banner of true revolutionary socialism; if it did this the followers of the Majority Socialists would gradually force their leaders to return to the right path, which would then make fusion possible, or, if the Majority Socialists continued their drift to the right, the masses

72. Various indications in *Vorwärts,* Nov. 15, 1918; Dec. 7, 1918 (m); a report of an assembly of the Berlin SPD, Dec. 17, 1919 (m); Dec. 20, 1918 (e). Also Friedrich Stampfer, *Erfahrungen und Erkenntnisse* (Cologne, 1957), p. 226.

73. These thoughts are explicit in *Vorwärts,* Jan. 13, 1919.

74. Ledebour in *Allgemeiner Kongress,* pp. 175–76.

75. *Leipziger Volkszeitung,* Dec. 27, 1918.

76. See the expression of Hilferding's private views in a letter to Kautsky, Sept. 8, 1918, Kautsky papers, D XII 632. The considerations advanced above indicate why it would have been nearly impossible for Haase and Dittmann to change parties after the Workers' and Soldiers' Congress in the hope of more effectively serving their goals in the SPD (as suggested in Rosenberg, *Geschichte,* pp. 50–52). The psychology and party dynamics of the situation made such a decision excessively unattractive for the leading Independents, who furthermore had not given up hope of bringing their own party under control again.

77. For example, *Freiheit,* Nov. 21, 1918 (e); Zietz, *ibid.,* Dec. 24, 1918 (m).

would gradually rally around the USPD standard and achieve unity there.

There remained possibilities of party collaboration, however, such as in the coming elections. The Magdeburg-Anhalt organizations of the two parties decided in November to conclude a political truce; a few days later the Erfurt USPD, the party's strongest organization in Thuringia, came out for joint lists in the National Assembly elections.[78] To be sure, the party conference on December 6 decided, with only one dissenter, against joint lists, which looked too like a preliminary step toward reunification;[79] but the idea of an all-out campaign against brother socialists was still repugnant. The Greater Thuringian party organization was still talking of joint lists after the Workers' and Soldiers' Congress, while other organizations and party journalists were advocating the looser form of electoral cooperation known as "tied lists."[80] The party took no public position on tied lists but does not seem to have discouraged them. What did discourage them, and most effectively, was the bitterness that arose between the two parties after the events of Christmas week in Berlin and the January disturbances in Berlin and other cities. These events were probably responsible for the fact that only six of the USPD's district organizations went into the elections in even this very mild form of comradeship with the SPD.[81]

The radicals in the party were unhappy with what they saw as a tendency toward political horse trading, about the emphasis the whole party was giving to the coming elections, and, most of all, that the elections were being held at all at this time. The latent discontent in the party first took a turn toward open revolt when the government announced its November 29 decision on a date for the voting. As related in an earlier chapter, the official USPD attitude toward the National Assembly originally was that the matter was not immediate and could for the present simply be ignored—a convenient doctrine that might have succeeded in glossing over the party's internal differences. The party executive gave no further guidance to the party, at least not publicly, until its manifesto

78. *Vorwärts*, Nov. 26, 1918; *Freiheit*, Nov. 30, 1918 (e).

79. See the resulting manifesto in *Freiheit*, Dec. 8, 1918; and Luise Zietz's motivation, *ibid.*, Dec. 24, 1918 (m). *Vorwärts*, Dec. 14, 1918 (m), reported rumors of a much larger minority in favor of joint lists.

80. *Vorwärts*, Dec. 23, 1918 (m); on "verbundene Listen" see Siegfried Nestriepke in *Der Sozialist*, Dec. 5, 1918, pp. 6–7, and a number of later articles in the same journal. The purpose of the device was to give one or the other of the cooperating parties a chance at an extra seat in a particular voting district from votes that might otherwise be wasted.

81. *Vierteljahrshefte zur Statistik des Deutschen Reichs*, 28 (1919), first supplement, 4–5. The six included Northern Bavaria, Thuringia, Halle-Merseburg, Hamburg-Bremen, and two rural districts. The arrangement resulted in no extra seats for either party.

of November 27.[82] Issued to rally support at a time when the Independents were under severe pressure from the Majority Socialists within the cabinet, this manifesto set forth the reasons why the National Assembly, though eventually a necessity for Germany, could not possibly be elected within the next few months. The party leadership took a stand on this compromise solution—which had the unfortunate effect of underlining its capitulation two days later, when the date of the elections was provisionally set for February 16. The surrender followed an ultimatum from the Majority Socialists and a hastily convened meeting of leading Independents; publicly the party could only hint at this background, emphasizing instead that the Independents had secured to the Workers' and Soldiers' Congress the right to reverse the cabinet's decision—an empty concession, as it turned out.[83] To have admitted openly the pressure of the SPD ultimatum would have been more likely to lead to an immediate party revolt against the coalition than to sympathy with the leaders' plight. As it was the decision, and the way its announcement was handled, served as powerful solvents on the bonds uniting the rank and file with the leadership.

A week later, on December 6, a gathering (probably a national party conference) was meeting in Berlin to discuss the party's policy in the coming election campaign when news came of the putsch attempt. To Ledebour these events were so obviously the consequence of governmental negligence and double-dealing that an argument broke out in the course of which he had to be restrained from a physical attack on his fellow party chairman, Haase.[84] This was a new low in intraparty amity. Ledebour's views were apparently not endorsed by the conference, but they were shared, at least in part, by a good many party members, principally, but not only, in Berlin. The reputation of the coalition government, and of the USPD leaders for continuing to take part, declined further than ever on the left.

The most prominent dissident element in the party at this point was still the Spartacists, who had despised the leaders and official policies of the USPD as weak and halfhearted even during the war. Regular Inde-

82. Text in *Freiheit*, Nov. 27, 1918 (m). This manifesto was quite probably the product of consultations with provincial leaders, perhaps in conjunction with the conference of state governments on November 25, which brought a number of prominent Independents to Berlin.

83. See Zietz's summons to an urgent meeting of the party leaders on Nov. 29, in the Barth papers, I, item 155; Zietz in USPD *Parteitag*, March 1919, p. 173; *Freiheit*'s comments in the issue of Nov. 30, 1918 (m).

84. Dittmann memoirs, pp. 895–96. *Vorwärts*, Dec. 14, 1918 (m), first published an account of the dramatic scene; Ledebour replied with a milder version in *Freiheit*, Dec. 15, 1918.

pendents were often exasperated by the Spartacists' total lack of loyalty toward their party and by their encouragement of recklessness among the workers; nevertheless many Independents tried to work with them, hoping to limit their irresponsible behavior and not wanting to see yet a third socialist party, especially not one to the USPD's left. When Liebknecht was released from prison in October 1918 he was actually invited to join the party executive, to which he replied, characteristically, that he could only consider the invitation if the USPD would go over completely to Spartacist principles and practice.[85] On November 9 the Spartacist leaders were prominent in the debates about entry into the government, and for a brief time they nearly had their way. Eventually, however, their counsel was ignored, and when the Spartacists also decided to boycott the Berlin executive council, they opposed the efforts of all factions of the Independents; Spartacist groups in most other cities took the same course.[86] The rift with the party grew steadily wider.

The Spartacist movement, however, was not large. At the time of the revolution it cannot have had more than a few thousand regular followers; only about ten of its people were delegates to the Workers' and Soldiers' Congress in December.[87] The Spartacists had built up a standing since 1914 that gave them influence beyond their numbers, and like the rest of the socialist movement they increased their membership before long; but on the basis of size they could have been of little significance—they could not have carried out a successful coup in any German city, and certainly not Berlin, except in alliance with other groups of the left. The Independents, with their close relations with Spartacus, recognized this weakness and never shared the exaggerated fears of the Majority Socialists about the Spartacist threat, especially since they knew that Liebknecht and Luxemburg had no enthusiam for putsches. A threat existed, nonetheless, though of a different sort. In Spartacist propaganda the leaders' sophisticated understanding of the revolution often took second place to passion, some of it disturbingly crude, which had the effect, not of warming up the whole working class toward a second revolution, but of overheating the extreme left.[88] All too many of the new members of the Spartacus League, perhaps the majority, were hotblooded young people or hyperradical riffraff, deserters and the like, people who could not be brought to accept discipline, restraint, or compromise.[89] There was a serious shortage of reliable leaders in the lower

85. Liebknecht's diary in *Illustrierte Geschichte,* p. 203.
86. Kolb, *Arbeiterräte,* pp. 144–45.
87. R. Müller, *Kaiserreich,* II, 204.
88. Kolb, *Arbeiterräte,* pp. 149–151, treats this problem at length.
89. Rosenberg, *Geschichte,* pp. 29–30; Richard Müller, *Der Bürgerkrieg in*

ranks who might have been able to direct the energies of the militants, and these latter came to regard every demonstration or strike as the possible start of the revolution; there was a danger of a putsch attempt by Spartacist followers, even if this was not wanted by the leaders, every time emotions ran high. Inevitably, the Spartacists became identified in the public mind with their more uncontrollable elements.

If the Independents tended to shy away from the heedless activities of many Spartacists, the latter in turn were far from comradely toward the party that was nominally theirs, and especially toward the policies of its leaders. *Rote Fahne,* the Spartacist newspaper, flayed the provisional government unreservedly from the start, declaring after a week that "nothing essential has changed in the state of the Hohenzollerns" and accusing the government of wanting to "liquidate" the revolution.[90] The executive council was spared attacks of this sort at first, only to be written off later as "the fifth wheel on the cart of a crypto-capitalist government clique" and as the "sarcophagus of the revolution."[91] The attack on the party as such was opened only at the end of November, after publication of the party's official position on the National Assembly. To the Spartacists, the incompatibility of the National Assembly and the revolutionary movement was axiomatic; the USPD's awkward attempt to combine the two was the last straw. On November 29 Rosa Luxemburg systematically and exasperatedly reviewed the history of the party, concluding that "Independent Social Democracy has been a child of weakness from the beginning, and compromise is the essence of its nature. . . . A party so constituted, suddenly confronted with the historic decisions of the revolution, was bound to fail miserably." She ended the article by calling for a party congress as the only possible way of setting things right.[92]

The demand for a party congress was, as we have seen, ignored by the party executive. The Spartacists' campaign of abuse, which took on personal overtones, and their increasingly provocative behavior after December 6, when they began to stage armed demonstrations, were not.[93] Not surprisingly, at the general assembly of the Berlin Independents on December 15 Haase called on the Spartacists to follow the logic

Deutschland: Geburtswehen der Republik (Berlin, 1925), pp. 86–87; Kolb, *Arbeiterräte,* pp. 146–47. For a milder version in a Communist source see *Illustrierte Geschichte,* p. 265.

90. *Rote Fahne,* Nov. 18 and 19, 1918 (articles by Luxemburg and Liebknecht).
91. *Ibid.,* Dec. 12, 1918.
92. *Ibid.,* Nov. 29, 1918; see also her earlier editorial on the subject, *ibid.,* Nov. 20, 1918.
93. On the armed demonstrations, see Emil Eichhorn, *Eichhorn über die Januar-Ereignisse* (Berlin, 1919), pp. 34–35.

of their views and leave the party, and the party press, previously embarrassedly reticent about Spartacus, took up the point.[94] The centrists, above all, regarded Spartacist views on the council system as unacceptable (as well as dangerous) and felt that the time had come to cut off the offending member, especially when voting at the general assembly showed that the Spartacists remained a small minority, even in Berlin.[95] The Spartacist leaders, however, were still unready to give up the advantages of being inside the party. They continued their efforts to force the executive to call a party congress, in the belief—which had some basis in events at the Workers' and Soldiers' Congress—that the USPD membership, then observing a loyal silence regarding its representatives in the government, would overthrow the coalition and repudiate the National Assembly if given the chance. This demand became an ultimatum on December 22; two days later the party executive refused, for the first time openly, on the grounds that to summon all the prominent figures of the party to Berlin would disrupt the agitation for the National Assembly.[96] The Spartacists then assembled their own conference in Berlin on December 29 and voted, with only three dissenters— one of them the shrewd organizer Leo Jogiches—to separate from the USPD.[97]

The following day the Spartacist delegates, reinforced by representatives of the previously separate left radicals of Bremen, Hamburg, and Dresden, met for the founding congress of what was to be the German Communist Party (KPD). It was not the uplifting occasion it should have been for Rosa Luxemburg and her associates. The formal leadership of the old group was accepted without question by the delegates, not so their ideas; the members of the congress showed a disturbing tendency to vote for the most left-leaning, radical-sounding policy without considering the realities of the situation or the needs of a political party. By a substantial majority they rejected the arguments of Paul Levi and

94. The general assembly is reported at length in *Freiheit,* Dec. 16, 1918 (m), and Dec. 17, 1918 (m). See the editorial in the first of these issues; *Leipziger Volkszeitung,* Dec. 16, 1918; and even the more radical Halle *Volksblatt,* quoted in *Freiheit,* Dec. 19, 1918 (e).

95. Rosa Luxemburg's resolution, which would have attracted much radical as well as Spartacist support, was defeated by a vote of 485 to 195. One purpose of the leadership in attacking the extreme left at this time may have been to weaken and tame the radicals by driving out the Spartacists (see Kolb, *Arbeiterräte,* p. 208), though there is no direct evidence for such an intention.

96. *Rote Fahne,* Dec. 24, 1918, and *Freiheit,* Dec. 24, 1918 (m).

97. The resolution on separation is in *Der Gründungsparteitag der K.P.D.: Protokoll und Materialien,* ed. Hermann Weber (Frankfurt on Main and Vienna, 1969), pp. 63–65. It is reported, *ibid.,* p. 9, that the other two negative votes came from Karl Minster (Mülheim) and Werner Hirsch (Cuxhaven); in Kolb, *Arbeiterräte,* p. 217n., that they came from Braunschweig delegates.

Rosa Luxemburg that participation in the National Assembly could bring important agitational benefits and voted to boycott the elections.[98] Only by a parliamentary maneuver were the delegates prevented from voting on the trade-union question; they would almost certainly have voted that all Communists must separate themselves from existing trade unions.[99] A spirit of violent action was in the air, enough to worry the leaders.[100] In all these attitudes, though most concretely in the parliamentary boycott, the new Communists were heedlessly flying in the face of prevailing working-class opinion, refusing to consider the need for alliance and adjustment. These characteristics were known in the polemics of the time as "sectarianism," and their effect was greatly to restrict recruitment to the new party. In consequence, the split, as Levi later admitted, had "scarcely any influence on the organization of the USP";[101] and the weak appeal of the Communist alternative relieved the force of the Independents' own crisis.

The separatism of the Spartacists was, however, only one of the USPD's internal conflicts, the most clear-cut but not the most dangerous. The strain was becoming intense between the impatient, activist groups in the party, often grounded in factory organizations, including the Berlin shop stewards, and the more cautious, passive party members, who were well represented in the leadership and thought in terms of long-range pursuit of socialism through means familiar from prewar Social Democratic practice. Whatever the incidental factors working to produce the behavior of the USPD delegation at the Workers' and Soldiers' Congress, the exasperation and intransigence displayed there genuinely reflected the sentiments of a growing part of the party. For these people, the policies of the party executive were blocking development of the revolution. This tension was to dominate the internal politics of the USPD for the next two years; in December 1918 it nearly caused a serious breach in the party.

In Berlin, where the break nearly occurred, the most ominous sign of the party crisis was the formal reconstitution of the wartime factory op-

98. *Gründungsparteitag der K.P.D.*, p. 135. Rühle was sponsor of the winning motion.

99. *Ibid.*, pp. 164–65. Bock, pp. 92–102, discusses the origins and significance of the issues defining the Communist ultraradicals at this congress.

100. According to later testimony, Jogiches and even Rosa Luxemburg were so upset by the congress that they spoke of abandoning foundation of a new party at that time; see Klara Zetkin in KPD *Parteitag*, April 1920, p. 58; Levi in *Die Internationale* (KPD), Dec. 1, 1920, pp. 42–43; Ruth Fischer, *Stalin and German Communism* (Cambridge, Mass., 1948), p. 79n.

101. Letter of Nov. 1920 to Fernand Loriot, Levi papers, P 126.

position—this time in opposition to the leadership of the USPD. The first recorded meeting of this group, since the revolution, occurred on December 14, after a week of conflict between the government and the executive council (which had until then occupied most of the time of the leading shop stewards).[102] The revival of their organization may have played some part in the radicals' dominance at the Congress that began two days later. The first appearance of the "Revolutionary Shop Stewards" before the public followed an assembly of its leaders on December 21 at which a resolution was unanimously adopted calling on the USPD party executive, in the tone of an ultimatum, to "summon a party congress, no later than the end of December, which shall determine the principles and tactics to be observed by the USP." The resolution also demanded

a clear separation from the Majority Socialists, immediate resignation of the USP members from the Ebert-Scheidemann cabinet in order to avert their expulsion from the USP, a resolute fight against the Majority Socialists in the coming elections, conduct of the election campaign in an antiparliamentary spirit, and an uncompromising proletarian-revolutionary policy.[103]

The party executive, doubtless feeling secure in its own evaluation of majority sentiment—especially after the Berlin general assembly of December 15—made no public reply beyond its brief notice, addressed to both the shop stewards and the Spartacists, that a party congress was impossible at such a time.[104]

In consequence, the shop stewards, and the party politicians closest to them, came very near to abandoning the USPD. When a Berlin party assembly met on December 28 to nominate the party's district list of candidates for the elections, the popular figures Däumig and Richard Müller refused to stand on the same list as Haase, thus giving the Berlin Independents a choice between them and the party leadership; party chairman Ledebour confused the issue further by joining them in their ultimatum.[105] The party was not ready for power plays of this sort, which

102. Pieck, I, 446–47. According to Ledebour (*Ledebour-Prozess*, p. 44) the shop stewards on Jan. 4 were "nahezu dieselben Personen" as those at the meeting of Nov. 2; we may assume that this was true also for their activities in December.

103. *Rote Fahne*, Dec. 23, 1918. This may have been the first time the name "Revolutionary Shop Stewards" was formally used; the comments of an editorial writer in *Freiheit*, Dec. 23, 1918 (e), make it clear that he had no idea what the group was.

104. *Freiheit*, Dec. 24, 1918 (m).

105. Account of the assembly, *ibid.*, Dec. 29, 1918; Ledebour gave an account of the background behind the move, *ibid.*, Jan. 3, 1919 (m), and in USPD *Reichskonferenz*, Sept. 1920, pp. 212–23; see also Däumig in USPD *Parteitag*, March 1919, pp. 263–64.

ran entirely contrary to Social Democratic tradition; in particular, the official local party leadership, itself very radical, at least in words, gave no support to the move. The assembly chose Haase, though it placed him only second on the list, behind the radical Police President Emil Eichhorn. The only effect of Müller's and Däumig's maneuver was to isolate the old shop stewards group within the party, at least for the moment.

At the assembly, Ledebour had expressed closer sympathies with the Spartacists, for all their faults, than with Haase; and the obvious next step for the shop stewards was to try to reach an accommodation in this direction. The curious halfheartedness with which this was attempted may reflect second thoughts after their rebuff in the Berlin assembly, as well as a certain resentment toward the Spartacists for having proceeded to found their own party without consultation;[106] in any case, the episode clearly illustrates the characteristic uncertainty of the shop stewards movement in matters of party politics. Two days of the Spartacists' congress—the founding congress of the Communist Party—were permitted to pass before the shop stewards made their approach. By this time the congress had adopted a political course sure to repel such men as Däumig and Ledebour; and the approach, when made, was consequently not serious, consisting of aimless discussion followed by the posing of obviously unacceptable demands.[107] Again the shop stewards came off badly; and this time Ledebour finally felt compelled to resign as party chairman.[108] The factory radicals, for all their revolutionary energy, clearly had no constructive ideas yet on party organization, and until they evolved such ideas they had no place to go.

And so the crisis, insofar as it threatened the structure of the USPD, passed with little damage done, thanks to the ineffectiveness of the two challengers from the left. The Spartacists took with them the party's Chemnitz organization and newspaper, thereby destroying the USPD in that district for nearly a year, and most of the Stuttgart membership, though none of the party apparatus there. In March an important minority defected in Braunschweig, and in April the whole Hanau organization. Elsewhere, apart from a few local branches (including Spandau), the USPD lost only small minorities from its organizations, mainly those

106. See the shop stewards' declaration in *Freiheit*, Jan. 3, 1919 (e); Ledebour in USPD *Reichskonferenz*, Sept. 1920, p. 213; R. Müller, *Bürgerkrieg*, pp. 86–88.
107. Account by Liebknecht in *Gründungsparteitag der K.P.D.*, pp. 270–80.
108. *Freiheit*, Jan. 3, 1919 (m). According to Däumig (USPD *Reichskonferenz*, Sept. 1920, p. 180) and Max Sievers (*Der Arbeiter-Rat*, 2 [1920], no. 19/20, 4), Ledebour, even after the failure of the talks with the Spartacists, still wanted to proceed with formation of a new party and had to be dissuaded by Däumig and others.

who had already thought of themselves as Spartacists.[109] Had the split divided the shop stewards from the USPD as well, the potential for the new party would have been much greater. The shop stewards movement in Berlin had its counterpart in many other large cities, with loose connections through the Metalworkers' Union. As in Berlin, the groups elsewhere were minorities, but minorities that included some of the party's most valuable activists; in such cities as Braunschweig and Düsseldorf they held great potential power. With a credible program and shrewd political leadership, they could have mounted a formidable threat to the established direction, or even the existence, of the USPD. Their lack of these assets, then and later, was important to the history of the party.

109. Günter Uebel, "Der gegenwärtige Stand der Erforschung des organisatorischen Aufbaus der KPD nach dem Gründungsparteitag," in *Die Gründung der Kommunistischen Partei Deutschlands* (Berlin, 1959), pp. 79–87. On Stuttgart, see Crispien in USPD *Parteitag,* Oct. 1920, pp. 96–97.

CHAPTER 7

Civil War (*January to May 1919*)

The tensions in Berlin ended in violence there in January, which spread to most of the important industrial areas of the country over the following months. It was systematic political violence, coming in part from radicals whose frustrations spilled over into attempts at a second revolution, in much larger part from the military operations of the Reich government, which was determined to reassert its authority and meet, or even forestall, force with force. Troops of the new Reichswehr moved up and down Germany suppressing all challenges to the authority of Berlin, whether violent or not. German fought German viciously in the streets, sometimes in pitched battle. In spite of their disorganized, sporadic quality, the conflicts of January–May deserve the title of civil war.

After the first conflicts in January, in Berlin and Bremen, the outcome could scarcely be in doubt. Among the workers only a relatively small number of militant radicals cared to engage in armed conflict. The government's new forces, though numerically small, were militarily adequate to deal with scattered, uncertain opposition, and they were growing; the balance of confidence quickly passed to the side of the government. By the end of January, the government's superiority in armed force was already evident; by March, any real hope of resistance was gone; in May, the last centers of defiance were eliminated.

Independent Socialists were in the thick of most of these losing struggles, and the experience was formative and traumatic for the party and its factions. Not that the party as such was heavily involved in the civil war; local party organizations, if involved at all, tended to play a subordinate role to council organizations, and the party executive had no part at all in the struggles (save as an outside, moderating force in a few instances). But the party was necessarily affected by the failure of all its factions' tactics to extend, or at least consolidate, the gains of the revolution. The careful efforts of responsible council leaders to make their organizations permanent power factors had as little success as heedless insurrection or stolid noncooperation; the government met all with military force. The government's policy was widely abhorred by the working

212

class, and even as it succeeded in the short run it activated new masses of support for the socialist left. But it blocked off, one after another, the revolutionary perspectives of Independents of all stripes. The end of the civil war found the USPD a rapidly growing party of radical protest but one whose role in the postrevolutionary development of Germany was less clear than ever.

First Confrontations: Berlin and Bremen

The first focus of events was Berlin, where the government (with Lequis' forces dissolved and the first small Free Corps only starting to assemble on the outskirts of the city) carried on through the ten days after Christmas in a condition of extreme weakness. It survived only because the leaders on the revolutionary side, even if they had been sure how little military support the government had, did not yet want to seize power. The revolutionaries knew that a radical seizure of power at that time would provoke the hostility of large numbers of Berlin workers, not to mention the rest of the city's population, and strong opposition from the rest of the Reich except a few large cities and industrial areas. It would mean civil war, in all probability a losing civil war. Such a rising would be equivalent to a putsch; and with the tide running strongly in the direction of still greater dissatisfaction, the revolutionaries could, it seemed, afford to wait.

In this tense situation any incident might set off uncontrollable reactions. On January 4, the Prussian government (whose Independent members had just resigned) attempted to dismiss Emil Eichhorn from his post as police president of Berlin. Eichhorn, a popular radical figure in Berlin who headed the USPD's list for the National Assembly elections, had tried to combine his (not very effective) command of the police with continued partisan activity, and had made himself widely mistrusted in the process.[1] The attempt to dismiss him was bound to make trouble; coming at a moment when so many frustrated revolutionaries were spoiling for a fight, it caused a week of violence in the capital that significantly changed the situation.

January 5 being a Sunday, the local USPD leadership (of which Eichhorn was a member) and the shop stewards called a mass protest demonstration.[2] The response was enormous, far larger than had been

1. His political partisanship was the main subject of a concentrated journalistic attack that opened suddenly on Jan. 1; see *Vorwärts,* Jan. 1–5, 1919. Eichhorn's disingenuous replies are in *Freiheit,* Jan. 2, 1919 (m), and Eichhorn, pp. 57–64. A letter to Barth (Barth papers, I, item 37) provides direct evidence that Eichhorn was assembling arms for the revolutionary cause while police president.
2. R. Müller, *Bürgerkrieg,* p. 30; Ledebour in *Ledebour-Prozess,* pp. 44–45; Eichhorn, p. 67; Pieck, I, 463–65; text of the appeal for demonstrations in *Freiheit,*

expected, and a part of the crowd unmistakably wanted to do violence to the government; by evening the radical leaders were considering whether something beyond protest should be attempted.[3] The decisive meeting, attended by the shop stewards en masse, by the whole local leadership of the USPD, and by Liebknecht and Pieck for the Communists, began under the powerful impact of the demonstrations and ended in a spirit of overconfidence.[4] It decided, not only to proclaim a general strike in protest against the attempt to dismiss Eichhorn, but also to resist his dismissal, by force if need be, and to use the opportunity, if it was presented, to overthrow the government. Operations were to be directed by a revolutionary committee under Liebknecht and Ledebour and Paul Scholze of the shop stewards.[5] Only six of the eighty or so persons present voted against such drastic measures. The dissenters, however, included Däumig and Richard Müller, who thereupon withdrew from the affair, convinced that it could only result in a disastrous setback for their movement.[6]

The events of the night of January 5 and the next day showed that Däumig and Müller had been right. The support of the garrison, enthusiastically promised to the insurgents, failed to materialize; even the People's Naval Division declared itself neutral.[7] The troops were no more anxious to fight for the government than to overthrow it until they saw which way the wind was blowing. But no serious attack was ever made on government buildings. The committee, disconcerted to find in the cold light of morning that the balance of forces was so unfavorable, failed to agree either on a plan of operations, offensive or defensive, or on a political program. All the important military operations on the

Jan. 5, 1919. For more extended treatments of the January disturbances in Berlin, see Erich Waldman, *The Spartacist Uprising of 1919* (Milwaukee, 1958), ch. 5, and Kolb, *Arbeiterräte*, pp. 223–32.

3. The rhetoric of the leaders doubtless had something to do with the mood of the demonstration; see their thoughtless use of the Spartacist catchphrase "Down with the Ebert-Scheidemann government!" in the original appeal, and Rosenberg, *Geschichte*, pp. 66–67.

4. On this meeting, see R. Müller, *Bürgerkrieg*, pp. 32–36; Ledebour in *Ledebour-Prozess*, pp. 50–53 and 86; Eichhorn, pp. 71–72; Pieck, I, 466–67.

5. Liebknecht's participation was not authorized by his fellow KPD leaders. As is now well known, official Spartacist participation in "Spartacus Week" was minimal and reluctant; see *Illustrierte Geschichte*, pp. 282–83; Pieck, I, 472–73. Waldman, esp. p. 192, uses the term "Spartacist uprising" in quotation marks in his text, if not in his title.

6. Some time later, replying to Ledebour's charge of desertion under fire, Däumig referred to the January adventure as "eine der hirnverbranntesten Erscheinungen . . . , die die deutsche Revolutionsgeschichte aufzuweisen hat"; USPD *Reichskonferenz*, Sept. 1920, p. 179.

7. R. Müller, *Bürgerkrieg*, pp. 32–33; Ledebour in *Ledebour-Prozess*, pp. 52–65.

insurgent side were carried out by small bands of fanatics under no one's control.[8] They occupied major newspaper buildings during the first night; lacking the authority to make them withdraw, the strike leaders were committed to holding these buildings, which constituted an unacceptable challenge to the government's authority but had no strategic significance.[9] Meanwhile, the streets were full of striking workers, who stood around until evening, waiting to be told how to help with the revolution and growing steadily more disillusioned.[10]

Ledebour's association with the shop stewards, not his party connection, led to his participation in the affair; the party executive had nothing to do with the enterprise in which its former chairman and its Berlin organization were caught up. The executive, in fact, regarded it as catastrophic. The revolutionary attempt was bound to fail, but it threatened to cost a great deal, in blood and in bitterness between socialist factions; so they quickly interjected themselves as mediators.[11] By evening of January 6 the two sides, each uncertain of its ability to dominate the situation by force, had declared themselves ready to negotiate.

For two days the floundering radicals' hopes rested on these talks.[12] The cabinet, however, quickly recovered from its original anxiety. The rebels' impetus was ebbing; Noske was gathering loyal troops (in the form of Free Corps) in the suburbs. The cabinet could feel sufficient confidence again to lay down rigorous terms for the rebels; indeed it was tempted to smash them once and for all. Accordingly it demanded evacuation of the newspaper offices, especially the *Vorwärts* building, as a precondition for negotiations on other issues. This demand the revolutionary committee scarcely had the power to grant, even had it dared to ask such a sacrifice of its followers; the committee retreated step by step, from one compromise offer to another, but it could not promise what the government asked. A stalemate had been reached. On the evening of January 8 the USPD mediators gave up.

8. Ledebour in *Ledebour-Prozess,* pp. 95–96; Eichhorn, pp. 72 and 80; R. Müller, *Bürgerkrieg,* pp. 42–46.

9. Ledebour in *Ledebour-Prozess,* pp. 64 and 86.

10. See the famous portrayal of the waiting masses in *Rote Fahne,* Jan. 14, 1920, with the litany, "Und die Führer berieten."

11. *Freiheit,* Jan. 7, 1919 (m); Dittmann in *Ledebour-Prozess,* p. 570; Dittmann memoirs, pp. 986–87.

12. The course of the negotiations can be followed in the minutes of the cabinet and the central council for Jan. 7 and 8, *Zentralrat,* pp. 225–34 and 250–63, and in *Freiheit,* Jan. 8, 1919 (m and e), Jan. 9, 1919 (m), and *Vorwärts,* Jan. 14, 1919 (m). See also accounts by participants: Dittmann in *Ledebour-Prozess,* pp. 570–82; Bernstein, *Die deutsche Revolution,* pp. 145–53; Dittmann memoirs, pp. 988–94; and *Vom I. Rätekongress zur Nationalversammlung: Die Tätigkeit des Zentralrates der sozialistischen Republik Deutschlands* (Berlin [1919]), pp. 19–20.

The small troops of armed radicals suffered a bloody fiasco as the government's forces moved in over the following days. The insurgent leaders, however, came out of the affair better. The workers responded to a final appeal; mass assemblies met in parks and factories on January 9 and 10 to demand renewed negotiations, not only to avert bloodshed but also to bring an end to the conflict within the socialist movement.[13] The central council, standing in for the government, held discussions with representatives of the demonstrators on January 10 and 11, by which time the problem of the newspaper buildings had been settled by force.[14] Against a background of violence, prospects for new talks could not be good. By shifting the ground of the discussions to socialist cooperation, however—which implied reconstruction of the government—the shop stewards and Berlin Independents were able, as the rebellion collapsed beneath their feet, to transform themselves from insurgents back into political organizations. The revolutionary committee did not meet again after January 9; the Communists withdrew their collaboration on January 10, when Liebknecht and Pieck were finally forced out by the Communist leaders who had disapproved of the enterprise.[15] KPD, USPD, and shop stewards all hoped to resume their old ways.

But circumstances had changed. The government was unwilling to return to the terrifying insecurity of the ten days after Christmas, especially with elections to the National Assembly scheduled for January 19, and it had the military power to assert itself. The storming of the occupied buildings was followed by formal occupation of the city by the first Free Corps, who were to pacify it before the elections. Some government troops were fully as brutal and unrestrained as the worst left radical extremists, and they had more opportunity to do violence with impunity. The bloodshed in the "pacifying" operation was out of proportion to anything the radicals had done; arbitrary arrests and executions went beyond anything known under the old regime at its harshest.[16] The Majority Socialist government disapproved of the brutality, particularly of the murder of Rosa Luxemburg and Karl Liebknecht on the night of January 15,[17] but since they depended on the Free Corps, there was little they could or dared do to restrain the troops. The incipient reign of ter-

13. *Freiheit,* Jan. 9, 1919 (m and e), Jan. 10, 1919 (e).

14. *Ibid.,* Jan. 10, 1919 (m), Jan. 11, 1919 (m), Jan. 12, 1919; *Zentralrat,* pp. 325–34.

15. Pieck, I, 472–73 and 475; *Illustrierte Geschichte,* pp. 282–83; declaration of Jan. 10 by the KPD, *Rote Fahne,* Jan. 13, 1919.

16. See Haase's judgment in a letter of Jan. 16, *Hugo Haase,* pp. 173–74.

17. Stampfer, *Erfahrungen,* p. 235; Arnold Brecht, *Aus nächster Nähe: Lebenserinnerungen 1884–1927* (Stuttgart, 1966), p. 234.

ror in Berlin ended within a week, but by then it had set a new tone for the revolution.

The Independents' efforts for renewed socialist collaboration could scarcely succeed in these circumstances; yet the case was pressed. The huge open-air assemblies of workers calling for socialist unity may, as some Majority Socialists suspected, have been less spontaneous than they seemed and more the result of organization by the Independents,[18] but a strong emotional drive for socialist brotherhood was felt in the factories as the full consequences of disunity became evident. Nor did the demand for unity come only from Berlin. Other cities experienced disturbances during the same January days—often sparked by the news from Berlin—and saw the same solution. In Munich, the leaders of the Bavarian USPD, including Eisner, declared themselves ready for reunification of the two parties.[19] In Hamburg, after large demonstrations, a unity commission was established.[20] Giving political form to these sentiments was another problem; but the ideal was very much in the air.

On January 13 a committee of the Berlin Independents (insurgents no longer) began serious discussions with the central council. The position of the council was anomalous. Formally, it enjoyed the right to appoint and dismiss members of the cabinet, and thus to reconstruct the government to the satisfaction of the Independents if it wished. Although made up entirely of Majority Socialists, among whom experienced party and trade-union officials predominated, its members had served most recently on workers' and soldiers' councils, not in national politics; such men were closer than the party executive to the thinking of ordinary party members and much more anxious to conciliate the workers and keep up good relations with the Independents. In December, the council would have preferred to maintain the socialist coalition; its support of Ebert, Scheidemann, and Landsberg on December 28 was reluctant. During the January disturbances, it loyally supported the government's measures, but it was restive. The council's attitude was one of the first concrete demonstrations of the disaffection that was growing quietly in Majority Socialist ranks.

In effect, though not formally, the precondition for any discussion of a possible common program was the central council's willingness to consider removing certain SPD leaders from the government; that the council showed as much good will toward the Independents as it did is there-

18. See, for example, Robert Leinert in *Zentralrat*, pp. 308 and 326. Cf. Pieck, I, 473.
19. *Freiheit*, Jan. 13, 1919 (m).
20. *Illustrierte Geschichte*, pp. 353–54.

fore noteworthy. Negotiations began on January 13 and continued for several days;[21] they were judged both important and promising enough for Haase to attend one session to make an urgent plea. But, although several members of the council would have liked to dispense with one or another of the cabinet members, the whole scheme was bound to break down on the solidarity of the SPD leaders. Replacing one would mean replacing all, and it would be impossible to find Majority Socialists of stature to put in their places—the same problem as had confronted the more skeptical members of the council on December 28. Nor would the council necessarily have wanted to accede to the Independents' wishes. The USPD's assumption that only the practices of such leaders as Ebert and Noske kept the two parties apart was shown up as inadequate; most thinking Majority Socialists, including the members of the central council, derived their party allegiance from the belief that the SPD was the more sensible and the USPD the more irresponsible party. The events of January had done nothing to persuade them otherwise.

In any case, the USPD, in full disarray, made a difficult negotiating partner. The talks almost came to an early end when the Independents made it clear that, while they wanted a purge of the cabinet, they were not offering to re-enter it, but only to cooperate with it.[22] And when, on January 15, the central council suggested that further discussions about personnel could only be pursued after a common program was agreed on, the Berlin party leaders took nine days to produce their proposals.[23] The central council then waited another five days before discussing them, by which time the moment had passed.[24] Replying to the Independents the council resigned its intermediary role and recommended "conducting these talks from party to party, since in fact only in this way can they promise success."[25]

The cabinet was kept informed of the course of the negotiations but seems not to have been diverted from its path toward the National Assembly and the restoration of order and governmental authority. Noske continued to collect troops—and to plan their use. On January 21 he informed the cabinet that the new military forces of the government totaled 22,000 and should reach 50,000 in two or three weeks. Of these, 10,000 were needed to assure control of Berlin, and a certain number would be sent to the eastern frontier; the balance, he said—without

21. The talks can be followed in *Zentralrat*, pp. 365–81 and 400–11; also *Freiheit*, Jan. 14, 1919 (e), for the session of Jan. 13; and *Vom I. Rätekongress*, pp. 21–23. Cf. the skeptical evaluation of these sessions in Flemming, p. 111.
22. *Zentralrat*, pp. 372 (Gustav Laukant) and 401 (Haase).
23. Text in *Freiheit*, Jan. 25, 1919 (m).
24. *Zentralrat*, pp. 517–18.
25. *Freiheit*, Feb. 4, 1919 (m).

eliciting comment from the rest of the cabinet—would restore order in Halle and Braunschweig (to ensure the security of the National Assembly in Weimar) and in Bremen.[26] The government was ready to take the military offensive against the strongholds of the left.

These strongholds had drawn the attention of the central government in the past two weeks. The conflict in Berlin had been followed closely throughout the Reich, and on the left with mounting anger, amplified by the general radicalization taking place in late December and early January.[27] The Republic of Braunschweig had demobilized all Reich military units in its territory (partly to prevent their use in Berlin), denied passage to government troops, and claimed the right to censor postal and telegraph communications through its lands; its workers' and soldiers' council was exceptionally hostile toward the Majority Socialist government in Berlin.[28] In Halle, where disturbances began about January 7, the soldiers' council disarmed troops that might be headed for Berlin, and serious clashes were only narrowly averted.[29] The same course was followed in Leipzig, another major rail center.[30] And Bremen, where revolutionary councils were already far down the path to achieving effective control, issued the most direct challenge of all when it proclaimed a soviet republic (*Räterepublik*).

The Bremen Soviet Republic was in part a kind of tragic misunderstanding, being founded on a premise (that the events in Berlin marked the opening of a second revolution) that any Berliner could see to be false the day it was proclaimed, January 10. But weeks of radical preparation lay behind the event.[31] As we have seen, in Bremen the orderly, unremarkable course of the revolution in November began to give way in December, as Communist influence grew, to a more radical conception of the role of the councils.[32] On December 12 the workers' and

26. Cabinet minutes for Jan. 21, *Regierung der VB*, II, 287–88. Noske told the cabinet on Jan. 28 that he would like to act against the Ruhr, too, but had not enough troops; *ibid.*, II, 344.

27. For a survey of the disturbances in other cities in January, see Drabkin, pp. 520–38; on Hagen, see Lambers, pp. 56–57; on Stuttgart, Keil, II, 133–39, Jakob Walcher in *1918: Erinnerungen*, pp. 548–52, and Willi Münzenberg, *Die dritte Front* (Berlin, 1930), pp. 274–81; on Erfurt, Willibald Gutsche, *Die revolutionäre Bewegung in Erfurt während des 1. imperialistischen Weltkrieges und der Novemberrevolution* (Erfurt, 1963), pp. 181–89.

28. *Freiheit*, Dec. 31, 1918 (m), Jan. 7, 1919 (e), Jan. 9, 1919 (e); IML Berlin, Reichskanzlei 8/17, pp. 80, 85, and 86, and 8/28, pp. 97 and 132; Anlauf, pp. 101–4.

29. Schulz, "Rolle und Anteil," pp. 145–48.

30. Fabian, pp. 44–45; Willy Langrock in *1918: Erinnerungen*, pp. 538–39.

31. For what follows see Breves, pp. 40–50; Kolb, *Arbeiterräte*, p. 330.

32. The left radicals in Bremen assumed the title of Communists on November 23, well before the founding of the KPD; it will be convenient to make the transition to the new designation at this point.

soldiers' council arrested bourgeois hostages, though it set them free after a day. After the Workers' and Soldiers' Congress in Berlin many more such events occurred. On December 21, the council seized the *Bremer Bürgerzeitung* and turned it over to the Independents; on December 24 and 27 two nonsocialist newspapers were forced to stop publication briefly. On December 24 the council voted not to recognize the Congress' decision supporting the National Assembly but to adhere instead to the council system. Four days later it decided to arm the workers—the Independents and Communists among them—a decision that led the Majority Socialists to withdraw from the council; arms were distributed on December 31, and on that day and the next two military units were surrounded by workers' forces and disarmed.

The Bremen workers' and soldiers' council had successfully arrogated to itself powers that most other councils had not dared to exercise or had been prevented from exercising and was well on the way to fulfilling the radical ideal of a council's revolutionary functions. The last step would be to dismiss the old Senate and take the administration of the city's affairs into the hands of the councils. The Communists began to press seriously for such a move, which, even if events in Berlin were the catalyst, was the logical consequence of the course on which the council had embarked.[33] Alfred Henke and his Independents, who had trailed rather than led in this process of radicalization, were well aware that Bremen was far ahead of the rest of the Reich and in danger of being isolated. Even in Bremen, the socialist left's control was not secure; the soldiers were not altogether happy with the course of events, and in new elections to the workers' council on January 6 nearly half of the carefully restricted electorate of 30,000 workers voted for the Majority Socialists (with the other half divided between the Independents and the Communists).[34] Even Johann Knief could see that prospects for a coup were not good and advised against it; but Knief was mortally ill, and his followers could not be held back.[35] The momentum established earlier could not be reversed, and when, on January 10, the Communists staged the demonstrations that led to a seizure of power, the Independents, who had not even been informed until the last minute, could do nothing but go along.[36]

33. Kuckuck, pp. 97–99.

34. Breves, pp. 59–60, gives the distribution of seats as 113 for the SPD, 58 for the USPD, and 59 for the KPD (slightly different numbers are given by Kuckuck, p. 64). The voting system is explained (tendentiously) in *Illustrierte Geschichte*, p. 338. There were also 30-odd soldiers in the new council, who thus held the balance of power.

35. *Illustrierte Geschichte*, p. 338.

36. Kuckuck, pp. 99–101; Karl Jannack in *Vorwärts und nicht vergessen*, pp. 180–181.

Despite the radicals' energy over the preceding weeks, the Soviet Republic of Bremen was a pathetic enterprise, comparable to the first soviet republic in Munich, three months later.[37] The Communists were slow to concede their error, but within a few days most of the soldiers and Independents (who, since the SPD had been excluded, made up a majority in the soviet institutions) were thoroughly alarmed by their own temerity. The elaborate new governmental structure introduced on January 10 remained a paper system. Martial law and censorship, decreed on January 10, were attacked by Henke three days later and rescinded on January 21. The leaders' decision of January 12 not to permit National Assembly elections in Bremen was reversed by the full workers' and soldiers' council the following day by a vote of 101 to 88. Henke had pointed out that prevention of the elections would be very unpopular, even among workers, and that Bremen, which was only "a tiny part of Germany," was in no position to challenge the rest of the Reich in such an important matter (by which he was understood to mean that military intervention was likely).[38] Such arguments implied that the seizure of power had been a mistake; from this point on, the council's main concern was "the search for a satisfactory way out."[39] On January 21, to restore the city administration's financial credit, the soviet government promised regular local parliamentary elections. Nothing remained of either the idealism or the practice of a soviet republic; but no one could take the last step of giving up the provocative claim to authority, and thus avert military intervention by Berlin.

On January 25, Noske commanded "restoration of order" in Bremen; the plan, as outlined to the Gerstenberg Free Corps two days later, was to enter the city, form a provisional government, disarm elements hostile to the government, and arrest the leading Communists.[40] This program, announced on January 30, shocked the socialist left, not only in Bremen but throughout the country. Noske's pretext, that the movement of food supplies from abroad through Bremen was endangered, was patently incorrect; the city had been quiet since January 21; its council government had made far-reaching concessions to normal political propriety and was prepared to make more, as it hastened to assure Noske, even to the extent of disarming the workers and resigning its powers.[41] This was not enough for Noske. Such a solution would have left the workers' and soldiers' council a potential power in the city and complicated Noske's

37. The following account is based largely on Kolb, *Arbeiterräte*, pp. 339–47, and Kuckuck, pp. 102–35.
38. See his speech in Breves, pp. 74–75.
39. Kolb, *Arbeiterräte*, p. 344.
40. *Wirren*, p. 106.
41. *Freiheit*, Feb. 3, 1919 (m).

relations with the new army units; worse, it would have suggested that the Berlin government was willing to compromise with threatening minorities.[42] Operations were delayed for a few days when the Hamburg soldiers' council, controlled though it was by Majority Socialists, threatened to mobilize its forces against Noske's operation.[43] When this danger had passed, the troops were sent in; predictably, given the temper of the troops and of the Communist workers in Bremen, the result was street fighting, serious bloodshed, and a wave of bitterness.

The action in Bremen confirmed the fears that the left-wing socialists had felt since the Free Corps had appeared during the Berlin troubles: the government was willing and able to employ force against challenges to its authority and its conception of Germany's democratic future. But Bremen also established a pattern of reaction and response. As Kolb puts it:

> The great majority of the workers wanted an end to the rule of the Communists in Bremen—but they did not want this action to be carried through by a "reactionary Free Corps"; Noske on the other hand was not satisfied with achieving a political goal, he wanted in addition a demonstration of the unconditional authority of the government—even at the price of a growth in the power of ultra-rightist circles and the alienation of many workers from the SPD.[44]

On both sides, a preoccupation with the government's new instrument of force was developing. The government, treating the army as a neutral power factor, had set out on the path of suppression of difficult minorities, on which it was not to hesitate again. The socialist left, though itself largely responsible for the atmosphere of violence that had led to resort to arms, was neither purposeful nor united enough to offer effective resistance; it was appalled that the controversies of the revolutionary period were to be settled with machine guns, and moreover that these guns were in the hands of military forces that they, unlike the government, recognized as a threat to progressive politics in Germany. The left could respond only with hatred and defiance, and the result was a further incitement of the government and its troops. The "Noske Era" of 1919 and 1920 had begun.

The General Strike Movement: The Ruhr, Halle, and Berlin

After the fall of Bremen, the civil war entered its second phase, different in important respects from the aimless insurrectionary spirit of the first. The general strikes that took place in the Ruhr, Central Germany,

42. Noske, *Von Kiel,* pp. 78–84.
43. Kolb, *Arbeiterräte,* pp. 345–46.
44. *Ibid.,* p. 345.

and finally Berlin between mid-February and mid-March were directed, ostensibly at least, toward limited goals, founded on carefully prepared organizations with broad support among the workers, and consciously designed to avoid violence. In these respects they foreshadowed the modus operandi of the radical left over the coming year and displayed the potential strengths and fatal weaknesses of the method.

The first and classic case was that of the miners of the Ruhr.[45] This region had not been particularly unruly during the first weeks after the revolution—in spite of the presence of strong, if scattered, concentrations of support for the Independents and groups farther to the left—partly because relations between Independents and Majority Socialists had not deteriorated as far as they had elsewhere and parity was often observed in local councils.[46] The origins of the miners' unrest were more basic: wages had lagged behind wartime inflation; food supplies were insufficient, in both quantity and quality; and the social tensions between workers and self-willed mine-owners were unusually severe. These factors had led to a series of fairly serious, if nonpolitical, strikes in August 1918.[47] The movement was interrupted during the fall but resumed for three weeks in December, this time with incidents of violence against both plant directors and workers unwilling to strike.[48] In early January 1919 the strikes were renewed, accompanied by more serious disorders, including putsches or putsch attempts in Dortmund, Gladbeck, Düsseldorf, and Duisburg during the week of the Berlin fighting.[49]

By this point trade-union and socialist leaders, who had had little part in the movement, were seriously worried. The trade unions were trying to abide by a collective agreement with the owners, made just after the revolution, and were in danger of losing large parts of their following;

45. The student of the complex affairs of the Ruhr has a difficult secondary literature to deal with. The two authors best versed in the events and politics of the coalfields interpret their material from opposed viewpoints; Spethmann, *Zwölf Jahre Ruhrbergbau*, takes the mine-owners' side, while Lucas, "Bergarbeiterbewegung" and *Märzrevolution im Ruhrgebiet*, vol. I (Frankfurt on Main, 1970), assumes the workers' point of view. The present account largely follows Oertzen's interpretation of the socialization movement in his *Betriebsräte* and his article "Die grossen Streiks der Ruhrbergarbeiterschaft im Frühjahr 1919," *Vierteljahrshefte für Zeitgeschichte*, 6 (1958), 231–62, but without adopting Oertzen's positive evaluation of the potential of the socialization movement. See also the useful study of Manfred Dörnemann, "Die Politik des Verbandes der Bergarbeiter Deutschlands von der Novemberrevolution 1918 bis zum Osterputsch 1921 unter besonderer Berücksichtigung der Verhältnisse im rheinisch-westfälischen Industriegebiet" (Ph.D. dissertation, University of Würzburg, 1965).
46. Metzmacher, "Novemberumsturz," p. 144; Kolb, *Arbeiterräte*, pp. 91–92.
47. Spethmann, I, 67–76.
48. *Ibid.*, I, 121–39; Lucas, "Bergarbeiterbewegung," pp. 29–105.
49. Spethmann, I, 158–72; Oertzen, *Betriebsräte*, p. 112; Kolb, *Arbeiterräte*, p. 315.

the leaders of all three working-class parties, including the Communists, felt their influence over their members slipping away. All disapproved of the trend toward aimless violence, and most were concerned about the economic effects of the loss of coal production. On the initiative of the Essen workers' and soldiers' council, and with special support from the Independents (to whom the idea seems to have come most naturally), they tried to shift the focus of the movement onto the single, political issue of socialization, in order to bring it into orderly channels.[50]

Socialization, to the Ruhr miners and their supporters among industrial workers, especially in the metalworking industry, meant not only a change in ownership but also workers' codetermination. The latter aspect originated in the pits and on the shop floor as spontaneous demands for freedom from oppressive direction by foremen and inspectors, rights for workers' committees, and a role in determining working conditions and work rules.[51] After the Workers' and Soldiers' Congress, these demands merged with the move for expropriation into a distinctive vision of socialization through workers' councils (or factory councils, as they were beginning to be called[52]). The vision was not quite syndicalist; ownership of the means of production was to pass to society in general, but the plants were to be administered internally by their councils and in larger economic matters by associations of the councils. Grass-roots "economic democracy" was the aim, and socialization through factory councils the route to it.[53]

This program the Majority Socialists, Independents, and Communists of the Ruhr adopted in January and pursued with imposing solidarity, all misgivings temporarily suppressed. The Majority Socialists, the strongest of the three parties, were the most reluctant; the remark that "unity was forced on the leaders" is especially true of them, but they collaborated loyally for over a month, even the skeptical trade unionists

50. On the motivation of the Independent leaders in the Ruhr, see Otto Brass's testimony in *Nationalversammlung*, vol. 326, pp. 325 and 333, and in *II. Kongress der Arbeiter-, Bauern-, und Soldatenräte Deutschlands am 8. bis 14. April 1919 im Herrenhaus zu Berlin* (Berlin, n.d.) (hereafter cited as *II. Rätekongress*), pp. 75–76.

51. Details in Oertzen, *Betriebsräte*, p. 111, and *Illustrierte Geschichte*, p. 313.

52. There is no good English equivalent for the German word *Betriebsrat;* not only a factory but also a mine, a hospital, a department store, even a university could be classified as a *Betrieb,* and under the *Betriebsräte* system the employees would elect a council to supervise the unit's economic life. The term "factory council," arbitrarily chosen over "works council," will be used here but should be understood in this broad sense. In practice, it was mostly mines and factories that took up the idea and elected such councils.

53. See the evaluation in Oertzen, *Betriebsräte*, pp. 127–32.

among them.[54] The Communists' support for the movement is less surprising; more remarkable about their role is the degree of discipline that their unruly followers, despite their lack of organization, showed until the middle of February. The Independents were most at home in a movement of this sort. They did not lead it, however; apart from a few localities they did not have the organization or standing in the Ruhr that they had in the Halle district or in Berlin, especially not in the Westphalian mining region.[55] The socialization movement in the Ruhr was a genuinely multiparty, even supraparty movement.

The first step was a conference in Essen on January 13, attended by delegates of councils and trade unions from the area. The delegates, including those of the Catholic unions, unanimously favored socialization of the mines and elected a "Commission of Nine," comprising three representatives from each party, to define the task, negotiate with the government, and carry the program through. A second conference a week later endorsed the first labors of the commission, again unanimously, and adopted a more elaborate set of program proposals. Meanwhile the strike movement tapered off, together with most of the political violence.[56] The immediate object of the parties was thereby achieved. The rest depended on the government in Berlin.

The government was in an awkward position as the socialization movement spread. There is no reason to suppose that the Majority Socialist cabinet of January had changed its mind about proceeding with socialization, and the coalition government that succeeded it on February 13 (which included ministers from the Democratic and Center Parties) had even less natural sympathy with the proposals. Few, if any, of the ministers in either government, whatever their feelings about taking industry into public ownership, could conceive of turning over management of one of the most important branches of the economy to workers' councils. Yet the movement in the Ruhr was too strong to be ignored; concessions would have to be made.

From mid-January until early March the government yielded step by step to threatening strike movements. Sometimes concessions were real;

54. The quoted phrase is *ibid.*, p. 122. On the role and motives of the unions, see Dörnemann, pp. 31–46.

55. Oertzen, *Betriebsräte*, pp. 125–27. The USPD's Westphalia district organization had 2,000 members in December 1918; *Freiheit*, Oct. 15, 1919 (e). Of the Ruhr cities in the Lower Rhineland district, only Essen had a strong (but not predominant) Independent organization; in Duisburg, Mülheim, and Hamborn, left radicals and syndicalists were as prominent as Independents; in fact, in this area these groups often cannot be distinguished from one another.

56. R. Müller, *Bürgerkrieg*, pp. 134–35; Oertzen, *Betriebsräte*, pp. 113–14 and 121–22; but cf. Spethmann, I, 173–75.

more often they were promises that were not kept, actions taken in response to pressure, a few critical days after the psychological moment had passed. The government's Social Democratic ministers used the vocabulary of the council movement, often in all sincerity, without meaning the same things the miners' leaders meant. Eventually the government adopted "socialization" and "factory councils" into its program, meaning by the former a sort of mixed system in which both workers and state would join management in controlling the operation of the mining industry, and by the latter an elaborated version of existing factory workers' committees that would still have no power to direct the firm in economic matters.[57] The government was never prepared to concede full expropriation of the mines or full workers' control; nor had there ever been any reason to suppose it would.

The miners wanted rapid action; they had been assured of it by their leaders, but they were getting only promises, in peripheral matters. On February 6 a third conference of the councils of the area issued an ultimatum: the government must accept the factory council system for the mines as drawn up by the Commission of Nine, assign to the councils the rights of supervision that they claimed, and recognize the authority of the Commission of Nine. If these demands were not met by February 15, "the workers will be forced to begin a general strike."[58]

As the strike deadline approached, the government began assembling troops nearby and stepping up pronouncements against anarchy and terror. On February 11 the new commanding general of the region had his soldiers' council arrested. There could be no doubt about what these actions meant, and tensions increased in the Ruhr.[59] At the same time, as the strike became imminent, even the unsatisfactory compromises offered by the government began to seem more attractive to some of the workers' leaders—to the Majority Socialists almost without exception, and to some of the Independents as well. At a conference in Weimar on

57. These are the principles of the later legislation, the origin of which is traced in Oertzen, *Betriebsräte*, pp. 153–69. Oertzen is surely mistaken, however, in supposing that more far-reaching legislation was ever possible from the National Assembly.

58. Text in *Die Sozialisierung des Bergbaues und der Generalstreik im rheinisch-westfälischen Industriegebiet* ([Essen], n.d.), pp. 33–34. This pamphlet is the report of the Commission of Nine, written some time in March.

59. The Ruhr cities (excepting Mülheim), unlike most Prussian cities, had never had permanent garrisons; the workers there had seen troops in peacetime only when strikes were suppressed and were exceptionally antagonistic to the military in any form. See Heinrich Teuber, "Beiträge zur neueren Geschichte der Arbeiterbewegung im Ruhrbezirk," *Sozialistische Politik und Wirtschaft*, 4 (1926), issue of Aug. 5 (unpaginated); Gerhard Colm, *Beitrag zur Geschichte und Soziologie des Ruhraufstandes vom März-April 1920* (Essen, 1921), pp. 13–16.

February 13 and 14 with delegates from the Ruhr and the Halle mining district, the government, though still rejecting most of the workers' demands, finally committed itself to legislation on some kind of socialization and on rights for a form of factory councils.[60] Meager though the concession was, in the circumstances it was bound to have some appeal.

Even before the report of the delegates to Weimar had been received, however, the movement in the Ruhr had begun to disintegrate. A conference on February 14 decided (not unanimously this time) to launch the general strike if the government did not rescind its military preparations against the Ruhr by February 17, regardless of progress on socialization.[61] So far from backing down, the army marched into Hervest-Dorsten, to the accompaniment of bloody street fighting. The infuriated radicals lost their self-control. Without waiting for a scheduled conference on February 18, extremists from the western Ruhr, including some Independents, assembled in Mülheim on February 16, voted the general strike, and set about trying to enforce it on their reluctant colleagues by force of arms at the pitheads.[62] The long-reluctant Majority Socialists and trade unionists reacted on February 17 by deciding to accept the government's concessions and resist the general strike.[63] At the conference the next day, amid ugly scenes, the Majority Socialists walked out, and the movement was split.

The conference proclaimed the threatened general strike; but with the Majority Socialists gone, the trade unions issuing counterpropaganda, and troops advancing, it had little chance. At its peak, slightly over half the miners were out on strike. This was not enough; in the circumstances it could lead to nothing but violence within the working class. There was some fighting between armed radicals and troops, but most workers showed no inclination to fight, and the resistance posed no serious problems for the army. Recognizing that they had failed, the Independents and Communists secured a conditional promise of military withdrawal—which was not honored—and brought the strike officially to an end on February 21, after only three days.[64]

The united movement had fragmented, failing at the critical moment;

60. *Die Sozialisierung des Bergbaues*, pp. 13–18; Oertzen, *Betriebsräte*, pp. 140–41.

61. Text in *Freiheit*, Feb. 18, 1919 (e).

62. Portrayed with some sympathy by Lucas, *Märzrevolution*, pp. 42–43; with hostility by Teuber (one of the leaders whose plans were upset by the extremists' action) in *Sozialistische Politik und Wirtschaft*, 4 (1926), issue of Sept. 23 (unpaginated).

63. *Die Sozialisierung des Bergbaues*, p. 23.

64. For the course of the strike and its conclusion see Spethmann, I, 211–45; R. Müller, *Bürgerkrieg*, pp. 137–39; *Freiheit*, Feb. 22, 1919 (e).

but the council advocates soon regrouped. The Commission of Nine remained in existence (without its Majority Socialist members) and at once set about rebuilding the council structure. Its success, in the face of obstruction from unions, Majority Socialists, and troops, is evidence of the hold the idea of councils had on the miners, even those who were not politically radical. By the end of March, the Independents and Communists, greatly aided by working-class outrage at the continuing aggressive actions of the military, had brought the movement to the point of attempting another strike, which began on April 1.

The April strike was far more successful; in spite of its one-sided political leadership, it was supported by a large number of politically moderate miners and at its peak embraced some 73 percent of the labor force in the mines.[65] For over three weeks it crippled coal production in the Ruhr. Its formal program was typical of the radical demands of the period, including recognition of the council system, disarming of the Free Corps and arming of the workers, and recognition of Soviet Russia;[66] but additional demands, for a six-hour shift and a 25 percent pay raise, clearly appealed most to the miners. In other words, though the strike was ostensibly a radical political movement, in reality it marked a return to an older style of labor conflict, but with the councils occupying the role of the trade unions. Politics came in only when the government tried to meet the crisis with martial law, a move that was deeply resented, led to street fighting, and probably prolonged the strike considerably.[67] The unions recognized the nature of the conflict by incorporating the six-hour shift into their own program (though reluctantly, as they felt the demand was irresponsible in view of the national shortage of coal). The government offered the strikers concessions only in practical economic matters, including a seven-hour shift and better food supplies for the area; and the new Reich commissioner in the Ruhr, the able Bielefeld trade unionist Carl Severing, was able to combine concession, exhortation, and repression to bring the strike to an orderly end.

Severing's purpose was to show the miners that negotiations brought better results than a strike. His success was sufficient to prevent further serious outbreaks of violence in the Ruhr for the remainder of the year. But politically the cost of fighting the socialization and strike movements

65. Spethmann, I, 280. Oertzen, *Betriebsräte*, p. 120, points out that this result was achieved with much less use of terror than in February, since the presence of government troops hindered the use of force against nonstrikers.

66. Text in *Freiheit*, March 31, 1919 (m).

67. R. Müller, *Bürgerkrieg*, pp. 140–41; Carl Severing, *1919/1920 im Wetter- und Watterwinkel: Aufzeichnungen und Erinnerungen* (Bielefeld, 1927), pp. 35 and 42–43.

had been high. The socialist miners' union was badly shaken, and its old leadership survived largely because so many radicals deserted it altogether.[68] The Independents' standing in the mining districts increased at the Majority Socialists' expense; in the Lower Rhineland cities on the margin of the Ruhr the Majority Socialists' losses were even sharper.[69] And memories, connections, and resentments remained alive among the workers to reappear in March 1920.

The socialization movement in the Halle district—second of the three important strike centers of February and March—was similar in its origins to that of the Ruhr. Indeed, there are indications that the Halle leaders imitated the Ruhr movement, both in focusing on the issue of socialization and in practical details of organization—as they appear to have imitated Berlin in their ideological development.[70] But there were important differences. Whereas in the Ruhr the whole movement was carried by the miners and the traditionally allied foundry workers, with little support from other branches of industry, in the Halle region all branches of industry and transport joined the miners, first in their demands and ultimately in their strike.[71] Second, while spontaneous pressure from the workers was an important element, the movement in the Halle area was less spontaneous than the Ruhr's, more receptive to direction from above, and much better organized.[72] Less violence occurred than in the Ruhr. Finally, the Halle movement was politically united not only because the parties were driven together by pressure from below, but also because one party, the USPD, was clearly dominant in the area.

The movement took its organizational form later than in the Ruhr—at the end of January—and with some hesitation.[73] Once begun, however, organization was rapid and purposeful. The idea of socialization was as popular in Halle as in the Ruhr; at least one plant was "socialized" by its workers on their own initiative early in February.[74] The influential

68. The radicals founded their own unionlike structure based on councils, the General Miners Union (*Allgemeine Bergarbeiter-Union*), which was of considerable importance in the Ruhr for a time; see Bock, pp. 132–39. On the unions themselves at this stage, see Dörnemann, pp. 55–73.
69. The USPD's Westphalia district (the eastern Ruhr, organized from Hagen) went from 2,000 members in December 1918 to 38,000 in October 1919; *Freiheit*, Oct. 15, 1919 (e). In the Düsseldorf-East voting district, which included the remaining Ruhr cities, the SPD vote fell from 25.7 percent in 1919 to 10 percent in 1920, its third lowest poll in the country.
70. Oertzen, *Betriebsräte*, pp. 135–36, 148, 151, and 152.
71. R. Müller, *Bürgerkrieg*, p. 142; Helga Schubert, *Der Generalstreik in Mitteldeutschland* (n.p. [1958]), p. 22.
72. Oertzen, *Betriebsräte*, p. 147.
73. *Ibid.*, p. 136.
74. *Ibid.*, pp. 138–39.

Independents, headed by Wilhelm Koenen, put their weight behind the movement, for they had agreed to coordinate the general strike toward which they were headed with the Ruhr and other cities. As Koenen described the plan, forty years later:

It was agreed that the decision for a general strike would be made in Halle on February 23 and take effect on Monday the 24th, that Leipzig and Thuringia were to make the same decision on the 25th and that the Ruhr would hold a great conference for the continuation of the general strike between the 23rd and the 25th. Berlin was to join on Friday the 28th and thereby cause the struggle to break out in all industrial regions. We were certain that, if this succeeded, we would not only force the government to its knees on the question of independent, freely elected factory councils, but that moreover the question of the officers' powers of command [vis-à-vis soldiers' councils] . . . could be solved, and the recognition of workers' and soldiers' councils, the release of political prisoners and similar democratic rights and liberties could be forced through by us.[75]

A series of general strikes on such a precise timetable was a difficult undertaking, even had the total impact not been greatly reduced by the premature collapse of the movement in the Ruhr and delays in Berlin. But the Halle district did its part; on February 23 a conference there rejected the government's concessions and proclaimed the general strike.

A united front of the three workers' parties was preserved not only throughout the preparatory stages, as in the Ruhr, but also in the proclamation of the strike.[76] Coordination between the various branches of the councils was likewise maintained. The result was the most impressive large-scale strike Germany was to experience until the Kapp Putsch in the following year. Not only the mines but also the great chemical plants, the metalworking industry, and the electricity stations that supplied Ber-

---

75. Koenen in *Zu einigen Fragen,* p. 37. From the nature of this detailed program (if we can trust Koenen's memory), it must have been adopted shortly before the expected outbreak of the strike in the Ruhr, probably when delegations from the Ruhr's Commission of Nine and from the Halle district were in Weimar to negotiate with government officials on February 13 and 14 (see Oertzen, *Betriebsräte,* pp. 140–41). Koenen names his principal collaborators as four of his fellow deputies to the National Assembly (which had opened in Weimar on February 6): Bernhard Düwell of Zeitz, Otto Brass of Remscheid, Curt Geyer of Leipzig, and August Merges of Braunschweig. He had also been in contact with Richard Müller since the Workers' and Soldiers' Congress in December and names as other allies Otto Geithner of Gotha, Walter Stoecker of Elberfeld (not Cologne as Koenen says), Franz Dahlem of Cologne, Robert Dissmann, Tony Sender, and Lorenz Breunig (misspelled Bräuning) of Frankfurt on Main, and Hermann Remmele of Mannheim. The USPD party executive was not informed. See also Koenen in *Vorwärts und nicht vergessen,* pp. 397–400.

76. At the conference of February 23, over half the delegates were Independents, a quarter Communists, and the rest Majority Socialists; Schubert, p. 21.

lin shut down.[77] More important, as the strike spread into Saxony and Thuringia, the railwaymen participated, isolating the government and National Assembly in Weimar. It was a model of the general strike— total, united, disciplined, and remarkably free from violence.[78]

For all this, the strikers' position was not strong. The strike failed to spread beyond the adjoining areas already mentioned. The government was securely protected by troops in Weimar and could afford to wait; it might choose to compromise, but it would not have to surrender. In fact, it chose to send troops into Halle, on March 1, and at the same time to offer a slightly improved version of its concessions of February 14.[79] The troops provoked violence where there had been none before and thereby caused fury and dismay, and ultimately the dissolution of the strike movement. The concessions were seized upon by the leaders as a way to bring the strike to an end, and though not all their followers were ready to accept so poor a result there was really no choice. The decision to end the strike was taken on March 5, the day the government's promises were received, and work resumed throughout the area between March 6 and 8.

As a satellite to Halle, Leipzig, too, had its general strike, from February 27 to March 10.[80] Like the great strike in Berlin that followed it, the Leipzig general strike was inspired as much by politics as by a spontaneous desire for strong factory councils, and its timing was dictated by a desire to join the Halle movement.[81] Unlike the Berlin Independents, the Leipzig USPD could proclaim the strike knowing that it would succeed so long as the party's followers supported it. Government troops never intervened; the strike leaders had less difficulty with the government than with Leipzig's bourgeoisie, which proclaimed a counterstrike of its own. But the strike lost its raison d'être when the movements in Halle and then in Berlin ended. When the exercise was terminated, it had done nothing more than demonstrate again the Leipzig USPD's hold over its working class and their alienation from what was happening outside their own secure island.

77. *Ibid.,* p. 23, with a comprehensive list.
78. Oertzen, *Betriebsräte,* pp. 144 and 148n.
79. The promises were made propagandistically on March 1, in the placard "Die Sozialisierung marschiert!" (facsimile in *Illustrierte Geschichte,* p. 374), formally on March 4 and 5 to various delegations (text, and draft legislation submitted to the National Assembly, in *Freiheit,* March 8, 1919 [e]). The government later claimed that its promises of March 4 went no further than those of February (that is, that it had yielded nothing to the pressure of the strike), but Oertzen, *Betriebsräte,* p. 146, agrees with Koenen that the later terms were an improvement from the strikers' point of view.
80. The best description is in Puchta, pp. 377–82.
81. Text of the strike call in *Leipziger Volkszeitung,* Feb. 26, 1919.

The general strike movement met its third and most crushing defeat in Berlin, in a five-day strike that began on March 3 and was followed by terrible reprisals by government troops. The defeat in the capital was crucial. It confirmed the failure of the general strike as a power factor in Germany's current circumstances and thereby marked the beginning of the end of the attempts at interparty cooperation at the factory level begun in January. In Berlin and elsewhere the political choices confronting working-class socialists became increasingly sharply defined, as political hopes for the councils were destroyed. These choices drove apart the Independents and the Majority Socialists, eventually to the point of rupture, and thus set the scene for a frustrating year of political ineffectiveness for the socialist left.

During the six weeks leading up to the Berlin strike, however, unity and legitimacy (in terms of the workers' councils) were guiding principles for the radicals.[82] They had learned in January that action ranging workers on opposite sides in roughly equal numbers (reflecting party strengths in Berlin) must be stillborn, and they turned to the council system to overcome this difficulty. After the January debacle, the factory radicals of the USPD transferred their activity from the shop stewards' conventicle to the successive general assemblies of the Berlin workers' councils.[83] There they proceeded forcefully but cautiously, respecting procedural niceties and avoiding any step that would split the movement along party lines. In this way they moved carefully toward a new challenge to the government.

The council movement in Berlin, ineffective during the first two months of the revolution, began to show more life in January. Berlin had many reasons for discontent, the most important being deteriorating food supplies and unemployment, which was rising rapidly, to a total of over 248,000 persons by the end of February.[84] The government's military measures were generating disquiet, even among leading Majority Socialist council figures.[85] And suspicion of Ebert and his cabinet mounted among the workers as the government moved toward a bourgeois-socialist coalition and "normal" parliamentary rule and as its draft legislation and constitutional proposals for the National Assembly became known. The militants of all parties resented the government's unresponsiveness to

82. R. Müller, *Bürgerkrieg*, pp. 149 and 151–53.
83. *Ibid.*, p. 208. The old shop stewards group never functioned again after the January disturbances, but its leaders—including Richard Müller, Ernst Däumig, Paul Wegmann, Heinrich Malzahn, and Paul Eckert—continued to work together in the council movement and remained the most active and important single element in the Berlin USPD, though without ever controlling its organization.
84. *Freiheit*, Feb. 26, 1919 (m).
85. For example, Albert Grzesinski (the later police president of Berlin) in *Zentralrat*, pp. 287–88.

even the workers' most modest claims to a place for their councils in local government or in the factories. In Berlin, unlike the Ruhr or the mining fields near Halle, this discontent could not be focused directly on the single issue of socialization.[86] But although it remained more diffuse, it concentrated on the institution of workers' control and was none the less strongly felt.

After mid-February, under the impact of the news from the Ruhr and later from Halle, the radical workers' excitement reached a peak. The leaders, too, felt the urgency of the situation; they could see the national economy, and thus the livelihood of their followers, collapsing because of what they regarded as the blindness of the politicians in Weimar to the real forces in society.[87] Once news of other strikes came, Däumig and Müller pressed for action in Berlin, albeit circumspectly, so as not to lose contact with their more hesitant colleagues. From the general assembly of February 26 onward, progress toward the strike was rapid and virtually unstoppable. The Majority Socialists had tried to prevent this assembly, and when it did meet they attempted delaying tactics; but their resistance was broken by the elections in the second session of the assembly, on February 28, when for the first time the Independents and Communists combined had a majority. When this assembly was continued on Monday, March 3, the strike had already begun in some of the more radical factories, and the Majority Socialist members of the workers' council bowed to the inevitable.[88] Their leaders said they opposed a general strike but would accept the will of the majority.[89] With that, the strike was assured; the slow, careful campaign of the USPD radicals seemed to have justified itself.

The strike's prospects, however, were poor from the start, partly because of the delay needed to bring the Majority Socialists into the enterprise. During this delay the strike in the Ruhr had collapsed and that in the Halle district, while still in progress, had become, since the arrival of Maercker's troops, no more than a show of defiance. Meanwhile, the government in Weimar had finally adopted policies calculated to undercut the appeal of the radicals. Scheidemann, who only a week earlier had told a newspaperman that "no member of the cabinet has any thought of incorporating the councils . . . in the constitution in any form,"[90] an-

86. R. Müller, *Bürgerkrieg,* pp. 148–49.

87. See R. Müller in the minutes of the executive council for Feb. 19, IML Berlin, 11/6, pp. 188–89, and in the minutes of the general assembly for Feb. 28, IML Berlin, 11/12, p. 155.

88. The Majority Socialists soon realized that the "spontaneous" premature strikes had been a device of the Independents; see Krüger in *II. Rätekongress,* pp. 92–93; and the admission in R. Müller, *Bürgerkrieg,* p. 154.

89. Minutes of the general assembly for March 3, IML Berlin, 11/13, pp. 34–35.

90. *Freiheit,* Feb. 26, 1919 (m).

nounced that the cabinet was determined to do just that. A plan for giving a share of management to the workers in industry was hastily put together and publicized. Berlin was placarded on March 2 with announcements that "Socialization is on the march!" Two days later it was "Socialization is here!" Such statements were hard to take seriously, but they did indicate that the government had awakened to the need to show some movement. The Berlin Majority Socialists had sent a delegation to Weimar the weekend before the strike, hoping to bring back something that could blunt the strike, and they had some success.[91] The government, having learned something from the two miners' strikes, was ready this time to drive a wedge among the strikers.

The Communists, too, were a continuing threat to the unity of the movement. They were not yet a large force in the workers' council, having formed their own separate group only on February 20, and in the general assembly on February 28 they received only 99 of the 770 votes and two seats in the executive council;[92] but they were intransigent. They had no sympathy with Müller's tactics of drawing the Majority Socialists into the movement and more than once nearly succeeded in disrupting the coalition as the strike approached. When the strike started the Communists broke ranks. Rather than "sit together with those people whom we are fighting to the knife" (the Majority Socialist members of the executive council) they withdrew from the council and thus from the strike leadership, promptly setting up a strike committee of their own.[93] While their leaders emphasized that this strike was not the decisive struggle for power, the temper of their following (and indeed the tone of the leaders) made the distinction difficult to observe.

The final blow to the hopes of the strikers came from circumstances in Berlin over which the socialist leaders had no control. The premise of the general strike was that there would be no resort to armed force, for in this area the government was immeasurably superior; but the strike leaders were unable to prevent violence breaking out in the city almost at once. The first incidents involved plundering, which different sources date as beginning either on the morning before the official strike call or in the evening following it.[94] Attacks on police stations in the north of

91. R. Müller, *Bürgerkrieg,* p. 154. See n. 79 above for the stages of the government's concessions.
92. *Rote Fahne,* Feb. 21, 1919; minutes of the executive council for March 1, IML Berlin, 11/7, p. 3.
93. Levi, in minutes of the executive council for March 3, IML Berlin, 11/7, p. 59; Caius [Levi], *Generalstreik und Noske-Blutbad in Berlin* (Hanau, n.d.), pp. 4–5.
94. See two contemporary accounts of violence in the strike, *Die Berliner Spartakus-Unruhen im März 1919* (Berlin, n.d.), pp. 3–6, and the USPD's *Die Wahr-*

the city followed.[95] On March 4, firing began on the square in front of the Police Presidium—it is uncertain how or why—and the day ended with the People's Naval Division and the Republican Soldiers' Guard ranged against units loyal to Noske. The strike leaders were helpless; these developments were a disaster for their cause, giving Noske a valid reason to send his Free Corps into the city and a pretext to portray the strike as a rebellion. Resort to arms was forced on the strikers.

The triumph of the radicals quickly turned to ashes. Preoccupied with problems of cohesion and tactics, they had begun their movement without even a program; the demands adopted by the general assembly on March 3 were paraphrases of those put forward by the Communists, a sure sign that no one else had given the matter any thought.[96] The next three days were spent trying, against great odds, to consolidate the general strike. On March 4 the Communists almost caused the break-up of the united front with a motion to expel the SPD from the strike leadership; the USPD-KPD majority in the general assembly would have passed the motion if Richard Müller had not misused his powers as chairman to prevent a vote.[97] On March 5, under heavy pressure, the printers' union finally fell into line, causing the Berlin press to shut down, the first progress since the strike started. On the next day, however, the united front fell apart. The Independent and Communist rank and file in the general assembly would not be talked out of proceeding to the extreme measure of shutting off the city's gas, water, and electricity supplies. The Majority Socialists, who had denounced the decision in advance, resigned from the strike leadership and shortly after left the general assembly.[98] The Berlin trades council, which had earlier supported the strike, changed sides, and the strike was dead; it only remained to bury it officially on March 8.

The end of the strike was not the end of the affair. Noske's troops had already entered the city; and whatever the desires of the radical leaders, a number of armed workers could not refrain from a suicidal response to the provocation. The result was regular street battles in the east of the city, during which government troops used aircraft and artillery; sporadic violence lasted for another week. In the middle of the fighting,

---

heit über die Berliner Strassenkämpfe (Berlin, 1919), p. 3. R. Müller, *Bürgerkrieg,* pp. 170–71, is confident that agents provocateurs were at work, though there is no evidence to support the charge.

95. These actions were probably led by organized Communists acting against party orders; see Pieck, II, 11.

96. *Rote Fahne,* March 3, 1919; *Dokumente und Materialien,* III, 289–90; minutes of the general assembly for March 3, IML Berlin, 11/13, pp. 48–50.

97. Minutes of the general assembly for March 4, IML Berlin, 11/13, pp. 77–79; R. Müller, *Bürgerkrieg,* p. 157.

98. R. Müller, *Bürgerkrieg,* pp. 158–59.

on March 9, Noske proclaimed full martial law in the city, with the additional provision that any unauthorized person found armed was to be shot on the spot. Great bitterness ensued, on both sides. The soldiers instituted an orgy of random killing; more than 200 arbitrary shootings allegedly took place and total deaths, including those from the street fighting, are reckoned to have been more than 1,200.[99]

Military terror could not end radicalism in Berlin—rather, it increased the radical trend—but it did suppress any tendency toward rebellion. Berlin was under a state of siege for the next nine months; assemblies were subject to permission, the socialist press to arbitrary bans; the Communist Party organization was virtually outlawed. More serious was the effect of the whole experience on relations between the Independents and the SPD in the workers' councils. Much as they disapproved of Noske's measures, the Majority Socialists were even more alienated from the socialist left. The general assemblies continued to meet, and the executive council to function, but both were crippled by a mutual suspicion that made decisions difficult. The experience of collaboration had been a bitter one for both sides. Serious cooperation was not to be possible again for another year.

Other Struggles and Final Phase

Radical action—and radical defeat—in the spring of 1919 followed a pattern. The impulsive assaults that marked the January troubles were partially, though never wholly, superseded by planned general strike movements, which required all the resources of the radical socialists and which they were often unable to control once action had begun. In the aftermath of the strikes, there was sometimes a relapse into disorderly discontent and "putschism," sometimes (as in the Ruhr) a resumption of strike activity but with sharply reduced political content, often just a decline into angry but helpless passivity. Meanwhile the strongholds of council rule fell one after another as government troops marched in and destroyed the remnants of the revolutionary regimes, often amid bloody fighting.

The extent and timetable of the essentially repetitive incidents in many cities can be indicated briefly. The conflict after January fell into two phases. The first, from the second half of February to mid-March, had

---

99. *Wahrheit über die Strassenkämpfe,* p. 26; *Wirren,* p. 103. Harry Kessler entered in his diary on March 8 (*Tagebücher,* p. 151): "Ein neues Element, das gestern und heute unheimlich gewachsen ist, kommt seit einigen Wochen, etwa seit der Ermordung Liebknechts, in die deutsche Revolution: das Element der Vendetta, der Blutrache, das in allen grossen Revolutionen schliesslich treibend wird und als letzte von den revolutionären Kräften übrig bleibt, wenn alle andren ausgebrannt oder befriedigt sind."

three sources: the government's extended military offensive after February 15, Kurt Eisner's assassination on February 21, and the strikes fostered by the radical Independents of the school of Koenen, Brass, and Däumig after February 22. Strikes and disorders ensued in most areas where the radical workers' movement was strong. In Gotha, occupied by troops on February 18, the workers responded with one of the longest general strikes on record, which lasted, in the principal factories, until March 8.[100] In Mannheim, where the news of Eisner's death provided the immediate impulse, a soviet republic was declared on February 22, and, though the hotheads were brought under control by the two socialist parties the following day, the city remained under council rule until the arrival of troops on March 6.[101] These actions were nourished by the example of the larger strikes in the Ruhr, Central Germany, and Berlin; in turn they helped encourage further strikes early in March—for instance, the miners' strike in Upper Silesia from March 5 to 15[102]—until the whole movement was ended by a combination of exhaustion, conciliatory gestures from the government, and the operations of Noske's troops.

The final phase came in April. Once again the working class seemed ready at last to offer effective resistance to oppressive authority, the principal impetus coming from the institution of the Hungarian Soviet Republic on March 21, a belief that Austria was on the verge of taking the same path, and the great miners' strike in the Ruhr that began on April 1. The miners of southwestern Saxony struck for nine days, starting on April 7, and for a time it seemed that Upper Silesia would follow suit.[103] Of the more important cities, Stuttgart had a general strike from March 31 to April 8, in origin much like the Berlin strike of four weeks earlier except that local Communists played a greater role, and Braunschweig a strike in the week following April 9; both ended in military suppression.[104] Amidst all this, and influencing some of it, there began the last and best known of all the local upheavals of the civil war, the theatrical Bavarian Soviet Republic in Munich.

Although Independent Socialists played a central role in Bavarian

100. Buchsbaum, pp. 145–60.

101. Adam Remmele, *Staatsumwälzung und Neuaufbau in Baden* (Karlsruhe, 1925), pp. 60–67; *Die Kämpfe in Südwestdeutschland 1919–1923*, Darstellungen aus den Nachkriegskämpfen deutscher Truppen und Freikorps, vol. 5, issued by the Kriegsgeschichtliche Forschungsanstalt des Heeres (Berlin, 1939), pp. 94–99.

102. Schumann, pp. 171–83.

103. *GdA: Chronik*, II, 63; Schumann, pp. 183–192.

104. On Stuttgart, see Wilhelm Blos, *Von der Monarchie zum Volksstaat*, 2 vols. (Stuttgart, 1922–23), II, 40–65; Walcher, in *1918: Erinnerungen*, pp. 552–57; *Die Kämpfe in Südwestdeutschland*, pp. 31–42. On Braunschweig, see Roloff, pp. 56–59, and Anlauf, pp. 107–14.

politics from Eisner's death to the Soviet Republic of April 7 (and
through the Soviet Republic's first phase), they gave no distinctive stamp
to the events of the period.[105] While in most North Bavarian cities (notably Nuremberg and Hof) the Independents had regular local organizations of the type familiar elsewhere in Germany, in Munich, the center
of events, the USPD had an ill-defined organization that differed from
the usual pattern. Local leadership passed at the end of February to
Ernst Toller, student, poet, and inspirational speaker, who is justly
described by a baffled Communist historian as "a somewhat eccentric
young man."[106] Toller, who had been a socialist of sorts for little more
than a year, was not a party man, and the organization he headed was
correspondingly loose. Many of the militants, especially those connected,
like Toller himself, with Munich's unofficial Revolutionary Workers'
Council, felt less allegiance to their party than to the loose alliance of the
revolutionary left whose principal figures, apart from Toller, were the
Communist Max Levien and the anarchists Gustav Landauer and Erich
Mühsam. A more traditional wing of the Munich party, exemplified by
Hans Unterleitner, was left leaderless by Eisner's death. The leading
Bavarian Independent was Joseph Simon, a sophisticated trade-union
leader and National Assembly deputy from Nuremberg, but there is no
evidence that he was able to consolidate any following in Munich.

The party organization was thus able to play little part in the political
turmoil of March and April in Bavaria. No more, however, was the
SPD; such a gulf had opened between the SPD leaders and the radicalized members, especially in Munich and Augsburg, that the party was
virtually crippled during the critical period. The result was that leading
Independents were projected into a position of artificial prominence as
mediators between the intimidated Majority Socialists and the activists
of the far left. First, despite intraparty opposition, they cast their lot
with the Majority Socialists' attempt to find a stable form of mixed government and avoid a soviet republic; Unterleitner and Simon accepted
ministerial posts in the new socialist government, established on March

105. The best account of the events from February through April is Mitchell,
chs. 9 and 10; see also Hans Beyer, *Von der Novemberrevolution zur Räterepublik
in München* (Berlin, 1957), Neubauer, *München und Moskau,* and two short
works useful for detailed chronology and the documents they reprint, Schmitt, *Die
Zeit der zweiten Revolution,* and Max Gerstl, *Die Münchener Räte-Republik*
(Munich, 1919). An evaluation from the point of view of a moderate Independent
(Paul Hertz) appeared anonymously as *Die Münchener Tragödie* (Berlin, 1919).
106. Beyer, p. 50. On Toller, see his autobiography, *Eine Jugend in Deutschland*
(Hamburg, 1963); Angress, "Juden," pp. 280–86 and 292–96; and Ernst Niekisch,
Gewagtes Leben (Cologne and Berlin, 1958), pp. 97–99, together with the affec-
tionate but cutting remark by Max Weber he records (pp. 90–91): "Gott habe in
seinem Zorn Toller zum Politiker geschaffen."

18, headed by the SPD's Johannes Hoffmann.[107] Then, when this government, too, was seen to be both powerless and purposeless, they joined the deliberations that resulted in the only remaining solution the socialist left could see, the proclamation of a soviet republic in Munich on April 7.[108]

The Munich Independents, as the largest socialist faction sure to support the enterprise warmly, were assigned five of the eleven seats in the cabinet of the soviet republic; at the same time, the Munich party leadership made its reluctance clear in a manifesto, and it is noteworthy that none of the leading Independents, not even Toller, cast his lot in with the new government.[109] The Majority Socialists, some of whose leaders had been involved in the preparations up to the last minute, ultimately withheld official support, as did the Communists; in the end, only the anarchist members of the government, Landauer and Mühsam, performed their ministerial tasks with conviction. That this regime, "in reality no government at all,"[110] lasted nearly a week was due only to the utter lack of any promising alternative. When it fell, to be replaced by a purposeful but hopeless Communist regime under Eugen Leviné, the Independents retired from center stage. They had gone as far as the politics of drift could carry them and left behind a situation that resulted in military fiasco for the radical workers, a week of white terror, and the end of all prospects of socialist progress in Bavaria.[111]

When Munich fell, on May 1, only one important stronghold remained to the revolutionaries: Leipzig. The city had caused little trouble; it was well managed by the revolutionaries, who were moderate in practice, securely supported by their well-organized followers, and apparently little inclined to jeopardize their local position by involving themselves

107. Beyer, pp. 56–58. According to Mühsam, pp. 27, 30, and 34, the decision was taken under the guidance of emissaries from the Berlin leadership. An opposition group in the party issued a manifesto disclaiming responsibility for compromises with the SPD; see Neubauer, pp. 43–44.

108. See the accounts of the critical meetings in Niekisch, pp. 65–71; Toller, pp. 89–90; Mühsam, pp. 42–43; P. Werner [Paul Frölich], *Eugen Leviné* (Berlin, 1922), p. 33; Rosa Leviné, *Aus der Münchner Rätezeit* (Berlin, 1925), pp. 13–16.

109. Gerstl, pp. 12–13 and 16–17; Toller, p. 90; Mitchell, p. 316; *Die Münchener Tragödie*, p. 58. Toller became involved in the soviet republic later, when he succeeded to the office of chairman of the Bavarian councils.

110. Mitchell, p. 311.

111. On the terror, see the USPD pamphlet, *Die Münchener Tragödie*, pp. 27–50, esp. the figures on pp. 46–48. Oddly enough, the USPD survived the disaster and was able to report a membership of 10,000 in Munich alone at the end of May; *Freiheit*, May 24, 1919 (m). In municipal elections the following month, the Independents won an absolute majority in Hof, exceeded the Majority Socialist vote in Munich, and showed the beginnings of strength in other cities (*Freiheit*, June 22, 1919); but it was henceforth an outsider with no influence in Bavarian politics.

in revolutionary adventures. Even their protracted general strike in support of the Halle and Berlin movements was an undramatic affair in which they followed rather than led, and the army left them alone for the time being. Not even Curt Geyer's accession during the strike to the chairmanship of the inner committee of the workers' and soldiers' council (in place of Seger) fundamentally altered the character of Leipzig's radicalism.[112] The change was accompanied, however, by intensified recalcitrance, and ultimately the council's refusal to adapt itself to the new political order sealed the city's fate. The formal grounds for intervention were Leipzig's refusal to apply the state of siege proclaimed by the Majority Socialist government in Dresden for the whole of Saxony on April 13. In May, with troops available after the end of the troubles in the Ruhr and Bavaria, the rule of the councils was finally suppressed, though bloodlessly—another illustration of Leipzig's disciplined radicalism.

General Maercker's troops entered Leipzig on May 11; this date marked the end of the civil war, and therewith the most activist phase of the postwar labor movement, at any rate until 1923. The past months had seen moments when the atmosphere had been almost revolutionary, as revolutionary perhaps as in the critical days of the previous November. This time, however, clear, practical goals and definite enemies (apart from the army) had been lacking and outside events had not dictated a timetable. The movement's leadership had been too diverse, too scattered, too vague in its purposes, and too little coordinated to meet the needs. As Heinrich Ströbel later wrote, "the revolutionary energy of the masses dissipated itself in uncontrolled strikes and wild convulsions which were stifled in blood by the new militarism."[113] With the revolutionary impulse disappeared also the revolutionary institutions themselves, the political councils on which the socialist left had placed such hopes. The immediate postrevolutionary period was over. The era that followed was, for the opposition socialists, a time of propaganda, organization, and preparation—a time of revolutionary politics but not of revolution.

112. See Puchta, pp. 376–82, and Beutel, pp. 403–8.
113. Ströbel, *Die deutsche Revolution,* p. 104.

CHAPTER 8

Adjusting to the Initial Defeat
of the Revolution (1919)

The conflicts of the spring of 1919 thus ended in outright defeat for the revolutionary camp, including the USPD. By the end of May, radical socialists had been deprived of most of their institutional bases of power.[1] And while left-wing socialism displayed disunity and confusion, the enemies of further revolutionary progress had shown confidence and strength. The parties of the center had put together a politically effective coalition of conservatives and democrats to oppose the radicals and built up a formidable military force. Six months after the revolution, four months after the outbreak of armed conflict, the socialist left was out of power, once again in political opposition to consolidated governmental authority.

The initial stabilization (or apparent stabilization) of the Weimar order, symbolized by the adoption of the Weimar constitution in August, could not hide the fact that a large, radical section of the working class remained outside the broad consensus on which the new parliamentary democracy would have to rest. The socialist left had been defeated, but not destroyed and certainly not persuaded. Moreover, a further broad section of the working class, not initially committed to advanced socialist ideas, was drifting away from the political center in the spring and summer of 1919, disillusioned by the government's inability to promote economic recovery and its timid handling of the business and bureaucratic elites, by the failure of the prosaic and imitative parliamentary system to satisfy democratic idealism, and by the excesses of Noske's military forces. Hundreds of thousands of new members flocked to the

---

1. By June, the Independents shared in the government of only three states: Braunschweig (a socialist coalition, under the SPD's Heinrich Jasper, which fell on June 19), and Reuss and Gotha in Thuringia. In each case, the government was based on a socialist majority (in Gotha an Independent majority) in the Diet, not on the councils. The only significant instance of continuing council rule was in Frankfurt on Main.

camp of the socialist left; revolutionary and potentially revolutionary sentiment survived and even hardened.

The Independents, at once defeated in their aims and reinforced in their antagonism to the existing order, had to assess their position in a new political situation. Their party, which had scarcely had a collective existence while its officials and activists were preoccupied with the revolution, needed to try to find a common purpose. For the USPD 1919 was above all a year of self-definition.

Growth

For the USPD as a party, rather than as a movement seeking power, the civil war was far from a disaster. The lost positions of power, to the extent that they had involved governmental responsibility, had been as much a burden as an advantage, for they had strained the party's unity and political idealism. Despite their talk of defending the partial gains of the revolution, the Independents' political outlook, like that of radical socialists everywhere, required that they have a broad, even dominant influence in government or none at all. They had not in fact enjoyed that degree of influence after the revolution, and the arguments that applied to the resignation of the three Independents from the provisional government in Berlin ultimately applied to every power position born of the revolution, since none could affect the overall course of German politics in 1919. The behavior of the Leipzig Independents illustrates the ideological strain involved; they risked their locally impregnable position by a futile show of defiance to higher authority and then quietly abandoned their offices.

The history and ideology (or ideologies) of the Independent Social Democratic Party suggest that the party's real role lay in opposition. So far as its power to attract support is concerned, this supposition appears to be borne out by the party's remarkable growth during 1919. Between January and October the number of members more than doubled, from about 300,000 to perhaps 750,000, and the growth continued.[2] Figures showing how this growth was distributed over the year are lacking, but it was probably especially vigorous in the spring. Elections in those months reflected the USPD's growth; nearly everywhere, it won a larger

---

2. USPD *Parteitag*, March 1919, p. 50; *Freiheit*, Oct. 17, 1919 (m). These figures have not been rounded off; the imprecision is in the sources. (The first occasion on which the party published an ostensibly accurate membership count to six figures was the Halle congress in Oct. 1920, at which the party split.) The 259 delegates at the Leipzig party congress that opened on Nov. 30, 1919, represented only about 647,500 members, presumably as of Sept. 30, and this is probably closer to the true figure for that date; see n. 4 below.

share of the poll than in January, making particularly impressive gains in relation to the declining Majority Socialist vote. In Berlin the USPD passed the SPD between the National Assembly elections in January and the municipal elections on February 23 to become the largest party in the city. In other large cities similar growth was recorded, the most spectacular instance being Munich, where the USPD went from just over 10 percent of the SPD vote in January to some 170 percent in June. *Freiheit's* circulation increased to over 200,000 in June, a remarkable number for a socialist newspaper.[3] The USPD during 1919 was rapidly acquiring far greater popular support than it had enjoyed during the revolution.

In the process of growth, the overconcentration of membership that had marked the early USPD was to some extent corrected. The party organization expanded within a year of the revolution from twenty-two to thirty-two districts, and by the end of September 1919 twenty of these had a membership of over 10,000.[4] The greatest single block of members was the 100,000 claimed by Berlin-Brandenburg, including 45,000 in Berlin City and as many again in the suburbs and adjoining areas.[5] Next in size was the Halle district, with 72,500 members, followed by Lower Rhineland with 62,500 and Thuringia with 50,000. Leipzig had a membership of 45,000, while the Hamburg area accounted for another 42,500 and Bavaria for 40,000. These seven districts (which included the familiar centers of Berlin, Central Germany [Leipzig, Halle, Thuringia], and the Düsseldorf area) claimed some three-fifths of the membership—still a high degree of concentration. Nevertheless, Halle's leap forward, to nearly three times the prewar SPD membership of the district, was significant, as was the new prominence of the Ham-

3. *Freiheit,* June 30, 1919 (m). The peak prewar circulation of *Vorwärts,* then the only socialist newspaper in Berlin, had been about 160,000; *Mitteilungs-Blatt,* Dec. 8, 1915.

4. Districts and membership figures are calculated from the list of delegates at the Leipzig congress. Delegation strengths at this congress were determined (unfortunately for the last time) by a simple ratio of one delegate to every 2,500 members (*Freiheit,* Oct. 17, 1919 [m]). (The reliability of computations based on delegation strengths is confirmed by the few districts for which independent membership information is available: Württemberg, Hamburg, Westphalia.) The membership figures used to determine delegations were presumably those of Sept. 30, 1919, since accurate figures were available, even to the leadership, only at the end of a quarter.

5. The Berlin-Brandenburg superdistrict consisted of four districts, Berlin City, Teltow-Beeskow (20,000 members), Potsdam IV (27,500), and Frankfurt on Oder (7,500); the administration of the four districts was largely centralized in Berlin, and here Berlin-Brandenburg is treated as a single district. *Informationsblatt,* Nov. 10, 1919, contains data from which the total membership can be broken down.

burg and Bavarian districts. And the regions of the country where the party was really weak had shrunk to relatively few: Silesia, Mecklenburg, the Prussian province of Hanover, Oldenburg, Hesse-Darmstadt, and the Rhineland south of Cologne. To have spread the USPD organization over so many additional regions of Germany in the eleven months since the revolution was a considerable organizational achievement.

The USPD's press, too, had expanded. At the beginning of the revolution the party had thirteen daily newspapers (the original fourteen minus the Düsseldorf *Volkszeitung*), three weeklies (in Berlin, Stuttgart, and Nuremberg), and Breitscheid's theoretical journal, *Sozialistische Auslandspolitik*. Before the end of 1918 the Düsseldorf paper had been recovered (also the Bremen and Braunschweig papers, but these only temporarily) and new newspapers had been founded in nine cities, including Berlin, Hamburg, Königsberg, and Munich;[6] at the Leipzig party congress at the end of the following year, Dittmann claimed fifty-five newspapers for the party.[7] The distribution of these papers was far from even: of forty-six party newspapers listed in August (the best official list for 1919), seventeen were in the old Central German stronghold, from Dresden westward through Thuringia; Westphalia still had only one newspaper, and in the previously mentioned weak regions the only papers available were those of Breslau and Hanover and such peripheral cities as Cologne and Frankfurt. Still, there were seven party papers in South Germany, eight for the territories from Magdeburg eastward (exclusive of Berlin), and papers in most of the significant North Sea and Baltic ports.[8] The party had also begun to supply the other publications that Social Democrats expected, such as a magazine for socialist women, a journal on municipal politics, a weekly pictorial supplement for the party press, and (from March 1920) a publication aimed at peasants and agricultural workers.[9] The provincial papers could draw on a press service after May 1919; *Referentenmaterial,* designed to provide party speakers with arguments for party policies, appeared regularly from December 1919. And Breitscheid's journal, rechristened *Der Sozialist,* had

6. Calculated from Robert Wheeler, "Bibliographie und Standortsverzeichnis der Unabhängigen sozialdemokratischen Presse von 1917–1922," *Internationale Wissenschaftliche Korrespondenz zur Geschichte der deutschen Arbeiterbewegung,* 6 (June 1968), 35–55. My figures omit the USPD paper in Chemnitz, which went to the KPD in January 1919.

7. Dittmann in USPD *Parteitag,* Nov.–Dec. 1919, p. 81. The number then remained quite steady until the division of the party the following October, at which time the USPD had about sixty papers; see below, ch. 12, n. 14.

8. List appended to *Haase's Anklagerede in der Nationalversammlung in Weimar* (Berlin, 1919), a pamphlet issued early in August 1919.

9. *Die Kämpferin, Die sozialistische Gemeinde, Die freie Welt,* and *Der Landbote.*

been joined by a further unofficial publication, *Der Arbeiter-Rat,* on the other wing of the party.

The USPD thus became during 1919 what it had not been at the revolution—a national party, even if not a balanced one, with an apparatus to support its continuing revolutionary aspirations. Yet the party's strength still had significant limitations, of which the increasing isolation of the socialist left from the rest of the political world was the most serious. The government's policy of repression combined with petty concessions, while it did not weaken the determination of the radicals or deter many previously uncommitted (and Majority Socialist) workers from supporting the USPD, did set limits to the appeal of radicalism. The experiences of the spring of 1919 had forced a choice on many workers and led to a polarization of allegiances that tended to leave the socialist left cut off except when an extreme crisis occurred to drive all workers together. Consequently the Independents relied for most of their growth on a pool of radicalized but uncommitted workers that, though far from exhausted in the middle of 1919, was of limited size short of some further great upheaval. The party became increasingly isolated, too, from potential allies, and this isolation set narrow limits to its opportunities for action—again short of a catastrophic development of some kind. The party was moving rapidly but not necessarily going anywhere. Not surprisingly a longing for some sort of dramatic upheaval grew on the left wing of the party, not only because action might be the harbinger of socialist revolution but also because it could help the party break out of its frustrating, circumscribed position.

Internal dissension also limited the strength of the party. The spectacle of conflict does not appear to have acted as an important restriction on party growth, no doubt because in most localities a particular tendency (not necessarily one of the wings) predominated and the infighting was kept within bounds. But numerical strength was an uncertain blessing if the party could not work together. Given the intensity of revolutionary politics, with its millenarian aspirations, and the frustrations imposed by circumstances, disagreements about both goals and tactics were inevitable. The continued cohesion of the party was in some ways as remarkable as its growth, but not great enough to allow the party's strength to be effective in action except on rare occasions. The dichotomy between formal power and practical ineffectuality thus marked the party's life throughout 1919 and on into the following year.

New Programs and Tactics

As 1919 began, the USPD conspicuously lacked a program. The leaders, at least, of the parties on either flank of the Independents, the SPD

and the KPD, knew what they wanted; the USPD did not. Nor were the aims of the different party factions much more clearly defined. The revolutionary alliance of the working-class parties had failed in Berlin by mid-January and was weakening nearly everywhere else, leaving the moderates without a concept; the council advocates were still on the defensive. The Independents knew that, with the National Assembly coming, they must find ways of advancing or at least consolidating the revolution quickly or they would lose the initiative. But a program still took some time to emerge.

As the civil war developed, all factions in the party reacted with bitterness. They saw the revolution being dismantled by the policies of the leading Majority Socialists in defiance of elementary rules of socialist behavior. Rather than embark on the socialist construction the revolution had made possible, the government had embarked on capitalist restoration; rather than alleviate the causes of unrest among workers, it had joined with the extreme right to suppress all expression of popular discontent. In the name of democracy the Majority Socialists had instituted reaction. These policies, according to the Independents, had driven the masses into rebellion and thereby caused bloodshed and lasting disruption of the country's economy. They had led to division of the socialist movement, the bearer of revolutionary progress, and obstructed socialist renewal at a time when the gains of the revolution were in danger of being dissipated.

The Majority Socialists were bitter in their turn about criticism they felt to be not only unfair but also irresponsible. At best, as they saw it, the Independents were drifting with a tide of irrational popular sentiment instead of helping to control it. By measuring the government's performance against an impossible standard, and prescribing policies that, although sometimes desirable, could not be implemented democratically, the Independents were inciting the alienated part of the working class to irresponsible acts that any government would have to suppress. It seemed to SPD leaders that the Independents criticized only those who tried to adapt their work to hard realities, never the utopian extremists who were the real source of violence. They thus forced the government to rely on military might and pushed the nation's industry toward the abyss. The Independents, in short, made it impossible for socialists to unite in the cause of progress.

The Independents never admitted the justice of any of these charges. To them, the troubles of the spring were the outgrowth of the masses' natural, legitimate, and historically necessary desire for socialism. Frustration of this desire caused the country's ills; the Independents were simply acting as spokesmen for the masses and thereby acting in the

interests of the country as a whole. There was no difference between factions on this point; *Freiheit* was as vehement about it as any radical. When the Halle strike broke out, the party's Berlin organ commented in tones of desperation that the movement had been *"provoked* by the government in the most insane fashion. . . . Only socialism, and not the miserable spirit of compromise that now inspires the government, can still save Germany."[10] The same sentiments could be heard from normally moderate party spokesmen in the National Assembly.[11] All sections of the party felt they were responding to a great historical crisis, not creating it. This feeling gave them a mission and, in the face of repression, helped force the party back into a kind of unity.

This was still a response, and not a program; but as the spring wore on a program began to emerge around the idea of the council system. Characteristically, the initiative came from the left; the left wing was probably not yet a majority in the party—indeed may never have been a majority, even in 1920, if the left wing is identified with Curt Geyer's or Ernst Däumig's rigorous views—but it was the driving force and was to remain so as long as it stayed in the party. Much of the party's energies were concentrated in this wing, in its factory radicals, big-city militants, and youthful intellectuals, and it probably also constituted a disproportionate share of the party's new recruits (especially in unruly areas such as the Ruhr and Halle) and thus increased the left's relative strength in the party. These men, the revolutionary conscience of the party, contended ceaselessly that the party must not just proclaim its revolutionary purposes but also adapt its thinking and practices to new times; eventually the party had to respond.[12]

In the process of being accepted, however, the original idea evolved into a kind of ambiguous slogan—also characteristic of the USPD. The principles of the council system amounted to an ideology standing apart from the party and in some respects in conflict with it. A large part of

10. *Freiheit,* Feb. 28, 1919 (m).

11. For example, Emanuel Wurm and Oskar Cohn; see *Nationalversammlung,* vol 326, pp. 646–47 and 718.

12. To this point the USPD's factional alignments have been discussed in terms of two broad, loose groupings, which we have labeled radicals and moderates (or centrists), it being understood that much of the party had no very clear allegiance to either. We must now make further distinctions. Within the broad radical tendency in the party there grew up during 1919 a narrower, purposeful faction with a sense of cohesion, which we shall call the left wing; while among the moderates those of most pronounced centrist or traditionalist views similarly came to feel themselves a kind of faction, hereafter called the right wing. From the fall of 1919, the left wing worked with some kind of informal but regular factional organization of its own; nothing similar is provable in the case of the right wing, but then they were much better placed in the regular party machine.

the middle ranks of the USPD, though sincerely radical in their own way, took up the idea of the council system without accepting its full consequences. Others, on the influential right wing of the party, set out to integrate the council system into the standard ideas and practices of the party, modifying their normal expectations as little as possible. The principles of the council system eventually carried the party, but only after they had come to have many shades of meaning. By adhering to these principles the party moved perceptibly to the left—but by no means to the position of its left wing.

The socialization movement and the general strikes of the spring earned the councils their central place in the thinking of the left wing. In November and December, while a few ideologues, including Däumig, had seen a new political and social principle in the councils, the everyday reality had been far from inspiring in many parts of the Reich, and the Independents' stubborn insistence on retaining the councils had generally not been backed with a developed vision of their potential. This potential first became apparent in January and February when the councils, especially in the Ruhr and Central Germany, emerged as the most spontaneous and promising expression of the radical feelings of the disappointed masses. The ideals of the council system rapidly gained support and began to take on their mature shape.[13]

Council supporters in the USPD during 1919 saw the council system as both "a goal *and* a way of reaching this goal."[14] While agitational considerations were certainly important in the propagation of the council idea, the councils were regarded, in the spring and summer of 1919, not so much as instruments of agitation or revolution, but primarily as valuable social institutions. The advocates of the councils believed in them both as a better form of political and economic order and as an effective way of organizing the working class for social progress even before the overthrow of capitalism. Many radical Independents became absorbed in the internal life of the movement as it sought to realize its principles of direct democracy and self-government (*Selbstverwaltung*) even while struggling to establish itself as a power factor in German politics. A shop-floor and pithead ideology, its ambiguity reflected the fact that most radical workers, while they had no conception of how to approach the final overthrow of capitalism, were ready to struggle for

13. The fullest discussion of this phase of the council movement is in Oertzen, *Betriebsräte*, esp. pp. 89–99; for its significance see also Kolb, "Rätewirklichkeit," pp. 165–67 and 176–78, who aptly characterizes the ideals as a "Räte-Mythos" (p. 178), and Reinhard Rürup, *Probleme der Revolution in Deutschland 1918/19* (Wiesbaden, 1968), pp. 45–47; also Tormin, pp. 104–5, where the symbolic significance of the councils is emphasized.

14. Oertzen, *Betriebsräte*, p. 89.

workers' rights and political influence. This struggle, which the radical socialists had helped organize into the socialization movement, was seen by many as the central form of the struggle for socialism, and the strikes of the spring were its expression. As Däumig wrote,

Give the proletariat genuine, tangible, and honest guarantees that it is no longer to be the object, but rather the subject of the state and the economic order, and you will see that order and confidence, desire to work and joy in work will take root again in the German people. The most significant guarantee consists in allowing the institution which the proletariat has created for itself out of its revolutionary impulse, the workers' councils, to come to full development, and not trying to strangle it by trickery and force.[15]

Even after hopes for rapid socialization had faded, the councils remained part of the immediate aspirations of the workers. Through the council movement to socialism: this was the watchword of the council advocates, pursuing in their traditional fashion the most practical activity available to revolutionaries operating directly among the masses.

Part of the appeal of the councils was that they promised working-class unity. At a time when workers were "splintered among parties, trade unions, and associations of all kinds," the council system could serve as "a *new organizational form* of the *whole* proletariat."[16] Däumig held that the councils were "the sole institution that can bridge the party differences that have become so sharp."[17] Nearly all council supporters on the USPD's left wing held that the councils must be independent of partisan rivalries if they were to be effective. This principle derived from the practice of the most powerful council movements, such as that in the Ruhr, where cooperation between members of different parties was much closer in the councils than elsewhere on the political scene. But even in the Ruhr members of workers' councils (including the Independents) had formed themselves automatically into party caucuses, and as partisan tensions grew councils frequently broke apart along party lines. Council advocates in the USPD, however, let themselves be diverted neither by such problems nor by the hostility of their party's leaders to the idea that the councils, rather than the party, were the most effective agent of revolution. The supraparty status of the councils continued to be a key element in their ideology.

The councils also provided, in theory, a way of circumventing the inadequacies of the trade unions. Here the problem was not division in the

---

15. *Der Arbeiter-Rat,* 1 (1919), no. 10, 4. See the similar contentions by Koenen (*Nationalversammlung,* vol. 326, p. 594) and Richard Müller (minutes of the general assembly for Jan. 31, IML Berlin, 11/12, p. 94).

16. Wilhelm Koenen, *Deutschlands sozialistischer Räteaufbau* (Halle, n.d.), p. 4.

17. Minutes of the general assembly for Jan. 17, IML Berlin, 11/12, p. 20.

movement—the unions survived even the postwar upheavals largely intact—but the continued conservatism of union leaders, who generally held to the principle of the national front and opposed strikes during the postwar economic crisis. The councils had no scruples about strikes, whether arising from economic or political grievances, and they had the advantage of being able to unite all workers of a particular plant regardless of craft—an old demand of the radical trade unionists. Consequently, in such restive regions as the Ruhr they sometimes temporarily supplanted the unions. Over the longer run, however, the unions were a rival that could be neither discounted nor destroyed. Most workers, whatever their grievances against the unions, could not conceive of doing without them, and the period was marked by great growth in union membership, from the prewar total of two and a half million to a peak of over eight million. The councils could not afford to be so intransigent toward the unions as to cut themselves off from the great organized masses of the working class, as the most extreme Communists did. They had to try to live with the unions, to work alongside and within them, and to hope that eventually they could impress the stamp of their movement on the unions.

Council advocates sought, also, to use the appeal of their system to break the workers' attachment to parliamentary democracy—an ambitious undertaking. The central concept to which they turned to explain their purpose was the "dictatorship of the proletariat," Marx's old, ambiguous term, which had been restored to currency by the Bolsheviks. Perhaps the radicals, as a minority movement aspiring to seize power, would have come to this idea later in any case, but at first they applied the term exclusively in connection with the council system. Däumig indicated the link: "In the council system we shall first prepare the dictatorship of the proletariat organizationally. With it we shall secondly conquer political power and thirdly, after the victory, carry through the dictatorship of the proletariat in the economic process as well as in the machinery of state."[18] Däumig found the two terms, council system and dictatorship of the proletariat, "synonymous";[19] and the dictatorship was thus invested with all the radical democratic idealism of the council idea itself. The council system was democracy on a limited base—even more limited in practice than in theory since the councils only really took root in mining regions and the larger factories, leaving not only the bourgeoisie but also large parts of the working class as onlookers; yet it was

18. Däumig in *Die Revolution: Unabhängiges sozialdemokratisches Jahrbuch für Politik und proletarische Kultur 1920* (Berlin, 1920), pp. 94–95.
19. USPD *Parteitag,* March 1919, pp. 95–96.

the only visible alternative to the stolid, unresponsive, and above all antisocialist, system of Weimar. Consequently the radicals accepted and propagated the notion of proletarian dictatorship with no apparent hesitation.

None of these ideas was unique to the USPD's left wing. The ideal of workers' councils in some form was held by a broad section of the socialist movement, not only by Communists and radical Independents but also by most moderate Independents, much of the Majority Socialist rank and file, and even a few leading members of the SPD.[20] What distinguished the council advocates in the USPD from their party leaders, and from the Communist leaders as well, was the exclusiveness of their emphasis on the councils. To them the future of the revolution was wholly bound up with the problem of developing the council system; party organizations, party politics, parliamentary activity, trade unionism—these became secondary matters except insofar as they affected the factory-level organization of the workers for the future tasks of revolution and the construction of socialism.

The party moderates' advocacy of the council system came more slowly and painfully and was never as complete. Ernst Däumig's radical democratic idealism, his confidence that the necessary structures would emerge of themselves, did not appeal to party men trained in orderly processes and instinctively valuing party organization—the outstanding achievement of the socialists to date. Nor could changing times entirely overcome the attachment of most moderates to the ideal of parliamentary democracy, which has been called "the only really concrete aim of the German labor movement" before 1918.[21] Such feelings were more than prejudices; they were rooted in the old Marxist Center's deep theoretical commitment to the orderly seizure of power by the representatives of the overwhelming majority of the German people. The council system was the negation of majoritarian revolution, not so much in its theory (though here it was ambiguous) as in its visible practice; and its exclusion of certain categories of citizens from the exercise of political rights was abhorrent.[22] Many socialists educated in the school of prewar SPD practice and Kautskyan principle thus found it difficult to accept the council system.

The approach of the centrist Independents to the councils was thus pragmatic rather than idealistic. The Independent leaders readily ac-

20. For Majority Socialist council theories, whose principal proponents were Max Cohen and Julius Kaliski, see Oertzen, *Betriebsräte,* esp. pp. 82–83 and 200–5.
21. Rürup, *Probleme,* p. 22.
22. Hilferding reiterated these points even as he came out for the permanent establishment of limited powers for the councils; *Freiheit,* Feb. 5, 1919 (m).

cepted the councils of the first revolutionary weeks (in principle, at least) as the legitimate expression of the will of the revolutionary masses and supported them as a counterweight to the retrograde tendencies of the provisional regime. Even Kautsky joined in assigning to the councils the important, if transitional, task of implementing popular control of the civil administration and the army pending a full-scale reform by the government.[23] But despite these attitudes, which were responses to a situation, there was for months no sign that the party leaders saw any permanent role for the councils.

The National Assembly and the general strike movement finally forced the party to find a policy. From this necessity emerged the USPD's distinctive proposal to "anchor" the councils in the new national constitution, that is, to secure a permanent place of power for them by defining their role in the constitution. As first elaborated by Hilferding, the proposal provided that a supreme workers' council, to be elected by yearly congresses of Germany's councils, should have the right to examine bills before they were submitted to the National Assembly, to place bills of its own before the Assembly, and to require a popular referendum if one of its bills were rejected in parliament or if it objected to a new law.[24] It would thus be a sort of second chamber of parliament with limited powers. The party executive and the National Assembly delegation adopted the idea at once as official party policy, though when they first introduced the scheme in the National Assembly it was greeted with laughter.[25] Even Däumig and Richard Müller accepted the proposal, though with visible distaste; at the party congress in March it became part of the USPD program.[26]

The Independents' adoption of this policy may fairly be called opportunistic, but opportunistic in a complex way. One motive was doubtless party cohesion; by giving specific and limited content to the council idea the program made it possible for the moderates to support the councils and thereby probably contributed to encouraging the new members who joined the party during the spring. But the scheme was also intended as serious politics. Some device was necessary to prevent the bourgeois majority in the new democratic institutions from whittling away the

23. Karl Kautsky, *Das Weitertreiben der Revolution* (Berlin [1918]), pp. 3–4.
24. "R.H." in *Freiheit*, Feb. 5, 1919 (m). The powers (if any) of the lower workers' councils were not specified; factory councils, with economic powers, were endorsed separately.
25. Manifesto of Feb. 8, *ibid.*, Feb. 11, 1919 (m); *Nationalversammlung*, vol. 326, p. 19.
26. *Freiheit*, Feb. 19, 1919 (m); USPD *Parteitag*, March 1919, p. 4.

gains of the revolution, as Breitscheid frankly stated; the Independents hoped to consolidate the revolutionary advances by means of united working-class pressure on the National Assembly and believed they had found the right policy to mobilize the workers in defense of the revolution.[27]

Within a few weeks the difficulties involved in the new policy were apparent. Theoretical justification for marrying the class-based, indirect electoral system of the councils to representative democracy founded on universal suffrage was hard to find; and ultimately socialists needed such a justification. Furthermore, though the Independents were aware that their demands had no chance in the National Assembly unless accompanied by extraordinary pressure from the masses outside, the proposal tended nonetheless to displace emphasis from the mass pressure onto the parliamentary proceedings, and as the radicals saw this they moved away from the idea. Mass pressure of the kind required never developed, and by the end of the spring workers' councils in the form familiar in the winter were all but dead. As Hilferding later noted, the scheme "was put forward in a quite definite situation in which one could still believe that the power of the working class would suffice to secure political rights for the workers' councils"; and that situation passed.[28] The idea of anchoring the councils in the constitution was thus but an episode in the party's career, whose memory is preserved in Lenin's ridicule.[29] By the summer, the debate on the councils had shifted ground; the right wing of the USPD, satisfying itself with warm words of support for the council idea, never again made specific proposals for giving reality to the councils.

With the councils barred from a share in governmental authority, the moderate Independents turned elsewhere; for, unlike the radicals, they were not inclined to withdraw from the national political scene and await the second revolution. But the way to power did not lie through a simple coalition with the SPD. The previous attempt to rule jointly with the Majority Socialists had been so disillusioning as to make it politically impossible for the USPD to ally itself with them again. Moreover, even together the two parties lacked a majority in the National Assembly, which precluded such a coalition for the SPD.[30] Some new way had to be

27. *Der Sozialist*, Feb. 7, 1919, pp. 83–84; also Hilferding in *Freiheit*, Feb. 5, 1919 (m), and Feb. 9, 1919.

28. *Freiheit*, Dec. 10, 1919 (e).

29. In his theses for the founding congress of the Communist International, in Comintern *Kongress*, March 1919, pp. 124 and 125, and in many later writings.

30. The exchange of notes in Weimar about the USPD's willingness to join the first regular government of the Republic was only political shadowboxing; see *Das Kabinett Scheidemann: 13. Februar bis 20. Juni 1919*, ed. Hagen Schulze, Akten

found in which the workers' movement could rally behind a reliably socialist government that could confirm the gains of the first revolution before they were altogether lost.

The new model formulated by leading Independents in the spring of 1919 was the principle of the "purely socialist government." The phrase became a slogan only in March and April, but the ideas behind it existed since the negotiations with the central council after the January fighting.[31] The thesis was that a socialist alliance neither should nor could grow out of a party deal but would result from an upsurge of working-class activism that would force the SPD out of its coalition with the bourgeoisie and into alliance with the Independents. Such unwanted Majority Socialist leaders as Noske and Scheidemann would be swept aside. The new government, drawing its authority directly from the masses rather than from the National Assembly, would proceed at once to implement a socialist program featuring socialization and a complete reform of the military and the bureaucracy.[32] The National Assembly would not need to be dispersed because it would have no choice but to accept the new order. Democracy, in effect, would be realized rather than overridden by the actions of an aroused class-conscious proletariat.

This schema for the takeover of power by the working class, which became quasi-official for the most statesmanlike moderates in the USPD, had the advantage of offering a way round the practical difficulties of an ordinary coalition with the SPD, but at the cost of abandoning the USPD's original realism about the importance of the regular party organizations in the revolution. Even some moderates were skeptical.[33] The notion was also evasive on the point of majoritarian democratic principle and thus unlikely to appeal to the SPD, while the radicals were apt to see it as calling for revival of the regime that had failed in December.[34] Expectations of a spontaneous groundswell of such force were, in any event, doomed to disappointment, at least during 1919, despite the urgency of the Independents' efforts.

Only once in these months was there even a glimmer of hope for the idea. The general strike in Berlin in March, which followed the two

der Reichskanzlei (Boppard on Rhein, 1971), pp. xxiv–xxv, and the notes published in *Freiheit*, Feb. 6, 1919 (e), and Feb. 7, 1919 (m).

31. See above, pp. 216–18. The original provisional government had referred to itself as "rein sozialistisch" in its program of Nov. 12, the earliest known use of the term.

32. See the program submitted to the central council by the Berlin organization of the USPD on Jan. 24, in *Freiheit*, Jan. 25, 1919(m); and Hilferding's program, *ibid.*, Feb. 9, 1919.

33. Editorial in *Leipziger Volkszeitung*, Feb. 12, 1919.

34. *Rote Fahne*, April 25, 1919.

other great general strikes and was marked by an undignified scramble by the government to head it off with concessions, was widely seen as heralding the bankruptcy of the existing government coalition. Leading members of the USPD were said to have met on the first day of the strike, March 3, and decided in principle that a new coalition with the Majority Socialists could be considered.[35] The following day, Haase had an interview with the practiced intriguer Brockdorff-Rantzau, foreign secretary in Scheidemann's government, and for several days thereafter an intermediary (Harry Count Kessler) shuttled between Rantzau and Hilferding trying to arrange an understanding.[36] Simultaneously, the central council, despairing of the government's ability to unite the workers behind it and pacify the country, resolved on talks with the Independents. Members of the council were ready to sacrifice all the Social Democratic ministers, though not Provisional President Ebert; but they no longer had the authority to impose such a solution.[37] The ensuing talks, about which we know very little, collapsed when the Weimar government mastered the strike movement and recovered its self-confidence.[38] The Independents had been cautiously willing, but the obstacles were too great.

Ultimately, the SPD was too much of a leaders' party to respond to the Independents' appeal. Unquestionably many in the Majority Socialist rank and file sympathized with the Independents' advocacy of stricter socialist policies; but these sympathies found expression in local organizations or in a limited flow of members to the USPD rather than in the national policies of the SPD. Party officials and party regulars, a relatively restricted group, nearly always stopped short of open rebellion against the leadership, no matter how great their dissatisfaction—the central council is a case in point. For most, the appeal of unity in principle was greater than the attractions of collaboration with the Independents in practice; for the USPD was seen as a party in which one faction encouraged disorders while the other failed to discourage them, a squab-

---

35. *Zentralrat*, pp. 269–70. Breitscheid had visited Brockdorff-Rantzau on March 2, perhaps on an exploratory mission; see Rantzau's declaration to his cabinet colleagues on March 12, in *Das Kabinett Scheidemann*, p. 41. It was later reported that Däumig strenuously resisted any approach to the SPD; *Das Kabinett Scheidemann*, p. 41n.

36. *Das Kabinett Scheidemann*, p. 41; Kessler, pp. 143–45, 146, 149, and 152; see also Treuberg, p. 283. Rantzau's serious interest in the talks, which he was careful to deny to his cabinet colleagues, is betrayed in a letter summarized in Elben, p. 116n. For the characterization of Rantzau, see Kessler, p. 105.

37. *Zentralrat*, pp. 757–65, *passim*. Unfortunately this source contains no information for the days after March 5.

38. See the accounts of Kessler's talks, with Rantzau on March 7 in *Das Kabinett Scheidemann*, p. 41n, and with Haase on March 9 in Kessler, p. 152.

bling, disunited party with a mainly negative approach to politics. When the SPD party congress met in June, therefore, the leaders were able to divert the strong sentiment for proletarian unity (felt especially by the Saxon and Thuringian locals) with a resolution laying down conditions the USPD would have to meet: "The party congress declares its readiness to enter into negotiations with the USPD about unity on the basis of the Erfurt Program as soon as the USPD unreservedly recognizes the principle of democracy and gives up all connections with the KPD, [the party of] putschist means and repudiation of all democratic principles."[39] This resolution not only successfully turned back a potentially awkward pressure group but also gave formal expression to a rift between the two Social Democratic parties that was to remain unbridgeable for many months.

The moderate Independents did not, however, abandon their hopes, any more than the radicals gave up their equally unpromising efforts to construct a functioning council system; for no other prospects seemed compatible with their socialist convictions. The Independents had become marginal to national politics by the summer of 1919, and no program promised much for them. The revolution was dead, living on in the aspirations of the socialist left, in the self-image and purposes of the Independent Social Democrats and the Communists, but with its prospects among the population depending after the spring on the Weimar political and economic order's incapacity for stability and effectiveness. The Independents, divided and disoriented, could do little more than wait.

Efforts at Unity: The Berlin Party Congress and After

The positions of council advocates and centrists represent, in broad terms, the party's two identifiable ideological approaches to the postrevolutionary situation, but the sentiments of USPD members in the spring of 1919 were more complex. Much of the party was neither radical nor centrist with any consistency. The bloc of members in the middle, including many people in leading positions, was open to the arguments of both sides according to the situation, though the circumstances of these months tended to influence their responses in an increasingly radical direction. This section of the party made it unruly and unpredictable, but also provided the cement that held the ideological factions together. Nowhere was this more apparent than at the USPD's first postwar party congress, which took place in Berlin from March 2 to 6.

39. SPD *Parteitag,* June 1919, p. 109. Unity resolutions submitted by a number of local party organizations may be found *ibid.,* pp. 74–75, 99, and 104–6.

This congress, taking place against the background of a general strike in Berlin and the continuing strikes in Halle and Leipzig, was not a quiet affair.[40] Conflicting diagnoses of the situation were aired at length, in a typical display of factionalism; moreover, while the principal speakers, Haase and Däumig, tried to get the party to look to the future, the debates concentrated on the past, especially on recriminations about the actions and omissions of November and December. Yet, with the leadership once again in opposition to the ruling powers, with the government apparently set on rolling back the gains of the revolution, with the Noske era in full swing and a civil war of sorts under way, the USPD was in little danger of falling apart. The risks involved in delaying the congress had been worthwhile for the party executive. Pressure of circumstances, the Social Democratic tradition of preserving outward harmony, and, above all, the uncertainties of the middle bloc of the party ruled the congress, leading to a series of compromise resolutions designed to unite the party for coming struggles.

The principal business before the congress was a new program, designed not to replace the Erfurt Program of 1891 but to supplement it for revolutionary times. The main speakers, Haase and Däumig, each presented a draft—a dangerous procedure since the two held views that were virtually irreconcilable. Haase's draft, accurately reflecting the position of the centrists, shone with revolutionary expectations and determination but contained almost no programmatic innovations, unless the idea of anchoring the councils in the constitution be counted as such. It centered on a list of practical demands, some of which were thought to be realizable through the National Assembly, though most were intended to give point to the party's agitation against the existing political order.[41] Däumig, in sharp contrast, offered a draft that would have committed the party to the propagation of the council system and direct preparations for the dictatorship of the proletariat, to the neglect of such traditional forms of party activity as elections and parliamentary work.[42] The ideological poles within the party could scarcely have been more clearly defined.

40. Halle and Leipzig sent only 4 delegates between them to the congress, out of the total of 176; Thuringia sent 7, and Bavaria (with transport strikes disrupting connections to Berlin) 4. The net effect was probably to weaken the left at the congress: the Halle organization was strongly radical; the Leipzig party at this point would probably have sent a good number of radicals; and the Thuringian and Bavarian delegations would have been divided. The Halle organization, with a membership approaching 60,000 (*Freiheit,* July 3, 1919 [e]), may have been the largest in the USPD at that date.

41. USPD *Parteitag,* March 1919, pp. 28–29.

42. *Ibid.,* pp. 30–31.

The last thing the congress wanted to do was to define the party's aims so clearly as to cause schism. Speakers who supported Haase tended to find his proposal a little old-fashioned and passive; Däumig's partisans found his program too provocative; Rudolf Breitscheid even managed to suggest that the two drafts were not really incompatible.[43] A committee was established to find a middle way; the next day it reported, unanimously and with great satisfaction, that it had managed to combine the two proposals. Haase gave the compromise his grudging endorsement; Däumig, however, though able to accept most of the revised proposal, rejected it because it qualified the idea of the dictatorship of the proletariat.[44] Despite Däumig's reaction, the delegates adopted the new program by an overwhelming majority.

The so-called Revolutionary Program of the USPD was a curious document, a product of its time and circumstances.[45] Several passages—that concerning the anchoring of the councils among them—became famous largely for their ambiguity. On the council system and the dictatorship of the proletariat the program said: "The Independent Social Democratic Party endorses the council system.[46] It supports the councils in their struggle for economic and political power. It aspires to the dictatorship of the proletariat, of the representative of the great majority of the people, as a necessary precondition of the realization of socialism." This passage might seem to endorse a soviet dictatorship, but the imprecision was sufficient (as it was also in other, related passages of the program) to allow supporters of a mixed system of parliaments and councils to subscribe to it. As for the term "dictatorship," the qualifying phrase about the great popular majority was more important to many party members than the term itself. The program's statement on means said: "To reach this goal [socialism], the USP employs all political and economic means of struggle, *including parliaments*."[47] Again the qualifying phrase proved vital, allowing the old-style Social Democrats for whom electoral agitation and parliamentary activity remained central to point to the statement in justification when reproached by the radicals. The program, in short, resolved none of the disputes within the party but merely covered them

---

43. *Ibid.*, p. 141. As pointed out in H. Stoecker, p. 190, the left-wing delegates failed at this congress to organize themselves into the purposeful faction that gave them so much leverage at the party congress the following December.

44. USPD *Parteitag*, March 1919, p. 264. Däumig was absent at the time of the vote but later declared that he would have voted against.

45. *Ibid.*, pp. 3–4.

46. " . . . stellt sich auf den Boden des Rätesystems"; this was the customary phrase, despite (or perhaps because of) its obscurity.

47. Emphasis in the original.

up with phrases; disagreement on how to interpret those phrases began almost at once.

From this point the congress appeared to be sailing toward a serene conclusion until the delegates, in the same spirit of purposeful harmony, elected Haase and Däumig joint party chairmen. Unexpectedly, Haase flatly refused to serve with Däumig and declined election. He could see no possibility of fruitful collaboration between himself and a man who had refused to stand on the same list of candidates in December and who had just rejected the party's new program.[48] Haase's act was unprecedented, and he was roundly criticized for it. But after some aimless debate a majority of the delegates made it clear that, of the two men, they preferred Haase, in spite of his disregard for the will of the congress. Däumig, never one to push himself forward, then withdrew his candidacy. The party was faced with the need to find a new cochairman, preferably one of a radical hue but acceptable to Haase.

The man finally chosen was Artur Crispien of Stuttgart. A party editor by profession, Crispien had been a leading figure in the hyperradical Stuttgart opposition during the war, when he had been generally considered a Spartacist.[49] He broke with the Spartacists while he was a minister in Württemberg's provisional government and drifted to the right in practice though not in rhetoric—his one speech at the party congress was vaguely syndicalist in tone.[50] He had not found a stable new political orientation. According to Dittmann's rather malicious account, Haase, who knew Crispien from the days when both were working in Königsberg, recognized the malleability of Crispien's views and believed him to be a manageable partner.[51] Given Haase's support and his own political past, Crispien's election was assured.

Selection of this lesser light from the provinces was possibly the most important decision of the congress, especially since the Independents, carrying on the Social Democratic tradition, were always reluctant to displace a high party official from his position. Crispien remained party chairman for three and a half years, until the party's reunification with the SPD. And, as Haase had predicted, he was not the strong radical the

48. USPD *Parteitag*, March 1919, p. 254.
49. See his own statement about his politics during the war in USPD *Parteitag*, Oct. 1920, pp. 81–82. There is no extended biographical treatment of Crispien; one must refer to entries in *Neue Deutsche Biographie* and Franz Osterroth, *Biographisches Lexikon des Sozialismus*, vol. 1 (Hanover, 1960). The fragmentary autobiographical sketches by Crispien preserved in ASD Bonn are of value only for his early career.
50. USPD *Parteitag*, March 1919, pp. 61–62.
51. Dittmann memoirs, p. 1032.

delegates presumably thought they were electing. His six months' apprenticeship under Haase, before the latter's death, seems to have impressed on him many of the centrists' habits of mind, above all their tendency to regard the party—with its apparatus, its election campaigns, its enclosed ideological world—as an end in itself. He remained verbally a radical in most matters, probably sincerely; he became the party's foremost crowd-pleasing orator, despite the poverty of thought that his speeches display to the reader; but in party matters Crispien, who became senior chairman on Haase's death in November, turned out to be a bulwark of the status quo.

The party congress finished its work by reshuffling the holders of the secondary leadership offices; the overall tendency was to introduce slightly more radical members, but not, so far as can be ascertained, outspoken council advocates.[52] This trend was typical of a congress at which the party middle, spurred to action by the dangers of conflict between the two wings, asserted itself and impressed its stamp on the debates, the program, and, in some measure, the party leadership. The middle tended to be more radical, more enthusiastic, and more activist than the moderates who had hitherto determined policy, and at this congress it succeeded in moving the party perceptibly off the old path. At the same time, it demonstrated its limited potential as a guiding faction. The middle had reacted, not led; the ideas had all come from the two wings, whose differences were only papered over by a compromise arrived at in the name of unity. The program satisfied none of the decisive elements in the party. The conflict would break out again.

For the time being, however, in the spirit of the congress attempts to bridge the differences in the party continued. We have little information on the internal affairs of the leading groups of the party between April and July, but enough to know that the two principal ones—those whom

52. As there were no debates on elections for associate members of the party executive or members of the auxiliary council and control commission, the motives behind the changes are unknown; but the voting (see USPD *Parteitag,* March 1919, pp. 265–66) provides some hints. Of the two associate members not reelected to the executive, Adolf Hofer apparently did not stand and Robert Wengels was elected to the control commission instead; their replacements, Julius Moses and Anna Nemitz, were prominent Berliners with views in the middle of the party spectrum. Of the three persons displaced from the auxiliary council, Lipinski (who had chaired the congress) was moderate; Dissmann radical but a party man; Paul Dittmann of Hamburg (brother of Wilhelm) was mortally ill and had not attended the congress. Their replacements, Herzfeld, Karl Kürbs of Halle, and Karl Kroepelin of Munich, were regarded as strong radicals. The election to the control commission was virtually uncontested, there being eight serious candidates for seven positions: the elderly radical Friedrich Geyer came eighth and lost his seat; in addition to Wengels, the newcomers were Konrad Ludwig of Hagen, a radical, and Adolf Schwarz of Mannheim, a moderate.

Rote Fahne on another occasion referred to as the Party-Independents and the Council-Independents[53]—made an exceptional effort to coordinate their activities. Who took the initiative we do not know, but presumably it was the party executive, shifted slightly leftward by the party congress and not wishing to lose contact with the still semiautonomous party left. But with the civil war approaching its unsatisfactory conclusion, all factions doubtless wanted to regroup for the new tasks they must confront. The Second Workers' and Soldiers' Congress, early in April, was used for extensive consultations between the party leaders and the leaders of its council wing, talks which, according to Richard Müller, produced "ideological clarity . . . to a certain extent."[54] The contacts were continued; the party conferences on May 11 (about the party's policy toward the Treaty of Versailles) and on June 22 and 23 (about the final crisis over the treaty) were attended by representatives of the council wing, identified as such—an innovation in party practice.[55]

One by-product of these contacts was the establishment of some fifteen small commissions to "work out guidelines for carrying out the political and economic tasks of socialism."[56] The commissions' assignments ranged from defense policy and foreign affairs to public health and art; members were predominantly from the council movement, though most commissions contained at least one representative of the executive or some other prominent Berlin intellectual. When they were established is not clear— possibly at the time of the Workers' and Soldiers' Congress in April or the party conference on May 11.[57] Their creation was not announced in *Freiheit* until June 12, and their membership not until July 2, by which time other newspapers had secured and published the list. Their purpose seems to have been to prepare a program for the socialist government that was expected to emerge soon as a result either of further revolutionary developments in the civil war or of the crisis over the peace. Such is the testimony of Müller and Barth, but the fact that all but one of the commissions apparently abandoned their labors before long and without reaching any result holds the same implication.[58] Only Däumig's commission on national defense continued its work, which, as Däumig obliquely

53. *Rote Fahne,* Sept. 15, 1920.
54. R. Müller, *Bürgerkrieg,* p. 210.
55. *Freiheit,* May 12, 1919 (m), and June 27, 1919 (m).
56. *Ibid.,* June 12, 1919 (e).
57. Bare hints in R. Müller, *Bürgerkrieg,* p. 210, and Barth, p. 149. The later date implies a connection with the prospects of a revolutionary crisis arising over the peace treaty.
58. Barth, p. 149. At the party congress in December Crispien mentioned that the commissions were still at work (USPD *Parteitag,* Nov.–Dec. 1919, p. 215), but there had long been no outward signs of their activity.

informed a later party conference, it conceived to be the construction of underground military cadres for the next revolutionary period.[59]

This period of intraparty rapprochement saw the election of Wilhelm Koenen and Walter Stoecker to the party executive as secretaries on July 27.[60] Koenen, aged thirty-three, had been district party secretary in Halle and a leading spokesman of the council system there; Stoecker, only twenty-eight, had barely emerged from the youth movement before 1914 and made his party career after the armistice as an able young editor of very radical views in Elberfeld.[61] Both were a full political generation younger than the next youngest member of the executive, the forty-four-year-old Crispien, who had been a party secretary as early as 1906. Dittmann implies that Haase and he agreed to the new appointments in the belief that the youthful radicalism of the two recruits would soon wear off.[62] If so, they were to be disappointed. Koenen later asserted that he and Stoecker had been "appointed as representatives of a particular tendency. . . . I was brought in as a representative of the council movement. So I must perform my work in this sense."[63] Neither of the two gave up any of his convictions. As the era of good feeling ended, it was discovered that the effect of this gesture toward the party left had been, not to tame it, but to bring the party conflicts, for the first time since Ledebour's resignation, into the party executive itself.

Purposeful Interlude: Versailles

Party cohesion during the late spring of 1919 was materially assisted by a critical episode that united the Independents by reviving the common antiwar purpose that had originally helped form the party: the campaign for acceptance of the Treaty of Versailles. The USPD was the only German party to maintain from beginning to end, from presentation of the treaty on May 7 until acceptance on June 23, that Germany would have to sign. The party was thereby exposed to exceptional pressures from outside; and, since its leaders and militants were determined to use all means to see that Germany signed, it faced intimidating tasks. Disagreements in detail were therefore kept below the surface while a united front was presented to the opposition. Perhaps partly for this reason, the campaign was one of the few times between the civil war and the party

59. USPD *Reichskonferenz*, Sept. 1920, p. 184; confirmed by Stolt, *ibid.*, p. 221. On the question of underground military preparations by the USPD in the winter of 1919–20, see below, ch. 10, n. 118.
60. *Freiheit*, Aug. 10, 1919.
61. On Stoecker, see the biography by his son Helmuth Stoecker.
62. Dittmann memoirs, p. 1037. This, after all, had happened to Dittmann himself.
63. USPD *Parteitag*, Nov.–Dec. 1919, p. 139.

schism at Halle that the USPD decisively influenced the course of events.

For once the Independents quickly arrived at a definite policy. Long before May 7 party members had been warned both that the treaty would be harsh and unpalatable and that it would have to be signed. Editorials in *Freiheit* and the *Leipziger Volkszeitung* and articles by Kautsky and Breitscheid took this line; Haase, Barth, and others privately held the same views.[64] When the terms were finally announced, the press was ready with urgent pleas against renewing the war. On May 11, at an unusually large conference in Berlin, the party officially adopted the policy that Germany must sign the treaty.[65]

The USPD's reasons were simple and cogent. In the words of the resolution adopted by the party conference:

Not signing means: the withholding of our prisoners of war, the occupation of our raw materials areas, the intensification of the blockade; means unemployment, starvation, mass deaths; means a terrible catastrophe, which more than ever will bring on the compulsion to sign. It is the proletarians who would suffer most frightfully from the consequences.[66]

Behind this statement lay more complex motives, which varied from person to person. Hilferding and *Freiheit,* for instance, were particularly concerned about the danger of a nationalist reaction that would destroy all chance of social progress; the USPD must make such a development impossible if it could.[67] Contrariness convinced many Independents that they could never enter a united national front with the bourgeoisie, headed by the Ebert-Scheidemann government; for some, this motivation was so strong that they would probably have opposed the government whatever it decided.[68] The decision was made easier for the Independents, too, by their conviction that Versailles would sooner or later go down with the entire bourgeois order. When Haase proclaimed to a skeptical National Assembly that the treaty could not last long because "the world revolution is on the march,"[69] he was articulating sentiments

64. *Freiheit,* April 22, 1919 (m), and April 23, 1919 (e); *Leipziger Volkszeitung,* May 3, 1919; Kautsky in *Freiheit,* April 24, 1919 (m and e); Breitscheid in *Der Sozialist,* April 28, 1919, pp. 249–54; Haase letter of April 22, 1919, in *Hugo Haase,* pp. 176–77; Barth, p. 148. Haase even told the cabinet his views, on April 3; *Das Kabinett Scheidemann,* p. 130.

65. *Freiheit,* May 12, 1919 (m).

66. *Ibid.*

67. Hilferding in *Annehmen—oder Ablehnen? Die Unabhängige Sozialdemokratie und der Friede* (Berlin, 1919), pp. 34–35. See *Freiheit*'s earlier complaint, April 22, 1919 (m), that the government was trying to arouse the "furor teutonicus" against the peace.

68. Such was the tone of Richard Müller's speech in the minutes of the general assembly for May 21, IML Berlin, 11/14, pp. 242–55.

69. *Nationalversammlung,* vol. 327, p. 1103.

that made it possible to accept with relative equanimity a treaty that the Independents knew to be a terrible obstacle to both German recovery and European peace.

The other two socialist parties did not see the issue as the USPD did. A sizable bloc of the SPD felt, for reasons similar to those of the Independents, that the treaty would eventually have to be signed; but official party policy supported the government in saying that the treaty was unacceptable, and within ten days the SPD dissidents fell into line.[70] The Communists' position was more obscure. The party's original manifesto on the subject concluded, after an exhaustive analysis of the probable consequences, that so long as the current government continued, acceptance or rejection of the treaty would be "equally fateful for the proletariat"; the treaty was unimportant; what mattered was the overthrow of the government.[71] As the political crisis intensified, the emphasis in KPD discussions turned more and more to how to exploit the tensions to create a new revolution. Only at the last minute, on June 20 or 21, did the central committee say that refusal to sign would have the more revolutionary effects—too late to affect the outcome.[72]

For once, the leadership and the party's left wing seem to have agreed on the proper course for the USPD to follow; but what drew the radicals into the common front may have been less the leaders' arguments than the preparations for action that were going on beneath the surface. We know few details. The party, or some organization connected with the party, had, we know, decided to proclaim a general strike if the German government should reject the treaty; Haase and Dittmann admitted as much to Chancellor Bauer after the crisis was over. According to the summary record of this conversation of June 27,

The party was [now] against a general strike. There had been talks on this question, and it had been agreed that a general strike would take place in case the government rejected the enemies' ultimatum. Since it had declared itself ready to sign the treaty, there had been a decrease in tension and the USPD had decided against a general strike.[73]

But we do not know who, if anyone, was to organize the general strike, when it was to be proclaimed, or what its goals were. Special prepara-

70. *Freiheit*, May 16, 1919 (m), and May 20, 1919 (m).

71. *Die Internationale* (KPD), May 30, 1919, pp. 28–32. The words of the quotation first appeared in an editorial in *Rote Fahne*, April 30, 1919.

72. A number of the later circulars may be found in the Levi papers, P 19; the last one, printed as a handbill, is in P 122. Rejection of the treaty was called for by the Communist International, whose views may have become known to the KPD only just before this last-minute change of front.

73. BA Koblenz, Reichskanzlei 2664, p. 20. See also the party executive's telegram, *ibid.*, p. 22.

tions for the strike seem to have been minimal. A new revolutionary organization, which the shop stewards and a number of party figures had been building since about March (and which was headed, so he tells us, by Barth), bent its efforts to the task; but as it was known to have been infiltrated by police agents, and as Barth had to resign after an egregious indiscretion early in June, it is unlikely that the Independents were relying on it.[74] More probably the party's intention was to proclaim the strike publicly and leave its organization to local factory leaders. So far as the timing of the strike is concerned, Barth seems to have doubted that the party would act immediately on the government's rejection of the peace terms and tried to prepare measures of his own; the KPD central committee apparently did not anticipate any immediate action at the time of its circular of June 20 or 21; and the USPD's press, including even Däumig's *Die Republik,* was warning the workers not to take ill-considered actions.[75] No definite plans may have been made in advance; the party held a special conference in Berlin on June 22 and 23, which again suggests that action was not imminent.[76]

The radicals conceived of any action at this time as a bid to seize power. Barth wanted to make the attempt in May without waiting for the government's decision on the treaty; but he was supported by the delegates of only a few cities.[77] Geyer, writing six months later, also testified to the radicals' readiness to seize power but indicated that there were differences in the party as to how this should be done. The radicals wanted a soviet republic, he implied, while Haase intended to aim for a socialist government on a quasi-parliamentary base such as the moderates had been advocating for months.[78] Such a division of purpose is exactly what might be expected among the Independents at this time, and Geyer's story makes it likely that in fact no goal for the general strike had been agreed on. Only the strike itself had been accepted, and probably only in principle.

The chances of a good response to a strike were excellent, of political success from it poor. Tension in Germany in the second half of June was high. One effect was a series of strikes and disorders, including railway-

74. Barth, pp. 137 and 150–55; mentioned also in R. Müller, *Bürgerkrieg,* p. 210, but unfortunately in no other source. Barth's indiscretion consisted of approaching Captain Pabst of the infamous Garde-Kavallerie-Schützen-Division about possible collaboration; see Barth, pp. 150–55; Noske, SPD *Parteitag,* June 1919, p. 207; *Freiheit,* June 12, 1919 (e), June 13, 1919 (m), and June 14, 1919 (m). This episode finished Barth's career as a high-ranking party figure, while his organization probably collapsed under police pressure not long afterward.
75. Barth, p. 154; Levi papers, P 122; *Republik,* June 22, 1919.
76. *Freiheit,* June 27, 1919 (m).
77. Barth, pp. 149–50.
78. *Das Forum,* Jan. 1920, p. 262.

men's strikes in Erfurt, Breslau, Berlin, and Frankfurt on Main, and food riots in Mannheim, Berlin, Hamburg, and Frankfurt on Oder, on which a general strike might have fed. But the military was at peak strength and spoiling for a fight. Rumors of preparations for a military dictatorship had been circulating at least since the beginning of May; the Independents assumed that such a move would be introduced or accompanied by a bloodbath among the workers, and they urged their followers to treat all who tried to agitate for violence among them as agents provocateurs. An exceptional crisis that mobilized the entire working class might reverse the balance of forces currently intimidating the leaders, especially if it were accompanied by complications on the frontiers to distract the army; but by traditional Independent reckoning the time was not ripe for a trial of strength.

Yet surely something would have been attempted, if not by the party then by sections of it or other radicals; and Germany would then have experienced another period of upheaval—though one that might have benefited the counterrevolution more than the revolution. An eventual clash was implicit in the confrontation over the immediate, inescapable issue of the peace terms and the consequences of not signing. Whatever the USPD's plans, its most important impact had been in breaking the united national front that the government needed to try to force the Allies to alter their terms. Once the break had been achieved, and the USPD's millions of working-class followers had rallied to its position, rejection of the treaty meant risking anarchy. This was the USPD's contribution to the final disposition of the war that had given birth to the party.

These events had an epilogue in the one-day demonstration strike of July 21. As conceived in the Allied countries, this strike was to be a protest against the Treaty of Versailles, and it had this character in Germany even though it was canceled in France, feeble in England, and often took the form elsewhere of a protest against Allied intervention in Russia.[79] At the same time it was a protest against German conditions, often against local military rule—a demonstration of defiance and a release of the last tensions remaining from June. It was remarkably successful. In spite of the party executive's delayed decision to recommend the action to the party and the somewhat ambivalent tone of its appeal, which called for rallies or demonstrations but scarcely mentioned strikes,[80]

79. On the origins of the international strike, and the character of the strike in other countries, see Wheeler, "Internationals," pp. 264–71 and 282.

80. Text in *Freiheit*, July 16, 1919 (m). Strikes may have been suggested privately to local leaders, prudence keeping the idea out of the executive's public appeal.

the majority of the largest German cities experienced greater or lesser demonstrative strikes on the appointed day and many other large cities and towns saw protest assemblies or public rallies.[81] The effect was impressive but had no impact and also no follow-up. Most of the party, to judge by its press, was pleased with itself, but did not try to repeat the action; while the party's real revolutionaries were depressed by the ineffectuality of such limited protest demonstrations and had no desire to repeat them.[82] This action was the last on this scale mounted by the party or the radicals during 1919 and marked the end of a phase.

Revolutionary Ebb Tide and the Independents

The first half of 1919 was an active time for radical socialists, as strikes, demonstrations, even bloody fighting took place and an early mobilization of the workers seemed possible. The second half of the year was very different. Active protest died away with the last flickers of the Versailles crisis. In August, Paul Levi told a Communist Party conference, "We have entered a creeping stage of the revolution and may no longer count on great mass movements."[83] By autumn, the "exhaustion" of the workers, and their lack of interest in action against the government, was a commonplace among Independents.[84] The various groups of Independents turned instead to the daily work that seemed most natural and most promising; in so doing they dramatized once again the divergencies within the party.

For the most distinctive group of radical Independents, quiet times meant renewed concentration on the council movement, almost to the exclusion of other concerns. The summer of 1919 was one of their most satisfying periods. After months of preparation, the Berlin executive council was finally able to produce a fully articulated organizational schema for a nationwide council system, to be built in the present as the basis for the future socialist state.[85] Perhaps their proudest achievement, this comprehensive, visible structure (on paper at least) gave intellectual reality to the council idea, filling a lack that the radicals believed had seriously hindered the development of the councils into an effective force. The chaos of differing systems, which led to overlapping competencies

---

81. Wheeler, "Internationals," pp. 275–80, gives a table of strikes and demonstrations, with analysis.

82. *Ibid.*, pp. 283–86.

83. "Protokoll der Reichskonferenz am 16.VIII.19. in Frankfurt a.M.," p. 1, in Levi papers, P 55.

84. Haase and Curt Geyer were in rare agreement on this point at the party conference in September; see *Freiheit*, Sept. 10, 1919 (m). The word used was "Ermüdung."

85. See *Der Arbeiter-Rat*, 1 (1919), no. 27, 7–10.

and mutual suspicions, could be ended by the new plan. The resulting unified structure, founded on the confidence of the factory masses, would be, they thought, a powerful force for revolutionary progress.

Nor did the organization remain entirely on paper. A series of national conferences of councils was held during the summer, with representatives attending from the central councils of three industries (shipyard workers, railwaymen, and inland shippers)—a welcome sign, since this form of organization was eventually prescribed by the Berlin guidelines. Other representatives came from the regional miners' councils of Halle and the Ruhr and from several of the largest cities, including Berlin, Hamburg, and Leipzig. On August 22 and 23, at a conference in Halle, these organizations joined together to coordinate their activities through a new Central Office of German Factory Councils, with Koenen, Däumig, and Curt Geyer as its leading lights.[86]

These achievements had not been without cost, the greatest being the damage done to the unity of the council movement. The strict, uniform organization toward which the Independents were striving in the councils required close agreement about the purposes of the councils; the effect in practice, though never in theory, was that the councils attached to the Independents' network became politically exclusive. As Richard Müller confirms, the Independents, "once they had the majority and the masses behind them," ceased to regard the sensibilities of their Majority Socialist colleagues.[87] In Berlin, for instance, the Majority Socialists, after months of futile protest over the antigovernment resolutions carried by the general assemblies, broke away to establish their own parallel council system for the city on July 16.[88] Delegates to a national conference during the summer were required to subscribe to "the council system and the dictatorship of the proletariat," which led some delegates to depart at once.[89] Even the Communists found the single-mindedness of their USPD colleagues exasperating at times. The emphasis on system instead of struggle was foreign to them,[90] and they fought against it, though the only effect was further to weaken the movement's unity.

The emphasis within the council movement had changed since the spring. Political workers' councils were dead in most of Germany, and though the system still prescribed both workers' and factory councils, the movement was now really concerned only with the latter. The Berlin

86. *Ibid.,* no. 27, p. 1, and no. 29, p. 2.
87. R. Müller, *Bürgerkrieg,* p. 211.
88. Text of their resolution in *Freiheit,* July 17, 1919 (m).
89. Oertzen, *Betriebsräte,* p. 162.
90. See, for instance, the bitter editorial in *Kommunistische Räte-Korrespondenz,* July 25, 1919, p. 2.

executive council had gradually abandoned its immediate political claims and converted itself into the local head of the Berlin factory council system. The choice was made explicit when the leaders set their sights on construction of a system of councils in the factories, reserving the political claims of the councils to a time when they should be powerful enough to re-enter the political scene.[91]

This course moved the councils onto territory to which others were trying to lay claim. One rival, to be discussed below, was the trade unions. Another was a government-sponsored system of factory councils. The government was after all going to redeem its promise of March to legalize factory councils—principally because leaving this popular institution in the hands of the radicals would be dangerous. The bill was still in the drafting stage during the summer, but enough was known about it for the radicals to reject it in advance; it would give the councils no substantial influence over the management of firms but would integrate them into a pyramidal structure whose higher levels were organized on the principle of collaboration between workers, management, and government.[92] Such terms were anathema to the radicals and only increased their determination to establish their own "revolutionary council system" as quickly as possible.

The government also moved against the radical council movement more directly. On August 23, Noske closed down the offices of the Berlin executive council, while also forbidding it to hold any factory elections under its new plan. From about this time council spokesmen began stressing that the councils were not just a grand social institution for the time of transition to socialism but also a revolutionary instrument. The thinking behind this emphasis was explained by Ernst Däumig. The purpose of directing attention to the economic side of the council movement was to reach the factory workers more successfully, "to drive the roots of the council system into all cells of the capitalist production process."[93] He and his colleagues intended

to set the revolutionary German council organization on so firm a foundation and construct it so broadly that the majority of the German proletariat is comprehended in it. . . . A council organization which does not base itself on *one* limited party but on the compact mass of the working population, and which must be revolutionary simply from the drive for self-preservation, is ultimately invincible.[94]

91. See Däumig's and Müller's statements, *Der Arbeiter-Rat,* 1 (1919), no. 27, 4 and 7.
92. For the vicissitudes of the bill in the drafting stages, see Oertzen, *Betriebsräte,* pp. 154–55.
93. *Der Arbeiter-Rat,* 1 (1919), no. 37, 3.
94. *Ibid.,* no. 28, p. 2.

The radical council advocates, despite their emphasis on the construction of a perfect system, never lost sight of the revolutionary purpose that had motivated that system. There may be some question about the suitability of their construct but none about the seriousness of the purposes it was designed to serve. The left-wing Independents grew steadily more extreme, rather than less, during the lethargic period of the late summer and fall. The revolution must come soon, they felt; Curt Geyer, for instance, wrote a notorious article predicting that the revolution would come within months, or even weeks.[95] As this feeling grew, the radicals became less and less tolerant of other Independents whose tactics were predicated neither on the expectation of immediate revolution nor on a determination to make revolution at any cost.

The trade-union movement provided an alternative opening for organizational work among the masses in the interests of radical socialist progress, and union work probably involved as many USPD militants (including many council supporters for part of their time) as did the council movement. Union activity was not associated at first with any party faction. All could join in the attempt to conquer these huge, unwieldy proletarian organizations and convert them into instruments of the class struggle.

The unions were a formidable barrier to radical aspirations. Under skillful established leaders and powerful bureaucracies, they would also be difficult to conquer and reform. There was, consequently, a temptation to try to circumvent the unions entirely, which had been one of the impulses behind the council system. But, unlike many Communists, most Independents did not turn their backs on the unions, despite the discouraging pace of change.[96] The unions had to be taken seriously. They not only comprehended a much larger part of the working class than the socialist parties (as they had done since the 1890's); they had also grown faster than the parties since the war, reaching a membership of about 6.4 million by September 1919.[97] By any reckoning, this was a much larger committed following than the radical council movement enjoyed. The two were not mutually exclusive; but if the working class was to be effectively mobilized under the banner of revolution, the support of the unions would be of inestimable benefit.

An attempt by a group defined by its politics to take over leadership

---

95. *Leipziger Volkszeitung,* Sept. 6, 1919.
96. See the resolution adopted at the party congress in March, which admonished party members not to abandon the unions but to work within them; USPD *Parteitag,* March 1919, p. 271. Only in special circumstances, as in the Ruhr, did substantial numbers of Independents turn their backs on the established unions.
97. *Freiheit,* Sept. 25, 1919 (e).

of the unions was something new in union history and was deeply resented by the leaders whose positions were challenged. The opposition had four aims: control of the leadership positions; abrogation of the *Arbeitsgemeinschaften,* the joint union-management machinery established immediately after the revolution in the interests of labor peace; a suitable place for the councils within or alongside the unions; and reorganization of the craft unions into industrial unions.[98] The variety of these aims rallied men with different priorities, including Richard Müller, who wanted to bring the unions under the influence of the council idea, and Arthur Lieberasch of Leipzig, whose concern was more generally to make the unions instruments of socialism.[99] Robert Dissmann, soon to give up his party secretaryship in Frankfurt to become the leading Independent trade unionist, was closer to Lieberasch's position. But radicals of many stripes worked more or less in harness during 1919 as the campaign was carried to a succession of union conferences.

The efforts of the opposition during the year were partially successful —not enough to make a reversal of union policies likely in the near future, but enough to make continued effort seem worthwhile. Greatest success was achieved at the local level. In Berlin, for instance, Independents headed branches of the most important unions and the local trades council. At the unions' national conferences, most of which took place in the late spring or summer, the opposition was strong enough to put through its resolutions in eight significant unions (including the Shop Assistants' and Textile Workers' Unions), though it did not always follow up this success by electing its own men to the leadership.[100] In half a dozen other unions (including the Transport Workers' and Woodworkers' Unions) the opposition was strong enough to command a third of the conference delegates. To be sure, the national trade-union congress that opened on June 30 gave the general commission a vote of confidence by the impressive margin of 445 to 179.[101] But the opposition's greatest triumph was still to come. The largest union of all, the Metalworkers, which included more than a fifth of all trade-union members, passed

98. Oertzen, *Betriebsräte,* p. 182. On the *Arbeitsgemeinschaften,* see above, ch. 4, n. 38.
99. The contrast is well drawn in Opel, pp. 88–90.
100. A useful survey of the conferences is Arthur Oswald, "Die freien Gewerkschaften im Jahre 1919," *Die Internationale* (KPD), Feb. 2, 1920, pp. 33–39. According to Rudolf Rettig, "Die Gewerkschaftsarbeit der Kommunistischen Partei Deutschlands von 1918 bis 1925 unter besonderer Berücksichtigung der Auseinandersetzungen mit den freien Arbeitergewerkschaften" (Ph.D. dissertation, University of Hamburg, 1954), p. 34, the USPD party executive set up an office to coordinate the opposition in the separate unions. For the re-election of their old officers by radical conference delegates, see Oertzen, *Betriebsräte,* p. 183.
101. *Freiheit,* July 2, 1919 (e).

into the hands of the opposition at its conference in October. The conference repudiated the wartime policy of the union and the *Arbeitsgemeinschaft* it had formed with the employers; a number of council supporters were taken into the leadership, including Richard Müller as editor of the *Metallarbeiter-Zeitung;* and Robert Dissmann was elected president.[102]

The long-term consequences of this victory and similar victories in other unions were not, however, exactly what had been anticipated. It would be more accurate to regard the unions as having captured the radical socialist organizers than the reverse. Specific policies, such as the *Arbeitsgemeinschaften,* could be repudiated; the tone of union relations with the government and employers could be altered; but the basic orientation of the unions toward piecemeal progress within the existing order was scarcely susceptible of change—at least not without further revolution. As the revolt declined, the opposition's seizure of power in the unions remained incomplete. The Independents remained a minority in the leading positions, and the principle of trade-union solidarity was strong enough to keep them from breaking ranks in order to pursue innovation. Those who could not tolerate the implicit restrictions drifted away or came into conflict with their colleagues, as did Richard Müller, who lasted only six months as editor of the *Metallarbeiter-Zeitung.* The rest of the Independent union leaders, following the pattern of all union leaders in the German socialist movement, gradually became a kind of autonomous group within the party that was not identified with existing ideological factions—Dissmann, the group's leader, was very radical on many issues—but tended, because of its concern for the interests of large formal organizations, to promote traditional, cautious behavior. This development in the party became important the following year.

The characteristic forms of activity for most of the moderate party leaders, insofar as they were not primarily trade unionists, and for Independents with no particular factional affiliation were those traditional to Social Democracy: work for local party groups, agitation among the uncommitted, preparation and execution of election campaigns, and—for those who had risen highest—participation in the work of an elected body. There was nothing exceptional in the USPD's practice in these fields during 1919. To the radicals, however, much of this work seemed irrelevant, and the fact that there was nothing exceptional about it—that it implied normalcy—was offensive to their sense of what the party

102. Opel, pp. 97–109; the principal resolution of the conference is in *Dokumente und Materialien,* VII/I, 129–30. For Dissmann's earlier career as an official of the Metalworkers' Union, see Appendix 4.

should be. By the end of the summer, loud, if vague, complaints from the left, primarily about the leaders' parliamentary activity, were audible.

The parliamentary work that most upset the radicals was that practiced in Saxony. Since the opening of the Saxon Diet in February, the state had been ruled by a minority SPD government that depended for the greater part of its legislation on the votes of the Independents—support that was usually "loyally" granted.[103] The legislative accomplishments of this regime were not inconsiderable, but the USPD was thereby involved in the petty work of the existing order. Worse still, from the radicals' point of view, was the unmistakable desire of the Saxon party leadership, especially Lipinski and Seger, to convert this collaboration into a formal government coalition. In February, only a month after the Independents had abandoned their revolutionary alliance with the Majority Socialists, the USPD Diet delegation had made a serious if unsuccessful attempt to come to terms with the SPD.[104] The USPD renewed the attempt in June, only four weeks after the SPD government had ordered the occupation of Leipzig; among the reasons for the failure of this bid was the SPD's refusal to lift the state of siege and find a place for the councils in the constitution.[105] The Saxon radicals, headed by Curt Geyer, opposed these attempts, which they regarded as treason to the revolution; but not until late September, amid the pressures of growing radicalism in the party, did the Saxon leaders give up efforts to form a government of socialist unity.[106]

There was nothing so offensive to radical sensibilities in the work of the USPD's National Assembly delegation. A socialist coalition government was not a possibility there. The party's numbers, in fact, were too insignificant for it to have much impact in practical affairs, so that use of the National Assembly as a platform for propaganda was the more natural course. Even had it not been, a resolution submitted by Däumig at the March party congress and only narrowly defeated reminded party leaders that many members were skeptical about the value of attempting positive work in the National Assembly.[107] With few exceptions, the In-

103. Lipinski, p. 17.
104. See the USPD's conditions of collaboration, and their eventual refusal, in *Leipziger Volkszeitung*, Feb. 24 and March 12, 1919; also Fabian, pp. 53–55.
105. Fabian, p. 73; and USPD-Sachsen *Landesversammlung*, August 1919, esp. the debate on pp. 68-117.
106. The reasons for the breakdown of negotiations are given in *Freiheit*, Sept. 24, 1919 (e), and Sept. 25, 1919 (m); also Fabian, pp. 73–74.
107. USPD *Parteitag*, March 1919, p. 251. Däumig's resolution provided that the only important parliamentary activity was the election campaigns, which must be exploited for the revolutionary incitement of the masses; the USPD's elected representatives were to use the parliamentary platform to expose reformists and

dependents in the Assembly did not take their duties there seriously; Luise Zietz stated proudly that the deputies had been intentionally lax about deliberations at the committee stage, preferring to carry on such party work as agitational tours even when the Assembly was in session.[108] Curt Geyer's charge that, so far from confining itself to revolutionary fanfares, the delegation, in customary Social Democratic fashion, submitted detailed amendments, for instance on the constitution, was accurate;[109] but the greater part of this work was essentially declamatory, aiming only at defining the socialist position on such legislation. With the exception of Saxony, therefore, the debate over parliamentary activity was not practically important; indeed, since few Independents opposed all participation in parliamentary bodies, and since the radicals were unable to define what was and what was not acceptable parliamentary behavior—it being essentially a matter of attitude, which could hardly be legislated—the controversy proved unusually futile.

Relations with the SPD were a further source of intraparty contention. As the forward movement of the revolution halted and the threat of reaction grew, part of the party turned again to the ideal of the united working class—if not through reunification of the two Social Democratic parties then through collaboration. The idea was put forward, tentatively and with conditions, by a number of party intellectuals and by a few party districts, most importantly Franconia.[110] From the Majority Socialist side, feelers were put out to Independent National Assembly deputies by Scheidemann, who, freed of governmental responsibilities, had resumed his position left of the center of his party.[111]

A significant number of Majority Socialists favored closer relations with the Independents at this time. The permanent, almost paralyzing struggles of the coalition government—which, however, few of them wanted to abandon—had revived the desire to find some way of giving more weight to socialist policies; perhaps, too, collaboration might slow the drastic defection of the SPD's following to the left. Above all, the Majority Socialists feared a military, monarchist reaction. Most SPD leaders, except those in the government, found the revival of militarism

bourgeois parties as enemies of the revolution and to further the extraparliamentary actions of the proletariat until bourgeois parliamentarianism was finally overcome by the council system. The resolution was defeated by a single vote.

108. *Freiheit*, Sept. 2, 1919 (m).

109. Article in *Leipziger Volkszeitung*, Sept. 6, 1919, and speech reported in *Freiheit*, Sept. 10, 1919 (m).

110. Prager and Breitscheid in *Der Sozialist*, Oct. 25, 1919, pp. 665–70, and Nov. 22, 1919, pp. 733–34; resolution of a conference for North Bavaria, *Freiheit*, Sept. 11, 1919 (e); and delegates at the party congress, USPD *Parteitag*, Nov.–Dec. 1919, pp. 92, 95, and 104–5.

111. Discussed in USPD *Parteitag*, Nov.–Dec. 1919, p. 262.

ominous; even *Vorwärts* was attacking Noske's minions, though not Noske himself.[112] Wolfgang Heine, the Social Democratic minister of the interior for Prussia, was so unsatisfactory that members of his party had approached another colleague about replacing him, without success.[113] The National Assembly delegation submitted a formal memorandum of grievances to the Social Democratic members of the government in November.[114] The SPD was in no danger of collapse; the activists wanted socialist but not radical policies, and the USPD did not attract them; the party's discipline still held them, and most protests were private. But a rapprochement with the socialist left would have been welcome.

The USPD could not afford even to consider closer relations with the SPD. Writing in September on the possibility of a joint government with the SPD, Curt Geyer called the Majority Socialists "our enemy and the enemy of the revolution like any other bourgeois party."[115] Only the extreme left felt this way; but the left as a whole was averse to any compromise with forces further to the right, and the strength of the left in the party was growing. By the time of the party congress in December, the party executive had abandoned its position of the spring rather than make an issue of what was in any case a remote possibility. Crispien, to whom a party-centered intransigence came naturally, stated the leadership's unalterable aversion for the "Noske-Socialists."[116] Hilferding had the last word. Unity between the socialist parties, he pointed out, was a wholly inappropriate subject for abstract discussion. It would come, some day, as the product of "a *particular political situation";* and the topic had best be left alone until then.[117]

Again the left had dictated the party's orientation, if only negatively. In the fall of 1919, the central facts in the life of the USPD were the growing aggressiveness of the left wing and the hearing its doctrines were gaining among the party's radicals. The focal point of the left wing's offensive was advocacy of the party's joining the Third International (which will be discussed in the following chapter), but it was advancing on all fronts. Both left and right had to admit the political lassitude of the workers and their disinclination to support actions involving risk or great effort; the tide was running against socialist hopes. For the left

112. See the frank debate recorded in the minutes of the SPD National Assembly delegation (IISH Amsterdam), Oct. 28, 1919, and Hermann Heidegger, *Die deutsche Sozialdemokratie und der nationale Staat 1870–1920* (Göttingen, 1956), pp. 315–18.

113. Carl Severing, *Mein Lebensweg,* 2 vols. (Cologne, 1950), I, 248–49.

114. Minutes of the SPD National Assembly delegation, Nov. 21, 1919.

115. *Leipziger Volkszeitung,* Sept. 6, 1919.

116. USPD *Parteitag,* Nov.–Dec. 1919, pp. 58–59.

117. *Ibid.,* p. 268.

wing, however, this situation necessitated greater efforts. The disintegration of the economy would ensure that a further chance for revolution arose soon; in the meantime, every nerve must be strained to keep the movement from being pushed back and to prepare it for its next opportunity. The party must find its way to clarity and intensity of purpose, putting aside distracting forms of activity, no matter how strong the traditions that sanctioned them. Only revolutionary agitation and organization mattered. Most of the broader group of radicals were not yet ready to cast off as much of their past as such left-wing rhetoric implied; but they were restless with the old prescriptions and increasingly open to suggestions of new ways to ensure the revolution on which their hopes were set.

The portents on the left of the party were disturbing to the right. Though few in the party were prepared to say, or perhaps even think, that the revolution might have ended for good, the moderates continued to value the traditional task of gathering proletarian forces in readiness for whatever might occur. Revolution might come soon or late; to base one's tactics on a particular assumption would be reckless. Moreover, the moderates seriously doubted the effectiveness of radical new prescriptions that challenged the traditions, not only of the party, but also of the working class. Large numbers of followers might be attracted by new organizational forms; but equally large, and probably larger, numbers would remain attached to the old. Social Democrats of the old school, even those who were quite radical, never marched off on a new course for which there was not demonstrable working-class support in the expectation that the workers would follow. The left, it seemed to the moderates, was asking the party to run the risk of detaching itself from the tendencies of the majority of the working class. If this happened, then even if the organized radicals succeeded in seizing power, they could hardly expect to hold it—or only by dictatorial means, including measures directed against the rest of their class. This would be the ultimate violation of Social Democratic principle and the end of the party as the right wing had known it.

But the left wing would not be denied. Curt Geyer and Stoecker put forward the left wing's position in developed form at the disputatious if inconclusive Berlin party conference of September 9 and 10, and the disappointments of the fall months only intensified their determination.[118] The single important strike movement of these months, a Berlin metalworkers' strike lasting about seven weeks, had been a failure, not least

118. The conference was reported fully in *Freiheit*, Sept. 10, 1919 (m), and Sept. 11, 1919 (m and e).

because of the lethargy of many workers; failure had been turned into fiasco by a last-minute attempt to elevate the movement into a general strike when there was not sufficient support.[119] The retrograde political trend became ever more evident, as the military and the extreme right grew bolder. These developments did not cause the left wing to think again; it merely became more bitter and dogmatic, and turned increasingly toward the idea of a minority dictatorship for the first stage of the coming revolution;[120] meanwhile, its support within the party continued to grow.

The showdown with the party leadership was expected to come at the party congress opening in Leipzig on November 30, which would set the party's future course. The well-organized radical faction came determined to end the ambiguity in the party's ideals and practice—in Curt Geyer's words, "to shape the party's Action Program in such a way that there would remain no possibility for the right to interpret it for their purposes."[121] But a party congress was home ground for the party leadership, which rose to the occasion with a pyrotechnic display of tactics, if not of straightforwardness. The party executive outmaneuvered the radicals by the simple expedient of submitting a draft program that met all the radicals' demands.[122] The program employed the radical shibboleths—council system and dictatorship of the proletariat—without qualification and endorsed the ideal of socialist democracy through the councils that Däumig and others had been preaching since the beginning of the year. It defined the transition to socialism much as a program written by the radicals would have done. None of its definite proposals lent itself to positive parliamentary work in bourgeois-democratic parliaments; all were designed to be implemented after the seizure of power and to serve purely as agitational guides in the present. The belligerent radicals found themselves pushing at an open door. They were denied their struggle; after a few minor amendments had been adopted, the congress unanimously approved the new Action Program.

This was a curious episode. Nobody could seriously suppose that the party had united overnight on the platform of its radical ideologues. Nothing in the past (or future) political behavior of many of those who voted for the Action Program suggests that they could have believed in the full implications of the formulas they had endorsed. These implications, however, were not spelled out, either in the program or in any

119. The best accounts are Däumig, *Der Arbeiter-Rat,* 1 (1919), no. 40, 2–7, and Opel, pp. 92–96.
120. See, for example, Curt Geyer's speech, *Freiheit,* Oct. 9, 1919 (e).
121. *Das Forum,* Jan. 1920, p. 264.
122. USPD *Parteitag,* Nov.–Dec. 1919, pp. 215–18.

other resolution of the congress (unless the resolution on the International be counted). The program was purely a statement of radical socialist principle and gave no guidance on how this principle was to be applied to the pressing tactical problems of the day; it did not even define the nature of the dictatorship of the proletariat beyond identifying it with the council system. The radicals doubtless assumed that their practice would follow necessarily from their principles. The moderates chose to believe otherwise. It must have been difficult for many men of the Kautskyan school to vote for this program, even in the name of party unity; it is certainly hard to imagine that Hugo Haase would have voted for it if he had still been alive.[123] But the moderates voted for it knowing that they thus earned full rights to interpret a program lacking any concreteness. Once again, and with even greater fanfare, the Independents had established a program without securing a common understanding of its relevance to party practice. The tendency of much of the party to overlook fundamental differences in the interests of false unity was never better demonstrated.

Yet unity of a kind was preserved—this time by accepting the formal perspective of the radicals. The party had suffered throughout 1919 from inchoate and conflicting doctrines. Acceptance of the Action Program gave it a coherent official doctrine with which to approach 1920, though whether this apparent consolidation of the party's purposes would really lead to greater effectiveness and advance the cause of revolution remained to be seen.

123. Hugo Haase died on November 7 of complications resulting from a bullet wound suffered a month earlier. His assassin, who was judged insane, had a private grudge against Haase, and the Independents' suspicion (for which there were no positive proofs) that the assassination might have had a political background was not investigated.

CHAPTER 9

Revolutionary Internationalism
and Consolidation of the Left
(August to December 1919)

In August the question of the USPD's international affiliations with other socialist parties had arisen to occupy a large share of the party's attention. The issue seemed innocent enough, for historically the International had had little impact on the policies or inner life of the German party. Before long, however, the problem of the International had developed into the foremost threat to the USPD's unity.

The issue was dangerous partly because it could not be avoided. The ideal of international solidarity permeated the party; both right and left insisted on the importance of international ties. Moreover, the problem admitted of only a very limited number of solutions; shifting, vague compromises such as the party used in dealing with the problem of the councils were not possible. And whichever solution was chosen, the decision would have consequences. Many in the party may have supposed, at least in the early stages of the debate, that a decision for the Third (Communist) International was essentially a declaratory gesture of solidarity; the two combative wings of the party were convinced otherwise from the start. Incorporation into the Bolsheviks' International threatened the centrists' conception of Social Democracy more than any other issue raised by their left-wing opponents. The advanced radicals, for their part, saw adherence to the bloc of parties united in the Comintern as an essential step in freeing their party from the drag of its Social Democratic past to pursue truly revolutionary activity. Finally, the issue was a godsend for the left wing. On this question, the right wing's position was weak (we shall see below that the centrist policy was difficult to uphold); rank-and-file sentiment tended toward the left; and an answer could not be fudged. Soon after the problem began to be seriously debated in the party, the left wing made the issue of adherence to the Third International its own, seeing in this cause a lever to force the old-style

279

Social Democrats out of command and set the party on a revolutionary course. Other concerns, especially the councils, continued to occupy the left wing, but the new issue became the distinctive weapon in their challenge for control of the party.

Emergence of the Problem of the International

Efforts to revive some organized expression of the international solidarity of the workers (after the Second International had failed to influence the general European situation at the outbreak of war or the war policies of member parties) have been mentioned above in the chapters dealing with the war, principally in connection with the Zimmerwald movement. These efforts, while they had revived some of the idealism of the international socialist movement, had been ineffectual—and could hardly have been otherwise under wartime conditions. At the end of the war, therefore, the problem of how to bring the international movement together again, and in what form, remained.

At the center of the problem as it originally presented itself was the question of unity: whether, after all that had happened in the socialist movement during the war, the International could or should be revived as the all-encompassing organization it had been before 1914. The wings —exemplified by the Bolsheviks and the governmental socialists of Belgium or Germany—had grown far apart; to imagine them once more comprehended within a single fraternal organization was difficult. But if there could not be complete unity, could there be a broad front solidified by the exclusion of one extreme or the other, or would there have to be more than one International?

The far left had already adopted the latter position during the war, either explicitly, as in Lenin's case, or by virtue of a program requiring the exclusion of a broad range of "social patriotic" parties (the Spartacist view). Most Independents, however, were not ready for the radical innovation in socialist tradition implied by a splitting of the international socialist movement. In the orthodox view, the International had never been so much an organization as an ideal—the international community of all workers. Schism was incompatible with such an ideal, and the future course of the movement would be hard to envisage if a split took place. Bernstein examined the consequences with a certain prophetic vision:

If one were to convert the national schisms into international ones, then not one or two but at least half a dozen Internationals would be necessary, which would make nonsense of the concept of the International and deprive the

cause of that inspired grandeur from which each separate national section before the war drew a great part of its strength.[1]

Furthermore, leading Independents were conscious that they and like-minded counterparts in other countries formed only a fraction of the international socialist movement, even at the end of the war. Conservative and patriotically inclined parties still predominated. In England, the Labour Party towered above the opposition factions; in Germany, the Majority Socialists lived up to their name; the leaders in Sweden, Denmark, Holland, and Belgium were distinctly conservative; while in Austria and Switzerland power was divided between factions. Only in France did the leadership of the party change hands during the war, with the opposition coming into control a few months before the armistice. Of the major established party organizations in Western Europe (and German socialists traditionally regarded themselves as Western Europeans), only those of Italy and Switzerland had taken an antiwar stand, and nowhere except in Sweden had a new party of even the USPD's modest influence appeared. Soberly calculated, the immediate prospects for a radical International were poor.

If, nevertheless, such an International were to be created, what would its powers be? As the Spartacists and others saw it, if the disgrace of 1914 were not to be repeated, the cohesion of the new International would have to be insured by imposing an absolute obligation on member parties to coordinate their policies, that is, to carry out the decisions of the International. The practical implications of such a principle were not clear; but the obligation to submit unconditionally to what a majority of foreign socialists might decide had never been a part of either the practice or the ideology of the SPD before the war. The currency of this new idea, whose force could not be denied, placed yet another obstacle in the way of centrist willingness to consider formation of a new International.

While the war lasted, the debate in the USPD (Spartacists apart) was muted. The party leadership (except for Ledebour) never supported the idea of carrying German party divisions onto the international plane but favored international contacts of all sorts, not only the Zimmerwald movement but also all attempts to revive the institutions of the Second International as instruments for peace. But resistance to this approach was already evident. Given the party's relations with the SPD, it was hard to envisage taking part in international gatherings where the SPD was admitted as an equal; cooperation with other parties that had di-

1. *Sozialistische Auslandspolitik,* June 27, 1918.

verged from the path of permanent opposition to the bourgeois state, or even gone so far as to enter bourgeois-dominated cabinets—according to former socialist conceptions, these constituted almost a new class of socialist parties—was equally difficult to imagine. The *Mitteilungs-Blatt*, Däumig's newspaper, thought the conflicts might necessitate a system of two separate Internationals;[2] but in most circles the discussion had not yet proceeded so far. There was no agreement on the left about the nature of a new International; from the start, even radical Independents were clearly not attracted to the idea of a centralized, powerful International able to dictate to its national sections. Ledebour was among those who objected most strenuously to this idea, as he made clear in anti-Spartacist polemics in the spring of 1916.[3] Ledebour's view was shared by the *Mitteilungs-Blatt*, which, while envisaging the future International as "a strictly organized *international party*," still placed great stress on the autonomy and free development of its member parties.[4] In effect, even the radicals were thinking of a revival of the International rather than a complete breach with the past, though a revival that would exclude the "reformists" and work in a new spirit.

The leadership was responsive. Renewal of the International as an integral part of socialism's hopes for the future would mean, at the very least, a disavowal of the worst excesses of chauvinism displayed by some socialists during the war; ideally, it would mean retrospective adoption of the USPD's view of the war, imposition of penalties on "social patriots" like the Majority Socialists, and guidelines for dealing with similar situations in the future. Thus the USPD entered postwar international negotiations with a strong commitment to a broad, inclusive International on the old model but also determined to force on the organization the point of view of a minority. With the eyes of an increasingly skeptical membership on them, the USPD's leaders could scarcely afford to compromise.

Not until well after the end of the war, however, did the problem become pressing for the USPD. At first, the Independents had more urgent concerns. They did feel that they were riding an international socialist wave, which they often called the world socialist revolution; they were quick to call up the vision of international working-class action, notably at the time of the signing of the Treaty of Versailles; and they sought to defend foreign socialist governments, such as the Hungarian Soviet Republic, against capitalist threats even if they did not support these regimes with enthusiasm. But little attention was paid to the forms and

2. *Mitteilungs-Blatt*, Aug. 19, 1917.
3. See the sources cited in ch. 1, n. 63.
4. *Mitteilungs-Blatt*, Sept. 15, 1918.

machinery of the International. Only in midsummer 1919 did the issue again become central for the USPD. Meanwhile, the shape of the problem had been defined by events in the spring.

The first postwar socialist conference met at Bern from February 3 to 10, with preliminary sessions starting in the last days of January.[5] The occasion was awkward for all concerned, not least the USPD. In the first place, it was questionable whether the party should have sent a delegation at all; there was widespread hostility in the ranks to sitting down around the table of friendship with nationalistic parties that had supported or even joined capitalist governments—above all the SPD.[6] Other parties, notably the Swiss and Italian socialists, the KPD, and the Bolsheviks, had boycotted the proceedings. Nor were the USPD delegates representative of rank-and-file party opinion; the principal spokesmen were Kurt Eisner, who went as a self-appointed Bavarian delegate concerned chiefly with the issue of war guilt, and Karl Kautsky, who was openly at odds with the drift of his party's domestic policies. Kautsky found the air of the revived International congenial and quickly found his way back to the center of things, unconcerned about what party followers at home might think. "The International," he reported later, "has arisen again."[7] But the party congress of March showed that the regulars thought very poorly of the whole affair; while no vote was taken on the Bern conference, Kautsky's report was criticized from the floor far more frequently than it was defended. Most Independents, determined to go it alone in Germany, transferred this uncompromising outlook to the international scene. The proponents of broad international unity faced a hard road.

Unity in the International could, in any event, only be had at high cost to the USPD. The Bern meetings had shown that parties of the USPD's general outlook were the weaker force in such gatherings. Substantively, the only conference action of which Independents could wholeheartedly approve was the extraction of a veiled confession by the German Majority Socialists that they had been guilty of supporting a government held by most foreign parties to have been responsible for the war.[8] Once this penance was done, however, the SPD, not the USPD, clearly fitted best with the general attitudes of the majority at the conference. For exam-

5. On the conference, see Wheeler, "Internationals," pp. 157–87, and "The Failure of 'Truth and Clarity' at Berne: Kurt Eisner, the Opposition and the Reconstruction of the International," *International Review of Social History*, 18 (1973), 173–201.

6. See the comments of Dissmann, Barth, Herzfeld, and Däumig, USPD *Parteitag*, March 1919, pp. 147, 149, 189, and 236.

7. *Ibid.*, p. 126.

8. *Ibid.*, pp. 120–21; Wheeler, "Berne," pp. 181–83.

ple, only with difficulty could the delegates be dissuaded from voting on a resolution condemning the Soviet form of dictatorship of the proletariat, which would certainly have passed.[9] The postwar International had a new majority of parties that had quietly left behind any oppositional, millenarian views they might have held and become committed to participation in the politics, and even the governments, of their respective states. The British Labour Party and the German Majority Socialists formed the axis of this new majority, supported by most of the parties of Scandinavia and the Low Countries. Events at Bern demonstrated that, in an International restored on an inclusive basis, the USPD would occupy, at least at first, the position of a relatively ineffectual left wing.

In spite of these awkward circumstances, and although their policy was a divisive force within the party, the more moderate party leaders continued to steer cautiously toward a solution within the revived Second International. Their reasons were partly ideological: the International should express the unity of the proletariat. This principle was dominant, if not absolute, for Kautsky; and in modified form it motivated Hilferding, who emerged as the leading advocate of the reviving International in the USPD. More important for most of Hilferding's colleagues were two other considerations: the desire (or duty) to have a practical impact on international socialism, and a Western orientation. The former was expressed by Haase upon his return from the April meeting of the permanent commission of the International in Amsterdam: "The Independent Social Democratic Party cannot remain isolated. It considers its task to be to unite the proletarians of all countries in a revolutionary spirit."[10] This tendency, and the Western orientation as well, were reinforced by the crisis over the Treaty of Versailles and the vision of the International that the Independents summoned up for the occasion. The conception is found in developed form in a leaflet circulated in the party to explain the leadership's controversial decision to send delegates to the Lucerne meetings in August. The USPD's task was "to help bring about the necessary clarification in the International." To achieve this:

It is necessary that the revolutionary standpoint of the German USP be represented vis-à-vis other parties. Nonparticipation would mean excluding ourselves from the possibility of influencing the stand of the proletariat in the Western countries. But it is precisely the position of the proletariat in the more highly developed capitalist countries of the West that is decisive for the future development of the revolution. Thus the interests of the revolution require that we do not cut ourselves off from the Western proletariat. . . .

9. Wheeler, "Berne," pp. 183–92.
10. *Freiheit,* May 4, 1919.

In the East the proletariat is already revolutionary, while spurring on the revolutionary moment in the West must be *our* task in the International.[11]

Implicit in such arguments was the consideration that the USPD had no real alternative. Until summer's end party leaders gave no serious thought to the new Communist, or Third, International, which was weak, distant, obviously dominated by the Bolsheviks, and allied with the despised German Communists.[12] Not only the Third, but any other breakaway International would almost inevitably offend against the Western orientation by having its center of gravity in Central and Eastern Europe. To work within the broader International for a time, while hoping for a change, was therefore better. Circumstances might change the attitude of some national parties, as had already happened in France and was happening in Austria; the Italians and others might return to the fold and strengthen the left wing. The Independents' experience of the changing balance of forces that a rapid growth of working-class radicalism had brought about within Germany encouraged hopes of a similar shift in the International. In any case, in view of the lack of any attractive alternative alignment, the only possibility seemed to be to suppress emotional objections and work in the only forum available.

Party leaders, however, were not immune to the left's influence, especially in choosing words in which to define their tasks. In the leaflet mentioned above, the future International was envisioned in a manner remote from the old orthodoxy:

The International, which must no longer be an International of preparations and demonstrations, must become a real international force and an International capable of action.

The International must work for the conquest of political power and the realization of socialism by means of the dictatorship of the proletariat.

The International must reject all opportunist endeavors and concentrate the social-revolutionary forces in all international matters concerning the workers. . . .

The parties adhering to the International must submit and subordinate themselves to international decisions.

The International is the supreme unifying and directing organ of all affiliated parties.[13]

11. "U.S.P.D. Referentenmaterial: Warum gehen wir nach Luzern?" Levi papers, P 122. This translation is my own; a translation of the entire text is in Wheeler, "Internationals," pp. 298–99.

12. In the leaflet cited in the previous note the Third International is dismissed in a single sentence.

13. *Ibid.;* "capable of action [*aktionsfähig*]" and "social-revolutionary" were key phrases in the arsenal of slogans with which Independents approached questions of the International.

Vague as this rhetoric was, some practical conclusions were inescapable. One, specified in the leaflet, was that there was no place in such an International for the SPD. Even Hilferding found it necessary to endorse this view:

An International that included the outspokenly reformist and nationalist groups would be so weak as to be useless for the proletariat. . . . [It] would be too compromising for socialists, would assist in misleading and deceiving the working class, and would be morally and practically incapable from the start of any energetic action.[14]

In effect the Independents were introducing into the International the principle of ideological exclusiveness. In defining a common ideological basis, the USPD was thrown back on the formulas with which it had (it hoped) fixed its own ideological position amid Germany's controversies: the council system and the dictatorship of the proletariat. These were not terms with universal appeal abroad, even among radicals, but the Independents knew of no other way to identify the category of parties on which the USPD's hopes for the future of the International rested.

In this state of divided purpose the party executive still clung to its connection with the International, though officially only on an exploratory basis. The party congress in March had given no mandate on this question; the party left, though hostile to the moderates' policy, did not yet have an alternative to suggest and was still largely preoccupied with domestic struggles. The executive therefore continued to allow Kautsky to represent the party in the bureau that the Bern conference had established. And in consultation with the auxiliary council and the control commission the executive decided to participate in the second preparatory conference of the International in Lucerne.[15]

The party's futile role at this conference, which met from August 1 to 10, 1919, was the last straw for critics of the party's international policy.[16] The party had gone with aggressive purposes: "to bring to bear the revolutionary standpoint of Independent Social Democracy, to take a stand against reformist tendencies, and to bring the counterrevolutionary attitude of the German Right Socialists before the forum of the International";[17] and the delegates (including Crispien and Hilferding) engaged in the rhetorical fireworks expected of them by their followers at home. But again the majority was against them; their only achievement was to rally an effective pressure group that prevented the majority from con-

14. *Freiheit*, July 24, 1919 (m).
15. *Ibid.*, July 30, 1919 (e).
16. Wheeler, "Internationals," pp. 303–7 and 312–28, examines the conference and the role of the Independents.
17. *Freiheit*, July 30, 1919 (e).

demning the policies of the Bolshevik government in Russia.[18] Otherwise, they returned with empty hands. The demand for expulsion of the SPD disappeared into a committee. The council system was not even seriously debated; indeed, for the sake of submitting a joint resolution with the French delegates the Independents let their specific formula fall and retired onto the principle of the "class struggle, which is to be carried forward without compromise with bourgeois parties."[19] Even this motion was unsuccessful. The meetings were dominated as before by the compromising mood of the practiced politicians of Western socialism.[20]

This was not the International to stir the emotions of Independent Social Democrats in the summer of 1919. Pressure on the party leaders to sever connections with it became intense. And at the same time increasing numbers of Independents came to take seriously the only existing alternative to the Second International: the Communist International.

The Third, or Communist, International began life early in March 1919.[21] Founded solely on the initiative of the Bolsheviks (specifically Lenin), with the purpose of offsetting any attractions the Bern conference of the regrouping Second International might have for radical sister parties, the new International in distant Moscow was at first quite unprepossessing. Circumstances were inauspicious: for most of 1919 the usual avenues of communication between Russia and the rest of Europe, and thus between the Bolsheviks and sympathetic parties, were closed. The so-called First Congress of the Comintern, meeting from March 2 to 6 in Moscow, was attended by few delegates from abroad and dominated by the Russians, with the aid of assorted Bolshevik recruits of other nationalities, many of them former prisoners of war. Under these conditions, establishment of a new, revolutionary International was little more than a gesture.

The gesture, however, had considerable appeal once news of it had seeped out of blockaded Russia. A number of East European socialist parties quickly declared their adherence, led by the larger of the Bulgarian socialist parties. Response was more limited at first in Western Europe, with few except splinter groups affiliating; but within six months

18. Hilferding, USPD *Parteitag,* Nov.–Dec. 1919, p. 311.
19. P. J. Troelstra papers (IISH Amsterdam), item 465.
20. See critiques of the party's failure at the conference by Curt Geyer, *Leipziger Volkszeitung,* Sept. 6, 1919, and Stoecker (at the September party conference), *Freiheit,* Sept. 11, 1919 (m).
21. There is a copious literature on the early years of the Comintern; the most detailed studies are James W. Hulse, *The Forming of the Communist International* (Stanford, Calif., 1964), and Branko Lazitch and Milorad M. Drachkovitch, *Lenin and the Comintern,* vol. 1 (Stanford, Calif., 1972); see also Franz Borkenau, *World Communism* (London, 1938), and E. H. Carr, *The Bolshevik Revolution,* vol. 3 (London, 1953).

the Norwegian party, a breakaway Swedish party, and the Italian Socialist Party had joined the Third International. The German Communists soon gave up their initial skepticism and joined. With the central authority of the International remote and ineffective, these admirers of the successful Russian revolutionaries could align themselves with the Bolsheviks, and even support Bolshevik views on international organization, without feeling the weight of centralized authority that was to alienate so many of them two years later.

At first the Independents were not much affected by the new International. Non-Communists paid little attention in advance, or for some time afterward, to its founding congress, which coincided with the USPD's March party congress, and until the end of the first phase of the revolution in May–June the Independents had other things to occupy them. Moreover, the leaders of the Third International made no effort to recruit the USPD—rather the contrary. The most bitter polemics of the First Congress were directed at the "Center," to which the whole of the USPD, left wing included, was explicitly consigned.[22] All the factional differences of the war and the revolution were raked up, not for the last time. The USPD's policy of anchoring the councils in the new constitution was ridiculed by Lenin, and Kautsky and Hilferding were singled out for damnation.[23] The Russian leaders took the hard line that the "revolutionary elements" in the USPD, meaning the workers, must and would abandon their party and become Communists; no attempt was made to differentiate among the leaders of the party, who were treated merely as different types of centrists.[24] Such a vehement attack by Comintern leaders on present and past USPD policies gave the party no incentive to pursue contacts with the new organization.

Not all USPD leaders felt themselves touched by the strictures of the Comintern; those with established sympathies for the Bolsheviks certainly did not. Though wounded by the sharp accusations from Moscow, older radicals, including Ernst Däumig, wrote them off as the result of a misunderstanding. And the party's new men, who were already trying to refashion the party in a new image and felt little responsibility for past policies, were not displeased at foreign intervention that seemed to support their own efforts to hasten change. Some prominent younger men in the party apparently saw the Third International as the issue that would lead their faction to dominance in the party and revive the revolutionary impetus in Germany. In the summer of 1919 this idea gained ground

22. See Comintern *Kongress,* March 1919, esp. pp. 166 and 191.
23. *Ibid.,* pp. 124–28.
24. *Ibid.,* p. 166.

within the radical section of the party, even among those, including Däumig and Koenen, whose principal concern remained the organizational problems of the workers' councils. Leadership of the campaign was assumed by a small number of younger men, the most prominent of whom were Walter Stoecker, newly a member of the party executive, and Curt Geyer of Leipzig.

The lines were first drawn in August and September, in connection with the widespread dissatisfaction over the USPD's participation in the Lucerne conference and the course of that conference. The proponents of the Third International found a ready audience, in that they seemed to offer a plausible alternative to the distasteful connection with the reformists in the Second International. For some Independents, the question seemed a simple choice between a suspect, weak, reformist International and "an International that takes its stand clearly on the council system, on the dictatorship of the proletariat."[25] In this spirit, and reflecting their long-standing admiration for the achievements of the Bolsheviks, the radical locals of Gotha and Halle adopted resolutions demanding immediate adherence to the Communist International.[26] The campaign had opened.

The issue was brought formally before the party for the first time in September, at the party conference in Berlin. Stoecker, as spokesman for the advocates of affiliation, delivered an address in which may be seen, although in primitive form, both the strengths and the weaknesses of the position the left was to take.[27] On the one hand, he spoke to his somewhat discouraged audience of the strength to be derived from international ties, these being understood in terms of an effective organizing structure—a way of thinking congenial to most Independents. From this point of view, the Second International was useless; "it would break down again in a crisis just as in 1914." In any case, an all-inclusive International was by then out of the question, he pointed out, because the Bolsheviks and their allies would never sit down with the reformist socialists; and since "we will have to reckon permanently with two Internationals," the choice of any revolutionary party ought to be obvious. On the other hand, Stoecker's attitude toward the program and pronouncements of the Third International, which he subjected to criti-

25. The *Hamburger Volkszeitung,* quoted in Horst Naumann, "Der Kampf des revolutionären Flügels der USPD für den Anschluss an die Kommunistische Internationale und die Vereinigung mit der KPD (unter besonderer Berücksichtigung der Hilfe durch die Kommunistische Internationale und die KPD)" (Ph.D. dissertation, Institut für Gesellschaftswissenschaften beim Zentralkomitee der SED, Berlin, 1961), p. 65.
26. *Ibid.,* pp. 64–65.
27. Stoecker's speech is reported at length in *Freiheit,* Sept. 11, 1919 (m).

cal review, suffered not only from incomplete information, which was understandable since little news was reaching Germany from Moscow, but also from serious misapprehensions about the views of Lenin and other Bolshevik leaders. Despite a number of criticisms of detail, he was persuaded, he said, that no essential differences divided the programs of the USPD and the Third International and that such differences as existed would be accommodated by tactical autonomy within the International. The founding congress' attack on the Independents was due, he said, to Russian ignorance of the USPD's March Action Program, then being adopted. In any case, "not only Moscow decides" in the International. Everything thus pointed to the desirability of immediate affiliation with the new International.

In rejecting the bold step advocated by Stoecker, Hilferding may have spoken for the majority of the conference (though no vote was taken).[28] He added a note that went beyond the familiar arguments for cooperation with the Western parties, however, in his vigorous skepticism about the Bolsheviks, and in this he was probably not followed by most delegates, especially when he suggested that the Bolshevik state might be "a sinking ship" from which one ought to steer clear. The argument led him to a prophetic understanding of what the Third International was to become, well before even the Bolsheviks really understood the implications of their creation. Unlike Stoecker, Hilferding was aware that "Russian Bolshevism *is* the Third International." He predicted that affiliation would mean subjection, that it would mean accepting not only the Bolshevik program but also Bolshevik methods, however inappropriate they might be to Germany. He singled out as objectionable the Bolsheviks' tendency to generalize their experience of civil war into a binding doctrine for other parties and to elevate the use of terror by a revolutionary government into a principle. But such arguments, however acute, were ahead of sentiment in the party, where a platonic pro-Bolshevik stand still seemed the easiest path. Besides, Hilferding's conclusions were negative. His own policy was to temporize, to open contacts with the Bolsheviks (for a purpose not stated) while awaiting the growth of a revolutionary spirit in Western Europe that would provide the basis for another, more acceptable revolutionary International. It was not a vision to carry away his listeners.

By September 1919, then, the more traditional forces in the USPD were already on the defensive over the International. The left wing had not yet made their case; but they were beginning to rally their potential

28. *Ibid.* Wheeler, "Internationals," p. 361, holds that the majority was probably on Stoecker's side; the evidence is inconclusive.

support, to carry their cause into the party assemblies and district conferences, and eventually to the party congress at the end of the year.

German Communists and the Comintern in Germany

When the USPD began turning uncertainly in the direction of the
Third International, two previously ignored actors became important:
the German Communist Party and the Communist International itself.
The Independents had generally been able to ignore the KPD because it
was largely invisible, or, to use Paul Levi's words, "nearly dead as far as
the public is concerned."[29] The party's troubles began in its first days. Its
opening congress struck an ultraradical attitude that was unlikely to have
wide appeal, and within two weeks came the crushing defeat of a hare-
brained rising in Berlin that was identified, however erroneously, with
the KPD. Three of the party's outstanding leaders were assassinated in
rapid succession, Rosa Luxemburg and Karl Liebknecht in January and
Leo Jogiches in March. The sketchy central organization of the party
was incapable of rallying even its natural supporters, some of whom—
for instance, in Hanau or Braunschweig—did not join the new party for
weeks or even months. And, most important, the new party, weak but
conspicuous, presented the perfect target for government repression. In
the wake of the March fighting in Berlin, both the central committee and
Rote Fahne fled the capital; they surfaced again in Leipzig a month
later, but the fall of Leipzig drove them on again.[30] From early May until
December the party was outlawed under the state of siege in Berlin and
other important sections of the country, its newspapers unable to appear
legally, its communications subject to constant disruption, its leaders
liable to arrest at any moment.

The KPD had difficulty, too, in finding its bearings. The party leaders
—headed from March 1919 by Paul Levi—were as little able to tie
their followers to a reasoned tactical line as they had been before the
founding congress.[31] Communists were active in all the more notorious
radical actions of the period, including the Bavarian Soviet Republic and
the terrorism in the Ruhr mines; while they had company in many of
these actions from other groups, including Independents, the Commu-

29. Circular of Nov. 28, 1919, by Hartstein [Levi], p. 4, Levi papers, P 19.
30. A chronology of the central committee's peregrinations is attached to a circular of March 4, 1920, Levi papers, P 129.
31. Gerhard P. Bassler, "The Communist Movement in the German Revolution,
1918–1919: A Problem of Historical Typology?" *Central European History*, 6
(1973), 236–39 and 274–77, argues that Communist rank-and-file behavior
springs from the movement's origin in a reaction to excessive structure and author-
itarianism in society and in the old party. On what follows see also Bock, pp.
112–17.

nists were identified in the popular mind as the perpetrators. They became tagged as "putschists," ready for violent action on any pretext, however ill-considered the time and place. The leadership fought this tendency, to the point of dissolving the party's paramilitary arm, the Red Soldiers' League;[32] but by the time the principle of restraint in matters of armed action was finally established—as much by circumstances as by guidance from the leadership—the party had a bad reputation.

Settlement of this problem only cleared the ground for theoretical and tactical disputes. The first was over parliamentarianism; a section of the party wanted to regard the founding congress' decision against participation in the National Assembly elections as a point of general principle, while the central committee reasserted its desire to use elections and the parliamentary rostrum for agitation.[33] The second issue—participation in trade unions—was even more pressing; Levi later called it a "life and death" matter for the party.[34] The dissidents, despairing of ever making headway in the old trade unions, urged formation of a new kind of union, based on factory councils, and called on their followers to abandon existing unions. This point of view was popular among party members, especially in Hamburg, Bremen, Berlin, and parts of the Ruhr,[35] but had little appeal for nonmembers, so that the Communists risked isolating themselves from the great mass of the workers and perhaps having their followers shut out of the factories by the powerful unions. The leadership, attracted by the idealism of the Hamburg scheme and impressed by members' enthusiasm, was slow to recognize the realities of the situation.[36]

While the KPD floundered, the Independents could view it with a combination of indifference, suspicion, and big-brotherly disapproval. Independent custom was to criticize the Communists on grounds, not of principle (since this would mean using the same arguments as the Majority Socialists), but of tactics. The USPD radicals, in particular, argued that their aims were identical with those of the Communists, but their

32. See the KPD notices, *Freiheit*, June 21, 1919 (e), and June 23, 1919 (e), according to which the League was dissolved "some time ago."

33. Bernhard Reichenbach, "Zur Geschichte der K(ommunistischen) A(rbeiter)-P(artei) D(eutschlands)," *Archiv für die Geschichte des Sozialismus und der Arbeiterbewegung*, 13 (1928), 120.

34. Report by Levi to the Comintern, *Berichte zum Zweiten Kongress*, p. 31.

35. The interesting case of one of the KPD's strongest locals, in Bremen, is discussed in Kuckuck, pp. 160–90.

36. See the critique in Alexandra Müller, "Die Spaltung in der Kommunistischen Partei Deutschlands," *Sowjet*, Dec. 1919, pp. 22–30. On the subject of the KPD's trade-union policy during 1919 see also Rettig, pp. 14–23, and Bock, pp. 122–32.

methods were more sensible and responsible; they hoped, in time, to detach the sounder Communists from their false ideas and lead them back into a broader proletarian unity. Meanwhile, even the left-wing Independents found the Communists unreliable allies, unwilling to share responsibility and always ready to break the common front and strike out on their own while blaming all failures on their former allies. Relations between the two parties remained poor.

Only in the autumn did the wavering leadership of the KPD adopt a firm line, which made its unexpected appearance at a party congress at Heidelberg in October. Levi's opening address set the tone by attacking all elements of the opposition—antiparliamentarians, opponents of the trade unions, and anticentralists, which were overlapping but not identical groups—as representing a single phenomenon, stigmatized as "syndicalism."[37] Theses were introduced that took the old, orthodox line and provided that members who could not accept them were to be expelled from the party.[38] It was a classic splitting operation, carried out without warning. The central committee had a bare but firm majority; after a bitter debate, the opposition was driven out.

The costs were great; perhaps half the party's membership was lost, and an internal crisis developed that lasted until the following summer and led to the formation of the rival Communist Workers Party (KAPD) in April 1920.[39] These costs were acceptable to the leadership because it had far-reaching aims in mind. In contrast to the party's hyperradicals, who seemed to be heading for a sectarian existence on the far left, the party leaders remembered that mass support must be won within the proletariat, as laid down in Luxemburg's Spartacist Program, if there was ever to be a successful revolution. The original expectation had been that such support would come during the continuing radical surge; but when the first revolutionary period ended, the problem of means had to be considered carefully. In cleansing their party of confused elements incapable of following a tactical line, the old Spartacists who made up the central leadership were convinced that they were not only laying a sound basis for their own party but also developing precepts to guide the entire international Communist movement in the

37. KPD *Parteitag*, Oct. 1919, p. 17; on the nature and roots of this syndicalism, see Bock, pp. 139–44.

38. KPD *Parteitag*, Oct. 1919, pp. 60–62. Among the first to be expelled were Otto Rühle of Dresden and Heinrich Laufenberg of Hamburg.

39. The party reported 106,656 members in October, probably an inflated figure; *ibid.*, p. 27. The official figure for July 1920 was 66,323; KPD *Parteitag*, Nov. 1920, p. 5. The membership probably dropped below 50,000 in the worst days before the Kapp Putsch; Rist, p. 86, gives a figure of 45,000 for the time of the Putsch. On the foundation of the KAPD, see Bock, pp. 225–28.

second, more difficult phase of the revolution.[40] From this perspective, the drastic measures of the Heidelberg congress were justified.

A second major motive for the split may have been a desire on the central committee's part to overcome the barriers between the Communists and the left wing of the USPD. Whether or not this thought was influential at the October party congress (there is no direct evidence), within six weeks thereafter it had become a dominant feature of the KPD's plans. The principle of appealing to the broader revolutionary masses could be implemented only by winning over the more radical elements of the USPD. Furthermore, some leaders (notably Levi) saw that aiming to absorb the radical Independents into the existing KPD as individuals and small units might not be the best idea. More realistic, and even more desirable, might be a policy of encouraging the USPD's left wing to win over the whole party, or at least the greater part of it, to Communist ideas, which would bring a massive bloc of support into the Communist camp and the Communist International all at once, together with the older party's authority, machinery, voters, and press.[41] Herein seemed to lie the fastest route to a mass revolutionary party (the KPD had perhaps 50,000 members after its split, the USPD had nearly three-quarters of a million and was growing); and the Communists' hopes were predicated on a massive following, especially so long as Rosa Luxemburg's view of revolution predominated. This policy, however, required an unpalatable degree of tolerance for the less-than-pure ideology of the left-wing Independents; and before the Leipzig party congress its only known exponents were Levi and, significantly, Karl Radek.[42] Levi, however, allegedly with the backing of the Comintern's new secret office in Berlin (the West European secretariat),[43] put his ideas into practice. Shortly before the Leipzig congress of the USPD, he established his first contacts with the leaders of its left wing—Stoecker, Brass, Koenen, and Curt Geyer—to consult on tactics at the congress and give assurances of

40. KPD *Parteitag,* Oct. 1919, p. 25, peroration of Levi's speech; article "Nach einem Jahr," *Rote Fahne,* Jan. 1, 1920.

41. Circular of Nov. 28, 1919, by Hartstein [Levi], Levi papers, P 19.

42. See Arnold Struthahn [Radek], "Die Unabhängigen und die Internationale," *Die Internationale* (KPD), Nov. 1, 1919, esp. pp. 291–93. Lenin, who later supported the Levi-Radek policy, was at this time still sharply hostile to the left-wing Independents; see his article of Oct. 1919 in *Die Kommunistische Internationale,* no. 3, esp. p. 29.

43. *Rote Fahne,* March 7, 1920. The West European secretariat was set up in the fall of 1919 under the leadership of the Polish Bolshevik Thomas (or Reich), whose recollections are the best source for its functioning; see Boris Nicolaevsky, ed., "Les premières années de l'Internationale communiste, d'après le récit du 'camarade Thomas,'" *Contributions à l'histoire du Comintern,* ed. Jacques Freymond (Geneva, 1965), pp. 1–27.

the International's good will.[44] These fraternal bonds were never fully broken, even by the vicissitudes of the following six months.

Karl Radek's favorable view of the USPD's potential was particularly significant. Radek, undoubtedly the best versed of the prominent Bolsheviks in German affairs, played a central role in International's dealings with the Germans from 1920 until the fiascos of 1923; but his views of the German situation were formed during 1919, while he was in prison and later under house arrest in Germany. He may have been the first to formulate the policy of attempting to work through the USPD's left wing to win that party to Communism; he was certainly the first to expound it publicly.[45] He was also among its most effective advocates— in his copious writings, his regular consultations with the German Communists and the West European secretariat, and his conversations with left-wing Independents.[46] Early in 1920 he carried the idea back with him to Moscow.

In Moscow the Communist International was showing the first signs of another development that became important for German socialists. The executive committee (ECCI) in Moscow, in practice a Russian institution, as Lenin and Zinoviev later admitted,[47] had at first limited its public pronouncements to fiery manifestoes and appeals for support for Soviet Russia and Soviet Hungary against aggressive foreign governments. There is little evidence that the International in its first months offered tactical advice even privately; its agent Thomas, for instance, came to Germany without such instructions, and as late as November he was sponsoring an international conference at which such matters were allegedly not even discussed.[48] The International, in fact, was initially the "propaganda society" that Zinoviev later called it,[49] and the relations of foreign parties with it were correspondingly free of friction. By the fall of 1919, though, the ECCI had started to lay down political guide-

44. USPD *Parteitag*, Nov.–Dec. 1919, pp. 133–34.
45. See the article by Radek cited in n. 42.
46. Otto-Ernst Schüddekopf, "Karl Radek in Berlin," *Archiv für Sozialgeschichte*, 2 (1962), 155–58 and 162; Nicolaevsky, p. 14; R. Fischer, pp. 206–7. Radek's most important writings on relations with the USPD, apart from the article already mentioned, are *Die Entwicklung der Weltrevolution und die Taktik der Kommunistischen Parteien im Kampfe um die Diktatur des Proletariats* (n.p., n.d.; preface dated Nov. 1919); the preface (dated Dec. 12, 1919) to his *Die Entwicklung der deutschen Revolution und die Aufgaben der Kommunistischen Partei*, 2d ed. (Hamburg, 1920); and (as Arnold Struthahn) "Der Parteitag der Unabhängigen," *Die Internationale* (KPD), Feb. 2, 1920, pp. 22–32.
47. See G. Zinoviev, *Bericht des Exekutivkomitees der Kommunistischen Internationale an den Zweiten Weltkongress der Kommunistischen Internationale* (Petrograd, 1920), p. 5.
48. Nicolaevsky, pp. 12 and 15.
49. Comintern *Kongress*, July–Aug. 1920, p. 237.

lines, albeit tentatively at first. The first recorded instance was in September, when the ECCI intervened in the dispute then raging among Communist parties about participation in parliaments and elections with a circular favoring participation as a necessary tactical measure.[50] An article by Lenin in October on German socialism and Communism went further.[51] The recommendations, however, were couched in the language of fraternal advice and hedged about with qualifications; they seem to have become known in Germany only after Levi had set his party on a corresponding course;[52] and for some months they remained the only instances of such advice. Yet they portended Russian impatience with the independent development of brother parties and a growing tendency to use the organs of the Communist International to urge Russian views abroad. They were the beginning of a "manipulative" stage in the Comintern's work,[53] the first foreshadowings of the future character of the Moscow International.

The Leipzig Party Congress

Meanwhile, the Independents, largely ignorant of these developments, were preparing for their own debates on the questions dividing them. The focus for these preparations was the party congress that had been anticipated since the party conference of September and that opened on the last day of November.

The debates leading up to the congress, and those at the congress itself, presented the arguments for and against the Third International in much the form they were to retain until the Comintern's second congress more than six months later.[54] The pro-Moscow side's position was familiar. The argument for adherence to the Third International was basically simple. Emotionally, it drew on the sympathy, even admiration, that most party members felt for the Bolsheviks and conferred on the Third International something of the aura the Bolsheviks enjoyed as successful revolutionaries. Ideologically, it pointed out the congruence between the principal aspirations of the radical Independents—dictatorship of the proletariat and government by councils—and the program of

50. *Die Kommunistische Internationale*, no. 3, pp. 71–74.

51. *Ibid.*, pp. 27–34.

52. The September circular was first published by the KPD in *Kommunistische Räte-Korrespondenz*, Dec. 1919, pp. 7–8, at about the time *Die Kommunistische Internationale*, no. 3, appeared in Germany.

53. Dan L. Morrill, "The Comintern and the German Independent Social Democratic Party," *Historian*, Feb. 1970, pp. 191 and 197.

54. For more detailed treatment of this debate and the factional maneuvering that accompanied it, see Wheeler, "Internationals," ch. 7, which draws on some thirty of the USPD's provincial newspapers.

the International and the aims of its member parties. By drawing the USPD together with parties of like mind in other countries, the International would help the party renew its energies, define its ideological commitments, and intensify its revolutionary work.

The right wing could scarcely answer these arguments; its part of the debate was conducted largely on a different plane, though there were some points of contact. Where the left wing saw ideological conformity between itself and the Bolsheviks, the moderates saw serious differences. The skeptics pressed a whole series of arguments deriving from the probable organizational consequences of affiliation with Moscow. Hilferding again put forward the most extreme formulation:

> The entire spirit of the Moscow International implies that one can belong to it only if one accepts its decisions, that above all one can belong to it only if one *follows the tactical directives* that proceed from this Third International, in which in reality, given the present composition, the Moscovites of course exercise a dictatorship. What Moscow means by an International capable of action is precisely that those actions which are decided there *must* be carried out by the other parties.[55]

There was little evidence for this charge at the time, but the suspicion was there. And in case the prospect of receiving tactical prescriptions from abroad was not repugnant enough, the opponents of the Third International were able to point to particular matters in which Moscow seemed likely to try to override foreign parties. The Bolsheviks, for example, emphasized the role of force (*Gewalt*) in the revolution, including civil war and even red terror, and this did not accord with the civilized—perhaps overcivilized—traditions of the Social Democrats; to many these principles seemed neither moral nor expedient.[56] The Comintern's tendency to flirt with syndicalists, as another group of useful revolutionary allies, similarly ran counter to rooted prejudices among Social Democrats.[57] Finally, the splitting of national labor movements implied by the nature of the Third International and virtually written into its program was seen by many as a grievous fault.[58]

There was, too, a widespread feeling among Independents that the Bolsheviks had been behaving badly toward them. The unilateral creation of a new International was resented: "It is not permissible for a part of the international labor movement to found an International, set

---

55. USPD *Parteitag*, Nov.–Dec. 1919, p. 317 (emphasis in the original). Hilferding even suggested that the Bolsheviks looked on their International as a mere tool of their own interests; *ibid.*, p. 321.

56. See, for example, Hilferding and Ledebour, *ibid.*, pp. 317 and 359–60.

57. The offending resolution of the Comintern is in Comintern *Kongress*, March 1919, p. 191.

58. Hilferding, USPD *Parteitag*, Nov.–Dec. 1919, pp. 322–23.

up a program and prescribe tactics which all the others are then supposed simply to put up with. The foundation of an International must be preceded by national and international debates and arrangements."[59] And most Independents were disconcerted by the invective regularly hurled at the party and all its works by the Comintern. The greatest share of this abuse was directed at Kautsky and disgusted not only those who, like Hilferding, still listened to their former teacher but also Ledebour.[60] For many Independents, accustomed to thinking of German socialists as leaders, not pupils, in the international movement, this vituperation reinforced a stiff party pride. A pro-Bolshevik delegate at the Leipzig congress sardonically summed up this attitude as "Deutschland in der Welt voran!"[61] and however exaggerated this accusation may have been the assumption of Russian priority in the International deeply offended a large part of the USPD.

The advocates of affiliation had to answer these questions. Hilferding's basic objection to the Third International, that there was a danger of having to accept dictation from the Bolsheviks, was simply denied, and in all good conscience; there was no direct evidence of such necessity at the time, at least not in Germany.[62] As for the dominance of the Bolsheviks, the Comintern's advocates tacitly accepted the undeniable fact that this was the case but argued that the adherence of the Independents and similar parties, such as the French party, would change the internal balance of the International and relieve it also of its East European character.[63] Under these assumptions, more specific objections to current views expressed by the International became secondary matters. They were not, however, brushed aside. Stoecker, too, was disturbed by the precipitate foundation of the International, by the tendency to ally with syndicalists, and by the overemphasis on the role of military force in the revolution; the Bolsheviks, he remarked, had made a lot of mistakes in their time.[64] He found the Bolsheviks' defamation of the USPD to be simply out of date, while Däumig declared that, in critical times, to be influenced by wounded honor or party pride was unworthy.[65] Revolutionary terror, the left repeatedly stressed, was not prescribed in any resolution or declaration of the International.[66] As for the role of vio-

59. Artur Crispien, *Die Internationale: Vom Bund der Kommunisten bis zur Internationale der Weltrevolution*, 2d ed. (Berlin, 1920), pp. 35–36.
60. USPD *Parteitag*, Nov.–Dec. 1919, p. 350.
61. Bertha Braunthal, *ibid.*, p. 377.
62. See, for example, Stoecker, *ibid.*, p. 333.
63. *Ibid.*, p. 340.
64. *Ibid.*, pp. 330–33.
65. *Ibid.*, pp. 331 and 370–71.
66. *Ibid.*, p. 334; Curt Geyer, "Nach dem Parteitag," *Das Forum*, Jan. 1920, p. 267.

lence and civil war in a revolutionary period, the supporters of the International accepted the Russian position, though in somewhat weakened form: to suppose that revolution could be carried through without a great deal of force and disruption would be foolish.[67] Here, evidently, the left wing sensed an issue on which the International could help them override the cautious and humanitarian traditions that were preventing the party from wholeheartedly committing itself to the revolutionary struggle.

The basic weakness of the left wing's case, and the reason why the pro-Moscow faction might capture control of the USPD but never be able to carry the party as a whole, lay in its response to the questions of Bolshevik dominance and Bolshevik methods. The positive arguments of the advocates of affiliation were simple and legitimate and could provide an effective framework for agitation in certain circumstances, that is, when impatience and the drive for change were very strong in the party, as at the end of 1919. But the USPD combined this sort of impulse in uneasy mixture with reliance on tradition; it was also an established political organization with a certain pride and a deadweight of self-interest. These factors, as much as or more than purely ideological reservations, limited the appeal of innovation within the party; and when the Third International later began to appear in its other guise, as a centralized, external authority with alien ways, conservative sentiments were quickly awakened in the party's members and especially its leaders. The advocates of the Third International never successfully evolved arguments to offset the coolness produced in their party, and particularly in its most influential quarters, by the conflict between German Social Democratic orthodoxy and the increasingly visible peculiarities of the Communist International.

Even at the end of 1919, an inkling of this conflict kept many in the party from enthusiastically advocating "going to Moscow"; and the position of the left wing was made more difficult by the skeptics' seeming room for maneuver. The Second International, most agreed, had nothing more to offer the USPD; but if, as Hilferding suggested and many others believed, the Third International had "no prospect of uniting in itself those great proletarian masses of the industrial West that are decisive for the revolutionary struggle,"[68] then the Independents must take an active role in creating something better.

Thus began the movement known as "reconstruction"; revolutionary parties turning their backs on the International of Bern and Lucerne

67. USPD *Parteitag*, Nov.–Dec. 1919, pp. 333–34.
68. From Hilferding's resolution at the congress, *ibid.*, p. 39.

need not bow to the Bolsheviks' fait accompli but might agree (with the Bolsheviks) on a reconstruction of the International to take better account of the views of the Central and West European parties. The goal, in Crispien's words, was to unite "all socialist parties which wage the independent class struggle in word and deed, which strive for the conquest of political power by the workers, which accept the basis of the council system, and which recognize the dictatorship of the proletariat as a necessary transitional measure for the phase between capitalism and socialism."[69] This scheme appealed to those who found themselves in the middle between Hilferding and Stoecker, for it meant breaking with the reformists without risking isolation; answering the hesitations of several West European parties, and thus making possible a more inclusive International of the left; and giving the united left-wing parties of West and Central Europe the leverage to combine with the Bolsheviks without being dominated by them. The flaws were that it implied mistrust of the Bolsheviks, which would give the far left pause, and complicated negotiations, which were not as attractive to many Independents as the inspirational appeal of the dramatic act of adherence. Most important, the Bolsheviks were in such a strong position that the undertaking could not succeed unless they cooperated. But since all other solutions to the problem of international affiliation also involved difficulties, reconstruction gained many supporters on the right and in the center of the USPD.

Such was the state of the debate when the Leipzig party congress assembled on November 30. The debate itself had been accompanied by a hard-fought struggle in the local and district organizations for delegate strength at the congress, coordinated at least to some extent from Berlin in the case of the left wing;[70] and the line-up of forces at the congress gave the radicals a majority for their efforts to change the party. The left wing was denied its struggle on the party program; only on the question of the International did it emerge as an organized faction. On this issue, however, it had a majority, if a slim one. Employing a practice not previously seen at USPD party meetings, Stoecker and his friends

69. Crispien, *Die Internationale*, p. 39. On the party executive's correspondence with other parties about the possible reconstruction of the International see the analysis in Wheeler, "Internationals," pp. 289–90 and 362–76.

70. See Curt Geyer's letter, read out by a hostile delegate at the congress; USPD *Parteitag*, Nov.–Dec. 1919, p. 136. On the struggle to secure a majority at the congress, see Wheeler, "Internationals," ch. 7. As always in such cases, a minority of the members took part in the decisions. Election of most delegates took place in assemblies, which were attended by only a fraction of the members; even in Leipzig, where the selection was by referendum, less than a quarter of the members voted (Wheeler, "Internationals," p. 412).

began collecting signatures for a proposed resolution on the International even before the debate began. When the resolution was submitted, still before the debate was under way, it had probably over 140 signatures, or just enough to control the vote on the issue.[71] This maneuver created an atmosphere of factional divisiveness that many delegates found increasingly unpleasant.

Thinking at the congress was not as polarized, however, as these conflicts would suggest. Only on the issue of the International did the left have a clear and unifying position, and only on this issue were a significant number of delegates under instructions from their electors to vote in a particular manner (a practice that was still rare at party congresses). The radical majority was a reality apart from this issue—if a division had occurred on the party program, the majority would have been larger since Dissmann, Henke, Ledebour, and others who were skeptical about the Bolsheviks, would have joined it.[72] But only on the question of the International was radical cohesion strong; on other issues there was more play for the party's traditional spirit of compromise, and the dominance of the radical faction was not always as secure as its left-wing leaders would have wished.

The debate on the International was given a peculiar tone by Hilferding's success, as quasi-official spokesman, in making official policy sound more conservative than it was. Hilferding belonged to the small minority who still wanted to attend the Geneva Congress of the Second International in February 1920, and though he spoke on this point personally, and not on behalf of the party executive, his preferences colored his speech.[73] His effectiveness was further weakened, in spite of the logic and force of his arguments, by his renowned skepticism about the immediate prospects of revolution—his proposed resolution ended with a call for the USPD to be willing to wait for a satisfactory International[74]—and by his thinly veiled dislike of the Bolsheviks. His address was, in short, not representative of moderate party opinion. The confrontation of his

71. No accurate count of signatures was ever given; nor are the names recorded. In the debate, a figure of 130–140 signatures was mentioned (USPD *Parteitag,* Nov.–Dec. 1919, p. 326); but it was generally agreed that the pro-Moscow side had demonstrated a narrow majority, so that, in view of the 280-odd votes eventually cast, this figure cannot represent the full support of the Stoecker motion. See the discussion in Wheeler, "Internationals," pp. 469–70.

72. At this congress a distinctive grouping of radicals began to emerge, allied with the right wing of the party on certain matters immediately affecting the party's autonomous development and established modes of operation. The case of Dissmann is noteworthy because of the influence he wielded as head of Germany's largest trade union.

73. USPD *Parteitag,* Nov.–Dec. 1919, p. 324.

74. *Ibid.,* p. 39.

views with Stoecker's served to give a false impression of severe polarization by overdramatizing party conflicts.

The debate was further confused by the decision to allow a third major address, by Ledebour, though eventually his stand led to a kind of solution. The former party chairman, with all his customary vigor, took a strong stand somewhere in between Hilferding and Stoecker. Ledebour despised Hilferding's unrevolutionary skepticism and his tolerance for reformists, but he balanced this with a strong suspicion of the Bolsheviks. For Ledebour, the two main arguments against attaching the party to the Bolsheviks were moral disapproval of the principle of terrorism and pride in the party's revolutionary past.[75] The Comintern, he said, was set up by the Bolsheviks for parties "modeled after their own party system," and he quoted chapter and verse to show that the Russians had repeatedly declared their intention of splitting and destroying the USPD.[76] Although his viewpoint was eccentric, Ledebour spoke from somewhere in the neighborhood of the reconstructionist program; and the effect of his speech was to reopen the possibility of a middle solution in a debate that had seemed to confirm the polarization of the delegates.

Following Ledebour's speech the congress recessed so that the factions could meet separately. The meetings went on all that evening and throughout the following day, when the congress did not meet until 6:30 P.M. We have little information about the debates in these sessions;[77] but the results were dramatic. Ledebour's speech had clearly aimed at influencing Stoecker's supporters, with whom he felt greater affinity, to abandon their insistence on immediate affiliation to the Third International and accept a more reserved approach in the form of negotiation between equals. What emerged from the discussions, however, was not an alliance of Stoecker's and Ledebour's supporters, but a new bloc of the right and center under the party executive—which, having stood in the background before, was still in a position to step in as mediator. The leaders of Stoecker's faction eventually, and with great reluctance, accepted the compromise as well; but many of their followers could not be held to the agreement.[78] Crispien presented to the reconvened plenary session a new resolution, comprising recognizable fragments from the original three competing resolutions cemented with new material drafted

75. *Ibid.*, pp. 359–60.
76. *Ibid.*, pp. 356 and 349–50.
77. What evidence there is, much of it from the provincial press, is assembled in Wheeler, "Internationals," pp. 483–87.
78. One reason was doubtless the definite instructions many of them had received from their electors. Crispien, *Die Internationale*, p. 45, calls this the major issue in the negotiations during the recess.

by Dittmann.[79] The executive had found a formula that the majority could accept.

The formula was, in effect, the reconstructionist program, which, although close to Ledebour's intentions, had not actually been advocated in any of the original speeches. This program involved only one definite obligation for the party: it was to cut its ties with the Second International.[80] Otherwise the requirements were vague and clothed in the familiar indeterminate rhetoric of the USPD:

> The USPD is in agreement with the Third International [in desiring] to realize socialism on the basis of the council system by means of the dictatorship of the proletariat. A proletarian International capable of action must be created by the union [*Zusammenschluss*] of our party with the Third International and the social-revolutionary parties of other countries.
>
> The party congress therefore charges the central committee to enter at once into negotiations with all these parties on the basis of the party's Action Program, in order to bring about this union and thus, [jointly] with the Third International, make possible a united proletarian International capable of action, [one] which will be a decisive weapon for world revolution in the struggle for the liberation of the working class from the chains of international capital.

The debate on Crispien's resolution was brief but bitter. Stoecker's supporters, dissatisfied with half measures and suspicious of the party executive, refused to join in a display of unity. They insisted on upholding Stoecker's resolution in opposition to Crispien's, though their support was beginning to crumble as a group headed by Kurt Rosenfeld split off in the name of party unity; when the vote came, Stoecker's resolution mustered only 114 votes, while 169 voted against.[81] The radicals' intransigence did, however, win a major point for their cause. By amendment from the floor, over protests from the party executive, a promise made in Crispien's speech was written into the resolution as a rider: "Should the parties of other countries not be inclined to enter the Mos-

---

79. Dittmann memoirs, p. 1070.

80. Text of the resolution in USPD *Parteitag*, Nov.–Dec. 1919, p. 369.

81. See the results of the roll-call vote, *ibid.*, pp. 388–91. The largest party districts split their votes almost evenly, 80 votes for the resolution, 78 against; Halle was solidly for it (27 votes, nearly a quarter of the total), Leipzig solidly against it, while the votes of the others (Berlin-Brandenburg, Lower Rhineland, Thuringia, Hamburg, and Bavaria) were each split fairly evenly. The votes to defeat the motion therefore came from the smaller organizations, none of which (ignoring single-member delegations) had a majority for the resolution with the exception of Pomerania and Silesia; and from the nondelegates with voting rights (party executive, auxiliary council, control commission, National Assembly delegation), who voted by 19 to 5 against the resolution. Few inferences can be drawn from these figures, however, since a number of supporters of the Stoecker resolution voted against it, honoring the compromise, and it is not known how these thirty or so votes are distributed among districts.

cow International with us, the adherence [*Anschluss*] of the USP is to be undertaken alone."[82] With this amendment, another sixty of Stoecker's supporters felt able to submit to the appeals for party unity, and the resolution passed by the deceptively impressive vote of 227 to 54.[83]

The last, and in some ways most important, item of business before the congress, election of party leaders, took place in the shadow of the debate on the International. The determined radical leaders intended to employ their strong—though, as we have seen, not infallible—faction organization "to put together the central committee of the party in such a way that its composition represents a guarantee of continued revolutionary development in the party."[84] The moderates resented not only the prospect of losing control of the party machine but also the procedure itself, which implied election according to factional loyalties defined by the unsatisfactory issue of adherence to the Communist International. But demands for elections could not be resisted. The congress adjourned for a night of factional maneuvering.

When it reassembled the next morning two lists of candidates were presented.[85] The left had plainly decided not to attempt a one-sided election and had put together a compromise center-left list for the twenty-five places that included only fourteen who had voted for the Stoecker resolution in spite of the compromise and only six who had gone on to vote against the party executive's resolution. Crispien and others of uncertain views also appeared on the list. The aims of the radicals, however, required them to exclude the principal bulwarks of the previous leadership, in particular Dittmann, Zietz, and the aged Wilhelm Bock of the control commission. The list put up by the moderates, hasty and incomplete, comprised mainly those whom the left had dropped,[86] and its proponents were able to play on the pathos of the situation. The delegates were susceptible to the moderates' appeals, and the left's majority proved fragile again. In the final voting, Dittmann, Zietz, Bock, Dissmann, and three others from the moderates' list were elected, displacing, among others, the rising extreme radical from Hamburg, Ernst Thälmann. All four of those who had appeared on both lists, including Crispien, were returned; if these four are counted as moderates, as they often proved to be, then the congress had chosen a leadership in which

82. *Ibid.*, p. 388.
83. The results of the roll-call vote on the Crispien resolution may be found *ibid.*, pp. 392–95. Among the Stoecker supporters who joined the majority on Crispien's resolution were Stoecker himself, Koenen, Brass, and the Hamburg delegate Ernst Thälmann. The intransigents included Däumig and Curt Geyer.
84. Curt Geyer, *Das Forum*, Jan. 1920, p. 264.
85. USPD *Parteitag*, Nov.–Dec. 1919, p. 416.
86. Dissmann explained the background, *ibid.*, pp. 426–27.

eleven of the twenty-six positions were held by persons whom the left must regard as unreliable. Both the party executive and the control commission were so evenly balanced between moderates and radicals that a single defection from among the radical members could give the moderates a majority. That such swing votes were sometimes there soon became apparent.[87]

The Leipzig congress thus came to an indecisive conclusion. To many people, including most outsiders, it had appeared to celebrate the triumph of the party's left wing. The left's leaders had shown that, at least on the issue of the International, they could rally a majority of the active party members to their side, and by focusing on this issue they had organized a majority at the congress. Their program had been adopted, even if it was proposed by others; they had forced the party to break with the Second International and seen it set on a course likely to lead to the Third; they had elected their nominees to a majority of the leadership positions in the party. Nevertheless, the right wing had not only survived but also succeeded in throwing its weight into the balance at critical junctures, using its old standing with the center of the party and appealing to the traditional sentiments of the center and moderate left. The USPD was by no means to be the sole preserve of the left wing in the months to come.

87. For a list of those elected, see Appendix 3. Zietz, Dittmann, Radtke, Dissmann, Henke, Bock, and Wengels were elected from the list of the moderates; the names of Crispien, Moses, Nemitz, and Agnes appeared on both lists.

CHAPTER 10

The Frustration of the Left
(December 1919 to April 1920)

The outcome of the party congress was received on the left with satisfaction, even with jubiliation.[1] The immobility that had plagued the party since the first weeks of the revolution seemed finally to have been overcome. In a fair political fight, the vigorous left wing had defeated the old guard on the most important questions, clarified the party's ideals, purged its leadership, and set the party back on the path of fruitful action. The USPD would at last be able to do full justice to the apparent revolutionary potential in Germany.

This reading of what had happened at Leipzig was not confined to the radical Independents; the harassed Communist leaders, for whom the apparent victory of the USPD left was a gleam of light in the darkness, held even higher expectations. In the view of the Communists, the so-called right wing of the USPD was "essentially only a small group of leaders,"[2] a clique whose positions of power enabled them to keep the party from developing in accordance with the necessities of the revolution. The left, however, was the masses, and by seizing the initiative at the party congress they had finally demonstrated their attainment of revolutionary maturity. Thus the congress was "a turning point in [the history of] the German labor movement," "a milestone in the development of the proletarian world revolution."[3] As Radek put it, "there is no longer anything dividing the Communist from the Independent proletarian masses"; "the Independents are on their way to becoming a Communist party."[4] Clearly, some hindrances still existed: the leaders of the

1. Curt Geyer, *Das Forum*, Jan. 1920, pp. 260–70; Max Sievers, *Der Arbeiter-Rat*, 1 (1919), no. 43, 1–2; Halle *Volksblatt*, quoted in *Freiheit*, Dec. 13, 1919 (m). But cf. the more skeptical reading of the radical *Gothaer Volksblatt*, quoted in Buchsbaum, p. 191.
2. *Rote Fahne*, Dec. 29, 1919.
3. *Ibid.*, Jan. 1, 1920; A. Struthahn [Karl Radek], "Der Parteitag der Unabhängigen," *Die Internationale* (KPD), Feb. 2, 1920, p. 22.
4. *Die Internationale* (KPD), Feb. 2, 1920, pp. 30 and 25.

left were not quite as advanced as their followers; they were "still in the process of clarification";[5] they had yet to apply the logic of their ideas to their practice in numerous ways, for instance by dealing with the renegades in the party—Kautsky, Hilferding, Dittmann, Ledebour. But now that the hold of the centrist leaders had been broken and the masses had shown their quality, the left-wing leaders would surely find the right paths, or be driven onto them. With these thoughts, the Communists opened an era of good feeling (or perhaps wishful thinking) toward the USPD.

A third group also took the results at Leipzig seriously—the intellectuals of the party's extreme right wing. Siegfried Nestriepke, a prominent journalist, demonstratively left the party, but without rejoining the SPD.[6] August Erdmann, a former Reichstag deputy living in Otto Brass's Rhineland, stayed with the USPD because he felt, like Nestriepke, that he could not belong to Noske's SPD; but his small faction more or less withdrew from party affairs to organize a pressure group with a band of dissident Majority Socialists.[7] The patriarch of the right wing, Karl Kautsky, nearly resigned from the party, going so far as to draft a statement of resignation;[8] although he never used it, he gradually withdrew from the party in all but the name, writing little for the party press after March 1920 for over a year.

But the group that continued to count most in the life of the USPD—the "small group of leaders" around Dittmann, Zietz, Hilferding, and often Crispien, and their considerable following in the party—did not regard the congress as having transformed the party. They had fought for their political lives at the congress, and in a fashion they had won. Their victory had involved subscribing to views that they did not really hold; but proposing and voting for the Action Program had been a victory in political tactics, since they had earned the right to construe it in their own way. They did not see the program as involving any direct practical consequences for their policies; indeed, their most common complaint about the congress was that it had given no guidance on what party members should do in daily politics.[9] The emergence of the left as a bloc was disturbing, but then the bloc had not actually held together at critical moments. Even the resolution on the International, with the exception of the amendment tacked onto the end, was acceptable to most

5. *Ibid.*, p. 25.
6. Koszyk, p. 234.
7. Letters from Erdmann to Kautsky of Jan. 5 and April 10, 1920, Kautsky papers, D X 252 and 253; DZA Merseburg, Rep. 77 Tit. 4040b Nr. 19, pp. 8–12.
8. Kautsky papers, A 95.
9. See the comments of the party's Leipzig and Düsseldorf newspapers, reprinted in *Freiheit,* Dec. 13, 1919 (m), and of the Munich paper, *ibid.,* Dec. 16, 1919 (e).

of the old leaders. The principle of compromise in the interests of party unity had generally prevailed, despite the fears of Hilferding and others that the right might be driven into leaving the party.[10] The same principle of compromise might be expected to rule among the new leaders. Consequently, the moderates were more relieved and resolute than despondent as the congress closed.

So far as the daily politics of the party were concerned, the right-wing leaders, practiced Social Democratic politicians and editors who still occupied many of the influential positions throughout the party organization, read the situation most accurately. The debates of the fall, and then the congress, had given the left wing a momentum that it could exploit for a time. But events broke this momentum, and without it the leaders of the left wing were no match for their counterparts on the right in a struggle over everyday policies. Yet the state of affairs before Leipzig could not return. At the congress, a number of leaders of the left had accepted positions of authority in the party. These men—above all Däumig, cochairman of the party with Crispien—could no longer act as the autonomous faction they had been before, with loyalties as much to the council system as to the party, and ignore the party when they disapproved of its work. They had responsibilities; the party was now theirs to an extent it had never been before. The decline of the councils after January 1920 only made this trend more pronounced. The left wing hoped that it had captured the party at Leipzig; certainly it had established itself as the preponderant faction; but it had also become more entangled than before in a still largely unaltered party. For a time it seemed that the party had captured it, absorbing some of its best men into the ponderous apparatus and binding them to majority decisions. A difficult time lay ahead for them.

Partly because of the radicals' absorption into positions of responsibility, partly because of external circumstances, the USPD enjoyed six months of relative stability, though not harmony, in its internal affairs. These were not happy months for the party: internal dissension continued, tending to impose political paralysis; and from the outside came severe government repression and then the provocation to armed conflict. But the factions were at least committed to working together, and they tried this in good faith. The party stood together, as the great "bearer of socialism in Germany"[11] and the hope of future revolution, as it had rarely done since November 1918; and it continued to grow.

10. Hilferding was frank about his fears only in retrospect; *ibid.,* Dec. 8, 1919 (m). See also the comments of the Dresden party paper, reprinted *ibid.,* Dec. 15, 1919 (e).
11. *Ibid.,* Dec. 8, 1919 (m).

Uncertainty on the International Scene

The first item on the agenda of the new party executive was the International. Given the composition of the newly elected leadership, and the strength of party feeling at the congress, the moderates had no chance either to interpret the congress resolution in a sense favorable to their own views or, for the moment, even to procrastinate. The first steps required by the resolution lay, in any case, along the path the old party executive had already begun to travel before the congress: bilateral discussions with sympathetic parties about a conference.[12] The executive consequently moved with dispatch and without dissension to carry out its mandate. Tentative discussions were held at once with the delegates of foreign parties who had come to the congress, and a few days later with others in Berlin. Even Radek was consulted, on December 10, and, though with reservations, showed himself not unfriendly to the USPD's hopes.[13] Encouraged by these talks, the party executive sent off, on December 15, a letter to nineteen foreign parties and groups—including the Third International and some parties that had already adhered to it —proposing an international conference, perhaps in February. To make the USPD's position clear, copies of the Action Program and the resolution on the International were enclosed. The party's aim was described in words echoing the party congress resolution: "to bring about a union of our party with the Third International and the social-revolutionary parties of other countries and thus, together with the Third International, to make possible an International with the potential for action."[14]

The first responses to these overtures were encouraging, especially those from the Scandinavians, who were anxious to sponsor such a conference as the USPD wanted.[15] However, it soon became evident that there would be difficulties. Numerous other parties were looking for a better, more radical international alignment, particularly now that the USPD's abandonment of the Second International had put an end to that organization's hopes of remaining reasonably comprehensive; but to coordinate them would not be easy. Some, like the Swiss, mistrusted the Bolsheviks and were willing to deal with them only with the greatest caution; others, like the Italians (now formally members of the Comin-

12. See Hilferding's account of these earlier contacts in USPD *Parteitag*, Nov.–Dec. 1919, p. 325; and Wheeler, "Internationals," pp. 362–76.

13. *Die U.S.P.D. und die 3. Internationale: Bericht des Zentralkomitees über die Ausführung des Leipziger Parteitagsbeschlusses* (Remscheid, n.d.), p. 3.

14. *Ibid.*, pp. 4–5.

15. *Ibid.*, pp. 5–7. A full survey of the USPD's attempts to arrange a conference, and the response they received, is in Wheeler, "Internationals," pp. 525–37, 550–53, and 567–68.

tern), admired the Russians and saw a slight in the USPD's proposed procedure. Still others, notably the French, needed time to work out their own inner conflicts and arrive at a policy. Most important, discussions with the other parties suggested that it was not going to be possible to treat the existing Third International, as the USPD moderates had envisaged, as simply one of the elements to be welded together into a new International. The Third International was the key to the situation.

This being the case, the efforts of the Independents were stalled for several months when no reply came from Moscow. A copy of the letter of December 15 had been sent to the ECCI "by an indirect postal route"; another went with Radek when he departed for Russia late in January.[16] The other parties replied during January and early February, at least on a preliminary basis; but there was no word from Moscow.

Some signs came from the Communist camp, if not from the Comintern, and at first these were encouraging. Stoecker had reported to the party congress in Leipzig that Levi promised the USPD ready entry into the Third International, which seemed to bear out the left's contention that Moscow, once properly informed, would recognize the USPD as a revolutionary brother party.[17] For the rest of December *Rote Fahne* pursued a cautiously friendly line toward the Independents, or, more accurately, toward the left Independents, whom it believed to control the party. The paper entertained the possibility of the USPD and KPD existing alongside one another in the Comintern, announced that Lenin's harsh views on the left Independents were out of date, and asserted that a high degree of tactical free play was available in the International.[18] Even Radek, as mentioned, did not discourage the Independents from their hopes of an honorable arrangement.

This was the honeymoon period of the USPD's relations with its Communist neighbors, the afterglow of the supposed victory of the left wing at Leipzig. So far as the Comintern was concerned, however, the signs were less encouraging. A circular issued by the Comintern's West European secretariat on January 15, 1920,[19] was stiff, sharply worded, and aggressive—very different from the markedly conciliatory draft unsuccessfully put forward by Levi.[20] Much of the circular was devoted to showing that the right-wing leaders of the Independents were shifty and treacherous and the left-wing leaders weak and uncertain in their deal-

16. *Die U.S.P.D. und die 3. Internationale,* p. 5.
17. USPD *Parteitag,* Nov.–Dec. 1919, pp. 134 and 341. Since Levi was not in a position to give such an assurance, Stoecker probably misunderstood him.
18. *Rote Fahne,* Dec. 15, 23, and 24, 1919.
19. Text in *Die Kommunistische Internationale,* no. 10, pp. 172–76.
20. Levi papers, P 126.

ings with the right; most of the rest to arguing that the USPD's proposed conference was wholly impractical. The circular brushed aside suggestions that the International interfered with brother parties and ended with the suggestion that the USPD should enter at once into bilateral negotiations with Moscow.

Leading Independents, of all factions, were now ready to follow this advice, since the Third International held the key to their plans;[21] but there was still no answer from Moscow to their letter. The party executive decided not to try to hurry the ECCI's reply but just to wait; fortunately the membership had more immediate concerns, and there was little pressure from below for speedy action. In February the party executive conferred with the auxiliary council and the control commission, which approved the decision to wait. All that could be done for the time being was to adopt in principle the plan of sending a delegation to Moscow, when the opportunity should arise, to discuss with the leaders of the Communist International the possible adherence of the USPD.[22]

Fiasco in the Council Movement and Resurgence of the Moderates

After the International, the other main issue for the USPD—one that absorbed far more of the party's activity both in the National Assembly and in the factories—was the fate of the councils. Though the congress had little to say on this subject, the delegates plainly expected to see this matter pursued by the party with more energy than before. This course was followed—until it led to disastrous defeat on January 13.

The USPD delegation in the National Assembly had not been very active in connection with the government's Factory Council Bill, deliberations on which were approaching their end; in fact, they had been demonstratively unconcerned with it, making no attempt to incorporate practical improvements at the committee stage.[23] This course had been dictated not by indifference to factory councils but rather by sensitivity to party feeling about parliamentary horse trading. The bill was, from the USPD's point of view, a bad bill, and the SPD's agitated efforts to squeeze concessions out of their coalition partners seemed a case study

---

21. On the official attitude expounded by Crispien in Switzerland late in January 1920, see Horst Naumann, "Die USPD und die Kommunistische Internationale: Zur Entsendung einer Delegation der USPD zum II. Weltkongress der KI," *Zeitschrift für Geschichtswissenschaft*, 19 (1971), 1036; *Die U.S.P.D. und die 3. Internationale*, p. 6; *Freiheit*, March 12, 1920 (m).

22. *Die U.S.P.D. und die 3. Internationale*, p. 6. There is some evidence that the USPD intended to send its delegation early in March but postponed the trip; see the discussion in Wheeler, "Internationals," pp. 563–64.

23. "Bericht des Parteivorstandes über das Geschäftsjahr 1919," p. 97, in SPD *Parteitag*, Oct. 1920.

in the futility of coalition with bourgeois parties.[24] The Majority Socialists, in turn, resented the Independents' failure to help, and attributed some of the bill's bad features to the absence of USPD members from committee votes.[25] But the USPD was saving its ammunition for the plenary sessions, where, although it could not hope to effect changes, its representatives could speak "out the window" to the masses.

The bill was indeed damaging to prospects for the kind of factory council movement the Independents had been seeking. It provided for only very limited powers for the councils at the factory level, much too limited for them to have any hope of serving as effective instruments of socialization, as the radicals wished. Moreover, white-collar and blue-collar workers were to be organized separately, in contrast to radical doctrine; elections were to be held at fixed intervals, not when changes were desired by the workers; and certain provisions effectively prevented organization of an independent council movement connecting factory to factory and region to region. At the higher levels of the proposed structure, real powers were provided, not for the councils, but for joint committees in which employers would also be represented. Finally, the bill's last clause abolished all rival workers' and factory councils, so that only the government's councils could have legal existence.[26]

Thanks to the delaying tactics of the Center Party and the Democrats, consideration of the bill dragged on past Christmas; an unusually forceful protest by the SPD delegation was required to get the other parties to agree to a special session of the Assembly, beginning on January 13, which should finally dispose of it.[27] By this time events had enabled the USPD to combine its agitation on the final stages of the bill with a revived council movement at the grass roots.

On December 6, the state of siege was ended in Berlin and other major cities of North Germany. In Berlin the effect was to release the council movement from the condition of suspended animation in which, despite the efforts of its leaders, it had been since September. Since the end of the state of siege coincided with a period of growing economic distress, as well as with the final agitation against the Factory Council

24. The efforts can be followed in the unpublished minutes of the SPD's National Assembly delegation, especially the meetings of Oct. 10, Nov. 21, and Dec. 15, 1919.

25. See n. 23 above.

26. See also the summary in Oertzen, *Betriebsräte*, p. 156. Examples of the Independents' critique are Curt Geyer, in *Der Arbeiter-Rat*, 2 (1920), no. 2, 2–7, and in *Nationalversammlung*, vol. 331, pp. 4249–62; and "W.K." [Wilhelm Koenen?] in *Freiheit*, Jan. 3, 1920 (m), and Jan. 7, 1920 (e).

27. See the minutes of the SPD's National Assembly delegation, Dec. 15 and 16, 1919.

Bill, it was possible to get the movement under way again without delay.

The ambitions of the council advocates had been in no way reduced by their experiences of the summer and fall. Indeed, the system as a theoretical construct had been refined during the months of forced underground work.[28] The structure had been modified to take more account of the trade unions, in such a way that the council system was to contribute to the construction of industrial unions. There would be no attempt to establish political workers' councils for the time being, but since the same basic factory unit was the foundation of both the political and economic council systems, political councils could be called into being, at least at the local level, on short notice. But the radicals' main work at this point was educational, an attempt to familiarize all workers with the practice and potential of the councils so that when the opportunity came later councils would be both generally accepted and immediately effective.

Neither Independents nor Communists appeared to be disturbed by the continuing SPD boycott of their council system; indeed, if the Reichstag election results of the following June are indicative of the relative strengths of the parties in January, perhaps the boycott was no longer of great significance in Berlin.[29] More important to the image of their movement, one of the Independents' first acts in the revived general assembly of councils in Berlin was to expel the Communists.[30] The Berlin Communists were undeniably a difficult group to work with; they belonged to the dissident wing of their party and had a pronounced tendency toward syndicalism. Their offense in the eyes of the Independent radicals was that they continued to regard the councils purely as organs of struggle and to see as their function a kind of direct action—"control of production," meaning attempts to take over operation of the factories. The Independents were not ready for this, wanting first to install their system, for the sake of its later revolutionary potential, and to bring it to the consciousness of the workers. From the Communist point of view, the concern for "system" shown by the "Independent pedants of the revolution" amounted to a disease; to try to establish exact structures before the revolution was utopian and only resulted in endless delay.[31]

28. For the organizational principles in finished form, and their rationale, see *Der Arbeiter-Rat*, 2 (1920), no. 1, 2–6.
29. In the June Reichstag elections, the USPD polled 42.7 percent of the Berlin vote, the SPD only 17.5 percent; among factory workers, the only place where councils were firmly established, the relative strength of the USPD is generally thought to have been even greater.
30. *Rote Fahne*, Jan. 6, 1920.
31. *Ibid.*, Dec. 16 and 20, 1919.

But the radical Independents were in a commanding position in such cities as Berlin, and they were sure of the perfection of their system; they preferred to dispense with the doubtful assistance of the Communists and go it alone.

As in the previous spring, revival of the councils was associated with a renewal of industrial unrest. The Ruhr miners were again involved, expressing their general grievances as a demand for shorter working hours; the extreme radicals among them, not content with a strike, began to propagate the idea of "direct action"—that is, leaving work after six hours—and sabotage.[32] This threat of another economically crippling coal strike coincided with a strike movement among the railwaymen of the Ruhr and elsewhere, potentially the most disruptive of all strikes. With two of its most important labor forces in a militant mood, the Ruhr began to show signs of political as well as economic decomposition once more. The Independents and Communists both intervened with political demands; petty violence began; in Hamborn a soviet republic was suddenly proclaimed again. The same trend was visible in Germany's other main coal-mining region, Upper Silesia; and among railwaymen a strike could easily spread much further still. From early January the Reich was on the verge of a general industrial crisis.

In this atmosphere, the USPD, the KPD, and the Central Office of German Factory Councils called for a mass demonstration before the Reichstag building as the National Assembly met on January 13 to discuss the Factory Council Bill. The origins and intentions of this demonstration are obscure. We know that the proposal was put through the party executive by the left majority, over the protests of the right, in two days of bitter discussion; and that the radicals and the other two organizations involved were following a scheme that had been formulated before the matter was brought to the full party executive.[33] These details suggest that there were plans going beyond the demonstration itself; but we do not know what they were. Prior consultations had been held in Halle, at a conference of factory council leaders, on January 7 and 8; a police report on these secret meetings surmised, plausibly, that the radicals hoped to encourage a general strike in conjunction with the railway and mining strikes.[34] Certainly the radicals were of a mind to seize power if the opportunity arose. Curt Geyer wrote at about this time: "The necessity of the dictatorship of the proletariat is becoming ever clearer, ever clearer too the necessity of realizing it in the *present* circumstances. To be ready for the seizure of power—that is the lesson of the develop-

32. Severing, *1919/1920,* pp. 121–23; Dörnemann, pp. 131–33.
33. Dissmann, USPD *Parteitag,* Oct. 1920, pp. 38–39.
34. *Ibid.;* BA Koblenz, Reichskanzlei 2118, p. 161.

ment of the political situation."[35] At least some of the leaders were prepared, as the government charged,[36] to see a total economic collapse if
this made a seizure of power possible. The demonstrations of January 13
may have been intended as the beginning of a movement toward a general strike or, as the SPD maintained, as the dress rehearsal for an attempt to overturn the government.[37] But there is neither evidence nor
reason to suppose that the radicals meant violence on January 13. There
was nothing of this tone in the appeal for demonstrations, whose rhetoric
of conflict was relatively subdued.[38] Violence against the National Assembly would hardly be an intelligent way to begin the overthrow of the
bourgeois order, and Berlin was full of Noske's troops. Whatever its
long-range motives, the demonstration must be seen as part of an on-
going struggle to mobilize the workers for action.

The question of the radicals' intentions is important because the demonstrations did not go as planned.[39] Worker response was excellent; by
early afternoon the huge square in front of the Reichstag building was
filling up with enthusiastic demonstrators. The crowd was peaceful, content to applaud the speakers provided by the Berlin council leaders, who
were in charge of the demonstration. But then the oratory was finished,
and the crowd was still there. The marshals had given no thought to
dispersing the crowd, by providing some finishing flourish such as a
resolution that the crowd could thunderously endorse and then know its
work was done. Instead, the crowd remained standing about. Then a part
of it began to press toward the building's entrances—led on by "criminal
elements" or agents provocateurs according to the viewpoint of the observer, but probably the same sort of men who had stormed *Vorwärts* a
year earlier. The pressure on the security policemen became dangerous.
Then a shot or two rang out (probably from the crowd, though this is
not certain), whereupon the security police opened fire with machine
guns. In a few minutes, 42 people lay dead, 105 more wounded, in the
bloodiest incident since the revolution.

A few hours later the government declared a state of siege over the

35. *Das Forum,* Jan. 1920, pp. 261–62. The article was obviously written before
Jan. 13.
36. In a letter of Jan. 31 to the Berlin trades council, BA Koblenz, Reichskanzlei
2531, p. 17.
37. Handbill, BA Koblenz, Reichskanzlei 2065, p. 26. Cf. the SPD's warning in
Vorwärts, Jan. 13, 1920 (m).
38. *Freiheit,* Jan. 12, 1920 (m).
39. The following account tries to find its way between two sets of contradictory
eye-witness statements, published in *Vorwärts* over the following several days and
in *Die Wahrheit über das Blutbad vor dem Reichstag 13. Januar 1920* (Berlin,
n.d.), which contains the material *Freiheit* would have published had the paper not
been suppressed. On the failure of the demonstration's organizers, see below.

whole of North Germany, and Noske, in putting the decree into effect, subjected the USPD to the most systematic repression it had ever experienced. The real reason for the state of siege decree, as government documents make unambiguously clear, was not the tension caused by the incident in Berlin but the desire to master the strike movement by clamping down on agitation and making special powers available to such officials as Reich Commissioner Severing in the Ruhr.[40] But the shooting in Berlin provided a useful pretext, with the government claiming that the radicals had only just been prevented from dispersing the National Assembly and seizing power.[41] And once this pretext had been adopted, persecution of the USPD, not just in the restive industrial districts but over most of North Germany, was natural.

For the next month or more, the USPD lived in a condition of semi-legality again in most of the country. The party itself was not suppressed, but its public activities were greatly impeded and some of its leaders harassed. A January 14 telegram from Noske to the military commanders said: "By order of the Reichswehr Minister, all Independent and Communist newspapers are to be suppressed or confiscated at once if they engage in incitement [*wenn sie hetzen*]."[42] On January 26 this order was supplemented: "Imposition of preventive detention on the editors actually responsible for objectionable articles is also recommended as a particularly effective measure against the inflammatory press."[43] Noske set an example by suspending publication of *Freiheit* before it could even report the demonstration; it remained under ban until February 9. Many other party newspapers—at least thirty-five in all—were similarly banned for a time before the period of repression was over.[44] General Maercker, in suppressing the *Leipziger Volkszeitung*, was especially candid about his reasons:

40. A government telegram of Jan. 13 to all state governments explaining its action makes this clear; BA Koblenz, Reichskanzlei 2699, p. 24. A further explanatory message from a high official on Jan. 20 fails even to mention the incident in Berlin; BA Koblenz, Reichskanzlei 2711, pp. 28–31.

41. See Chancellor Bauer's speech on Jan. 14, *Nationalversammlung*, vol. 331, pp. 4203–6.

42. BA Koblenz, Reichskanzlei 2531, p. 46.

43. *Ibid.*

44. A list of twenty-eight papers suppressed at one time or another can be found in the USPD's *Referentenmaterial*, Feb. 15, 1920, pp. 106–7, and a further seven are cited in: *Referentenmaterial*, Feb. 1, 1920, p. 103; *Informationsblatt*, Jan. 22, 1920; StA Dresden, MdI Nr. 11016, p. 12; and StA Magdeburg, Rep. C20 Ib Nr. 4778, p. 33, and Nr. 4791, p. 16. There may have been others. The papers listed are concentrated in the Ruhr and Lower Rhineland, Saxony (five papers), the Halle district (all four papers, from Jan. 19 to March 1), Thuringia, and Prussia east of the Elbe.

It needs no demonstration that it is altogether incompatible with the security of the Reich when, in a newspaper with a wide readership, everything coming from the government or its official representatives and other organs is deliberately and consciously disparaged. An end must be made to this, and in the circumstances it can only be done by prohibiting the printing, publishing, and sale of the *Leipziger Volkszeitung* in any form.[45]

Public strike agitation by the party's followers was made impossible, and the activities of the council organizers were greatly hampered. Däumig, chairman of the party, was among those arrested and held for several weeks. A report from Berlin claims that branch assemblies of the party were arrested en masse and carried off in trucks.[46] The KPD suffered even more—*Rote Fahne* appeared only once between January 14 and February 27, and a party congress at the end of February was broken up by the police—but it enjoyed the advantage of being ready to return to an underground life at any moment. Against the strike movement, the prime object of the decree, the state of siege proved very effective. The incipient railway strike was brought under control within a few days by the threat of mass dismissals and arrests; the miners' movement never got properly under way, and a policy of implicit threat combined with concessions and exhortation introduced the most productive period in the history of the Ruhr mines since the war.[47]

The effects of this experience on the USPD were dramatic. Outwardly, the party showed only the fury toward the government that might be expected and argued its innocence. Inside the party, however, the moderates were up in arms. The council people, at their own demand, had had the management of the demonstration and had neglected the most elementary rules of crowd control.[48] The effect had been, in the words of a Majority Socialist handbill, to "drive the unfortunates onto the guns" of the security police.[49] Further, the result of the action had been that the party press was threatened with ruin.[50] At a party conference on

45. *Mitteilungen des Landesvorstandes und der Bezirksleitung für den Bezirk Leipzig der Unabhängigen Sozialdemokratischen Partei Sachsens,* Jan. 24, 1920.
46. USPD, Bezirks-Organisation Berlin-Stadt, *Jahresbericht für die Zeit vom 1. Oktober 1919 bis 31. März 1920* (Berlin, n.d.), p. 8.
47. The decline of the strike movement in the Ruhr, to its virtual extinction by Jan. 15, can be followed in reports in BA Koblenz, Reichskanzlei 2118, pp. 151–96; also Severing, *1919/1920,* pp. 114–15 and 124–31, and Dörnemann, pp. 139–47.
48. Dittmann memoirs, pp. 1078–79, contains a detailed presentation of this point. See also Ströbel, *Die deutsche Revolution,* pp. 178–81, and Prager, pp. 214–15.
49. BA Koblenz, Reichskanzlei 2065, p. 26.
50. The USPD's press enterprises had large fixed expenses, such as salaries, that did not cease when the papers failed to publish, so suppression was not only a political hardship but also a direct economic threat. See the anxious comments in

January 28, these resentments and more surfaced. At such a conference, composed mainly of high party functionaries and editors, the moderates had a natural majority; and frustrated right-wing spokesmen seem to have exploited their opportunity to put the radicals on the defensive. They had had enough of the left wing's preoccupation with immediate revolution and wanted to shake the party free of tactics that ignored other possibilities. Seger and Lipinski of Leipzig, together with Unterleitner of Munich, appear to have led the attack. Even the bland *Freiheit* summary of Crispien's speech gives a hint of the tone:

> Tactics must be followed that reckon with the real power relationships and do not nourish fantastic hopes of an overnight collapse [of the social order]. The political party must have the leading role and the right of decision about all its actions. . . . The inclination to follow Communist groups in their tactics must also be overcome.[51]

Such arguments were mixed with strong language about the "incompetence" of the radical leaders. The latter's reply is unknown; certainly they found no support for the idea, held by some radicals, that "we find ourselves in the same situation as in October 1918."[52] The conference ended by adopting resolutions intended to ensure more control over the councils by both the party and the trade unions.

The right wing's counteroffensive had carried the day; the left wing came away feeling that a large part of the party had abandoned the Leipzig program.[53] Hilferding, who was known for his skepticism about the current possibilities for revolution, was apparently at the peak of his influence in the party executive in this period.[54] In December he had written that political developments since November 9, 1918, had meant a "marked *weakening of socialism* as a whole"; and he held to these views throughout the upheavals of the winter and spring.[55] Crispien, too, had become convinced during the autumn that, while current circumstances might allow the proletariat to seize power, they would not be

Mitteilungen des Landesvorstandes und der Bezirksleitung für den Bezirk Leipzig der Unabhängigen Sozialdemokratischen Partei Sachsens, Jan. 24, 1920.

51. On this conference, see *Freiheit,* Feb. 9, 1920 (e), which contains a summary of Crispien's speech and the decisions of the conference, and Paul Wegmann, *Der Arbeiter-Rat,* 2 (1920), no. 8, 5–6, which supplies other details.

52. Handbill signed by the Berlin executive council, Levi papers, P 122.

53. Wegmann, *Der Arbeiter-Rat,* 2 (1920), no. 8, 5; the *Augsburger Volkswille,* quoted in *Freiheit,* Sept. 3, 1920 (m).

54. According to Koenen and Stoecker in USPD *Parteitag,* Oct. 1920, pp. 29 and 49. Hilferding attended sessions of the executive in his capacity as editor of *Freiheit* but had no vote. During much of this period (from January 19 to March 4) Däumig was in prison; among the remaining eleven members of the executive only five were strong radicals.

55. *Freiheit,* Dec. 11, 1919 (m); Koenen in USPD *Parteitag,* Oct. 1920, p. 29.

able to retain it.[56] Such thinking was gaining ground on the right wing of the party. It followed that the task of the moment was to avoid direct confrontation with the government and concentrate on the arduous task of bringing full socialist consciousness to the working class, much as Social Democracy had tried to do before the war—but with the expectation that revolution was nevertheless not so very far off. The results were constricting for the leaders of the left wing.

At the same time, the left wing suffered what was perhaps its most damaging blow. The combination of Noske's measures and the new Factory Council Law effectively killed what remained of the revolutionary council system; as a Communist noted, nothing was left but the diagrams.[57] As "W.K." wrote in *Freiheit,* in a kind of obituary, the council idea had been an agitational success for the party but a failure as a system:

The call for the election of their own revolutionary factory councils was actually carried through by the workers and white-collar employees only in a few regions of Germany. However much the movement progressed intellectually, in the greater part of Germany the proletariat still lacked the energy to elect independent factory councils extralegally against [the will of] the employers.[58]

The Independents even had to give up earlier plans to elect councils on their own model in rivalry with the councils established by the Factory Council Law.[59] There was no choice but to submit to the law's provisions and devote the party's efforts to winning a controlling voice in the new councils so as to give them at least a revolutionary spirit and preserve what potential remained for political action. Plenty of opportunity remained for agitation and organization in this arena, and the radicals kept on with the task; but it was a poor shadow of the work that had inspired them through the first year after the revolution.

If the left wing had lost its apparent ascendency in the party organization, the right wing had not gained a majority for its preference, a somewhat more aggressive version of the old Social Democratic tactics. The result was that reaching any decision was difficult. On the question of the campaign for support in the new factory councils, for instance, the party executive was conspicuously silent, and the trade unions were able

56. *Freiheit,* Oct. 15, 1919 (m); report of his conversation with Frossard, BA Koblenz, Reichskanzlei 2664, pp. 48–49.
57. *Kommunistische Räte-Korrespondenz,* Jan. 22, 1920, p. 2. Kolb, "Rätewirklichkeit," pp. 165–66, calls the Factory Council Law a "first-class state funeral" for the council system.
58. *Freiheit,* Feb. 13, 1920 (e). "W.K." is presumably Wilhelm Koenen.
59. The plans were not discussed openly; but see the interesting account in a KPD circular, Levi papers, P 105.

to take the lead.[60] And Hilferding's proposal of a "sliding wage scale" (a sort of escalator clause to combat the continuing inflation) involved the executive in weeks of argument; agreement could not be reached, and the party remained without an economic policy.[61]

In all of February and early March, the party executive issued a strong statement on only one of the issues of the day: the Entente's demand for the extradition of supposed war criminals to stand trial before an Allied court. When the German government replied intransigently and international conflict appeared imminent, all the old antinationalist, pacifist instincts in the party were aroused, exactly as in the Versailles crisis of the previous spring. The party executive condemned the injustice of the Allies' proposed procedure and reprimanded the German government for not having acted against its own war criminals in good time, but after all possible means of conciliation had been exhausted, said the executive, Germany must sacrifice a few individuals rather than permit war to break out.[62]

There was nothing exceptional in this statement, which was consistent with past party policy. But many had supposed the party to have become a different entity, so that the very ordinariness of its response to the crisis was exasperating—the more so since the left wing either accepted the policy or kept its objections to itself. The Communists, in particular, found this action a betrayal. The possibility of stirring up a revolutionary crisis might have existed; the USPD had passed it by. Its action was characterized as "the evasion, the deliberate blunting, of revolutionary situations from the fatal consciousness of not being equal to them."[63] Since the left wing was unable to prevent or openly oppose such party actions, Communists could have no further feeling of community with it. On February 25, at its third party congress, the KPD voted to cut the ties it had established in December and ceased trying to work with the radical Independents.[64]

The Party Executive and the Kapp Putsch

Nothing could have been better chosen to demonstrate the operation of the party's new internal dynamics than the great national crisis of 1920, the Kapp Putsch, which broke out on March 13. In spite of the

60. See the complaints of Viktor Stern, *Der Arbeiter-Rat*, 2 (1920), no. 10, 2–3.
61. According to Stoecker, USPD *Parteitag*, Oct. 1920, p. 49. The suggestion was raised for discussion in an editorial in *Freiheit*, Jan. 3, 1920 (e), and disappeared from the columns of the paper in the middle of February.
62. Manifesto in *Freiheit*, Feb. 11, 1920 (m). In the end the Allies did not insist on their demands.
63. *Die Internationale* (KPD), Feb. 25, 1920, p. 6.
64. KPD *Parteitag*, Feb. 1920, p. 8.

great general strike, in which the party had a prominent part, this was not a glorious episode for the USPD. The party was less passive, in principle at least, than in earlier crises, and its relations with the council movement showed the effects of the changes of the winter; moreover, at one point it came close to breaking out of its habitual sterile isolation. But the party members' most enduring memory of those two weeks seems to have been a feeling of helplessness. The party leadership had been paralyzed by uncertainty and dissension; decisive action, even definite proposals, were all but impossible, and when the great moment had passed little seemed to have been gained for the cause of socialism.

The possibility of a military coup d'état had been in party leaders' minds at least since May of the previous year. They did not, it seems, expect one at just this point—only a few weeks before, Crispien and Hilferding, still reacting against the radicals' tendency to see revolutionary opportunities around every corner, had ridiculed suggestions that a coup might be imminent.[65] But when it occurred, the party executive did not hesitate, at least on the first step. It immediately appealed for a general strike.[66] At this stage, before party leaders realized that the Bauer government had survived and would continue to be a factor in the situation, the demands of the hour seemed simple. The party summoned the workers to a struggle "for freedom! . . . for revolutionary socialism! Against military dictatorship! Against white terror! Against the restoration of the monarchy!"

The USPD was not alone in calling for a general strike. Even before the USPD acted, an appeal had gone out over the signatures of President Ebert, the six Social Democratic members of the Reich government, and Party Chairman Wels; the text had been communicated by telephone to some twenty of the largest cities in the country.[67] Though the origins of

65. Stoecker, USPD *Parteitag*, Oct. 1920, p. 49. The work of the party executive during the putsch was felt to have been so unsatisfactory that no fewer than seven of its twelve members were moved to make revelations about it during the recriminations of the fall; we owe much of our knowledge to this circumstance.

66. Text in *Handbuch für die Wähler der Unabhängigen Sozialdemokratischen Partei, Reichstagswahl 1920*, 3 vols. (n.p., n.d.), I, 51; a slightly different form in Karl Brammer, *Fünf Tage Militärdiktatur* (Berlin, 1920), pp. 66–67. According to Zietz, USPD *Parteitag*, Oct. 1920, p. 63, the appeal was drafted at a hasty morning meeting of those members of the executive who could be found, before the response of the other parties or the trade unions was known; by early afternoon it had been printed and sent off to other cities.

67.   *Arbeiterklasse siegt über Kapp und Lüttwitz*, ed. Erwin Könnemann, Brigitte Berthold and Gerhard Schulze, Archivalische Forschungen zur Geschichte der deutschen Arbeiterbewegung, vols. 7/I–7/II (Berlin, 1971), I, 117–18; Franz Krüger, *Diktatur oder Volksherrschaft? Der Putsch vom 13. März 1920* (Berlin, 1920), p. 7; Paul Löbe, *Der Weg war lang: Lebenserinnerungen*, 2d ed. (Berlin, 1954), p. 98.

this document are unclear, the general strike was as natural and automatic a response for the SPD as for the USPD in the face of a military coup.[68] Even more significant, the trade unions supported the same policy—the central organizations of the liberal and Catholic unions as well as the two federations of socialist unions, the ADGB (the old organization under a new name) and its new white-collar partner, the AfA. The two socialist federations, in their first appeal, emphasized the threat to the eight-hour day, collective bargaining, and similar trade-union achievements as much as the threat to the Republic.[69] But the fact that the great national unions felt compelled to recognize the connection between political developments and their own traditional interests was perhaps the most important single development of the strike against Kapp. The unions were becoming politicized.

Only the KPD central committee opposed acting against the putsch. Its first manifesto, aimed more at the old government than at Kapp and Lüttwitz, leaders of the putsch, announced that

the revolutionary proletariat . . . will not lift a finger for the democratic republic, which was only a sorry mask for the dictatorship of the bourgeoisie.

The bourgeoisie now exercises its dictatorship directly, through its old familiar masters, the heroes of 1914: that is the only change.[70]

This kind of sectarian behavior, and bad judgment, had given the Communists a bad name in the past among left Independents, and Levi, in prison, was almost desperate with exasperation.[71] To be sure, this March 13 directive of the central committee was generally ignored by the party in the provinces—was burned, according to one source[72]—and the leadership reversed itself the next day; but the initial response had left its mark, undermining the KPD's chance to exercise influence in the central strike leadership and delaying its recovery from the troubled period of the split.

The USPD next had to decide on its relationship to the other leading forces of the strike, a problem that occupied the leadership throughout March 13. At a meeting in the morning with representatives of the SPD and trade unions, the Independent spokesmen were dubious about the

68. See the discussion in Johannes Erger, *Der Kapp-Lüttwitz-Putsch* (Düsseldorf, 1967), pp. 193–94.

69. Text in *Arbeiterklasse siegt über Kapp*, I, 118–19.

70. Text *ibid.*, I, 120–23; for the background see J. Walcher, "Die Zentrale der KPD (Spartakusbund) und der Kapp-Putsch," *Die Kommunistische Internationale*, 7 (1926), 392–93, and Erwin Könnemann and Hans-Joachim Krusch, *Aktionseinheit contra Kapp-Putsch* (Berlin, 1972), pp. 175–84.

71. See his letter of March 16 to the central committee, in *Die Kommunistische Internationale*, no. 12, pp. 147–50.

72. R. Fischer, p. 126.

USPD's willingness to collaborate with a party they regarded as largely responsible for the situation.[73] In an afternoon meeting,[74] however, the representatives of the USPD appeared ready to consider an alliance if their conditions were accepted: the strike must not be conducted in support of the "Ebert-Bauer-Noske" government, since "no worker could be expected to enter a general strike on its behalf"; the workers must be armed (a point on which the Independents themselves were apparently divided); and the goal of the dictatorship of the proletariat must be acknowledged. The SPD's reply was surprisingly accommodating. It too wanted a reconstruction of the government to include the Independents while dropping Noske and perhaps other Majority Socialist ministers; it could also support arming the workers if proper precautions were observed. It would not, however, accept the principle of dictatorship; this was not wanted by the great majority of the people, and to proclaim such a goal would drive the whole bourgeoisie into the Kappist camp and lead to a long and bloody struggle that would end in defeat for the workers. The Independents withdrew once again for consultation. When they returned in the evening they had decided to stand on their Leipzig Action Program, and the possibility of collaboration was therefore closed, at least for the time being.[75]

Consequently, not one but two strike committees were established in Berlin. The first, with more national importance, represented the ADGB and the AfA and remained in close contact with the SPD. The second was set up by the national and local leaderships of the USPD, the Berlin trades council, and the Central Office of Berlin Factory Councils,[76] with the later addition of the KPD; this composition gave it exceptional influence over the workers of Berlin.

The USPD's direct participation in the leadership of a mass action was new in the party's history and shows how much the balance between party and councils had shifted during the winter. The party's radicals might have been expected immediately to elect and organize factory delegates and to confer the leadership on them, as the KPD demanded and as happened in other cities; but they did not. The presence of Ehrhardt's ruthless troops in the city made such a plan very hazardous; but

73. Wels in SPD *Parteiausschuss,* March 1920, p. 2.

74. *Ibid.,* pp. 2–3; Krüger, pp. 7–8.

75. Wels in SPD *Parteiausschuss,* March 1920, p. 3; Krüger, p. 9; Legien in *Vorwärts,* April 8, 1919 (e); report of a commission of the Second International that chanced to be in Berlin at the time, Troelstra papers, 479, p. 7. According to Zietz, Däumig threatened to resign if the USPD joined the SPD in organizing the strike; USPD *Parteitag,* Oct. 1920, p. 64.

76. This central office was the successor to the old Berlin executive council, and is not to be confused with the Central Office of German Factory Councils in Halle.

the decision was more a matter of policy, as is shown by a letter from the Central Strike Committee (as the USPD's group was called) replying to the KPD's demand for factory elections: "It cannot be admitted that factory and workers' councils proceeding from immediate elections are the proper organs for the direction of this struggle. They would mean the exclusion of the party executive from the leadership of the struggle."[77] Koenen and others did call for election of workers' councils, but apparently not until the evening of March 16, when Kapp's regime was already tottering. The party executive decided against the idea, and the radicals had to settle for reviving the revolutionary factory council system instead.[78] This institution had much less immediate political potential, and it took time to organize (the first branch assemblies met on March 21, the first general assembly on March 23); its purpose, in fact, was to "win positions of power in order to have means of pressure against the government."[79] The party itself was to maintain active control at the top.

Apart from the councils, we know little about the issues considered inside the party executive in the early days of the strike. All seem to have agreed that it would not be possible to establish a successful soviet republic[80]; beyond this, reaching agreement on anything was difficult. The executive's public declarations during the first several days were unanimous, but long, wearying meetings were needed to achieve unanimity, one of them lasting from 7:00 P.M. until 6:00 A.M.[81] Such time-consuming discussions meant that the USPD was slow in reaching a position on important matters and that the results were unpredictable. No one could speak for the party when a new issue arose, and discussions with other organizations often had to be interrupted while the Independents assembled separately to seek agreement among themselves. The party tended to be driven back onto its least common denominator, permanent opposition and rhetorical extremism; so difficult was the process of making novel or constructive decisions that even those that were made lacked the force of conviction. The party was important in the conduct of the general strike; but its role in attempts to find new solutions as the country emerged from the strike was distressingly weak.

There were only brief moments during the strike when the USPD

77. Quoted by Paul Frölich, *Die Internationale* (KPD), June 24, 1920, p. 21. The date of the message, to judge from a mention in a KPD circular of March 22 (*Arbeiterklasse siegt über Kapp,* I, 218), was probably March 14.
78. Koenen, USPD *Parteitag,* Oct. 1920, pp. 46–47.
79. From a speech by Crispien, *Freiheit,* April 3, 1920 (m).
80. *Ibid.;* Zietz, USPD *Parteitag,* Oct. 1920, p. 21.
81. Stoecker, USPD *Reichskonferenz,* Sept. 1920, p. 155.

seemed to know what it wanted, and these came toward the end. Its second appeal, on March 14, made no mention of arming the workers or the dictatorship of the proletariat; the party had retreated to the neutral observation that "bringing down this dictatorship is a necessary stage in the struggle for the complete emancipation of the working class and the victory of revolutionary socialism."[82] A day or two later it had arrived at the opposite rhetorical extreme, in words that are worth quoting for their calculated ambiguity:

The working class is not conducting this struggle in order to help restore the Bauer-Noske government to power.
    This government is finished!
    Finished as well is the National Assembly, which has supported the policies of the government and bears the same responsibility for the coup by Kapp and Lüttwitz.
    The goal of our struggle can only be to put an end for ever to the rule of the reactionary bourgeoisie and the Junkers, of the dictatorship of the saber.
    The working class must fight until it has won power!
    Arise to purposeful struggle under the banner of revolutionary socialism!
    Arise to liberation from all oppression and exploitation, and for the establishment of a socialist community!
    Down with reaction! All power to the working class![83]

The tone suggests an appeal to proceed to a dictatorship of the proletariat through the council system, as the Leipzig program prescribed; yet the text is remarkable for the absence of both these slogans; the idea of arming the workers, and hints on means of reaching the goal are also missing. Alternatively, the passage can be construed as a highly provocative way to call for election of a new Reichstag and formation of a workers' government—which is doubtless closer to what such party leaders as Hilferding wanted it to mean. In fact, the leadership was not serious about either of these courses, as later developments were to show; it was offering incitement without direction because the party did not yet know where it wanted to go.

    The only certain point in the declaration is the decision to bring down the Bauer government and prevent its replacement with another basically bourgeois government. In terms of practical politics, this decision pointed toward attempts to form a workers' government—one based on the socialist parties and the unions, including the nonsocialist (Catholic and liberal) unions. Independents had been the first to suggest this course, on March 13, but had since let the idea drop. It arose again on March 17, the day

82. *Dokumente und Materialien*, VII/I, 219–20.
83. *Freiheit*, March 16, 1920 (special issue). The declaration probably emerged from the long meeting of March 15–16 mentioned by Stoecker in USPD *Reichskonferenz*, Sept. 1920, p. 155.

of Kapp's fall, when Carl Legien of the ADGB was seeking some rational solution to the crisis. This time it caused fierce controversy in the party executive.[84] Many USPD leaders were in no mood to talk to the SPD and trade unions at all; this was Crispien's position, and Däumig threatened to resign from the party if it reached agreement with the SPD.[85] On the other side, the warmest supporter of a workers' government was Wilhelm Koenen, who seems to have had in mind an initially parliamentary regime including representatives of the nonsocialist unions that would then develop a more satisfactory basis of power in a council system.[86] He found allies, though lukewarm ones, in Stoecker, Rosenfeld, and Hilferding, who favored trying the idea though they had little faith in it. The views of others, though not recorded, were apparently even more indefinite. With this line-up the party executive could not possibly act. The next day Crispien changed his mind and went off to find Legien; but by then the trade unions had set off on another path.

On the day Kapp resigned, March 17, the parties and trade unions involved in the strike began to consider future moves. The strike could not simply be broken off by fiat; most workers were convinced that the Weimar system was ineffective against the militarist and monarchist reaction and that drastic reforms in its personnel and practices must be made. As Franz Krüger, leader of the Berlin SPD, put it, "The parties and trade unions do not have the power to call an end to the general strike unless the working class can be sure that the power of reaction in the country and in the state is broken in every respect."[87] Krüger's words were more than a statement of fact; even conservative Majority Socialists saw an opportunity to exploit this wave of popular feeling in the interests of their own long-standing demands. At the same time, the trade unionists and Majority Socialists were anxious to bring the strike to an end as soon as possible, partly because it was damaging the economy, but more because there was a danger of leadership passing into the hands of extremists and the situation degenerating into civil war. In their negotiations with the government, the union leaders pressed far-reaching demands; but their determination to seize the chance to trans-

---

84. Wilhelm Koenen, "Zur Frage der Möglichkeit einer Arbeiterregierung nach dem Kapp-Putsch," *BzG*, 4 (1962), 347–49, supplies most of the details. Cf. Koenen in USPD *Parteitag*, Oct. 1920, p. 47, and Zietz, *ibid.*, pp. 64–65.

85. Däumig's intransigence was known outside the party, too; see Pieck, KPD *Parteitag*, April 1920, p. 38. The unusual alliances within the party executive on this question were of very brief duration; the usual factional alignments reappeared within a few days.

86. Koenen is not explicit on this point, but it is implied by a number of comments in his article, pp. 346–48.

87. From the minutes of a meeting of March 18, printed in *BzG*, 8 (1966), 273.

form the Weimar state was undermined by their desire to reach some sort of constructive agreement with the greatest possible speed.

On March 18, the socialist unions issued a manifesto saying that the strike would continue until their demands were met; at noon on the same day they began talks with the government and the majority parties about these demands.[88] The temper of the times is reflected in the radicalism of their detailed program.[89] The unions demanded "decisive influence . . . on the reconstruction of the governments of the Reich and the states and on the development of new legislation in economic and social policy," as well as a share in the purge of all soldiers or officials who had taken part in the putsch or lent their services to the Kapp regime; dismissal of all reactionary officials and a few unpopular ministers, including Noske; dissolution of all counterrevolutionary military formations, with the "organized workers" taking over the security services; and, finally, a number of specific, far-reaching items of social legislation, including "socialization of mining and electricity production." In long, difficult negotiations with representatives of the government and its three constituent parties the union leaders pushed their demands through. Some of the sharper edges were filed off in the course of the talks; but the eight-point agreement that resulted was still a remarkable document.[90] If even a few of its major points had been implemented, the face of Weimar democracy might have been changed—not necessarily in a desirable way, in view of the powers claimed by the unions. With these promises in hand, the unions felt they could count on bringing the strike to an end. On March 20, a few hours after the eight-point agreement was concluded, they published the text of the agreement and "declare[d] the general strike at an end as of today."[91]

But the trade unionists had miscalculated. The eight points were only paper promises, and the ominous presence of the nonrepublican (though not necessarily counterrevolutionary) military could be felt everywhere. The agreement had no immediate effect for the Berlin workers skirmishing from time to time with the Free Corps on the outskirts of the city, for the Ruhr working-class forces lined up against the Reichswehr, for the Halle workers who had lived under a military dictatorship since the beginning of the putsch. Moreover, with communications and train services restored (since the evening of March 17 in most areas) workers in different cities were being made aware of the extent of their common

88. Krüger, pp. 25–26.
89. Text in *Arbeiterklasse siegt über Kapp,* I, 175–76.
90. Text in *Vorwärts,* March 22, 1920 (e). A ninth point assured the workers that Ministers Noske and Heine would resign.
91. *Ibid.*

struggle. Finally, in going ahead without the parties—that is, without the USPD—the unions had overestimated their strength.

Some Independents were tempted to go along with Legien, in order to avoid an open split. On March 20, the day the ADGB and the AfA issued their call to end the strike, open conflict developed in the central strike leadership, with Crispien and Hilferding favoring joining the call and Koenen and other members of the executive opposed.[92] Crispien and Hilferding seem to have carried the majority; but the following day, when the first authentic news arrived from the Ruhr, they changed their minds rather than abandon the comrades there who were obviously in a dangerous position.[93] The decision to continue the strike was communicated on March 21 to the council assemblies, which emphatically endorsed it.

The Independents, meanwhile, had finally acted, calling for election of factory councils and then a general assembly of Berlin councils.[94] At the same time, in response to the trade unions' announcement of their demands, the USPD formulated its own demands:

1. The dissolution of all counterrevolutionary mercenary armies. Dissolution of all military, civil, and police formations, of the citizens' guards [Einwohnerwehren] in city and countryside, of the Technical Emergency Service, of police troops. Disarmament of the bourgeoisie and landowners. Establishment of a revolutionary guard.
2. Immediate ending of the state of emergency and release of all political prisoners. Judgment of all counterrevolutionary putschists by revolutionary people's tribunals.
3. Immediate beginning of socialization, especially of the mines.[95]

On March 21 these demands were elaborated in a manifesto of the Central Strike Committee giving detailed guidance on how to ensure that the workers penetrated and controlled all the armed forces of the state and calling on workers everywhere to elect factory councils, supervise their factories, shops, or places of business, and take over control and distribution of food supplies.[96]

At this late date, the USPD was beginning to give practical effect to its goals. The demands were on two levels. Some, concerning the state of

92. Koenen, USPD Parteitag, Oct. 1920, p. 29.
93. Ibid.; Crispien's speech, Freiheit, April 3, 1920 (m).
94. The appeal was published on March 19 (Arbeiterklasse siegt über Kapp, I, 205–7) but the decision seems to have been made on March 17 (see the KPD circular ibid., I, 219).
95. Ibid., I, 206–7. The demands had been formulated at least a day earlier; they were read out by an Independent trade unionist at the negotiations of March 18; see the minutes in BzG, 8 (1966), 270.
96. Placard, Levi papers, P 54.

emergency, political prisoners, and revolutionary tribunals, were directed at the government and were in this respect similar to the efforts of the trade unions. The difference was that a visible beginning could be made on each of them within a few days; and the intention was to continue the strike until then.[97] The other proposals were directed at the workers, calling on them to take matters into their own hands and assure themselves of effective power positions in the factories and cities where they could do so. Thereby they might be able to achieve further gains, perhaps even abrogation of the Factory Council Law.[98]

This tactic, however, could not be successful if it was supported only by the followers of the socialist left; if an opportunity ever had existed for the USPD to exploit the situation without regard for the Majority Socialists (which is unlikely), it had passed. The strikes could not be continued for long, even in Berlin, against the will of the unions and the SPD. Consequently, when Legien approached the USPD again, apparently on March 21, about a joint solution, the party executive was ready to negotiate.[99] Legien was adamant that the course on which he had already begun, a solution by agreement with the government parties, must be pursued, even though it had not succeeded at the first try; he was, however, ready to see the question of a workers' government opened at the same time. This time the USPD was prepared at least to discuss the possibility.

In these talks the question of a workers' government took second place. This, it seems, was the intention even of the Independents.[100] They were ready in principle; they sketched out a program for such a government, including certain basic socialist measures, and they committed themselves to accepting representatives of the nonsocialist trade unions into the government.[101] But there is no doubt that participation in such a government would have been embarrassing for the Independents, given the mood of many of their followers, and this may well account for their lack of enthusiasm. The SPD delegation ratified the plan, subject to the agreement of the Center Party and Democratic delegations,[102] which, predictably, was not forthcoming.

The possibility of such a government continued to be discussed for a

97. *Ibid.*
98. Crispien speech, *Freiheit*, April 3, 1920 (m).
99. Koenen, USPD *Parteitag*, Oct. 1920, pp. 29–30; Däumig speech, *Freiheit*, March 24, 1920 (m); Krüger, p. 30; see also Walcher, "Die Zentrale," pp. 398–402, on the background.
100. See Crispien's offhand remarks at a meeting with representatives of the two socialist delegations on March 22; *BzG*, 8 (1966), 278.
101. *Ibid.;* "Bericht," p. 13, in SPD *Parteitag*, Oct. 1920.
102. "Bericht," p. 13, in SPD *Parteitag*, Oct. 1920; Varain, p. 178.

few days by the socialist parties and the unions, even after the end of the strike; but the idea was really dead. Its realization depended on the bourgeois parties being intimidated enough to permit a class-based government and the socialist parties being certain of their common purpose. The first condition obtained, if at all (which is unlikely), only during the early days of the crisis; the second, if at all, only near its end. The venture was thus chimerical. Even without these problems, the USPD would probably never have acted on its professed willingness to participate in such a government. The left-wing members of the party executive have not informed us how they felt at the time, but it is hard to believe that they could have tolerated a government on Legien's model, that is, a modified parliamentary government; if they ever did agree, they backed off almost at once. Two days after negotiations with the National Assembly delegations failed, the USPD was speaking of a "socialist workers' government," a term not conducive to collaboration with the nonsocialist unions; two days later, according to Däumig, party policy had returned to the "purely socialist government" of the previous spring.[103] Crispien confirmed this view officially some weeks later, having earlier explained that the essence of such a government would be Independent predominance and the Independent program.[104] This way of thinking was equivalent to abandoning the notion. The idea remained only as a memory of a moment when a majority of the party leaders had been ready, or nearly ready, to come out of their isolation and try to influence the development of the Republic.

The issue of improving the government's guarantees to the strikers was treated separately. What the USPD's demands were is not recorded; all we know is that, not surprisingly, they were met only in part.[105] The formal promises of the government were nonetheless of some importance:

1. that the troops in Berlin will be withdrawn to the line of the Spree;
2. [that] the intensified state of emergency will be terminated at once;
3. that the armed workers, especially in the Ruhr, are not to be attacked;
4. [that] there shall be talks with the trade union organizations about incorporation of workers into the security forces in Prussia.[106]

A majority of the party executive decided, "in view of the fact that the united [strike] front had been broken by the decision of the large trade unions," to join the SPD and the unions in calling for an end to the

103. Party declaration in *Freiheit*, March 25, 1920 (m); Däumig speech *ibid.*, March 28, 1920.
104. *Ibid.*, April 18, 1920 (m), and April 3, 1920 (m).
105. Däumig's speech *ibid.*, March 24, 1920 (m).
106. *Ibid.*, March 23, 1920 (e).

strike on the basis of these concessions and the earlier agreement with the governing parties. A minority dissented vigorously but in vain.[107] At midnight on March 22, the SPD, USPD, ADGB, AfA, and Berlin trades council signed the appeal for an end to the strike; should the government renege on its promises, they undertook to consider a renewal of the strike later.[108]

Däumig had the thankless task of presenting the decision of the five organizations, with which he disagreed, to an assembly of the "revolutionary factory councils" on March 23, the first since the Independents had decided to sponsor the election of councils six days earlier.[109] The Communist Party, represented by Wilhelm Pieck, urged that the strike be carried on until the goals of a workers' government and general election of workers' councils were achieved.[110] The whole assembly was in fact reluctant to abandon the strike with so little accomplished and with their proletarian brothers engaged in life-and-death struggles elsewhere in the Reich. But almost all delegates from the industries and trades of the city reported that the strike was on the verge of crumbling unofficially, whatever the assembly might decide. The final decision, by a narrow majority, was that the strike should be "interrupted" (Däumig's recommendation)—interrupted, not brought to an end.

The idea of renewing the general strike, by command either of the trade-union and party leaderships or of the revolutionary factory councils, was a will-o'-the-wisp. The unions and the parties had obviously given up the idea within a week. They continued to meet from time to time, well into April, to measure the government's actions against its undertakings and, when necessary, to issue demands. But the demands were not accompanied by ultimata; and only the forceful demand that the government extend its own ultimatum to the Ruhr workers met any government response.[111] Berlin radicals, of course, took renewal of the strike as a serious duty, particularly when the government sent troops against the Ruhr. The factory council assemblies at the end of the month passed resolutions that were belligerent but limited to calling for strike

107. Däumig speech *ibid.*, March 24, 1920 (m). According to H. Stoecker, p. 227, the minority was Stoecker, Däumig, Koenen, Rosenfeld, and Geyer (who, however, was not a member of the party executive).

108. *Freiheit*, March 23, 1920 (e).

109. Extensive report of the assembly *ibid.*, March 24, 1920 (m).

110. The KPD leadership, having abandoned its sectarian position of March 13, resolved on March 23 to encourage the USPD to enter a workers' government by promising that the KPD would observe "loyal opposition" to such a government; text of their declaration in *Rote Fahne*, March 26, 1920. See Walcher, "Die Zentrale," pp. 398–404, and Könnemann and Krusch, pp. 324–29.

111. Text in *Freiheit*, March 31, 1920 (e).

preparations in the factories.[112] When fighting resumed in earnest in the Ruhr, in the first days of April, the councils in Berlin were strangely quiet. They met again only on April 8, and only to vote that there was not enough general support for a strike.[113] The movement in Berlin was over.

The Kapp Putsch, Working-Class Militancy, and Armed Action

Critical as they were for the development of the USPD, the attempts of the socialist leaders in Berlin to find political solutions to the crisis were not the central part of the experience of the party's following in the days of the putsch and its aftermath. For a large part of the German working class, these were days of direct local confrontation with the armed forces of reaction. Certain regions saw armed proletarian action of a kind Germany had not known even during the civil war of 1919— and has not, on the whole, seen again. These armed actions, the bloodiest of the postwar period, marked the high point of the German workers' disciplined aggressiveness. The working class was united and passionate; and if the gains for the workers were meager at best, the memory of the actions undertaken remained a force in radical socialist politics for years.

The German working class in these years always summoned up far more energy, and achieved more unity, in defense against counterrevolution than in efforts to overthrow capitalism; and the particular circumstances of the Kapp Putsch created a stark confrontation of the workers with their most hated enemy, the military.[114] The military units of most of the north and east of the country either openly declared their allegiance to the Kapp regime or tacitly accepted the coup, at least provisionally; in either case they were hostile to the general strike with which the workers greeted the putsch, and still more hostile to any signs of proletarian action against the state, whoever might be in charge in Berlin. In several cities clashes occurred between hostile crowds and military units in the first days of the putsch; deaths were reported from Frankfurt on Main on March 13, from Leipzig and Kiel on March 14, from Leipzig, Berlin, and Dresden (the worst case of all with fifty-nine dead) on March 15.[115] In many other towns and industrial regions, workers and military remained in passive, sullen opposition; in some, the workers

112. *Ibid.*, March 28, 1920, and March 31, 1920 (e).
113. *Ibid.*, April 9, 1920 (m).
114. The enemy was principally the regular army (including the remaining Free Corps) but included its auxiliaries (*Zeitfreiwilligen*), local citizens' guards, and the Prussian security police.
115. See the collection of wire-service dispatches, DZA Merseburg, Rep. 90a D Tit. I 1 Nr. 29, vol. 1; for Dresden see also Fabian, p. 78.

actively armed themselves. Often only an incident was needed, sometimes the collapse of the Kapp regime supplied the impulse, for the workers to move to settle accounts with the army. Before the crisis was past, armed engagements between the two sides had occurred not only in the cities of the Ruhr, the best-known case, but also in at least twenty-six other places.[116]

The Independents commonly played a significant role, sometimes a dominant role, in these actions; but whether or not the party organization as such became centrally involved seems to have been a function of locality and personalities. If there was any central direction from Berlin through the party organization we know next to nothing about it.[117] Even the parallel illegal organization that the radical forces in the party had apparently been trying to build since the previous December cannot have functioned in any coherent way since there is no trace of it in the accounts of even the most careful investigators of the fighting and no signs of any coordination between the regions where fighting occurred. Locally, for instance in Halle or Hagen, the efficiency with which leading Independents were able to muster an armed force suggests prior preparation, albeit through some network other than the party itself; and there is some direct evidence to support this suggestion.[118]

116. See the map in *Arbeitereinheit siegt über Militaristen* (Berlin, 1960), facing p. 32. This map is concerned only with armed engagements and omits places where the army fired on crowds but the workers did not attempt armed struggle. In such places (including Dresden, Cassel, Königsberg, and Nuremberg), feeling against the army must often have run fully as high as where it was expressed in fighting.

117. There are reports of emissaries from Berlin turning up in Hagen (Westphalia) and Guben (Lusatia) on March 14; see Lucas, *Märzrevolution*, p. 152, and *Unter der roten Fahne: Erinnerungen alter Genossen* (Berlin, 1958), p. 179. Emissaries were the only possible means of communication, since telephone connections with Berlin were broken off in the first hours after the putsch; but normal means of travel, such as trains, also quickly came to a halt.

118. For instance, Colm, pp. 56–59. The Prussian Staatskommissar für Ueberwachung der öffentlichen Ordnung reported on Jan. 8, 1920, with plausible detail, that radical delegates at the USPD's Leipzig congress (on the initiative of the Berlin shop stewards) had set up a secret, illegal network to prepare and execute working-class actions; though a number of party officials were involved (the names were given), the party executive was to have no official knowledge of the scheme. See StA Magdeburg, Rep. C20 Ib Nr. 4790, p. 36. There are additional reports that, if genuine, confirm the existence of such an organization; one dated Jan. 14, 1920, StA Magdeburg, Rep. C20 Ib Nr. 4788, p. 15, and one dated July 16, 1920, DZA Potsdam, RMdI 12258, pp. 238–39. See also USPD *Reichskonferenz*, Sept. 1920, pp. 184 and 221, where Däumig and Georg Stolt seem to refer to such an organization. If it existed, its only opportunity for action during 1920 (after which nearly all of those named in the evidence joined the Communists) was the Kapp Putsch, but it plays no role in, for instance, Lucas' detailed account of events in the Ruhr in his *Märzrevolution*. Perhaps the period of persecution after January 13 disrupted it in the early stages of its development.

Anger was the dominant working-class response and was by no means confined to the ranks of the parties of the socialist left. Some of the greatest violence occurred in places where the USPD's following was not conspicuously large—Kiel, the Cottbus-Senftenberg area southeast of Berlin, the rural areas of Mecklenburg. But most of the outstanding instances of conflict—the pitched battles in the streets of Leipzig and Halle, the regular military campaigns fought near Halle, in western Thuringia, and in the Ruhr—took place in parts of the country where the working class was primed by its traditions and its daily political fare for active hostility to the existing order. These were Independent strongholds, and here the Independents underwent an experience as harsh as that of the leaders in Berlin.

One of the first places where fighting broke out was Leipzig.[119] On Sunday, March 14, a large demonstration of aggressive but still peaceable workers who were marching on the central city was suddenly met with gunfire from a force of auxiliary troops. Overnight the city found itself divided into two armed camps, with an army unit and its auxiliaries defending the inner city and a force of armed workers (estimates of its size range from 600–700 to 3,000) attempting to press in from the outside.[120] The emergence of this workers' force appears to have been spontaneous, or at least independent of any political leadership; once it had formed, however, the USPD (in the person of Lipinski) and the trade unions established a leadership organ to give it political direction.[121] An armed stalemate developed, and Lipinski, hearing of the collapse of the Kapp regime on March 17, entered into a compromise agreement with the military in the hopes of extricating the workers from the situation without further bloodshed. Some of the armed workers, indignant at the terms of the compromise, renounced their official leadership and carried on with Communists at their head; the result was that the victorious military concluded their campaign on March 19 by burning down the proud center of the Leipzig labor movement, the House of the People, and created a residue of impotent bitterness.

In the neighboring district of Halle, events unfolded quite differently. Here, too, the district executive of the USPD took the initiative in calling the general strike on March 13, but then—because of arrests and a particularly aggressive Reichswehr unit in Halle—the city was quiet for

119. On Leipzig, see Hans Block, *Freiheit*, April 1, 1920 (m); Könnemann and Krusch, pp. 96–101 and 200–2; *Arbeiterklasse siegt über Kapp*, I, 342–48; Willi Langrock in *Arbeitereinheit*, pp. 106–20.

120. Estimates in *Illustrierte Gechichte*, p. 489, and *Arbeitereinheit*, p. 114.

121. There is some evidence that Lipinski tried to minimize the influence of the Communists at all points. See for instance *Arbeitereinheit*, pp. 106–20; Schunke, p. 40.

several days while the movement spread through the towns and country-side of the district beyond.[122] Starting on Monday, March 15 (the first full day of the strike), the workers of several towns and coal fields set out to arm themselves (commonly by raiding the supplies of the citizens' militia) and disarm or drive off whatever military forces might be in their area. The first reported skirmishes took place near Bitterfeld on that day; two days later a regular engagement with Reichswehr troops oc-curred there, ending with the withdrawal of the latter. There were battles in the Zeitz area on March 16 and 17 and at Schkeuditz on March 17, all ending in the disarming or withdrawal of the military; and on March 17 an attack on Eisleben by an armored Reichswehr train was driven off in a full day of fighting.

Only at this point did the city of Halle re-enter the picture. The army had remained in control in Halle while Kapp ruled in Berlin, and even thereafter, until, on March 18, armed workers attacked the city from the south. By the following day the "battle of Halle," one of the bitterest and most protracted of the period, was well under way. The workers' forces, including men from all over the district and even further afield, closed in on the city from three sides, driving the army and its auxiliaries out of the working-class districts and back on their strong points in the inner city. From these, however, a day of bitter fighting on March 21—"bloody Sunday"—failed to dislodge them. On the following day the workers' Independent and Communist leaders, apparently fearing inter-vention by further forces from Berlin, agreed to a settlement, and the fighting was soon at an end. The strike, however, was not; the workers, dissatisfied with the settlement, persevered, and in many parts of the dis-trict work did not begin again until March 27 or even later—later than anywhere else in the Reich.

The very different conditions of socialist radicalism in the neighbor-ing cities of Leipzig and Halle are illuminated again by the events of the putsch. In Leipzig, USPD leaders and their trade-union allies dealt with a fundamentally disciplined working class, and by taking care not to lose touch with the most activist of the city's workers they were able to act as the official leadership of the movement on most occasions—but with the intention of restoring orderly conditions when opportunity offered. The regular labor organizations of the city thus maintained a kind of control, and the organizational form remained central to the movement's pur-poses. In the Halle district, by contrast, the force and real raison d'être

122. The particulars in this account are from Schunke's valuable study, which however tells us little about the leadership of the workers or such underlying or-ganization as there may have been; and from two authoritative USPD sources re-printed in *Arbeiterklasse siegt über Kapp*, I, 434–43 and 453–58.

of the party lay in the scope of the activist, grass-roots movement over which it presided; even when the formal organization was decapitated by arrests, the party's followers were ready and able to go into action. How such activist readiness was prepared and arranged we do not know, but plainly it was, and had been since soon after the revolution, the focus of the party's activity. The Halle party, accordingly, can reasonably be called a revolutionary party, as revolutionary as German Social Democrats of this era knew how to be; while the Leipzig party represented, not the drive toward radical change, but the element of continuity in the German socialist tradition.

Southwest of Halle and Leipzig lay Thuringia, another center of armed conflict.[123] Conditions here were very diverse, since Thuringia, though on the eve of unification (except for the Prussian territories) into a single Thuringian state, still consisted of eight separate political entities, seven of them petty republics of variegated political coloration. Two, Reuss and Gotha, which still had Independents in their governments, were centers of some of the fiercest fighting in the area. In Gera, capital of Reuss, the local Reichswehr unit attempted to depose the government; instead the workers overcame the soldiers in a day of hard fighting on March 15—the proudest moment of the revolutionary epoch for the Gera labor movement.[124] In Gotha, ruled by a government of radical Independents who derived their authority from a popular majority, a burst of militant activism merged with the anti-Kapp spirit of the workers of the nearby Thuringian Forest; roving organized bands of armed workers in the southwest corner of Thuringia engaged in large-scale regular combat of a particularly bitter sort.[125] The district remained isolated, however, from other centers of armed action—its influence did not extend even as far as Erfurt—and within two weeks of the outbreak of the putsch, without major incident, the conflicts petered out.

In the Ruhr, the troubles accompanying the putsch were longer-lasting and presented a more difficult political problem for all concerned than anywhere else in the Reich.[126] Predictably, given its endemic industrial conflict and widespread political radicalism, the Ruhr was one of the

123. The best overall survey of the conflicts in Thuringia is Könnemann and Krusch, pp. 102–8 and 205–15.
124. *Der Märzputsch im Volksstaat Reuss: Nach amtlichem Material dargestellt vom Reussischen Presseamt* (Gera, n.d.).
125. On Gotha, see especially Buchsbaum, pp. 250–88; Witzmann, pp. 22–24; *Arbeiterklasse siegt über Kapp*, II, 502–13.
126. Lucas, *Märzrevolution*, gives a detailed account of the first week of the Ruhr conflict; Spethmann, II, 76–276, is unbalanced and politically biased but full of facts. See also especially Colm; Severing, *1919/1920*, pp. 134–205; and (for the USPD center at Hagen) Lambers, pp. 98–122. The key documents are in *Arbeiterklasse siegt über Kapp*, vol. 2, section 8.

most disorderly regions of the country. Furthermore, resentment against the military ran as high here as anywhere, though the army was, relatively speaking, very weak.[127] This resentment and the Ruhr's history of violence were the ingredients for unusually serious conflict.

In many cities of the Westphalian part of the Ruhr, unlike Halle or Berlin, for instance, the absence of Reichswehr units meant that nothing stood in the way of a spontaneous political response to the putsch. Local action committees were established in many places, some originating in the initiative of the workers but all composed in the end of representatives of the parties.[128] Some of the rhetoric of the workers' front was extreme; in Elberfeld, for example, the Lower Rhineland district leaders of the three socialist parties combined to issue a manifesto calling for a dictatorship of the proletariat, a council system, and immediate socialization.[129] In practice little of this was attempted; the uniting force was less far-reaching programs of this sort than a determination to resist the reactionaries, in particular the hated army. In a number of towns where action committees intimidated or virtually supplanted the regular authorities, they contented themselves with declaring a state of emergency and suppressing newspapers that had seemed to support Kapp. In some, however—Hagen, Bochum, and a few smaller towns—the workers armed themselves, seizing and distributing the weapons intended for the local police or citizens' guards.[130] Attempts by such local leaders as USPD district secretary Konrad Ludwig of Hagen to restrain them were in vain. Most of the Ruhr workers, whatever their party, meant business.

Meanwhile Reichswehr units in the area (largely unreconstructed Free Corps) demonstratively welcomed the new regime;[131] and General von Watter, regional commander in Münster, misjudging the situation, set some of his units in motion toward areas where an insurrectionary spirit was suspected. The armed workers responded aggressively. At the town of Wetter on March 15 a Free Corps detachment was surrounded (largely by workers from Hagen) and, after several hours of battle, forced to surrender. The same night, insurgent forces surrounded another detachment of the same Free Corps in another town, receiving its surrender the next morning. Through such victories, and by disarming

127. See ch. 7, n. 59.
128. The patterns are examined in Lucas, *Märzrevolution*, pp. 119–44. The preferred constellation seems to have been an alliance of all three workers' parties. Where this could not be arranged, the Independents in the Ruhr (unlike those in Leipzig) seem to have invariably chosen to side with the Communists rather than the SPD in the early days of the crisis.
129. Facsimile in *Arbeitereinheit*, facing p. 33.
130. Lucas, *Märzrevolution*, pp. 148–63.
131. *Ibid.*, pp. 104–7; Colm, pp. 21–27.

the citizens' guards of the smaller towns, the workers' forces soon acquired a proper arsenal of small arms.[132] The example was followed elsewhere. On March 16 a larger Free Corps unit was badly mauled by a workers' army while trying to march out of the district; two days later, the Westphalian part of the Ruhr was entirely free of Reichswehr troops, all having been disarmed by the workers or withdrawn from the area. There remained troops in the Rhenish part of the Ruhr and a large body of security police in Essen; but when the latter city fell on March 20, after a three-day battle, no regular armed forces were left in the district.

Only as this conflict developed did it become clear to the insurgents that their actions had placed them in an exposed political position, however secure their local hegemony. The putsch was over, and the Ruhr workers confronted not an illegal, counterrevolutionary regime but the constitutional government of the Reich. Commanding General Watter, whose ambivalent response to the putsch had contributed to the violence, was once again the authorized agent of a legal government. The military units that had demonstrated their sympathy for the putsch on March 13 and 14 were once again, although unchanged, legitimate organs of the state; resistance to them, previously a democratic act, had become rebellion. And behind this confusing turn of events lay the knowledge that the government could ultimately assemble enough troops —indeed was already assembling them—to crush the isolated socialist strongholds of the Ruhr.

Clearly the enterprise must be liquidated; and, as elsewhere, the only hope of doing this in an orderly fashion was to secure concessions from the government—above all, guarantees against renewed military excesses. Since the issue was, and remained, primarily the workers' hatred of the army, the political front among the workers' parties in the Ruhr was remarkably firm. The Independents had the lead; at the first area-wide conference of the three socialist parties, held in Hagen on March 20, they had a slight overall majority of delegates, the remainder being about evenly divided between KPD and SPD.[133] This conference started the process of establishing a political position from which to negotiate with the Reich government and began by proclaiming firmly, and unanimously, that there had never been any intention of setting up a dictatorship of the proletariat in the Ruhr. The conference's demands, also unanimous, were nearly all directed toward the central issue of the con-

---

132. Colm, p. 29; Konrad Ludwig, "Der Kapp-Putsch im Ruhrgebiet," *Der Sozialist*, March 12, 1921, p. 226.

133. Ludwig in *Der Sozialist*, March 12, 1921, p. 229; Lambers, p. 110. On the USPD's role in general and especially on its Hagen command, see Colm, pp. 74–76 and 103–6.

flict: dissolution of the old armed forces of the state and their replacement by a new, reliable, republican, worker-dominated military force.

The conference set the movement on a course that made negotiations with Reich Commissioner Severing possible in Bielefeld on March 23 and 24.[134] The first item of business there was an armistice, which, since neither side wanted to settle the conflict by force of arms, was readily arranged. The second day's talks produced the text known as the Bielefeld Agreement, signed by Severing and Minister of Posts Giesberts for the government and by representatives of all three socialist parties of the Ruhr.[135] Its core was the eight points of Legien's March 20 agreement with the governing parties, which were taken over unaltered. A second group of points set up guidelines for disarming the workers and disbanding the local action committees while establishing regular local security forces in which the workers should have a predominant share. Prisoners were to be released and the state of emergency ended; an amnesty was promised. Finally: "If these agreed points are loyally observed, there will be no entry of the Reichswehr into the Rhenish-Westphalian industrial area."

For the Independents and other relatively moderate forces among the Ruhr leadership, the Bielefeld Agreement was the key to ending the affair without a bloody fiasco; but the problem was to enforce it among the intransigents. The Majority Socialists and the trade unions began to drift out of the picture while the Independents and some of the Communists strove to gain acceptance for the agreement.[136] Their efforts were vain, however, where they mattered most, in the Red Army (as it was now called). By this time, the most important segment of the workers' forces was under a command center in Mülheim that was dominated by syndicalists and dissident Communists; like the Red Army in the last days of the Munich Soviet Republic, these forces obeyed no politician's orders. A united front was restored, briefly, when the government issued an ultimatum on March 28, which showed that it regarded the Ruhr workers' derelictions as having invalidated the Bielefeld Agreement. A few days later, political unity had disintegrated again. When the cautious advance of the Reichswehr began, it met only scattered resistance. The last of the socialists' illusory gains from the upheaval of the putsch days had crumbled away.

The collapse of the de facto workers' rule in the Ruhr meant the end

---

134. Described in Severing, *1919/1920*, pp. 174–80, and Spethmann, II, 147–60.
135. Text in *Arbeiterklasse siegt über Kapp*, II, 781–85. The signatories did not include representatives of the Red Army leadership in Mülheim, of the syndicalist trade unions of the Rhenish part of the Ruhr, or of the more radical part of Communist opinion.
136. Severing, *1919–1920*, pp. 182–84.

of the most violent of all the postwar crises. To call it a moment of potential revolution would be misleading; the workers' readiness for violence was focused on certain limited, fairly concrete aims—above all on disarming the reactionary armed forces—and not on the overthrow of capitalism or any other major political goal. Their resistance to Kapp and the army was an episode, and one from which little direct benefit issued to either the workers or the revolutionary cause. Yet the readiness of so many workers to take up arms stiffened the revolutionary resolve of the radicals again and produced a new flurry of debate about how to prepare for the next occasion. The putsch thus helped to exacerbate the tensions within the labor movement, and the concomitant crisis of purpose, and to set the scene for the troubled summer that followed.

CHAPTER 11

Toward Schism (April to October 1920)

The six months from April to October were the USPD's last as a united party. The prospect of schism did not hang oppressively over the party before the end of August; the possibility was there, but the party had long since learned to live with that and had its own ways of dealing with the danger. The late spring and summer was an ordinary (which is not to say uneventful) period in the party's life, dominated first by the Reichstag elections, then by the trade-union offensive over the councils and workers' direct action. The simmering problem of the Third International was worrisome but not central—until suddenly, in the last week of August, an immediate choice was forced upon the party and schism was inescapable.

The possibility of a split had hung over the party for so long that most party leaders on both sides accepted within about ten days, though not without bitterness, that the moment had arrived; the debate leading to formal separation on October 16 at the Halle party congress took a mere seven weeks and might have been concluded earlier without significantly altering the result. Yet for all the months of debate that had already taken place on the question of the International, the choice when it came was difficult for some, for the issue was posed in an unexpected form, focusing on the Twenty-One Conditions for admission to the Comintern. Consequently, the lines of division, among leaders and members, did not follow the usual USPD pattern. The schism did not leave the right wing in impotent isolation, as had seemed likely at the end of 1919; instead, the left wing, albeit with a much increased following, was separated from the rest. What remained was not a broken faction, a set of generals without an army; it was the stuff of a party. The USPD would continue to exist.

Aftermath of the Kapp Crisis

The importance of the Kapp Putsch and its outcome for the German political right and the Weimar political system have often been analyzed;

less often recognized is how significant the crisis was for the history of the German labor movement. The period did not mark a caesura; for most socialists, of all stripes, the politics of the late spring and summer of 1920 were a continuation of the phase that had begun in the summer of the previous year, not something new. In many quarters, however, a new urgency was felt. The crisis had the effect of forcing tactical choices that had long been postponed, a process of crystalization set in. And for the USPD, crystalization was dangerous.

The most immediate visible changes in orientation within the labor movement occurred on its right wing, especially in the trade unions. The actions of union leaders during and after the putsch were significant, for they were a belated response to the threat of schism that had been building up for over a year. The unions' traditional constituency, the socialist working class, was divided into mutually antagonistic parties, each with its claim to influence in the unions; much of the union rank and file was impatient with the official leadership over such issues as the *Arbeitsgemeinschaften* with the employers, and further challenges to the leadership could be expected. Moreover, the factory councils, now legally established but nonetheless often controlled by radicals, constituted potential competition. In March and April 1920 union leaders began to see that aggressive political action could help to preserve the unions, indeed could positively enhance the unions' position by establishing them as an active working-class force capable of rising above crippling party divisions. In everyday politics the unions could only destroy themselves by taking sides, but in extraordinary situations, when the mass of the active working class was looking for unified leadership, the unions were well placed to meet the need. In such situations over the next few years, the initiative of the trade unions played an important part in the workers' united front, indeed made such fronts possible. The unions' political role proved to be the most important socialist innovation resulting from the putsch.

A sense of the need for change was strong in the SPD as well; and, given the SPD's position as a pillar of the Weimar order, the slight but noticeable alteration in the party's orientation in the following months was of particular significance. The change can be characterized as a renewal of the party's conception of itself as a socialist and working-class party, at the expense of its recent emphasis on assuming a share of responsibility for the governance of the Republic. The impulse to change came in part from political calculation, forced on the party by evidence —above all, the drastic losses suffered in the Reichstag elections on June 6—that it was in danger of losing its mass working-class support.

In part, too, it came from a kind of rebellion of the Reichstag delegation, middle-rank leaders, and party militants in the aftermath of the Kapp Putsch.[1] The victims of this brief, peculiar revolt were not members of the party leadership (headed at this date by Hermann Müller and Otto Wels), or even the SPD's participation in the government, but a number of party members in high government posts who were felt to have shown the worst kind of insensitivity to the workers' interests and blindness toward growing reaction. Gustav Noske, Wolfgang Heine, Albert Südekum, and August Winnig, all hardliners of the party's right wing, had been elevated to the upper levels of the party by its war policies, had held some of the most important government posts during the revolution, and were now discarded as the SPD turned back toward its roots in the working class. Since none of them was ever either readmitted to party favor or re-elected to his parliamentary seat, their dismissal may be said to have begun the process of stripping off the party's extreme right wing. For the moment, this was the only tangible result of the rebellion; but the new trend was confirmed when the party withdrew from the government after the Reichstag elections. The SPD never entirely returned to the class-bound, interest-group politics in which it had been reared by the prewar political system, but neither had it entirely discarded the old attitudes. The reinforcement of such tendencies at this point had an impact ultimately on the course of Weimar politics, and more immediately on the SPD's relations with the USPD.

The impact of the Kapp Putsch on the KPD is more difficult to evaluate, in that the party's affairs were in a tangled state both before and after.[2] Many members felt that the central leadership had failed badly during the crisis, and this feeling helped spur the dissidents into forming a new party, the Communist Workers Party (KAPD), on April 3, as well as producing an ideological dispute inside the KPD about the permissibility of encouraging (though of course not participating in) a workers' government. In some areas (notably Chemnitz), however, the party had performed creditably during the period of activism. It gained, too, from the ending of Noske's policy of rule by state of siege; after Kapp the party could operate more openly than at any time since its foundation. It was able to resume a slow growth, to a membership of 66,323 on July 1 and 78,715 on October 1. But nothing in this modest

1. See Scheidemann, *Memoiren,* II, 399–412; Alfred Kastning, *Die deutsche Sozialdemokratie zwischen Koalition und Opposition 1919–1923* (Paderborn, 1970), pp. 28–32.
2. See especially Bock, pp. 225–28, and Ossip K. Flechtheim, *Die KPD in der Weimarer Republik,* 2d ed. (Frankfurt on Main, 1969), pp. 148–51. The membership figures are from KPD *Parteitag,* Nov. 1920, p. 5.

growth opened new perspectives for the party; its hopes still depended on forces outside the party itself—on the USPD.

In the USPD, the crystalizing effect of the events of March and April was to be seen especially in the increased frustration of the left wing. The general strike had been an extraordinary demonstration of working-class power—but no one had found a way to exploit this power to achieve tangible gains, let alone revolution. The tendency of the left wing, and an increasing number of activist rank-and-file members in the factories, was to blame the party, its leadership, traditions, and organization. The party's real revolutionaries understood more clearly than before that if the party continued to ride with events, rather than try to force the pace, no revolution would occur. The essential radical core existed among the German workers—or so the left thought, and in the spring and summer of 1920 they had some evidence to support their view. But without firm leadership the masses could not find their direction quickly and accurately enough to seize their opportunities. The party had been poorly led during the crisis weeks.[3] The party executive had produced directives hesitantly and too late, directives that had produced no concrete results. Furthermore, the central organs of the party had lost touch with the provinces, making coordinated action impossible; this observation raised organizational questions to which, however, no one had an answer at the time. In short, dissatisfaction with the outcome of the promising revolutionary movement focused on some of the fundamental characteristics of the USPD—its awkwardness, its fuzziness of purpose, its decentralized authority. Few radicals had suggestions for changing this state of affairs; indeed, they thought they had overcome it the previous December. That they had tried, and their efforts had failed, however, only made them the more receptive to suggestions of solutions from elsewhere.

The right and much of the center of the party experienced less frustration because expectations had always been lower. This part of the party had a role it understood, even if the revolution were long delayed—the role of organizer and educator of the working-class movement in opposition to capitalist society. The evidence of the past year had shown them that many workers were relapsing into apathy and the balance of forces tipping more and more in favor of the bourgeoisie. From this perspective, the performance of the masses in the general strike was pure gain, a spontaneous, vigorous, and above all united demonstration of

3. This was tacitly conceded even by the right wing during the extensive debates on the subject at the party conference and party congress in the fall, though they assigned the blame differently. See, in particular, the debates on the party executive's business report, USPD *Parteitag,* Oct. 1920, pp. 19–65.

determination to act for the vital interests of the working class. Like the left wing, the right was reactivated by its experiences. Its conclusion, however, was different: the united front was the impressive element. The strike had shown that the way forward lay through actions by the whole working class in fundamental class interests, a united front of the proletariat on the basis of the class struggle (in a sense like that understood by the old centrists).

Working-class activism during the summer had the effect of reinforcing the divergent tendencies in the labor movement and, especially, the USPD. First, the summer months were remarkable for the revival among a part of the workers of the same spirit of direct action as had been the hope of the radicals in February and March 1919. Renewed by the experiences of March 1920, this spirit showed itself, first, in a spontaneous tax revolt against the new withholding tax on wages, which disrupted industrial life in Saxony and the Düsseldorf area and even led to a general strike in Stuttgart at the end of August;[4] second, in the better-known attempt of the transport workers to interdict munitions shipments to Poland during her war with Soviet Russia.[5] The transport workers' movement, which was at its peak in August, appealed to various constituencies in the labor movement. The radicals saw their revolutionary expectations confirmed in the courageous action of the workers, in the widespread popular sympathy for Soviet Russia that it expressed, and in the symptoms of collapse of the postwar settlements, indeed of capitalism itself, that the war appeared to display; the Communists, indeed, declared that the time was ripe for a revival of the revolutionary workers' councils—a premature judgment, as the dissolution of the movement in September made clear.[6] The moderate Independents, on the other hand, while also glad to see the workers in action, were most impressed by the broad working-class unity the movement expressed at its peak; the cooperation of parties and unions first seen in the days of the Kapp Putsch re-emerged, becoming established, the moderates hoped, as the normal working-class weapon for dealing with such situations. Whether in fact the movement had any effect on the outcome of the war (ultimately favorable to Po-

4. StA Dresden, MdI Nr. 11077, pp. 1–3, 7–8, 52, 54, and 59–60; *GdA: Chronik,* II, 92; *Die Kämpfe in Südwestdeutschland,* pp. 61–67; Keil, II, 214–18. The movement has not been studied, and we know little about its full extent, its dynamics, or its conclusion.

5. See Hans-Werner Schaaf, "Der Widerhall des polnisch-sowjetischen Krieges von 1920 in Deutschland" (Ph.D. dissertation, University of Halle-Wittenberg, 1963), and summary accounts in Friedrich Stampfer, *Die vierzehn Jahre der ersten deutschen Republik* (Karlsbad, 1936), pp. 186–87, and Prager, pp. 220–21.

6. See the stage-by-stage emergence of the policy in *Rote Fahne,* Aug. 10, 19, 21, and 27, 1920.

land), is unclear; eventually it dissolved in acrimony, but for several critical weeks in August and September it was the focal point of socialist politics.

The second major concern of the labor movement during the summer was the protracted struggle between the trade unionists and the factory radicals for control of the new, legally instituted council system. The old autonomous radical councils were dead, killed by the Factory Council Law; but the radicals turned to the new councils, determined "that the factory councils [must] take from the law everything that can be taken from it, and that, supported and driven on by the working masses behind them, they [must] prepare the way for socialism in the production process, without regard for the limiting clauses [of the law]."[7] The councils would continue to develop into "compact, unified organizations of struggle," leading the great political actions of the working class with the assistance of the parties and revolutionary trade unions.[8] But the unions, even those controlled by Independents, were in no mood to accept the role of auxiliaries to the radical factory councils. Even Dissmann regarded control of the councils as "a question of life and death for the trade unions."[9] The councils could not be allowed to interpose themselves between the workers and their unions, or the latter would forfeit their authority, even their raison d'être. Union leaders resolved instead that, "in order to put the activity of the factory councils at the service of the community . . . the factory councils are to be built into the overall organization of the trade unions."[10]

When the conflict came to a head in July and August, the position of the unions, with their powerful organizations and discipline and their much broader base, proved by far the stronger. By the end of July, even in such a radical center as Berlin the council supporters were insisting that their leaders find some compromise with the unions; while in Halle, where the radical councils more or less had their way, success was at the cost of repeated defections by fragments of the movement to the trade-union camp.[11] The settlements reached differed from city to city, but nearly everywhere the trade unions won important powers over the councils, most particularly the right to control their finances. By August 11 the ADGB and AfA felt secure enough to summon a national conference of factory councils for early October; at this conference the superior authority of the unions was confirmed.

7. Däumig, *Der Arbeiter-Rat,* 2 (1920), no. 15, 1.
8. See the resolution adopted by a Berlin council assembly in May; *ibid.,* no. 17, p. 3.
9. Speech reported in *Freiheit,* July 8, 1920 (e).
10. See the circular printed in *Der Arbeiter-Rat,* 2 (1920), no. 19/20, 8.
11. *Freiheit,* July 22, 1920 (e); Schulz, "Rolle und Anteil," p. 230.

The affair seriously aggravated tempers as the summer progressed. The radicals were frustrated yet again; the existing institutions of the labor movement seemed less adequate than ever to express their revolutionary aspirations, and even the "revolutionary" unions had turned against them. The Independent trade unionists, too, retained bitter memories of the struggle. The party executive and auxiliary council had attempted to intervene in the conflict when it was nearly over; moreover, they had taken the councils' side—in the last majority mustered by the left.[12] Dissmann made it clear to the party conference a week later that neither he nor any other self-respecting trade unionist would accept directives from the party in matters affecting the vital interests of the unions.[13] The Independent trade unionists were (by the very nature of their jobs) union men first and socialists (though often radical socialists) second; particular policies, or their attitude toward broader political issues, might distinguish them from their Majority Socialist colleagues, but their solidarity with the trade union movement was dominant. Party considerations could not be allowed to interfere. Robert Dissmann and his associates entered the battle over conditions of entry into the Communist International with their mistrust sharpened by the summer's work. Their conflict with the council advocates had almost reached the point of open breach; their determination to be free of party dictation had also hardened. Union leaders certainly had reasons going beyond doctrine on councils and party supremacy to reject the Third International; but the distinctive, highly visible role the trade unionists played in the controversy of the autumn was probably caused at least partly by the conflicts of the summer.

Not all Independents were centrally involved in these conflicts, nor in the direct action of these months. Intense concern with doctrinal, tactical, and organizational differences kept the wings of the party in a state of tension, but as far as can be ascertained many members were content for the time being simply to support the mass party of socialist opposition without worrying about the longer perspective. They were the cement holding the party together. As long as they fulfilled this function, the party seemed unchanged; and it still grew.

Apogee: The Elections of June 1920

On June 6, elections were held for the new Reichstag, elections on which the party set great hopes and which demonstrated the impressive

12. *Freiheit*, Aug. 27, 1920 (m).
13. USPD *Reichskonferenz*, Sept. 1920, pp. 138–39; USPD *Parteitag*, Oct. 1920, p. 40.

support the USPD had assembled since the National Assembly elections seventeen months earlier. For nearly two months, preparations for the elections, and then the consequences, dominated the official life of the party.

Considering the ill repute in which elections and parliamentarianism were held on the left wing of the party, such a concentration of effort might seem anomalous. In fact, however, election campaigns were still taken for granted by most of the membership, and they were what the party's machinery did best; no objection to the expenditure of party resources on elections had a serious chance of being heard. The party leadership bridged its differences with rhetoric, intended to counteract excessive faith in the benefits to be gained from parliamentary successes. The election manifesto, published as early as April 20, is a case in point.[14] Its core was the program for a workers' government that *Freiheit* had published on March 25; but this time there was no mention of a workers' government as the goal of the election. Instead, the manifesto proclaimed:

We know that these demands cannot be realized merely through work in parliament, which itself bears a great share of the guilt for the revival of the counterrevolution. Our power and strength lie above all in the activity of the masses, who must continually work to influence the shaping of political conditions.

Voters! The election campaign must bring a sweeping, energetic reckoning with the counterrevolutionaries, pseudodemocrats, and pseudosocialists, with all class enemies of the proletariat! It must muster the forces of socialism, must show that the will to socialism has seized the masses of the working people in city and countryside.

Such rhetoric made little difference to the conduct of the campaign, beyond minimizing cooperation with the "pseudosocialists" of the SPD; but the hostilities of an election campaign could be expected in any case to have driven the parties apart again. Otherwise, the campaign seems to have been carried on by traditional methods and with the traditional Social Democratic enthusiasm.

Not that it was conducted everywhere in precisely the spirit laid down in the party executive's manifesto. In some places, the party struck a more radical tone; a conference of the Hamburg district in April, for example, declared that "for the revolutionary socialist masses the bourgeois parliament is only an institution designed to uphold the rule of the bourgeois state against the assault of its oppressed class."[15] Ernst Thälmann,

14. *Freiheit,* April 20, 1920 (m). Dittmann was the author.
15. Naumann, "Die USPD und die Kommunistische Internationale," p. 1040.

chairman of the Hamburg city organization, told an assembly on May 2: "We are going into parliament for the same reason as into the trade unions. We intend to bring revolutionary spirit to the masses. . . . We must say to the masses, the participation of our revolutionary fighters in the Reichstag can only succeed by remaining in touch with street actions."[16] But this impeccable expression of revolutionary socialist principle was not heard everywhere. The *Leipziger Volkszeitung* was perhaps most outspoken at the other extreme, declaring that "the working populace now has it in its hands to conquer political power through the elections."[17] Party speakers in the Leipzig area were instructed to emphasize socialization, an emphasis that might encourage rapprochement of the socialist parties and the formation of a workers' government.[18] Even Crispien, in an article distributed widely to party speakers, addressed himself hopefully to the prospect of a socialist government, clearly thinking that one might emerge from the elections.[19] Yet these were probably minority viewpoints. More representative of the organization as a whole, perhaps, was the purely party-centered viewpoint laid down in a resolution of a district conference for Potsdam IV:

[The conference] categorically demands a principled waging of the Reichstag election campaign. Regard for the need for joint actions against reaction with the proletarian organizations standing right and left of the USPD must not hamper an emphatic presentation of the final goals of revolutionary socialism. The guide for the conduct of our campaign is therefore under all circumstances the [Leipzig] Action Program of the USPD. No precept of the socialist world view may be neglected in order to win seats. Only in this way will it be possible to win the masses of the proletariat for revolutionary socialism and the continuation of the social revolution.[20]

Whatever the local tone, the campaign seems to have been very effective. To be sure, the working-class parties failed to win a majority in the

---

At this conference the district removed the last of the moderates from leadership positions, completing the consolidation of the most radical district organization in the party.

16. *Ibid.;* see the similar statement by the *Gothaer Volksblatt*, quoted in Buchsbaum, p. 301. According to Ströbel, *Die deutsche Revolution*, p. 166, the left wing wanted the party to demand an advance commitment from all its candidates not to attempt any positive legislative activity if elected; the party executive did not adopt this policy.

17. Quoted by Koenen, USPD *Reichskonferenz*, Sept. 1920, p. 73.

18. *Material für die Redner der U.S.P.D. zur Reichstagswahl 1920* (n.p., n.d.). This leaflet was apparently a Leipzig product but may have had wider distribution in the party.

19. *Referentenmaterial des Zentral-Komitees der U.S.P.D.*, Sondernummer 1920 Nr. 1, pp. 24–27.

20. *Informationsblatt*, May 6, 1920.

new Reichstag—their combined 42.1 percent of the vote was in fact smaller than their 45.5 percent in January 1919—and a socialist government was thus no nearer than before.[21] But for the USPD it was a spectacular victory. In the 32 election districts where voting took place (there was no voting in East Prussia, Upper Silesia, or Schleswig-Holstein, where plebiscites were still to be held to determine frontiers[22]), the USPD received 4,896,095 votes, more than twice as many as they had won throughout the country in January 1919; their share of the total poll rose from 7.6 percent to 18.8 percent. The SPD was still the stronger party, with some 700,000 more votes and 21.6 percent of the total poll; but having lost nearly half its support of January 1919, it could take little comfort in this fact. The Communists, with 1.7 percent of the vote, showed themselves to be a negligible factor nationally; only two Communist deputies entered the new Reichstag. The Independents, having become the second strongest party in the country, sent eighty-one.

The election returns also show that the USPD's influence was much more widespread than it had been a year earlier; in only four of the thirty-two voting districts did it fail to win a seat. Yet, encouraging as this was, the bulk of the party's strength remained concentrated in the areas in which the party had had its start. Almost exactly half of the USPD's vote came from eight districts that had earned the party nineteen of its twenty-two seats in 1919: the three making up Berlin and its vicinity, where the party polled nearly a millon votes (to half a million for the SPD); the two districts covering the industrial area of Düsseldorf and the Ruhr; and Halle, Leipzig, and Thuringia. With the exception of the Westphalian Ruhr (the Arnsberg district), the USPD outpolled the SPD in each of these eight districts; but nowhere else in the country, apart from Düsseldorf-West, did they manage this. The only other districts in which the party won as many as three seats—Braunschweig, Franconia, Chemnitz, Dresden, and Magdeburg—adjoined its Central German strongholds; these regions accounted for another sixth of the party's vote. The USPD's voter concentration was far greater than the Majority Socialists'.

It would be advantageous to compare these voting statistics with contemporary membership statistics; unfortunately, the available information does not permit this. We have a 1920 membership figure of 893,923,

21. See the table in Appendix 1.
22. Until elections could be held, the National Assembly deputies for these districts continued to sit, which added 19 deputies to the SPD's parliamentary strength but none to the USPD's. When voting was held in East Prussia and Schleswig-Holstein in February 1921, the rump USPD gained two seats; Upper Silesia did not vote until November 1922, after the reunification of the two Social Democratic parties.

apparently for September,[23] but no way of breaking the total down into districts since the party used a standard other than reported membership in assigning seats for the party congress in October.[24] Of the scattered district data available for 1920, some figures relate to March 31, some to June or September; they are, therefore, not strictly comparable, and the relative size of the district organizations cannot be reliably determined.[25] Some shifts in relative size may have occurred since September 1919; the Leipzig district organization, for instance, experienced a 25 percent growth during the winter of 1919–1920,[26] while the Berlin-Brandenburg and Thuringian organizations grew more slowly, the former from about 100,000 to 112,000, the latter from about 50,000 to 57,268.[27] Then came a further rapid general rise in membership after the Kapp Putsch and during the election campaign; in Saxony this growth stopped during the summer, but whether this was a general phenomenon we do not know.[28] Probably the year's growth in membership left the large organizations about as predominant in the party as they had been in September 1919; the only districts that may have joined the giants of over 40,000 members were Western Westphalia and East Prussia.[29]

The centers of USPD strength were the great industrial cities and regions. In only two of the electoral districts dominated by major industrial towns (Breslau and Hamburg) did the USPD fail to get at least two-

23. Zietz in USPD *Parteitag,* Oct. 1920, p. 24. The total is allegedly based on the latest reports, that is, presumably those for the quarter ending Sept. 30; but these cannot all have been available when Zietz spoke, on Oct. 12, so the figure must either have elements of approximation or rely on earlier data.

24. The seats were assigned not by reported membership but by payments to the party executive on account of party dues; this method was adopted in an attempt to force recalcitrant districts (above all Hamburg) to pay up their arrears. The most striking result was that the Leipzig district was grossly overrepresented, its 72,000 members sending nearly as many delegates (55) as the much larger Berlin-Brandenburg organization (58); a wealthy district, Leipzig could apparently afford subsidies for the party executive in addition to obligatory payments. To what extent other districts were over- or underrepresented seems impossible to determine.

25. The greater part of the available figures, and estimates to fill in the gaps, are given in Wheeler, "Internationals," p. 800.

26. Calculated from tables in USPD-Sachsen *Landesversammlung,* Sept. 1920, pp. 8–9. Several adding errors need correction before the tables can be used, and there are indications that the first column, allegedly for Jan. 1, 1920, actually contains figures for Sept. 30, 1919; at least this is true for Leipzig, see *Halbjahrs-Bericht des Vorstandes und Sekretariats des Sozialistischen Vereins der U.S.P. Gross-Leipzig* (n.p., 1919), p. 5.

27. The figures are for Sept. 30, 1919, and March 31, 1920, in both cases. The September figures are those calculated above in ch. 8 (see n. 4); those for March are from *Informationsblatt,* July 7, 1920, and Pöhland, p. 385n.

28. USPD-Sachsen *Landesversammlung,* July 1921, p. 16.

29. For Western Westphalia, see the estimate of 45,000 in Wheeler, "Internationals," p. 800. For East Prussia, see the official figure of 40,000 recorded in a police report in DZA Merseburg, Rep. 77 Tit. 1810 Nr. 18, p. 207.

thirds of the SPD vote; in Berlin City, Leipzig, Halle, and Düsseldorf-East, the Independents overwhelmed the Majority Socialists by margins greater than two to one (five to one in the case of Halle). Further breakdown of voting results to isolate the cities and mining districts within electoral districts would probably only further emphasize the trend; for instance, the USPD outpolled the SPD in the great cities of Stettin, Bremen, Dortmund, Stuttgart, and Munich, though the Majority Socialists had the larger vote in the district surrounding each city.[30]

This pattern of USPD strength can be variously interpreted. *Freiheit* thought that

Independent Social Democracy has increasingly become *the* party of the German working class in the centers of German industry. . . . The Right Socialists, apart from particular great cities like Hamburg and Breslau where there are special causes at work, have done better in general in the less industrially developed parts than in the more advanced. Their petty bourgeois stamp has become even stronger, while the nucleus of the working class supports our party.[31]

Polemic apart, this observation is probably true, as we have seen, and the support of industrial workers was a legitimate source of pride to Independent Socialists. The implication of the statement, however—that the support of the industrial nucleus of the working class was somehow especially significant—was only a half-truth. It could never be more than half-true for a party most of whose leaders—including the editors of *Freiheit*—thought of the party's constituency as the whole of the working class in the broadest sense, that is, the great majority of the German population. The factory proletariat, however important strategically, was only a fraction of this working class; the party was still supported by only a small part of the German people. Its electoral success thus left untouched its old tactical and theoretical problems.

The elections also reflected a general polarization of political forces in the country. Just as the socialist vote had shifted dramatically toward the left, so had the nonsocialist vote sought out the more conservative parties. The strength of the Democrats was halved, while Stresemann's People's Party, the Democrats' neighbor to the right, tripled its voting strength in the Reichstag, and the Nationalist Party enjoyed large gains. The Center Party was weakened, though not so much by the voters as by

30. See the tables in *Statistik des Deutschen Reichs*, 291/II. A correlation of voting results with occupational data would be of considerable interest.
31. *Freiheit*, June 7, 1920 (e). The reference to special circumstances in Hamburg probably reflects *Freiheit*'s disapproval of the hyperradical leadership of the local USPD; in Breslau the problem was a well-established local SPD, under Paul Löbe, which kept its distance from the more unpopular policies of the national leadership.

the breaking-away of the Bavarian wing to form its own Bavarian People's Party with a much more conservative orientation. The Independents, with satisfaction, identified the trend as an "intensification of the antagonisms between the classes."[32] Again the observation is true, and the Independents, through their efforts to "secure the fruits of the revolution" or to encourage a second one, had done their part to promote class antagonism. But again the inference was misleading; for the socialists, even including the "pseudosocialists," had gathered only slightly over 40 percent of the voters to their side of what threatened to become a terrible gulf within the nation. On the other side stood an increasingly determined bourgeoisie—and the army.

The election returns also had immediate political consequences. The voters' repudiation of the parties of the center had deprived the Weimar government coalition of its parliamentary majority. However difficult the cooperation of the Weimar coalition parties may sometimes have been, the grouping had a certain logic to it and a tradition reaching back into the war years. No other likely coalition, broad enough to encompass a majority of the Reichstag, was available. Consequently a series of government crises arose to plague national politics throughout the remaining years of the Republic and to draw the USPD increasingly into the "swamp" (as the radicals called it) of parliamentary bargaining.

The first of the series posed no particular problem for the USPD. When Chancellor Hermann Müller approached the party on June 11 about joining the government, he could only have been intending a coalition in which bourgeois parties would also be represented; and by common consent among Independents such cooperation was out of the question.[33] Furthermore, Müller's offer could be assumed not to be serious, merely a preliminary gesture before the SPD withdrew from the compromising responsibilities of government to lick its wounds.[34] The Independents' reply, delivered within four hours of Müller's inquiry,[35] was still noteworthy for its intransigence. The party, it said, was not interested in taking part in any government, even a workers' government, that grew out of political bargaining: "Should the necessity of a socialist government arise from the development of the revolution the USPD can consider as a transitional measure only *a purely socialist government* in which it has the majority,

---

32. *Ibid.*
33. Müller's letter, *ibid.*, June 12, 1920 (m).
34. *Freiheit,* July 2, 1920 (m), published the confidential circular of the SPD party executive laying down party tactics after the election. See also the notes (undated) on a joint meeting of the Majority Socialist deputies and the party committee after the elections, Carl Giebel papers (ASD Bonn), box II, folder 3, pp. 210–15; and Kastning, pp. 53–58.
35. According to Müller, p. 210 in the SPD meeting cited in n. 34.

exercises the decisive influence, and in which its program provides the basis for [government] policies."[36] The full extent of the withdrawal from the advanced position of the Kapp days is evident here, trumpeted forth with postelectoral overconfidence. So extreme was the position adopted that it caused some dissatisfaction among party followers, as can be seen from the number of assemblies and explanatory manifestoes on the subject that the leadership felt were necessary.[37] It settled the issue, however, in a negative sense, for the time being.

The question of participation in state governments arose simultaneously, and here the answer was less automatic. The Saxon government (Majority Socialists and Democrats) was unstable and might have to be replaced at any moment; a government had to be formed for the new state of Thuringia (which included all the petty dukedoms of that area but not the Prussian lands); and Braunschweig also faced the necessity for cabinet-building in which the USPD might be called on to play a part. The party executive, speaking through Dittmann, was anxious that the issue in these states be approached as "a question of political expediency" and not with the full rigor of socialist dogma; the state governments, after all, had become mainly administrative organs, and there was useful socialist work to be done, even if local dictatorships of the proletariat were out of the question.[38] Much of the party seems to have been receptive to this distinction, but little came of the apparent opportunities in the summer of 1920. The Saxon government survived for another six months; the Thuringian parliament, where the bourgeois parties had a majority of one over the socialists, did not resolve its crisis until new elections were held a year later.[39] Only in Braunschweig did political negotiations lead eventually, on June 22, to the formation of a coalition socialist government headed by the USPD's Sepp Oerter, who, though as aggressive as ever, had somehow swung around to the right wing of his

---

36. *Freiheit*, June 12, 1920 (m). Dittmann was the author; according to him, Stoecker wanted a statement that the USPD would take part only in a government based on the council system, but this went too far even for Däumig. See USPD *Parteitag*, Oct. 1920, p. 127.

37. See, for instance, *Freiheit*, June 18, 1920 (m), which contains a party manifesto, an article, and a report of a speech by Crispien on the subject; also *Informationsblatt*, July 7, 1920, and Prager, p. 219. It has been suggested that the USPD's relatively poor showing in the Mecklenburg state elections at the end of June was caused by the defection of voters who disapproved of the party's sterile attitude toward a socialist government; see Heinz Meiritz, "Die Herausbildung einer revolutionären Massenpartei im ehemaligen Land Mecklenburg-Schwerin unter besonderer Berücksichtigung der Vereinigung des linken Flügels der USPD mit der KPD (1917–1920)" (Ph.D. dissertation, University of Rostock, 1965), pp. 168–69.

38. *Freiheit*, June 11, 1920 (e).

39. Witzmann, pp. 41–46.

party. Oerter's participation in straight parliamentary bargaining and his willingness to grant parity to the smaller Majority Socialists outraged the party's left wing and embarrassed the party executive;[40] but as the only instance of its kind, and in one of Germany's secondary states, it did not greatly exercise the party during the summer.

Thus did the great electoral victory of the USPD run into the sands, having, as far as anyone could see, done nothing to advance the cause of socialism in Germany. Little more than the lively consciousness of strength, if strength unutilized, remained. The elections had been a period of united endeavor for the USPD, an isolated moment of pride, nothing more.

Negotiating with the Third International

While these developments were taking place, the issue of adherence to the Communist International was relatively quiescent. The Comintern itself was largely at fault: the ECCI's reply to the USPD party executive's letter of December 13, 1919, was received in Berlin on April 9, 1920, nearly four months later.[41] The reasons for the delay remain mysterious.[42] While it lasted, however, the prospect of joining the Communist International necessarily receded from the forefront of the USPD's concerns. Only in June did the issue become central again; and not until the end of August was it clear that the party would split over the problem.

The ECCI's letter, dated February 5, 1920, confirmed the worst fears of the Independents.[43] It was offensive even in its outward form, being addressed first "to all the workers of Germany," then to the leadership of the KPD, and only in small print to the party executive of the USPD. The content was still worse. Couched in the harsh polemical tone that Lenin made famous, the bulk of the letter was an enumeration of the past and present failings of the USPD, in terms that indicated the correct policy in each case. The attack was directed explicitly at the party's right-wing leaders; but while this distinction appeared to spare the party left, the implication that they had been collaborating complaisantly with a clique of traitors to socialism was inescapable. The argument was entirely Bolshevik and set out what amounted to a sketch of all the major

40. Roloff, pp. 72–73; Zietz, USPD *Parteitag*, Oct. 1920, p. 65.
41. *Die U.S.P.D. und die 3. Internationale*, pp. 5 and 7; see also ch. 10, above.
42. The possible reasons are discussed in Wheeler, "Internationals," pp. 549–50 and 564–65.
43. The text cited here is that of the pamphlet published by the West European secretariat as *Der Leipziger Kongress der U.S.P. und die Kommunistische Internationale* (n.p., 1920). For the origins of the letter in theses drafted by Lenin, see Wheeler, "Internationals," pp. 544–548.

decisions of the Second World Congress of the International, six months in advance.

The points made in the ECCI letter may be regrouped for discussion according to their impact on the USPD. First came a comprehensive indictment of the party's history since its foundation, which is worth quoting at length to illustrate the substance and tone of the charges. The section concentrates on

the opportunistic right-wing party elements, which are inclined to acknowledge all manner of things verbally, but which hinder the actual development of the revolution in every way. These opportunistic "centrists" held the proletariat back from all mass actions during the imperialist war, supported the traitorous line of the defense of the bourgeois "fatherland," denied the necessity of an illegal organization, shied away from the thought of civil war. At the start of the revolution they entered a joint government with the open betrayers of the working class, the Scheidemanns, sanctioned the infamous expulsion of the Berlin embassy of the Russian proletariat, and supported the policy of breaking off diplomatic relations with the Soviet state. Since the beginning of the German revolution these right-wing leaders of the "Independents" have preached an Entente orientation and opposed the alliance of Germany with Soviet Russia with all their strength. . . .
At first they totally rejected the dictatorship of the councils and held completely to the position of bourgeois democracy. Then they began to preach a mixture of councils and constituent assembly (Hilferding's plan). Until now they have swung from one to the other, when what was needed was action. Their literary representatives (Kautsky) . . . find no better occupation than to spread the dirty babble of Russian and other counterrevolutionaries about the Russian revolution.[44]

The qualities of the whole letter are illustrated here. From the radical point of view, the criticism was powerful and well founded, though weakened by misstatements (about mass actions during the war and adherence to bourgeois democracy). But the important issues were jumbled together with relatively petty matters (especially matters affecting Soviet Russia); and the tone was one to which Independents were not accustomed. As later comments by Independents show, passages like this did little for the Comintern's cause, even with the party's left wing.

The ECCI spoke more accurately to the needs of the radical Independents when it attacked weak or controversial points in the party's current theory and practice. The letter warned, for instance, that it was utopian to expect the seizure of power to be accomplished by the "majority of the people" and without drastic disruption of the economy. It stressed "the necessity of breaking the resistance of the exploiters by force" and the inevitability of civil war.[45] It argued that "socialization"

44. *Der Leipziger Kongress*, pp. 4–5.
45. *Ibid.*, p. 6.

was a misleading concept that encouraged reformist illusions and concealed the need for violent struggle against the capitalists. It pointed out that the present "bourgeois-democratic liberties" were, for any trained Marxist, an obvious fraud and called for more reliance on illegal, underground organization. In short, the letter demonstrated how the traditional moderate, pacifist, nonviolent views of the party were preventing adoption of an active revolutionary policy. In their place the International preached a harsh, violent vision that was foreign to the USPD's heritage but appealed, at least in the abstract, to a growing number of frustrated radical workers who were moved by the harsh, violent reality of the times around them.

A third category of arguments, mixed in among the others, preached Russian doctrine and experience to a wholly unprepared German audience. On the doctrinal side, the clearest example is Lenin's theory of the role of the workers' aristocracy in imperialism, to which hardly anyone in Germany subscribed; this theory was used in the letter to explain the entire international situation, and the USPD was criticized for not applying it.[46] On the practical side, the Independents were urged to agitate in the army and among agricultural workers and poor peasants. The party was told it must "shatter" the existing government apparatus when it took power; and it must use not only force but terror against its enemies while establishing the new state. Such advice could only meet with incomprehension or hostility—and establish the ground on which the centrists of the USPD could later launch an effective counterattack.

Not surprisingly, the ECCI firmly rejected the idea of reconstructing the International along the lines proposed by the Independents. Other considerations apart, the people who would lead such an endeavor were unacceptable: "We absolutely refuse any collaboration with the right-wing leaders of the Independents and the Longuetists, who are drawing the movement back into the morass of the yellow Second International."[47] It followed (without being stated in so many words) that the USPD would have not only to reform its theory and practice but also to disembarrass itself of many of its current leaders. There was no mention of a split, or of expulsions, but these were obvious consequences of the Comintern's position. One organizational point was made explicit: the final goal was union of the USPD with the KPD. The USPD should

46. *Ibid.*, esp. pp. 13–14. The locus classicus of Lenin's doctrine is his *Imperialism, the Highest Stage of Capitalism.*
47. *Der Leipziger Kongress,* p. 19. The "Longuetists," or followers of Jean Longuet, were a French socialist faction regarded by the ECCI as analogous to the German centrists. "Yellow"—a much-used term in Comintern invective—refers in trade-union usage to a management-run union; by extension, a yellow socialist group is one that serves the interests of the bourgeoisie.

send a delegation to Moscow at the first opportunity to discuss these matters.

This letter began the breakdown of the tenuous unity that had prevailed in the party executive on the issue of the International since December. The consequences of the Comintern's recommendations for such men as Dittmann and Crispien were clear: the prudent line of advance for which they stood would be abandoned, and their careers in the party would probably be ended. More important, the leaders attacked directly by the ECCI were joined by others who were put off by the style or the substance of the Comintern's answer (or perhaps by the suspicion that Moscow's conception of a centralized, effective International would involve intolerable interference in the USPD's affairs). These groups together made up a majority of the executive. Their immediate reaction was to procrastinate; with the party busy trying to pull itself together after the Kapp Putsch, and national elections not far away, the time was inauspicious for a full-scale party controversy on the issues raised by the ECCI's letter. Consequently, over the protests of the Comintern's supporters in the party executive, the letter was simply suppressed for six weeks. Not until May 20 was it circulated to the party press, and most party newspapers did not print it until after the elections on June 6.[48]

But procrastination could only be a stopgap response. The letter could not be kept secret; in fact, the Communist press published it as soon as it saw that the Independents were hesitating. Most of the enthusiasts for the Third International in the USPD rank and file were not seriously put off by the ECCI's tone; and many among the more sober radicals comforted themselves that they could negotiate away the harsher, more "Russian" aspects of the policies the ECCI was attempting to impose. The skeptics in the USPD were thus cornered, caught between Moscow and their own membership. As they read the letter, Moscow had served notice that it intended to extirpate moderate influence in their party if it could, presumably by amputating at least the right wing; yet such a prospect had not so far caused any significant defection from the pro-Moscow camp. To come out against the Third International, to try to reverse the policy adopted at Leipzig, would, therefore, isolate the moderates within the party, deprive them of influence when critical decisions about the International were being made, and facilitate their expulsion later on. Finally, no alternative International was in prospect. Even

48. *Die U.S.P.D. und die 3. Internationale,* pp. 10–13. Stoecker proposed a draft reply to the ECCI on April 14, but the executive repeatedly delayed acting on it; USPD *Parteitag,* Oct. 1920, p. 49. See Crispien's and Koenen's comments on Stoecker's letter *ibid.,* pp. 58 and 59.

Hilferding is said to have concluded that the party had no alternative but to join the Moscow International.[49] The moderates were certainly not prepared to submit to Russian insults and interference without a struggle, as they showed later in the official party reply to the ECCI; but for the time being they preferred to discuss their fears and reservations as little as possible in public. Tactically, they took up a strong defensive position on the principle of unity, always a powerful emotive force in the party. Party cohesion might defeat Russian hopes of splitting the USPD and make the whole party's admission to the International possible; once in, it could hope to use its strength to resist interference and even, with the aid of similar Western parties, to alter the policies of the International.[50]

The united front was successfully maintained, with the somewhat reluctant assistance of Stoecker and other radicals in the party leadership, up to the departure of the delegation for Moscow in July. The first meeting of the party executive with the auxiliary council and control commission, on May 11, made no decisions. Three weeks later, a telegram from Radek attempting to prod the party into some response elicited only a bland reply, over Däumig's signature, explaining that the party's inaction was the result of the election campaign and a shortage of newsprint.[51] But nearly two months had passed since receipt of the ECCI letter; the election campaign was over; nothing had occurred in the meantime to make the party's dilemma any easier; and pressure from both the Comintern and radical USPD members made further procrastination impossible.[52] Consequently, when the West European secretariat of the Comintern invited the Independents to send a delegation to Moscow to coincide with the Second World Congress of the Communist International, scheduled to start on July 15, the party executive, in a note of June 11 to the secretariat, announced that it had decided to adopt this course.[53]

The next problem was how to deal with the negotiations. In the remaining month before the departure of the delegation, two important decisions were reached. The first, taken at a further meeting of the auxiliary council and control commission with the party executive, on

49. According to Däumig, USPD *Reichskonferenz*, Sept. 1920, p. 51.
50. See, for instance, Crispien, *ibid.*, p. 7.
51. *Die Kommunistische Internationale*, no. 11, pp. 213–15; *Die U.S.P.D. und die 3. Internationale*, pp. 12–13.
52. The ECCI, before receiving notice of the USPD's decision to send a delegation, addressed an appeal over the heads of the party leaders to the radical local and district organizations, asking them to send their own deputations; *Die Kommunistische Internationale*, no. 12, pp. 324–26.
53. *Die U.S.P.D. und die 3. Internationale*, p. 13.

June 19, defined the basic negotiating posture of the party. In the words of the official summary released by the meeting:

In accordance with the resolution of our Leipzig party congress there was full unanimity that our representatives in Moscow are to negotiate as fully equal partners [Gleichberechtigte] concerning the union of our party with the Third International on the basis of our Action Program, preserving the autonomy of our party in its internal affairs and in its tactics but with strict recognition and observance of the goal and the principles which the International adopts.[54]

The Independents, in other words, were determined not to approach the Comintern congress as supplicants.

This determination was even more apparent in the USPD's written reply to the original ECCI letter. This reply, we are informed, was drafted in haste, shortly before the delegates set out for Moscow,[55] and Stoecker and Däumig, who signed it with the rest, later found it a source of considerable embarrassment. It took a lofty tone, giving no hint that the USPD might be in a weak position vis-à-vis the Russians. The party, it said, had no apologies to make for its past. Indeed, the charges against the so-called right-wing leaders were "the product either of malicious distortion of the facts or of insufficient knowledge of the revolutionary process in Germany."[56] The ECCI's letter

constructs, on the basis of inaccurate, untrue allegations, a caricature of the so-called right-wing leaders, then identifies these "right-wing leaders" with the whole leadership of the USP and, by attacking the policies attributed to them, attacks the policy of the whole party; and finally it crowns this whole edifice with the conclusion, contrary to all Marxist theory, that a proletarian mass party which determines its own leadership and direction [could] permit a leadership that was directly in conflict with its real will and aspirations.[57]

The history of the USPD needed no justification since it expressed the will of the revolutionary German workers; the idea that it was just the work of right-wing leaders was pure invention. As for the theoretical issues raised by the ECCI, the charges rested on a failure to understand the views of the USPD and their context; the required innovations—use of terror, proclamation of civil war in advance, destruction of the entire state apparatus—were products of purely Russian conditions. Indeed, in the passage on the peasantry, the ECCI's letter represented a "relapse

---

54. *Ibid.*, pp. 13–14. Hilferding formulated this reservation, which was accepted unanimously; USPD *Reichskonferenz,* Sept. 1920, p. 110.

55. Comintern *Kongress,* July–Aug. 1920, p. 250.

56. *Antwort an das Exekutivkomitee der Kommunistischen Internationale durch das Zentralkomitee der Unabhängigen Sozialdemokratischen Partei Deutschlands auf das Schreiben vom 5. Februar 1920* (n.p., n.d.), p. 5.

57. *Ibid.,* p. 9.

into petty-bourgeois modes of thought that have long since been overcome."[58]

In the process of concentration of the proletarian forces, their schooling and
preparation and the continued intensification of revolutionary energy, it is of
no benefit to the proletariat of Germany if, instead of objective lessons from
the Russian revolution, it receives as recommended guidelines rigid theoretical formulas and schematic methods which ignore the different content of the
social upheaval in other countries. Such a state of affairs is not only likely
to make more difficult the concentration of all parties that endorse the proletarian dictatorship and the realization of socialism, it also contains the
danger that the development of the revolution in the individual countries
could be hampered by the adoption of foreign models and precepts.[59]

This declaration does credit to the independent spirit of the USPD,
though the party leaders can hardly have appreciated how the letter
would appear to the Bolsheviks—as is shown by the fact that all members of the party executive, including Stoecker and Däumig, endorsed it.
Stoecker's and Däumig's approval was reluctant, however, which meant
that if the Bolsheviks challenged the letter's formulations the left wing's
feelings of solidarity would be dangerously strained. And solidarity was
the only card the Independents had to play in Moscow. The imposing
delegation that left on July 13 for Russia was composed of four of the
most influential men of the party: the two party chairmen, Crispien and
Däumig, and two of the four party secretaries, Dittmann and Stoecker.
But despite the protestations of unity, this delegation was all too obviously
chosen with factional considerations in mind: the supporters of affiliation and the doubters were equally represented. The story of the group's
stay in Moscow is primarily one of attempts to preserve a united front
against Bolshevik efforts to drive a wedge into the ranks of the party.

No more unfavorable context for the USPD's negotiations could be
imagined than the Second World Congress of the Comintern.[60] The goal
of the congress, as determined in advance by the Bolsheviks, was to organize and discipline member parties into "one single Communist party
that has sections in different countries."[61] As Zinoviev wrote before the
congress, "The Communist International must extend itself into *a firm,
centralized, international proletarian organization* which must possess
not only a perfectly clear program but also *precise tactics and a fully de-*

58. *Ibid.*, p. 15.
59. *Ibid.*, pp. 14–15.
60. The principal source for the motives and actions of the USPD delegation in
Moscow is the reports delivered by the four delegates to the party's conference in
September; USPD *Reichskonferenz*, Sept. 1920, pp. 4–72. For the congress as a
whole, see Comintern *Kongress*, July–Aug. 1920, and the secondary accounts in
Hulse, chs. 9 and 10, and Carr, pp. 187–208.
61. Comintern *Kongress*, July–Aug. 1920, p. 111.

veloped and distinct organization."[62] And the Bolshevik leadership had the congress fully in hand. The tone of the meetings was infused with admiration for them, especially since in these inspiring weeks the Red Army was driving back the threatening Polish invasion and carrying the war toward Warsaw. The Bolsheviks were virtually certain of a majority for their proposals on any issue, though they sometimes resorted to maneuver and behind-the-scenes persuasion in order to secure maximum support. Whatever measures the Russians decided on for taming new applicants for membership would certainly be approved.

The Bolshevik policy toward the Independents showed itself early; in Zinoviev's words, the aim was "to separate the two wings of the German USP."[63] Only rarely could this aim be openly stated, and all four Independents resisted the idea whenever it was put forward; but the Bolsheviks' dealings with the Independents from their very first talks must be understood as part of an attempt to split the delegation. In the circumstances, the only wonder is that the delegation held together as long as it did. A first crack appeared almost at once, after a meeting on July 21 in which the ECCI launched a probing operation focusing on the USPD's formal reply; the four Independents managed to agree on their responses, but Däumig and Stoecker, though not denying that they had freely signed the letter, let it be known that they were no longer in full agreement with it.[64] Thereafter, however, things seemed to take a turn for the better. The locus of the debate shifted to a committee of the congress dealing with conditions of entry into the International; and here the tone of the deliberations gave hope that the Independents might yet succeed in bringing the party intact into the International. All the USPD delegates attended the committee sessions regularly, and they found that— especially when they presented unanimous protests—they could often carry their point.[65] A draft list of eighteen conditions for membership, which adhered closely to the line of thought of the ECCI's February letter, was softened step by step. In the plenary sessions of the congress the USPD continued to be treated with suspicion or contempt, often without distinction of wings, but it seemed that the Independents might still attain their goal with no worse penalty than a few weeks of humiliation.

The delegation, however, was not far from the breaking point. The two pairs of delegates roomed separately and often moved in different circles when not at work; meetings of the four to concert policy were

62. Zinoviev, *Bericht an den Zweiten Weltkongress,* p. 38.
63. *Die Kommunistische Internationale,* no. 13, p. 155.
64. See the accounts by Crispien and Stoecker in USPD *Reichskonferenz,* Sept. 1920, pp. 7–10 and 65–66; and Comintern *Kongress,* July–Aug. 1920, p. 250.
65. According to Crispien, USPD *Reichskonferenz,* Sept. 1920, p. 207.

awkward or acrimonious.[66] Each side felt confirmed in its prior judgments by the experience of the congress. Crispien and, especially, the stubborn Dittmann still resented the Comintern's abuse, suspected the intentions of the Bolsheviks, and felt the gulf between the International and the traditions of the USPD. They could not, however, afford to abandon their posture of seeking an accommodation, for the Russians, after all, had not yet closed the door to agreement. Their position, therefore, embodied in a draft declaration of August 6, was that the conditions of membership could form the basis for future negotiations between the party and the ECCI but that the Independents had the right to expect less hostile, more understanding treatment from the Comintern.[67] In contrast, Däumig and, especially, Stoecker found the milieu of the Comintern one in which they could quickly learn to live.[68] They were embarrassed by the reserved attitude of their colleagues, preferring to associate themselves with the warmer, more hopeful feelings of other delegates. Though their distaste for the conditions of membership differed from that of Crispien and Dittmann only in degree, they continued to regard such details as secondary to the main purpose of revitalizing the German revolutionary movement through association with the Communist International. Less stiff-necked than the others, they had come around to admitting the justice of many of the Russian criticisms of their party. Accordingly, as they said in their own draft declaration, they were prepared to work in the USPD for acceptance of the conditions and entry into the International.[69]

Perhaps these differences could have been papered over by a compromise formula; but the opportunity never arose, for the Russians suddenly changed the situation by a kind of parliamentary coup. Bypassing the established drafting subcommittee, the leadership of the congress produced another version of the conditions of membership, restoring the original terms in all their severity.[70] All the dogmas that the Independents found offensive or irrelevant—on civil war, on terror, on agitation among the peasants—were to be strictly imposed on parties wishing to affiliate. The list of reformists who must be expelled had been expanded to in-

66. Crispien, *ibid.*, pp. 6 and 15–16.
67. Text *ibid.*, p. 27; Dittmann's handwritten original is in Dittmann papers, folder: Moskau-Reise der USPD-Vertreter 1920.
68. See the excerpts from Stoecker's letters of July 23 and 28 to his wife, H. Stoecker, pp. 230–31.
69. USPD *Reichskonferenz*, Sept. 1920, p. 27.
70. Comparison of the ECCI's original draft (*Die Kommunistische Internationale*, no. 12, pp. 10–15) with the final form (Comintern *Kongress*, July–Aug. 1920, pp. 388–95) shows how slight the changes were. See also Meyer's commentary, Comintern *Kongress*, July–Aug. 1920, p. 657.

clude Hilferding as well as Kautsky. Moreover, new conditions were added. One provided that the leadership bodies of parties applying for membership must have at least a two-thirds majority of members who had favored affiliation even before the Second World Congress. Another required with brutal clarity that all persons in these parties who voted against the formal conditions of membership—the Twenty-One Conditions—must be expelled.

Dittmann and Crispien could not possibly accept such conditions, which were unambiguously intended to crush such men as themselves. Däumig and Stoecker, however, were prepared to make the leap of faith. At a meeting with the ECCI on August 9, while Dittmann and Crispien were politely evading any statement on what they intended to do, the two left-wing Independents committed themselves without any spoken reservation to accept the Twenty-One Conditions and work for their acceptance by the party.[71] The Comintern had accomplished its purpose at last. The USPD delegation was visibly split, and it could be predicted that the party would split as well. The leaders of the two factions on the wings of the party were divided publicly on an issue on which compromise was impossible because it was an issue defined and pressed on the party from outside and deliberately formulated for divisive effect. The wings of the party had been pulling apart for some time under the influence of their previous choices and commitments, the logic of their ideals and interests, and their different perceptions of events. But the bonds of unity had previously been strong; even if some of those on the wings wondered if unity was not an obstacle to their purposes, a large middle bloc of the party—including radicals as well as moderates—was unwilling to countenance a split. Now, abruptly, a single issue became crucial, and outside pressure made it impossible to evade the conflict. In this situation, schism was inescapable.

Schism

On August 23 the delegates arrived home from Russia. The following day the party executive decided to summon a preliminary party conference for September 1 to hear the report of the delegates and open discussion in the party. The day after, August 25, *Freiheit* published the full text of the Twenty-One Conditions; and the following day it opened its columns to the arguments of both sides, starting with an article by Däumig. Soon the debate was under way.

71. Accounts of this meeting are in *Die Kommunistische Internationale*, no. 13, p. 156, and USPD *Reichskonferenz*, Sept. 1920, pp. 28–33. There is a hint of private uneasiness in Stoecker's letter of August 4 to his wife, quoted in H. Stoecker, p. 232.

To call it a debate is somewhat misleading, for the two sides tended to conduct their campaigns on different levels. The left wing,[72] by and large, stood on the position it had arrived at a year earlier: association with Soviet Russia and its successful revolutionary leaders was self-evidently desirable for the German revolutionary movement, a step that would bring moral and eventually practical assistance to the cause of revolution in Germany. Events of the past year had given additional force to these sentiments, which had been embodied in the official aims of the party since the Leipzig party congress. The recent attention paid to Soviet Russia's struggle with Poland had tended—again with official party blessing —to revive militant sentiments of solidarity with the Russians, and these could be exploited in favor of affiliation with the Communist International.

There was more to the arguments of the advocates of affiliation than just reliance on sentiment; the Twenty-One Conditions required justification. For this the ideologues of the left wing relied on the dogmatic assumption that "we have now entered the stage of acute civil war."[73] Stoecker believed "that the question of international civil war will confront us very soon, and that very soon we will face the decisive power struggle with the bourgeoisie."[74] If so, then Daumig's conclusion followed, that the proletariat needed "a strictly organized structure with military discipline," or, in Adolph Hoffmann's words, a "dictatorship— even in our own ranks."[75] In effect, the leaders of the left wing, most of whom had no natural affinity for the type of party prescribed by the

72. The designation of the two camps presents problems. It is argued below that the advocates of affiliation to the Third International under the Twenty-One Conditions comprised (as far as the articulate levels of the party were concerned) the left wing and some other radicals, the arguments used (not always with conviction) being those of the left wing. The other side, however, comprised not only the ideological centrists and committed moderates, along with those of moderate tendencies from the middle of the party, but also a substantial number of outspoken radicals; while special attention will be given to the position of the moderates and centrists, by no means all of the arguments advanced from this side can be classified as right-wing. The quality shared by the members of this group was simply opposition to entering the Third International under the Twenty-One Conditions. While, therefore, the one side can be referred to as the "left wing," on the understanding that its base in the party was broader than such a designation implies, the other side must be referred to by more circumstantial phrases, such as "the opponents of affiliation."

73. Däumig's speech was reported in *Freiheit*, Sept. 13, 1920 (e). The abrupt emergence of this argument suggests consultation among the spokesmen of this camp about what line to put forward—probably with guidance from the ECCI; see below, p. 374.

74. USPD *Reichskonferenz*, Sept. 1920, p. 69. For similar statements by Koenen and Curt Geyer, see *ibid.*, pp. 72 and 77; by Adolph Hoffmann, *Freiheit*, Sept. 21, 1920 (m).

75. *Freiheit*, Aug. 26, 1920 (e), and Sept. 21, 1920 (m).

Bolsheviks, explained the necessity of the International's program by positing an emergency situation for which it was presumably fitted. The supposition that the final struggle would come shortly was reinforced by the events of the summer, the excited state of the radical workers, and, perhaps most of all, by the Bolsheviks; it was readily taken up by dedicated rank-and-file revolutionaries, who had long been waiting for their moment. However, to the extent that the leaders of the left wing relied on this argument, they committed themselves to fruitless and dangerous activism; moreover, they showed that they had not faced the long-term implications of the organizational form they had been asked to adopt.

If the Conditions had been milder, many of them would have been positively attractive to the supporters of affiliation. The USPD had been so unsuccessful as a revolutionary force that the rigor and purposefulness of Bolshevik doctrines had a degree of real appeal. They would replace the loose, ineffectual party structure of the past with a strict centralization, the crippling conflict of wills with common purpose, hesitation and delay with positive policies, wordy moralism with quasi-military ruthlessness. Most left-wing spokesmen preferred not to examine the full implications of these doctrines or assumed that the party would be able to adapt them to its needs; in particular, almost all of them failed to face the fact that they were being asked not just to reform the USPD but to form what was effectively a new party with the KPD.[76] But the desire for change was so strong among the exasperated, frustrated radicals that they were happy to accept guidance from the world's most successful revolutionaries on how to reorganize their party.

None of the prominent leaders of the left wing seem to have understood the full import of the Twenty-One Conditions. Stoecker probably came closest. He was both more outspoken and more systematic than others when he wrote of

this miserable spirit of passivity and the remnants of pacifist illusions that still haunt the minds even of otherwise radical comrades. We must completely clear away this spirit of seeing only the difficulties and hindrances, so enervating and restrictive for the revolutionary forward impulse of the German working class, and emphatically demonstrate the distortion of the revolutionary methods of Marxism into Kautskyan economic fatalism, with which most of our right-wing leaders are also tinged. Especially in an epoch like the present one, when we are faced fairly certainly with grave, decisive conflicts with the bourgeoisie in the near future, it is important to cultivate the Marx-

76. See, for example, the critique in Buchsbaum, p. 342, of the otherwise very radical Gotha party's attitude. But cf. the acerbic comment of the Hamburg newspaper on its party's struggles to survive: "Man muss zur rechten Zeit zu sterben wissen"; quoted in *Freiheit,* Sept. 14, 1920 (m).

ist revolutionary offensive spirit again in the forward-driving German proletarian masses and ruthlessly to combat the feeble passivity of the right wing.[77]

The theme of the "offensive spirit" recurred many times in Stoecker's
utterances in this period.[78] He had also adopted other ideas from the International; in fact, he was one of the few to endorse every clause of the
declarations of the Second World Congress.[79] He condemned "petty-
bourgeois and pacifist prejudices in the questions of force and terror,"
preached the necessity of a vanguard of the proletariat, and accepted
the idea of the International as "the international general staff of all national proletarian armies."[80] Stoecker did not foresee the extent of his
party's later subordination to the Bolsheviks; but in this, too, he was representative of the most thoroughgoing and honest proponents of adherence.

Stoecker was the youngest member of the party executive, and the few
other leading figures who seemed both to sense and to approve of what
the party was being asked to do were also young. Among them were
Werner Scholem of Halle; Franz Dahlem of Cologne (who was greeted
at the party conference with a shout of "Dummer, grüner Junge!");
Curt Geyer, though he showed some insecurity on the question of Russian dominance; and Ernst Thälmann, chairman of the Hamburg party
organization, whose followers formed the firmest and most Communist-
minded bloc among the local party organizations that moved from the
USPD to the KPD.[81] By no means all their allies in the campaign were
certain about the course they had chosen. Däumig's arguments, for instance, tended to be defensive—dogged rather than confident. He had
made his choice on the basis of long-standing admiration for the Russians, dissatisfaction with the USPD's course, and a belief that the revolution must come soon; but he was patently uneasy about the split and
avoided defending the Twenty-One Conditions in detail.[82] Koenen, who

77. *Kommunistische Rundschau*, Oct. 1, 1920, p. 3.
78. See *Freiheit*, Sept. 13, 1920 (e); USPD *Parteitag*, Oct. 1920, p. 137.
79. *Freiheit*, Aug. 30, 1920 (e).
80. *Ibid.*, Sept. 13, 1920 (e), and Aug. 30, 1920 (e).
81. USPD *Parteitag*, Oct. 1920, pp. 44–45 and 50–52; USPD *Reichskonferenz*,
Sept. 1920, pp. 77–79 and 93–96. Scholem was 24, Dahlem and Geyer 28, Stoecker
29, and Thälmann 34. Robert Wheeler has been able to show that there was a general age difference between the supporters and opponents of the Comintern at party
congresses—the former being 5.4 years younger on the average at the Leipzig
congress, 7.3 years younger at Halle; see "German Labor and the Comintern: A
Problem of Generations?" *Journal of Social History*, 7 (1973–74), pp. 304–21.
82. USPD *Reichskonferenz*, Sept. 1920, pp. 37–52; *Freiheit*, Aug. 26, 1920 (e),
and (speech reported) Sept. 6, 1920 (e); USPD *Parteitag*, Oct. 1920, pp. 98–113.
The reservations were made explicit in USPD *Reichskonferenz*, Sept. 1920, pp.
43–44, 50, and 188.

approved of the Conditions completely, minimized the alterations they would bring to the life of the party.[83] Adolph Hoffmann rested his case on the immediacy of the final crisis of the old order.[84] Other certified radicals, including Alfred Oelssner and Otto Brass, experienced a period of uncertainty before joining their comrades of the left. All these men were largely committed by their past to choose the more radical course and go with Soviet Russia; and the pressure of their customary following in the party helped them over any difficulty in the choice.

For the other side, the issues were different. The principal arguments of the opponents of affiliation concerned the party's "autonomy"—the reservation that the party executive, at Hilferding's suggestion, had adopted before the delegates left for Moscow.[85] The Twenty-One Conditions were themselves a remarkable interference in the party's affairs; and the opponents were quick to see that the decisions of the Second World Congress laid the foundation for permanent direction of the German party from Moscow. The issue was emotional, exploitable as propaganda against the Third International; the *Hamburger Volkszeitung* had grounds for expecting "a furious explosion of party chauvinism."[86] The *Leipziger Volkszeitung* denounced the idea of "unconditional merger with the KPD and subjection to the leadership of this party"; Hilferding, more aptly, observed that the Conditions might as well have frankly subordinated member parties directly to the Bolshevik central committee.[87] "The dictatorship of one brother party over other brother parties"[88] was so contrary to Social Democratic tradition that the idea encountered immediate, emotional resistance.

But more than emotion was involved. Both Ledebour and Hilferding argued that the idea of directing German party affairs from Moscow (or anywhere else abroad) could not possibly work, that only trusted representatives of the German working class, in close, regular contact with the workers' activities, could understand the appropriate forms for the movement or follow the mood of the workers accurately enough to prescribe action.[89]

Central direction, even from abroad, might have some rationale if one assumed that international civil war was about to break out; but this

83. Article from the Halle *Volksblatt* in *Freiheit*, Aug. 29, 1920; and USPD *Reichskonferenz*, Sept. 1920, pp. 73–75.
84. *Freiheit,* Sept. 21, 1920 (m).
85. See above, p. 360.
86. Quoted in *Freiheit,* Aug. 31, 1920 (m).
87. Quoted *ibid.,* Aug. 26, 1920 (e); *ibid.,* Sept. 10, 1920 (m).
88. Fritz Kunert, USPD *Reichskonferenz,* Sept. 1920. p. 75.
89. USPD *Reichskonferenz,* Sept. 1920, p. 80; *Freiheit,* Sept. 10, 1920 (m). The *Leipziger Volkszeitung* argued similarly; quoted in *Freiheit,* Aug. 26, 1920 (e).

part of the left wing's arguments was attacked by the other side. In its milder form, the attack rested on the old principle of the Independents (and the German Communists) that the party must not stake everything on one possible turn of events but must prepare for all eventualities.[90] The "go-for-broke" policy of the Comintern's spokesmen, as Hilferding called it,[91] was contrary to all Social Democratic instincts. Furthermore, it was dangerous. Dittmann repeatedly predicted that the promises made to the radical workers in the course of the conflict in the USPD would eventually come back to haunt the left-wing leaders. The result could be local putschism, such as was already reviving in the fall of 1920; or the leaders, under pressure from their whipped-up followers, might feel compelled to start an action in which "the German proletariat is driven onto the machine guns of the Reichswehr and the counterrevolution."[92] Russian pressure made pointless violence more likely; for, in Dittmann's estimation, the Bolshevik attitude was that "the Germans must make a revolution at all costs."[93] In distant Moscow, the Bolsheviks, unable to appreciate German conditions, might give the command for what would prove to be, not a successful revolution, but a bloodbath.[94]

Such arguments also reflected the continued skepticism of party moderates about the prospect of immediate revolution. Only Crispien seems to have been willing to try to demonstrate by argument that conditions were unfavorable for a successful seizure of power;[95] but the same point was implicit in many other arguments used by the opponents of adherence. For over a year the party's policy had been dominated by the judgment that the counterrevolution held the initiative, had the stronger forces, and was looking for the chance to crush the workers' movement once and for all by violence. Empirical evidence that the spirit of the masses had changed sufficiently to let the initiative pass to them was thin, consisting mostly of the growing radicalism of some industrial workers. Moderate Independents had never believed in the possibility of willing an action into existence without prior evidence of broad mass support; and it seemed to them that their antagonists were trying to press this feat upon them.

More fundamentally, most of the critics of the Twenty-One Conditions felt that the practices Moscow was trying to force on the party were

90. For example, Dittmann, USPD *Parteitag,* Oct. 1920, pp. 116 and 118.
91. *Ibid.,* p. 184; "Vabanque-Spiel" was his term.
92. *Ibid.,* p. 130; speech reported in *Freiheit,* Sept. 14, 1920 (m). The quotation is from USPD *Reichskonferenz,* Sept. 1920, p. 63; see also p. 209 (Crispien). There is an implied reference here to the events of January 13, 1920, in Berlin.
93. USPD *Reichskonferenz,* Sept. 1920, p. 55.
94. For example, Hilferding, *ibid.,* p. 111.
95. *Ibid.,* pp. 208–9.

wrong whether revolution was at hand or not. Hilferding and Crispien in particular delivered impassioned statements of Social Democratic principle concerning the limited role of leadership in a mass socialist party, according to which the free, autonomous individual worker, and not the leadership, was both the raison d'être of the party and its principal motor.[96] Others felt that Bolshevik discipline was an offense against human dignity, and thus against the very purposes of socialism. More specifically, many argued that the German workers, having been educated to think otherwise, would never accept a centralized, essentially uncontrollable leadership for any length of time; the very idea was a chimera, wholly unsuited to German conditions.[97] As Crispien put it, the party was being asked to commit "suicide" in the eyes of the German workers.[98]

But it was the imminent split that angered the moderate and middle sections of the party more than any other consequence of the Twenty-One Conditions. For misconceived, self-seeking, ultimately frivolous reasons—as they saw it—the Bolsheviks and their agents were "carrying schism from land to land" across Europe.[99] In Germany they were destroying "the greatest and strongest social-revolutionary party of the world,"[100] and to no purpose. A united workers' movement had not been the sole or overriding goal even of the opponents of Moscow, as the continued separate existence of the USPD had shown; but, both theoretically and emotionally, proletarian unity had an important place in their beliefs. What was now happening to the USPD was almost a crime in the eyes of those who had given years of their lives to the party, and, for the more far-seeing, a crime not only against the Independents but against the working class. The orthodox USPD program for eventual unity had called for isolating the intransigent, irresponsible Communist fringe while achieving a common front with the SPD—on the USPD's terms, of course. Such a plan was invalidated, at least for the near future, by the coming creation of a mass party of "maximalists" and the accompanying reduction in the weight of the socialist center. The split was disorienting for the moderates; this fact helps to explain the overtones carried by the charge of "splitting," one of the most frequent and effective of the charges made against the left.

The charge of splitting was also leveled against the International's pro-

96. Crispien, *ibid.*, p. 204; *Freiheit*, Aug. 28, 1920 (m); Hilferding, *Freiheit*, Aug. 29, 1920, Sept. 13, 1920 (e), and USPD *Parteitag*, Oct. 1920, esp. pp. 181–83.
97. Hilferding, *Freiheit*, Aug. 29, 1920.
98. *Ibid.*, Aug. 27, 1920 (m).
99. Crispien, *ibid.*, Sept. 23, 1920 (m).
100. Hilferding, *ibid.*, Aug. 29, 1920.

gram in trade-union affairs. The Second World Congress had stopped short of calling for a Communist-sponsored trade-union movement, for much the same practical reasons as had motivated the KPD's change of front on the subject a year earlier; it had, however, founded its own embryonic trade-union international—the International Council of Trade Unions—to compete with the International Federation of Trade Unions at Amsterdam. The implications of this new institution for the united front of the German trade unions, if any should pass into Communist hands, were undeniable—though denials were attempted.[101] Within each country the Communists were not to abandon the existing trade unions, unless forced out by the intolerant or excessively reactionary policy of the leaders, but they were to form Communist cells within the unions; given the attitudes of the German trade-union leaders this course guaranteed conflict or expulsion. The Communist International had set itself to challenge the united power of the established unions at a time when the importance of trade-union unity was especially strongly felt— a piece of tactlessness beyond repair.

Most of these ideological or emotional factors in the debate emerged quickly; there was little change in the substance of the controversy in the month before the party congress met on October 12. The period was full of drama, nevertheless, as intrigue and factional maneuvering took place in the party organization, with vehement conflict in the press and party assemblies.[102] Across the country, struggles were going on for control of local and district organizations and, most important, delegates' seats at the coming party congress. The party was dividing into two camps, but the fate of many of the objects of their struggle, including the majority at the congress, was not decided until the last days before the congress, and in some cases not until afterwards.

Whether the party membership made up its mind quickly or slowly is impossible to know; most of those who did take a position probably decided fairly soon, and the party executive's action in calling the party congress earlier than they need have done suggests that this was their estimation. Certainly the higher party functionaries and the editors of the party press decided fairly rapidly, if often with severe internal con-

101. See the articles by *Freiheit*'s trade-union editor, R. Seidel, in the issues of Sept. 9, 1920 (m), and Sept. 12, 1920; Dissmann's speech was reported *ibid.*, Oct. 8, 1920 (m and e); Crispien in USPD *Reichskonferenz*, Sept. 1920, p. 203. One who attempted a reply was Richard Müller, *Freiheit*, Sept. 11, 1920 (m).

102. For a careful presentation of the debate and voting results in each party district, taken from the provincial press, see Wheeler, "Internationals," pp. 679–733.

flicts. The decision of some who hesitated for a time, including Alfred Oelssner of Halle and Friedrich Geyer of Leipzig, was always likely to be for Moscow. Kurt Rosenfeld's delayed decision for the other side was more surprising. Only a few were still undecided at the last minute, so far as we know. Among them was Emil Höllein of Jena, an energetic radical who was nevertheless so depressed by the prospect of a split in the party that he evolved a scheme whereby the party would accept the Twenty-One Conditions "in principle," convert itself to a centralized revolutionary party more or less along the lines prescribed in Moscow, and then approach the ECCI again with an application for membership. This proposal was actually adopted by a subdistrict conference in Jena; when it failed to gain support in the party at large Höllein went with the left wing into the Third International.[103] More significant was the case of Otto Brass. The day before the party congress opened, he was still trying to persuade a conference of the Lower Rhineland district to declare for adherence in principle while trying for a renegotiation of terms; when his proposal lost, he opted for the left and the company of most of his followers and associates.[104] Among the few waverers who finally decided the other way was Paul Hennig, editor-in-chief of the Halle *Volksblatt,* who tried to devise ways in which the party might escape a split (along the lines of Höllein's proposal) and went to the party congress (as an observer) still uncertain, only to decide there to remain with the opposing minority.[105]

It became apparent quite early in the conflict that most party officials and journalists were inclined to reject the Conditions. By the time the party conference began on September 1, Franz Künstler had committed himself against the Conditions, thus giving the opponents a majority in the party executive; after Kurt Rosenfeld's similar but more hesitant decision, only four of the executive's twelve members—Däumig, Stoecker, Koenen, and Adolph Hoffmann—were for affiliation. Konrad Ludwig's vote gave the opponents a majority in the control commission; on the auxiliary council the left wing, despite the defection of Karl Kürbs of Halle, retained a four-to-three majority, with the result that this body was conspicuously bypassed whenever possible in the decisions of the following weeks. At the September party conference itself, to judge from partial indications (no votes were taken), the majority was hostile to the Twenty-One Conditions. The party press was equally one-sided; Däu-

103. Pöhland, pp. 449–50 and 453.
104. *Freiheit,* Oct. 15, 1920 (e). The respected elderly radical Joseph Herzfeld was also against accepting the Conditions as late as Oct. 4, because they would cause a split; Meiritz, p. 182. He eventually chose to go with the left wing.
105. Wheeler, "Internationals," pp. 689–93; Dittmann memoirs, p. 1203.

mig and his associates estimated that four-fifths of the party papers were against them.[106]

Such a division in the upper ranks of the party was produced by the somewhat unusual factional alignment in reactions to the Twenty-One Conditions. The right wing alone did not control such a high proportion of the party machinery, let alone the press; but in the face of the threat to the autonomy and organizational integrity of the USPD the party's moderates were reinforced by members from the middle and even the left of the party. Ledebour's adherence to the anti-Moscow cause was no surprise in view of his well-known suspicion of the Bolsheviks' intentions and his pride in the USPD's revolutionary past. But that Kurt Rosenfeld, Fritz Kunert, Karl Kürbs, and even Karl Liebknecht's brother Theodor (whose name was demonstratively placed at the head of the opponents' list for the voting in Berlin) should have joined them showed that the Conditions were not producing a clean split along the line that might have been expected. These men had supported the Stoecker resolution at the preceding party congress and continued to regard themselves as representatives of the USPD's radical left, even as supporters of the Third International; but they could not stomach the Twenty-One Conditions. Their views were similar to those of Brass or Höllein—a group of them issued an appeal on October 6 calling for a declaration "in principle" for affiliation to the Third International and renegotiation of the Conditions[107]—but they found the existing Conditions an insuperable obstacle. Such a reaction by leading figures in the party turned what might have been a fairly even contest on this level into a one-sided decision against Moscow.

The left wing's strength lay not so much inside the party apparatus, though in such important districts as Hamburg and Halle it had this advantage on its side, as in the enthusiastic support of many of the party's local functionaries and militants, especially those who were bound together by what remained of the council system. The left wing thus had to improvise an informal organization to assist its disconnected supporters, even though factional organization offended against party tradition and served to emphasize the coming split, about which the advocates of the

106. *Freiheit*, Oct. 3, 1920 (e). This estimate was impressionistic; in fact, the left wing came away with twenty-one of the party's sixty or so papers (see ch. 12, nn. 14–16).

107. *Ibid.*, Oct. 6, 1920 (e). The signatories were Heinrich Knauf, party secretary in Gera; Fritz Kunert of Berlin, Reichstag deputy from Halle; Kurt Löwenstein, Reichstag deputy from Teltow-Beeskow; Gerhard Obuch of Düsseldorf, deputy in the Prussian Diet; Kurt Rosenfeld; Willy Scholz of Erfurt, district party secretary for Thuringia; and Mathilde Wurm of Berlin, editor of *Die Kämpferin*.

Third International preferred not to talk. The left wing circulated its own bulletin to its leading supporters and supplied services, such as model resolutions for use in local assemblies.[108] On October 1 it began publishing a theoretical journal, boldly named *Kommunistische Rundschau,* as a rival to Breitscheid's *Der Sozialist.* By the time of the party congress it seems to have had a functioning apparatus to set against the official party organization, most of which it would lose when the split came.

The left wing also had support from the International—probably including financial support, which would explain its publishing ventures. The broad outlines of the campaign had been agreed upon by Däumig and Stoecker, in consultation with Levi and the Bolsheviks, before they left Russia.[109] Of the German Communists, Levi in particular was anxious to give all the assistance he could, though it seemed expedient that his association with the left wing's campaign should not be visible.[110] On September 6 the KPD issued a confidential circular to its organizations laying down that "the Communists have the task of being of assistance to the comrades in the USPD in their schism."[111]

In general, the association with the KPD and the prospect of future merger with it were an embarrassment to the left-wing forces in the USPD and were mentioned as little as possible. The Communist Party had a bad name with most Independents that was rooted in long-standing prejudices and found confirmation in that party's recent practice. In the latter stages of the campaign against munitions shipments to Poland, the KPD had set out on its own sectarian course, the most notable feature of which was a demand for immediate election of political workers' councils—an idea that was regarded as merely silly by most Independents.[112] On September 17 the KPD took a step that was positively offensive to the USPD left wing: it changed its name from "KPD (Spartacus League)" to "KPD (Section of the Third International)."[113] This formula was laid down in the Twenty-One Conditions, and Communist spokesmen later claimed that the party was simply adjusting to the rules of the International;[114] the move was generally understood, however, as asserting the KPD's priority in its connection with Moscow and implying that there

108. *Freiheit,* Sept. 14, 1920 (m).
109. According to Levi, "Bericht über die Verhandlungen in Moskau," delivered to the KPD's expanded central committee on Aug. 25, Levi papers, P 27.
110. *Ibid.;* Heckert gives an account of Levi's activity at the time in *Die Kommunistische Internationale,* no. 19, p. 86. One instance of consultations was brought to light in USPD *Reichskonferenz,* Sept. 1920, p. 176.
111. Pöhland, p. 447n.
112. See n. 6 above; and *Freiheit,* Aug. 20, 1920 (m).
113. *Rote Fahne,* Sept. 21, 1920.
114. Pieck, KPD *Parteitag,* Nov. 1920, p. 22.

was already a Communist Party in Germany, which the Independents could join if they liked.[115]

While these maneuvers by the KPD were an annoyance to the pro-Moscow Independents, they did not seriously affect the left wing's superior position in the campaign for the allegiance of party members. The inevitability of the division of the party into two irreconcilable camps was brought home to party leaders at the conference in early September. Thereafter, the two sides increasingly directed their efforts toward making sure that the division would be as favorable as possible to their interests. The left wing, as we have seen, organized a vigorous campaign, but it was the other side that was on the offensive. The case for the Third International had been stated—indeed, rather embarrassingly overstated—by the Russians in their earlier communications and again in the theses of the Second World Congress and the Twenty-One Conditions. The active membership was believed to be generally sympathetic to the Third International, probably even more so than a year earlier; the left wing's task was to consolidate this support into voting strength while fighting off attempts by the opponents to reverse members' sympathies. The opponents, on the other hand, had to convince the party rank and file that an important change had occurred, that, contrary to earlier party policy, it was no longer desirable to join with the Bolsheviks in the Third International (or at least not on present terms). The task was difficult, and it made the opponents aggressive.

The opponents of affiliation at least had the advantage of controlling the central organs of the party apparatus, and they made use of their organizational leverage. The key decisions of the party executive date from the middle of September. The first was to advance the date of the party congress by two weeks, to October 12; the second, to insist that the delegates be elected by the membership at large by secret ballot on a proportional system, rather than by assemblies of the local party organizations.[116] The minority in the executive objected so strenuously to these two steps as to publish a declaration of protest in *Rote Fahne*.[117] The division of the party was plain for all to see.

115. For example, Eugen Prager, *Freiheit*, Sept. 21, 1920 (m). The move was criticized as tactless even by Zinoviev (*Die Kommunistische Internationale*, no. 15, p. 402).

116. A third decision—to set an arbitrarily tight deadline for the districts to pay up arrears in dues in order to qualify for full delegation rights—was eventually modified. Seven districts (Bavaria, Frankfurt on Main, Hamburg, Hesse-Waldeck, Magdeburg, Middle Rhineland, and Zittau), which would have had a single delegate apiece under the party executive's original decree, eventually cast 60 votes at the congress, 44 for the Twenty-One Conditions and only 16 against. The case of the outstanding delinquent, Hamburg, was only settled at the congress.

117. *Rote Fahne*, Sept. 22, 1920.

Moving the date of the party congress may not have been intended as a tactical ploy; Kurt Rosenfeld argued that the purpose was to shorten the period when the party would be paralyzed by conflict.[118] Nor did the change in date confer any advantage on the opponents of the Conditions. The provision for direct election of delegates by the members, however, was almost certainly prescribed because the anti-Moscow forces expected to gain by it, and gain they did. The great strength of the Third International's cause lay in the enthusiasm of its supporters among party activists—those who would dominate indirect elections where party sentiments were otherwise fairly evenly divided. In Berlin City, for instance, assemblies held in eighteen wards in mid-campaign were dominated in all but one case by supporters of Moscow, sometimes by huge majorities; but when the balloting took place the vote was close, the pro-Moscow side winning twelve delegates and the opponents eleven.[119] The Hamburg party organization, the most ruthless of those on the left wing, even altered its statute to avoid holding direct elections[120]—though in the end it was forced into line by the party executive.

Except in a few districts, which could not affect the result, delegates were thus elected from competing lists and were wholly committed in advance. At least a week before the congress opened it was clear that, despite the maneuvers of the party executive and the one-sided stand of the party press, the opponents had fallen short of a majority.[121] On the first morning of the congress, *Freiheit* estimated that there were about 220 delegates in favor of affiliation to 158 against.[122] No more than about ten delegates can have changed their votes during the proceedings; Prager's estimate of two or three is more likely.[123] There was thus little

118. *Freiheit,* Sept. 22, 1920 (e).
119. *Ibid.,* Oct. 5, 1920 (m).
120. *Ibid.,* Sept. 25, 1920 (m).
121. Only a little more than a quarter of the party members voted; according to a widely accepted calculation, the result of the voting in the districts was 144,000 in favor of accepting the Twenty-One Conditions and 91,000 against. See *Mitteilungsblatt für die Anhänger der III. Internationale in der U.S.P.D.,* Oct. 20, 1920.
122. The final vote at the congress was 237 to 156; most of the increase in the majority's vote can be attributed to the admission of certain disputed delegations by majority vote of the congress.
123. Prager, pp. 224–25. Zinoviev, *Zwölf Tage in Deutschland* (Hamburg, 1921), p. 11, claims that the left wing's majority grew from 50 to 80 during the congress; even if this was so, about half of the increase came from the admission of disputed delegations, so that the number of delegates who changed their vote would be something under ten. If we could accept the signatures appended to the two resolutions (as printed in USPD *Parteitag,* Oct. 1920, pp. 70–73) as precisely reflecting the division of sentiment before the proceedings began, then the number changing their votes would be two (one in each direction); but in fact we have no firm evidence that the lists were closed before the debate.

or no suspense on the central issue; the victory of the left wing and the survival of a strong minority were both certain.

The pattern of the results in the districts showed how the factional balance had changed since the Leipzig congress and suggested the regional strength each side might hope to take with it after the split.[124] At Leipzig, it will be recalled, the Stoecker resolution was defeated by the votes of the party leadership, the National Assembly delegation, and the smaller organizations, with the larger districts splitting their votes almost evenly. At Halle, however, the party leadership and Reichstag delegation could not vote (the Leipzig congress having ruled that they should have only a deliberative voice at future congresses), and this cost the opponents of the Conditions a potential 62 votes to only 25 for the other side. This time, the smaller districts (the 22 organizations with fewer than 40,000 members) divided their votes almost evenly, with the anti-Moscow vote of the smaller Saxon districts (14 to 3) almost offsetting the margin the rest of the small districts gave to the left-wing cause. Thus the largest districts, accounting for almost three-quarters of the delegates, provided nearly all of the left wing's final 81-vote margin. The large districts split into two camps; the first was made up of Berlin-Brandenburg, which voted by only 29 to 27 for the Third International, and Leipzig, which voted 36 to 19 against; the second included the remaining seven districts —Halle, Lower Rhineland, Thuringia, Hamburg, Bavaria, Western Westphalia, and East Prussia—the sum of whose votes was 134 for the Third International and 41 against. The Halle and Lower Rhineland districts together provided a 53-vote margin for the left wing—34 to 9 and 39 to 11, respectively. On the other side, Leipzig and the rest of Saxony together with Berlin-Brandenburg supplied 77 votes for the anti-Moscow forces, or almost exactly half of their total; elsewhere, only Bremen (with its satellite district, Oldenburg–East Frisia), Braunschweig, and two single-member districts (West Prussia and Danzig) gave a majority of their votes to the opponents of the Twenty-One Conditions. The pattern was disturbing for the opponents. If the actual lines of fracture in the party followed those of the congress vote, the future USPD would be a very imbalanced party indeed. The opponents had at least some votes in every important district except the Middle Rhineland to go with their great strength in Berlin and Leipzig; but clearly the remaining organization might find itself reduced to a small, struggling remnant in much of the country, including such former strongholds as the Halle district, the Lower Rhineland, and perhaps Thuringia. The party could probably survive on this basis, but its prospects would not be impressive.

124. The following analysis is based on a comparison of the roll-call vote (USPD *Parteitag,* Oct. 1920, pp. 257–61) with the delegate list.

Despite its foregone conclusion, the congress in Halle was dramatic. The delegates of each faction—sitting on opposite sides of the central aisle—were passionately convinced of their positions, and emotional outbursts were the order of the day. The delegates of the pro-Moscow side were generally better behaved. The only danger, from their point of view, was that the minority might find some excuse to break up the congress before its conclusion and hence deprive the majority of some part of the legitimacy of its triumph; they therefore disciplined their followers and conceded small points to the minority.[125] The opponents of the Conditions appear to have had no deliberate intention of disrupting the congress; but neither did they have any reason to restrain themselves. The rowdiest scenes occurred when the delegates of the minority, exasperated by a long, abusive speech by the Russian Lozovski against the International Federation of Trade Unions in Amsterdam, began a concerted uproar under the leadership of Dissmann, finally forcing Lozovski to abandon his speech.[126]

But incidents were exceptional. In the main, the congress' proceedings moved inexorably toward their appointed end, with passion but without disturbance. The oratorical centerpieces were a four-and-a-half-hour speech by Zinoviev and a reply of almost equal length by Hilferding; each had great impact on the morale of supporters of the speaker's position but no effect at all on the vote. After only perfunctory debate, the congress proceeded to the long, solemn process of a roll-call vote, and soon the party congress of the USPD had officially voted, by 237 to 156, to accept the Twenty-One Conditions and join the Third International.

Thereupon Artur Crispien was recognized by the chairman. What happened then is best told in the words of the minutes of the congress:

Comrades! As chairman of the German Independent Social Democratic Party and by decision of the party executive of the German Independent Social Democratic Party I declare:

A part of this party congress has accepted the Twenty-One Conditions of admission prescribed by the Third Communist International. This part (shouts of Aha!) is consequently obligated under articles 16 and 17 of the Conditions [and] article 3 of the Statutes of the Communist International to enter the German Communist Party, Section of the Third Communist International, as already constituted on the basis of the decisions of the Communist International, and adopt this name. (Shout: Who says that?). . . .

They have thereby dissolved their organizational bonds with the members of the party who adhere to the Leipzig Action Program and want to remain in the present organization of the USPD. By adopting the Däumig-Stoecker motion this assembly has ceased to be a party congress of the USPD. (Dis-

125. Zinoviev, *Zwölf Tage*, p. 13; Stampfer, *Die vierzehn Jahre*, p. 198; Dittmann memoirs, p. 1182.
126. USPD *Parteitag*, Oct. 1920, pp. 223–24; *Freiheit*, Oct. 16, 1920 (m).

order. The delegates of the right leave the hall with three cheers for the USPD. Shouts, whistling from the balcony. The delegates of the left sing the Internationale.)[127]

Crispien and his followers assembled in another hall in the city the following day and reconstituted the party. The division of the USPD was now formal and definitive.

The left wing had won; they had mustered a coherent, aggressive majority in the USPD and displaced the old guard from the leadership— although at the expense of a split that cost them most of the party's organizational resources and much good will among the workers. The Comintern had been successful, too, after its fashion; its assault on the uneasy equilibrium of the most significant centrist-led party in Europe had destroyed that party in its old form and would bring a mass of new members into the camp of the German Communists. But the schism had its odd features, and even at the moment of triumph for the left wing and the Comintern, as nearly half the seats on the floor of the congress emptied following Crispien's declaration, there were doubts about whether the result was beneficial to the revolutionary cause. The aim of the Comintern's splitting operation, endorsed—albeit often with reservations —by the left-wing Independents, had been to discard the centrist elements in the leadership of the USPD and whatever small following they might have and attract the masses of the party rank and file into the Communist camp so as to form a mass revolutionary party. The first half of the program had been carried out; but the instrument used, the Twenty-One Conditions, had been so blunt and imprecise a tool that not only the centrists but also most of the leaders of the party middle and even significant sections of the left had been lost as well. The Comintern was no doubt prepared to bear this loss; but whether the movement could alienate such a large part of the established leadership of the socialist left and still rally the masses was far from clear. The coming months, as the two sides competed for the allegiance of the former USPD membership, were to show that forcing a decision, and moreover an organization-oriented decision, on the USPD from outside might have destroyed a rival but had not ensured assumption of the rival's assets.

The division of the USPD also altered the revolutionary perspective of the German left in a manner that was of dubious benefit to the cause.

127. USPD *Parteitag,* Oct. 1920, p. 261. The published proceedings of the Halle congress exist in two versions, one recording the rest of the proceedings of the left wing after the split, the other the remaining session of the seceding rump USPD. The two are typographically identical in their title pages and in pp. 14–260. Since the citations in this book are, in all but one case, from the portions that the two versions have in common, the notes make no distinction; the sole exception is the above quotation, which is from the left-wing version.

After a protracted shaking-down period, the expanded KPD emerged as a tightly organized Leninist party of sufficient strength to have a real, though very slight, chance of seizing power under ideal conditions. That such conditions did not occur before 1945 was due not least to poor party leadership, characterized by misdirection from afar, mindless application of Bolshevik methods, involvement in Russian factional disputes, repeated schism, and rejection of the ablest independent-minded socialists —all characteristics that were foreshadowed, though not inevitable, in the autumn of 1920. This slim and misperceived possibility of Communist revolution was bought at the cost of destroying what prospects existed for socialist revolution in the old sense—seizure of power, not by a self-directed vanguard organization, but by the masses of the proletariat. Such a conception of revolution had predominated in the old USPD, and so long as strong Social Democratic elements and strong activist proletarian elements were united in a single organization there had remained at least the faint hope of an effective challenge to the bourgeois order without resort to Bolshevik methods. This hope expired with the breakup of the USPD. For the regrouping remnants of the party, this was the ultimate disaster of Halle, and it shaped the remaining two years of the party's life.

CHAPTER 12

The Rump USPD (October 1920 to June 1922)

Halle opened a new epoch for the Social Democratic left in Germany. Since its recovery from the first revolutionary months, this part of Social Democracy—incorporated in the USPD, though ultimately losing control of the party—had devoted itself to assembling and guiding the activist elements of the working class, hoping to turn rising dissatisfaction into a powerful drive toward socialism. The premise of this work had been the unity of the activist elements of socialism (the Communists could be largely ignored); its form had been the expanding organizational framework of the USPD. With Halle, the premise was undermined, the form destroyed. The party was in a new situation, in which prospects for fruitful left-wing Social Democratic activity were in jeopardy.

The party survived, though reduced from what had previously appeared to be the leading position in German socialism to a kind of dangerous middle position with more clearly defined parties on either flank. On the left, the attractions of Communism had been neutralized by the bitterness of the split. This antagonism was not necessarily permanent, however, especially if the Communist Party should shed its more obviously offensive features (above all its dependence on Moscow); for many in the USPD still felt it somehow improper to belong to any other party than that of the extreme left. More serious in the immediate circumstances was the temptation from the right. With the division of the USPD, and particularly after the failure of the United Communist Party (VKPD) in 1921 to make itself a real mass party, the SPD was by far the largest political organization of the working class and on those grounds alone had a strong attraction for other Social Democrats. The SPD had again become, in a sense, *the* party of the proletariat for non-Communists. The USPD's separate existence needed explanation more than ever.

With its impressive size and rapid growth things of the past, the USPD had to find its raison d'être elsewhere, in hostility to the political course

381

of the other two parties, reinforced by doctrine and habit. The Communists and Majority Socialists gave unintentional assistance, without which the USPD might have given up the fight much earlier than it did. In February 1921, the VKPD experienced a disruptive party crisis, and in March it embarked on a sectarian political line; both factors helped to repel possible USPD sympathizers. The Majority Socialists chose September 1921, a time of dawning rapprochement with the Independents, to replace the old Erfurt Program with a more reformist document, while simultaneously accepting the idea of a coalition with the right-wing People's Party. Yet hostility, habit, and doctrine were a weak foundation in relatively quiet times for a small working-class party seeking support among workers with a strong tradition of class unity. In the two years of life remaining to it the USPD could never feel secure.

Splitting and Reconsolidation

The Halle congress did not produce an immediate, neat division of the USPD. On the contrary, the regrouping on the socialist left was an agonizing, drawn-out process, and it was months after the congress before the last local organizations had chosen sides and the last problems of ownership of local party assets had been resolved. The construction of a unified party out of the remnants of the old took even longer. Some six months passed before conditions in the USPD were settled enough to allow the party leadership to think of other matters, and more than a year before a party congress was summoned to celebrate the survival and continuing mission of the USPD.

The immediate problem after Halle was not survival; so long as the solid Leipzig organization and such large blocks of members as those in Berlin and Thuringia adhered to the USPD the loyalty of smaller groups elsewhere in the country would hold and the party would continue to exist. However, as the factions pulled apart after the congress, it was questionable for a time whether the party could maintain the numbers and organizational cohesion, the credibility and operating effectiveness that were necessary if it was to keep its remaining members for long and hold out some prospects of a renewal of strength. In the end it succeeded, but with little margin to spare.

The principal advantage of the Right USPD[1] in the struggle for the allegiance of members and lower levels of the organization was its predominance in the party's official positions, including the press. Only four

---

1. In the months immediately after the Halle congress, before the left wing united with the KPD to form the VKPD, there were two Independent Social Democratic Parties, which, following contemporary usage, we shall call the Right USPD and the Left USPD.

of the twelve members of the party executive decided for the Twenty-One Conditions, and the Right USPD leaders were therefore able to hold onto the central offices and treasury. In the districts the same situation often obtained: in Berlin, where the vote had divided evenly, the whole apparatus with one exception among the numerous party secretaries stayed with the Right USPD; in Magdeburg, also an evenly divided district, the press and district leaders were all on the anti-Moscow side; and this happened in individual cities, such as Düsseldorf, as well. Even in the Halle district, the leaders of two of the eight subdistricts opted for the Right USPD. Among parliamentarians the trend was, if anything, stronger. Of the eighty-one members of the Reichstag delegation, only twenty-two left-wing dissidents were lost; the left's share was larger in the Prussian Diet (ten of the twenty-four) but still a minority, while in Braunschweig, Bavaria, Saxony, and Württemberg substantial majorities of the Diet deputies remained with the Right USPD. So far as the press was concerned, in Thuringia, whose delegates at the Congress had voted for the Twenty-One Conditions by twelve to four, seven of the ten party papers remained with the rump party; and in Bavaria, whose delegates had voted eleven to four with the left wing, three of the four papers went with the Right USPD. At the top, the balance of party opinion worked strongly in favor of the continued existence of the USPD.

The assets of the other side were those they had converted into victory at Halle, reinforced by the momentum of that victory and the legitimacy it had conferred. The warm popular sympathies for the Bolsheviks were still there, as was the enthusiasm of the militants over the conversion of their party into a party of action after the repeated frustrations of the past two years. The left too had its solid organizational strongholds, notably in Hamburg, the Halle district, and parts of Rhineland-Westphalia; more important, the nature of this side's appeal enabled them to assemble a following—notable for its activism if not always for its size—nearly everywhere, even in the face of a hostile leadership and press. The aggressively dissatisfied part of the German working class, with a sizable bloc of fellow travelers, was coalescing under their leadership, as they had hoped. It only remained to see how large this following was and whether the means could be found for sweeping along with it the broader masses of the German working class in a movement aimed at seizing power.

How members' loyalties divided is difficult to determine. The best figure for the number of Independent Socialists who chose the party of the Third International is probably that which can be derived from a private VKPD circular of January 15, 1921. The circular estimates VKPD membership at 449,700; if the 78,715 KPD members reported as of

October 1, 1920, are deducted, the result suggests an increment of about 370,000 former Independents.[2] For the USPD there is a somewhat problematic membership breakdown in a circular of April 6, 1921, which gives a total membership figure of 360,648 or, to use a corrected figure, 339,951.[3] Given that the party membership as of September 1921 was later reliably quoted at 300,659,[4] a figure on the order of 340,000 or perhaps somewhat less for the early months of the year is probably acceptable.

From these figures, a picture of what happened to the membership of the old USPD begins to emerge. The picture does not quite accord with the well-known three-way division suggested by Walter Rist (300,000 to each of the competing sides and a similar number into "indifference," that is, abandonment of socialist party membership altogether).[5] In the first place, early in 1921 the number of former Independents accounted for by the remaining USPD and the VKPD was probably about 700,000; this figure is close to 80 percent of the presplit membership if we accept the announced estimate of 893,923 members, and more than 80 percent if this optimistic estimate is reduced (as it probably should be) by some tens of thousands.[6] The number of dropouts grew as the year went on. The USPD declined to 300,659 on September 30, 1921, and 290,762 on (apparently) June 30, 1922.[7] Membership of the VKPD also dropped, falling precipitously in the second quarter of 1921, to the point where there can hardly have been 120,000 former Independents enrolled as dues-paying Communists in September.[8] By then, fully half of the former

2. Levi papers, P 99; KPD *Parteitag*, Nov. 1920, p. 5. Stoecker's estimate of 428,000 Left Independents just before the merger with the KPD was clearly optimistic, while Pieck's later estimate that the VKPD gained 300,000 former Independents presumably discounts membership losses in the spring of 1921. See VKPD *Vereinigungsparteitag*, Dec. 1920, p. 327; *Jahrbuch für Wirtschaft, Politik und Arbeiterbewegung 1922/23*, p. 643.

3. The circular (without its date) was printed in *Vorwärts*, June 13, 1922, more than a year later; the date was supplied by *Freiheit*, June 15, 1922. I have made two corrections. One substitutes verified figures for the five Saxon districts as of March 31 from USPD-Sachsen *Landesversammlung*, July 1921, pp. 17–18. The other is necessitated by the impossibly high estimate of 15,000 given for Eastern Westphalia, where the USPD had about 3,000 members before the split (according to Stoecker, VKPD *Vereinigungsparteitag*, Dec. 1920, p. 325); I have followed Wheeler's suggestion ("Internationals," p. 801) and reduced the figure by a factor of ten on the assumption that an extra zero was added in error.

4. USPD *Parteitag*, Jan. 1922, p. 130.

5. Rist, p. 88.

6. See ch. 11, n. 23. The previously mentioned VKPD circular of Jan. 15, 1921, gave a figure of 800,000 for the membership of the old USPD. This estimate is probably low, but the true figure may have been closer to this than to 900,000.

7. USPD *Parteitag*, Jan. 1922, p. 130; USPD-SPD *Parteitage*, Sept. 1922, p. 127. The latter source does not give the date of the membership count, which may refer to the close of the business year on March 31 or to some other date.

8. The dues-paying membership of the KPD (the "V" having been dropped in

Independents had disappeared from the rolls of the parties of the socialist left; but that was a consequence of events some time after the split
itself.

There is no hard evidence to tell us how many of the former Independents who turned their backs on both of the successor parties returned to the SPD. Comments from all sides suggest that it was a common phenomenon, but nothing is known of its magnitude; the fairly
stable membership figures of the SPD (1,180,208 in March 1920,
1,221,059 in March 1921[9]) could conceal as many as 100,000 recruits
from the USPD, but there is no way of knowing. Whatever the number,
it did not include any prominent figures.[10] On the distribution of the
USPD's former voting support, however—which does not necessarily
correlate with membership movements—much can be learned from the
elections to the Prussian Diet on February 20, 1921. Comparison of the
results of this election with voting in the same area (which comprised
more than half the Reich) in the Reichstag elections of June 1920 shows
that the Independents lost 1,993,000 votes, or just over two-thirds of
their former total, while the Communists gained 916,000 and the Majority Socialists 551,000; the remaining 526,000 votes were lost to the
socialist camp altogether.[11] Here, then, the SPD managed to sweep up
only about half the debris of the party realignments to its left. The decline in the total socialist vote was a sign of the times; many workers
apparently withdrew from political involvement in these months. Elections in Saxony in November, in the middle of the division of the USPD,
nearly cost the workers' parties their majority; in Bremen in January the
socialist majority was lost. None of the workers' parties could take comfort from this development.

Taking as a basis the VKPD membership table for January and the
USPD membership table for March, we can determine roughly where the
USPD was hardest hit by the split.[12] In Hamburg, the 42,000 members

---

August) was then 180,443; see n. 50 below. In a party with the rapid membership
turnover of the KPD, the total by September would have included tens of thousands of new members who had belonged to no party in 1920.

9. "Bericht des Parteivorstandes über das Geschäftsjahr 1920/21," p. 10, SPD
Parteitag, Sept. 1921.

10. Two well-known Independents, Heinrich Ströbel and Siegfried Nestriepke,
rejoined the SPD in 1920, but in both cases before the schism at Halle.

11. *Preussische Statistik,* 251/I, 76–77. These calculations omit East Prussia and
Schleswig-Holstein, since no vote was held there in June 1920.

12. Crude totals for the increases in VKPD membership can be derived by sub-
tracting the prefusion membership of the KPD as of Oct. 1, 1920, from the VKPD
membership of Jan. 1921; the USPD membership is taken from the circular of
April 6, 1921 (see nn. 2 and 3 above). Difficulties arise when the three sources do
not use the same district boundaries; in such cases other comparisons are used.

before the schism melted away to 1,400; in the Halle district, the figure dropped from 82,000 to 15,000; in the Lower Rhineland, from 86,000 to 25,000.[13] The VKPD in these districts claimed, respectively, 40,000, 67,000, and 55,000 members (in each case nearly all from the USPD), accounting for over a third of the VKPD membership at that time. The USPD was reduced to impotence again in Silesia, Mecklenburg, Hanover, and the Middle Rhineland. In South Germany, except for northern Bavaria, they were devastated; in Württemberg, the Communist gains were four times as big as the remaining USPD, in Baden twice as big. The division was more nearly equal in Bavaria, Western Westphalia, Pomerania, East Prussia, Magdeburg-Anhalt, and, most important, Berlin-Brandenburg. In Thuringia, the remaining Independents had the edge by 35,911 to 23,150; in Frankfurt on Main they had a similar margin; and they carried the day convincingly in the traditional strongholds of Bremen and Braunschweig and all of Saxony.

The elections of February 1921 confirm this picture for Prussia. The rump USPD's vote exceeded the VKPD's in nine of the twenty-three electoral districts: the four making up Berlin and Brandenburg (and together supplying 41 percent of the total USPD vote in these elections), the adjacent electoral districts of Magdeburg and Pomerania, the Prussian territories in Thuringia (Erfurt), and two rural districts lying within the spheres of influence of Bremen and Braunschweig. The USPD's following exceeded that of both other working-class parties only in the small Erfurt district. The Communists had the largest vote only in the Halle district and Düsseldorf-East (the heart of the Lower Rhineland), but their level of support was more uniform, making them the better balanced of the two left-wing parties.

The USPD newspapers, some sixty in number at the time of the Halle congress,[14] did not, as has already been indicated, divide along the lines of the old party's membership or voting support. Only about twenty-one papers, or approximately a third, passed into the hands of the Left Independents; for various reasons, mainly financial losses, several of these were closed down, and only about fourteen were still publishing for the VKPD in January.[15] The USPD's losses included three of the five papers

13. The preschism memberships are from Stoecker, VKPD *Vereinigungsparteitag*, Dec. 1920, p. 323; *Die Internationale* (Left USPD), Oct. 27 and 29, 1920. the USPD spoke a year later of having had 50 papers before the split (USPD *Parteitag*, Jan. 1922, p. 130). More than 56 party newspapers, however, can be identified just before the schism; a final total is probably impossible to establish because of the prevalence of obscure and ephemeral local editions of larger papers (*Kopfblätter*).

14. The largest recorded estimate is 56, in the VKPD circular of Jan. 15, 1921;
15. The total of 21 results from the collation of three lists: *Freiheit*, Oct. 27, 1920 (m); VKPD *Vereinigungsparteitag*, Dec. 1920, p. 327; and the VKPD cir-

in the Lower Rhineland, three of the four in the Halle district, two important papers in Thuringia (Jena and Gotha), and the entire party press in Württemberg and the districts mentioned above as especially weak (Silesia, Mecklenburg, Hanover, and the Middle Rhineland).[16] The USPD also had to shut down papers that had lost their economic base and reduce others to the status of local editions of stronger papers; nevertheless, it did better than the Left Independents, carrying on at least thirty-two of the old newspapers and founding new ones (even in such hopeless places for its cause as Gotha, Hamburg, and Solingen) until it had forty-eight at the end of 1921.[17] In this most visible expression of organizational solidity the USPD had apparently survived the crisis remarkably well.

Within a year of the split, in fact, the strenuous efforts of USPD leaders had rebuilt a party that, in organization and other externals, was a simulacrum of the old one. By January 1922 the party organization was functioning in all districts (thirty-two as then defined) and claimed a credible membership of 300,659. With a full array of publications, adult education courses, and other specialized offerings, the USPD still strove to be the complete Social Democratic party, though a chronic shortage of funds imposed limitations.[18] It retained its democratic innovations, especially those relating to party congresses—proportional representation of districts, direct election of delegates, denial of a vote to those who attended ex officio—and prided itself on its internal democracy in contrast to the leadership-dominated parties on either side of it. The parliamentary strength of the party remained formidable, both in the Reichstag and wherever elections had not been held since the schism. The USPD seemed the same, only somewhat smaller.

Yet everything was subtly different. The renewed strength of the party's internal administration, which was, if anything, more effective

---

cular of Jan. 15, 1921. The last-named lists 13 papers as of January but omits the Jena *Neue Zeitung,* which was certainly still publishing.

16. The full list of cities where the party paper is known to have been lost is: Augsburg, Breslau, Cassel, Cologne, Danzig, Eisleben, Essen, Gleiwitz, Gotha, Halle, Hamburg, Hanover, Jena, Karlsruhe, Merseburg, Remscheid, Rostock, Saarbrücken, Solingen, Stuttgart, and Suhl.

17. The VKPD circular of Jan. 15 names 34 USPD newspapers then publishing (one of which [Wilhelmshaven] had in fact succumbed by that time, while another [Cassel] may have been a new foundation rather than a legacy from the old party) and notes (without naming them) that there were many new *Kopfblätter.* The figure of 48 was given in USPD *Parteitag,* Jan. 1922, p. 131.

18. Among the early signs of strained finances were the conversion of the weekly supplement to the party press, *Freie Welt,* into a drab, pictureless page in newspaper format (January 1921) and the end of the semimonthly publication aimed at rural areas, *Der Landbote* (September 1921).

than before, and the exaggerated weight of the parliamentary delegations meant a degree of leadership power that the USPD had hardly known before, certainly not since the party executive's policies during the revolution isolated it from a large part of the membership. Finances played a role here; few of the party districts were able to support themselves fully on the level to which the party aspired, so that the central treasury, drawing on the resources of the remaining strong districts, had more weight than before. More importantly, the most fractious districts of the old party were stripped away by the split, and the remainder tended to huddle together and accept a common leadership, controlling their internal divisions (which had not disappeared) and managing to live a fairly sedate internal life. Under such circumstances, powers tended to devolve on full-time leaders; this tendency had been evident in the old SPD as well as in the current Majority Socialist party, and the USPD experienced the same thing in 1921 and 1922.

Nor, despite carefully cultivated appearances, was the USPD still a fully national party. In the spring of 1921, Saxony, with nearly 80,000 members, made up just under a quarter of the party's total strength; Saxony, Berlin, and Thuringia accounted for almost half; and the addition of the two large Rhenish-Westphalian districts brought the accounting up to 60 percent.[19] Such concentration had been unknown in the USPD since the end of the war. Apart from the areas mentioned, only Bavaria, Halle, Frankfurt on Main, Bremen, Braunschweig, and Pomerania had as many as 10,000 members. In most of the rest of the country, the party was negligible; in such great cities as Hamburg and Stuttgart it was reduced to a faithful few. The USPD had shrunk back into its early centers of strength and was henceforth dominated by them.

Nor was it likely that further growth would change the party's condition, whatever party optimists might say.[20] The stabilization of the truncated, over-concentrated USPD had been a defensive action; the laborious recreation of a national apparatus deceived no one outside the party. The two recognized forms of positive action by working-class parties— parliamentary politics and factory activism—found their principal expression in other parties. The USPD, however excellent its Marxism, was seen by all too many as representing abstentionism without prospects, and a powerful party could no longer be built on this basis. It could perhaps serve as a bridge for the tendencies in the other two

19. For the source of the figures see n. 3 above.
20. For instance, the chairman of the Berlin organization, Richard Krille, USPD *Parteitag,* Jan. 1922, pp. 109–10.

parties that it saw as complementary rather than mutually exclusive. But it had to operate in fields of force set up by others; it was no longer a national force in itself.

Image and Purposes of the Party

In its reduced circumstances, the party had more need than ever of a political position to identify itself with in the minds of the workers; survival depended on its establishing a clear profile that would set it off from both Communists and Majority Socialists and underline the need for its continued existence. For a time it seemed that the USPD might succeed in finding and holding a common line. With most of its intractable left wing stripped away, and the remainder of the party conscious of the need for cohesion, the USPD throughout 1921 displayed a formal unity of purpose that had few if any parallels in the party's past. Only in the spring of 1922 did it become evident that this outward unity masked serious internal strains.

The basis for the common front of 1921 was a somewhat unexpected factional alignment; power resided, not in the right wing, as might have been anticipated, but in a broad middle coalition. Incorporating many from the middle ranks of the old party and some moderates, this coalition tended to blunt the initiatives of the remaining wings while holding the party as close as it could to the center of gravity established in party tradition—the radicalized center of gravity of 1920. This bloc, which encompassed views ranging from Robert Dissmann's on the left to Wilhelm Dittmann's on the right, was held together by attachment to the party and its past in a defensive reaction to the party's current difficult position. Artur Crispien, still party chairman and located somewhere near the center of this bloc, was perhaps its truest representative, with his rhetorical belligerence, practical caution, and overriding commitment to the integrity of the party as the standard-bearer of an ill-defined but deeply felt socialist radicalism.

The first work of this bloc (the wings acquiesced in its leadership for the time being) may be seen in the results of the rump party congress in Halle after the split. The decision made here, a natural one in the circumstances, was not to permit the split to make any difference to the party's ideological posture. The party clung to its identifying characteristics of the year preceding the split, professing to be the same party that had made such remarkable strides during that year but without the crypto-Communists who had been trying to divert the party from its proper course. The campaign against the Twenty-One Conditions had been

fought as a defense of the party status quo, and for the time being not even the right wing was inclined to risk redirecting the party's efforts— particularly with the adherents of the Comintern watching for evidence that the centrists in the USPD had never been more than halfhearted revolutionaries and had been held to an energetic course only by the pressure of the old left wing.[21] In any case, the remaining members and leaders might not tolerate any tampering with established policies. Consequently, in another of the USPD's traditional displays of united purpose, the rump party congress at Halle adopted a manifesto reaffirming the old platforms and shibboleths: the Leipzig Action Program of December 1919, the class struggle, abhorrence of any coalition with the bourgeoisie, the dictatorship of the proletariat, and the revolutionary spirit of the party.[22] Only one familiar element was missing; although factory councils still had a prominent place in the manifesto, the "council system" was gone and was never to play an important part again in the USPD's thinking, for its active supporters in the party had largely been stripped away by the split.

For most of the middle bloc of the USPD, the commitments undertaken at the rump Halle congress were sincere. Its members had found, and believed the party had found, a secure doctrinal footing in a version of the "pure opposition" of prewar orthodoxy combined with the revolutionary vision that had taken hold after the war. This doctrine defined the USPD in contrast to both the Majority Socialists, who had fallen into the error of supposing that socialism could be materially advanced in alliance with the bourgeoisie, and the Communists, who were attempting to bring on revolution by sheer determination without a rational understanding of social processes.[23] The USPD was thus the only party of scientific socialism, of the class struggle conducted in a way to bring maximum benefits to the workers; this in itself sufficed to justify the party's continued existence.

Such an ideological orientation, whatever its merits in the abstract— and it was as an abstract, ideological conception that it united the disparate elements of the middle bloc—still needed to offer some vision of

---

21. See, for example, Stoecker's prediction at Halle that the right wing would quickly find its home in the SPD; USPD *Parteitag*, Oct. 1920, p. 140.

22. Text in *Freiheit*, Oct. 18, 1920 (e).

23. Most clearly expressed by a leader of the left wing, Ledebour, in USPD *Parteitag*, Jan. 1922, pp. 90–91. See also the manifesto of the congress, *ibid.*, pp. 3–7, esp. p. 5; and the short, quasi-official formulation by Dittmann in an article written early in September 1921 (Maximilian Müller-Jabusch, ed., *Politischer Almanach auf das Jahr 1922* [Berlin, n.d.], p. 113): "die auf dem Boden des wissenschaftlichen Marxismus stehende proletarische Massenpartei Deutschlands, die sowohl den Nurreformismus wie den Putschismus verwirft."

socialist action. In the USPD's reduced circumstances, this need could no longer be fulfilled by such simple assumptions as that the party's revolutionary moment would come or that the Independents could some day coerce the Majority Socialists into joining them in a purely socialist government. To be sure of one's socialist correctness was satisfying but not sufficient for many Independents, not when five-sixths of the organized socialists were in other parties. The USPD was in the middle, and if this position was not to become a threat to the party's cohesion it must be used as an opportunity. The prospects of possible action were therefore attached to the potential of a united front.

Though the term 'united front' is historically associated with the Communist Party, in 1921 and 1922 the USPD was par excellence the party of united-front tactics. The explicit goal of party policy from the moment of the split was to find programs that would override ideological differences and bring the three parties together in a struggle for the essential requirements of the German proletariat.[24] In the classic manner of united-front tactics, the proposed programs had to be rooted in the immediate needs of the working class in order to appeal so strongly to the members of all proletarian parties that their leaders would feel obliged to overlook their mutual suspicions and collaborate in throwing the united weight of the labor movement into the struggle. Such actions might create broader unity in the proletarian movement, with errant brothers to the right being recalled to the class struggle, those on the left to reality. At very least, they should bring real political or economic gains for the workers, and in a way consistent with the furtherance of the class struggle.

The first of these programs put forward by the Independents as a prospective rallying point for the members of all three parties centered on socialization, that is, nationalization of the nation's mines in accordance with the minority report of the official socialization commission the previous summer. Hilferding had been a coauthor of the report, and his influence launched the issue as the USPD's first try at assembling a united front.[25] Hopes of achieving a measure of socialization through government action, even under the existing political order, had never entirely died on the right wing of the party, and when, during the summer of 1920, the reactivated trade unions and the SPD (in opposition again since the Reichstag elections) began to show interest in the issue, prospects for action were suddenly improved. Barely taking time to draw

24. The point appears already in the manifesto of the rump congress at Halle; *Freiheit*, Oct. 18, 1920 (e).

25. On Hilferding's conception of socialization and his work in the socialization commission, see Gottschalch, pp. 170–79.

breath after the split, the USPD launched a full-scale campaign for socialization.[26]

Beyond the limits of the USPD, the campaign achieved success neither in legislation nor in encouraging a broad proletarian front. Legislative success depended on mobilizing the working class to the point that either a socialist majority was elected or part of the existing nonsocialist majority intimidated—a return to the thinking behind the idea of a purely socialist government. But socialization and the complex of lesser economic issues could not arouse this kind of fervor, or, if they could, the small USPD was no longer able to employ them effectively without help. The SPD remained skeptical; its interest in socialization was mostly theoretical, while the practical possibilities of parliamentary politics occupied its attention. The VKPD was contemptuous of attempts to squeeze socialism out of the existing capitalist order, much as the left wing of the old USPD had been.[27]

But within the USPD, the campaign was a success, both in expressing a characteristic method and in defining a suitable field of activity for the party. The method, a return to the prewar orthodoxy of the left Center but with radicalized rhetoric, was to combine pursuit of real political and economic goals with encouragement of mass action on their behalf as the only way to breach the capitalist wall. As it had before 1914, this tactic synthesized the divergent activist and practical tendencies of the party. And the notion underlying the socialization campaign—that the USPD, by concentrating on the real, practical needs of the working class, could play a critical role in restoring class unity on the basis of class struggle—was a rallying point for the USPD, if not for the class as a whole. All Independents shared this vision, which became the central point of their agitation in their remaining two years as a significant party.

Despite the success of such official, unifying policies, real differences still remained within the party, expressed at first as tendencies but later in ominous factionalism. The USPD still had its wings, and if neither could dominate the party at this point they threatened to provoke further debilitating conflicts.

That the USPD would continue to have a left wing had been predictable since the Comintern's harsh policies divided the radicals of the old

26. Socialization figured prominently in the manifesto of the rump congress and occupied much editorial space in *Freiheit* over the following months. That this approach was accepted even in the party's more radical quarters is shown by the Halle *Volkszeitung* (USPD successor to the lost *Volksblatt*), for instance in the editorial of Jan. 3, 1921.

27. See *Freiheit*'s complaints in the issues of Oct. 27, 1920 (e), Oct. 31, 1920, Nov. 6, 1920 (m), and Nov. 17, 1920 (m).

party. Since many radicals adhered to the middle bloc, the remaining left wing in the shrunken USPD was not large, but it was active, and it was headed by two members of the party executive, Georg Ledebour, serving as party chairman again,[28] and Kurt Rosenfeld. This wing was distinguished by a genuine conviction that the revolution was still in progress and by a strong sympathy for the Communists, though not for the current Moscow-dominated VKPD leadership. For these men, the USPD was still a revolutionary party in a very direct and urgent way, and the truncated USPD's inability to carry the revolutionary movement alone only made them more determined to extend the party's influence.

This small left wing became the guardian of the party's orthodoxy, not least because it generally had the emotional support of much of the party's less single-mindedly revolutionary middle bloc if the party's revolutionary heritage was in question. Ledebour still saw the USPD—a unique tower of true socialism between the heresies of opportunism and adventurism—as having a grand historical mission.[29] In practice, the left wing tended to lean more in the direction of the Communists, as fellow proletarian activists, than the Majority Socialists. Kurt Rosenfeld, for instance, had been one of the leaders of a last-minute attempt to find a compromise that would allow a united USPD to enter the Communist International; and after Halle he wanted the party's international policy still to concentrate on achieving an alliance with Moscow.[30] Ledebour, through all the VKPD's troubles of 1921 and 1922, continued to think of the Communists as revolutionary comrades from 1918 who had been temporarily led astray.[31] In a party whose movement to the left had been abruptly halted, this group still pulled to the left; and this inclination set them apart.

If the party had stopped moving to the left, it did not immediately, after adjusting to the requirements of its new position, show signs of moving to the right. Those who, like Karl Kautsky, had expected the remainder of the USPD quickly to adopt a centrist position were disappointed.[32] Kautsky, in fact, although facing less hostility from fellow Independents than before the split, was still isolated in the party, and probably remained in it only because he sensed an opportunity to urge

28. The split removed the two issues that had divided Ledebour from the left wing of the party before Halle (unconditional affiliation to the Third International, and the council system as an exclusive political method) and he at once found his natural position in the remaining left wing.

29. USPD *Parteitag*, Jan. 1922, pp. 90–91.

30. *Freiheit*, Oct. 6, 1920 (e), and Nov. 2, 1920 (m).

31. USPD-SPD *Parteitage*, Sept. 1922, p. 154.

32. Kautsky, *Mein Verhältnis*, pp. 14–16.

it toward reunification with the SPD.[33] But on this point he received almost no open support. Whatever the right wing of the USPD may have thought about reunification, and there is little evidence on the point, this was not its battle cry. Rather, Hilferding, Breitscheid, and like-minded colleagues accepted the settlement arrived at by the rump party for the sake of unity, welcomed the renewed emphasis on practical problems, and set out to increase gradually the party's involvement in the great issues of the day.[34]

If the strength of the left wing was its energy and its appeal to the party's revolutionary tradition, the right wing could rely on equal energy, a contrasting but effective appeal for involvement in immediate issues, and a strong base in the party apparatus. The USPD's premier newspapers, *Freiheit* and the *Leipziger Volkszeitung,* and its theoretical journal, *Der Sozialist,* all supported the right wing; so did the party organization in Leipzig (and thus in Saxony as a whole), Braunschweig, and a few other significant cities. More important, there were many others in party positions and in the parliamentary delegations who, if they did not identify themselves with the right wing, were open to its thinking on particular matters. The right wing provided most of the innovative thinking in the party after Halle, in particular Hilferding, in the area of fiscal and economic issues (the focus of German domestic politics in this period), and Breitscheid, in the field of foreign policy.[35] Hilferding's success in getting the party to adopt socialization as its first united-front slogan was a case in point; at a critical moment for the party, he and his associates were ready with a policy when others were still in a state of shock. Ten months earlier, when Hilferding had advanced the idea of a sliding wage scale, a cause that could have been as popular as socialization, the left wing had been strong enough to block it and keep the party's eyes fixed on revolution.[36] This was no longer the case, or not until 1922, when fears arose that Hilferding's policies might jeopardize the very existence of the party; until then, the strong-minded and inventive part of the right wing could provide the specific content for the framework generally agreed on

33. *Ibid.,* p. 15; Kautsky, "Die Einigung," *Der Sozialist,* Sept. 3, 1921, pp. 761–72.

34. On Breitscheid's views after Halle, see Peter Pistorius, "Rudolf Breitscheid 1874–1944: Ein biographischer Beitrag zur deutschen Parteiengeschichte" (Ph.D. dissertation, University of Cologne, 1968), p. 191. Though Breitscheid did not urge reunification, he was prepared at least to mention the possibility; see *Der Sozialist,* Feb. 26, 1921, p. 170.

35. On Breitscheid's foreign policy views during 1921 and 1922, see Pistorius, pp. 242–50.

36. See ch. 10, n. 61.

for party action and thereby, very gradually, prepare the party for a normal political role.

In the controversies accompanying the evolution of factions in the rump USPD, the International, oddly enough, played little part. With the road to a comprehensive revolutionary International blocked, the sense of urgency declined. At the same time, for those whose interest in the International was undiminished, the USPD's success in achieving an international affiliation that accurately reflected its own policies removed a possible source of conflict within the party. This was the International Working Union of Socialist Parties—probably best known by the sarcastic Communist name, the 2½ International.

The Vienna Union (as it was known in English-speaking countries) was the outgrowth of the talks the USPD had held intermittently, since the fall of 1919, with fellow refugees from the Second International. Differences of approach and practical problems delayed the summoning of a conference for over four months after the Halle congress;[37] when the delegates assembled, in Vienna at the end of February 1921, the organization they established was a reasonably coherent and, from the standpoint of the USPD, highly satisfactory association. It avoided calling itself an International; in the words of its Statutes, the Vienna Union was "not an International, comprehending the entire revolutionary proletariat, but a means to the creation of such [an International]."[38] Its chosen task was to "unify the activity of the affiliated parties, inaugurate joint actions, and encourage the formation of an International which will include the entire revolutionary proletariat."[39] With a membership that included the regular socialist parties of France, Switzerland, and Austria, minority parties from Britain (the Independent Labour Party) and Germany, and most of the small socialist parties of the East European countries, the Vienna Union could hope to play a role of some importance in the international working-class movement.[40]

The Vienna Union set out to mediate the international differences within the proletariat in a way that was entirely satisfactory to the bulk of opinion in the USPD. If anything, the Vienna Union's version of attaining unity through action was more purist than the USPD's, in that

37. On the background, see André Donneur, "Histoire de l'Union des Partis socialistes pour l'action internationale (1920–1923)" (Ph.D. dissertation, University of Geneva, 1967), pp. 47–83; and Wheeler, "Internationals," pp. 759–73.

38. *Protokoll der Internationalen Sozialistischen Konferenz in Wien vom 22. bis 27. Februar 1921* (Vienna, 1921), p. 113.

39. *Ibid.*

40. For full membership lists of the Vienna Union see *Nachrichten der Internationalen Arbeitsgemeinschaft Sozialistischer Parteien* (hereafter cited as *Nachrichten*), Sept. 1921, p. 16, and July 1922, p. 4.

the Union steadfastly refused to collaborate with either the Second or the Third International alone, even temporarily; when one or the other would not agree to a broad front, the Union preferred to do nothing and await a better opportunity. Inasmuch as the Communists remained unapproachable throughout 1921, the Union was at first condemned to solitary action or at best parallel action; in April 1921 it met in Amsterdam simultaneously, but not jointly, with the leaders of the Second International and the International Federation of Trade Unions and participated at arm's length in the formulation of an international socialist program for reparations.[41] Far more than the USPD, the Vienna Union symbolized the desire for broad proletarian unity through common action; but the rigidity of its insistence on *total* unity made its agitation, no matter how vigorous, ultimately sterile. Ledebour, the leading Independent representative in the executive of the Vienna Union, might strongly support such a policy, and the mass of party members might emotionally approve it, but it was unlikely to assist the USPD with present problems of German politics.

The USPD, then, managed to find its footing again in 1921 with a strong enough sense of purpose to make continuation of the party possible. It had found, at least temporarily, a position similar to that it had occupied a year earlier, though without the self-confidence that had gone with a sense of limitless growth and without the powerful leftward tendency imposed by a vital left wing. Determined, but necessarily also circumspect, the reduced USPD established itself at a point on the socialist spectrum, slightly to the right of where it had been before, that seemed to promise party unity and some prospect of action. Whether political circumstances would permit the party a stable, effective life along the lines suggested by this first settlement remained to be seen.

Vicissitudes of the VKPD

As indicated above, the USPD's relations with other working-class parties were central to its experience after the schism, a fact the party itself recognized in its adoption of united-front tactics. On the one side, the problem was old and well understood; the SPD was a known quantity, and the USPD's relations with it, though altered in significant respects by the changed balance between the parties, were still largely defined by a history of some years. On the other flank, however, the rump USPD faced a new party whose qualities could at first only be surmised but with whom the Independents must compete for the allegiance of the USPD's old constituency. The process of self-definition of the

41. An extended account of these meetings, *ibid.*, April 1921, pp. 1–8; and in Donneur, pp. 141–43.

new United Communist Party therefore had great impact on the role of the rump USPD. Fortunately for the Independents, for nearly a year this process took a course yielding maximum benefits to the party interests of the USPD.

The amalgamation of the Left USPD with the old KPD did not go smoothly. Part of the trouble arose from the formation of a new, combined leadership group in which the former Independents had the greater numbers but the old Communists tended to exercise ascendency on the basis of their priority as Communists and members of the Third International.[42] Still more important was the spirit in which the former Independents, both leaders and, particularly, followers, came to the new party. The USPD, in one of its aspects, had been the party of aggressively dissatisfied factory workers and miners; this sector of the party moved to the VKPD with a sense of liberation. They wanted action, and they expected to have it in the new party. Such a frame of mind was very much to the liking of some of the old KPD leaders and, especially, the representatives of the Comintern; both groups saw the conversion of the German Communist movement into a mass organization as presenting an opportunity for immediate mass action. Those VKPD leaders— headed by Paul Levi, whose relations with the Comintern had been deteriorating since the summer[43]—who rejected this perspective as one-sided and dangerous could not stem the tide. And so began the process that led to the March Action of 1921 and a fiasco for the Communist cause in Germany.

During the period of preparation for its "revolutionary offensive" the VKPD became very difficult for other parties to work with.[44] This was in any case a time of bitterness between it and the USPD, but relations were worsened by the Communist determination to push every action to

42. In the new VKPD leadership (the outcome of detailed negotiations), the former Independents had a slight numerical edge in the central committee, with eight of the fourteen seats; in the body where the district organizations were represented they held at least twenty-three of thirty-nine seats. See the lists in VKPD *Vereinigungsparteitag,* Dec. 1920, pp. 270–71.

43. On the crisis in the old KPD leadership, see KPD *Parteitag,* Nov. 1920, pp. 25–29; Nicolaevsky, pp. 18–21; Richard Lowenthal, "The Bolshevisation of the Spartacus League," in *St. Antony's Papers Number 9: International Communism,* ed. David Footman (London, 1960), pp. 43–50; with a somewhat different perspective, Marie-Luise Goldbach, *Karl Radek und die deutsch-sowjetischen Beziehungen 1918–1923* (Bonn–Bad Godesberg, 1973), pp. 70–84. See Lowenthal's classic account also for what follows, together with Werner Angress' more detailed *Stillborn Revolution: The Communist Bid for Power in Germany, 1921–1923* (Princeton, 1963).

44. On the emergence of the doctrine of the "revolutionary offensive," see esp. Lowenthal, pp. 46–47.

its limits, in violation of normal socialist tactical considerations. The Communists' cell-building activities in the trade unions were a further aggravating factor.[45] The Levi wing's simultaneous attempt to broaden the movement's revolutionary base with united-front tactics did not alter the effect of the VKPD's work. When Levi's famous Open Letter of January 8 was published, proposing joint action with other labor and socialist organizations, the USPD party executive, with little resistance from the left wing, flatly rejected the offer as dishonest.[46]

The VKPD's first tentative ideas of a united front were a casualty of intraparty conflict at the end of February, when Levi fell from office. Levi's fall was not unexpected; what turned the affair into a crisis was the simultaneous resignation of Clara Zetkin and four of the eight former Independents in the central committee—Däumig (the other cochairman of the party), Brass, Hoffmann, and Curt Geyer.[47] The shock of this episode left the reconstituted central committee searching for a policy to restore members' faith in the leadership.[48] They were in the right frame of mind to be led by Comintern emissary Bela Kun into the irresponsible adventure known as the March Action.

The essence of the March Action, as it was later described by an admirer, was that "the party went into battle without concerning itself over who would follow it."[49] It was a classic attempt to create mass action by sheer act of will. Outside the area where the action started —the Halle region, and especially the Mansfeld mining district, where the confrontation of workers and Prussian police had genuine passion behind it—few, even among its members, followed the party into battle. Rather than break off the contrived operation, the leadership increased the pressure on members and used all the means it could think of, including sabotage and faked bomb attacks on Communist property, to bring

45. See Rettig, pp. 57–58 and 68–78.

46. *Rote Fahne,* Jan. 8, 1921; *Freiheit,* Jan. 13, 1921. The reply in *Freiheit* is accompanied by a note that only a short discussion was needed for the executive to agree on it. Some local organizations of the USPD responded favorably to the Open Letter at first, but they soon fell into line.

47. Geyer, who was in Moscow at the time, resigned only when he returned to Germany, but his action was in solidarity with the others and over the same issues.

48. In the new leadership, Stoecker was elevated to the chairmanship (with Heinrich Brandler), but only until the party congress in August, when he was not re-elected to the central committee despite his loyalty. Of three former Independents appointed in February to fill vacancies, two (Max Sievers and Paul Wegmann) followed the Levi group into opposition later in the year.

49. Arkadi Maslow, *Die Internationale* (KPD), June 1, 1921, p. 254. The fullest account of the March Action and its background is Angress, *Stillborn Revolution,* chs. 4 and 5. See also Levi's classic polemic, *Unser Weg: Wider den Putschismus* (Berlin, 1921); Lowenthal, pp. 57–64; and Willy Brandt and Richard Löwenthal, *Ernst Reuter: Ein Leben für die Freiheit* (Munich, 1957), pp. 151–60.

other workers out on strike. The results were still meager, but a bloody failure was turned into a shameful fiasco.

The central committee refused to admit error, even after the heat of the action was over and the mistakes were plain for all to see. The leadership clung to the theory of the revolutionary offensive, even as the party melted away beneath its feet (membership declined from 450,000 members early in the year to 180,443 in the summer).[50] Levi, in despair, campaigned publicly against the policies of the central committee; but the latter, after rallying sufficient support from the inner cadres of the party, answered his charges by expelling him and such outspoken associates as Curt Geyer. Levi's support among prominent Communists, some of them, including Brass, still in the party, grew to formidable proportions; at its peak, Levi's breakaway faction, the Communist Alliance (KAG), comprised fifteen of the twenty-six Communists in the Reichstag.[51] The central committee remained adamant, putting up a stiff front even against the Comintern, which, after Lenin's intervention in the late spring, abandoned the doctrine of the unilateral offensive and turned to united-front tactics; even after the Third World Congress of the Comintern in July made the change of front obligatory, the German party, at its congress in August, showed its recalcitrance while paying lip service to the new policies. Not until October did Moscow's unremitting pressure begin to show results in the German party's attitude; and by then the KPD was a much smaller, more narrowly based party than it had been at the beginning of the year.

In this process the KPD (as it was known again after August) ceased to be a mass party as that term had previously been understood. This change was only partly the result of the drastic decline in regular membership; defectors tended not to go to another party, such as the USPD, but to stand aside, still accessible to the influence of the KPD even if not belonging to it.[52] The most significant change was rather that the

50. Angress, *Stillborn Revolution*, p. 217n. An even smaller figure (157,168) can be found in Pieck, II, 262. The official figure given in the summer of 1921 was 359,613; but the smaller totals are based on actual dues-paying membership, which is the only acceptable standard.

51. The fifteen were Berthelé, Brass, Däumig, Düwell, Eichhorn, Fries, Curt Geyer, Friedrich Geyer, Hoffmann, Levi, Malzahn, Plettner, Reich, Teuber, and Wackwitz (all but Levi being from the Left USPD after Halle). For their later fate see n. 105 below.

52. The USPD, whose membership was probably declining slowly during 1921, cannot have taken in more than a small fraction of the Communist defectors; indeed, local parties sometimes resisted readmission of former comrades who had spent time in the VKPD (*Mitteilungsblatt des Bezirksverbandes Berlin-Brandenburg der Unabhängigen Sozialdemokratischen Partei Deutschlands* [hereafter cited as *Mitteilungsblatt*], July 8, 1921). The few available figures indicate that only

KPD had become a cadre party, responsive not to the membership at large but only to the inner circles—and, of course, the International. In the course of the crisis, these inner circles had been purged of the great majority of those who still held to a radicalized Social Democratic vision or were otherwise resistant to the idea of a dictatorial, centralized party and International; specifically, the party had cast off most of the upper leaders inherited from the Left USPD. What remained was a younger, more pliable group of leaders; men of equal devotion to revolutionary socialism but more receptive to direction; in many cases men whose active political careers dated from the war and the revolution, who did not need to discard old centrist habits because they had never had them.[53] The party that emerged was a far more wieldy instrument in the hands of its leaders, ultimately in the hands of the Comintern; but it was becoming the peculiar, slightly alien, encapsulated KPD of the later years of the Weimar Republic.

The KPD became a more formidable machine at the same time that it lost its residual appeal for Social Democrats; but during the more hectic stages of the change in 1921 the advantage was all with the Independents. After March 1921 the USPD was for some months without a serious rival to the left. This gap materially aided the rump party's consolidation, which dates especially from these months;[54] at the same time, it temporarily weakened the whole revolutionary cause in Germany and hence the position of the USPD's left wing, which was deprived of an outside reference point to put against the right's attention to daily politics. In this way it made possible the course of action the party followed during the middle of 1921.

Relations with the SPD: Rapprochement and Rebuff

In the middle of 1921, with the Communists sunk in sectarian, "ultra-left" policies and a damaging internal crisis, the USPD found itself more susceptible to the attraction of the one remaining massive proletarian party, the SPD. While specific events and opportunities precipitated the rapprochement of these months, the USPD's actions reflected its strong

small numbers were involved; in Düsseldorf only 243 by November, for instance (*Volkszeitung* [Halle], Nov. 28, 1921).

53. Hermann Weber, *Die Wandlung des deutschen Kommunismus,* 2 vols. (Frankfurt on Main, 1969), II, 29–31, discusses the length of service of the leading Communist officials of the mid-1920's, showing that while half of them had formerly been Independents hardly any had held responsible positions in the SPD before the war; half had not even been SPD members before 1914. The median age of Weber's sample was under 35 in 1927; *ibid.,* II, 26. Several further purges had had their effect before 1927, but the process was under way in 1921.

54. According to Dittmann in Müller-Jabusch (1922), p. 113.

desire, inherent in the search for a united front, to bring the proletariat together again as an effective force in national politics. In the summer of 1921 the problem of a united front resolved itself into the question of relations with the Majority Socialist party; and it seemed for a time that the party was close to solving this question.

The rapprochement between the two parties was parliamentary in origin and began in May, at the time of the international crisis over Allied reparations demands. The timing was favorable; the USPD was just starting to recover its equilibrium, aided by the troubles of the Communist Party, and, with Independents able to agree readily among themselves on the issue, the party had unusual freedom of movement.[55] Foreign affairs was the one area in which the policies of the party leadership had never wavered from the day of the party's foundation; once again, as in June 1919 and February 1920, they used their "revolutionary pacifism" to try to prevent a pointless but dangerous resistance to Allied demands. The international crisis was accompanied by a government crisis that eventually resulted in the replacement of the all-bourgeois Fehrenbach cabinet by a bourgeois-socialist Weimar coalition headed by a leader of the Center Party's left wing, Josef Wirth. The Wirth government, for all its faults, was probably the most liberal government of the Weimar period; its advent facilitated a change in the USPD's attitude toward the Weimar state that was of the greatest importance for the remainder of the party's history.

USPD leaders wanted to see the crisis resolved without hostilities or economic catastrophe, such as would have been brought on by an Allied occupation of the Ruhr. As at the time of Versailles, they formulated the issue as a simple choice—accept or refuse—and favored acceptance of the Allied ultimatum.[56] But the more important question raised by this crisis, and only partially answered at the time, was the extent to which the party was prepared to participate in an honest attempt at what was becoming known as "fulfilment"—a genuine effort to meet Germany's obligations under the treaty—and thus become, however informally, a part of the government's regular support in the Reichstag.

In the course of the crisis came the customary inquiry from the Majority Socialists about the Independents' readiness to join a new cabinet and the customary USPD refusal. This time, however, the refusal had a different tone, being phrased as a counterproposal of an all-socialist

55. There are signs of preliminary disagreement about the crisis in the brief, unrevealing minutes of the USPD Reichstag delegation, April 20–23, 1921; the differences did not, however, disturb the outward unity of approach the party showed during the crisis.
56. *Freiheit,* May 10, 1921 (m).

government; the suggestion, adopted by unanimous vote of the Independent delegation, was moreover phrased so as to indicate serious intent.[57] Three days later the party executive reinforced the impression of serious willingness to contribute to positive politics with the publication of a ten-point program that consisted principally of demands that could actually have been implemented by a moderate socialist government.[58] And on June 4 they took the important step of voting their confidence in the new government.[59]

The decisions of May and June established a momentum for the party, though not an irreversible momentum, as time was to show. Wirth's minority government required the support of either the Independents or Stresemann's People's Party to pass its measures. The USPD repeatedly supported Wirth's attempts to establish an open, conciliatory foreign policy; but it found in time that its appreciation of the course Wirth was pursuing had further implications. On other measures, too, the USPD's vote could be vital to the passage of government bills, and hence to the survival of the government. Breitscheid, whose influence in the Reichstag delegation was growing, identified the problem from the start: "Again and again we will face the question whether we should prefer a cabinet of the right to the present cabinet."[60] He went on to suggest that there might be an occasion when they would; but once the Wirth cabinet had confirmed its sincerity and courage, contributing to its overthrow, without exceptional provocation, would not be easy.

This remarkable progress toward direct political participation was not achieved without resistance. We know little about the opposition inside the party at this point, save that by July there was sufficient discontent for the VKPD to think of exploiting it.[61] The opposition found some expression in the more radical provincial papers. The Halle *Volkszeitung,* for example, greeted Wirth with the observation that "regarded historically, the new government represents a further retrograde force and a renewed strengthening of the power position of the bourgeoisie"; but the Halle paper, at least, swung into line when the Reichstag delegation com-

57. *Ibid.,* May 10, 1921 (e); minutes of the USPD Reichstag delegation, May 10, 1921, morning meeting.
58. *Freiheit,* May 14, 1921 (m).
59. See the elaborate explanation of this step, *ibid.,* June 5, 1921. The text of the motion of confidence had to do with the government's foreign policy, which made the decision possible.
60. *Der Sozialist,* May 21, 1921, p. 459.
61. See the VKPD circular of July 15, 1921, in *Dokumente und Materialien,* VII/I, 520–21; and the comments of Curt Geyer, by this date a dissident Communist, in *Sowjet,* June 15, 1921, pp. 120–22.

THE RUMP USPD 403

mitted itself to supporting Wirth.[62] Rosenfeld and Ledebour were among the dissatisfied leaders; but for the time being the tactic of rapprochement had the upper hand, and so long as the policies connected with it appeared to be bringing tangible gains without outright sacrifice of principle the minority was impotent.

The tentative progress toward political involvement on the national level had a more vigorous counterpart in Independent activity in those states where the electorate, despite the vicissitudes of the postwar socialist movement, still gave a majority to the working-class parties. In these states—Braunschweig, Saxony, and Thuringia—the ideal of a purely socialist government was realizable without the long-awaited mass action, and in each state the Independent leadership—distinctly right-wing in Braunschweig and Saxony, right of center in Thuringia—was oriented toward this possibility. To the radicals, a parliamentary government of this sort was unappealing just because it was independent of mass action and might lead the USPD into subjection to Majority Socialist hesitancies or, worse, into an attack of "parliamentary cretinism"—the belief that bourgeois democratic institutions could be important for the realization of socialism. In the old united USPD the question of whether the party ought to exploit such opportunities when they arose had thus been controversial. The Braunschweig leadership, under Sepp Oerter, had gone ahead in June 1920, despite private expressions of disapproval from national leaders.[63] The prospect of similar developments in Saxony and Thuringia, however, caused heated debate in high party circles before the split.[64] After the schism, in December 1920, the possibility became reality in Saxony, with Lipinski and Fleissner resuming the ministerial careers they had given up in January 1919; and within a year, in October 1921, the same development took place in Thuringia. Thus by the fall of 1921 the USPD was a government party in three German states.

Of course there was no real analogy between these all-socialist governments in the states and the kind of government possible in Berlin. The governments of Saxony, Thuringia, and Braunschweig were true labor governments; each held a mandate from the populace, albeit by the slimmest of margins (one or two seats in each Diet); and each was dependent for its majority on the votes of the Communists, who refused to join the cabinet but exercised considerable pressure on it. Consequently, all three governments were vigorous, at least in spurts, in carrying out

62. *Volkszeitung* (Halle), May 12, June 3 and 6, 1921. On June 3, the day before the vote of confidence, the newspaper was still hostile to the Wirth government, but three days later it had changed its tone.

63. See above, pp. 354–55.

64. According to *Die Internationale* (Left USPD), Nov. 10, 1920.

their programs. They could not address such overriding political issues as socialization, foreign policy, the military, or national tax policies, but there was much they could do regarding state and local taxes, education, the position of the Church, and a broad range of issues of social policy.[65] These were the first (and last) regular socialist governments of the Weimar Republic, and they created a legacy to which the movement could appeal in later agitation.[66] More important for our purposes, they also established a habit of cooperation between the two Social Democratic parties in three of the USPD's most important strongholds.

On the Reich level, this kind of collaboration was not available to the Independents. Rather, the rapprochement with the SPD was expressed in collaboration on particular issues, of which the most important was the question of how to raise the money needed for reparations. The policy advocated by the socialists in the summer of 1921 was to place the main burden on the nation's real assets (agricultural and urban land, industrial and banking capital) by assigning a fixed share of their ownership, and thus their profits, to the Reich; such a source of income would be immune to the inflation that was vitiating other tax revenues, and, even better, it would relieve the general populace of the direct taxes that were the only other option.[67] This policy, known as *Erfassung der Sachwerte* (roughly, drawing on real assets), was launched into political debate by an SPD minister in the Wirth government, Minister of the Economy Robert Schmidt; but the full program failed to win cabinet approval in June, and a reduced program died there early in August.[68] Thereupon the two Social Democratic parties made the idea the center of their agitation. The USPD was serious enough about it to be willing to negotiate with the SPD and ADGB even under the latter's condition that the KPD (which in any case scorned the idea at the time) be excluded from discussions—the first recorded joint talks since the USPD adopted its united-front policies.[69] And through all the difficulties of the fall,

65. For the legislation of the socialist Saxon government, see Lipinski, pp. 18–31, and Fabian, pp. 99–126; for Thuringia, Witzmann, pp. 58–83; for Braunschweig, Roloff, pp. 93–94.

66. The socialist government in Braunschweig fell on May 4, 1922. The Saxon and Thuringian socialist governments lasted into 1923, undergoing some changes in personnel and ultimately (in October 1923) the entry of Communist ministers, whereupon the Reich government intervened and brought them to an end.

67. There are simple explanations of the complicated policy in Stampfer, *Die vierzehn Jahre,* p. 231, and Ernst Laubach, *Die Politik der Kabinette Wirth 1921/22* (Lübeck, 1968), p. 62; also *Freiheit,* June 1, 1921 (m).

68. Laubach, p. 62.

69. The USPD approached the SPD and ADGB on August 23; reported in an SPD circular of Aug. 30, 1921, in the library of the ASD Bonn, catalogued under Otto Wels' name.

until January 1922, the drive for *Erfassung der Sachwerte* remained a bond between the two parties.

Such instances of collaboration, or adoption of parallel courses, were still far from providing the impetus needed for reunification of the two Social Democratic parties. The SPD was still a member of a coalition government with bourgeois parties, and, however much sympathy the Independents might have for Wirth's policies, only the extreme right wing of the party was ready to consider a coalition role for the USPD; coalition politics therefore remained a substantial barrier between the parties.[70] Nor was there yet any sign of the mass action that the Independents awaited as the necessary background and impulse for a true, as opposed to formal, unification. Nevertheless, by July reunification was being openly discussed, for instance by Scheidemann in *Vorwärts* on July 3. The USPD party executive quickly responded with a statement holding out no hopes of early unification;[71] but at the same time, the executive urged closer collaboration between socialist groups wherever possible, and in some places, for instance Elberfeld, the two parties reached alliance agreements (*Arbeitsgemeinschaften*) that were generally recognized as the prelude to merger.[72]

Then, at the end of August, the necessary mass action seemed to have come, in response to the assassination of former Minister of Finance Matthias Erzberger, a leading representative of the republican camp. For the first time since the Kapp Putsch, the lower classes seemed lifted out of their lethargy by an explosion of wrath directed against the reactionary forces in the country. The trade unions quickly seized the lead, as was becoming customary. They first approached the government, alone, with demands for the suppression of reactionary groups, then joined with the SPD to organize mass pressure in support of the demands, and finally brought in the USPD as well.[73] The latter, whose initial reaction to the situation had been instinctively radical,[74] agreed to join in the action, even though the KPD was to be excluded, and adjusted its attitude accordingly; the KPD commented that the party's "attitude differs

70. Kautsky had been ready to see his party approach unification by entering a coalition government with bourgeois parties as early as April 1920; see the manuscript "Schliesst die Reihen!" Kautsky papers, A 89, esp. pp. 9–21. For his views in 1921, see the article "Die Einigung," *Der Sozialist*, Sept. 3, 1921, pp. 761–72.
71. *Freiheit*, July 9, 1921 (m).
72. *Volkszeitung* (Halle), Aug. 5, 1921.
73. Stages recorded in the circular mentioned in n. 69 above: substance given also in Gotthard Jasper, *Der Schutz der Republik* (Tübingen, 1963), p. 35.
74. See the manifesto by the party executive, *Freiheit*, Aug. 28, 1921.

from [that of] the SPD only in tone and scarcely in degree."[75] Given the background of the summer, the occasion seemed one that might bring the SPD and USPD together for good.

Dittmann, for one, according to his later testimony, was ready for such a conclusion and believed it would have followed had it not been for the actions of the USPD's partners.[76] For example, pressure was brought on the government privately, for the most part, so that, despite the undeniable excitement of the workers, the quality of mass action so important to the Independents was vitiated by back-room negotiations. Moreover, even right-wing Independents were displeased by both the manner (presidential decree) and the substance of the government's response to the threat from the right; while the Majority Socialists, as members of the government coalition, were necessarily restrained in their criticism.[77] Even so the Independents might have been ready to draw some organizational conclusions from the united front had it not been for decisions taken by the SPD at its party congress (held in Görlitz from September 18 to 24).

Two decisions of this congress made it impossible for the rightward-leaning part of the USPD to hold the party on its earlier path. First, the SPD adopted a new program to replace the Erfurt Program of 1891, felt by the Majority Socialists to be no longer relevant to their tasks. This step had been planned since the previous year's party congress, and the draft had been published as early as July; it cannot, therefore, have been designed as a deliberate slap at the Independents, but it was felt as such. The tone of the Görlitz Program is conveyed by its opening sentences: "The German Social Democratic Party is the party of the working populace in the cities and countryside. It strives to unite all manual and intellectual producers who depend on the proceeds of their own labor . . . into a community of action for democracy and socialism."[78] In effect, the program formalized the reformist tendencies of the SPD; to the Independents, for whom the Erfurt Program still had a kind of sacred importance, the congress' action was a crime against the heritage of Social Democracy and the doctrine of class struggle, and thus a new divisive element.

The second decision, of more practical import, deepened the disillusion. Majority Socialist leaders had recently felt cramped by a party policy that would not allow coalition with Stresemann's People's Party,

75. KPD circular of Aug. 29, *Dokumente und Materialien*, VII/I, 568.
76. See his reminiscences, *Freiheit*, Sept. 20, 1922.
77. See Breitscheid, *Der Sozialist*, Sept. 17, 1921. The fullest account of the government and party negotiations that accompanied the crisis, and their results, is Jasper, pp. 35–61.
78. SPD *Parteitag*, Sept. 1921, p. iii.

generally regarded among socialists as the party of heavy industry; this restriction they had removed by the congress.[79] There were good reasons for this policy change, involving circumstances in the Prussian Diet as well as the SPD's position in a Reich government that depended part of the time on People's Party votes. But it was obnoxious to the Independents; we have Breitscheid's word for it that "there is no Independent who would approve of or even tolerate the collaboration of socialists and the party of heavy industry."[80] Above all, the action showed how little importance the SPD attached to the rapprochement that had been under way. Many Independents were bound to interpret the resolution as Kurt Rosenfeld did: "The SPD prefers the great coalition [with the People's Party] to the unification of the proletariat."[81]

This check was fatal to the momentum toward unity. It did not, at first, affect the USPD's attitude toward its responsibilities in the Reichstag; indeed, when it was approached again, during a cabinet crisis in October, about participating in the government, its reply was conciliatory, proposing a program so mild that the SPD was able to accept it.[82] The party's moderation had a tactical purpose; the USPD had no intention of becoming involved in a government coalition and only wanted to force the SPD into an awkward position vis-à-vis its coalition partners.[83] But the party was a further step away from sterile rhetorical opposition; and three weeks later it helped a new Wirth cabinet into existence with another vote of confidence. Meanwhile the socialist front in the state governments continued unaffected—indeed the Thuringian government was formed during the weeks of disillusion over Görlitz—but the SPD's desire to turn this collaboration into a formal alliance in Saxony was unanimously rejected by the USPD's state executive with bitter references to Görlitz.[84] A parallel (rather than joint) agitation for *Erfassung der Sachwerte* also continued, but since the Communist Party adopted the same slogan in October the idea no longer created a special bond between the two

79. Text *ibid.*, pp. 576–77. The resolution does not directly mention coalition with the People's Party, but this implication had been made explicit in the debate.

80. *Der Sozialist*, Sept. 24, 1921, p. 835. Breitscheid, as a leading figure of the party's right wing, could speak with authority. He went on to write angrily of the "complete political obtuseness" of thinking that the defense of the Republic or the *Erfassung der Sachwerte* could be undertaken by a government including members of the People's Party.

81. USPD *Parteitag*, Jan. 1922, p. 107.

82. *Freiheit*, Oct. 2, 1921 (m). On the origins of the reply, see minutes of the USPD Reichstag delegation, Oct. 1, 1921 (two meetings).

83. According to Dittmann, USPD *Parteitag*, Jan. 1922, pp. 71–72.

84. *Mitteilungen des Landesvorstandes der Unabhäng. Sozialdemokratischen Partei Sachsens*, Oct. 1, 1921, pp. 1–4. The USPD was willing, however, to engage in regular private talks with the SPD about particular issues.

Social Democratic parties. Such bonds were not all loosening, but few were becoming tighter after September 1921.

The retrograde tendency in the USPD's relations with the Majority Socialists was demonstrated and confirmed at the Independents' party congress in January. The rebuff of the autumn had blocked off the one promising prospect the party had had, leaving the leadership without direction; in these circumstances the executive led the not-unwilling delegates back to a program that at least had the appeal of being traditional, the principles of the Leipzig Action Program of December 1919. All that was interesting in this retreat was the emphasis. The keynote of the congress, established in Dittmann's opening speech, was that "the coalition policies of the Right Socialists are the main factor that divides the proletariat, are the main hindrance to the unification of the proletariat."[85] The attack on coalition with the bourgeoisie was hardly novel; what was new was raising this problem to the status of *the* great barrier of principle between the two Social Democratic parties. The emphasis represented a retreat from the USPD's position immediately before Görlitz; then, as the bitter reaction to Görlitz shows, many Independents were tacitly coming to believe that somehow the SPD's participation in a coalition with moderate bourgeois parties need not be an absolute obstacle to unity. At the same time, concentration of hostility on a single point of SPD behavior (other objections were renewed too, but not with the same force) meant that only a single wall stood between the two parties. To all appearances the wall was very sturdy, for it was founded on the basic principle of the class struggle. But the choice of this formulation suggested that the perspective of the past summer lingered on even in its negation. Unification of the parties could not be expelled again from the USPD's outlook.

In other respects, the congress that marked the end of the first year of the rump party was curiously empty. Apart from the question of coalition policy—over which any dissidents held their tongues—no serious issues were discussed; Hilferding even cancelled the speech he was to have given on tax policy because of the controversy it would have provoked.[86] Instead, the party took its stand foursquare on the policies it had inherited from the past, spelling these out in a comprehensive new manifesto; thereby it produced the kind of self-congratulatory unity Inde-

85. USPD *Parteitag*, Jan. 1922, p. 74.
86. See the comments of Hilferding's close associate, Paul Hertz, *Der Sozialist*, April 22, 1922, pp. 254–55. The Halle *Volkszeitung* had expected the congress to be full of invigorating controversy, which shows that the party was fully aware of its internal conflicts; see the issues of Jan. 6 and 7, 1922.

pendents always liked to see at their congresses.[87] The major purpose served by the congress was thus to demonstrate that the USPD still had an emotional coherence and a platform to justify its existence. For the moment, but for the moment only, Independents could forget that this platform was as ambiguous as ever and, after the experience of the previous summer, no longer wholly credible.

Drift and Conflict

Before long the party was finding that rhetorical displays of unity at the congress in January had solved none of its real problems. The spring of 1922 brought a succession of wearing conflicts, some of them inside the party, some between it and its socialist neighbors. The USPD's morale, insofar as it had been lifted by the congress, fell again sharply in the following months, to the point that by the end of the spring the continued existence of the USPD was once again in question.

Throughout these months the party was engaged in an inconclusive struggle about its fundamental orientation. The general tendency was to drift to the left. The failure of the party's movement toward rapprochement with the SPD had the effect of driving its middle bloc back onto the safe ground of class-conscious opposition; and two further factors reinforced the trend. First, the erosive effect of continuing inflation on the workers' standard of living and level of employment was reviving signs of activism in the working class. Second, the Communist Party at long last re-emerged as an active factor on the political scene, thus giving force again to the program of the left wing of the USPD. Even as the party drifted to the left, however, the contrary pull of the incipient commitments of 1921 continued to be felt, at least among leading cadres— less in the matter of relations with the SPD, which continued to deteriorate for some months after January 1922, than in the party's sustained support of the Wirth government.[88] Only the right wing, strengthened in its belief by the developments of the previous summer, was consistent in this respect, and its increasing stubbornness produced several small party crises, though without converting the party back to its former political line. But the party never entirely lost the sense that relations with the Majority Socialists offered the best hope for a wider socialist unity; and when crisis came in June this idea could be taken up again at once.

87. See the manifesto in USPD *Parteitag*, Jan. 1922, pp. 3–7.
88. At the end of January the SPD, in order to make an agreed fiscal policy possible for the governing coalition, had abandoned its insistence on *Erfassung der Sachwerte* and accepted a compromise tax program based on other principles, which most Independents took as a further betrayal.

If the USPD had had only the SPD to contend with in the summer of 1921, in the following spring it had the tension of a two-way pull. Indeed, as far as the politically active part of the proletariat was concerned, the KPD made the running in the first five months of the new year. During the period October 1921–January 1922 the Communist Party liquidated its two most immediate liabilities, its stubborn adherence to the "offensive tactic" that had brought on the March Action and its prolonged party crisis. Persistent pressure from the Comintern, which had gone over to united-front tactics at its Third World Congress in July 1921, led to resolution of the first problem, as the new line was forced on the KPD by stages in October and November.[89] The party crisis took longer to resolve, not least because *Vorwärts* began publishing late in November KPD documentation on the expedients it had adopted to try to prolong the March Action, which thus became widely known for the first time. Ernst Friesland, general secretary of the party since August, formed the active center of a new wave of outspoken opposition within the party, while Levi's KAG moved beyond its parliamentary role to set up a national organization to encourage Communist opposition. Party leaders moved rigorously against the dissidents, and their policy of wholesale expulsion, beginning in January 1922, finally brought the party's internal difficulties to a temporary conclusion.[90]

Part of the USPD had been waiting eagerly for signs of effective vitality in the KPD, and when these first appeared, in the form of a heavily qualified proposal for a "workers' government" at the time of the cabinet crisis late in October 1921, there was a quick response. The USPD officially turned its back on the KPD's proposals on learning that the Communists proposed not to participate in such a government but only to offer support from the outside;[91] but the program points raised by the KPD at the same time, including *Erfassung der Sachwerte,* offered the chance of joint agitation outside parliament. A modest united-front movement opened in November with a general assembly of factory councils in Berlin, the first in many months, at which Rosenfeld appropriately acted as USPD spokesman; and the USPD party executive, through Ledebour, informed the KPD central committee that, although the

89. See Arnold Reisberg, *Lenin und die Aktionseinheit in Deutschland* (Berlin, 1964), esp. pp. 85–125. This East German work makes use of internal Communist Party documentation.

90. On the "Friesland crisis" see Brandt and Löwenthal, pp. 185–204, and Angress, *Stillborn Revolution,* pp. 208–19. Friesland himself had additional reasons (stemming mainly from Comintern interference in the daily operation of the party) for moving into opposition, but the broader crisis derived principally from the *Vorwärts* revelations.

91. Reisberg, pp. 108–9.

ADGB and SPD refused to have relations with the Communists, the USPD proposed to maintain relations in both directions and try to bring the hostile wings of the labor movement together.[92]

This rapprochement fell a casualty to the Friesland crisis in the KPD, but soon another united-front movement was set in motion from a different quarter—the Vienna Union. The original cautious proposal of the bureau of the Vienna Union, meeting on December 17 and 18, 1921, was to hold an international conference on the subject of reparations, to be attended by all socialist and Communist parties of the countries concerned regardless of their international affiliations.[93] Such a conference had little appeal to the German Communists, who used it, however, to launch their own more grandiose plan of a world workers' congress, that is, a full world conference of the three Internationals.[94] This broader notion, with the support of a full-scale propaganda campaign from the Comintern, became the focus of the united-front ideal in Germany in the months to May. In January the bureau of the Vienna Union felt encouraged enough to suggest a meeting of the executive committees of the three Internationals to explore the possibility of a world congress, as desired not only by the Communists but also by some of its own members, notably Ledebour.[95] Late in February it persuaded the reluctant leaders of the Second International to attend a meeting of the three executives.

The conference (held in Berlin April 2 to 5, 1922) and the month following it were the high-water mark of the united-front campaign. The conference itself was acrimonious, but agreement was reached on calling for an international workers' demonstration on April 20 to symbolize the direction of its efforts, and a Commission of Nine was established for further deliberations.[96] In Germany the result was a period of good feeling between Independents and Communists that lasted for several weeks. The SPD participated in only the most minimal way, going so far as to boycott the demonstrations of April 20. During these weeks, enthusiasm ran high among the socialist left and was reinforced, initially at least, by the unexpected conclusion on April 16 of the Treaty of Rapallo be-

92. *Ibid.*, pp. 123–24.
93. *Nachrichten*, Jan. 1922, pp. 1–2.
94. Reisberg, pp. 133–34.
95. *Nachrichten*, Feb. 1922, pp. 1–2; on the background see Donneur, pp. 162–65. Reisberg, p. 134, tells us that Ledebour and Rosenfeld met privately with representatives of the Third International in January to assure the latter of their support for a world congress; but they admitted they were far from sure of carrying their party with them on this point.
96. See the report of the meetings, published as *The Second and Third Internationals and the Vienna Union* (London, 1922); and Donneur, pp. 187–223.

tween the Reich and Soviet Russia, which normalized relations between the two countries.[97] But it could not last. Soon even the optimists realized that the Second International saw no reason to proceed further with the rapprochement; though it carefully avoided giving definite cause for the breakup of the front—leaving it to the impatient Communists to disrupt the Commission of Nine, on May 22—its attitude doomed the enterprise to failure. And without the framework of a three-way alliance the USPD's relations with the KPD quickly cooled. Except in terms of its long-range promise, a united front with the hyperenergetic, ruthless Communists had been an uncomfortable experience, for the Communists' idea of appropriate behavior within such a front included continued abuse of the other parties and sudden presentation of programmatic demands that were designed to ensure that the KPD had a more radical image than its partners. Even radical Independents were weary of the KPD as allies by the end of May, and the spirit of active collaboration was, for the time being, dead.[98]

The episode had consequences. During the campaign for a world congress of the three Internationals the German Communist Party finally found its feet again; even after the collapse of the common front in May the Communists were a formidable force on the socialist left, searching incessantly for issues with which, in the guise of united-front action, to undercut the appeal of the Social Democratic parties. For the USPD too, the campaign was revitalizing, particularly at the local level, where the demonstrations of April and May were often conducted with real enthusiasm. Ultimately, however, the experience was empty or negative for the Independents. The united-front campaign was an unusually abstract one, never having specific content on issues of German domestic policy, and finally disappointing. Part of the rank and file may have been radicalized; but for the leaders the lesson seems to have been that the KPD in its new guise was nearly as difficult to deal with as it had been a year earlier. A three-way unification of the German proletariat was no closer.

The cause of unity enjoyed one success during these months (though a small one and controversial in the USPD) in the accession of the bulk of Paul Levi's KAG to the USPD in March and April 1922. At the time of the KAG's formal foundation as a national group in November 1921, with the future of the existing KPD leadership uncertain, it had seemed

---

97. An example of the enthusiasm of the more radical Independents for Rapallo may be found in the editorial comment of the Halle *Volkszeitung,* starting on April 18. The leadership's attitude was more reserved, increasingly so with time; see Laubach, p. 215.

98. See, for instance, *Volkszeitung* (Halle), May 22, 1922.

to have a real chance of not only collecting the various splinters cast off by the KPD since the March Action but also exercising leverage that could ultimately force the KPD into what the dissidents saw as effective policies. Accordingly it was designed not as a party but as a pressure group, with members both outside and inside the KPD.[99] The ensuing months, however, rather than witnessing the further disintegration of the Communist Party, saw its recovery, still in a form unacceptable to the dissidents; the leaders of the KAG, who included fifteen Reichstag deputies, failed to assemble the hoped-for following among the masses at the same time as they lost their last foothold in the KPD apparatus with the expulsion of the group around Friesland and Brass. By the time of the KAG's second conference, on January 29, 1922, hopes of forcing reform on the KPD were clearly vain. The group turned instead toward a closer association with the USPD.[100]

Though we know little about the KAG's approaches to the USPD, they were plainly not well received at first. The KAG was headed by the man felt to be principally responsible for the Communist policy of splitting the party in 1920; and his associates and followers included many former Independents divided from the USPD since Halle by a gulf of bitterness—Däumig and Curt Geyer among them.[101] Moreover, association with the KAG, let alone KAG merger into the USPD, might possibly change the balance of factions to the advantage of the left wing. Ledebour was in favor of taking in the KAG as a "valuable stage on the road to unity," a sign that the USPD was the "nucleus of unity [*Einigungskern*] of the revolutionary socialist proletariat";[102] but the majority of his colleagues seem to have been unenthusiastic. On February 9 the USPD Reichstag delegation rebuffed what was probably the first attempt by the KAG to arrange joint assemblies or demonstrations.[103] The party

99. See the resolution of its founding conference in *Unser Weg*, Dec. 1921, p. 415, and Levi's editorial, *ibid.*, pp. 405–14; also Bernd Dieter Fritz, "Die Kommunistische Arbeitsgemeinschaft (KAG) im Vergleich mit der KPO und SAP" (Ph.D. dissertation, University of Bonn, 1966).

100. The spirit of the KAG in January 1922 emerges from the correspondence of its secretary, Max Sievers; see Levi papers, P 63 and P 99. On the conference of Jan. 29, see the KAG circular of Jan. 31, *ibid.*, P 99.

101. The bulletin of the Berlin party characterized the expelled Communists as "die Erledigten und Gestrandeten"; *Mitteilungsblatt*, Oct. 5, 1921, p. 1. Däumig edited the KAG's bulletin but otherwise played only a secondary, rather withdrawn political role after leaving the KPD, apparently because the collapse of his aspirations for the German proletariat left him "a spiritually broken man" (Dittmann memoirs, p. 1236; see also the obituary by P.L. [Paul Levi], *Freiheit*, July 6, 1922). He died in July 1922 at the age of 55.

102. Article in *Mitteilungsblatt*, March 1, 1922, pp. 1–2.

103. Minutes of the USPD Reichstag delegation, Feb. 9, 1922. See also the KAG circular of Feb. 16, Levi papers, P 99, which still had no progress to report.

conference of February 22 took a reserved position on merger, offering the KAG only the possibility of entering the USPD as individuals. Having failed to arrange corporate union with the USPD, the KAG had no choice; on March 24 it announced its intention of dissolving itself and accepting the USPD's terms.[104]

The adherence of most members of the KAG cannot have meant a large accession of strength for the USPD—a few thousand members, not more. The potential effect of the development lay elsewhere, in its symbolism (as Ledebour had suggested) and in the eleven new members it brought the Reichstag delegation, one of the ruling institutions of the USPD.[105] In both respects the adherence of the KAG tended to confirm the more leftward orientation of the party since January and thereby contributed to what was becoming an enervating party crisis.

The divergencies in the party, so carefully ignored at the congress in January, began to find open expression only a month later. The first incident was a parliamentary one, in itself without direct consequences but remarkable as the first open assertion of right-wing dissatisfaction with the party's course. Early in February a brief but bitter railway strike occurred, which the Communists attempted to turn into a general political strike and which was brought to an end only by means of extraordinary government measures based on the principle that state employees had no right to strike.[106] The bitterness spilled over into the Reichstag debates, which ended with Wirth demanding a vote of confidence for his handling of the strike.[107] The USPD had not expected such a move; its spokesmen had been harshly critical and could hardly retreat at this point. In almost permanent session during February 14 and 15, members of the delegation debated their stand, deciding in the end that they must vote against the motion of confidence, even though the arithmetic of party alignments suggested that their votes might bring down Wirth's government, which they still preferred to any visible alternative.[108] But when the vote was held, thirteen of the Independent deputies, including

104. *Freiheit,* March 24, 1922 (m); also minutes of the USPD Reichstag delegation, April 3, 1922, where the adherence of the new members is reported.
105. The eleven new adherents were Brass, Däumig, Düwell, Fries, Curt Geyer, Friedrich Geyer, Adolph Hoffmann, Levi, Plettner, Teuber, and Wackwitz; four other KAG members (Berthelé, Eichhorn, Malzahn, and Reich) remained apart, rejoining the KPD delegation in the fall (Berthelé and Eichhorn as full members, the other two as associates). All of the eleven who joined the USPD (except Däumig, who had died in the meantime) followed the party majority into the SPD in September, but none except Levi was ever elected to the Reichstag again.
106. Severing, *Lebensweg,* I, 339–46; Stampfer, *Die vierzehn Jahre,* pp. 239–42.
107. On the complicated parliamentary situation, see Laubach, pp. 155–57.
108. Minutes of the USPD Reichstag delegation, Feb. 14 and 15, 1922.

Breitscheid and Seger, defied discipline and absented themselves.[109] Thirteen abstentions might have provided the margin necessary to save the cabinet, but they proved not to have been needed.

The significance of the episode lay in how it was viewed—with delight by those looking for signs of dissolution in the USPD, and with consternation by many of the members themselves. The more radical elements in the party were furious over what they called a "barefaced breach of discipline" and even an "attempt to split the delegation"; initially only five party papers were willing to defend or explain the action of the thirteen.[110] The party executive felt compelled to place the question of their colleagues' breach of discipline before a party conference on February 22; before the event, however, Dittmann (probably acting for the executive) circulated an article arguing that the minority was acting in accordance with its established rights, the same rights as those the minority had claimed for itself during the war.[111] The conference thus wound up instead debating the delegation's decision to vote against Wirth, with representatives of the majority arguing that the overthrow of the Wirth government could only be beneficial to the cause of proletarian unity in that it would force the SPD into opposition.[112] In the end, the conference supported the delegation's stand by a large majority and took no action against the minority, so that the controversy, or "party crisis" as at least one party paper called it,[113] ended after a week with no change having taken place. But the party had had a scare—a sign of the malaise it had hitherto managed to keep hidden.

A month later, two further incidents, again minor and transitory, illustrated the dissatisfaction on the party's right wing. The first and most important was the resignation of almost the entire editorial staff of *Freiheit*. Formally, the resignation occurred because a majority of the party executive and the auxiliary council and control commission found the paper to have deviated consistently from the official party policies laid down in the manifesto of the recent party congress, particularly

109. See Breitscheid's account, *Der Sozialist,* Feb. 18, 1922, pp. 97–99; a list of the deputies involved is in *Freiheit,* Feb. 16, 1922 (e). Eleven more deputies were absent on other business, an unusually large number; a few of these, though probably (to judge by the list of names in *Freiheit*) not more than four or five, might be suspected of having arranged business in order to avoid having to vote against Wirth. On the whole episode, see also Kastning, pp. 94–95.

110. *Volkszeitung* (Halle), Feb. 17, 1922. The five papers were those of Berlin, Bremen, Leipzig, Nuremberg, and Plauen; *ibid.,* Feb. 20, 1922.

111. *Ibid.,* Feb. 21, 1922.

112. *Freiheit,* Feb. 23, 1922 (m); *Der Sozialist,* March 18, 1922, pp. 192–93; *Volkszeitung* (Halle), Feb. 23, 1922.

113. *Volkszeitung* (Halle), Feb. 20, 1922.

with respect to tax policy, Hilferding's specialty.[114] In fact, it followed from bitter attacks on Hilferding in the party executive by Crispien and Ledebour, who charged that *Freiheit* was attempting to undermine the independence of the USPD by aligning its policies with those of the SPD in preparation for reunification. Hilferding asserted in return that the financial policies he advocated, though unpalatable, were essential in the inflationary conditions then prevailing and that this consideration was his sole motivation; he resigned from *Freiheit* rather than allow himself to be the focus of the confused factional conflicts of the directionless party.[115] Dittmann, the party's man-of-all-work, was reluctantly forced to step in as editor-in-chief, and, not surprisingly in the circumstances, *Freiheit* became the most colorless of newspapers. The change was accomplished quickly and smoothly, almost without controversy[116]—a strange end for the old *Freiheit,* whose braking influence on the party's radicalism over the years had been of such incalculable importance.

The second incident, the resignation from the party of Paul Brühl and Wilhelm Schüning, took place the same week but had no immediate effect. Brühl was the important figure, a former chairman of the Berlin party organization, member of the Reichstag and treasurer of the USPD delegation, and associate member of the party executive. His dissatisfaction with the party's course had been evident at least since February, when he joined Breitscheid in abstaining on Wirth's vote of confidence; but his resignation was provoked by a purely local matter, the party's intransigent stand on a municipal fiscal issue in Berlin, where he was a full-time city official. The nature of the dispute guaranteed that hardly anyone would follow him out of the USPD and (a few months later) into the SPD; but his was the first important defection from the party since the split after the Halle congress, a worrying sign.

Whether there was a link between the *Freiheit* affair, Brühl's defection, and the third important party event of the end of March, the KAG's decision to enter the USPD, is unclear, but some measure of interconnection is likely; certainly all expressed, in their different ways, the mood of the party. The party seemed, to outside observers in mid-spring, to be growing steadily more radical, not least because of the wave of demonstrations in April and early May.[117] Hermann Müller of the SPD said the

---

114. *Freiheit,* March 26, 1922, and March 28, 1922 (m).

115. Dittmann memoirs, pp. 1275–76. Hilferding had been a full member of the party executive since January, and his position there was not affected by his resignation from *Freiheit.*

116. See Paul Hertz (one of the former editors) in *Der Sozialist,* April 22, 1922, pp. 252–55; Koszyk, pp. 150–51.

117. For example, the military intelligence report of April 20, 1922, referring

change in the USPD amounted to Crispien's having assumed the leadership and found it much harder than before to know what the party's attitude would be on matters before the Reichstag.[118]

Yet such a view of the USPD's position was misleading. The party had drifted to its more radical stance for want of a better policy; it could easily drift in the other direction again, and indeed to some extent began to do so after its estrangement from the Communists in May. The significant aspect of the USPD's life during the spring was not the doctrinaire attitudes it displayed but the malaise that accompanied them.

Pressures on and within the USPD had built up gradually to the danger point. The most evident focus of these pressures had been and remained the Reichstag. The party's position as a part-time de facto bloc partner in the government coalition, although almost inevitable, given the alignment of forces, could satisfy neither the right wing, which was exasperated at the party's refusal to accept the consequences of its role, nor the radicals, who were placed under considerable ideological strain. The situation repeated itself in a number of state and local parliaments, as the party's ambivalence toward the uses of parliamentary democracy continued to take its toll. The consequence was a latent threat of schism —and further schism would finish the USPD as a serious force.

As if this were not sufficient cause for worry, the party's organizational strength was slowly but distinctly declining. This problem was not specific to the USPD, being a function of the workers' general withdrawal from the political involvement of the first postwar years, aggravated by the need to keep raising party dues and newspaper subscription rates in order to keep up with inflation.[119] However, the USPD was the most vulnerable of the three working-class parties; compared to the SPD it was seriously overextended, because it sought to keep up the appearance of being the old, nationally important USPD, and unlike the KPD it had no foreign resources with which to support its pretensions. The party press was particularly affected; exact information on circulation and finances was supressed as a matter of policy as the party neared its end, but it was symptomatic that *Freiheit* was not only reduced to a single issue daily

---

to the "victory of the more radical wing" in the USPD; BA Koblenz, Reichskanzlei 676, p. 111.

118. At a meeting of party leaders on June 17, 1922; BA Koblenz, Reichskanzlei 1020, p. 32.

119. For example, the Berlin organization, which had exacted dues of 10 pfennigs a week from its male members in 1914 and only 20 pfennigs as recently as the beginning of 1920, had raised its dues by stages to 30 marks a month just before reunification. The first issue of *Freiheit* cost 10 pfennigs, the last 6 marks.

but also sold its offices and printing operation.[120] The membership decline cannot be fully documented either, though clearly everyone was aware of it. The party's constituency was being reduced to its existing following in districts where it was the established workers' party, or shared this distinction (as in Saxony and Berlin), and a scattered membership among the shrinking number of radical, non-Communist workers and intellectuals who still saw a place for a middle party in the socialist camp. The USPD was looking, even to its supporters, more and more like a holding operation rather than a party with a future.

To be sure, one had to be close to the USPD to sense this mood. To outward appearances the party remained what it had been a year earlier, the second largest socialist party of Germany, with a broad-based organizational strength, strong parliamentary delegations, an important if informal position among the government's supporters, ministerial posts in the cabinets of two important states (the socialist government of Braunschweig fell in May), and a key role as mediator when the opportunity for socialist unity should present itself. More closely examined, however, the party was weary from internal as well as external conflicts and sensed the weariness of the working-class masses; it was less sure of its purposes than it liked to pretend, and uncertain of the future. There were still energetic leaders and militants in the party who could not be depressed by such moods and continued along their paths with determination. But uncertainty was more widespread than determination; and this fact determined the party's response to the crisis that came upon it in June.

120. See Koszyk, p. 150.

CHAPTER 13

Reunification (June
to September 1922)

On the morning of June 24, 1922, Foreign Minister Walther Rathenau was brutally assassinated by a band of young right radicals. The murder had extraordinary repercussions. Between June and October, as a result of the crisis caused by Rathenau's death, republican institutions enjoyed a significant increase in strength, attracting new political commitments from the left and the moderate right; at the same time, the Republic's parliamentary system reached a point of virtual paralysis with the polarization of republican parties and the breakup of the most promising government of the early Republic. In the middle of these developments the USPD abruptly decided to end its independent existence.

The murder of Rathenau was the most serious in a series of political assassinations that were challenging the authority of the republican system, and response to this event thus reflected accumulated concern and frustration.[1] Furthermore, Rathenau's death brought to the surface the long-standing tensions produced, particularly in the Social Democratic parties, by the unsatisfactory political situation. The SPD's actions during the crisis reflected its settled conviction that this time socialist unity was the highest priority; accordingly, the Majority Socialists not only smoothed the way for the Independents at every turn but, in the interests of reunification, were even willing to jeopardize their membership in Wirth's coalition. As for the Independents, when reunification came, it brought, amid all the practical and ideological satisfaction, even among the still widespread doubts, a sense of relief.

The first reaction of republican politicians to the assassination was fury. The chain of murders had grown too long and reached too high into the government; moreover, Rathenau, for all his personal peculiarities,

1. Liebknecht, Luxemburg, and Eisner had been murdered during the revolution; more recently, a series of assassinations of leading politicians (starting with Karl Gareis, leader of the Independents in the Bavarian Diet, in June 1921 and including Erzberger, mentioned above) pointed to systematic political murder by right-wing conspiratorial groups.

had been regarded by the center and the left in the Reichstag as a man of unusual perception, honesty, and determination, a sincere republican, and one of the pillars of Wirth's cabinet. At the same time, there were grounds for anxiety. On the one hand, the murder might be the signal for a general mustering of the forces of reaction, even a putsch.[2] On the other, the working class and its leaders might be spurred to one of their periodic outbursts, with the prospect of violence in the streets, socialist attempts to win dominance over the government, and even revolution.

The government's initial counteraction, in both its moral and practical aspects, showed concern for working-class sentiments. Although the emergency decrees issued within a few hours of the murder, under Article 48 of the constitution, were generally received with disappointment by the socialists, they did incorporate, in a number of respects, earlier socialist proposals and went far beyond previous laws against monarchist subversion.[3] More important were the words spoken, especially the chancellor's. Rising to the occasion, Wirth addressed himself to the crisis with force and dignity that did full justice to the anger of all republican forces, including the socialists.[4] Wirth's speeches—especially that of June 25, when he proclaimed to the Reichstag, arm pointing, that the "enemy is on the right!"—did more than anything else to make it possible for the two Social Democratic parties to seek a resolution of the crisis through government action and legislation, that is, within the existing parliamentary system.

Among working-class organizations the immediate response was to think of forming a united proletarian front. As it happened, the triennial conference of the ADGB was in session in Leipzig when news of the assassination arrived. The conference immediately adopted a resolution condemning the outrage, identifying it as part of "a new planned attack on the existence of the Republic" and demanding "really decisive measures" from the government rather than just the words that had followed earlier killings. To give weight to this demand, the conference scheduled a "joint work stoppage . . . and the staging of mighty public demonstrations" for the following Tuesday, June 27.[5] Once again the trade unions had seized the initiative, even more quickly than before, and to an extent they held this initiative throughout the coming weeks.

No one doubted that the ADGB's call would have great appeal among

2. See Dittmann in *Reichstag*, vol. 355, pp. 8035–36; Viscount d'Abernon, *An Ambassador of Peace*, 3 vols. (London, 1929), II, 53.
3. Texts in *Reichstag*, vol. 355, pp. 8037–39; see the commentary in Jasper, p. 59.
4. *Reichstag*, vol. 355, pp. 8034–35 and 8037; vol. 356, pp. 8054–58.
5. Text in *Freiheit*, June 25, 1922.

the workers, and the three working-class parties, together with the AfA on behalf of the white-collar unions, quickly associated themselves with the planned demonstrations. The idea of a united mobilization of the workers caught on at once. Its first fruits were a number of locally organized demonstrations the next day, a Sunday, in Berlin, Leipzig, and elsewhere, in which bourgeois speakers and crowds also took part. Though sizable, these demonstrations were notable not so much for their numbers as for their emotion.[6] That afternoon, the national leaderships of the ADGB, the AfA, and the three working-class parties sent a joint delegation to the chancellor with "some of the most urgent demands" for measures against the right. Mass mobilization was well under way.[7]

Odd man out in this front was the Communist Party. The Communist leaders saw at once that events were creating the united front of the working class that they had been pursuing with dogmatic ineffectuality for months, and they quickly circulated their proposals to the leaders of the other two parties.[8] Apart from the demand for a general strike, which was soon dropped, their proposals ran in the same general direction as the immediate wishes of the two Social Democratic parties and the trade unions—mobilization of the masses in support of stringent police action, dramatic purges, and radical reform. But the Communists were too isolated and distrusted to gain lasting advantage from their early initiatives. They won formal and equal membership in the councils of the united front, but on grudging and conditional terms; as Crispien privately explained after consultations with SPD leaders, "We will act jointly with the Communists at the present time so long as the Communists honorably, together with the other parties, support the jointly agreed demands."[9] This condition, as understood by the Social Democrats, did not permit the Communists to act separately or to criticize their partners; frustrated, the Communists remained in the alliance for only a little over a week.

Except for the Communists, the leaders of the different elements of the united front seem to have been able to collaborate with little friction. On June 27, the day of the nationwide demonstration strike, they made public a set of demands, addressed to the Reichstag and the government,

6. Stampfer, *Die vierzehn Jahre,* p. 265; Sender, p. 197.

7. Minutes of the USPD Reichstag delegation, June 25, 1922; *Freiheit,* June 26, 1922; Künstler speech, *Freiheit,* June 28, 1922.

8. Reisberg, pp. 157–58. The USPD delegation received a letter with five proposed demands, then another letter with eight more, and two other demands orally; minutes of the USPD Reichstag delegation, June 24, 1922, evening meeting. There are two recorded texts: BA Koblenz, Reichskanzlei 2708, p. 6, and *Dokumente und Materialien,* VII/II, 100–1.

9. Minutes of the USPD Reichstag delegation, June 24, 1922, evening meeting.

that were to serve as the common program of all five signatory organizations, including the KPD.[10] The demands called, in great detail, for complete prohibition of active or verbal expressions of "monarchist or antirepublican" sentiment; dissolution of all organizations with such a viewpoint; a purge of the state bureaucracies, including the Reichswehr and the courts, to eliminate "monarchist or antirepublican elements"; establishment of a special court with competence to deal with such cases; introduction of a Reich police force to act where individual states failed; and various reforms in criminal procedure to make convictions easier to obtain. Separately the parties also called for an amnesty for political prisoners, including the railwaymen sentenced after the February strike of that year. These far-reaching demands seem to have reflected the real desires of the signatories, a sign of how intense the crisis was felt to be. Although the Independents consistently referred to the program as their "minimum demands," whereas, on the basis of past experience, the unions could be expected to settle for much less than their original demands, for the moment the united front was unusually firm.

The mustering of the working class in the nationwide demonstrations of June 27 was impressive. Carefully organized though they were, the demonstrations plainly expressed genuine sentiments. The demonstrators showed by their numbers that the workers wanted decisive measures against the counterrevolution, and by their spirit that the ideal of proletarian unity was once again uppermost in their minds. In effect they gave a mandate to the organizations that had sponsored the demonstrations to continue working together to impose their program on the government. Three days later, with working-class agitation continuing and the government still not taking a strong stand, the five organizations called repeat demonstrations for Tuesday, July 4.[11] This time even greater crowds were involved, and, despite precautions, the action ended in violence in several cities; there could be no doubt about the strength of popular feeling.[12] The repeat demonstrations also led to the Communists' abrupt expulsion from the united front in Berlin when they were unable to restrain themselves from issuing additional demands above and beyond those of the joint leadership.[13] Partly because of the KPD's departure, no

10. Text in *Freiheit,* June 28, 1922.

11. *Ibid.,* July 1, 1922. The trade unions were the driving force behind this second day of demonstrations, while the SPD, fearing growing radicalism, followed only with reluctance; see the comments of Otto Braun, BA Koblenz, Reichskanzlei 1867, p. 99, and Adolf Braun in a letter to the Breslau *Volkswacht,* July 8, 1922, Löbe collection, 8, p. 24.

12. See the survey of the demonstrations, BA Koblenz, Reichskanzlei 1867, p. 143. The worst incidents, in Zwickau, lasted several days and caused several deaths; see StA Dresden, MdI Nr. 11106a, pp. 152–53 and 245–63.

13. *Freiheit,* July 7 and 9, 1922. The breach in Berlin was followed by similar

further nationwide demonstrations were held, and in most areas the popular drive to radical action began slowly to fade. But the volatile emotions of the masses continued to be a political factor well into July.

Against the background of the workers' obvious restiveness and their ready response to a united-front movement, USPD leaders argued out their future program. The debates were by no means confined to the tactics of the mass pressure being publicly exerted by the joint committee of the united front. The Reichstag delegation served as the main forum for evolving USPD policy over the next three weeks; accordingly, ideals of mass action were mixed with other considerations ranging from the practical problems of current legislation (for instance the pending grain bill)[14] to the composition of an effective cabinet to deal with the crisis. The faith of the majority of deputies in the efficacy of mass pressure alone was obviously not great.

The Independents were unanimous in taking the counterrevolution seriously. Moreover, many saw defense of the Republic as an overriding necessity, an ironic position given the hostility the Independents had shown earlier to nearly every institution of the Republic. As declared "social revolutionaries," the Independents believed that the Republic was an intermediate political form that must be transcended; but the revolutionary ardor of most had cooled enough to allow them to recognize the Republic's merits and possibilities—especially when the only likely alternative was some form of autocracy. The Republic seemed the most suitable base for the further propagation of socialist principles, the system in which the open politics they preferred could be practiced without hindrance. It permitted the socialist parties and trade unions to develop with relative freedom and offered more opportunity for social legislation than any imaginable reactionary regime. In short, "the Republic" had acquired much the same complex of associations as "democracy" had had for Kautsky in his polemic against the Bolsheviks, with added emotional force because the Republic was being threatened from the right.[15]

---

developments in most other parts of the country. In a few places the three-way alliance continued; it was confirmed, for instance, in Düsseldorf and Thuringia some ten days later (*ibid.*, July 15, 1922). By the end of the month, however, it appears to have been dead everywhere.

14. The liveliest political issue for the socialists just before the crisis broke out had been the bill to hold down the price of bread by means of state grain purchases, a last vestige of wartime price controls on foodstuffs; until the bourgeois parties decided to acquiesce, in the last days of July, this issue threatened to divide the republican bloc along class lines. See Stampfer, *Die vierzehn Jahre*, p. 256.

15. On July 13, 1922, the USPD delegation voted to declare Constitution Day (August 11) a national holiday; Pistorius, p. 199, singles out this act as symbolizing the final conversion of the Independents into supporters of the Republic.

For the defense of the Republic all Independents could agree on the use of their traditional tactics, mobilizing mass pressure on the government; but only a few still believed this could be sufficient. For the others, including most of the leaders, the crux appeared to lie in decisive use of government power. Mass pressure could move the government off dead center, experience had shown, but it could not move a body of moderate and conservative men to carry radical measures through with energy; nor could it ensure continuation of positive action once the pressure ceased. In June 1922 many Independents were in a frame of mind to consider radical measures not only desirable but necessary; and such measures, they felt, required a new, more decisive government. The only way the cabinet could acquire new, more radical members and still maintain its parliamentary majority was to include Independents—the solution recommended at once by many party leaders.

This logic was responsible for the odd circumstance that the USPD's first debates after the murder concerned not proletarian unity, as might have been expected, but the question of whether the USPD should agree to enter the Reich government. Only six months before, rejection of coalition with the bourgeoisie had justified the continued existence of the party. Yet this shibboleth was the first to be challenged as the USPD settled down to a new wearying round of controversy over its future.

The issue arose on the evening after Rathenau's death, at the Reichstag delegation's second meeting of the day.[16] Levi revived the familiar but empty notion of a government of "socialists, trade unions, and perhaps also Center Party workers"; the idea roused little enthusiasm and among the party's major figures only Ledebour seems to have found it a plausible solution. Dittmann then advocated entering the present government provided that the cabinet was constituted in proportion to the parliamentary strength of the parties (which would have given the two Social Democratic parties a majority) and that a joint political program was adopted that went beyond passage of a law for the defense of the Republic; he added that of course such a government could only be "transitional," since it would soon break up on its own inner tensions and lead to a "purely socialist" government and new elections. Dittmann's qualifications were unreal but gave his proposal enough respectability that others could follow their inclinations and support it with fairly good consciences. Those who spoke against the step included such able and influ-

16. The account that follows is based on the minutes of the USPD Reichstag delegation, June 24, 1922, evening meeting. *Freiheit* made no mention of the discussions until it reported a speech by Franz Künstler on the subject on June 28; but *Vorwärts* knew of the subject of the Independents' deliberations on June 25. See also Kastning, pp. 97–98.

ential members as Robert Dissmann, Tony Sender, and Kurt Rosenfeld; but most of those who spoke supported Dittmann. Crispien ended the meeting by announcing that the leadership would try to find out from the SPD what the terms of entry into the government were likely to be.

When the delegation renewed its debate two days later a strange feeling of inevitability had already set in. The opponents, though they mustered their arguments cogently, knew they were fighting a losing battle; and Dittmann even proposed that a special party conference be convened the following weekend to consider the matter—by which he plainly meant that it should ratify the views of the majority of the delegation.[17] On June 27 came the first feelers from the SPD.[18] A letter of July 1 then formally requested the USPD to discuss entry into the government;[19] and the same day the delegation met to vote on the matter, as did the party executive, auxiliary council, and control commission. The deliberations are not recorded, but the round of sessions ended the next day, July 2, with a full conference at which the momentous decision was approved.[20] Crispien then informed the SPD that: "In view of the present exceptional situation we are ready to negotiate with your party, together with the trade union organizations, about the question of the entry of our party into the Reich government."[21]

This rapid progress toward coalition occurred in spite of having not only party tradition but also many of the best arguments against it. Except on the unlikely assumption of lasting radical pressure from the populace, the vision of great USPD influence in a coalition government was illusory, as the SPD's experience since 1919 indicated. To hope in existing circumstances that the Center Party and Democrats would agree to a socialist majority in the cabinet was unreasonable; even if they did, the Independents, as the smaller and less strategically placed party, would be the junior partner to the SPD. Later tentative negotiations showed that the Independents might get two seats in the cabinet—hardly a decisive number.[22] Furthermore, the ministries they would be given, Reconstruction and probably the Foreign Office, were not the best from which to fight reaction. In short, the USPD inside the government was

17. Minutes of the USPD Reichstag delegation, June 26, 1922.
18. According to Crispien, *ibid.,* June 28, 1922. For the thinking of high-ranking Majority Socialists at this point, see the letter from Justice Minister Radbruch to his wife on June 27, 1922, in Gustav Radbruch, *Briefe* (Göttingen, 1968), p. 82.
19. Printed in *Freiheit,* July 6, 1922. The date, not given in *Freiheit,* is supplied by a copy of the letter in ASD Bonn, collection: Verschiedene Originalbriefe und Dokumente, item 24.
20. Resolution of the conference, *Freiheit,* July 6, 1922.
21. *Ibid.*
22. According to Rosenfeld, *Freiheit,* Aug. 25, 1922.

unlikely to enjoy enough additional influence to balance the loss of its advantages (particularly in agitation) as an opposition party. To enter the cabinet meant to send members to sit around a table with such detested figures as Reichswehr Minister Gessler, Transport Minister Groener (the former general), and Minister of the Economy Hermes; and it meant giving up the agitational position that the unnatural alliance between socialists and bourgeoisie was responsible for the failings of the system.

Moreover, the decision of the party conference provoked dissension in the party. A fairly large minority of the conference, twenty-six out of sixty-five, voted to uphold the party's established practices;[23] and in the aftermath critical resolutions were adopted at meetings of the local functionaries of the influential Düsseldorf, Dresden, and Frankfurt on Main organizations.[24] These militants had seen enough of party conferences in the past to protest vigorously against the use of such an unrepresentative body to make fundamental alterations in the party's policies—a complaint that was certainly justified. The party press, to judge from the editorials reprinted in *Freiheit* and the Halle *Volkszeitung,* was prepared to accept the new policy, but often with skepticism. The large Leipzig local organization—which with Berlin was the backbone of the party— supported the decision in its functionaries' assembly and even suggested that it might lead to reunification of the parties.[25] But in pushing through the breach with tradition the leadership clearly risked not carrying all the membership with it.

The basic and predictable flaw in the scheme was that the SPD's bourgeois coalition partners had no intention of agreeing, in part because the Independents were unattractive as coalition partners but even more because two Social Democratic parties would dominate the coalition as the SPD alone had not been able to. A coalition in which one partner was predominant was unappealing enough in any case; but only under extreme circumstances—such as those of February 1919—was such a coalition acceptable when the partner was the socialists, who were not yet regarded as a fully normal and legitimate political party. The more the socialists sought to mobilize the trade unions and their followers outside parliament, the less inclined were the parties of the bourgeois middle to accept the SPD's wishes for the future of the coalition.

In the first days after the murder prospects for USPD entry looked promising simply because the parties of the middle were in no position

23. According to Kunert, *Volkszeitung* (Halle), July 24, 1922.
24. *Freiheit,* July 6 and 8, 1922.
25. *Ibid.,* July 7, 1922.

to take a strong stand against the socialists so long as the popular reaction seemed capable of turning into rebellion if it were provoked. In these days the grain bill was finally reported from committee and passed in a compromise form favorable to the workers' interests. The Center Party and Democrats seemed generally passive in the face of events, and on July 1 the SPD executive formally told the USPD that it believed the opposition of its coalition partners to Independent participation could be overcome.[26] But when the Independents, the following day, reported their wish to negotiate about entry, the latent resistance began to show itself. On July 6 the Center Party and Democrats addressed a joint formal inquiry to the conservative People's Party about their possible entry into a republican coalition, obviously as a counterweight. The People's Party, accepting the conditions laid down—unambiguous commitment to the Republic, a law for the defense of the Republic, and a rational foreign policy—at once agreed.[27]

This move was a turning point for the socialists. They had set out to give the government a more decisively socialist orientation in good faith, if with unreasonable optimism. Now this path was blocked. If USPD entry into the government depended on coalition with those questionable republicans, the People's Party, then the exercise lost its point for the Independents. The SPD, in turn, could not accept the People's Party without rupturing the renewed brotherhood with the Independents; with little visible wavering, they chose the path of socialist solidarity.[28] This solidarity was the sole tangible result of the USPD's painful reappraisal of its coalition policy. It is difficult to escape the conclusion that it was a major, though unspoken, reason for the difficult step being taken.

The first two weeks of July saw the consolidation of this new alignment of the parties in the Reichstag as the socialist parties (usually without the Communists) joined together in opposition to the bourgeois parties (usually without the Nationalists). Not that the battle lines were clearly drawn; the government coalition remained together, though with its members having to consult outside allies at every turn parliamentary business was greatly complicated. The major issue of these weeks was the draft law for the defense of the Republic, and nothing could more effectively have drawn the two Social Democratic parties together. Both wanted a much stronger law than the government's draft (prepared by the Social Democrat Radbruch as justice minister) and stronger than what was obtainable; there was, therefore, little occasion for conflict of views on details. The two delegations coordinated their proposals for

26. See n. 19 above; also Ledebour, USPD-SPD *Parteitage,* Sept. 1922, p. 150.
27. *Freiheit,* July 8, 1922.
28. Declaration of July 9, *Vorwärts,* July 11, 1922 (m).

amendments and their presentations in the Reichstag committee deliberations. The USPD sent Levi and Rosenfeld, two of its best legal minds and most articulate spokesmen, into the fray, and the Majority Socialists gave them full support.

The socialists' efforts were not, however, successful. As representatives of the socialist working class they had two special goals: a general amnesty for political prisoners, most of whom were socialists and Communists convicted in a dubious manner by a partisan judiciary; and a guarantee that the new strict laws were for application only against the threat from the right, a wish that stemmed from mistrust of the judges and bureaucrats who would apply the law. On the latter point the socialists received verbal assurances from ministers but failed to get a guarantee written into the law; in fact, the final draft of the law specified defense of the Republic in its existing constitutional form, which could be easily interpreted as outlawing efforts to convert the state into a soviet republic.[29] On the question of amnesty, dealt with in a separate bill debated at the same time, the socialists obtained some concessions, though the result was not as sweeping as they would have liked. In matters where special socialist interests were less directly involved, little heed was taken of their desire for thoroughgoing reform of administrative practices, a purge of monarchists from the judiciary and civil service, and strict laws against the propagation of antirepublican views.[30] Indeed, in these areas socialist demands were so extreme that they amounted to outlawing the political views of a good part of the population and making second-class citizens of those holding them. For the socialists the emergency was great enough to justify such measures; but the other parties, having recovered from their first alarm, saw no need for extreme measures and preferred to depart as little as possible from the assumption that normalcy should obtain in political life. Normalcy included retention of experienced civil servants; the inviolability of the judiciary; considerable freedom of speech, even for monarchists; and a federal system in which decisive police powers remained with the states. It was also assumed that leftist revolution was at least as strong a danger as rightist reaction. Accordingly, the laws, while of considerable use as weapons against subversion, did not promise the suppression of the antirepublican right that the socialists desired.

The final vote on the laws came on July 19; long before then, however, the socialists had foreseen the outcome and had considered their

29. Jasper, pp. 70–71.
30. The committee stage of the bill can be followed in *Freiheit,* July 7 to 11, 1922.

response. The most dramatic response available to them, which could have been achieved by joining the Communists and Nationalists to form a majority in the Reichstag against the laws, was to bring down the government and force a dissolution of the Reichstag. The possibility of dissolution had been discussed among the parties from the beginning of the crisis, while the republican front was still a unit; and indeed an election fought on the basis of the party alignments of late June might have delivered the most effective blow possible to the isolated radical right. But there were doubts from the start about the wisdom of such a course. The republican bloc was not really firm, and neither wing (certainly not the Independents) believed in fighting an election in harness with representatives of the opposing class. Dissolution would also have ended all pending legislation, including the grain bill and the law for the defense of the Republic. Moreover, the Independents in particular had to face the fact that new elections, even if they strengthened the republican camp, would cut their own party's strength, for their present seventy-one seats reflected the glories of June 1920 rather than the situation of 1922. No definite evidence exists that the Independents opposed dissolution on these grounds, despite the belief of the chairman of the SPD delegation, Hermann Müller, that they did;[31] but an awareness of political realities probably helped keep them from actively advocating that solution.

With the division of the republican bloc along class lines in early July, the prospect of elections took on new meaning. An election campaign fought along class lines had much more appeal for many Independents, and the halfhearted attitude of the bourgeois parties toward the dangers of monarchist reaction provided an issue. Popular feeling was still running high and was reflected even in the trade unions, where as late as July 9 Leipart of the ADGB was thinking of a general strike.[32] Majority Socialist leaders, however, opposed a dissolution. An election campaign in such circumstances and along such lines would be bitter, possibly even violent; it might harm the Republic more than serve it and would certainly widen the gulf between the socialist right and the bourgeois left more than most Majority Socialists wished. It also might easily widen the division between the two Social Democratic parties.[33] Moreover, with the compromise grain bill accepted, what issues were the socialists to raise? The desire to find seats in the government for two Independents

31. BA Koblenz, Reichskanzlei 1020, p. 36; Eduard David papers (BA Koblenz), Nr. 19, diary entry for July 13, 1922.
32. According to Julius Moses, in minutes of the USPD Reichstag delegation, July 10, 1922. Leipart (successor to Legien) seems to have been influenced by a meeting of the executive committee of the International Federation of Trade Unions in Berlin that day; see *Freiheit,* July 11, 1922.
33. Dittmann memoirs, p. 1282.

would certainly not serve.[34] Few seem to have thought that the socialists could win an election; to force one would therefore be more a demonstration than a practical act, and the Majority Socialists, and a growing number of Independents, had lost their enthusiasm for dramatic demonstrations without practical effect.

With the crisis building up after July 10, the Majority Socialist delegation made the clever move of leaving the decision about a dissolution to the Independents, promising to follow their lead.[35] Their calculations were correct; a majority of the USPD delegation no longer had the heart to fight the good fight regardless of the consequences, even though this course was recommended by some of their most prominent leaders, including Ledebour, Rosenfeld, and even Dittmann. But failing a dissolution, some other dramatic move must be made. Similar considerations to those bearing on the question of dissolution eliminated the idea of a general strike. Only a parliamentary solution was left, and on July 14 the two Social Democratic delegations announced tersely that they were entering into a formal alliance binding them to joint action in all Reichstag affairs.[36]

Oddly enough, the USPD seems to have hoped that a formal alliance of the two delegations would force the other coalition parties to take the Independents into the government.[37] This was a miscalculation; the Center Party and Democrats instead drew closer to the People's Party, forming their own alliance the following month. The real significance of the action lay elsewhere; from the day the SPD-USPD alliance was announced, it was obvious to all socialists that full reunification of the two parties was not only feasible but had become practically certain. In effect, the decision of July 14, though no one would admit it at the time, was to give up hope of determining the immediate course of events and withdraw to consolidate the forces of the socialist working class.

This second and final turning point in the socialist response to Rathenau's murder was less abrupt than it seemed. Reunification of the socialist movement was the ultimate goal of all united-front actions such as that which followed the assassination; everyone knew this, though it

34. See Levi's analysis, *Freiheit,* July 21, 1922.
35. According to Rosenfeld, *ibid.,* Aug. 25, 1922.
36. *Ibid.,* July 15, 1922. In the USPD delegation, between two-thirds and three-quarters of the deputies present supported the step, in the SPD delegation only three voted against it; Ledebour, USPD-SPD *Parteitage,* Sept. 1922, p. 150, and Alfred Grotjahn, *Erlebtes und Erstrebtes: Erinnerungen eines sozialistischen Arztes* (Berlin, 1932), pp. 240–41 (Grotjahn was one of the three).
37. Rosenfeld, *Freiheit,* Aug. 25, 1922; Ledebour, USPD-SPD *Parteitage,* Sept. 1922, p. 150.

was impolitic to be explicit on the point. In the crisis of June 1922 the aim of socialist unity was closer to the surface than usual. There must have been many who, like Dittmann, immediately concluded that this time the united front with the SPD must lead to a reunited party;[38] unfortunately for purposes of analysis, most of them, Dittmann included, kept their views to themselves. The *Leipziger Volkszeitung,* with its customary outspokenness (exceptional in the party), declared on June 26 for both entry into the government and reunification; Dittmann's *Freiheit,* however, said nothing editorially until August 27. Evidence that there was a deliberate drive toward unification from the first days after Rathenau's death is, therefore, slim; yet the peculiar twists in the policies of the socialist parties between June 24 and July 14 become more rational if they are understood as guided by a determination to move toward reunification without ever openly indicating the goal.

Not all the leaders had necessarily thought so far ahead. The change in the USPD's policy on coalitions had a genuine impulse behind it— the desire to join actively in an important task. Perhaps only a few saw that abandoning their stand against coalitions abolished at a stroke the single major issue separating the two parties, thereby not only making unification possible but also disposing of the rationale for separate existence.[39] More must have realized that the spirit of unity was so strong during the weeks of the demonstrations that any organizational measures beyond the formation of the united front would release powerful pressures for the leaders to compose their differences once and for all. The USPD's decision to join the SPD in the government, had it succeeded, would have amounted to such a measure; critics of the action had pointed this out in advance. The formation of the parliamentary alliance was almost certain to have the same effect.

As with the earlier decision to enter the government, the alliance met a mixed response in the USPD. This time negative reactions were fewer and less hostile, partly no doubt because the issue of entry into the government faded into the background at the same time. Yet the news was hardly received with enthusiasm, judging from the response of the party press. Still less was there ready acceptance of the idea that the alliance meant reunification. The first comments either avoided direct mention of the possibility of reunification or indicated that the prospect was still distant; the Düsseldorf *Volkszeitung,* for instance, observed that "a lasting unification of the proletariat is only possible on the foundation of a common, principled socialist basis of struggle and program for struggle. This,

38. Dittmann memoirs, pp. 1281–82.
39. See Levi, *Unser Weg,* Aug. 15, 1922, p. 299.

however, is not yet present."[40] Even in Saxony, where (except in the Dresden district) sentiment for socialist unity was stronger, a statewide party conference immediately after formation of the alliance heard few speakers advocate early organizational fusion with the SPD.[41]

Within days, however, opinion began to change, partly because passage of the unsatisfactory Law for the Defense of the Republic on July 19, followed by a long parliamentary recess, left socialists with little to address themselves to except unity, partly perhaps because a declaration of July 19 had hinted at the leadership's intention to pursue further negotiations with the SPD, for a purpose that was left vague but could only be an approach to organizational unity.[42] As early as July 16 a resolution of a party conference of the Frankfurt on Main district, which was hostile to the party's course in recent weeks, recognized "that the majority decision of the national conference of the USP and the decision of the Reichstag delegation to form an alliance with the SPD will necessarily lead in a very short time to the absorption of the USP into the SPD" and based future policy on this assumption.[43] On July 20 a conference of 1,200 functionaries of the Berlin organization voted by a large majority for a resolution endorsing steps toward reunification; a unanimous resolution of the Berlin-Brandenburg organization's governing committee referred forthrightly to "fusing" the two parties.[44] The party press, too, began to refer to unification as the likely if not necessarily immediate outcome of the existing relationship between the two Social Democratic parties. Hesitancy and scattered resistance were still expressed; but with the bulk of the articulate strata of the party accepting reunification as inevitable, the idea can be said to have triumphed.

In spite of this, on the whole, encouraging response, the party executive embarked on further steps with caution. The leaders' actions after July 14 proceeded in a straight line toward unification with the SPD but were conducted almost entirely out of the sight of the members until the last days of August. The process was carefully managed. The majority of leaders seem to have made up their minds and to have had no further doubts; members' feelings had been tested, and the leaders were satisfied that they would be followed by most of the party. They could not be un-

40. Quoted in *Freiheit,* July 19, 1922.
41. USPD-Sachsen *Landesversammlung,* July 1922. The principal resolution of the conference, however, mentioned among the reasons for endorsing the alliance the fact that it "smooths the path to a union of the socialist parties"; *Freiheit,* July 20, 1922.
42. *Freiheit,* July 20, 1922.
43. *Ibid.,* July 19, 1922.
44. *Ibid.,* July 22 and 24, 1922. The word was "verschmelzen."

aware, however, that some members were hostile and many more reluctant. The task was, therefore, to complete reunification as smoothly and uncontroversially as possible and to minimize the loss of members or apparatus to the dissidents who might choose to remain outside the reunited party.[45]

A negotiating committee was quietly appointed in late July and held a preliminary meeting with its counterpart from the SPD on July 28.[46] There may have been some hesitation at first about the wisdom of proceeding rapidly. Their need for a vacation was surely not the only reason the three leading USPD negotiators, Hilferding, Crispien, and Dittmann, left Berlin and let the talks languish for most of August.[47] August, however, was a catastrophic month for Germany, and events continued to work for reunification. During the Reichstag recess the conservative Bavarian government defied several provisions of the new Law for the Defense of the Republic, and the Reich government chose to settle the conflict by negotiation, in the process negotiating away some important provisions of the law; this new success for the spirit of reaction strengthened the sense of defensive unity among the workers. The accelerated inflation brought on by the crisis also had its effect. The *Frankfurter Zeitung* estimated that the cost of living rose by 52.5 percent between July 1 and August 1.[48] Party revenues, especially newspaper revenues, could not be increased at the same rate; there are signs that *Freiheit* was on the verge of going under.[49] Whether or not the financial problems of the USPD had strengthened desires for reunification earlier on—and there is no direct evidence that they had—the impact of the inflation of

45. For an expression of the need to move cautiously, see the letter from Paul Hertz to Dittmann, Aug. 11, 1922, Dittmann papers, Kasten: Originalbriefe, Dokumente, Photokopien, item 38.

46. The first recorded step was a letter from the SPD party executive on July 22, mentioned in the USPD's reply of July 25 (copy in ASD Bonn, collection: Verschiedene Originalbriefe und Dokumente, item 23). The meeting of July 28 was reported in a terse notice in *Freiheit,* July 29, 1922. The USPD's negotiators were Hilferding, Crispien, Dittmann, Franz Künstler, and Konrad Ludwig, representing the full range of views in the party short of Ledebour's intransigent opposition to unification.

47. Letter from Adolf Braun (one of the SPD negotiators) to Kautsky, Aug. 2, 1922, Kautsky papers, D VI 402.

48. *Freiheit,* Aug. 15, 1922.

49. Letter from Emil Rauch to Dittmann, Aug. 16, 1922, Dittmann papers, Kasten: Originalbriefe, Dokumente, Photokopien, item 45; notice on an increase in subscription price, *Freiheit,* July 28, 1922; report of the Verlagsgenossenschaft, *Freiheit,* July 19, 1922. Ernst Drahn, "Zur Quellenkunde einer Pressegeschichte der Sozialisten (Marxisten) Deutschlands," *Jahrbücher für Nationalökonomie und Statistik,* 132 (1930), 407, claims that *Freiheit* had a circulation of only 10,000 during the summer of 1922. In the course of July, 144 German newspapers and periodicals ceased publication; *Freiheit,* Aug. 31, 1922.

July and August meant that if reunification was to come it should come without delay.[50]

Thus, when negotiations finally began in earnest they were conducted with almost indecent haste. On August 25 and 26, the party executive at last assembled the auxiliary council and control commission to sanction negotiations for reunification.[51] On August 29 the two sets of negotiators met, officially for the first time, to decide on procedures; on September 4, in a single session, they agreed on an Action Program for the reunited party.[52] The more difficult problems of fusing the two organizations and disposing of their assets took longer. But little time was available even for these matters, for the SPD party congress was scheduled to meet in Augsburg on September 17, which fixed a terminus ad quem. All the serious negotiations for the fusion of two major political parties were compressed into a period of less than three weeks. Inevitably, a great deal was left to be settled later—another sign that the leaders of the two parties regarded unification as an all but accomplished fact even before it was ratified by the two party congresses.

Progress was not achieved without resistance. Only a few leading figures in the USPD set their faces against reunification, but they included two members of the party executive, Kurt Rosenfeld and the intractable Georg Ledebour. Within a week of the formation of the parliamentary alliance with the SPD, the leading opponents met and resolved to carry on the USPD even if the majority should decide for reunification[53]— though how many would follow them was unclear. Ledebour's group was influenced not only by ancient grudges and resentments that made it difficult for them to conceive of becoming members again of the party of Ebert and Noske, but also, and more importantly, by their profound commitment to the mission the USPD had been proclaiming since Halle, to unite the proletariat, the whole proletariat, on the basis of the class struggle. No matter how strong its support, a unification arrived at through the manipulations of two party executives was not this unity. It would not include the Communists (though admittedly waiting for them might mean a long delay); and it would have been brought about by the

50. One former Independent (Fritz Bieligk) later judged that imminent financial disaster was a leading motive for reunification at this time; Fritz Bieligk et al., *Die Organisation im Klassenkampf* (Berlin [1931]), p. 56.

51. *Freiheit*, Aug. 27, 1922.

52. *Ibid.*, Sept. 5, 1922.

53. Police report of July 24, 1922, DZA Merseburg, Rep. 77 Tit. 1809 Nr. 5, p. 47. One outspoken opponent of unification, Fritz Kunert, refused to go along with this decision, stating that he would acquiesce if a party congress decided against him; see *Volkszeitung* (Halle), Sept. 4, 1922.

calculated dealings of the leaders, not generated by the impatient masses. In Rosenfeld's words:

> Only the fire of the class struggle can weld the socialist parties into a unity. Only when this has occurred, when the parties have reached agreement on the methods of the class struggle, can the organizational fusion of the parties come about.
>
> Just because I desire the unification of the proletariat, I am against the *present* unification of the two socialist parties.[54]

The Ledebour-Rosenfeld group could make a number of points in attempting to influence those who did not share their own intensely ideological approach to the issue, but most of them were based on the single argument that the supposed merger of the USPD and the SPD in fact meant "the absorption [*Aufgehen*] of the USPD into the SPD."[55] Such an effect was to be expected when one partner was so much larger than the other; and there were signs in advance that the ideals for which the Independents had fought would be difficult to uphold in the larger party. The most egregious sign, from the point of view of the rebellious left wing, was the new Action Program, generally understood to have been drafted principally by Independents.[56] This document made no reference to the dictatorship of the proletariat or the problem of coalition governments. The term "class struggle" appeared in the preamble, but as a whole the document constituted nothing more than a vigorous program of social reform. The contrast with the two previous USPD Action Programs could hardly have been more marked.

The leadership was ready with answers to all such objections; and though these answers were not always very satisfactory they were delivered in a tone that showed that the majority was sure of its cause. The fundamental problem with Ledebour's position was that it obviously would not attract enough followers to give his group the leverage to reunite the proletariat—or indeed to carry out any ambitious program. No matter how good the cause, if it rallied only a few tens of thousands, then a separate organization was a mistake; there was no place for what Hilferding called "sect politics with a fine revolutionary program."[57] Levi and most of the former members of the KAG saw this readily enough and stayed with the majority.[58] To defend the Action Program was more

54. *Freiheit*, Aug. 25, 1922.
55. Ledebour, USPD-SPD *Parteitage*, Sept. 1922, p. 153.
56. Text in *Vorwärts*, Sept. 6, 1922 (m). On its origins, see Dittmann memoirs, p. 1283.
57. *Freiheit*, Sept. 14, 1922.
58. See Levi's speech, *ibid.*, July 21, 1922, and his article in *Unser Weg*, Aug. 15, 1922, pp. 293–300. Only two widely known Independents who were former members of the KAG remained with Ledebour after reunification: Paul Wegmann,

difficult, given its contrast with party traditions; but at least the USPD could claim to have squeezed a recognition of the class struggle out of the Majority Socialists, who thereby suspended their Görlitz Program.[59] As for the problem of being submerged within the SPD, the leaders could offer only exhortations; party members must enter upon this venture in the spirit of creating a new party, not a merger of two old ones, and must have the self-confidence to believe that their ideals and program would prove the stronger in the long run.[60]

This last point was the central issue for that large body of members who were unenthusiastic about reunification but had no intention of remaining apart from what was evidently a mass movement of the party, however ill-advised. The spokesman for this group was Robert Dissmann. Dissmann had struggled "very passionately" against the course adopted by the party since June,[61] as he observed party leaders shedding their professed principles and steering for unification with a party he mistrusted, but he never gave serious thought to remaining in a tiny splinter party. His group was determined, however, not to sacrifice its political identity but to march into the united party with banners flying—in effect, to enter it as a coherent faction, both to provide mutual support within the unsympathetic environment they foresaw, and to form the base for an attempt to convert the united Social Democratic Party to their own ideals. Most concretely, they meant to make it clear in advance that the party decision of July 2 did not affect their long-standing objection to coalition government.

Such were the alignments when the USPD assembled at Gera, in Thuringia, on September 20 for its last congress. The leadership had carried its campaign to obtain the maximum majority for reunification into the local election of delegates by providing—in contrast to the voting before Halle—that minorities should go unrepresented.[62] The fact that only 9 of the 192 delegates voted against the merger is therefore no guide to the division of party sentiment. Since figures on the voting locally were not generally published—another piece of careful management by party officials—there is no way to make a better estimate; plainly, however, the intransigents were in a minority nearly everywhere. The effect desired by party leaders had been created; apparently with

---

successor to Däumig's Reichstag seat in July, and Oskar Rusch, deputy in the Prussian Diet. Both were former colleagues of Ledebour on the Berlin executive council during the revolution.

59. Crispien, USPD-SPD *Parteitage*, Sept. 1922, pp. 134–35.
60. See speeches by Levi and Hilferding, *Freiheit*, July 21 and 22, 1922.
61. Dissmann, USPD-SPD *Parteitage*, Sept. 1922, pp. 157–58.
62. *Ibid.*, p. 154.

near unanimity, the USPD was ready to merge itself into a reunited Social Democratic Party.

These final debates were not a glorious end for the party—they could hardly be so. The delegates of the majority were either apprehensive about the future or embarrassed about the past, and very much aware of having acted as much under the pressure of events as from high idealism. Such feelings precluded rhetorical accomplishments; even Crispien could not rouse his listeners. The only real fire in the proceedings came from the tiny minority, who could do nothing but rail. In Ledebour they had the man for the task; bitterly he poured out his feelings: "The break with the revolutionary past of our party: that is the denial of our principles, that is the suicide of the USPD";[63] "It is a frightful crime that you propose to commit against the workers' movement."[64] But the delegates were not listening.

Dissmann's group provided a few spirited moments. Its members did not have to reproach themselves with unfaithfulness to their past, and they offered a rallying point for the uncertain future. Their stand was embodied in a proposed resolution that members of the USPD would profess in their future roles in the SPD, as they had in the past as Independents, a commitment to the class struggle and the rejection of all forms of alliance with the bourgeoisie.[65] Such importance was attached to this declaration that it was submitted to the congress in spite of a warning from the party executive that its adoption would probably cause the SPD to repudiate the unification agreements, and it gained the signatures of over half of the delegates—though the party executive was eventually able to sway a sufficient number of the signatories for the resolution to be turned into a declaration of a part of the congress, without a vote being taken.[66] For a majority of the congress, as this episode demonstrated, the moment of unity required a reassertion of fundamental principle; but unity remained the overriding consideration. In the end, even Kurt Rosenfeld took this view; at the last moment, after the voting had been held, he joined Kunert in bowing to the will of the majority, leaving Ledebour with only six followers among those present at the congress to help him organize the sad remnants of the USPD and carry on.[67]

63. *Ibid.,* p. 146.
64. *Ibid.,* p. 167.
65. Text *ibid.,* p. 131; see also Sender, pp. 200–1.
66. See the accounts of this episode by Dissmann and by Hilferding (supported by Crispien), SPD *Parteitag,* 1924, pp. 135 and 136. Just how much the SPD leaders resented this declaration is shown by Otto Wels' words two years later; *ibid.,* pp. 125–26.
67. The six included Theodor Liebknecht (Berlin) and Gerhard Obuch (Düsseldorf), both deputies in the Prussian Diet; Heinrich Rau (Gleiwitz), the leading Independent in Upper Silesia; and three little-known delegates from Westphalia.

One last moment of enthusiasm was felt, not at Gera, but at Nuremberg, where many of the USPD delegates gathered with delegates from the Majority Socialists' Augsburg congress on September 24. The moment of unification was expressed symbolically as the aged Wilhelm Bock of the USPD control commission and the even more aged Wilhelm Pfannkuch of the SPD party executive, both veterans of the days of the first socialist unity congress in 1875, advanced from opposite sides of the stage to shake hands and embrace.

This emotional moment, a milestone in the history of the German socialist movement, marked the inglorious death, after five and a half years, of the Independent Social Democratic Party.[68] Many leading Independents had known for over a year, and most thoughtful members at least since the failure of the three-way united front in May, that the life expectancy of their party was not great, however sound the theoretical reasons for its existence. The manner of the party's demise—negotiated merger into the SPD—was not the end for which they had hoped and prepared themselves but a last resort, the only form of broader unity available in the summer of 1922 when the pressure, popular and practical, to act was so great. Once the party leadership had taken the first steps, the rest of the leading cadres in the party, willingly or unwillingly, recognized that the wearying struggle for USPD independence was over and acquiesced in the inevitable, often with ill grace, but definitely. Ledebour's alternative—a new schism, a new rebuilding, a new struggle for survival on even more unfavorable terms—had little appeal for those who had struggled to so little effect in the two years since Halle. Reunification offered at least a respectable escape from the prospect of continued decline. Independent Social Democracy accordingly dissolved itself into the broader, more secure unity of the United Social Democratic Party.

68. For a discussion of the surviving splinters that carried on the name, see the Epilogue.

Epilogue

The great majority of the members of the USPD joined the United Social Democratic Party (VSPD) during the fall of 1922.[1] The path back to the old party—for this was really the meaning of unification—was made easier for the Independents by a sad irony: the suddenly increased strength of the socialist coalition partner brought down Wirth's government at last. As it was succeeded by a nonparty cabinet, the VSPD was relieved, at least formally, of governmental responsibility, and the worst struggles over the question of coalition were postponed. This result was not what the leaders of either socialist party had wanted; their ideal was continuation of the old coalition but with the socialists promoted to dominance; but the Center Party and Democrats were not prepared to be as self-effacing as the new assertiveness of the socialists required. As they had warned during the summer, they demanded the right to bring in their own reinforcements, the People's Party—which in the circumstances the socialists could not possibly tolerate. The status quo had been upset by the unification of the socialists, and there was too much class consciousness, as well as party egotism, on both sides for a new balance to be found. This sad end to the campaign to strengthen the Republic may, however, have strengthened the cohesion of the newly united party.

How much of a role was played by new members from the USPD in defining the Social Democratic position that helped lead to this impasse is unclear. A number of the old Majority Socialists felt that the atmosphere of the party changed abruptly; David, for instance, noted in his diary that the former majority-minority relationship within the SPD

1. Figures published in 1924 show that 206,065 members of the USPD became members of the VSPD; SPD *Parteitag,* 1924, p. 16. The 1922 membership of the USPD was 290,762 (see ch. 12, n. 7 on the ambiguities of this figure); the discrepancy reflects partly losses suffered before September, partly the defection of persons who dropped their socialist membership altogether at the time of reunification, and partly the establishment of Ledebour's splinter party. Not many are thought to have joined the Communist Party.

Reichstag delegation on grain bills was reversed at the first meeting of the united delegation.[2] Noske and Heine were both bitter about the effects of reunification—which, indeed, made it impossible for either to regain his earlier position in the party.[3] Certainly the adherence of the Independents did nothing to reverse the party's tendency, evident as early as 1920 and again in the recent crisis, to cling to its working-class constituency and show ambivalence about governmental responsibility.

Overall, however, the former Independents were not numerous enough to bring about a real change in the posture of the SPD, and they therefore had individually to choose between assimilating to the main body of the party or forming part of a permanent and fairly ineffectual opposition. The former national leaders of the USPD adapted easily to the new milieu, though generally remaining somewhat left of center in the party. Crispien and Dittmann sank into the honorable posts accorded them in the joint party executive (chairman and secretary respectively) and never again played a distinctive role in socialist affairs. Hilferding and Breitscheid, the two outstanding intellectuals of the USPD, had the most impressive careers, Hilferding as editor of the party journal, *Die Gesellschaft,* and twice minister of finance, Breitscheid as the party's principal foreign policy spokesman and later also chairman of the Reichstag delegation. Others became district secretaries and influential officeholders and carried on their work entirely in the spirit of the united party.

Still others, however—and apparently they made up much the greater part of the former Independents—remained true inside the SPD to the ideology of their old party and consequently found themselves constituting a more or less distinct left wing. It may be an exaggeration to say that the SPD before the reunification had "no left wing worthy of mention,"[4] but the arrival of the Independents certainly provided the Social Democratic left in the 1920's with its backbone and most of its outspoken members (particularly on the issue of participation in a coalition).[5] The first center of this opposition was Paul Levi, who found his

2. David papers, Nr. 19, entry for Oct. 2, 1922; see also Keil, II, 269–70.

3. Gustav Noske, *Erlebtes aus Aufstieg und Niedergang einer Demokratie* (Offenbach on Main, 1947), pp. 228–29 and 248; Wolfgang Heine, "Politische Aufzeichnungen" (BA Koblenz, Kl. Erw. 371–9), pp. 229–32; also Grotjahn, pp. 239–42.

4. Hanno Drechsler, *Die Sozialistische Arbeiterpartei Deutschlands* (Meisenheim on Glan, 1965), p. 1.

5. Of the 55 Reichstag deputies whom Günther Arns identifies as belonging to the left-wing faction in the SPD delegation in the controversy over the great coalition in autumn 1923, 49 were former Independents; see "Die Linke in der SPD-Reichstagsfraktion im Herbst 1923," *Vierteljahrshefte für Zeitgeschichte,* 22 (1974), pp. 197–202. (Arns counts only 47, but he omits Karl Kirchmann and Levi.)

métier at last as publisher of an opposition journal within the massive socialist party; from 1927, the focus was the semimonthly *Klassenkampf*, edited by Max Adler, Kurt Rosenfeld, Max Seydewitz, Heinrich Ströbel, and (from 1928 until his death early in 1930) Levi, all of whom, with the exception of Seydewitz, were from the Independent camp.[6] At party congresses, most of the spokesmen for the left were former Independents, notably the two leading trade unionists of the old USPD, Siegfried Aufhäuser (of the AfA) and Robert Dissmann. Even though the left could regularly claim between a quarter and a third of the delegates at party congresses, their influence on party policy was severely restricted; the majority never conceded them representation in the party executive, and indeed the executive periodically showed signs of paranoia about the party left.[7] The radicals had to be satisfied with their local power bases, of which the most important, revealingly, were Saxony, Thuringia, Halle, and Berlin.[8] The capture of the Saxon party organization by the left—former Independents plus radical Majority Socialists—provoked the party's only serious internal crisis between reunification and the onset of the final spasms of the Republic.[9]

When the left wing took more distinct shape after 1928, in a period when the party was first a member of a coalition government (this time a great coalition including the People's Party) and then committed to supporting the conservative Brüning government, the preponderance of old Independents in the faction became even clearer. Of thirteen Social Democratic deputies who abstained on the Müller cabinet's first vote of confidence in 1928, eleven had identifiable political pasts, and of these ten had been Independents.[10] On a similar occasion in December 1929, twenty-eight deputies absented themselves; of the twenty-five whose political history is known, twenty-two were former Independents.[11]

6. Drechsler, pp. 1–2 and 21–33. Seydewitz came from the radical left wing of the Saxon Majority Socialists, as did Erich Zeigner, the Saxon minister president in 1923. Max Adler, an Austrian, had been closely associated with the USPD. Ströbel is a rare example of an extreme right-wing Independent (he left the party in 1920 disgusted with the left) who took up a position on the left inside the SPD.

7. Richard N. Hunt, *German Social Democracy 1918–1933* (New Haven, Conn., 1964), pp. 228 and 237–38. For the attitude of the party executive, see, for instance, Wels' speech, SPD *Parteitag*, 1924, pp. 125–26, where, inter alia, Wels attributed the executive's difficulties with the left wing to the disloyal behavior of former Independents.

8. Hunt, p. 81.

9. *Ibid.,* pp. 210–21; Fabian, pp. 185–90. This crisis ended in a local schism in which the Saxon right, largely concentrated in the Dresden district, broke away to form a new party (which never attained any importance).

10. List in Drechsler, p. 34 (where fourteen abstainers are mentioned but only thirteen names given); investigation of previous party memberships by the present author.

11. *Ibid.,* p. 52.

In March 1931 came the first definite breach of discipline by nine deputies; apart from Seydewitz, who led the group with Rosenfeld, all were
former members of the USPD.[12] Among the six who broke away to form
the Socialist Workers Party in October 1931, only Seydewitz had not
been a member of the USPD. Thus while only some of the leading figures among former Independents in the SPD belonged to the militant left
wing, and while only a fraction of this left wing (and a bare handful of
those who had played important roles in the USPD) defected to the
Socialist Workers Party, the link between the socialist outlook of the
USPD and that of the later Social Democratic left is evident.

When a part of the Social Democratic left passed into the Socialist
Workers Party in 1931, it found itself reunited with old comrades—
those who had remained with Ledebour in 1922. The departure of the
majority of Independents into the United Social Democratic Party had
not meant the end of the USPD. Many thousands could still be rallied to
the banner of "revolutionary socialism" as traditionally understood by
the USPD radicals, refusing to be absorbed as tiny minorities into the
great parties on either side and continuing to respond to Ledebour's
vision:

> It is our task to drive toward common actions of all the proletarian orga-
> nizations until, in the fire of these common actions, both the Communist
> Party, which has now become a dependent instrument of the Moscow dicta-
> torship, and the simple-mindedly opportunistic VSPD are inflamed
> with the same fundamental revolutionary socialist conviction. This common
> fundamental conviction will then inevitably weld together the two neighbor-
> ing parties and ourselves into the great unitary proletarian party, which will
> bring us the final victory of socialism.[13]

This mission was out of all proportion to the strength of the recalcitrant
Independents; as long as the continuing economic and political crisis of
1922–1923 gave color to revolutionary hopes, however, the USPD had
a certain amount of support. In May 1924 the party received nearly
250,000 votes in the Reichstag elections.[14] Thereafter it declined rapidly
but did not expire, for parties sustained by the sort of impassioned sectarianism that characterized the splinter USPD are apparently almost
incapable of dying.

Even before its delayed decline, the splinter party's prospects were
never bright. The old USPD leaders, by then very experienced in party

12. *Ibid.*, p. 62.
13. Manifesto in the first number of *Klassenkampf*, Oct. 4, 1922. This weekly
paper was published in Berlin with Ledebour as editor.
14. In these elections the VSPD won over six million votes, the KPD over three
and a half million.

splits, had seen to it that the entire press and upper bureaucracy of the party, with insignificant exceptions, remained loyal to the majority decision for fusion. All sections of the party organization above the level of the smallest local subdivision (*Ortsgruppe*) were held, and even at the local subdivision level only a few went to the recalcitrants—several in the Rhineland and Westphalia, only one in Berlin, and none in Leipzig.[15] As for the members, the majority went willingly, if not always enthusiastically, into the united party, and the party bureaucracy used all the means at its disposal (not always admirable means[16]) to turn its genuine majority into something approaching unanimity. Even many of the most reluctant could see that the USPD would never again be a significant political force and were thus willing to go along. Of the nine dissenters at the Gera Congress, two (Kurt Rosenfeld and Fritz Kunert) announced that they would bow to the majority decision; three weeks later another of the nine, with a fellow member of the USPD's provisional executive, bowed to local pressure and followed the same path.[17] The momentum of reunification was not to be stemmed; so much was it taken for granted, even by those who regretted it, that in March 1923 Theodor Liebknecht admitted that "even today the news that the party continues to exist has not yet penetrated everywhere."[18] Potential members found it difficult to take the party seriously; consequently the party found it hard to grow.

The circumstances in which the leaders of the splinter USPD, under Ledebour and Liebknecht as chairmen, attempted to preserve the party, or more accurately to rebuild it from the ground up, were thus far from promising. They can hardly have inherited more than 30,000 or 40,000 of the old party's 300,000 members. Even this following—to judge from scanty evidence—was spread across the whole country and was nowhere very strong; most of the old USPD's centers of strength had groups who were willing to carry on the struggle rather than be absorbed into what they saw as the great, shapeless, and virtually unreformable VSPD, but these groups were neither large nor cohesive.[19] Only in a few places, notably Berlin and Düsseldorf, did the remaining USPD have something like a firm nucleus of support; in Berlin, the core was formed by remnants of the radical metalworkers' movement, who stood by their old

15. *Klassenkampf*, Oct. 4, 11, and 18, 1922.
16. See, for instance, *ibid.*, Oct. 18, 1922 (admittedly a biased source).
17. USPD-SPD *Parteitage*, Sept. 1922, p. 173–74; and *Klassenkampf*, Oct. 18, 1922.
18. USPD *Parteitag*, March–April 1923, pp. 2–3.
19. See the issues of *Klassenkampf* for Oct. 1922; and the results of the May 1924 Reichstag elections in *Statistik des Deutschen Reichs*, vol. 315/I, pp. 6–7.

comrade Ledebour.[20] Nor was there unanimity in political views, as time was to show. Among the leaders whose political histories can be discovered, the majority had been Independents uninterruptedly since the party's birth; but former Independents who had served a spell in the VKPD after 1920 were also well represented, and the group even included old Spartacists (Carl Minster, a prominent founding member of the KPD, among them). By remaining in the USPD after September 1922 all had shown a high degree of political stubbornness. It was not a secure alliance.

If the USPD remained marginally a force to be reckoned with during 1923,[21] the crisis conditions of that year, which loosened the German party structure generally and frustrated all normal political reckoning, were responsible. But the solvent effects of the general crisis affected the USPD, too. The issue was resistance to French occupation of the Ruhr. The party executive took a narrow, purist line that avoided nationalist diversions and concentrated its attack on the German government, thus repudiating the passive resistance in the Ruhr; an indignant minority, however, found the official line sectarian and argued that the proletariat should fight all capitalists everywhere (including the French capitalists in the Ruhr) and oppose the violation of German self-determination. The latter policy was of course also necessary for any united front of the workers' parties. The minority—primarily Berliners, headed by the party's two remaining Reichstag deputies, Ledebour and Paul Wegmann —carried their disagreement to the point of resigning from all party offices and eventually from the party itself.[22] Despite this ominous manifestation of the fissiparous tendencies of a small, intense sect, and the loss of the USPD's most famous personality, the split did not greatly harm the party; in the Reichstag elections of May 1924 the USPD received 235,000 votes, to 26,000 for the Socialist League, as Ledebour's faction called itself.[23]

In the elections of May 1924, the last of the centrifugal elections of the postwar crisis and the USPD's last big day at the polls, the party won no seats in the Reichstag (its votes were too scattered); further elections in December increased the strength of the moderate parties and cut

20. According to Anna Siemsen, in Minna Ledebour, ed., *Georg Ledebour: Mensch und Kämpfer* (Zurich, 1954), p. 24.

21. See the references to USPD participation in important conferences in the Ruhr and Berlin during 1923 in Angress, *Stillborn Revolution*, pp. 300 and 370.

22. See USPD *Parteitag,* March–April 1923, esp. pp. 5–22 and 44; and *Jahrbuch für Wirtschaft, Politik und Arbeiterbewegung 1923/24,* pp. 604–5.

23. A 1925 estimate of relative membership strengths suggests 10,000 for the USPD and 3,000 for the Socialist League; *Jahrbuch für Wirtschaft, Politik und Arbeiterbewegung 1925/26,* pp. 56 and 759–60.

back the USPD vote to 99,000. In 1928 the party's vote fell to under 21,000, in 1930 to under 12,000. The following year, defectors from the SPD founded the Socialist Workers Party in an attempt to reopen an independent class struggle and overcome the political paralysis of the two large workers' parties. Since the new party had much the same aims, and indeed some of the same leaders, as the old USPD and apparently better prospects than the small factions, both the remaining separate descendants of the USPD threw in their lot with it, ending their independent existence at last.

In spite of the adherence of some of the most vigorous and perceptive elements of the socialist left (among them the young Willy Brandt), the Socialist Workers Party was an egregious failure and played no role in the final crisis of the Weimar Republic. The new party experienced factional conflict that makes the USPD's pale by comparison; and it was formed at a time when the spirit of the socialist movement was generally defensive rather than, as it had been in 1917–1920, aggressive. In addition, as the historian of the new party notes, "the memory of the fate of the USPD obviously continued to have its effect" on those who might have been attracted to it.[24] In retrospect, the years of the USPD recalled to the minds of the socialist left many moments of which they could be proud, especially the war period and the early struggles of the revolution; but they also recalled the experience of disunity, protracted fruitless tension, and ultimate failure. Tamed and disillusioned, and divided from their fellow activists in the Communist Party, left-wing socialist leaders and militants in the 1930's were reluctant to repeat the experience of ten years earlier and separate themselves again from what was still the mother party of the Social Democratic labor movement in Germany, grounded in the strongest traditions of the German working class and expressing their ultimate hope for reordering society through class unity. The role of left socialists within such a party might be frustrating, sad, at times embittering, but the role had a long history that gave even left-wing socialists a place in the slow, uncertain, but perhaps ultimately hopeful historical progress of the German working class.

Committed to the vision of a free and equal society, achieved through the agency—indeed on the initiative—of a united, class-conscious proletariat, the socialist left had given their best to the struggles of 1917–1920. The struggle against the war, though ineffectual, had been perhaps their finest moment. Then had come the revolution, which they saw as the opening of their era but which turned into something altogether different. Their exertions had done little to clear the path for socialism but had not

24. Drechsler, p. 160.

been entirely without effect. They had helped identify the problem of the revolutionary months as the conflict between socialism and capitalism and thereby helped to carry over into the Republic attitudes that cut across what in retrospect appears the true conflict of the period, the struggle between democratic and authoritarian elements. The ideology of the class struggle, however much it might mask fundamentally democratic beliefs in particular instances, was a factor in the corrupting circumstances accompanying the birth of the Republic and preventing its consolidation. The concept was rooted in the historical development of the German people and could not be altered (or perpetuated) by the actions of a few score party leaders or newspaper editors; but the radical socialists in the USPD were its leading spokesmen in that era. If anything, they intensified this side of their agitation after the revolution, in a vain attempt to seize on a vanishing situation on which they had rested their hopes and an equally vain attempt to prevent the final disruption of their camp. After 1920, stripped of their activist allies by the expansion of the Communist movement, the left-wing socialists were forced back into the posture that had defined them before the war—an attitude of radical expectancy with tendencies to negative intransigence; an attitude of waiting. A separate party was of no assistance in a period of waiting, rather the contrary; and so the Social Democratic left found its home again in the mother party, a reduced and chastened minority whose moment had once come and had passed them by.

The Socialist Share of the Poll in Major Elections, 1919 to 1921

The names used for the voting districts in the 1920 and 1921 elections are the official ones (with a few explanatory notes added in parentheses). In the 1919 elections the districts had no official designations; the names used here are those of the equivalent districts of 1920, with similar names invented for the five districts (nos. 2, 8, 15, 16, and 37) that had no counterpart in 1920.

Rough comparisons between the district results in the different elections are possible in most cases. Apart from small boundary changes, the districts in the first two tables are similar, except that districts 15, 16, and 37 in the 1919 elections were redrawn to make four districts (nos. 15 through 18) in 1920. The Prussian districts of 1921 are precisely the same as in the Reichstag elections in fifteen cases; districts 13, 17, and 19 exclude small areas of non-Prussian territory embraced in the corresponding Reichstag districts; districts 10, 12, 14, and 16 exclude larger territories, with a loss of more than 20 percent of the former population, so that comparisons are questionable; and district 21 was expanded to include the Prussian exclave of Sigmaringen.

The sources for the tables are: *Statistisches Jahrbuch für das Deutsche Reich,* 1919 and 1920, and *Statistisches Jahrbuch für den Freistaat Preussen,* 1921.

Table 1. Percentage of votes for SPD and USPD lists, elections to National Assembly, January 19, 1919

	SPD	USPD
1. East Prussia	46.1	5.0
2. West Prussia	29.1	5.1
3. Berlin	36.4	27.6
4. Potsdam I	41.9	14.9
5. Potsdam II	35.8	15.5
6. Frankfurt on Oder	52.5	0.7
7. Pomerania	41.0	1.9
8. Posnania	16.4	—
9. Breslau	48.2	0.1
10. Oppeln (i.e. Upper Silesia)	32.7	4.9
11. Liegnitz	50.2	0.0
12. Magdeburg	58.3	3.0
13. Merseburg (i.e. Halle)	16.3	44.1
14. Schleswig–Holstein	45.7	3.4
15. West Hanover–Oldenburg	28.0	4.3
16. East Hanover–Braunschweig	43.0	6.6
17. Westphalia–North	30.6	2.1
18. Westphalia–South	41.3	5.1
19. Hesse–Nassau	41.0	3.8
20. Cologne–Aachen	25.5	0.6
21. Koblenz–Trier	22.6	—
22. Düsseldorf–East	25.7	18.7
23. Düsseldorf–West	26.9	0.8
24. Upper Bavaria–Swabia	32.8	3.7
25. Lower Bavaria–Upper Palatinate	25.8	0.5
26. Franconia	36.4	6.1
27. Palatinate	37.9	1.6
28. Dresden–Bautzen	50.9	5.1
29. Leipzig	20.7	38.6
30. Chemnitz–Zwickau	58.7	6.3
31./32. Württemberg	35.4	2.7
33. Baden	34.8	—
34. Hesse–Darmstadt	44.3	1.9
35. Mecklenburg	49.7	—
36. Thuringia	34.6	22.5
37. Hamburg–Bremen–Stade	46.0	8.6
Total	37.9	7.6
	(11,509,048 votes)	(2,317,290 votes)

Table 2. Percentage of votes for SPD, USPD, and KPD lists, elections to Reichstag, June 6, 1920

	SPD	USPD	KPD
1. East Prussia		(election not held)	
2. Berlin	17.5	42.7	1.3
3. Potsdam II	17.4	29.7	1.3
4. Potsdam I	20.6	30.2	1.3
5. Frankfurt on Oder	24.8	14.4	1.0
6. Pomerania	20.7	16.7	1.2
7. Mecklenburg	37.0	9.7	1.0
8. Breslau	36.1	6.6	—
9. Liegnitz	32.2	10.4	1.0
10. Oppeln (i.e. Upper Silesia)		(election not held)	
11. Magdeburg	33.6	19.2	1.1
12. Merseburg (i.e. Halle)	8.8	45.2	1.6
13. Thuringia	15.4	30.6	1.9
14. Schleswig–Holstein		(election not held)	
15. Hamburg	38.4	15.1	0.5
16. Weser–Ems (incl. Bremen)	17.4	16.1	2.0
17. East Hanover	27.3	10.7	0.5
18. South Hanover–Braunschweig	28.0	19.2	0.5
19. Westphalia–North	21.9	8.0	1.5
20. Westphalia–South	20.8	19.7	1.5
21. Hesse–Nassau	27.3	12.3	1.5
22. Hesse–Darmstadt	30.3	12.2	0.5
23. Cologne–Aachen	20.0	8.3	—
24. Koblenz–Trier	12.1	5.6	—
25. Düsseldorf–East	10.0	32.8	1.2
26. Düsseldorf–West	13.5	13.8	5.1
27. Upper Bavaria–Swabia	15.8	11.9	3.2
28. Lower Bavaria–Upper Palatinate	10.2	9.3	2.1
29. Franconia	17.4	16.6	1.0
30. Palatinate	24.3	10.8	0.8
31. Dresden–Bautzen	27.4	21.4	1.2
32. Leipzig	9.1	42.1	2.0
33. Chemnitz–Zwickau	31.8	17.2	9.2
34. Württemberg	15.9	12.8	3.2
35. Baden	20.1	10.9	1.5
Total	21.6	18.8	1.7
	(5,616,164 votes)	(4,896,095 votes)	(441,793 votes)

Table 3.   Percentage of votes for SPD, USPD, and VKPD lists, elections to Prussian Diet, February 20, 1921

	SPD	*USPD*	*VKPD*
1. East Prussia	24.0	5.7	7.0
2. Berlin	22.7	20.3	11.6
3. Potsdam II	21.6	13.3	7.2
4. Potsdam I	27.3	12.4	8.3
5. Frankfurt on Oder	31.9	6.2	2.8
6. Pomerania	29.4	4.7	3.3
7. Breslau	39.9	0.9	2.5
8. Liegnitz	39.7	1.9	2.6
9. Oppeln (i.e. Upper Silesia)	(election not held)		
10. Magdeburg	41.3	7.6	3.9
11. Merseburg (i.e. Halle)	10.6	11.3	29.8
12. Erfurt	11.0	17.8	11.1
13. Schleswig–Holstein	37.1	3.2	6.0
14. Weser–Ems	19.1	5.3	2.5
15. East Hanover	32.5	4.1	3.8
16. South Hanover	40.8	2.1	3.5
17. Westphalia–North	22.2	2.6	5.5
18. Wesphalia–South	25.0	7.3	9.5
19. Hesse–Nassau	31.7	4.2	4.2
20. Cologne–Aachen	19.4	1.0	5.4
21. Koblenz–Trier	11.6	0.5	2.3
22. Düsseldorf–East	14.5	9.2	16.6
23. Düsseldorf–West	14.3	3.8	10.0
Total	26.3	6.6	7.4
	(4,295,305 votes)	(1,076,498 votes)	(1,211,749 votes)

APPENDIX 2

Membership of USPD Reichstag and National Assembly Delegations

Members of the USPD Reichstag Delegation, April 1917–November 1918

Original members of the SAG
  Eduard Bernstein (Breslau-West)
  Wilhelm Bock (Gotha)
  Otto Büchner (Berlin IV)
  Oskar Cohn (Nordhausen)
  Wilhelm Dittmann (Remscheid)
  Friedrich Geyer (Leipzig-Land)
  Hugo Haase (Königsberg)
  Alfred Henke (Bremen)
  Joseph Herzfeld (Rostock)
  Georg Horn (Dresden-Altstadt)
  Fritz Kunert (Halle)
  Georg Ledebour (Berlin VI)
  Theodor Schwartz (Lübeck)
  Arthur Stadthagen (Niederbarnim)[1]
  Karl Wilhelm Stolle (Zwickau-Crimmitschau)[2]
  Ewald Vogtherr (Stettin)
  Emanuel Wurm (Reuss j.L.)
  Fritz Zubeil (Teltow-Beeskow)
Joined the SAG in April 1916
  Karl Ryssel (Borna)

Joined the USPD delegation in May 1917
  Adolf Albrecht (Calbe-Aschersleben)

Joined the USPD delegation in July 1917
  Gustav Raute (Eilenburg)

Joined the USPD delegation in September 1917
  Joseph Simon (Hof)

  1. Died Dec. 5, 1917; seat lost to the SPD in the ensuing by-election.
  2. Died March 11, 1918; seat lost to the SPD in the ensuing by-election.

Joined the USPD delegation in December 1917

Alwin Brandes (Halberstadt)
August Erdmann (Dortmund)
Heinrich Hüttmann (Cassel)
Hermann Jäckel (Plauen)

Members of the USPD National Assembly Delegation, February 1919–May 1920

Names are organized by electoral districts and follow the order of the electoral list:

3 (Berlin): Emil Eichhorn, Hugo Haase,[3] Gustav Laukant, Luise Zietz
4 (Potsdam I): Paul Brühl
5 (Potsdam II): Fritz Zubeil
13 (Merseburg): Fritz Kunert, Gustav Raute, Wilhelm Koenen, Bernhard Düwell, Anna Hübler
16 (East Hanover–Braunschweig): August Merges[4]
22 (Düsseldorf-East): Lore Agnes, Otto Brass
26 (Franconia): Joseph Simon[5]
29 (Leipzig): Friedrich Seger, Friedrich Geyer, Curt Geyer
36 (Thuringia): Wilhelm Bock, Emanuel Wurm,[6] Oskar Cohn
37 (Hamburg-Bremen-Stade): Alfred Henke

Members of the USPD Reichstag Delegation, June 1920–September 1922

Names are organized by electoral districts and follow the order of the electoral list. Names in italics are of members who joined the VKPD; an asterisk indicates members who returned to the USPD delegation in April 1922. One name is missing from the list; Paul Levi, a member of the USPD delegation from April to September 1922, was not elected as an Independent.

2 (Berlin): Luise Zietz,[7] *Emil Eichhorn*, Georg Ledebour, Artur Crispien, Julius Moses, *Adolph Hoffmann*,* *Heinrich Malzahn*
3 (Potsdam II): Fritz Zubeil, *Ernst Däumig*,* [8] Kurt Löwenstein, Franz Künstler
4 (Potsdam I): Rudolf Breitscheid, Paul Brühl,[9] Frida Wulff, Wilhelm Staab
5 (Frankfurt on Oder): Franz Kotzke, Maria Karch
6 (Pomerania): Ewald Vogtherr, August Horn
7 (Mecklenburg): *Joseph Herzfeld*
9 (Liegnitz): Anna Nemitz
11 (Magdeburg): Alwin Brandes, Wilhelm Dittmann, Adolf Albrecht

3. Died Nov. 7, 1919; succeeded by Richard Herbst.
4. Resigned his seat in Feb. 1919; succeeded by Karl Aderhold.
5. Election declared invalid in Nov. 1919; seat passed to the SPD.
6. Died May 3, 1920; succeeded by Kurt Rosenfeld.
7. Died Jan. 27, 1922; succeeded by Wilhelm Hoffmann.
8. Died July 4, 1922; succeeded by Paul Wegmann.
9. Resigned from the USPD delegation in April 1922.

12 (Merseburg): Fritz Kunert, *Wilhelm Koenen, Bernhard Düwell,** Gustav Raute, *Marie Wachwitz**
13 (Thuringia): Wilhelm Bock, Heinrich Mehrhof, Kurt Rosenfeld, Mathilde Wurm, *Emil Höllein*
15 (Hamburg): *Hermann Reich*
16 (Weser-Ems): Alfred Henke
17 (East Hanover): *Wilhelm Bartz*
18 (South Hanover–Braunschweig): *Carl Eckardt,* Karl Aderhold,[10] August Karsten
19 (Westphalia-North): Josef Ernst
20 (Westphalia-South): Konrad Ludwig, *Heinrich Teuber,** Walter Oettinghaus, Heinrich Pieper
21 (Hesse-Nassau): Robert Dissmann, Toni Sender
22 (Hesse-Darmstadt): Georg Beckmann
23 (Cologne-Aachen): *Philipp Fries**
25 (Düsseldorf-East): Lore Agnes, *Otto Brass,** Hermann Merkel, Julius Rosemann, Paul Sauerbrey
26 (Düsseldorf-West): *Walter Stoecker*
27 (Upper Bavaria–Swabia): Hans Unterleitner, *Wendelin Thomas*
29 (Franconia): Joseph Simon, Hans Seidel, Fritz Soldmann
31 (Dresden-Bautzen): Hermann Fleissner, Johannes Schirmer, Paul Ristau
32 (Leipzig): *Friedrich Geyer,** Friedrich Seger, Richard Lipinski, Karl Ryssel
33 (Chemnitz-Zwickau): Hermann Jäckel, Bernhard Kuhnt, Friedrich Puchta
34 (Württemberg): *Hermann Remmele,* Anna Ziegler
35 (Baden): Adolph Geck, Adolf Schwarz
National List (June 1920 elections): Lorenz Breunig, Paul Hertz, *Curt Geyer,** Hans Mittwoch, *Georg Berthelé,* Arno Bruchardt, *Hans Plettner**; (February 1921 elections): Siegfried Aufhäuser, Heinrich Hüttmann

10. Died June 20, 1921; succeeded by Wilhelm Voss.

The Party Leadership

The sources of the following lists are generally published reports of party congresses. The ordering of names under each office follows that of the sources; where not alphabetical it reflects the number of votes received by the candidates, in descending order.

Elected at the Party Congress of April 1917

Party Executive.[1] Hugo Haase, Luise Zietz, Adolf Hofer, Robert Wengels, Wilhelm Dittmann, Georg Ledebour,[2] Gustav Laukant, [Ernst Däumig][3]

Auxiliary Council. Sepp Oerter (Braunschweig), Robert Dissmann (Frankfurt on Main), Alfred Henke (Bremen), Paul Dittmann (Hamburg), Willi Grütz (Remscheid), [Hermann Fleissner (Dresden)],[4] Friedrich Schnellbacher (Hanau), [Otto Brass (Remscheid), Richard Lipinski (Leipzig)][5]

Control Commission. Wilhelm Bock (Gotha), Friedrich Geyer (Leipzig), Josef Windau (Bochum, later Zeitz), [Lore Agnes (Düsseldorf)],[6] August Karsten (Aschaffenburg, later Hanover), Karl Liesegang (Berlin), [Adolph Geck (Offenburg)][7]

Elected at the Party Congress of March 1919

Party Executive. Chairmen: Artur Crispien, Hugo Haase;[8] Secretaries: Luise Zietz, Wilhelm Dittmann, [Wilhelm Koenen, Walter Stoecker];[9] Associates: Gustav Laukant, Anna Nemitz, Julius Moses

1. The party executive (this time only) determined its own division of functions; Haase and Ledebour became cochairmen, Dittmann and Zietz paid secretaries, and Hofer, Wengels, and Laukant associate members.
2. Resigned his position in Jan. 1919.
3. Coopted into the party executive about April 1918 to replace the imprisoned Dittmann; resigned again in (apparently) Nov. 1918.
4. Replaced the elected Paul Banse (Halle), who stepped down so that Saxony could be represented in the auxiliary council.
5. Both added to the auxiliary council before the next party congress, Brass presumably as a replacement for Grütz.
6. Replaced the elected Clara Zetkin (Stuttgart), who was unable to serve.
7. Added to the control commission after he resigned from the SPD in May 1917.
8. Died Nov. 7, 1919.
9. Coopted into the party executive in July 1919, with the approval of the auxiliary council and control commission.

Auxiliary Council.   Hermann Fleissner (Dresden), Otto Brass (Remscheid), Alfred Henke (Bremen), Sepp Oerter (Braunschweig), Joseph Herzfeld (Berlin), Karl Kürbs (Halle), Karl Kroepelin (Munich)

Control Commission.   Lore Agnes (Düsseldorf), Adolph Geck (Offenburg), Konrad Ludwig (Hagen), Wilhelm Bock (Gotha), Robert Wengels (Berlin), August Karsten (Hanover), Adolf Schwarz (Mannheim)

Elected at the Party Congress of November–December 1919[10]

Party Executive.   Chairmen: Artur Crispien, *Ernst Däumig;* Secretaries: Luise Zietz, Wilhelm Dittmann, *Walter Stoecker, Wilhelm Koenen,* Hermann Radtke; Associates: *Adolph Hoffmann,* Franz Künstler, Julius Moses, Anna Nemitz, Kurt Rosenfeld

Auxiliary Council.   *Otto Brass* (Remscheid), *Johann Baier* (Nuremberg), *Paul Böttcher* (Leipzig), Robert Dissmann (Frankfurt on Main), Alfred Henke (Bremen), *Joseph Herzfeld* (Berlin), Karl Kürbs (Halle)

Control Commission.   Lore Agnes (Düsseldorf), Wilhelm Bock (Gotha), *Philipp Fries* (Cologne), *Max König* (Dresden), Konrad Ludwig (Hagen), *Hermann Remmele* (Stuttgart), Robert Wengels (Berlin)

Elected at the Party Congress of October 1920—Right USPD

Party Executive.   Chairman: Artur Crispien, Georg Ledebour; Secretaries: Wilhelm Dittmann, Luise Zietz; [Treasurer: Konrad Ludwig];[11] Associates: Paul Brühl, Franz Künstler, Julius Moses, Anna Nemitz, Kurt Rosenfeld, Karl Schneider, Mathilde Wurm

Auxiliary Council.   Robert Dissmann (Frankfurt on Main), Franz Donalies (Königsberg), Alfred Henke (Bremen), Heinrich Knauf (Gera), Karl Kürbs (Halle), Richard Lipinski (Leipzig), Konrad Ludwig (Hagen),[11] Toni Sender (Frankfurt on Main), Joseph Simon (Nuremberg)

Control Commission.   Lore Agnes (Düsseldorf), Wilhelm Bock (Gotha), Georg Fuchs (Magdeburg), Max Güth (Kiel), August Karsten (Hanover), Adolf Schwarz (Mannheim), Robert Wengels (Berlin)

Elected at the Party Congress of October 1920—Left USPD

Party Executive.   Chairmen: Ernst Däumig, Adolph Hoffmann; Secretaries: Walter Stoecker, Wilhelm Koenen, Otto Gäbel, Bertha Braunthal; Associates: Emil Eichhorn, Curt Geyer, Richard Müller, Martha Arendsee, Paul Schindler

Auxiliary Council.   Otto Brass (Remscheid), Hermann Remmele (Stuttgart), Alfred Oelssner (Halle), Joseph Herzfeld (Berlin), Ernst Thälmann (Hamburg), Paul Noack (Offenbach on Main), Josef Staimer (Nuremberg)[12]

---

10. Names of members who voted in Oct. 1920 for adherence to the Third International under the Twenty-One Conditions are italicized.

11. Taken into the party executive as treasurer during 1921.

12. Some sources give, in Staimer's place, Johann Baier, also of Nuremberg.

Control Commission.   Philipp Fries (Cologne), Friedrich Geyer (Leipzig), Minna Reichert (Berlin), Hans Plettner (Hanover), Guido Heym (Suhl), Max Heydemann (Königsberg), Heinrich Teuber (Bochum)

Elected at the Party Congress of January 1922

Party Executive.   Chairmen: Artur Crispien, Wilhelm Dittmann, Georg Ledebour; Secretaries: Luise Zietz, Franz Künstler; Treasurer: Konrad Ludwig; Associates: Richard Krille, Julius Moses, Paul Brühl,[13] Anna Nemitz, Mathilde Wurm, Rudolf Hilferding, Kurt Rosenfeld

Auxiliary Council.   Franz Donalies (Königsberg), Heinrich Knauf (Gera), Peter Berten (Düsseldorf), Franz Peters (Halle), Friedrich Seger (Leipzig), Joseph Simon (Nuremberg), Alfred Henke (Bremen), Bernhard Menke (Dresden), Robert Dissmann (Stuttgart), Toni Sender (Frankfurt on Main)

Control Commission.   August Karsten (Peine), Robert Wengels (Berlin), Wilhelm Bock (Gotha), Lore Agnes (Düsseldorf), Max Güth (Kiel), Adolf Schwarz (Mannheim), Georg Fuchs (Magdeburg)

13. Left the party in April 1922.

Biographical Sketches

Emil Barth (*1879–1941*). Born in Heidelberg. Worked as a tinsmith in a number of cities, after 1904 in Berlin. Active anarchist from 1908 to 1910; transferred his activities to the Metalworkers' Union in 1911 and later to the SPD. During the war an early member of the factory opposition; then war service, ending just in time to succeed R. Müller as leader of the shop stewards in February 1918. After his role in the provisional government returned to his trade, with part-time service as party speaker and organizer. From 1921 to 1924 a leading official of the union-sponsored factory council headquarters for Berlin, then a minor employee of the SPD. In 1933 returned to manual labor until his death.

Eduard Bernstein (*1850–1932*). Born in Berlin. Attended *Gymnasium,* then worked in banks until 1878. A Social Democrat from 1872; editor of the principal party newspaper in emigration, 1881 to 1890; remained abroad until 1901. Engels' literary executor, editor of Lassalle's works, author of many historical and theoretical works; principal exponent of Marxist revisionism in the SPD. Opposed the war once it took on the appearance of a war against England instead of tsarist Russia; also objected to the party's growing dependency on the government. Thereafter close to Kautsky, an old friend from before the revisionist controversy. Alienated by the growing radicalism of the USPD in 1917 and 1918 but active in the work of the Reichstag delegation. During November and December 1918 served as undersecretary in the Reich Treasury Ministry. Rejoined the SPD late in December 1918 but retained his membership in the USPD until the latter ruled out dual membership in March 1919. During 1919–1920 chief sponsor of an organization attempting to bring about reunification of the two socialist parties. Reichstag member, 1902–1907, 1912–1918, and 1920–1928.

Otto Brass (*1875–1950*). Born in Wermelskirchen. Filemaker by trade. From 1903 to 1905 official of the Remscheid workman's sick fund, then business manager of the socialist newspaper there. By the end of the war had established himself as the most influential Independent leader in Rhineland-Westphalia; in contact with the Berlin radicals around Däumig and R. Müller at least since the Workers' and Soldiers' Congress in December 1918; sponsor of but also moderating influence in the strikes of February and April 1919. Hesitant adherent to the Communist International just before the Halle

457

congress; resigned from the VKPD central committee with Levi and Däumig in February 1921; protested the March Action; expelled from the KPD in January 1922; returned to the USPD with the KAG in April 1922. Member of the National Assembly, 1919–1920, of the Reichstag, 1920–1924. In the later twenties a publisher in Berlin; spent the Nazi years in detention; active after the war in East Berlin, where he died.

Rudolf Breitscheid (1874–1944). Born in Cologne. Earned a doctorate in political economy, worked as a newspaper editor and official of a democratic pressure group. Cofounder in 1908 of Theodor Barth's Demokratische Vereinigung, cochairman 1908–1912; after this party's feeble showing in the 1912 elections went over to the SPD. Worked for Friedrich Stampfer's article service, then in May 1915 founded his own *Sozialistische Auslandspolitik,* which became *Der Sozialist* after the revolution, with Breitscheid as editor and principal editorialist. Held local public office in Berlin from 1914; unsuccessful Reichstag candidate for the USPD in Niederbarnim, March 1918; Prussian minister of the interior during the period of the provisional government; entered the Reichstag June 1920. Principal foreign policy spokesman of the USPD Reichstag delegation, 1921–1922, then of the reunited party; from 1928 cochairman of the Reichstag delegation. Always mistrusted by the USPD left, never held major office in that party. Emigrated in 1933, handed over by the Vichy authorities to the Gestapo in 1941, died in Buchenwald during a bombing attack.

Artur Crispien (1875–1946). Born in Königsberg. Painter by trade, with some attendance at art school. From 1902 a party employee; editor in Königsberg and Danzig; 1906–1912 party secretary for West Prussia; served intermittently on the executive committee of the Socialist International. In 1912 called to Stuttgart as editor-in-chief of the *Schwäbische Tagwacht*. Associated himself there with the dominant radical faction, joined them in opposing the war and entering the Spartacist camp; dismissed from the newspaper in November 1914, edited the weekly *Der Sozialdemokrat,* spent some months in jail. As member of the provisional government in Württemberg after the revolution, moved rapidly away from his former Spartacist comrades. Elected cochairman of the USPD in March 1919 as a supposed radical and remained in this post until reunification; member of the party's delegation to Moscow in July and August 1920. Popular speaker in socialist assemblies, active in the affairs of the International and the Vienna Union. In 1922 became third cochairman of the reunited SPD with principal responsibility for relations with the International but little influence on the party's domestic policies. Emigrated in 1933 to Switzerland and died there.

Ernst Däumig (1866–1922). Born in Merseburg, attended *Gymnasium* in Halle. From 1887 to 1898 served in the German army and the French Foreign Legion. After 1901 an editor on socialist newspapers in Gera, Halle, and Erfurt; active in socialist education programs. In 1911 called to Berlin as editor on *Vorwärts;* again active in education and other local socialist programs. Opposed to official party policy from the start of the war, won increasing importance among the editors; after dismissal in November 1916

became leading editor of the weekly substitute paper, the *Mitteilungs-Blatt*. An early supporter of Bolshevik rule in Russia. Party secretary in the USPD central office from about April to about November 1918; member of the inner councils of the shop stewards movement from summer 1918. Leading radical intellectual of the Berlin executive council, soon leading USPD spokesman for the council movement and editor (from January 1919) of *Der Arbeiter-Rat*. Left-wing candidate for cochairman in March 1919 but election blocked by Haase; gained the position in December 1919. Member of the Reichstag from 1920 until his death. Member of the party delegation to Moscow. After unification of his wing of the USPD with the Communists, became cochairman of the VKPD, but resigned with Levi in February 1921; served on the national committee of the KAG and as editor of its weekly paper. Rejoined the USPD in April 1922, died without playing any further role.

Robert Dissmann (1878–1926). Born in Hülsenbusch, a Rhenish village. Machinist by trade. Became a full-time trade-union official in Elberfeld-Barmen in 1900 at age 22; from 1905 to 1908 Metalworkers' official in Frankfurt on Main. Then party service: party secretary in Hanau, 1908–1912; district secretary for Frankfurt on Main, 1912–1917; USPD district secretary for Southwestern Germany (Frankfurt on Main, Hesse, Baden, Palatinate) from 1917 to November 1919. Nearly elected to the party executive in 1913 as candidate of the left. Returned to trade-union service in November 1919 as chairman of the Metalworkers' Union. Member of the Reichstag from 1920 until his death. After 1922 a leader of the inner-party opposition in the SPD. An exceptionally effective organizer and administrator in both the party and the union; in politics an outspoken radical, to be found on the left wing on nearly every issue except those affecting trade unionism or ultimate party loyalty.

Wilhelm Dittmann (1874–1954). Born in Eutin, near Lübeck. Carpenter by trade. From 1899 to 1904 party editor in Bremerhaven and Solingen; then party secretary in Frankfurt on Main until 1909, when he returned to Solingen as editor-in-chief. Prominent young radical in the last years before the war, member of the Reichstag since 1912. Joined the opposition early in 1915; founding member of the SAG. Party secretary in the USPD central office from April 1917 until January 1922, then cochairman of the party. Imprisoned from February to October 1918 for addressing a crowd during the January general strike. Close follower of Haase. As a member of the provisional government became permanently associated with the more cautious wing of the party, but retained his position in the party executive even at the time of the radical triumph in December 1919. Member of the USPD's delegation to Moscow in summer 1920. Editor of *Freiheit* from March to September 1922, after the ouster of Hilferding. After 1922 served as party secretary in the SPD central office; never again associated with the left. In emigration after 1933 but returned to work in the party archives in Bonn in his last years.

Emil Eichhorn (1863–1925). Born in Röhrsdorf, Saxony. Had several

years of education beyond the usual for a workingman's son but became a mechanic in the metalworking trade. Joined the SPD in 1881; became a full-time party editor in Dresden in 1893, then in Mannheim after 1900. Most prominent during his Mannheim years when he was member of the Baden Diet, member of the Reichstag (1903–1912), and for a time party secretary for Baden. Moved to Berlin in 1908 as head of the SPD's press bureau. Organized illegal publications for the opposition in 1916; then head of USPD press bureau after the split. From August to November 1918 leading employee of the Soviet press agency Rosta in Berlin. Police president of Berlin November 1918 to January 1919, then in hiding until August. Member of the National Assembly, 1919–1920, of the Reichstag from 1920 to his death. Went to the VKPD with the left wing of the USPD; belonged for a time to Levi's KAG but without ever actually leaving the KPD. One of the handful of leading prewar Social Democrats to become loyal Communists for more than a brief period.

Kurt Eisner (1867–1919). Born in Berlin, son of a successful businessman whose circumstances deteriorated during Eisner's childhood. Four years of university, literary and philosophical interests. From 1890 to 1897 held a variety of journalistic positions with democratic publications. In 1898 joined the *Vorwärts* staff; from 1900 to 1906 effectively the principal editor; resigned when the party executive determined to radicalize the paper. From 1907 to 1910 editor-in-chief of the party paper in Nuremberg; after 1910 ran a private press service on cultural affairs and Bavarian parliamentary affairs from Munich. Known in the party as a Kantian revisionist in ideological matters, a specialist in literary developments and foreign policy (rare in the old SPD). Originally supported the war but became convinced from published documents that Germany bore heavy responsibility for it; his opposition took on the character of an ethical crusade to purge Germany of her sins. Founder and inspirer of the tiny Munich USPD, organizer of the revolution there, then Bavarian minister president until his death in February 1919.

Hermann Fleissner (1865–1939). Born in Dresden. Carpenter by trade. Active in party and cooperative movement since 1884 and trade unions since 1886. Left his trade in 1896 to serve as a reporter for the Dresden party paper; an editor on this paper, 1900–1917; editor-in-chief of the USPD's Dresden newspaper after the war. Held local government office, then member of the Saxon Diet, 1909–1920. When the party conflict broke out, was district chairman and its representative in the SPD party committee; continued in the same positions in the USPD; it appeared for a time that his influence would win the district for the opposition. Minister in the Saxon provisional government. From December 1920 until January 1924 Saxon minister of education. Reichstag deputy, 1920–1933. Spent the first year of the Third Reich under arrest. Most radical of the triumvirate (including Lipinski and Seger) of the Saxon USPD.

Curt Geyer (1891–1967). Born in Leipzig, son of a grand old man of Saxon Social Democracy, Friedrich Geyer. Earned his doctorate in history in

1914. After brief editorial stints in Leipzig and Nuremberg, became editor-in-chief of the Würzburg party paper in 1915; lost this job at the time of the split and rejoined the *Leipziger Volkszeitung*. As an effective radical agitator became probably the most prominent (though not the most powerful) Independent Socialist in Leipzig during the revolution; leading figure of the workers' council, USPD spokesman at the Workers' and Soldiers' Congress in December 1918, member of the National Assembly. After summer 1919 lost influence in Leipzig to the entrenched right wing under Lipinski and Seger, but continued as a national leader of the council movement. One of the first to advocate adoption of Bolshevik methods in Germany. In May 1920 transferred his activities to the more congenial Hamburg environment as editor of the hyperradical *Hamburger Volkszeitung*. Coeditor of the pro-Moscow journal *Kommunistische Rundschau* from October to December 1920, and later member of the VKPD's central committee. Took Levi's side in the conflicts of February and March 1921, became an outspoken critic of the party leadership; member of the KAG, then the USPD and the reunited SPD. Relatively subdued career in the reunited party; no Reichstag seat after 1924; *Vorwärts* editor 1924–1933. Editor of the party paper in exile for a time. Did not return to Germany after 1945.

Hugo Haase (1863–1919). Born in Allenstein, East Prussia. University training in Königsberg followed by law practice there. Made his name in legal assistance to the poor and as defense attorney in political trials. Member of the Reichstag 1897–1906 and again after 1912. As a leading member of the orthodox Marxist faction in the party, he was Bebel's and Kautsky's choice to succeed Paul Singer as cochairman of the party in 1911. Held this position until March 1916. Opposed to official party policy from the start of the war, but kept his views private until the spring of 1915; under constant attack from the party majority thereafter, but never wavered. Cochairman of the SAG and of the USPD from its foundation until his death; cochairman of the provisional government in November and December 1918. Continued his law practice throughout; never accepted a salary from the party. The only national leader of general authority the USPD ever had; his death by assassination in November 1919 helped set the party leadership adrift.

Alfred Henke (1868–1946). Born in Altona. Cigarmaker by trade. Came to Bremen in 1901 as a junior editor, from 1906 editor-in-chief of the *Bremer Bürgerzeitung*. In this capacity instrumental in the gradual creation of a left radical majority in the Bremen SPD; but drew back somewhat from left radicalism after 1910, especially after election to the Reichstag in 1912. One of the original fourteen opponents of war credits in the delegation; after some wavering followed Haase rather than Liebknecht within the opposition. Leader of the centrist faction in Bremen, hard pressed from right and left; lost the newspaper to the Majority Socialists in December 1916, the party organization to the left radicals. USPD district secretary for the North Sea coast in 1917–1918. Chairman of the Bremen workers' and soldiers' council, presided unwillingly over the Bremen Soviet Republic. Editor again from the end of 1918 until 1922. Prominence in the party declined after the end of

the war, though a member of the auxiliary council continuously from the birth of the party until reunification. Henke specialized in municipal affairs and in 1922 took a local government job in Berlin. Member of the Reichstag in every session from 1912 to 1932 and of the National Assembly in 1919–1920.

Joseph Herzfeld (1853–1939). Born in Neuss in the Rhineland. Son of a manufacturer, after *Gymnasium* worked in various firms and banks in Düsseldorf and New York; Columbia Law School, 1878–1880, followed by five years of law practice in New York; from 1885 to 1887 law study in Germany, ending in a doctorate, then established a practice in Berlin. Joined the SPD in 1887. Member of the Reichstag for Rostock, 1898–1906, 1912–1918, and 1920–1924. A quiet and unassuming man, he was a dedicated socialist and agitated tirelessly in his constituency and throughout Mecklenburg. Opposed to the war from the outset, founding member of the SAG and USPD. Supported adherence to the Comintern and remained loyal throughout the party crises of 1921, and also later in the twenties, when he was active chiefly for the *Rote Hilfe*. Died in emigration in Switzerland.

Rudolf Hilferding (1877–1941). Born in Vienna. Doctorate in medicine in 1901 but made his name early as a Marxist economist with *Herr Böhm-Bawerk and the Close of Marx's System* (1904) and *Finance Capital* (1910). Came to Germany to teach at the party school but forced out of this by the police; for a year on the staff of Kautsky's *Neue Zeit*, then in 1907 an editor of *Vorwärts*. By 1914 leading political editor of *Vorwärts;* opposed official party policy while seeking to avoid an open rift. Conscripted into the medical service of the Austrian army in May 1915, worked in field hospitals for the rest of the war. Editor-in-chief of *Freiheit* from November 1918 to March 1922, made it the best of the socialist papers in Berlin. A skeptic by nature and a political tactician by inclination, he stood distinctly on the right wing of his party; eloquent in the anti-Bolshevik cause, made the principal reply to Zinoviev at the Halle congress; influential in the party executive as an ex officio nonvoting member, from January 1922 as an elected member. In the reunited party, a member of the party executive, editor of the theoretical journal *Die Gesellschaft*, shaper of the 1925 party program. Reich minister of finance, 1923 and 1928–1929. Active in the socialist emigration after 1933. Died in the hands of the Gestapo in a Paris prison.

Adolph Hoffmann (1858–1930). Born in Berlin. Engraver, later gilder, by trade, but worked in a variety of jobs. From 1890 to 1893 editor of socialist papers in Halle and Zeitz, thereafter bookdealer in Berlin. Known as "Ten Commandments Hoffmann" for his attack on Christianity as practiced by the propertied classes. Berlin city councilor, 1900–1928, member of the Prussian Diet, 1908–1921, and of the Reichstag, 1904–1906 and 1920–1924. Chairman of the Berlin SPD, then of the USPD organization, 1916–1918; co-chairman of the Left USPD in October and November 1920; member of the VKPD central committee until his resignation with Levi in February 1921. Returned via the KAG to the USPD and eventually the SPD.

Karl Kautsky (1854–1938). Born in Vienna. University education. Wrote

for the socialist press from 1875; in the years of the Anti-Socialist Law edited émigré publications in Switzerland and England; founded the theoretical journal *Neue Zeit* in 1883. During these years trained himself in Marxism, partly in direct consultation with the founders, and made himself the most authoritative spokesman of second-generation Marxism. Largely responsible for the text of the Erfurt Program of 1891; leader of the attack on Bernstein's revisionism; guardian of the orthodoxy of the German party and the International (in close collaboration with August Bebel). Influence declined after Bebel's death (1913) and especially after the war issue divided him from both the right and the extreme left. Lost his platform in 1917 with dismissal from *Neue Zeit*. Close to Haase in 1915–1918, but disapproved of the leftward turn taken by the USPD toward the end of the war; in particular argued against uncritical admiration of Soviet Russia and Bolshevik methods. In the provisional government was undersecretary in the Foreign Office, with special responsibility for publishing documents on the outbreak of the war, and also chairman of the Socialization Commission. After the Leipzig congress in December 1919 virtually withdrew from USPD affairs and nearly resigned. Spent the second half of 1920 in Menshevik Georgia. Resumed activity in the rump USPD, seeking to promote reunification with the SPD. After reunification had a place of honor but no party position, so moved to Vienna and played no direct role in the German party after the 1925 program.

Wilhelm Koenen (1886–1963). Born in Hamburg. Commercial training, worked for a time in the socialist book store in Kiel and remained active in the affairs of the Shop Assistants' Union even after he moved on to other work. From 1907 to 1910 reporter for socialist papers in Kiel and Königsberg, then in 1911 after a course in the party school became an editor of the Halle *Volksblatt*. Rapidly established himself there; by 1914 was member of the party's district executive, deputy chairman of the Halle trades council, and chairman of the district youth committee. During the war the newspaper was cautiously centrist, and Koenen worked primarily through other channels (partly underground) to radicalize the workers. Dominant in the Halle shop stewards' committee that organized strikes in August 1917; conscripted into the army in consequence. After the revolution was the outstanding spokesman and organizer of the council movement in the Halle district; as such elected to the National Assembly in January 1919 and coopted into the party executive as secretary the following July; also retained his leading position in the council movement as chairman of the provisional Central Office of Factory Councils, and kept alive his ties with the Halle district. Member of the Reichstag 1920–1932. Joined the VKPD, served as secretary in its central committee, and was one of the few former Independent leaders who never wavered in their loyalty to the party during the crises of 1921. Survived the party conflicts of the 1920's, though usually occupying less eminent positions than in the USPD. Spent the Nazi years in emigration in the West; after 1945 held high positions in the Soviet Zone and East Germany; no political influence after 1953, but an elder statesman.

Georg Ledebour (1850–1947). Born in Hanover. Business education, but

soon turned to private tutoring and then activity in democratic circles, including the press. In 1891 joined the SPD and worked as editor in Berlin and Dresden. Elected to the Reichstag in 1900, earned his living as a free-lance writer and lecturer. By 1914 one of the senior members of the delegation, known as a passionate and articulate controversialist. One of the most bitter opponents of official delegation policy from the start of the war. Cochairman of the SAG and of the USPD from its foundation. Entered the circle of the shop stewards before the strike of January 1918, remained with them in the Berlin executive council, and served as cochairman of the revolutionary committee in the January disturbances of 1919 in Berlin. Fell out with Haase, especially over the policies of the provisional government, resigned his party office on January 1, 1919. In jail from January to June 1919, acquitted triumphantly at his trial. His views on the importance of parliamentary activity and on the Bolshevik use of terror cut him off from the advanced radicals, his natural allies, later in 1919 and 1920. At the rump congress in Halle he was again elected cochairman of the party. Thereafter consistently opposed any reunification that would exclude the Communists. In September 1922 led the remains of the USPD, but resigned at the end of 1923 over the party's attitude toward the Ruhr occupation. His Socialist League of 1924–1931, a small group of the faithful, was absorbed into the Socialist Workers Party at the latter's foundation. From 1933 until his death lived in Switzerland.

Richard Lipinski (*1867–1936*). Born in Danzig. Commercial training, worked as a shop assistant, then from 1891 to 1901 as editor in Leipzig, thereafter as bookdealer and writer in the same city. Founder or cofounder of a number of trade unions and friendly societies for shop assistants and party employees during 1890–1910; exceptionally active organizer. Member of the Reichstag, 1903–1906 and 1920–1933. District chairman of the SPD from 1907, of the USPD, 1917–1920, of the SPD again from 1923. Minister in the Saxon provisional government from November 1918 to January 1919; chairman of the USPD delegation in the Saxon Diet, 1919–1920; from December 1920 to February 1923 Saxon minister of the interior. Essentially an organization man, the most powerful Independent in Saxony, and one of the party's few regional bosses.

Richard Müller (*1880–?*). Born in Weira, Thuringia. Metalworker by trade. Rose as functionary of the Berlin metalworkers; in 1914 was the elected leader of the lathe operator's branch, apparently the highest-ranking of those who took the dangerous course of opposition to the *Burgfrieden* and the war. A sober and authoritative figure, the unquestioned leader of the shop stewards. Called up just before the strike of April 1917, freed at the insistence of the strikers; called up again after the January 1918 strike, released in October to stand for a Reichstag seat. Joined in the revolutionary preparations, resumed leadership of the shop stewards when Barth joined the provisional government, served as cochairman of the Berlin executive council from its formation until its dissolution in August 1919. An adherent of Däumig's views on the function of workers' councils. Served as editor of the Metalworkers' weekly newspaper in Stuttgart after Dissmann's election as

chairman, but was forced out in June 1920 after policy differences with the leadership. Went with the left wing to the VKPD and served in the trade-union section of the central office. Opposed the March Action and the policies of the Moscow Trade Union International; forced out of office late in 1921, apparently out of the party early in 1922. His later career is unrecorded.

Sepp Oerter (1870–1928). Born in Straubing, Bavaria. Bookbinder by trade. A leading anarchist editor until about 1910, with the interruption of an eight-year jail sentence. By 1914 an established Social Democrat of the left wing. Served as editor in Braunschweig in 1916 and established himself there; elected to the auxiliary council at the USPD founding congress. In the months after the revolution the dominant member of the provisional government in Braunschweig, and in Braunschweig socialism in general for the next three years. After February 1919 associated with the policy of collaboration with the SPD, outspokenly opposed to the Twenty-One Conditions; minister president of Braunschweig from June 1920 to November 1921, when he was forced out after evidence of questionable acceptance of favors. Left the party as a bitter man; said to have thrown in his lot with the Nazis later.

Kurt Rosenfeld (1877–1943). Born in Marienwerder, West Prussia. Earned a doctorate in law, settled as a lawyer in Berlin in 1905. Prominent as a defense lawyer in political trials, radical and a friend of Rosa Luxemburg, city councilor from 1910. Spent the war years in the army. Minister of justice in the Prussian provisional government after the revolution, elected to the Prussian Diet in February 1919, to the Reichstag in 1920, where he remained until 1932. In December 1919 elected to the party executive of the USPD as a radical; refused to accept the Twenty-One Conditions but continued as a radical gadfly in the party executive after the Halle congress; nearly refused to follow the party majority at the time of reunification. Became a leader of the left wing of the SPD, cofounder of *Der Klassenkampf* in 1927. In 1931 cofounder and cochairman of the Socialist Workers Party. Spent his years of emigration in the United States, where he died.

Friedrich Seger (1867–1928). Born in Wollbach, Baden. Tailor by trade. Active in the SPD and his trade union from 1887; in the 1890's held positions in the Tailors' Union; from 1901 an editor of the *Leipziger Volkszeitung*. Member of the Leipzig party leadership from 1893, of the district party leadership from 1905; member of the city council from 1911, of the Saxon Diet, 1915–1918, and of the National Assembly and the Reichstag from 1919 until his death. His specialty was municipal affairs, and he had exceptional local influence; lost the effective local leadership to Curt Geyer during the spring of 1919 but recaptured it with Lipinski's support. The Leipzig party and newspaper thereafter followed the Seger-Lipinski policy of moderation, and the two men were a formidable force in party councils in Berlin as well. Seger's career was unaffected by reunification; he continued to share in the domination of the Leipzig party.

Tony Sender (1888–1964). Born in Biebrich, on the Rhine. Finishing-school education, followed by commercial training. Worked in an office in

Frankfurt on Main, then in Paris, 1910–1914, then as office manager in a Frankfurt firm until 1919. Close political associate of Robert Dissmann during and after the war. Prominent in the revolution in Frankfurt, became principal editor of the USPD's new newspaper there in February 1919. In 1920 invited by Dissmann to become chief editor of the Metalworkers' Union's factory council magazine, a post she held until 1933. Like Dissmann considered herself a left-wing socialist but rejected the Comintern's conditions of entry; drafted the declaration of principle that made it possible for reluctant persons like herself to return to the united SPD in 1922. Member of the Reichstag, 1920–1933. Emigrated in 1933, to the United States in 1935. In America a prominent speaker and writer, leader of socialist émigré groups; 1941–1944 worked for the OSS, then for UNRRA; later a representative to the UN Economic and Social Council from the AF of L and the International Confederation of Free Trade Unions. The highest-ranking woman Independent to work her way up in general political activity rather than in the women's movement.

Joseph Simon (1865–1949). Born in Schneppenbach, Lower Franconia. Shoemaker by trade. Active in party and trade-union affairs from 1885, worked his way up into management positions in the shoe industry, then in 1900 became chairman of the Central Union of German Shoemakers with offices in Nuremberg. From 1907 secretary of the International Shoemakers' and Leather Workers' Union; attended the International Socialist Congresses in 1904, 1907, 1910, and 1912. Member of the Bavarian Diet, 1907–1918, of the Reichstag, 1912–1918 and 1920–1932, and of the National Assembly in 1919. Joined the opposition early in 1915, the USPD only in September 1917 when his constituency organization (Hof) transferred its allegiance. A member of Hoffmann's Bavarian government in March and April 1919, but avoided involvement in the soviet experiment. Spoke in the Reichstag mainly on trade-union or Bavarian affairs in his years as an Independent. Twice arrested by the Nazis, politically active in reconstruction in Nuremberg after the war.

Walter Stoecker (1891–1939). Born in Cologne. Commercial training, then editorial work in Kiel and Cologne, followed by two years of private study and then war service from 1915 to 1918. In November 1918 became a prominent member of the Cologne workers' and soldiers' council; in December appointed editor on the new USPD paper in Elberfeld; elected to the Prussian Diet in January 1919. In July coopted into the party executive as an additional secretary; kept his radical views and at the party conference in September and party congress in December 1919 was the principal advocate of joining the Communist International. A member of the delegation to Moscow; accepted the Twenty-One Conditions unreservedly and helped lead the campaign for acceptance by the party; coeditor of *Kommunistische Rundschau*. Secretary in the VKPD central committee, after Levi's resignation served as cochairman with Brandler, loyal throughout the ensuing crises but not re-elected to the central committee at the party congress in August. For the rest of the Weimar years held important regional jobs, intermittently

a member of the central committee, from 1924 to 1932 chairman of the KPD Reichstag delegation. Arrested in February 1933; died in Buchenwald of typhus, one of the few prominent Independents to die a loyal Communist.

Heinrich Ströbel (1869–1945). Born in Bad Nauheim. *Gymnasium* education. From 1892 to 1900 editor on Social Democratic newspapers in Kiel and Cassel, from 1900 to 1916 editor on *Vorwärts,* thereafter free-lance writer. His socialism had a strong ethical imprint; noted as a feuilletonist. Member of the Prussian Diet, 1908–1918. A strong opponent of the war from the start. Member of the Prussian provisional government. During 1919 a critic of the unconciliatory policies of the radical Independents; left the party in the summer of 1920 and returned to the SPD. Member of the Reichstag, 1924–1932, a leading figure in the party's radical opposition faction and coeditor of *Der Klassenkampf;* also a leader of the German Peace Society, in which capacity he briefly served as cochairman of the Socialist Workers Party in 1931 before resigning from the new party. From 1933 to his death lived in Switzerland.

Ernst Thälmann (1886–1944). Born in Hamburg. A transport worker by trade, but also held a variety of other jobs before 1914. SPD member from 1903, member of the Transport Workers' Union from 1904 and of its local committee from 1908, in both party and union an outspoken radical. From 1915 to 1918 at the front. During the revolution and the following year rose to the chairmanship of the Hamburg USPD because of his vigor and his great popularity among radical workers there. He and his associates made the Hamburg party the most tightly disciplined and most ruthlessly radical of all USPD branches; it was readily assimilated into the VKPD and suffered relatively little from the crises of 1921. Thälmann was a strong supporter of the central committee during these crises; later became associated with Ruth Fischer and Arkadi Maslow, rising with them to leadership of the party in 1924. He was kept on as representative leader of the party after the fall of the Fischer faction in 1925 and survived all later crises. Member of the Reichstag 1920–1933. Arrested in March 1933 and suffered eleven and a half years of imprisonment before being shot in Buchenwald.

Luise Zietz (1865–1922). Born in Bargtheide in Holstein. Trained as a kindergarten teacher, from 1892 an organizer and agitator for Social Democracy with special interest in social policy and women's affairs. In 1905 taken into the party executive; in 1908 became full-time party secretary there. Retained this position until 1917, when she took up the same office in the USPD, holding it until her death. A fiery speaker who preached revolution in the weeks leading up to November 9, she nevertheless tended to vote with the moderates on the divisive issues within the party executive. Member of the National Assembly and the Reichstag from 1919 until her death.

Sources

Note on Materials on the USPD

The bibliography of particular episodes or problems presented in the text appears in the notes; it will not be repeated here. What follows is a discussion of the material from which a history of the USPD and its milieu must be written and a survey of the literature bearing on the party and on left-wing socialism in the German revolutionary period.

For over half a century the standard, and only, published history of the USPD has been Eugen Prager's *Geschichte der U.S.P.D.: Entstehung und Entwicklung der Unabhängigen Sozialdemokratischen Partei Deutschlands* (Berlin, 1921). This work has been of considerable service to historians, for Prager not only assembled the basic story of the party from the press and party congress reports but also reprinted many important declarations and programmatic statements in extenso. But in other respects his work has long been in need of correction. An official party history, written by one of the editors of *Freiheit,* its aim was to bolster the morale of the members; it provides almost no information not already in the public domain; and it expresses the entirely conventional outlook of a moderate Independent Socialist, with party shibboleths taking the place of analysis. Furthermore, over half the book is devoted to the days of opposition, before the USPD was even founded, and barely a quarter to the party's history after the November revolution.

One reason why a better account has not been attempted for so long is no doubt the weakness of the archival documentation. The files of the USPD were combined with the archives of the Social Democratic Party after reunification in 1922, and together they were lost during the Third Reich (except for a few special collections); probably they were burnt to keep them out of Nazi hands. All that has survived of the USPD's internal records is a single minute book of the Reichstag delegation. Nor do private papers, where they are available, help much to make good the loss. Ledebour's private archive, said to have been outstanding, was left behind in Berlin in 1933 and never recovered. Haase's papers perished in a Hamburg warehouse during the Second World War. Of the five men who served as chairman during the party's five years of existence, only Wilhelm Dittmann left any considerable collection of papers relating to the period in question; a part of these papers,

held in Moscow, has not been opened to Western scholars, and what is available in Bonn is disappointing. Only Kautsky left a rich collection, but Kautsky's days as a leader of the party were over before the end of the war and there is, therefore, little information about the inner workings of the party after 1918 in his papers. Henke's papers are interesting for the early wartime opposition, and Barth's for his months in the sun in 1918 and 1919; the other collections left by Independents are of minimal value for the subject of this book. The total yield is not great, especially for the postwar years—a few letters or manuscripts of interest, copies of party leaflets, and an occasional circular or other record of internal party business.

A greater quantity of unpublished material on the wartime opposition and the USPD is to be found in the files of government authorities, above all in the reports of the political police. For the war period, in particular, when radical socialism was forced to operate largely in private or even underground, police reports are an essential supplement to press accounts; by about 1916 police sources were good, so that many reports will stand up to scrutiny; moreover, the reports are copious enough to make cross-checks possible. The postwar police material is much scantier (as regards the USPD—it is very full on the KPD), much less reliable, and also less accessible because of the archival policies of the Ministry of the Interior of the GDR. Very rich material, albeit on a limited part of the total subject, may be found in the files of the provisional government, which have been preserved intact. Other information—official reports on strikes and other incidents in which the USPD or its followers were involved, estimates by the government parties of the USPD's parliamentary strategy, some direct communications from the USPD leaders or records of meetings in which they took part—though also of use, is more scattered. In total, the material in government files, though often disappointing, adds an essential dimension to our knowledge of the USPD.

The historian of the USPD is not well served by memoirs, not surprisingly since so many leading Independents either suffered a violent end (Eisner and Haase, later Hilferding, Breitscheid, and Thälmann) or died abroad. Only Dittmann wrote a detailed autobiography, which remains unpublished in the IISH in Amsterdam; much of the tale it tells is already familiar, but it contains useful details and characterizations of colleagues. The only other full self-portraits have the merit of recording the authors' particular outlooks but tend to vagueness in matters of political detail; they are Toni Sender's *The Autobiography of a German Rebel* (New York, 1939), Ernst Niekisch's *Gewagtes Leben* (Cologne and Berlin, 1958), Ernst Toller's *Eine Jugend in Deutschland* (Amsterdam, 1938; Hamburg, 1963), and Peter Berten's *Lebenslauf eines einfachen Menschen* (Düsseldorf, 1958). Karl Kautsky's *Mein Verhältnis zur Unabhängigen Sozialdemokratischen Partei*, 2d ed. (Berlin, 1922), illuminates the party's history from the position of an unregenerate old-style centrist. Emil Barth's *Aus der Werkstatt der deutschen Revolution* (Berlin [1919]) is a pungent work and unexpectedly reliable if the bombastic self-importance of the author is discounted. Emil Eichhorn's *Eichhorn über*

die Januar-Ereignisse (Berlin, 1919), by contrast, has a modest and ingenuous air but is mendacious on critical issues. Richard Müller's *Vom Kaiserreich zur Republik,* 2 vols. (Vienna, 1924), and *Der Bürgerkrieg in Deutschland: Geburtswehen der Republik* (Berlin, 1925) are half memoir and half historical account and very valuable in both respects. There is only slight memoir content in Walter Oehme's two works, *Damals in der Reichskanzlei* and *Die Weimarer Nationalversammlung* (Berlin, 1958 and 1962), or Carl Herz's *Geister der Vergangenheit,* 2 vols. (Haifa, 1953). Georg Ledebour's and Wilhelm Koenen's recollections are recorded in a number of places, Ledebour's most notably in his opening speech in Georg Ledebour, ed., *Der Ledebour-Prozess* (Berlin, 1919), Koenen's in his contribution to *Zu einigen Fragen der Novemberrevolution und der Gründung der Kommunistischen Partei Deutschlands: Protokoll der theoretischen Konferenz der Abteilung Agitation-Propaganda der Bezirksleitung der SED-Halle* [Halle, 1959]. Finally, for Hugo Haase we have, not a memoir, but a selection of his letters and papers published by his son: *Hugo Haase: Sein Leben und Wirken,* ed. Ernst Haase (Berlin-Fichtenau, n.d.).

Nor did the Independents particularly distinguish themselves in writing the history of this period. Apart from Prager, only Ernst Lorenz wrote on the history of the party itself, in his *5 Jahre Dresdner USP: Ein rückschauendes Betrachten anlässlich des fünfjährigen Bestehens der Partei* (Dresden [1922]); like Prager, he devoted half his brief book to the days before April 1917. Of those who wrote more generally about the revolutionary period, Eduard Bernstein's *Die deutsche Revolution* (Berlin, 1921) is distinguished by its author's characteristic detachment and honesty, while Heinrich Ströbel's *Die deutsche Revolution: Ihr Unglück und ihre Rettung* (Berlin, 1920; 3d ed. 1922) is more engagé but covers more than the three months of Bernstein's account (Bernstein had deserted the USPD before writing, Ströbel was on the verge of doing so). Richard Lipinski's *Der Kampf um die politische Macht in Sachsen* (Leipzig, 1926) carefully smooths over the intrasocialist disputes that made up so much of socialist politics after 1918. Felix Fechenbach wrote a moving little memoir-biography of his mentor, *Der Revolutionär Kurt Eisner: Aus persönlichen Erlebnissen* (Berlin, 1929). Apart from these, there is nothing.

Fortunately, the USPD's own publications were copious and are fairly well preserved. Robert Wheeler's invaluable "Bibliographie und Standortsverzeichnis der Unabhängigen sozialdemokratischen Presse von 1917–1922," *Internationale Wissenschaftliche Korrespondenz zur Geschichte der deutschen Arbeiterbewegung,* 6 (June 1968), 35–55, offers a substantially complete listing of 138 Independent Socialist newspapers and periodicals (many of them ephemeral), naming, in all but 24 cases, libraries where at least a few copies of each may be examined. Alfred Eberlein, *Die Presse der Arbeiterklasse und der sozialen Bewegungen,* 5 vols. (Berlin, 1968–69), is less complete for the USPD press but gives the whereabouts of nearly all known surviving party congress reports, annual business reports, and the like. This material, widely scattered and only now beginning to be exploited by scholars, is fundamental

to all work on the Independent Socialist Party and forms the basis of this book.

In view of the constant interaction of the USPD with its two sister socialist parties, the deficiencies of the evidence on the USPD can be remedied to some extent by material relating to the SPD and the KPD. The SPD's archives were almost wholly lost, and those of the KPD are inaccessible in East Berlin; but the press of both parties is available, and there are more autobiographies and private papers relating to these parties than to the USPD. Paul Levi's papers are far more instructive than any surviving papers from Independent hands, as are the papers of numerous Majority Socialists, including Carl Severing and Hermann Müller. Wilhelm Pieck's memoirs of the revolution, printed in his *Gesammelte Reden und Schriften,* vol. I (Berlin, 1959), are of considerable interest. The Majority Socialists excelled in memoirs, of which the most valuable for the study of the USPD are Philipp Scheidemann's *Der Zusammenbruch* (Berlin, 1921) and *Memoiren eines Sozialdemokraten,* 2 vols. (Dresden, 1928), Hermann Müller's *Die November-Revolution: Erinnerungen* (Berlin, 1928), and Carl Severing's *1919/1920 im Wetter- und Watterwinkel: Aufzeichnungen und Erinnerungen* (Bielefeld, 1927). There are many others as well.

Finally, a number of published collections of documents bear on our subject. Among the most important are two East German publications: *Die Auswirkungen der Grossen Sozialistischen Oktoberrevolution auf Deutschland,* ed. Leo Stern, Archivalische Forschungen zur Geschichte der deutschen Arbeiterbewegung, vols. 4/I–4/IV (Berlin, 1959), and *Dokumente und Materialien zur Geschichte der Deutschen Arbeiterbewegung,* issued by the Institut für Marxismus-Leninismus beim Zentralkomitee der SED, of which vols. 1–3 of series 2 and vol. 7 (no series) (Berlin, 1957–58 and 1966) are relevant. The selection in these volumes has a strong didactic purpose, but the materials appear to be faithfully reproduced and are exceptionally useful. Of the numerous valuable publications of the Commission for the History of Parliamentarianism and Political Parties in Bonn, the most pertinent are *Die Reichstagsfraktion der deutschen Sozialdemokratie 1898 bis 1918,* ed. Erich Matthias and Eberhard Pikart, 2 vols. (Düsseldorf, 1966), and *Die Regierung der Volksbeauftragten 1918/19,* ed. Susanne Miller with Heinrich Potthoff, 2 vols. (Düsseldorf, 1969); both works have fine introductions by Erich Matthias. The massive report of the Reichstag committee investigating the origins of the "collapse" of autumn 1918, published as *Die Ursachen des Deutschen Zusammenbruches im Jahre 1918,* series 4, 12 vols. (Berlin, 1925–29), contains much testimony and documentation; there is other testimony in the published reports of the numerous political trials of the period (of which the most important for the USPD is *Der Ledebour-Prozess,* which has already been mentioned). Of general utility is the vast collection, *Ursachen und Folgen: Vom deutschen Zusammenbruch 1918 und 1945 bis zur staatlichen Neuordnung Deutschlands in der Gegenwart,* ed. Herbert Michaelis, Ernst Schraepler, and Günter Scheel, 14 vols. (Berlin, n.d.). There are many collections of documents on more specialized subjects but

The English language historiography of German socialism in the revolutionary period is distinguished by Carl E. Schorske's *German Social Democracy, 1905–1917: The Development of the Great Schism* (Cambridge, Mass., 1955), a fine book that is still the starting point for most thinking on German socialism in this period and also an excellent introduction to the origins of the USPD. A. Joseph Berlau, *The German Social Democratic Party, 1914–1921* (New York, 1949), is well researched, sympathetic to the Independents, and intermittently incisive, but its evaluations are eccentric. A. J. Ryder, *The German Revolution of 1918: A Study of German Socialism in War and Revolt* (Cambridge, 1967), based on his dissertation on the USPD (London, 1958), is an attractive work but slight. Lastly, two good regional studies contribute to our understanding of the revolution: Allan Mitchell, *Revolution in Bavaria, 1918–1919: The Eisner Regime and the Soviet Republic* (Princeton, 1965); and Richard A. Comfort, *Revolutionary Hamburg: Labor Politics in the Early Weimar Republic* (Stanford, 1966). Both offer not only careful research but also new insight into the dynamics of the revolutionary period—perhaps the most important contribution foreign scholars can make to the study of German history.

Principal Sources Consulted (exclusive of books and pamphlets)

Private Papers and Unpublished Memoirs

Emil Barth papers (ASD Bonn)

Eduard Bernstein papers (IISH Amsterdam)

Artur Crispien, "Erinnerungen—Fragmentarische Manuskripte" (ASD Bonn)

Eduard David papers (BA Koblenz)

Wilhelm Dittmann papers (ASD Bonn)

Wilhelm Dittmann, untitled memoirs (typescript in IISH Amsterdam)

Edmund Fischer papers (DZA Potsdam)

Carl Giebel papers (ASD Bonn)

Wilhelm Groener papers (BA-MA Freiburg)

Wolfgang Heine, "Politische Aufzeichnungen" (BA Koblenz, Kl. Erw. 371–9)

Alfred Henke papers (ASD Bonn)

Harold Hurwitz collection, in the possession of Dr. Hurwitz, Berlin

Karl Kautsky papers (IISH Amsterdam)

Otto Landsberg papers (BA Koblenz, Kl. Erw. 328)

Georg Ledebour papers (ASD Bonn)

Arnold Lequis papers (BA-MA Freiburg)

Paul Levi papers (ASD Bonn; formerly in the Library for Political Studies, New York)

Paul Löbe collection (DZA Potsdam)

Hermann Müller papers (DZA Potsdam)

Heinrich Scheüch papers (BA-MA Freiburg)

Kurt von Schleicher papers (BA-MA Freiburg)

Carl Severing papers (ASD Bonn)

P. J. Troelstra papers (IISH Amsterdam)
Clara Zetkin collection (IML Berlin)

State Archives

Deutsches Zentralarchiv, Potsdam
  Reichskanzlei, 1914–1919
  Reichsamt (from 1919, Reichsministerium) des Innern, 1914–1922
  Reichskommissar für Ueberwachung der öffentlichen Ordnung, 1920–1922
  Reichs- und Staatskommissar für gewerbliche Fragen (Severing), 1919–
    1920
Institut für Marxismus-Leninismus, Zentrales Parteiarchiv, Berlin (material
on long-term loan from DZA Potsdam)
  Reichskanzlei, 1914–1919
  Reichsamt (from 1919, Reichsministerium) des Innern, 1914–1922
  Reichskommissar für Ueberwachung der öffentlichen Ordnung, 1920–1922
Bundesarchiv, Koblenz
  Reichskanzlei, 1919–1922
  Reichssicherheitshauptamt, files containing police material from the early
    1920's
National Archives Microcopy T-120
  Auswärtiges Amt, 1919–1920
  Neue Reichskanzlei, Sammlung Prof. Dr. Holborn
Deutsches Zentralarchiv, Historische Abteilung II, Merseburg (archives of
Prussian authorities)
  Ministerium des Innern (Rep. 77), 1914–1922
  Auswärtiges Amt (Rep. 81), 1914–1919
  Geheimes Zivilkabinett (2.2.1), 1914–1919
  Preussisches Staatsministerium (Rep. 90a), 1918–1921
  Ministerium für Handel und Gewerbe (Rep. 120), 1914–1921
  Finanz-Ministerium (Rep. 151), 1915–1922
  Preussischer Landtag/Landesversammlung (Rep. 169), 1918–1922
  Deutscher Bevollmächtigter für den Abstimmungsbezirk Oberschlesien
    (Rep. 171), 1920–1921
  Preussischer Staatskommissar für Volksernährung (Rep. 197), 1915–1918
Staatsarchiv Dresden (archives of Saxon authorities)
  Ministerium des Innern, 1914–1922
  Kreishauptmannschaft Leipzig, 1914–1920
  Polizeipräsidium Zwickau, 1916–1922
  Kriegsarchiv/Kriegsministerium, 1915–1918
  Staatskanzlei, 1920–1922
Staatsarchiv Magdeburg (archives of the authorities of the Prussian Province
of Saxony)
  Oberpräsidium Magdeburg, 1918–1922
  Regierung Magdeburg, 1914–1917
  Regierung Merseburg, 1914–1922
  Oberbergamt zu Halle, 1918–1921

Staatsarchiv Potsdam (archives of the authorities of the Prussian Province of Brandenburg and of the Berlin police)
    Polizeipräsidium Berlin, 1914–1918
    Regierung Potsdam, 1914–1922

Unpublished Minutes of Meetings

Protokolle des Vollzugsrats der Berliner Arbeiter- und Soldatenräte (IML Berlin, 11/1–11/10); meetings from Nov. 11, 1918, to Aug. 18, 1919
Protokolle der Vollversammlungen der Arbeiter- und Soldatenräte von Gross-Berlin (IML Berlin, 11/11–11/14); meetings from Nov. 19, 1918, to June 6, 1919
Protokollbuch vom 24. Aug. 1917–20. Aug. 1919 (IISH Amsterdam); meetings of the SPD Reichstag and National Assembly delegations
Untitled book of minutes of the SPD National Assembly delegation, from Sept. 25, 1919, to Jan. 15, 1920 (IISH Amsterdam)
Protokoll der Fraktion der U.S.P. (IISH Amsterdam); one volume, meetings of the Reichstag delegation from June 21, 1920, to July 13, 1922

Newspapers and Periodicals

Der Arbeiter-Rat, Feb. 1919 to Dec. 1920 (complete); weekly, ed. Ernst Däumig
Das Forum, 1918 to 1922; roughly monthly, ed. Wilhelm Herzog
Die freie Welt (later Freie Welt), May 1919 to Sept. 1920; weekly illustrated supplement to the USPD press
Freiheit, Nov. 15, 1918, to Sept. 29, 1922 (complete); usually twice daily, ed. Hilferding, from April 1922 ed. Dittmann
Informationsblatt of the Berlin-Brandenburg district of the USPD, Nov. 1919 to Nov. 1920 (complete); approximately monthly, bulletin for party functionaries
Die Internationale, 1919 to 1921; irregular, later biweekly, official theoretical journal of the KPD
Die Internationale, Oct. 27 to Dec. 31, 1920 (complete); daily, Berlin organ of the left USPD
Jahrbuch für Wirtschaft, Politik und Arbeiterbewegung, 1922/23, 1923/24, and 1925/26; Comintern publication
Klassenkampf, issues of Oct. 4, 11, and 18, 1922. Weekly, ed. Ledebour, for what remained of the USPD
Die Kommunistische Internationale (Berlin-Hamburg edition), nos. 1 to 22; irregular, official journal of the Comintern
Kommunistische Räte-Korrespondenz, June 13, 1919, to Feb. 13, 1920 (with gaps); irregular
Kommunistische Rundschau, Oct. to Dec. 1920 (complete); ed. Däumig, Curt Geyer, and Stoecker, for the Left USPD
Korrespondenz Anna Geyer, Sept. to Nov.(?) 1920; press service for the pro-Moscow Independents, later the Left USPD
Leipziger Volkszeitung, Jan. 1917 to June 1919; daily

Mitteilungen of the Leipzig district executive of the USPD, or the Saxon state executive, or both; title varied repeatedly; 1917 to 1922; irregular, bulletin for party functionaries

Mitteilungsblatt des Bezirksverbandes Berlin-Brandenburg der Unabhängigen Sozialdemokratischen Partei Deutschlands, Dec. 1920 to Sept. 1922 (complete); approximately monthly, successor to the *Informationsblatt*

Mitteilungs-Blatt des Verbandes der sozialdemokratischen Wahlvereine Berlins und Umgegend, 1914 to Dec. 1918; monthly bulletin, then, from Nov. 1916, a weekly newspaper ed. Däumig

Mitteilungsblatt für die Anhänger der III. Internationale in der U.S.P.D., issues of Oct. 12 and 20, 1920; predecessor of *Die Internationale* (Left USPD)

Nachrichten der Internationalen Arbeitsgemeinschaft Sozialistischer Parteien, April 1921 to June 1923 (complete); irregular, bulletin of the Vienna Union

Neue Zeit, July 1914 to Sept. 1917; weekly, ed. Kautsky

Partei-Mitteilungen für die Organisationen der Unabhängigen Sozialdemokratie Deutschlands, Bezirk Waterkant, Aug. 11, 1917 (only number)

Referentenmaterial, Nov. 1919 to March(?) 1921; approximately biweekly, material for the use of party speakers

Die Republik, Dec. 3, 1918, to June 24, 1919 (complete); daily, ed. Wilhelm Herzog in association with Däumig

Rote Fahne, Nov. 1918 to Feb. 1921 (used selectively); daily, KPD central organ

Sowjet, May 1919 to June 1921 (complete); approximately monthly, from May 1921 ed. Levi, converted into *Unser Weg*

Der Sozialist, Nov. 1918 to Sept. 1922 (complete); weekly, ed. Breitscheid

Sozialistische Auslandspolitik, Jan. to Nov. 1918 and scattered earlier issues; weekly, ed. Breitscheid; press service for the opposition, later unofficial theoretical journal of the USPD; converted into *Der Sozialist*

Unser Weg, July 1921 to Sept. 1922; semimonthly, ed. Levi, successor to *Sowjet*

USPD Material, July(?) 1921 to 1922; irregular, successor to *Referentenmaterial* for party speakers

Volksblatt für Halle und den Saalkreis, 1914 to Sept. 1918; daily

Volkszeitung (Halle), Jan. 1921 to Sept. 1922; USPD's successor to the lost *Volksblatt*

Vorwärts, 1914 to 1922 (used selectively); central organ of the SPD

Minutes of Congresses and Conferences

USPD

Protokoll über die Verhandlungen des Gründungs-Parteitages der U.S.P.D. vom 6. bis 8. April 1917 in Gotha. Appendix: Bericht über die Gemeinsame Konferenz der Arbeitsgemeinschaft und der Spartakusgruppe vom 7. Januar 1917 in Berlin. Ed. Emil Eichhorn. Berlin, 1921.

Protokoll über die Verhandlungen des ausserordentlichen Parteitages vom

2. bis 6. März 1919 in Berlin. Berlin, n.d.

Protokoll über die Verhandlungen des ausserordentlichen Parteitages in Leipzig vom 30. November bis 6. Dezember 1919. Berlin, n.d.

Protokoll der Reichskonferenz vom 1. bis 3. September 1920 zu Berlin. Berlin, n.d.

Protokoll über die Verhandlungen des ausserordentlichen Parteitages in Halle vom 12. bis 17. Oktober 1920. Berlin, n.d.[1]

Protokoll über die Verhandlungen des Parteitages in Leipzig vom 8. bis 12. Januar 1922. Leipzig, n.d.

Parteitag der Unabhängigen Sozialdem. Partei Deutschlands: 30. März bis 2. April 1923 im Bürgersaal des Rathauses zu Berlin. N.p., n.d.

USPD, Regional

Berichterstattung über die Verhandlungen der Landeskonferenz der U.S.P. Badens vom 15. und 16. Februar 1919 zu Karlsruhe. Karlsruhe, n.d.

Protokoll vom Bezirksparteitag der Unabhängigen Sozialdemokratischen Partei des Niederrheins am Samstag, den 26. und Sonntag, den 27. April 1919 in Elberfeld. N.p., n.d.

Protokoll über die Verhandlungen der ausserordentlichen Landesversammlung der Unabhängigen Sozialdemokratischen Partei Sachsens, abgehalten am 10. und 11. August 1919 im Volkshaus zu Leipzig. Leipzig, 1919.

Protokoll über die Verhandlungen der ausserordentlichen Landesversammlung der U.S.P. Sachsens, abgehalten am 23. April 1920 im Volkshaus zu Leipzig. Leipzig, 1920.

Protokoll über die Verhandlungen der ordentlichen Landesversammlung der U.S.P. Sachsens, abgehalten am 12. und 13. September 1920 im Volkshaus zu Leipzig. Leipzig, 1920.

Protokoll über die Verhandlungen der ordentlichen Landesversammlung der U.S.P. Sachsens, abgehalten am 9. und 10. Juli 1921 im Volkshaus zu Leipzig. Leipzig, 1921.

Landesversammlung der Unabhängigen Sozialdemokratischen Partei Sachsens am 15. und 16. Juli 1922 im Gewerkschaftshaus zu Plauen im Vogtl. Leipzig, 1922.

USPD-SPD

Protokoll der Sozialdemokratischen Parteitage in Augsburg, Gera und Nürnberg 1922. Berlin, 1923.

SPD

Protokoll der Reichskonferenz der Sozialdemokratie Deutschlands vom 21., 22. und 23. September 1916. N.p., n.d.

Protokoll über die Verhandlungen des Parteitages der Sozialdemokratischen

---

1. The two versions of this work, both containing (typographically identical) minutes of the proceedings up to the point of the split but differing in most of their other contents, have identical title pages. See ch. 11, n. 127.

Partei Deutschlands, abgehalten in Würzburg vom 14. bis 20. Oktober 1917. Berlin, 1917.

Protokoll der Parteikonferenz in Weimar am 22. u. 23. März 1919. Berlin, n.d.

Protokoll über die Verhandlungen des Parteitages der Sozialdemokratischen Partei Deutschlands, abgehalten in Weimar vom 10. bis 15. Juni 1919. Berlin, 1919.

Sitzung des Parteiausschusses am 30. und 31. März 1920. N.p., n.d.

Protokoll über die Verhandlungen der Reichskonferenz der Sozialdemokratischen Partei Deutschlands, abgehalten in Berlin am 5. und 6. Mai 1920. Berlin, 1920.

Protokoll über die Verhandlungen des Parteitages der Sozialdemokratischen Partei Deutschlands, abgehalten in Kassel vom 10. bis 16. Oktober 1920. Berlin, 1920.

Protokoll über die Verhandlungen des Parteitages der Sozialdemokratischen Partei Deutschlands, abgehalten in Görlitz vom 18. bis 24. September 1921. Berlin, 1921.

Sozialdemokratischer Parteitag 1924: Protokoll mit dem Bericht der Frauenkonferenz. Berlin, 1924.

KPD

Der Gründungsparteitag der KPD: Protokoll und Materialien. Ed. Hermann Weber. Frankfurt on Main and Vienna, 1969.

Bericht über den 2. Parteitag der Kommunistischen Partei Deutschlands (Spartakusbund) vom 20. bis 24. Oktober 1919. N.p., n.d.

Bericht über den 3. Parteitag der Kommunistischen Partei Deutschlands (Spartakusbund) am 25. und 26. Februar 1920. N.p., n.d.

Bericht über den 4. Parteitag der Kommunistischen Partei Deutschlands (Spartakusbund) am 14. und 15. April 1920. N.p., n.d.

Bericht über den 5. Parteitag der Kommunistischen Partei Deutschlands (Sektion der Kommunistischen Internationale) vom 1. bis 3. November 1920 in Berlin. Berlin, 1921.

Bericht über die Verhandlungen des Vereinigungsparteitages der U.S.P.D. (Linke) und der K.P.D. (Spartakusbund), abgehalten in Berlin vom 4. bis 7. Dezember 1920. Berlin, 1921.

Bericht über die Verhandlungen des 2. Parteitages der Kommunistischen Partei Deutschlands (Sektion der Kommunistischen Internationale), abgehalten in Jena vom 22. bis 26. August 1921. Berlin, 1922.

Other

Allgemeiner Kongress der Arbeiter- und Soldatenräte Deutschlands vom 16. bis 21. Dezember 1918 im Abgeordnetenhause zu Berlin: Stenographische Berichte. Berlin, n.d.

II. Kongress der Arbeiter-, Bauern- und Soldatenräte Deutschlands am 8. bis 14. April 1919 im Herrenhaus zu Berlin: Stenographisches Protokoll. Berlin, n.d.

Der I. Kongress der Kommunistischen Internationale: Protokoll der Verhandlungen in Moskau vom 2. bis zum 19. März 1919. Hamburg, 1921.

Der zweite Kongress der Kommunist. Internationale: Protokoll der Verhandlungen vom 19. Juli in Petrograd und vom 23. Juli bis 7. August 1920 in Moskau. Hamburg, 1921.

Protokoll der Internationalen Sozialistischen Konferenz in Wien vom 22. bis 27. Februar 1921. Vienna, 1921.

The Second and Third Internationals and the Vienna Union: Official Report of the Conference between the Executives, held at the Reichstag, Berlin, on the 2nd April, 1922, and following days. London, 1922.

Index to References

Full reference to each work will be found on the page indicated.

481

Index

ADGB: and factory councils, 346; and Kapp Putsch, 322, 323, 326-27, 328, 331; USPD cooperation with, 404, 420-23; *see also* Trade unions

AfA, 346, 421; identified, 322; and Kapp Putsch, 322, 323, 328, 331; *see also* Trade unions

Albrecht, Adolf, 38n, 72, 174

Anhalt, 181, 201n

Army (later Reichswehr): debate on uses of, 151-54, 187, 191-92, 193-94, 195-96; excesses of, in civil war, 216-17, 236, 239; in fighting of March 1920, 327, 332-40; popular resentment of officer corps of, 150, 186; problem of demobilizing, 150-51; socialist fears of counterrevolution by, 152-53, 185-86, 222, 266, 274-75, 321, 332; used against radical centers in civil war, 212-13, 215, 216-17, 218-19, 221-22, 226-28, 231, 234-36, 236-37, 239, 240; workers' hatred of, 212-13, 222, 226n, 332-33

Auer, Erhard, 158, 160, 161

Aufhäuser, Siegfried, 441

Baden, 76, 181, 386

Barth, Emil: career, 457; characterized, 104; in provisional government, 126, 141, 144, 148, 184; resigns from provisional government, 195-98; and shop stewards, 105, 106, 120; and socialization, 191, 192; in Versailles crisis, 263, 265; at first Workers' and Soldiers' Congress, 190n, 191, 192

Bauer, Gustav, 264

Bavaria: elections in, 160-61, 181, 239n; and Law for Defense of Republic, 433; revolution and provisional government in, 116-17, 156-61; soviet republic of, 237-39

—— (district), 76, 217, 257n, 303n, 375n; membership in, 243-44; in rump USPD, 383, 386, 388; supports Twenty-One Conditions, 277, 383

——, northern (Franconia): and socialist unity, 51, 77-78, 274; USPD strength in, 160, 238, 250, 386

Bebel, August, 19, 29, 30

Berlin, 183; councils in, 121-23, 133, 139, 140, 180-81, 229, 233, 236, 346 (*see also* Executive council); disturbances of January 1919 in, 212-17; elections in, 243, 350, 352; influence of, on provinces, 155, 161, 219; Kapp Putsch in, 327, 328, 331-32; in KPD, 292; revolution in, 119-21; shooting of January 1920 in, 314-15; strike of March 1919 in, 230, 232-36; violence in, 185, 194-95, 213-17, 234-36, 314-15; wartime strikes in, 57, 83, 89-91; *see also* Shop stewards movement

—— (party): as bulwark of rump USPD, 382, 383, 418, 426; character, 43, 47-48, 69-70, 206-7, 209-10, 213-18; left radical and Spartacist influence in, 28, 45, 47-48, 50, 62; membership, 67-68, 243, 351; in reunified party, 441; supports reunification, 432; and trade unions, 271; in USPD after 1922, 443-44; and *Vorwärts* affair, 49-50, 78; in voting before Halle party congress, 376; in wartime opposition, 47-48, 49-50, 51n, 52, 68; *see also* Berlin-Brandenburg

Berlin-Brandenburg (district): on Communist International, 303n, 377; membership, 243, 351; in rump USPD, 386, 388; supports reunification, 432

485

WITHDRAWN FROM
JUNIATA COLLEGE LIBRARY